The Criminology Theory Reader

THE CRIMINOLOGY THEORY READER

Edited by Stuart Henry and Werner Einstadter

NEW YORK UNIVERSITY PRESS

New York and London

NEW YORK UNIVERSITY PRESS
New York and London

© 1998 by New York University

Library of Congress Cataloging-in-Publication Data
The criminology theory reader / edited by Stuart Henry and Werner Einstadter.
  p. cm.
Includes bibliographic references and index.
ISBN 0-8147-3550-9 (cloth : alk. paper). — ISBN 0-8147-3551-7 (pbk. : alk. paper)
1. Criminology. 2. Crime. I. Henry, Stuart. II. Einstadter, Werner J.
HV6025.C747   1997   97-40403
364—dc21   CIP

New York University Press books are printed on acid-free paper,
and their binding materials are chosen for strength and durability.

Manufactured in the United States of America

10 9 8 7 6 5 4 3 2

Contents

Biological and Psychological Theory

Ecology Theory

Strain and Subcultural Theory

Differential Association and Social Learning Theory

Neutralization and Social Control Theory

Labeling and Social Constructionist Theory

New Directions: Critical Theory

New Directions: Feminist Theory

New Directions: Postmodernist and Constitutive Theory

New Directions: Integrated Theory

Foreword

Robert J. Bursik, Jr.

The book you are about to read is as much a tribute to the emergence of modern criminological theory as it is a collection of important articles that appeared in the journal *Criminology* between 1986 and 1996. Stuart Henry and Werner Einstadter have done an excellent job of compiling a representative selection of articles from this period that span the many fields and theoretical orientations that are found under the multidisciplinary umbrella of criminology. In doing so, they have captured the richness and complexity of the criminological enterprise, and the key role that *Criminology*, the official journal of the American Society of Criminology (ASC), has played in that effort.

This collection also is a tribute to institutional survival. While its contemporary status as a cutting edge, first tier journal now is generally taken for granted (as Henry and Einstadter note in their Introduction, it arguably may be the most important of its kind in the world), a lot of us remember clearly when this was not the case. In fact, according to an early editorial comment of Simon Dinitz, the journal just barely made it past Volume 3 (1965) because a significant proportion of the Society's membership felt that its potential was extremely limited and that it was too great a drain on the Society's limited economic resources. Luckily for us, the Executive Committee voted to maintain its support.

The history of the journal's development into one of the premier outlets for criminological theory and research is a fascinating story. *Criminology* originated as *Criminologica*, a newsletter edited by Charles Newman for the then fledgling ASC. The mission of the journal began to shift significantly when Walter Reckless, then President of the ASC, moved the editorial offices to the campus of Ohio State University, under the direction of Dinitz. Although a large number of theory and research papers by most of the important criminologists of the time appeared in the Dinitz volumes, *Criminologica* still occupied a relatively minor niche in the field.

I believe this was due to three reasons. First, at that time the *Journal of Criminal Law, Criminology and Police Science* was recognized as far and away the most prestigious placement for original work, and I suspect that it was the first choice of publication outlets for most people in the field. Second, *Criminologica* still seemed unsure as to its mission. While some excellent papers were being published, it still took quite a while to completely shed its origins (and, as a result, its reputation) as a newsletter. Thus, an ongoing series called Across the Desk (a catalog of institutional developments and personnel changes in the field) continued to be a regular feature of the journal for several years, as did a column on Law Enforcement Education. Finally, to be honest, it was not an especially attractive journal physically, especially in comparison with *JCLCPS*. Nevertheless, there is no question that *Criminology* as we know it would not exist without the pioneering efforts of Newman and Dinitz.

Several major improvements to the journal were made during the years of C.Ray Jeffery, who took over from Dinitz at Volume 7 (1969). First, and most noticeably, the name of the journal was changed to *Criminology*. Second, Sage Publications took over the physical production of the journal during Volume 8. The covers were now very professional looking, the pages were printed on glossy stock, and the editor and editorial board were listed at the front of each issue. At least in appearance, it now could compete with *JCLCPS*. Finally, Jeffery published the first formal editorial policy and statement of style requirements. By Volume 10, under the guidance of Jeffery, the reputation of *Criminology* had improved to the point where it was being abstracted in a number of major outlets.

Charles Newman, who resumed the editorial duties after Jeffery, continued to build upon these improvements. The use of anonymous reviewers was a standard practice by Volume 12, and the first formal statement of criteria was published, that is papers should represent original contributors to knowledge. Donal MacNamara and Edward Sagarin (the only joint editors of the journal) succeeded Newman, and were the first to publish a special issue of *Criminology* devoted to a single theme (New Perspectives in Criminology, Volume 15, February 1978). While this decision seems to be fairly innocuous, it set the precedent for perhaps the most controversial set of events involving the journal. James Inciardi, who became editor during Volume 16, devoted a special issue of Volume 19 (1979) to radical criminology, which led to a great deal of concern from both radical/critical criminologists and more conservative elements of the ASC alike. In fact, the backlash from radical criminologists was so strong that a proposal for the Society to sponsor a "counterissue" was presented to the general membership of the ASC in a referendum (where it was defeated). Perhaps it didn't help that Inciardi was the first editor to announce the necessity of a $10 processing fee!

In the years following, the reputation of *Criminology* continued to grow. However, many members of the ASC continued to submit papers to the journal only if they had been rejected by other more prestigious outlets, a tendency lamented by Charles Thomas in his first formal statement as the new editor (Volume 19, No. 3). By the end of his term (Volume 22, 1984), he obviously was very angry at his perceived lack of success in changing this pattern, for in his outgoing statement as editor he identified by name a set of highly influential criminologists who he felt were especially guilty in this regard. In retrospect, I feel that Thomas significantly overstated the case, for a large number of still widely cited papers were published during his period. But I also believe that it is true that at the best, the journal still was perceived by many as being at the second tier of excellence.

The end of Thomas's term as editor represented the end of the ASC's agreement with Sage. Although the Society considered signing a new contract with John Wiley & Sons, an arrangement that was mutually satisfactory did not develop. The ASC therefore decided to once again self-publish the journal, subcontracting the printing. It was with the February issue of Volume 23 (1985), at the beginning of the editorial term of Joseph Weis, that the journal acquired the physical appearance that continues to this day.

While the journal's quality continued to improve during the Weis period (and some papers published during his tenure as editor are included in this volume), I believe that the jump to undisputed first tier status occurred after Doug Smith was named editor in 1988 (Volume 26). Smith streamlined the editorial process and for the first time the journal adopted the APA guidelines for nonsexist language. He also expended a great deal of effort convincing the ASC membership that *Criminology* was in fact a first tier journal. All these efforts paid off, and submissions to the journal increased by over a third in a very short time. Charles Tittle took over from Smith in 1992 (Volume 30), working hard to successfully maintain the high quality of the journal. It is my opinion that under the leadership of Smith and Tittle the original version of the American Society of Criminology came to full fruition.

In the process of compiling an excellent collection of theoretical articles from the journal, Henry and Einstadter have produced a lasting and fitting tribute to the hard work of Newman, Dinitz, Jeffery, MacNamara and Sagarin, Inciardi, Thomas, Weis, Smith, and Tittle. It was my privilege to become the newest member of this group in April 1997, when I assumed the responsibilities for the journal. I guarantee you that a copy of this book will be prominently displayed in our offices to remind us of the great tradition we have inherited.

Preface

An essential part of criminological education is that students read actual journal articles, as well as textbook accounts. This book brings together a selection of the best theory articles published during the decade 1986–96 by Criminology, the Journal of the American Society of Criminology. Modeled on Richard Abel's *The Law and Society Reader* (New York University Press, 1995), *The Criminology Theory Reader* was approved in 1996 by the Executive Board of the American Society of Criminology (ASC), under its then president, Freda Adler. It is supported by the contributing authors who have agreed to forfeit any and all royalties to the ASC's Minority Scholarship Fund.

Drawing articles from a professional journal has the advantage that each has been through a rigorous academic peer review process before being accepted for publication. This process typically requires the author(s) to revise and vastly improve their ideas. Peer reviewed articles represent the foremost work in the profession. They typically avoid repeating already established ideas, except as introductions to new developments.

Criminology is recognized as the leading professional criminology journal in the United States and arguably, the world. It is received by over 2,600 academic criminologists, four times a year, as part of their membership in the professional association. Many criminologists consider the journal their first choice when submitting articles for scholarly publication. Through *Criminology* readers are exposed to a range of theoretical work and ideas which are represented in the articles we have selected.

As with all anthologies of this type, it was necessary to be highly selective. Guided by space limitations we have included only those works we feel best illustrate the theoretical frameworks presented. Moreover, since journal articles are written for professional criminologists rather than students, we have undertaken the task of substantially editing and abridging the originals to be more readily consumable by a student readership. At the same time we have attempted to retain their structural and conceptual integrity. Although the authors have read and accepted our editing, students are encouraged to consult the originals in order to confirm or resolve any questions that our edited version may have raised.

While we have provided an introductory overview and summary introductions to the sections, this book is intended to be used in conjunction with a theory text. We hope that you find it a rich and useful resource for understanding criminological theory.

We thank the following people for their help, advice, and support at various stages of this project: Niko Pfund, Tim Bartlett, Rick Abel, Ronald Pipkin, Sara Hall, Freda Adler, and Martha Weber. We would especially like to thank the contributors for their tolerance and co-operation and we reaffirm *their* thanks to people too numerous to mention here, who assisted them in their original articles for *Criminology*.

About the Contributors

Robert Agnew is Professor of Sociology at Emory University in Atlanta, Georgia. His research focuses on the causes of delinquency, particularly strain, social learning, and social control theories. He has conducted empirical research on general strain theory and recently published two articles on this subject in Volumes 6 and 7 of the *Advances in Criminological Theory* series.

Ronald L. Akers is Professor of Sociology and Criminology and Director of the Center for Studies in Criminology and Law at the University of Florida. He is **past president of the American Society of Criminology** and **past president of the Southern Sociological Society**. He is author of *Criminological Theories* (1997), *Drugs, Alcohol and Society* (1992), and *Deviant Behavior: A Social Learning Approach* (1985) and numerous journal articles and book chapters.

Piers Beirne is Professor of Sociology and Legal Studies at the University of Southern Maine. His recent books include *Inventing Criminology: Essays on the Rise of "Homo Criminalis"* (1993), and (with James Messerschmidt) *Criminology* (1995). In addition to his current research on animal abuse, Professor Beirne is the founding editor of the journal *Theoretical Criminology*.

Michael L. Benson is an Associate Professor in the Department of Sociology at the University of Tennessee. He has recently completed a book (with Francis Cullen) on local prosecutors and corporate crime entitled *Prosecutors in Community Context: A Study of Local Enforcement of Corporate Crime*. He is currently investigating theft from patients in nursing homes.

Thomas J. Bernard is Professor of Criminal Justice and Sociology at Pennsylvania State University. He recently edited (with Richard McCleary) *Life without Parole, by Victor Hassine* (1996), and coauthored (with Jeffery B. Snipes) the 4th edition of *Theoretical Criminology*, originally written with the late George B. Vold.

Robert J. Bursik, Jr. is Professor of Criminology and Criminal Justice at the University of Missouri-St. Louis and is the current editor of *Criminology*. Most of the themes addressed in his paper are discussed in more detail in *Neighborhoods and Crime* (1993, with Harold Grasmick). His current research focuses on the linkages between local neighborhoods and political structures.

Avshalom Caspi is Professor of Psychology and H. I. Romnes Faculty Fellow at the University of Wisconsin, Madison. He received the **1995 Distinguished Scientific Award** for Early Career Contribution to Psychology from the American Psychological Association. He is the associate editor of the *Journal of Personality*.

William J. Chambliss is Professor in the Department of Sociology at the George Washington University. He is past **President of the American Society of Criminology** (1988) and won the **Lifetime Achievement Award** from the ASC's Division of Critical Criminology in 1995. Among Professor Chambliss's numerous books dealing with law, crime, and their interrelationship with the political economy, is *On the Take: From Petty Crooks to Presidents* (1978) and the classic work (with Robert Seidman) *Law, Order and Power* (1982). His latest publications include: *Exploring Criminology* (1988); (with Thomas Courtless) *Criminal Law, Criminology and Criminal Justice* (1992); and (with Marjorie Zatz) *Making Law: The State, The Law, and Structural Contradictions* (1993).

Ronald V. Clarke is Dean of the School of Criminal Justice at Rutgers University. He was previously the Head of the British Home Office Research and Planning Unit, where he played a major role in the development of both situational crime prevention and the British Crime Survey. He is editor of *Crime Prevention Studies* and his most recent edited books include *Preventing Mass Transit Crime* (1996) and (with Marcus Felson), *Business and Crime Prevention* (1997).

Derek B. Cornish, after working in the British Home Office Research and Planning Unit, joined the London School of Economics where he teaches criminology and psychology in the Department of Social Policy and Administration. His research interests include the study of criminal decision making in relation to crime commission, and the evaluation of rehabilitation programs. He has published articles on the procedural analysis of offending and is writing a book about the rational choice perspective.

Werner J. Einstadter is Professor Emeritus of Criminology and Sociology at Eastern Michigan University. He has published on critical theory, privacy, and corrections, including (with Neal Shover) *Analyzing Corrections* (1988). His latest book (with Stuart Henry) is *Criminological Theory: An Analysis of Its Underlying Assumptions* (1995).

Malcolm M. Feeley is Professor of Law and former Director of the Center for the Study of Law and Society at the University of California at Berkeley. He is the author of numerous books and articles. His book, *The Process Is the Punishment* (1979), received the **American Bar Association's Silver Gavel Award** and was cited as one of the best books in the past five years by the **American Sociological Association's Criminal Justice Section**. His most recent book is *Judicial Policy-Making and the Modern State* (1997).

Marcus Felson is Professor of Sociology at Rutgers University. He is a specialist in the study of routine activities as well as social trends and cycles. His research includes large statistical models, developing the routine activity approach to crime rate analysis, and studying tangible social change. He is the author of *Crime and Everyday Life: Insights and Implications for Society* (1994) and is coeditor (with Ronald Clarke) of *Routine Activity and Rational Choice* (1993), and *Business and Crime Prevention* (1997).

Diana H. Fishbein is a Research Scientist in the High Intensity Drug Trafficking Area (HIDTA) Research Program funded by the Office of National Drug Control Policy at the University of Maryland. She taught for several years in the Criminal Justice Department, University of Baltimore, and has been a researcher at the Addiction Research Center at the University of Maryland Medical School. Her publications have been on the psychological and biological aspects of antisocial behavior. Recently she authored (with Susan Pease) *The Dynamics of Drug Abuse* (1996).

David O. Friedrichs is Professor of Sociology and Criminal Justice at the University of Scranton. He is the author of *Trusted Criminals: White Collar Crime in Contemporary Society* (1996) and of some sixty articles and essays on such topics as legitimation of legal order, radical/critical criminology, victimology, violence, and narrative jurisprudence. Currently he is editing a volume on state crime for the International Library of Criminology.

Michael Gottfredson is Professor of Management and Policy, Law, and Sociology at the University of Arizona. Professor Gottfredson has coauthored (with Travis Hirschi) *A General Theory of Crime* (1990), and coedited *The Generality of Deviance* (1994). He has also published (with Don Gottfredson) *Decisionmaking in Criminal Justice* (1988).

John M. Hagedorn is Assistant Professor of Criminal Justice at the University of Illinois-Chicago. He has been the Principal Investigator of a five-year National Institute on Drug Abuse study of patterns of drug use and the structure of drug dealing among inner-city gangs. He is the author of *People and Folks: Gangs, Crime, and the Underclass in a Rustbelt City* (1988), and *Forsaking Our Children: Bureaucracy and Reform in the Child Welfare System* (1995).

John E. Hamlin is an Associate Dean of the College of Liberal Arts at the University of Minnesota-Duluth. His criminological research interests include social control, rape, and criminological theory. He is currently working on a delinquency text with Nick Tilley.

Stuart Henry is Professor of Sociology and Criminology at Eastern Michigan University. He has authored or edited fifteen books, most recently (with Werner Einstadter) *Criminological Theory: An Analysis of Its Underlying Assumptions* (1995), and (with Dragan Milovanovic) *Constitutive Criminology: Beyond Postmodernism* (1996). His introductory criminology text (with Mark Lanier) entitled *Essential Criminology* is being published in 1997.

Travis Hirschi is Regents Professor of Sociology at the University of Arizona. He is author of the classic work on control theory, *Causes of Delinquency* (1969). He coauthored (with Michael Gottfredson) *A General Theory of Crime* (1990), and (with Hanan Selvin) *Delinquency Research: An Appraisal of Analytic Methods* (1967, 1996) and coedited (with Michael Gottfredson) *The Generality of Deviance* (1994).

Richard C. Hollinger is Associate Professor of Sociology at the University of Florida and holds a joint appointment in the Center for Studies in Criminology and Law. He is the author (with J. P. Clark) of *Theft by Employees* (1983). His research has focused on various forms of occupational crime and deviance in the workplace. He has recently edited *Crime, Deviance and the Computer* (1997).

Robert F. Krueger is a postdoctoral fellow at the University of Wisconsin, Madison. His research focuses on personality and psychopathology.

Lonn Lanza-Kaduce is an Associate Professor of Sociology at the University of Florida. He also holds a joint appointment in the Center for Studies in Criminology and Law. His recent research has examined the phenomenon of drunken driving, police-citizen encounters, and juvenile justice policies, especially those related to transfer to adult court.

John H. Laub is Professor in the College of Criminal Justice at Northeastern University and Visiting Scholar at the Henry A. Murray Research Center of Radcliffe College. He is former editor of the *Journal of Quantitative Criminology*. His research interests include theories of crime and deviance over the life course, juvenile justice, and the history of criminology. He is the coauthor (with Robert J. Sampson) of *Crime in the Making: Pathways and Turning Points Through Life* (1993) which received the **Michael J. Hindelang Book Award from the American Society of Criminology**, the **Outstanding Book Award from the Academy of Criminal Justice Sciences**, and the **Distinguished Scholar Award from the American Sociological Association's Crime, Law, and Deviance Section**.

Daniel Maier-Katkin is Professor and Dean of the School of Criminology and Criminal Justice at Florida State University. In 1991, he was a Fulbright Fellow and Visiting Professor at the Institute of Psychiatry, University of London. That work and several of his published articles have focused on infanticide and, particularly, the murder of young children by their mothers.

Dario Melossi teaches criminology at the School of Law at the University of Bologna, Italy, after a long period in the United States doing research and teaching at various campuses of the University of California. He is a coauthor of *The Prison and the Factory* (1977), and author of *The State of Social Control* (1990). He has published many articles on the theory of law, the state, and social control. His latest research focuses on the current building of a European polity, with particular attention to issues of social control and social exclusion.

Dragan Milovanovic is a Professor of Criminal Justice in the Department of Criminal Justice, Sociology and Social Work at Northeastern Illinois University. He has published fourteen books as well as over one hundred other articles. His latest books include: *Postmodern Criminology* (1997) and (with Stuart Henry) *Constitutive Criminology* (1996). He also edited

Legality and Illegality: Semiotics, Postmodernism and Law (1995), (with Marty Schwartz) *Intersections of Gender, Race, and Class in Criminology* (1996), and (with Brian MacLean) *Thinking Critically About Crime* (1997). He is the past editor of *Humanity and Society, The Journal of Human Justice*, and *The Critical Criminologist*. In 1993 he received the **Distinguished Achievement Award from the Division on Critical Criminology of the American Society of Criminology.**

Terrie E. Moffitt is Professor of Psychology and H. I. Romnes Faculty Fellow at the University of Wisconsin, Madison. She received the **1993 Distinguished Scientific Award** for Early Career Contribution to Psychology from the American Psychological Association. She coedited (with S. A. Mednick and Steven Stack) *Biological Contributions to Crime Causation* (1987).

Robbin S. Ogle is Assistant Professor of Criminal Justice at the University of Nebraska at Omaha. She has authored four articles on women and homicidal behavior and several pieces on organizational perspectives on corrections. She is currently completing an article on changes to self-defense law for use by battered women who kill their abusers, based on her theory of female homicidal behavior.

Nicole Hahn Rafter, a Professor of Criminal Justice at Northeastern University, has published books on prison history, gender and criminal justice, international developments in criminology and eugenics. Her latest work, *Creating Born Criminals* (1997), is a social history of biological theories of crime. In addition she is writing books on crime films and on mobbing, the phenomenon of ganging, and group terrorism.

Joseph H. Rankin is Professor of Sociology and Head of the Department of Sociology, Anthropology and Criminology at Eastern Michigan University. His research interests include the etiological study of delinquency and behavioral problems in children, especially as they relate to the family. He is currently completing a book (with Edward Wells) on families and crime.

Gary E. Reed is a Ph.D. candidate in Sociology at Boston University. He is currently pursuing his dissertation research on the connections between management training and corporate deviance. His areas of interest include law and society, environmental crime, and white-collar crime.

John Rosecrance was Assistant Professor in the Department of Criminal Justice at the University of Nevada, Reno, prior to a permanently disabling accident. He conducted many investigations into judicial decision making, probation and parole systems, and gambling behavior. During Dr. Rosecrance's brief career he published more than thirty five journal articles and two books: *The Degenerates of Lake Tahoe: A Study of Persistence in the Social World of Horse Race Gambling* (1985) and *Gambling without Guilt* (1988). At the time of his accident Dr. Rosecrance was revising a completed manuscript on probation and parole. He resides at home with his wife in Santa Barbara, California.

Robert J. Sampson is Professor of Sociology at the University of Chicago and Research Associate at the Ogburn-Stouffer Center for the Study of Social Organization. He is the coauthor (with John H. Laub) of *Crime in the Making: Pathways and Turning Points Through Life* (1993), which received the **Michael J. Hindelang Book Award from the American Society of Criminology**, the **Outstanding Book Award from the Academy of Criminal Justice Sciences**, and the **Distinguished Scholar Award from the American Sociological Association's Crime, Law, and Deviance Section**. A 1996 article (with John Laub), "Socioeconomic Achievement in the Life Course of Disadvantaged Men: Military Service as Turning Point, circa 1940–1965" appeared in the *American Sociological Review*.

Pamela S. Schmutte is a graduate student in developmental psychology at the University of Wisconsin, Madison. Her current research focuses on psychological well-being.

Martin D. Schwartz is Professor of Sociology at Ohio University, and a former **President of the Association for Humanist Sociology**. The author and editor of seven books and some sixty research articles or chapters, Professor Schwartz has published mainly in the area of violence against women. Most recently he authored (with Walter DeKeseredy) *Contemporary Criminology* (1996), and *Sexual Assault on the College Campus: The Role of Male Peer Support* (1997), and (with Lawrence F. Travis) *Corrections: An Issues Approach*, 4th ed. (1997). In addition he has edited (with Dragan Milovanovic) *Race, Class and Gender: The Intersections* (1996), and *Researching Sexual Violence Against Women* (1997).

Phil A. Silva is Director of the Dunedin Multidisciplinary Health and Development Research Unit and a Research Fellow of the New Zealand Health Research Council. He received the **Order of the British Empire** in 1994 for his contributions to the study of children's health and development.

Jonathan Simon is Professor in the School of Law at the University of Miami. During 1996–97 he was Visiting Professor of Law at New York University and during 1997–98, will be Visiting Professor of Law at Yale Law School. His articles have appeared in *Law & Society Review* and *Law and Social Enquiry,* and other journals. His book *Poor Discipline: Parole and the Social Control of the Underclass: 1890–1900* (1993) received the **Distinguished Book Award, given by the American Sociological Association**. His latest research is on governance through crime.

Sally S. Simpson is an Associate Professor of Criminology and Criminal Justice and Graduate Director at the University of Maryland, College Park. Her research interests include corporate crime and gender, race, class and crime intersections. She is the author of over twenty publications, including *Why Corporations Obey the Law* (1997). She also serves as the **Executive Secretary** of the **American Society of Criminology**.

Rodney Stark is Professor of Sociology and Comparative Religion at the University of Washington. He is the author or coauthor of eighteen books and more than one hundred papers, primarily in the areas of religion, crime, and deviance. His most recent books include *The Rise of Christianity* (1996) and (with William Sims Bainbridge) *Religion, Deviance, and Social Control* (1997).

Magda Stouthamer-Loeber is Associate Professor of Psychiatry and Psychology at the University of Pittsburgh. She is Co-Director of the Pittsburgh Youth Study. She coauthored (with W. B. van Kammen) *Data Collection and Management: A Practical Guide* (1994).

Andrew Szasz is an Associate Professor in the Department of Sociology at the University of California, Santa Cruz. Professor Szasz has published articles on regulation, worker safety and health, hazardous waste policy, and the toxics movement. His book, *Ecopopulism: Toxic Waste and the Movement for Environmental Justice,* won the **Association for Humanistic Sociology's** book award for 1994–95. Currently he is doing research on the environmental aspects of social inequality.

Terence P. Thornberry is a Professor at the School of Criminal Justice, University at Albany, SUNY. His books include *From Boy to Man—From Delinquency to Crime: Follow-up to the Philadelphia Cohort of 1945* (1987) and *Developmental Theories of Crime and Delinquency* (1997). His current research interests focus on developing and testing an interactional theory of delinquency and crime. He is the Director of the Rochester Youth Development Study.

Bryan Vila is Associate Professor in the Administration of Justice Program in the Department of Political Science at the University of Wyoming. His primary research interests include criminology theory development, interdisciplinary research, and police performance. Before becoming an academic, Dr. Vila—who has a Ph.D. in ecology—spent seventeen years in law enforcement: nine years as an urban street cop and supervisor in Los Angeles, six years as a police chief helping the emerging nations of Micronesia develop innovative law enforcement strategies, and two years in federal law enforcement. Recent publications include (with Cynthia Morris) *Capital Punishment in the United States: A Documentary History* (1997), and articles on nurturant crime control strategies, police performance, and (with Lawrence Cohen) "Crime as Strategy: Testing an Evolutionary Ecological Theory of Expropriative Crime" (1993).

L. Edward Wells is Professor of Criminal Justice, Illinois State University. His research interests include social-psychological models of delinquency and crime, juvenile victimization, and family factors as they relate to delinquency and rural criminal justice. He is coauthor (with R. Weisheit and D. Falcone) of *Rural Crime and Rural Policing* (1994). Professor Wells is currently completing a book (with Joseph Rankin) on families and crime.

Peter Cleary Yeager is Associate Professor in the Department of Sociology at Boston University. He has published research in the areas of corporate lawbreaking, environmental law, and ethics in corporate management. His books include the classic (with Marshall Clinard) *Corporate Crime* (1980), and, most recently, *The Limits of Law: The Public Regulation of Private Pollution* (1991).

Introduction: Criminology and Criminological Theory

Stuart Henry and Werner Einstadter

Criminology has been defined as the "systematic study of the nature, extent, etiology, and control of law-breaking behavior" (Henry, 1996:236). Its subject matter "seeks to establish empirical knowledge about crime and its control, based on qualitative and quantitative research that forms a basis for understanding, explanation, prediction, prevention, and criminal justice policy" (1996:236).

Since the term "criminology" was first coined by the Italian Raffaele Garofalo in 1885, controversy has surrounded its content and scope: Is the subject scientific? Is it an autonomous discipline? Is it value-neutral? Can its applied approach, driven by the desire to control crime, ever be considered critical? Answers to these questions have been complicated by criminology's disciplinary fragmentation, its relative failure to recommend effective crime reduction policies, its not uncommon support for policies that inflict harm, and its reliance on government for funding.

The core components of criminology include:

(1) definition and nature of crime as harm-causing behavior;
(2) descriptions and classification of different types of criminal activity, from conventional crimes of property theft and personal violence to corporate and government crime;
(3) statistical analysis of the extent, incidence, patterning, and cost of crimes, including estimates of hidden or unreported crime, based on surveys of victims and self-report studies of offenders;
(4) profiles of typical victims and offenders, including corporate law violators; and
(5) analysis of crime causation.

1

Less agreement exists about whether the subject of criminology should also include victimology, the sociology of law, criminal justice, and penology. In the United States the inclusive term "criminal justice" generally refers to studies of the crime control practices, philosophies, and policies used by police, courts, and corrections. This collection of articles focuses on the fifth aspect of the criminological enterprise, the analysis of crime causation. It examines the range of theoretical explanations about why people commit crime. As such it involves us thinking seriously and clearly about crime. A necessary precursor to thinking seriously about crime is to go beyond the limits of commonsense and popular cultural views of crime and criminals.

Debunking Commonsense Myths about Crime and Criminals

Theorizing in criminology is an arduous and beguiling task. Perhaps more than any other phenomenon, the subject matter of crime is engulfed by myths that abound in popular explanation. Myths are typically based on media and political exaggerations and distortions of single incidents that come to represent whole categories of events or types of people (Cohen and Young, 1980; Surette, 1992; Barak, 1994). Often they involve gross omissions and stereotypical classifications based on simple differences. For example, African American males commit most violent crimes, only if we leave out corporate violence, domestic violence, and abuse by white males; young people commit most property crime, only if we omit occupational crimes in the workplace by mature adults; theft is financed by fences, only if we exclude consideration of the "bargains" purchased by legitimate businesses; Japan has a low crime rate only if we ignore its government's corruption, corporate bribery, and its patriarchal abuse of women; organized crime is responsible for drug trafficking only if we forget that money laundering requires the complicity of "legitimate" business and that hidden governments have used drug trading to finance covert foreign military adventures. Typically such myths are loaded with moral clarity *only* by allocating pure doses of good and bad to individuals, groups, and social types. As soon as we appreciate the spectrum of grays between the polar opposites of "black" and "white," myths begin to dissolve.

Thus it is not the case that the majority are honest and a minority are dishonest, but that the majority are somewhat dishonest. To put it more concretely, in the example of fencing, "it is not the case that one species of actor, 'the fence,' buys stolen goods, whereas another 'the businessperson' buys legitimate ones . . . [but] that businesspersons buy cheap goods in order that they may sell at a profit; a greater or lesser proportion of their purchases may be illicit" (Henry, 1977:133). Myths about crime must be overcome and some have attempted to debunk them (Pepinsky and Jesilow 1984; Kappeler, Blumberg, and Potter, 1993; Bohm and Haley, 1996). It is here that carefully crafted theory can provide considerable insight. Debunking myths, as a prelude to why criminological theories are important, can unlock an Aladdin's cave of insight and understanding about why people harm others through criminal acts. However, even when criminologists go beyond the taken for granted and popular accounts they often do not agree about which explanation is correct. Part of their disagreement arises out of the diverse disciplinary roots of academic criminology.

Criminological Theory as a Multidisciplinary Social Science

Criminology is a multidisciplinary social science. It uses explanatory frameworks derived from a variety of other disciplines in its attempt to explain crime and criminality. In particular it draws from economics, philosophy, biology, genetics, psychiatry, psychology, anthropology, geography, sociology, political science, history, and linguistics (Einstadter and Henry, 1995:26). Each of these different disciplines contributes its own domain assumptions, theories, and methods to the study of crime. In so doing, criminology displays a healthy tension between "competitive isolation," whereby different theories compete for criminological attention and empirical validity, and "synthetic integration," in which one or more disciplines are merged into new and superior theoretical frameworks (Messner et al., 1989; Bernard and Snipes, 1996).

A continuing source of controversy is criminology's disciplinary integrity: whether together its diverse theoretical perspectives constitute an independent academic discipline, whether they are merely subfields or special applications of established disciplines, or whether criminology is interdisciplinary. If interdisciplinarity is understood to be the integration of knowledge into a distinct whole, then criminology is not yet interdisciplinary. In spite of recent attempts to shift the emphasis toward a more integrated model (Messner et al., 1989; Barak, 1998), the predominant tendency of contemporary theory is toward *limited* integration. Indeed, criminology still shows a "considerable indifference and healthy skepticism toward theoretical integration" (Akers, 1994:195). However, there is sufficient independence of the subject from its constituent disciplines, and an eclectic accommodation to the diversity of their different contributions, to prevent criminology from being subsumed under any one of them. For this reason criminology is best defined as *multidisciplinary with limited integration*.

Part of the reason for its multidisciplinary nature is that unlike the physical sciences, criminology does not bury its theoretical corpses; it warms them over and revives them. Dominant perspectives are never completely replaced as empirical evidence points to newer and more trenchant ways of explaining accumulated anomalies (Kuhn, 1970). Rather, older perspectives often provide the underlying assumptions for newer emerging ones. Thus, for example, eighteenth-century classical theory's rational economic assumptions are incorporated into twentieth-century social control, rational choice, and routine activities theory; 1960s labeling and symbolic interactionism are incorporated into 1980s social constructionism, which itself is embodied in some forms of feminist and postmodern explanations. This is not meant as criticism but to point out that criminology is a dynamic unfolding discourse of explanatory frameworks.

At present there is no overriding theory that explains the phenomenon of crime in all its myriad shapes and guises. Certain theorists with a penchant for the term "general," have claimed such ability for their theoretical constructions (Gottfredson and Hirschi, 1990; Agnew, 1992; Vila, 1994). Some have tried to explain all crime with their insistence on the centrality of particular concepts, such as "social control" (Gibbs, 1989). Others have attempted to do so through "theoretical absorption," rendering their theory ever free from "hostile takeover" (Akers, 1994:186). Others object that it is premature to label the search for generality futile (Tittle, 1985). As the diversity of essays in this collection reveal, there is considerable dispute and controversy concerning claims toward both integration and generality.

Nor should we be surprised by criminology's inner conflicts. Criminology deals with an ambiguous subject matter, diverse behavior, and nothing if not difference. Once it is acknowledged that crime is a legal concept imposed on behavior rather than deriving from it, and that segments of the population are socially differently constituted as young, old, men, women, African American, Hispanic, "baby boomers," "late bloomers," "yuppies," "buppies," and Generation X, then it is perhaps overly ambitious, if not naive, to imagine such "general" explanatory potency. Just because laws define behavior as harmful does not mean those engaged in various forms of harm creation are similarly motivated, or subject to similar conditions or circumstances. Even if some mainstream criminologists argue that "slight differences" in crimes or criminality can be ignored for the purposes of theory construction (Tittle, 1985), others, notably some feminists and critical theorists, disagree. Perhaps some theories are better at providing an approach to a clearer understanding of certain facets of crime and criminal activity than others, and this collection strongly reveals such differential explanatory power. For such reasons we might agree with Gibbons (1994:196–97) that "progress toward more powerful etiological formulations lies in the direction of theories tied to, or focused upon specific forms of lawbreaking" and that to explain lawbreaking in all its forms, the criminological enterprise is better served by "the more modest goal of developing a 'family of theories'." Indeed, the history of criminological thought has seen this family grow and become very extended.

The Scope and Diversity of Criminological Theories

Criminology has shifted its emphasis from the search for a single cause of crime, common in the nineteenth century, to a recognition that crime is the outcome of multiple causes, either in combination or interaction, to the view held by recent postmodernist criminologists that crime may not be caused as coproduced by the interrelationship of society's component parts with its totality, and that the search for crime causation is futile. Equally problematic is the question of whether criminology should be based on one general theory of human behavior or several. From its economically rooted origins in the eighteenth-century Enlightenment philosophy of Cesare Beccaria (1735–95) and Jeremy Bentham (1748–1832), through the early anthropological and bio-psychiatric formulations of Italian School foundationalists Cesare Lombroso (1835–1909), Raffaele Garofalo (1852–1934), and Enrico Ferri (1856–1928), and on into its Freudian-influenced early-twentieth-century psychoanalytical period, criminology has been characterized by both theoretical dominance and disciplinary diversity. Having shared the biologically based "positivistic" ground, early American criminal anthropologists such as Arthur MacDonald (1893), Charles Henderson (1893), and Henry Boies (1893, 1901), and constitutional theorists such as Ernest Hooton (1939a, 1939b), and William Sheldon (Sheldon et al., 1940, 1949) were displaced, first in the early twentieth century by psycho-analytical personality theories of delinquency (Healy and Bronner, 1926; Aichhorn, 1935; Abrahamsen, 1944; Friedlander, 1947), and in the mid-twentieth century by the sociological approach, heralded by the Chicago school's cultural ecology, reflected in the 1940s work of Clifford Shaw and Henry McKay (1942).

Chicago school sociologists, inspired by nineteenth-century French Cartographic School statisticians Adolphe Quetelet (1831) and Andre Guerry (1833), showed that biological explanations alone could not account for why certain geographical areas of a city showed consistent patterns of crime, even when their populations changed.

By the 1940s and 1950s a variety of sociological theories of criminal behavior emerged. These ranged from the Durkheimian-influenced structural-functional sociology of Robert Merton's (1938) "strain" or "anomie" theory, which saw crime as an illegitimate response to the unequal distribution of resources, through Edwin Sutherland (1939) and Donald Cressey's (Sutherland and Cressey, 1955) social learning theory of "differential association," Thorsten Sellin's (1938) culture conflict theory, and the many subcultural theories of delinquency such as those by Albert Cohen (1955), and Richard Cloward and Lloyd Ohlin (1960).

In different ways these sociological explanations demonstrate that crime was more than simply individual choices governed by the pain and pleasure principle, as early classicists had allegedly asserted, and was more than could be explained by individual differences in biology or personality, as the early positivists had claimed. Crime was shown to be shaped by sociocultural, structural, and organizational forces.

The predominance of structural and cultural explanations in American criminology began to be challenged in the 1960s by socio-psychological influences emphasizing active social processes over both deterministic structures and internal forces. From its roots in Gabriel Tarde's (1886) "imitation theory," Albert Bandura (1973, 1977) established "social learning" as a major explanatory framework for violence. This went beyond the simplistic and mechanistic "operant conditioning" model of B. F. Skinner (1953) and superseded the criminal personality theory of Hans Eysenck (1964; Eysenck and Gudjonsson, 1989), and Samuel Yochelson and Stanton Samenow's (1976, 1977; Samenow, 1984) "criminal thinking patterns" theory. In criminology, Ronald Akers (1985) has done the most to develop this social learning approach by integrating ideas from psychology with Sutherland's principles of differential association.

Theories locating the cause of crime in a lack of intelligence or in insanity were further undermined by the neutralization and control theories of David Matza (1964) and Travis Hirschi (1969). They convinced criminologists that socialization processes or their negation could be important enough to free any ordinary citizen from moral and legal conformity, and extensions of control theory have been the most empirically tested in the discipline.

Less proven but no less influential on 1970s American criminology was the labeling theorist's idea that crime was actually made worse by criminal justice agencies' attempts to control it through the dramatic negative effect the system could have on individual self-identities. The "new deviancy theory," as the labeling perspectives of Howard Becker (1963), Edwin Schur (1965, 1971, 1980), Erving Goffman (1959, 1963), and Thomas Scheff (1966) were called, showed how criminal and deviant careers were shaped progressively over time. It was not long before conflict, radical, and critical criminology, reflected in the works of Austin Turk (1966, 1969), William Chambliss (1964, 1975b; Chambliss and

Seidman, 1971), Richard Quinney (1973, 1977), Ian Taylor, Paul Walton, and Jock Young (1973, 1975), were building on the early Marxist ideas of Willem Bonger (1916) to suggest that it was not just agents of government that caused additional unnecessary crime but the whole capitalist system which was "criminogenic." This "new criminology" argued that powerful social classes, and even the capitalist state, were committing more and worse crimes through corporate pollution, faulty product manufacture, bribery, fraud, and corruption, while punishing the less powerful for expressing their resistance to the system, albeit through property and violent crimes against society.

By the 1980s and into the 1990s it had become clear that not only was the merit in these ideas limited, especially in their romantic call for socialism as the solution to the crime problem, but that criminology was uncertain about any of its particular theories, at least not certain enough to discount any one of them. The result was new research, new theoretical developments, and new empirical studies testing the whole range of theories and resurrecting and revising those previously discarded. Even radical theories were no longer uniformly radical, but more self-critical, separating under the weight of feminist, anarchist, realist, and postmodernist criticism into a variety of "constitutive criminologies." Indeed, some leading feminist criminologists such as Carol Smart (1990) and humanist criminologists such as Harold Pepinsky (1991) and Stanley Cohen (1988) even questioned the value of academic criminology as a professional enterprise.

In spite of such calls, the decade 1986–96, covered by this book, bears witness to the continued vibrancy of criminological theory, as new turns are made to old explanations and fresh ideas burst forth. Classical theory has been expanded into rational and situational choice theory through the works of Ronald Clarke and Derek Cornish (Cornish and Clark, 1986a, 1987). Similar rational choice assumptions about human nature have been adopted by Michael Gottfredson and Travis Hirschi (1990) in their development of a general theory of crime; yet they also recognize the importance of self-control through family socialization. Rational choice has also been merged into a routine activities ecology theory by Marcus Felson (1987; Clarke and Felson, 1993; Felson and Cohen, 1980), although the implied shift toward a risk-managed society has been criticized by Malcolm Feeley and Jonathan Simon (1992).

Merging and integrating are central themes that permeate the new criminologies of the past decade, as the seemingly contradictory assumptions of rational choice, biological predispositions, and personality traits have been combined with other behavioral and social science by James Q. Wilson and Richard Herrnstein (1985), and some of these principles have informed Robert Agnew's (1992) revised strain theory.

Social ecology and social disorganization have also been revisited and reinvigorated through the work of Rodney Stark (1987) and Robert Bursik (1988a, 1988b), and communities have again become a main focus of criminological attention by Robert Sampson (1987a; Sampson and Groves, 1989) who, with John Laub (Laub and Sampson, 1993; Sampson and Laub, 1993), also gave birth to a new integrated approach examining turning points in the life course. Critical and feminist ideas have fought for a place within this rejuvenated mainstream criminology, and through the works of William Chambliss (1975b; 1979; 1988a), Meda Chesney-Lind (1989), Kathleen Daly (1990, 1992, 1994; Daly and Chesney-Lind, 1988), Sally Simpson (1989, 1991), John Hagan (1989b; Hagan et al., 1985), and James Messerschmidt (1986, 1993, 1997), have gone beyond simple class conflict to consider the interrelationships between class, gender, race, and ethnicity. These multiple dimensions of stratification are now seen as critical forces in shaping crime and criminal justice. Going beyond interactionist and labeling theory via social constructionist and postmodernist turns, Stuart Henry and Dragan Milovanovic (1991, 1994, 1996) have begun to focus on the central role of power and difference through their constitutive theory of crime. And once again, the explorations in integration of those like Delbert Elliott (Elliott et al., 1979, 1985), Terence Thornberry (1987b), and most recently, Brian Vila (1994) and Gregg Barak (1998), reassert the importance of taking a holistic approach to the study of crime and criminality.

Criminological Theory, Historical Context, and Criminal Justice Policy

Clarifying the nature of crime as harm, analyzing the causes of harm creation, and recognizing the variety of interrelated influences on and directions of criminological thought is of the greatest importance, for criminological theories have implications for social policy designed to deal with crime. Thus the stance of a particular theoretical emphasis has practical consequences for theory-based policy. Obviously, if a theory suggests that crime is caused by the interaction of genes and environment, then a logical policy would be to confine the potential criminal before he/she can cause any harm or find a means to either alter the genes, compensate for them through learning new behaviors, or restrict the kind of environment to those where criminal behavior ceases to become manifest. If, however, crime is found to be the result of poverty and relative deprivation, then policies that affect the just distribution of goods are more logical than those dabbling with genes. Unfortunately, the connection between criminological theory and policy is never that simple.

Theories are not constructed in a vacuum but are developed in a historical and political context. They reflect the confluence of the ideologies of their time. These are embedded in various schools of thought or approaches which become the dominant frameworks of logic in building theoretical statements at a particular historical period. Certain forms of explanation achieve greater popularity or become more fashionable than others. This means that while theories may have social policy implications, they have no chance of implementation unless they have political currency. The sociopolitical context sets limits on theoretical potential. For example, the recent policy of "three strikes," a simplistic notion based upon a baseball metaphor that has a "getting tough" sound of locking up repeat offenders for long periods of time, has gained popularity even though it has little, if any, effect on rates of crime. The policy is based on the belief that hard punishment deters crime. What is overlooked is that punishment, its perception, and its use and implementation are parts of a complicated process of social control that may have unexpected outcomes. Indeed, most contemporary criminal justice policy continues to be based on such ideas as "getting tough," "need for more police," "longer sentences," "boot camps," and "punk prison." These catch phrases and their accompanying "sound bites" may have political appeal but lack theoretical relevance. However, they are acceptable in a conservative political climate.

This does not imply that theories never challenge existing conditions and approaches dealing with crime. Indeed they do. It only means that they are not given credence unless the historical moment can provide the appropriate social nutrient. Consider the 1970s calls for decentralized community justice (Danzig, 1973; Fisher, 1975). These became policy possibilities in the 1980s not because of the inherent logic of humane justice, but because of the fiscal crisis of the state and the perceived need to cut the costs of institutional incarceration (Abel, 1982). Typically policy makers seek theoretical justification for short-term policies based on false assumptions designed more to appease the voting public than on long-term solutions tailored to deal with the problem.

Nevertheless, it would be a mistake to think that theory and policy are isolated from one another. Both influence and are interactive with one another, as several of the contributors to this volume demonstrate. Indeed, Lilly, Cullen, and Ball (1989:14) warn us not to decontexualize criminological theory, for "changes in theory that undergird changes in policy are themselves a product of transformations in society. . . . [E]xplanations of crime are intimately linked to social context . . . . [It is] only when shifts in society occur that theoretical models gain or lose credence and in turn, gain or lose the ability to justify a range of criminal justice policies." The central importance of theory to an understanding of crime and crime control through criminal justice policy is crucial and must be understood by all those entering the profession, whether as criminologists, researchers, or practitioners.

The Profession of Criminology and Resources for Further Study

A criminologist is someone whose professional training and occupation focus on the study of crime and its control, and whose primary income derives from that activity. Criminologists use a variety of methods of research to study crime, including documentary records, surveys, interviews, direct observation, ethnography, and experimentation.

In the United States there are over 1,000 academic programs in criminology or criminal justice, over 100 graduate programs, and 22 doctorates in criminology. Over 3,000 professional criminologists are employed by universities, research institutes, and by government and private agencies. Academic criminology is served by two professional societies: The **American Society of Criminology (ASC)** has over 2,600 members, two-thirds of whom are also members of the other professional association the **Academy of Criminal Justice Sciences (ACJS)**, which has over 3,200 members, including 600 student-members. Both hold annual conferences and have special topic area divisions. The ASC publishes the journal *Criminology*, which tends to publish theoretical and empirical articles about crime. The ACJS publishes the journal *Justice Quarterly* which tends to publish articles about criminal justice. However, their overlapping membership is reflected in these journals' interwoven interests and concerns and each makes regular forays into the other's domain. In addition to these journals, criminologists publish their work in numerous other professional journals, including *Crime and Delinquency, The Journal of Research on Crime and Delinquency, Social Problems, The Journal of Criminal Law and Criminology, Deviant Behavior, Law and Society Review, Social Justice, Crime, Law and Social Change, Theoretical Criminology,* and *Critical Criminology*.

Apart from pursuing higher education and becoming a professional or academic criminologist, undergraduates training in criminology and criminal justice in the United States are no longer restricted to law enforcement corrections, probation, and parole. Nowadays they typically go on to work as practitioners in a range of diverse settings such as loss prevention, corporate security, legal research, human services, substance abuse counseling, domestic violence counseling, and the numerous federal and state enforcement positions and regulatory agencies, including immigration, food and drug inspection, fraud investigation, wildlife conservation, alcohol, tobacco, and firearms investigation, as well as the more familiar FBI. Guides to criminal justice careers for college graduates include: DeLucia and Doyle's (1994) *Career Planning and Criminal Justice*, and Henry's (1994) *Inside Jobs: A Realistic Guide to Criminal Justice Careers for College Graduates*.

The Readings in This Book

The readings in this anthology are organized according to the various theoretical groupings into which they fall. These are not hard and fast categories and it would have been possible to place some into other categories. However, as presented we believe they represent a sample of what is best in contemporary criminological theory. Before each of the eleven sections we shall briefly outline the course of development of the group of theories that the section represents. This is not presented wholly chronologically for, as we have already noted, criminological theories appear and reappear throughout the history of criminological thought. Thus what we describe here is designed simply to orient you as a student of criminology toward the representative selection of articles we have made and the structure of their presentation in this text. We have provided a detailed analysis of the content of each of these theoretical frameworks in *Criminological Theory: An Analysis of Its Underlying Assumptions* (Einstadter and Henry, 1995) and the overview presented at the beginning of each section is derived partly from this source.

The full complement of essays presented in this volume represents the sweep of the decade 1986–96 in criminological theoretical development as represented in the journal *Criminology*. Mirroring the content and direction of the sociohistorical period and the culture of the moment, some of the essays reflect a reversion to the past in attempts to reshape older theoretical statements to encompass modern trends. On the other hand, there are also bolder moves to understand the modern/postmodern condition by new formulations without totally abandoning those theoretical accounts that have lasting explanatory power.

A Note to Readers

Aside from the politics and personalities of *Criminology*'s editorship as outlined in Robert Bursik's Foreword to this book, as a student reading this volume you may get the impression that criminological theory is a complete and finished product. Not so. Although the articles selected here are tightly argued and cover a diversity of perspectives, they are the product of a long series of tough decisions, decisions that have shaped their content. These decisions are part of the making of criminological their content. These decisions are part of the making of criminological theory that begins when criminologists decide to submit their work to the journal. From here, the editor must decide which three criminologists across the nation are qualified to give an independent evaluative assessment of, among other things, the contribution the article makes to the field. The editor then selects some of these "peer reviewers" for their particular expertise, others for their general criminological knowledge, and yet others for their reputations at delivering timely evaluations. It is the rare criminologist who combines all three of these qualities! To eliminate bias, the reviews are done anonymously; neither author nor reviewer knows the identity of the other.

When the reviews are in (which can take four to six weeks), the editor sends the reviewer's comments back to the contributing author for his or her consideration. If the editor accepts the article, it is scheduled for production which includes copy editing, proofing, and printing, all of which can take up to a year. More typically, however, submitted articles are returned with a "revise and resubmit" request, or an outright rejection, with a suggestion of an alternative place that the author might send his or her article.

In the case of a revision request, the author must decide to which of the reviewer's comments (and these may fundamentally disagree!) he or she should respond, how best to do it, and even whether to go to the trouble. Criminologists' egos are notoriously sensitive to criticism and part of the editor's job is to mediate between reviewer and author. Indeed, in some cases authors have been known to take reviewer comments, revise the article, and send the improved version to another journal! Yet others may not even revise their article but send it to another journal, repeating that process until some journal accepts it "as is."

In the event that the article comes back to the same journal the editor sends it back to the original reviewers who must decide if the author's revisions have met their concerns. If satisfactory, the reviewer recommends acceptance; if not he or she may recommend further revisions, again at the risk of alienating the contributor. Some articles eventually go round this process two or three times before finally making the pages of the journal.

So what about the articles in this book? As we have already mentioned, they have been through additional stages of selection and editing. The result appearing here is, like criminology itself, a study of ideas in the making, a work in progress, and one that you are about to join as you select which articles to read, and which are more convincing. As you do so, think about the process we have just described, and put yourself in the author's place. How might you have developed these ideas differently? What would you add and what do you want to know more about? In doing this you will actively engage in the criminological enterprise, and participate in making criminology come alive. Perhaps one day you will develop your ideas to the point of submitting an article to *Criminology* and join the ranks of those reflected in this milestone of understanding of crime causation.

Classical and Rational Choice Theory

Introduction

Classical theory, rooted in the eighteenth-century Enlightenment philosophy of individual rights and free choice, was originally a radical reaction to pre-Enlightenment criminal justice policy and practice, seen by classical reformers as arbitrary, corrupt, harsh, and unjust. It valued the preservation of social order over the rights of individuals. Based on economic principles of costs and benefits, classical theory considers people free to choose criminal behavior; it is to be controlled by costs built into the criminal justice system. These costs or consequences were to be so structured as to be proportionate to the harm caused by the offense but only sufficient to deter future offending. The response of the system was to be swift and certain to be effective.

The principal advocates of classical theory, Cesare Beccaria (1735–95) and Jeremy Bentham (1748–1832), are represented here by Piers Beirne's (chap. 1) critical analysis of criminologists' representations of Beccaria's rational assumptions. Often lost in textbook simplifications that equate classical theory with free choice, Beirne alerts us to the causal force of feelings and sensations viewed as motivators by these prescientific criminologists. Beirne rejects the notion that Beccaria was a humanist as he has been often presented, and points instead to the influence of Scottish scientific determinism in his writing, undermining even the existence of a classical era in criminology and foreshadowing later positivistic assumptions in criminology.

In the twentieth century similar rational choice assumptions to those attributed to the classical era were rediscovered. This time they focused on situational opportunities to commit crime. The assumption was that pleasure-seeking, self-interested, rational humans make individual choices about their future behavior by weighing not only the consequences of criminal justice sanctions should they get caught, but also the barriers and costs in situations and circumstances of criminal opportunity. Thus rational and situational choice theory argues that by manipulating various factors in the environment it is possible to "harden targets" and reduce victimization. A closely related theory, also relying on rational choice assumptions, is routine activities theory. (See Ecology Section.)

A major problem for rational choice-based theory is the criticism, particularly from positivists, that if potential offenders are independently motivated, environmental manipulation and "target hardening" will simply displace the crime. For example, drug dealers displaced from street corners may move into crack houses to continue their crime. A defense against this argument is provided here by Derek Cornish and Ronald Clarke's (chap. 2) article. In addition to extending the application of rational choice theory to policies based on situational crime prevention through structuring criminal choices, the authors draw on evidence to demonstrate that, at least in the short- to medium-term, switching crimes or locations does not necessarily occur. They call for continued vigilance to frustrate the easy exercise of crime choice, simultaneously with the pursuit of long-term solutions to criminal motivation.

A far-reaching application of the classical rational choice assumption is made in the article by Travis Hirschi and Michael Gottfredson (chap. 3). Although known for his social control theory (see chap. 16), and more recently for their theory of self-control (Gottfredson and Hirschi, 1990), in this 1989 paper Hirschi and Gottfredson apply rational choice principles to white-collar crime, in their attempt to develop a general theory of crime. They argue that all crime is motivated by rational self-interest and they seek to demonstrate how patterns of white-collar crime have important features in common with ordinary crime. They argue that it is a mistake to assume that white-collar crime is different. They reject the claim by critical theorists that white collar crime exposes the false assumptions of traditional theory, arguing instead that its presence reinforces some of these early analyses and may be explained as any other form of criminality by their general theory principles. As shall be seen later (chap. 17), some have criticized this general theory, especially its applicability to corporate or organizational crime.

Inventing Criminology: The "Science of Man" in Cesare Beccaria's *Dei delitti e delle pene* (1764)

Piers Beirne

In previous work I have tried to uncover the process of concept formation in the early history of criminology (Beirne, 1987a, 1987b, 1988; Beirne and Hunt, 1990). I have argued that the conceptual and explanatory origins of positivist criminology cannot adequately be understood either as mere representations of the power relations peculiar to modernity or as unmediated expressions of the epistemological divisions wrought by state practices in the asylum, the clinic, and the prison. I have also argued that the key concepts and discursive techniques of positivist criminology did not develop as logical or even inevitable products of scientific development. Rather, they emerged within the domains of penality and the statistical movement, which, during the Restoration (1814–30) in France, coincided in the issue of the regulation of the "dangerous classes." Positivist criminology was originally a multifaceted nineteenth-century discourse based on economism, biologism, and mental hereditarianism; its chief objects ("criminal man," "criminality," and "criminal character") were demarcated by epistemological boundaries dividing the "normal" from the "pathological." By the term "positivist" criminology, I refer to a discourse about crime and criminality predicated on the belief that there is a fundamental harmony between the methods of the natural and the social sciences. This discourse views its observational categories as theory independent, and it can assume several forms, each of which can be more or less appropriate as a method of inquiry (Beirne, 1987a:1141n3).

Like most other scholars (e.g., Vold and Bernard, 1986:10–15), I have always uncritically assumed the truth of the hallowed distinction between positivist criminology and classical criminology, the dominant discourse about crime that preceded it. Classical criminology was a mid-

Edited and abridged from *Criminology*, Volume 29(4):777–820 (1991).

to late-eighteenth-century discourse couched in the rhetoric of classical jurisprudence; its chief object, as found in the works of Beccaria, Bentham, Romilly, and others, is held to have been the construction of a rational and efficient penal calculus directed to the actions of the volitional legal subject. Some scholars nowadays suggest that because concepts such as "crime," "criminal," and "criminality" were absent from their epistemological universe, classical criminologists such as Beccaria and his followers were not representative of a criminology of *homo criminalis* as such. Rather, because their concepts were directed to *homo penalis* their labors should be categorized as either "classical penology" or "administrative penology" or even "a theory of social control" —their work "is essentially the application of legal jurisprudence to the realm of crime and punishment, and it bears no relation to the 'human sciences' of the nineteenth century that were to form the basis of the criminological enterprise" (Garland, 1985:14–15; see Foucault, 1979:102; 1988; Pasquino, 1980:20–21; Taylor et al., 1973:2–3).

In this chapter, I reconsider the merits of Beccaria's key classical text *Dei delitti e delle pene (Of Crimes and Punishments*—henceforth, *Dei delitti*) of 1764. I do so not only because descriptions of classical criminology invariably focus on its author, the shy and enigmatic member of the Milanese patriciate Cesare Bonesana, Marchese di Beccaria (1738–94), but also because the discursive objects of Beccaria's famous treatise have been persistently misrepresented. First, I claim that in the past two hundred years the predominant images of *Dei delitti* have been constructed more in terms of its practico-juridical effects in Europe and colonial America than in terms of its actual discursive features. I argue, second, that the persistent misrepresentation of the arguments of *Dei delitti* is actively encouraged by the ambiguity of many of Beccaria's own positions and by the obscure and secretive style of much of his prose—common in the dangerous publishing conditions during much of the Enlightenment—making the nature and intended objects of Beccaria's discourse difficult to discern. Third, I demonstrate that the chief object of *Dei delitti* is the application to crime and penality of the "science of man," a deterministic discourse implicitly at odds with conventional assumptions about the exclusively humanist and volitional bases of "classical criminology." Thus, I fundamentally challenge the existing interpretations of the context and object of Beccaria's book and cast doubt on the very existence of a distinctive "classical criminology." It is a corollary of my argument that those modern-day criminologists who adhere to models of human agency based on "free will" and "rational choice" must look to some discourse other than Beccaria's to discover their intellectual ancestry.

Images of *Dei delitti*

The first copies of *Dei delitti* were printed in Livorno, Italy, and circulated anonymously in the summer of 1764. Beccaria's short treatise of 104 pages, written in just ten months at the suggestion of his friend and colleague Pietro Verri, was an instant and dazzling success. The first Italian edition was quickly followed by two others and then in 1765, a widely-read French translation. By 1800 there had been no less than twenty three Italian editions, fourteen French editions and eleven English editions (three printed in the United States). Clearly, Beccaria's proposals for the reform of criminal law appealed to a large cross section of educated society. His disciples included Gustavus III of Sweden, Catherine II of Russia, and Empress Maria Theresa of Austria; lawyers and legal philosophers in England like William Blackstone (1769; Beattie, 1986:555–57; Lieberman, 1989:209) and Jeremy Bentham (1776; Halevy, 1928:21; Hart, 1982:40–52); republican revolutionaries in colonial America such as Thomas Jefferson and John Adams (Wills, 1978:94; Kidder, 1870:232); and, most important, the *philosophes* in France. Among the *philosophes*, Beccaria's ideas were highly esteemed by such luminaries as d'Alembert, Diderot, Helvétius, Buffon, and Voltaire (whose glowing *Commentaire sur le livre des délits et des peines* was appended to Beccaria's text).

Although *Dei delitti* was received with rapture by a large majority of the *philosophes*, who unanimously endorsed Beccaria's humanitarianism, some disagreed with either the direction or extent of his specific proposals for reforming criminal law. Against Beccaria's reticence about the legality of suicide, for example, Voltaire explicitly denied that it was a crime. Against Beccaria's complete opposition to torture, Diderot and others argued that it was justified for the discovery of a guilty party's accomplices. Others protested Beccaria's absolute opposition to capital punishment. Moreover, according to the dour Melchior Grimm (1765a:424), Beccaria's proposals were "too geometrical," implying a narrow emphasis on probabilism and mathematics (see also Ramsay, n.d.:55). Worse still, among many jurists in Italy and France, *Dei delitti* immediately became an object of derision and scorn. Beccaria's novel ideas about torture, capital punishment, and equality before the law were condemned as highly dangerous and his book was condemned for its extreme rationalism and placed on the papal *Index Prohibitorum*, where it remained for almost two centuries.

Notwithstanding some later retributivist objections to Beccaria's utilitarianism voiced in Germany, the initial furor over *Dei delitti* gradually gave way to a stock of complacent assumptions about the intentions of its author, principally that the key ideas in *Dei delitti* can be understood in terms of their practical effects. An unmediated and necessary association is held typically to exist between Beccaria's intentions, formulated in his text, and their more or less successful appropriation for the eighteenth-century practice of criminal law and criminal justice. Since then, most, if not all, sociologists and historians of penology (e.g., Gorecki, 1985:67–68; Jones, 1986:33–57; Mueller, 1990) have read backward from the effects of the written word to Beccaria's intentions, assuming it was primarily a humanist project inspired by the French *philosophes* and motivated by the author's humanitarian opposition to the arbitrariness and barbaric cruelty of European criminal justice in the mid-eighteenth century. They also assumed it had as its chief objects the reform of judicial irrationality (including judicial torture and capital punishment) and the institution of a utilitarian approach to punishment based on a calculus of pleasure and pain. In concert, these assumptions have led to the conclusion that Beccaria was the founder of classical criminology (e.g., Matza, 1964:3, 13), marked as it is by a penal calculus based on the doctrine of the social contract and couched in the rhetoric of the free legal subject.

This has been challenged by recent studies that have attempted to scrutinize the ideological content of *Dei delitti*. Foucault (1979:73–103, 1988) has argued that neither Beccaria's classical criminology nor its effects were the projects of genuinely enlightened or humanitarian reform but were two among many artifacts peculiar to a new disciplinary power. Following Foucault, the radical pioneering role usually assigned Beccaria within classical criminology has been contradicted, and he has been viewed as allegedly far more conservative than other Enlightenment theorists because he deliberately equivocated on such dangerous issues as materialism and spiritualism (Jenkins, 1984; see also Roshier, 1989:16–18). Beccaria is held to have been a champion of aristocratic values that, in his native Lombardy, had been deeply penetrated by the ideology and interests of capitalist agriculture and the new bourgeoisie (Humphries and Greenberg, 1981:224). Beccaria's liberalism, it is claimed, responded to a fundamental difficulty of postfeudal societies: how to prevent the criminality of the masses while masking the fact that the criminal law preserved a class system based on social inequality? Beccaria's solution to this problem is portrayed as a popularization of the legal doctrine "equality before the law," a bourgeois fiction that, simply by doctrinal fiat, lodges criminal responsibility at the level of the individual (Weisser, 1979:133–38). Even Beccaria's intervention in judicial history has been dismissed as a fairy tale, his humanism ridiculed because he did not know that the process of abolishing judicial torture had already been initiated through a decisive transformation of the medieval law of proof (Chadwick, 1981:98; Langbein, 1976:67–68). His attempts to reform the criminal law have therefore been described as fundamental only to the myth of rational sentencing replacing arbitrary injustice (Hirst, 1986:152–55; see also Newman and Marongiu, 1990; Young, 1983).

Many of these assessments of the discourse in *Dei delitti* assume that Beccaria's arguments and ideological presuppositions can be understood more or less exclusively in terms of their manifest effects. Beccaria's intervention in criminal jurisprudence, for example, continues to be regarded as (1) "humanist" because it opposed the barbaric practices of the *ancien régime*, (2) as "revolutionary" because it was in the vanguard of the Italian Enlightenment in exposing religious intolerance, or (3) as "conservative" because it did not travel as far down the road of materialism as others undoubtedly did at that time.

Dei delitti, however, shares with many Enlightenment treatises a lack of clarity. I will suggest that the vivid humanism in the forty seven rambling chapters of *Dei delitti* masks some of Beccaria's other arguments. Accordingly, neither the structure nor the content of Beccaria's discourse should be taken at face value. To understand how and why this is so, something must be known of the conditions of production of *Dei delitti* as a text of the Enlightenment.

Reading *Dei delitti* as a Text of Enlightenment

A key feature of Italy's Enlightenment was how backward its practitioners believed it to be compared with that of other countries in Europe. "This backwardness was ascribed," Woolf (1979:75) has recorded, "to the stifling effects of the 'official' counter-reformist culture in Italy, to a conformist mentality which led to acquiescence in the teachings of churchmen and lawyers, an acceptance of scholasticism, superstition and curialism" (see also Gross, 1990:258). In matters of religion, science, politics, and economics, the intellectual universe of the *illuministi* was one in which transgressions of the permitted bounds of discourse invited more or less severe censure either from the papacy or from the tiny political cliques that ruled each state.

In Beccaria's Milan, the state of Lombardy was subject to the political and economic dominance of the enlightened Austro-Hapsburg ruler Maria Theresa. Under Austrian rule, various aspects of social life in Lombardy were somewhat more liberal than elsewhere in Italy. Maria Theresa had loosened the influence of the Church (Roberts, 1960:38) and her representative in Lombardy had enacted a variety of liberal inroads into social and intellectual life, including toleration of debate and discussion by reform-minded *illuministi*. Beccaria himself was a member of the Milanese *illuministi*. These were typically government officials who sought to create a model bourgeois society that combined spiritual and moral regeneration with and through the materialist advantages of economic growth. However, far from being simple "thermometers of bourgeois opinion," these Milanese reformers envisioned a well-ordered hierarchical society whose reconstruction would emanate from an enlightened state administration that, although working in alliance with such other powers as the papal administration, could dominate all other power blocs and would include all men of property and education (Klang, 1984:41–46). For the *illuministi*, the problem, both intellectual and organizational, was how this collective dream could be implemented.

This problem was the chief focus of a literary club of Milanese reformers with whom Beccaria mixed, whose members included the Verri brothers Pietro and Allesandro, the economist Gian Rinaldo Carli, the ecclesiastical law expert Alfonso Longo, and the mathematicians Paolo Frisi and Luigi Lambertenghi. In 1762 their ideas began to be published in their critical literary journal. Beccaria himself was undoubtedly motivated to join the club, and then to compose *Dei delitti*, by his discomfort with the lack of reforms in Lombardy in the domain of criminal law and the administration of justice and also with the continued burden of censorship of the written word. Throughout the Enlightenment, in Italy especially, its practitioners employed ubiquitous trickery to defeat the censor and the police and, in Beccaria's Lombardy, to avoid the prying eyes of the Inquisitorial Council of Ten and to avoid trouble (Maestro, 1942:54–55). Everyday ruses were devised simply to allow heretical, seditious, or egalitarian ideas to be transmitted to the reading public. As with *Dei delitti*, these included anonymous authorship, phoney places of publication, secret printing presses, and an underground network for the distribution and sale of books and pamphlets. Numerous other ploys were designed to cover the truth with a thin veil that would protect a text from hostile eyes (see Darnton, 1979, 1982).

Few works of Italian *illuminism* were able to escape such textual deformities, and the style and content of the arguments in *Dei delitti* suffered from them too. As a result, a serious difficulty in understanding the arguments of *Dei delitti* is that, like many other Enlightenment texts, it employed an array of devious textual practices which relied on the cautious dictum that it is better to be a secret witness of the Enlightenment than a posthumously acknowledged martyr. Thus, the stated objects of Beccaria's protestations in *Dei delitti* were not the despotic monarchies of contemporary Italy but those of the "state of nature" and classical Rome and Greece (1764:15, 45, 49, 53), and his angry remarks on religious intolerance are utterly devoid of clear temporal and empirical referents. Moreover, in what was more than simply a casual failure to document his sources, Beccaria's text is virtually bereft of intellectual bearings, which, had he openly pointed to them, would have allowed his readers the privilege of observing more clearly the precise mast to which he chose to nail his colors. Thus, Beccaria referred to no contemporary sources other than the general works of Hobbes and Montesquieu.

Enlightenment and Enlightenments

It is not easy to generalize about the eclectic ideas of that period from the middle of the seventeenth century to the last quarter of the eighteenth century dubbed "the Age of Enlightenment." It can perhaps be said that all members of the Enlightenment affirmed their belief in the principles of reason, the precision of the scientific method, and the authority of nature; but because there was enormous disagreement about each one of these beliefs, this says little of real substance. Moreover, there was not just one Enlightenment but several, and in France, Italy, Holland, Germany, Sweden, Russia, England, Scotland, colonial America, and elsewhere, there existed diverse and sometimes quite incompatible notions of the content and direction of enlightenment.

The objects in Beccaria's text reflected this diversity of opinion. As Beccaria himself suggested, it was in "the choice of expressions and the rapprochement of ideas" (1766:863) that the power of his text resided. His attempted rapprochement occurred with respect to two chief ideas which in concert testified to the fact that the belated Italian Enlightenment was unusually under the influence of foreign authors. One was the humanism of the French *philosophes*; the other was the largely unacknowledged influence of the embryonic "science of man" in Scotland.

The Humanism of the French Philosophes

Beccaria openly acknowledged his profound indebtedness to the humanist writings of the French *philosophes*, on one occasion claiming to "owe everything to French books" (1766:862), specifically to d'Alembert, Diderot, Helvétius, Buffon, and Hume (1766:864). Among the *philosophes*, it was Montesquieu (1748) who exerted the greatest influence, even though Montesquieu is full of misgivings and contradictions about the problem of free will and determinism.

The influence of the *philosophes* can with reasonable confidence be discerned in the spacious antechamber to Beccaria's edifice, and it is lavishly decorated with their humanist rhetoric. First, Beccaria inherited from Montesquieu a desire to disentangle and then sever criminal law and justice from religion. In arguing for the supremacy of the rule of law in human affairs, Beccaria thus rejected any claim that the laws that regulate social relationships derive from Divine Will. For him, it was imperative that sin be demarcated from crime, spiritual powers from temporal powers, and ecclesiastical bodies from secular courts. For Beccaria, crime—"I do not address myself to sins" (1764:73)—is not a theological concept but a social one. Thus, he wrote, "the true measure of crimes is . . . *the harm done to society*. This is one of the palpable truths which one needs neither quadrants nor telescopes to discover" (1764:17).

A second way in which French humanism was manifest in Beccaria's text lay in his rejection of the cruel physical pain inflicted by the judiciary on suspects and on convicted felons. He drew a stark contrast between "the indolence of the judge and the anguish of someone accused of a crime—between the comforts and pleasures of the unfeeling magistrate . . . and the tears and squalid condition of a prisoner" (1764:36). His strictures here were directed almost exclusively, however, at the practices of judicial torture and capital punishment. Thus, "the torture of the accused while his trial is still in progress is a cruel practice sanctioned by the usage of most nations" (1764:29). In a comment on the popular and crowd-pleasing manner of disposing of witches and heretics, Beccaria declared that "rational men" object to the distasteful spectacle of "the muffled, confused groans of poor wretches issuing out of vortices of black smoke—the smoke of human limbs—amid the crackling of charred bones and the sizzling of still palpitating entrails" (1764:72). Yet Beccaria (1764:48–49) argued that capital punishment is justified if (1) an incarcerated citizen is still a threat to society, (2) a citizen's mere existence could produce a revolution dangerous to the state, or (3) a citizen's execution deterred others from committing crimes. Elsewhere Beccaria confessed that he would deem himself fortunate if, "in the course of upholding the rights of men and invincible truth, I should contribute to saving an unhappy victim of tyranny or of equally pernicious ignorance from suffering and from the anguish of death, then the blessings and tears of that one person overcome with joy would console me for the contempt of all humanity" (1764:23).

Although it was a major impetus to the aims in Beccaria's text, the humanism of the *philosophes* was not at all the sole feature of its discourse. Indeed, at times Beccaria's humanism seems only an incidental feature that was grafted almost in ad hoc fashion to other, more significant arguments in *Dei delitti*. Although humanism asserted itself in elegant passages that disavow the physical brutality of criminal law and that adopt a charitable position bent on ameliorating economic inequality, the depth of its textual penetration must not be exaggerated. This is unremarkable, though, if only because the *philosophes* themselves did not often address in their own writings the issues of penality raised in *Dei delitti.* Even in the case of those *philosophes* who did address issues of criminal law and punishment, their textual structure resembled unkempt mazes rather than the systematic treatise of Beccaria.

The principal discursive inspiration behind Beccaria's treatise is to be found, I suggest, in the ideas of Enlightenment authors developed in Scotland.

The "Science of Man" in Scotland

I have suggested that, because the publishing conditions in Lombardy were so fraught with danger, Beccaria was forced to conceal some of the intellectual influences on *Dei delitti* and, moreover, some of the arguments within it. Nevertheless, with typical Enlightenment flourish, Beccaria attached to his text a deliberate clue of extraordinary significance for unlocking the aims of his work. Preceding the text, and prominently displayed on the frontispiece of each of the six editions of *Dei delitti* personally authorized by Beccaria, is an epigram (originally in Latin) from one of the first purveyors of Enlightenment ideas, Francis Bacon (1561–1626): "In all Negotiations of Difficulty, a Man may not look to sow and reap at once; But must Prepare Business, and so Ripen it by Degrees" (1632:283).

The placement of Bacon's epigram must be mentioned not least because of Beccaria's use of it as an introduction to his text. As an introduction, it directs the reader to another dimension of Enlightenment thinking, the powerful presence of which in *Dei delitti* has largely been overlooked (Wills, 1978:149–51) but which was, I suggest, its central thrust and one that Beccaria had very good reason to hide from Catholic censors. This is the drift toward a science of man that had been inaugurated by enlightened English philosophers such as Bacon himself, and by Newton and Shaftesbury, and after them by Locke. Later, it was developed even more forcefully in the civic tradition of Scottish authors such as Hutcheson, Hume, John Millar, Adam Ferguson, and Adam Smith. Indeed, in a letter of April 6, 1762, Pietro Verri described his young friend Beccaria as "a profound mathematician . . . with a mind apt to try new roads if laziness and discouragement do not suffocate him" (cited in Maestro, 1942:53). Given the virulent Anglomania that gripped the Italian devotees of the Enlightenment, it is only to be expected that Beccaria should have been compared with some English theorist. But it is most interesting that the comparison was not with a legal reformer, such as William Blackstone, but with the great scientist Isaac Newton; the most affectionate and admiring nickname given Beccaria by his friends was "Newtoncino"—little Newton (Gay, 1966:12).

It is instructive now to consider Beccaria's other early writings, which, against *Dei delitti*'s bright reception, have generally been ignored. This is unfortunate because, although Beccaria's other writings did not exert much influence, they provide a broader view of his concerns at the time he wrote *Dei delitti*. Prior to the publication of *Dei delitti*, Beccaria published two short tracts, each of which yields some details as to the direction of his thought. In his first work, he (Beccaria, 1762a) addressed the economic problems of the Milanese currency. This essay drew its inspiration from Hume, Sir William Petty (Schumpeter, 1954:298), and especially, he admitted (Beccaria, 1762a:8), from Locke; here Beccaria (1762a:8) specifically referred to the influence of Locke's work on his monetary analysis. In another essay, Beccaria (1762a) creatively used algebraic formulae to analyze the costs and benefits of the crime of smuggling; here his main question was "given that a certain proportion of smuggled goods will be seized by the authorities, what is the total quantity that smugglers must move to be left with neither gain nor loss?" His answer to this question was probably influenced by his reading of Jonathan Swift's satirical Gulliver's Travels (1762b:164).

It has never been properly acknowledged that, like several other continental adherents of the Enlightenment (e.g., Helvétius, 1758; Jaucourt, 1751; see also Wood, 1989), Beccaria was inspired by the ideas of the founder of the Scottish Enlightenment, philosopher Francis Hutcheson, and his pupil Hume (whose "profound metaphysics" he praised generously: Beccaria, 1766:865). One of Beccaria's (1765:169) early essays, for example, shows the unmistakable influence of Hutcheson's (1725a:48–51) idea of the beauty of theorems. The influence of Hutcheson on Beccaria's *Dei delitti* far transcends the communality of discursive practices often engaged in by Enlightenment writers. When Beccaria introduced *Dei delitti* with the enigmatic sentence "Mankind owes a debt of gratitude to the philosopher who, from the despised obscurity of his study, had the courage to cast the first and long fruitless seeds of useful truths among the multitude!" (1764:3; see also Scott, 1900:273–74), he was referring to Hutcheson, who had explicitly termed himself "an obscure Philosopher" (Hutcheson, 1725b:vii).

Nearly every page of *Dei delitti* is marked by Hutcheson's towering influence on Beccaria's thinking. It is found in the common metaphors used in *Dei delitti* and in Hutcheson's (1755) *System of Moral Philosophy*; these metaphors are taken from such diverse fields as theology, law, architecture, Newtonian mechanics, and geometry. Hutcheson's influence is also found in the extraordinary correspondence between key recommendations in Beccaria's *Dei delitti* and those in Hutcheson's *System*. Careful comparison reveals that whole sections of *Dei delitti* either restate or develop the proposals for law and criminal justice in Hutcheson's *System*.

Among the most important of these are those that refer to property as the basis of the social contracts (see Hutcheson, 1755:Bk. II, chap. 6:319–22; Beccaria, 1764:7); the definition of crime (Hutcheson, 1755:Bk. II; chap. 15:86–87, "injury"; Beccaria, 1764:17, "harm"); the uniformity of laws (Hutcheson, 1755:Bk. II; chap. 15:101–2; Beccaria, 1764:11–12); the simplicity of laws (Hutcheson, 1755:Bk. III; chap. 9:322–23; Beccaria, 1764:12–13, 75); the harm inflicted by corrupt public servants and magistrates (Hutcheson, 1755:Bk. II; chap. 15:88–89; Beccaria, 1764:78); the compensatory use of fines (Hutcheson, 1755:Bk. II; chap. 15:88–91; Beccaria, 1764:39–40); the deterrent nature of punishment (Hutcheson, 1755:Bk. II; chap. 15:87, 93–94; Bk. III; chap. 9:333; Beccaria, 1764:23, 33, 47, 50, 74–75); the proportionality of punishment to crime (Hutcheson, 1755:Bk. III; chap. 9:331–38; Beccaria, 1764:14–16, 23, 46–47, 55, 64); and opposition to judicial torture (Hutcheson, 1755:Bk. II; chap. 15:97; Bk. III; chap. 9:337–38; Beccaria, 1764:29–33, 70–72).

But my chief intention here is not to document in detail the remarkable identity in the respective penal recommendations of Hutcheson's *System* and those of Beccaria's *Dei delitti*. Rather, it is to show that just as much of the specific content of Beccaria's famous treatise is taken from Hutcheson's (1755) *System* so, too, is much of the structure of its argumentation. As discussed below, Beccaria's treatise must thus be placed in a trajectory radically different from the "classical" one conventionally accorded it. In the same way that Hutcheson's *System* contained a progeny of useful truths otherwise known to Beccaria as the new "science of man" so, too, did Beccaria aspire in *Dei delitti* to apply this science to the field of crime and punishment.

The Science of Man in *Dei delitti*

Some of the arguments of *Dei delitti* embodied a deterministic discourse that seems decidedly at odds with the classic dependence on free will that is commonly attributed to *Dei delitti*. Among Enlightenment thinkers this discourse was denominated loosely and was signified by such terms as Pascal's *esprit géométrique* and, after mid-century, the Scottish civic tradition's "science of man." Beccaria himself variously referred to it as "geometry," "moral geography," "political arithmetic," "number," and the "science of man." Woven within Beccaria's stylistic eloquence and his passionate humanism is a strong reliance on the discursive use of determinist principles derived from the science of man.

Several key features of the science of man are plainly recognizable in *Dei delitti*. Chief among them are the doctrines of utilitarianism, probabilism, associationism, and sensationalism. The doctrine of utilitarianism operated for Beccaria as a core justificatory argument for establishing "the right to punish" and it is positioned prominently at the very beginning of the text. With it Beccaria attempted to forge linkages, as had Hutcheson before him, among the rule of law, justice, and the economic marketplace. Beccaria employed probabilism, associationism, and sensationalism throughout *Dei delitti*, and he wielded the three doctrines in concert as mechanisms with which to advance various technico-administrative aspects of his chosen penal strategies (or "how to punish").

The Right to Punish

The point of entry into Beccaria's discourse about penal strategies is provided by his subscription to an economistic form of social contract theory based on utilitarianism and secured through the rule of law. *Dei delitti* begins with a utilitarian argument for "the greatest happiness" cast in the specific context of a plea for the supremacy of the rule of law. Whereas in the past, according to Beccaria, law had most commonly been the instrument of the passions of a few persons, "the impartial observer of human nature [would] grasp the actions of a multitude of men and consider them from this point of view: *the greatest happiness shared among the majority of people*" (1764:3). The happiness of "a few illustrious persons" is something Beccaria derided as tyranny (1764:43). Beccaria attached the condition that if all individual members are bound to society then—as opposed to the original warlike state of nature—society is likewise bound to all of them by a binding contract of mutual obligation.

> This obligation, which reaches from the throne to the hovel and which is equally binding on the greatest and the most wretched of men, means nothing other than that it is in everybody's interest that the contracts useful to the greatest number should be observed. Their violation, even by one person, opens the door to anarchy. (1764:9)

Beccaria harnessed his declared utilitarianism to two mechanisms. The first is the rule of law: "the true foundations of the happiness I mentioned here are security and freedom limited only by law" (1764:62). For Beccaria, law is the condition by which "independent and isolated men, tired of living in a constant state of war and of enjoying a freedom made useless by the uncertainty of keeping it, unite in society" (1764:7). As will be discussed, Beccaria urged that criminal law especially should have various features of formal and substantive rationality including clarity, logical inclusiveness, and predictability. Beccaria's plea for the rule of law emerged largely as a result of his disenchantment with Catholic theocentrism, ecclesiastical courts, and inquisitorial practices. Law and justice must develop apart from the activities of religious policing:

> It is the task of theologians to establish the limits of justice and injustice regarding the intrinsic goodness or wickedness of an act; it is the task of the observer of public life to establish the relationships of political justice and injustice, that is, of what is useful or harmful to society. (1764:5)

Moreover, Beccaria asserted that those who believe that the intention of the criminal is the true measure of crime are in error because crime can only be measured by "the harm done to the nation" (1764:16) or "to the public good" (1764:15):

> Given the necessity of men uniting together, and given the compacts which necessarily result from the very clash of private interests, one may discern a scale of misdeeds wherein the highest degree consists of acts that are directly destructive of society and the lowest of the least possible injustice against one of its members. Between these extremes lie all actions contrary to the public good, which are called crimes . . . . (1764:14–15)

For the achievement of his declared utilitarian objective, Beccaria envisaged a second mechanism, namely, the economic marketplace. In this respect, he believed that the juridico-political basis of the modern state should be secured not through such feudal relics as theocentrism and the divine right of kings, but through the utilitarian principles of large-scale, bourgeois commodity exchange. The free economic agent and the subject of law are, indeed, one and the same individual; the atomized individual who "thinks of himself as the center of all the world's affairs" (1764:8) is an economic agent simply reconstituted in juridical terms. Thus, Beccaria argued that although "commerce and the ownership of goods" are not the goal of the social contract, they can be a means of achieving it (1764:66); "*common utility*," in other words, is "the basis of human justice" (1764:16). Beccaria was enthusiastic about the "quiet war of industry [that] has broken out among great nations, the most humane sort of war and the kind most worthy of reasonable men" (1764:3), and he praised "easy, simple, and great laws . . . that require only a nod from the legislator to spread wealth and vigor" (1764:66). Indeed, the surest way of securing the compliance of individuals with the law of their nation is to

> improve the relative well-being of each of them. Just as every effort ought to be made to turn the balance of the trade in our favor, so it is in the greatest interests of the sovereign and of the nation that the sum total of happiness . . . should be greater than elsewhere. (1764:62)

Given this relationship, Beccaria's concept of crime as "what is harmful to society" is likewise intimately linked to the economic marketplace (see also Wills, 1978:153–54; Zeman, 1981:20). For Beccaria, the social contract entails that all citizens surrender a portion of their liberty to the state, in return for which the state protects their right to security and tranquility; "there is no enlightened man who does not love the open, clear, and useful contracts of public security when he compares the slight portion of useful liberty that he has sacrificed to the total sum of all the liberty sacrificed by other men" (Beccaria, 1764:76). The sum of all these portions of liberty is thus a "deposit" that no citizen can ever "withdraw" from the "common store" or from the "public treasury" (1764:7, 34), and therein lies the basis of the state's right to punish its subjects:

> The mere formation of this deposit, however, [is] not sufficient; it [has] to be defended against the private usurpations of each particular individual . . . . Tangible motives [are] required sufficient to dissuade the despotic spirit of each man from plunging the laws of society back into the original chaos. (1764:7)

Crime is thus an offense against both law and economic intercourse. Accordingly, when in *Dei delitti* Beccaria referred to particular crimes, he only emphasized crimes against property, including theft, counterfeiting, bankruptcy, smuggling, and indolence. He especially condemned political indolence (which "contributes to society neither with work nor with wealth" 1764:41–42) and "timid prudence" (which "sees only the present moment" 1764:66). At several points in his discussion of punishment, moreover, he invoked a symmetry between the aims and conditions of penal servitude and those of the marketplace. One feature of this symmetry is described as "the faint and prolonged example of a man who, deprived of his liberty, has become a beast of burden, repaying the society he has offended with his labors" (1764:49). Elsewhere, he urged that "the most fitting punishment [for theft] . . . is the only sort of slavery that can be deemed just: the temporary subjugation to society of the labor and the person of criminal" (1764:40).

How to Punish

It is not my concern here to outline each of Beccaria's chosen penal strategies but to show how his argumentation regarding them again demonstrates his adherence to various aspects of the new science of man. Chief among those aspects were the loosely defined doctrines of probabilism, sensationalism, and associationism.

PROBABILISM

Beccaria's attempt to apply "probability" and "number" to matters of punishment derives from his dependence on the ideas of wise governance held by Locke and Hutcheson rather than by the French *philosophes*.

Near the beginning of *Dei delitti*, Beccaria asserted his intention of "going back to general principles" (1764:34) to uncover the rampant political and judicial errors "accumulated" over several centuries. In a sense, his search for these principles reflected an abhorrence of uncertainty. Thus, he objected to "arbitrary notions of vice and virtue" (1764:4). Sometimes, he complained, "despotic impatience" and "effeminate timidity" transform "serious trials into a kind of game in which chance and subterfuge are the main elements" (1764:24), and he derided "the errors and passions that have successively dominated various legislators" (1764:15). Such errors included the useless tortures "multiplied" with prodigious and useless severity; the punishment of crimes that are "unproven"; and the horrors of a prison, "augmented" by "uncertainty" ("that most cruel tormentor of the wretched" (1764:4). Simultaneously, Beccaria bemoaned the unhappy fact that, unlike "the symmetry and order that is the lot of brute, inanimate matter" (1764:74), "turbulent human activity" and "the infinitely complicated relationships and mutations of social arrangements" are impossible to reduce to a "geometric order devoid of irregularity and confusion" (1764:74–75):

> It is impossible to prevent all disorders in the universal strife of human passions. They increase at the compound rate of population growth and the intertwining of public interests, which cannot be directed toward the public welfare with geometric precision. In political arithmetic, one must substitute the calculation of probability for mathematical exactitude. (1764:14)

Beccaria's advocacy of probability extended as well to each stage of the criminal justice system, including the clarity of the law itself, judicial torture, witnesses and evidence, jurors, and sentencing practices.

Beccaria urged that only a fixed and predictable law could provide citizens with personal security and liberate them from judicial arbitrariness. Thus, "the greater the number of people who understand the sacred law code and who have it in their hands, the less frequent crimes will be, for there is no doubt that ignorance and uncertainty concerning punishments aid the eloquence of the passions" (1764:13). The law itself must be unambiguous because only with "fixed" and "immutable" laws can citizens acquire personal "security": "this is just because it is the goal of society, and it is useful because it enables [citizens] to calculate precisely the ill consequences of a misdeed" (1764:12). Moreover,

> when a fixed legal code that must be observed to the letter leaves the judge no other task than to examine a citizen's actions and to determine whether or not they conform to the written law, when the standard of justice and injustice that must guide the actions of the ignorant as well as the philosophic citizen is not a matter of philosophic controversy but of fact, then subjects are not exposed to the petty tyrannies of many men. (1764:12)

For minor and less heinous crimes, moreover, there should be a statute of limitations that relieves citizens of "uncertainty" regarding their fate; but such time limits "ought not to increase in exact proportion to the atrocity of the crime, for the likelihood of crimes is inversely proportional to their barbarity" (1764:56).

Beccaria's subscription to the doctrine of probabilism clarifies how *Dei delitti* viewed judicial torture. Beccaria opposed the practice of using torture for interrogation on humanist grounds but if this "humanism" connotes a condemnation of the infliction of physical pain on others, then it contradicts Beccaria's vigorous support for noncapital corporal punishment "without exception" for crimes against persons and for crimes of theft accompanied by violence (1764:37, 40). This apparent paradox can be resolved by stressing that Beccaria articulated his opposition to judicial torture on the basis that it is an inefficient method of establishing the "probability" or the "certainty" of the guilt or innocence of the accused. Accordingly, "the problems of whether torture and death are either just or useful deserve a mathematically precise solution" (1764:23). Elsewhere, Beccaria added that it is "a remarkable contradiction in the laws that they authorize torture, yet what sort of interrogation could be more *suggestive* than pain?" (1764:71):

> The outcome of torture, then, is a matter of temperament and calculation that varies with each man in proportion to his hardiness and his sensitivity, so that, by means of this method, a mathematician could solve the following problem better than a judge could: given

the strength of an innocent person's muscles and the sensitivity of his fibers, find the degree of pain that will make him confess himself guilty of a given crime (1764:31).

In place of judicial torture, Beccaria recommended "the real trial, the 'informative' one, that is, the impartial investigation of facts which reason demands" (1764:34).

In respect of witnesses and evidence, Beccaria argued that to determine the guilt or innocence of a defendant more than one witness is necessary because, if one witness affirms the guilt and another denies it, "there is no certainty" (1764:24; see also Locke, 1689, 1:309). A witness is credible if he is "a rational man" and his credibility increases if his reason is undisturbed by a prior relationship with either the defendant or the victim. "The credibility of a witness, therefore, must diminish in proportion to the hatred or friendship or close relationship between himself and the accused" (Beccaria, 1764:24). The credibility of a witness also diminishes significantly as the gravity of the alleged crime increases or as its circumstances become more "improbable" (1764:24–25). The credibility of a witness is virtually nil in cases that involve making words a crime: "[it is] far easier to slander someone's words than to slander his actions, for, in the latter case, the greater the number of circumstances adduced as evidence, the greater are the means available to the accused to clear himself" (1764:25). Somewhat inconsistently, Beccaria also held that to the degree that "punishments become moderate, that squalor and hunger are banished from prisons, and that compassion and humanity pass through the iron gates . . . the law may be content with weaker and weaker evidence to imprison someone" (1764:54).

For Beccaria, there exists a "general theorem" that is most useful in calculating with certainty the facts of a crime, namely, the "weight of evidence." In unfolding the aspects of this theorem, he argued that (1) when different pieces of factual evidence are substantiated only by each other, the less certain is any one fact; (2) when all the proofs of a fact depend on one piece of evidence, the number of proofs neither augments nor diminishes the probability of the fact; and (3) when proofs are independent of each other, then the probability of the fact increases with each new witness (1764:25). Moreover, Beccaria deemed it ironic that the most atrocious and obscure crimes—that is, "those that are most unlikely"—are the hardest to prove. Such crimes are typically proved by conjecture and by the weakest and most equivocal evidence; it is as though "the danger of condemning an innocent man were not all the greater as the probability of his innocence surpasses the likelihood of his guilt" (1764:58). That is not to say that there are not some crimes that are both frequent in society and difficult to prove—such as "adultery" and "pederasty"—and, in these cases, "the difficulty of establishing guilt takes the place of the probability of innocence" (1764:58). Finally, because the respective probabilities of "atrocious" crimes and of lesser offenses differ greatly, they must be adjudicated differently: for atrocious crimes the period of judicial examination "should decrease in view of the greater likelihood of the innocence of the accused . . . but with minor crimes, given the lesser likelihood of the innocence of the accused, the period of judicial investigation should be extended, and, as the pernicious consequences of impunity decline, the delay in granting immunity from further prosecution should be shortened" (1764:57).

Finally, Beccaria offered some brief comments on jurors and on sentencing practices from the perspective of probabilism. About jurors, he recommended, without explanation, that when a crime has been committed against a third party "half the jurors should be the equals of the accused and half the peers of the victim" (1764:27). About sentencing practices, he warned that "certainty" ought to be required for convictions in criminal cases and that if geometry "were adaptable to the infinite and obscure arrangements of human activity, there ought to be a corresponding scale of punishments, descending from the most rigorous to the slightest" (1764:15).

Many of the strategies in Beccaria's penal calculus, including his key concept of deterrence, are derived not from geometry or probabilism as such, but from the doctrines of associationism and sensationalism.

ASSOCIATIONISM

Beccaria's penal calculus rested on the view that it is better to prevent crimes than to punish them. This can only occur if the law forces potential criminals to make an accurate "association" of ideas between crime and punishment. "It is well established," Beccaria claimed, along with Hume and Helvétius, "that the association of ideas is the cement that shapes the whole structure of the human intellect; without it, pleasure and pain would be isolated feelings with no consequences" (1764:36). Following Hume, Beccaria urged that associated ideas must be in a position of constant conjunction and that they must comprise a relation of cause and effect. Beccaria characterized the nexus of the desired association between crime and punishment in many ways, such as "deterrence" (1764:33), "intimidation" (1764:23, 29) and "dissuasion" (1764:23), although at some points he also took a retributivist position toward criminals (Young, 1983). The key properties of the association between crime and punishment are condensed in the following formula, which is the concluding sentence of *Dei delitti*, now appropriately enshrined as the original statement of the principle of deterrence:

in order that any punishment should not be an act of violence committed by one person or many against a private citizen, it is essential that it should be public, prompt, necessary, the minimum possible under the given circumstances, [and] proportionate to the crimes. (1764:81; emphasis in original)

Elsewhere, Beccaria expanded most notably on the need for prompt, mild, and proportionate punishment. Beccaria believed that the shorter the time period between a crime and chastisement for it "the stronger and more permanent is the human mind's association of the two ideas of crime and punishment, so that imperceptibly the one will come to be considered as the cause and the other as the necessary and inevitable result" (1764:36). Delay thus serves only to sever the association between the two ideas. Moreover, the temporal proximity of crime and punishment is of paramount importance if one desires to arouse in "crude and uneducated minds the idea of punishment in association with the seductive image of a certain advantageous crime" (1764:37). Second, Beccaria argued that to achieve its intended effect the intensity of a punishment should exceed the benefit resulting from the crime and that, in its application, punishment should be "inexorable," "inevitable," and "certain" (1764:46–47). Cruel punishments, insofar as they destroy the association between law and justice, therefore undermine the aim of deterrence. Finally, on proportionality, Beccaria warned that "the obstacles that restrain men from committing crimes should be stronger according to the degree that such misdeeds are contrary to the public good and according to the motives that lead people to crimes" (1764:14, 15). This is so because, if two unequally harmful crimes are each awarded the same punishment, then would–be miscreants will tend to commit the more serious crime if it holds greater advantage for them. If punishments are disproportionate to crime by being tyrannical (i.e., excessive), then popular dissatisfaction will be directed at the law itself—"punishments will punish the crimes that they themselves have caused" (1764:16). For this reason, Beccaria suggested that some punishments might even be considered crimes (1764:17, 51). Further, in arguing that "punishment . . . should conform as closely as possible to the nature of the crime" (1764:37), Beccaria implicitly attempted to link the argument about the proportionality of crime and punishment with the desired association among ideas about the type of crime (e.g., theft), form of punishment (penal servitude with forced labor), and virtue of industriousness.

In the context of Beccaria's use of the doctrine of associationism, it is worth returning briefly to his opposition to capital punishment. It is fair to suggest that Beccaria opposed capital punishment not because he thought it cruel, which he did, but because it did not serve the new penal objective of deterrence. (Only much later did he [Beccaria, 1792:739–40] argue that the rights of an accused are violated by the death penalty because, once an execution had been carried out, there is no "possibility" of reversal even after proof of innocence.) He argued instead that a life sentence is a sufficiently intense substitute for the death penalty and that it includes all the necessary ingredients needed to deter the most hardened criminal. "Neither fanaticism nor vanity survives among fetters and chains, under the prod or the yoke, or in an iron cage . . . a lifetime at hard labor" (Beccaria 1764:50). It was thus not the severity of punishment that, for Beccaria, had the greatest impact on a would-be criminal but, besides its other characteristics, its duration:

> If someone were to say that life at hard labor is as painful as death and therefore equally cruel, I should reply that, taking all the unhappy moments of perpetual slavery together, it is perhaps even more painful, but these moments are spread out over a lifetime, and capital punishment exercises all its power in an instant. And this is the advantage of life at hard labor; it frightens the spectator more than the victim. (1764:50)

SENSATIONALISM

A third hallmark of the science of man engraved in *Dei delitti* is the doctrine of sensationalism. In Beccaria's discussion of the nature of honor, for example, the presence of this doctrine is indicated by a Newtonian metaphor:

> How miserable is the condition of the human mind! It has a better grasp of the most remote and least important ideas about the revolutions of the heavenly bodies than of the most immediate and important moral concepts, which are always fluctuating and confused as they are driven by the winds of passion and guided by the ignorance that receives and transmits them! (1764:19; see also Halévy, 1928:57)

This "ostensible paradox'" will disappear, Beccaria (1764:19) continued, only when one considers that

> just as objects too close to one's eyes are blurred, so the excessive proximity of moral ideas makes it easy to confuse the large number of simple ideas that go to form them. Wishing to measure the phenomena of human sensibility, the geometric spirit needs dividing

lines. When these are clearly drawn, the impartial observer of human affairs will be less astonished, and he will suspect that there is perhaps no need for so great a moral apparatus or for so many bonds in order to make men happy and secure.

These two passages betray the influence on *Dei delitti* of the doctrine of sensationalism, which, in the course of his unheralded book on aesthetics, Beccaria (1770:81–93; see also Beccaria, 1766:866) explicitly acknowledged having taken from works by Locke and Condillac. Locke's sensationalism tended to suggest that all things painful are by definition bad and all things pleasurable, good. His original discussion of the doctrine of hedonism—the pleasure/pain principle—occurred within the framework of sensationalism. Condillac developed Locke's doctrine of sensationalism, positing that the human mind is at birth a *tabula rasa* which operates through sensations. Like Locke, Condillac (1754:338) championed the rigidly materialistic conclusion that "man" is simply what he has acquired through his sensations.

It is difficult to imagine a doctrine more hostile to the doctrine of free will than sensationalism. When Beccaria applied it to criminal justice, sensationalism effectively displaced the volitional subject of Catholic theology and, thereby, denied any active role in human society for the Supreme Being. Beccaria was so fearful of the censor precisely because his text implied that human agents are no more than the products of their sensory reactions to external stimuli. His text, replete with probabilism, associationism, and sensationalism—all directed to the new objective of deterrence—is resolutely opposed to any notion of free will. *Dei delitti* contains a concept of volition, but it is a determined will rather than a free will: "sentiment is always proportional to the result of the impressions made on the senses" (1764:25). The penal recommendations of *Dei delitti* are not at all predicated, therefore, on the notion of a rational calculating subject who, when faced with inexorable punishment, will weigh the costs and benefits and choose to desist from crime. In this discourse, punishments ("tangible motives") have "a direct impact on the senses and appear continually to the mind to counterbalance the strong impressions of individual passions opposed to the general good" (1764:7).

Sensationalism intersects concretely with Beccaria's chosen penal strategies in three ways. First, it is an extra ground on which judicial torture must be rejected. Beccaria insisted that, in terms of their respective results, the only difference between judicial torture and other ordeals, such as fire and boiling water, is that the former appears to depend on the will of the accused and the latter on a purely physical act. To this he responded that speaking the truth amid convulsions and torments is no more a free act than staving off the effects of fire and boiling water except by fraud. Every act of our will is always proportional to the strength of the sense impressions from which it springs. . . . (1764:31)

Sensationalist claims were also inserted into Beccaria's arguments about the nature of deterrence. During his discussion of the appropriateness of prompt punishment, for example, he argued that "[the] gravity-like force that impels us to seek our own well-being can be restrained only to the degree that obstacles are established in opposition to it" and that "remote consequences make a very weak impression" (1764:14, 64). Effecting a link with probabilism, he argued that "experience and reason have shown us that the probability and certainty of human traditions decline the farther removed they are from their source" (1764:13). Effecting yet another link, this time with associationist claims, he reflected that

the magnitude of punishment ought to be relative to the condition of the nation itself. Stronger and more obvious impressions are required for the hardened spirits of a people who have scarcely emerged from a savage state. A thunderbolt is needed to fell a ferocious lion who is merely angered by a gun shot. But to the extent that human spirits are made gentle by the social state, sensibility increases; as it increases, the severity of punishment must diminish if one wishes to maintain a constant relation between object and feeling. (1764:81)

Finally, Beccaria attached his belief in sensationalism to a variety of nonpenal strategies designed to manipulate and channel sense impressions into law-abiding actions. While penal strategies tend to operate swiftly and dramatically on their subjects, nonpenal strategies are designed as positive mental inducements that operate slowly and calmly at the level of custom and habit, or at what is nowadays known as the domain of "socialization." Thus, Beccaria suggested that in order to prevent crimes, "enlightenment should accompany liberty" (1764:76). What precisely he meant by this recommendation is not very clear, but perhaps it was "education," an instrument whose importance he also stressed (1764:76–79), as did such thinkers as Montesquieu, d'Alembert, Helvétius, Rousseau, and Charles Pinot Duclos. He warned that "the most certain but most difficult way to prevent crimes is to perfect education" (1764:79).

From the "Science of Man" to *Homo Criminalis*

> Morality, politics, and the fine arts, which are respectively the
> sciences of virtue, of utility, and of beauty, have a greater identity of
> principles than can be imagined: these sciences all derive from one
> primary science, the science of man; it is hopeless to think that we
> will ever make rapid progress in fathoming the depths of these
> secondary sciences without first immersing ourselves in the science
> of man. (Beccaria, 1770:71)

In addition to the contemporary protestations (Grimm, 1765a, 1765b;
Ramsay, n.d.) that Beccaria's treatment of penal questions in *Dei delitti*
was "too geometrical," others of the period understood the protoscientific
intentions of *Dei delitti* and valued it for that very direction. To the
French mathematician and *philosophe* Condorcet, for example, Beccaria
was one of a select group of scholars whose works, since the time of
Locke, had advanced the moral and social sciences; the application of "the
calculus of . . . probabilities" to the understanding of human societies
(1795:178; see also Baker, 1975:193). Blackstone observed that Beccaria
"seems to have well studied the springs of human action" (1769:4:17), and
he emphatically placed Beccaria's "humane" reform proposals within the
rubric of a new discourse of crime and penality that emerged in Britain
in the 1760s and that stressed investigation of the "causes of crime,"
deterrence, and the correction of offenders.

Indeed, attached to Beccaria's discourse on penal strategies, there is
present in *Dei delitti* a very rudimentary attempt to forge some key
concepts of an embryonic criminology. Those concepts include "crime,"
"criminal," and "causes of crime." Quite apart from his innovative
approach to the understanding of crime ("the harm done to society"),
Beccaria also attempted to identify the criminal as something other than
a mere bundle of illegalities. This concept of a criminal operates in
concert with and is burdened by Beccaria's humanism and his advocacy
of legal rationality, yet it marks a movement away from a single-minded
focus on how to punish *homo penalis* to a wider "criminological" concern
with understanding the situation of *homo criminalis*. An example of this
movement occurs when, during an impassioned tirade against unjust laws,
Beccaria (1764:51) inserted the following words into the mouth of "a
scoundrel":

> What are these laws that I must respect and that leave such a great
> distance between me and the rich man? . . . Who made these laws?
> Rich and powerful men who have never deigned to visit the squalid
> hovels of the poor, who have never broken a moldy crust of bread

among the innocent cries of their famished children and the tears of their wives. Let us break these bonds that are so ruinous for the majority and useful to a handful of indolent tyrants; let us attack injustice at its source.

At several other points in his text, as well, Beccaria indicated that criminals and criminal behavior should be understood causally, in material and social terms, rather than purely individualistic ones. He suggested, for example, that "theft is only the crime of misery and desperation; it is the crime of that unhappy portion of humanity to whom the right of property . . . has left only a bare existence" (1764:39). It is difficult to know how much to invest in Beccaria's reasoning in passages such as these, other than to say that he seems keen to position illegalities in a quasi-social context. Similarly suggestive reasoning is directed to the crimes of adultery (1764:58–59), pederasty (1764:60), and infanticide "by a woman" (1764:60).

It must also be said that *Dei delitti* even contains an adumbration of a "dangerous class." This is visible at several points. Thus, Beccaria spoke philosophically of wanting to disabuse those "who, from a poorly understood love of liberty, would desire to establish anarchy" (1764:18) and who are inclined toward "a desperate return to the original state of nature" (1764:47). These unfortunates he described as "the credulous and admiring crowd" (1764:39), "a fanatical crowd" (1764:47), "a blind and fanatical crowd, pushing and jostling one another in a closed labyrinth" (1764:77) that "does not adopt stable principles of conduct" (1764:7). In crowds there resides a "dangerous concentration of popular passions" (1764:22) that is akin to the sentiments in "the state of nature . . . the savage" (1764:74). Ultimately, *Dei delitti* teases its audience with a presociological view of the relation between crime and social organization:

Most men lack that vigor which is equally necessary for great crimes and great virtues; thus, it seems that the former always coexist with the latter in those nations that sustain themselves by the activity of their governments and by passions working together for the public good, rather than in countries that depend on their size or the invariable excellence of their laws. In the latter sort of nation, weakened passions seem better suited to the maintenance rather than to the improvement of the form of government. From this, one can draw an important conclusion: that great crimes in a nation are not always proof of its decline. (1764:58)

Conclusion: Whither Classical Criminology?

Less by way of conclusion to this essay than as an invitation for further exploration, several implications must now be drawn about the place of *Dei delitti* in the intellectual history of criminology.

First, I have not disputed the conventional view that Beccaria's advocacy of humanism and legal rationality are important features of his treatise. Rather, I claim that neither the method of *Dei delitti* nor its object can be understood in terms of those tendencies alone. An altogether different tendency, veiled and incompletely developed, actually comprised the kernel of Beccaria's discourse—the application to crime and penality of key principles in the science of man. It is in the framework of that new science that the two major themes of *Dei delitti* (the "right to punish" and "how to punish") are couched as, too, are Beccaria's advocacy of deterrence and his opposition to capital punishment and judicial torture.

Second, contrary to prevailing opinion, the discourse of *Dei delitti* was not erected on the volitional subject of classical jurisprudence, or "free will" as it is often termed. Although Beccaria's view of volitional conduct is not clear in *Dei delitti*, it is possible that, like many of his contemporaries in the eighteenth century Enlightenment who saw in this no contradiction, he subscribed to a notion of human agency simultaneously involving "free" rational calculation and "determined" action. But the concept of an unfettered free will must be relegated along with humanism to the margins of *Dei delitti*. The warriors and wretches who inhabit its pages are not volitional agents but creatures trapped in a web of determinism. The potential criminals in Beccaria's schema "act" like automata; in effect, they are recalcitrant objects who must be angled, steered, and forced into appropriate and law-abiding behavior. But this is only to be expected of a discourse that relies on rigidly deterministic principles concretely manifest in the specific doctrines of probabilism, associationism, and sensationalism. As such, at the very least, the position of *Dei delitti* in intellectual history does not and cannot lie at the center of classical criminology as it is conventionally understood. Nor, however, despite the temptation to focus on Beccaria's predilection for the science of man, should it be placed, however precariously, at the beginning of the tradition to which it is commonly opposed, namely, positivist criminology. Beccaria's utterances on crime and penality were never intended—nor could they have been—to inhabit the same positivist terrain as that so eagerly tenanted a century later by his compatriot Cesare Lombroso.

Finally, the very category of a distinct "classical" period in criminology must be reconsidered. "Classical criminology" was not the creation of Beccaria, Bentham, and others, but the retrospective product of scholarly self-aggrandizement. As an identifiable set of assumptions about crime and punishment, classical criminology was not actually denominated as such until the 1870s, and then by another generation of Italian theorists—positivist criminologists such as Lombroso, Garofalo, and Ferri. These thinkers were keen to distance their invention of a scientific criminology from that of Beccaria's "outmoded discourse of free will," either because they failed properly to understand the arguments of *Dei delitti* or, more likely, because it did not suit their own interests to do so. Yet if the discourse of *Dei delitti* is not couched in the rhetoric of classical jurisprudence, if its chief object (the construction of a rational and efficient penal calculus) is not directed to the actions of volitional subjects but to those of automata given by the science of man, and if humanism is a minor rather than a major feature of this discourse, then what is left of the classical edifice? Perhaps very little.

2

Understanding Crime Displacement:
An Application of Rational Choice Theory

Derek B. Cornish and Ronald V. Clarke

The model of the offender as a decision maker underlies much criminological work recently undertaken by psychologists, economists, and sociologists of deviance (Clarke and Cornish, 1985; Cornish and Clarke, 1986a). The "rational choice" perspective assumes that offenders seek to benefit by their criminal behavior. This involves decision making and choices, constrained by time, cognitive ability, and information, resulting in a limited rather than normative rationality. Our rational choice theory was founded on the premise that decisions and factors affecting them vary greatly at different stages of decision making and among different crimes. Thus, when analyzing criminal choices there is a need to be crime-specific and to treat decisions relating to the various stages of involvement in crimes, such as initial involvement, continuation, and desistance, separately from decisions relating to the criminal event, such as target selection (Clarke and Cornish, 1985; Cornish and Clarke, 1986a).

A Rational Choice Perspective on Crime Displacement

Our emphasis upon criminal decision making was intended to provide a general framework for thinking about the prevention and deterrence of crime. Our interest in rational choice theory arose out of work on "situational" crime prevention—a range of preventive measures, including defensible space architecture, target-hardening, and neighborhood watch. These were designed to reduce the opportunities for committing specific kinds of crime and to increase the risks for potential offenders (Clarke, 1983). Despite evidence of its utility, critics argue that preventive

Edited and abridged from *Criminology*, Volume 25(4):933–47 (1987).

measures which increase the difficulties of a particular crime will merely result in criminal activity being "displaced" to other targets, times, places, or types of crime (Reppetto, 1976; Gabor, 1981). Crucial here is the belief that, to the offender, many if not most crimes are functionally equivalent. This view derives from the traditional positivist assumption that offending is a product of enduring criminal drives or dispositions (Cornish and Clarke, 1986b).

In contrast, situational approaches argue that displacement is far from inevitable and occurs only under particular conditions. Rational choice theory assumes that offenders respond selectively to characteristics of particular offenses—to their opportunities, costs, and benefits—in deciding whether or not to offend. Also questioned is the notion of criminal "energies" which have to be displaced into alternative actions. If frustrated from committing a particular crime, offenders are not compelled to seek out another crime nor even a noncriminal solution. They may simply desist from any further action at all, rationalizing loss of income: "It was good while it lasted"; "I would have ended up getting caught"; and so on. Such an analysis is consistent with empirical research which points to the contingent nature of displacement. For example, the fitting of steering column locks to *all* cars in West Germany in 1960 brought about a 60 per cent reduction in car thefts, whereas their introduction to only new cars in Great Britain displaced theft to the older, unprotected vehicles (Mayhew et al., 1976). Again, while a variety of security measures dramatically reduced airliner hijackings in the early 1970s (Wilkinson, 1977), a police "crackdown" on subway robberies in New York City displaced robberies to the street (Chaiken, et al., 1974).

However, research analyzing crime patterns is likely to yield limited information about displacement. Just as reductions in target crimes resulting from situational prevention may be modest and invisible, so evidence of displacement may remain concealed within the aggregate crime statistics. On its own, such research fails to provide an adequate explanation for the occurrence or absence of displacement. Given these problems, additional ways of investigating displacement are needed, such as studies focusing upon offenders' own explanations for their decisions and choices.

The Concept of Choice-Structuring Properties

A more promising approach to the study of displacement is suggested by rational choice theory's emphasis upon the need to adopt a crime-specific focus when attempting to explain or prevent criminal behavior. Rather than assuming that potential offenders are fueled by a general disposition to offend which makes them relatively indifferent to the nature of the offense they commit, the rational choice perspective asserts that specific crimes are chosen and committed for specific reasons. Decisions to offend are influenced by the characteristics of both offenses and offenders, and are the product of interactions between the two. Thus, the final decision to become involved in a particular crime is the outcome of an appraisal process which evaluates the relative merits of a range of potential courses of action, comprising all those thought likely in the offender's view to achieve his or her current objective (for example, for money, sex, or excitement).

It follows that an understanding of the factors which the offender takes into account when performing this rudimentary cost-benefit analysis is necessary. These factors relate both to offense and offender characteristics but, for the present, can be usefully viewed as those *properties* of offenses (such as type and amount of payoff, perceived risk, skills needed, and so on) which are perceived by the offender as being especially salient to his or her goals, motives, experience, abilities, expertise, and preferences. Such properties provide a basis for selecting among alternative courses of action and hence effectively *structure* the offender's *choice*. The characteristics of offenses which render them differentially attractive to particular individuals or subgroups (or to the same individuals and groups at different times) have therefore been termed *choice-structuring properties*. It follows that the readiness with which the offender will be prepared to substitute one offense for another will depend upon the extent to which alternative offenses share characteristics which the offender considers salient to his or her goals and abilities. A recognition of the contingent, crime-specific nature of criminal decision making therefore has important implications for an understanding of displacement.

In the absence of information from offenders, some a priori selection of properties thought likely to be salient to offender decision making has to be made. For illustrative purposes, this is attempted later in the paper in relation to two broad groups of offenses—those of theft involving cash and of illegal substance abuse (Table 1). The concept of choice-structuring properties was first employed, however, in the attempt to clarify policy issues relating to gambling and suicide (Cornish and Clarke, 1989).

In the case of gambling (Weinstein and Deitch, 1974), choice-structuring properties such as number and location of gambling outlets, frequency of events on which bets can be made, time elapsing before payment of winnings, range of odds and stakes, degree of personal involvement, skills needed or perceived, and "nerve" required, were employed to identify forms of gambling more or less designed to encourage high degrees of involvement and to attract the participation of particularly susceptible individuals (Cornish, 1978). In Britain, the widespread provision of "betting shops" in prime urban locations enables off-course gambling in the afternoon. These premises offer a vast range of simple and complex betting strategies, a feeling of personal involvement and challenge fostered by the exercise of handicapping skills, and an atmosphere of "action" encouraged by rapid events and payouts, other gamblers laying bets and collecting winnings, and live television commentary—a combination of properties which provides an environment designed to encourage continuous gambling. The contrast with the choice-structuring properties of lotteries is significant: lotteries are held relatively infrequently, involve lengthy periods between staking and payout, offer the minimum of personal involvement, little scope for social interaction or the exercise of skill (real or perceived), a limited range of odds and bets, and very long odds against winning. The prime attraction to their adherents, therefore, is the possibility they offer of a big "windfall" for very little initial outlay. "Numbers," on the other hand, while ostensibly rather similar to the lottery, offers a wider variety of staking levels and odds, a larger number of events and swifter turnaround, greater perceived scope for the invocation of personal luck, and more social interaction—features which go some way to explaining why attempts to promote lotteries as legal alternatives to the numbers racket have proved unsuccessful (Kaplan and Maher, 1970).

It is in examples like these, where activities are examined in some detail, that the value of choice-structuring properties in clarifying the unique constellations of motives, opportunities, rewards, and costs offered by different forms of gambling becomes evident. Attention to these parameters also suggests a means of controlling participation in potentially dangerous forms of gambling through regulation of these properties, as has occurred in the monitoring and controlling of certain forms of legalized betting and gaming such as bingo, and gaming machines (Hess and Diller, 1969; Cornish, 1978).

In the case of suicide, properties of the various methods such as the degree of prior planning, courage required, pain or distastefulness of method, extent of disfigurement, time taken to die when conscious, scope for second thoughts, and chances of intervention, were used to explain why, when deprived of more acceptable methods, people do not always turn to other means of killing themselves. Domestic gas, for example, used to have particular advantages as a method of suicide: it was painless, very widely available, required little preparation, was highly lethal (death could take place in less than half an hour), was not bloody, and did not disfigure. These features help to explain how the detoxification of domestic gas—a method that had formerly accounted for over 50 per cent of all suicides (Kreitman, 1976; Kreitman and Platt, 1984; Clarke and

Mayhew, 1988)—brought about a 35 per cent decline in the national rate of suicide in Britain during the 1960s. Some population subgroups such as the elderly and the less mobile may have found these advantages particularly compelling; there is evidence, for example, that suicidal women are more attracted by self-poisoning and more repulsed by violent and bloody methods (Marks, 1977).

Since the needs and circumstances of particular subgroups may make certain methods uniquely attractive, then, it seems likely that reducing opportunities to use particular methods need not simply result in displacement to others, but can bring about genuine gains in the prevention of suicide deaths. Thus, an apparently obvious alternative to gassing, such as overdosing, which might appear to offer many of the same advantages, may nevertheless be subject to disadvantages which limit its viability as a substitute; for example, access to the most lethal drugs may require the cooperation of a doctor, or long-term planning and the faking of relevant symptoms, in order to build up sufficient quantities, while the range of more accessible nonprescription drugs may be either less lethal or, in the case of other alternatives such as domestic poisons, more painful to ingest (Clarke and Mayhew, 1988).

Choice-Structuring Properties of Crimes

Identifying an activity's unique blend of choice-structuring properties emphasizes its distinctive features and facilitates comparison between different activities. But, because crimes are heterogeneous behaviors, the basis on which crimes should be grouped for comparison is not clear. Since displacement across behaviors chosen for widely differing purposes is unlikely, however, specifying the goals of offending could provide the primary criterion for selecting the crimes to be compared. Thus, crimes whose main purpose appears to be to obtain money might be analyzed together, while those whose goal is sexual satisfaction would need to be separately analyzed. Some a priori determination—later refined by empirical research—of the purposes being served by particular offenses will therefore need to be made before they are grouped together in order to analyze their choice-structuring properties. Although many crimes may serve a mixture of goals, one of these will usually be dominant. This will provide the appropriate criterion for analysis, the remaining subsidiary purposes taking on the role of further choice-structuring properties for the particular offenses being compared.

For the sake of simplicity, it has so far been assumed that individuals choose only from among criminal alternatives when seeking to achieve their goals. But, given the range of noncriminal alternatives available to offenders, confining comparisons of choice-structuring properties to *criminal* means alone may seem restrictive. A crime such as drunken driving, for example, whose purpose is very specific and temporary (i.e., the need to get home after drinking) and in relation to which alternative crimes are few or none, illustrates the point that for some crimes most, if not all, of the alternative means being compared will be noncriminal. Here displacement will usually be directed to legal behaviors: alternatives to drunken driving may be to call a cab, use public transportation, or walk, rather than to persuade an equally drunk companion to drive the car instead. Notwithstanding this example, it seems intuitively more likely that criminal behavior will usually be contemplated only after legitimate means have been foreclosed or rejected. Drunken driving, it could be argued, is a special case since one of the effects of alcohol may be to short-circuit this usual sequence. Under these circumstances, the capacity of otherwise law-abiding citizens to consider the long-range consequences of their actions may be temporarily impaired, and this may lead them to entertain criminal actions much sooner (Campbell and Gibbs, 1986:126, 177). If criminal means are usually only considered at a later stage, this may suggest that they have something in common with each other and that these features provide some justification for limiting comparisons to crimes alone. But, while this meets the above objections, it also opens the door again to the very dispositional explanations of offending that the rational choice perspective was designed to challenge, since it suggests explanations in terms of offender characteristics, such as the tendency to select means which offer immediate gratification of needs, regardless of the consequences for others. Consequently, the preference at this stage is to defend confining comparison to crimes alone, not because criminal behavior is inherently different from other behaviors, but on pragmatic grounds: it is the possibility of displacement to other crimes which constitutes the major problem for crime-control policy.

Before embarking on a more detailed discussion of their application to the problem of crime displacement, it may be useful to provide hypothetical lists of the choice-structuring properties of two quite different offense groupings: those designed to yield cash (e.g., burglary, theft with or without contact, shoplifting, mugging, bank robbery, fraud, tax evasion, and auto theft); and those concerned with the ingestion of illegal substances (such as marijuana, opiates, LSD, cocaine, "crack," amphetamines, barbiturates, and volatile substances).

As can be seen from Table 1, while specifying the dominant purpose and confining comparisons to criminal means takes one some way toward the goal of drawing up lists of choice-structuring properties, the resulting groupings of offenses will usually be rather broad. While it may be tempting to try for somewhat narrower arrays of offenses, such as those

Table 1. Choice-Structuring Properties of Two Offense Groupings

Theft Involving Cash

Availability (numbers of targets; accessibility)
Method (e.g., pickpocketing vs. fraud)
Cash yield per crime
Expertise
Planning (pickpocketing vs. bank robbery)
Resources (transport; equipment)
Solo vs. associates
Time involved
Cool nerves (bank robbery vs. computer fraud)
Risks of apprehension
Severity of punishment
Physical danger
Instrumental violence
Confront victim (mugging vs. burglary)
Identifiable victim
Social cachet (safecracking vs. mugging)
"Fencing"
Moral evaluation

Illegal Substance Abuse

Availability (glue vs. prescription drug)
Awareness (knowledge of doctors or pharmacists)
Social cachet (cocaine vs. heroin)
Solitary vs. social
Knowledge/skills (heroin vs. marijuana)
Technical equipment (heroin)
Dangerousness (crack vs. marijuana)
Primary method (injecting vs. smoking)
Different forms of substance
Psychological effects
Number, type, and severity of side effects
Dependency
Length/intensity of "high" per dose
Financial costs
Legal penalties
Detectability
Interference with everyday tasks
Moral evaluation

sharing a common modus operandi, this may be unhelpful when estimating the likelihood of displacement since it may result in the omission of important choice-structuring properties. In turn, their omission may make it difficult to explain, for example, why burglars who prey on distant affluent suburbs would never consider breaking into apartments in their neighborhood; why the shoplifter might be reluctant to contemplate mugging; or why the computer fraudster might give up crime entirely if it became too difficult to continue his frauds. In the course of his investigation of robbers' decision making, for example, Feeney (1986) notes the surprising fact that many of them thought burglary too unpredictable and risky.

Similar considerations apply to offenses of illegal substance abuse. An analysis of their choice-structuring properties indicates that different substances provide different experiences, and this—together with considerations of availability, cost, risk, expertise required, and social context of usage—suggests that displacement and escalation among substances may be more limited than is usually thought. Information from opiate abusers, for example, suggests that a desire to join a specific drug culture of users may be an important determinant of initial involvement (Bennett, 1986); an alternative culture such as that represented by teenage glue sniffing may be seen to offer rather different, and less attractive, experiences in terms of social cachet, excitement, and alternative life style. In addition, the specific psychological effects of the drugs themselves may restrict substitutability: today's energetic, acquisitive "yuppie" cocaine user may typically be of similar social background to the 1960s cannabis-using hippie, but the effects of cocaine may be more in tune with modern life-styles and aspirations than those produced by cannabis.

Choice-structuring properties may also highlight similarities between apparently different behaviors. For example, crimes such as burglary on a public housing project, in a middle-class suburb, or in a wealthy enclave may, *for some offenders*, have fewer attractive properties in common than apparently different offenses, such as burglary or mugging, committed in their own neighborhoods. While the latter offenses may involve different skills or risks, these may be counterbalanced by the advantages of offending within familiar territory. For these reasons, again, the most appropriate level of analysis for choice-structuring properties would seem to be at the most general level consistent with the likelihood of displacement.

Since the lists in Table 1 derive from a rational choice perspective on offending, they both concentrate upon the opportunities, costs, and benefits of the various alternatives being compared. The properties listed are not necessarily those taken into account by the offender, who may not be fully aware either of the range of properties involved or of the part they play in his decisions. Rather, the properties listed have been selected on a priori grounds as being of most relevance to the task of comparing offenses and, hence, of establishing the likely limits of displacement within each offense grouping. Thus, there is likely to be more displacement between particular theft offenses where they share similar profiles of choice-structuring properties—for example, where the likely cash yield per crime is comparable, where similar skills and resources are required, and where the physical risks are the same. In contrast, where the profiles differ, this may clarify why displacement is unlikely to occur. Lastly, some choice-structuring properties may have a more pivotal role to play in decisions concerning displacement. It is generally accepted, for example, that some offenders will not contemplate crimes which involve the use of violence.

Little is known at present about offender decision making, and because of this the above lists may need modifying in the light of empirical research. But even at this stage such lists should provide a useful tool for those involved in crime prevention. By directing attention to those features of crimes which make them attractive to particular groups of offenders, such an approach will make it easier for policy makers to anticipate the direction and amount of any displacement to other forms of crime. In the past, for example, uncritical and often hidden assumptions that illegal substances are equivalent in their attractiveness and effects may have had damaging effects upon policy formation through the tendency of these assumptions to encourage preoccupation with the inevitability of displacement and escalation. Careful attention to choice-structuring properties of different activities, however, will enable the accuracy of assessments to be improved about the likely costs and benefits of undertaking new crime prevention initiatives in relation to specific forms of crimes. The lists will also alert policy makers to action that needs to be taken in order to forestall criminal displacement or even to facilitate displacement to noncriminal alternatives. Finally, lists of choice-structuring properties should assist in the evaluation of crime prevention initiatives by helping to orient the search for displacement.

Choice-Structuring Properties and Offender Perceptions

Table 1 attempts to provide a comprehensive list of the salient ways in which crimes with similar goals differ from each other. Although policy makers require such comprehensive information in order to think constructively about displacement, it should not be assumed that offenders will utilize the data in a similar way. As mentioned above, they may lack information about the full range of offenses that could satisfy their goals, they may be unaware of the extent to which available opportunities have structured their choices, they may be ignorant of all the costs and benefits of the different offenses, and they may assign particular importance to certain choice-structuring properties (such as eschewing the use of violence, or restricting selection of victims to those of particular socioeconomic or ethnic groups), which then come to exert a disproportionate influence upon involvement and displacement decisions. Moreover, in practice, offenders may not always take into account the full range of properties. For example, the choice-structuring properties listed in Table 1 are mainly relevant to an individual's initial decision whether or not to get involved in a particular crime. They may have rather less application to more immediate decisions relating to the commission of a particular offense (or what may be termed the criminal "event"), although a similar comparison process—albeit using a different and more restricted range of properties—undoubtedly takes place when potential targets or victims are being compared. The present lists would become more salient again when, having committed the offense, the offender had to decide whether to continue with a particular form of crime or to desist. Last, as a result of the experience of committing the offense in question, further choice-structuring properties may become apparent to the offender and existing ones may assume a different value. Thus, the degree of steady nerves required may only become apparent once a mugging has been attempted.

As well as exemplifying one of the major premises of the rational choice perspective—that the offender's decision-making processes will tend to display limited rather than normative rationality—the above points also illustrate the dynamic nature of criminal decision making. Thus far it might well appear that a rather passive role has been assigned to choice-structuring properties in that it has been implied that offenders' needs lead them to search out suitable criminal opportunities in their environments. But, as the term implies, choice-structuring properties may often play a more active role in generating offending. Some of the opportunities may offer a constellation of properties sufficiently attractive to provide a temptation to crime, as is often argued to be the case with petty offenses such as shoplifting. These points underline the threefold distinction made by Maguire (1980) and by Bennett and Wright (1984) among offenders who seize, search for, or create opportunities. It is also clear that, as well as specifying features of behaviors (kinds of gambling, methods of suicide, types of crime), choice-structuring properties implicitly specify salient characteristics of the actor, such as his or her needs, preferences, personal characteristics, and perceptions. In other words, the term "choice-structuring property" is a relational concept designed to provide an analytic tool for increasing an understanding of the interaction between personal variables and arrays of behaviors—in the case of crime, to specify more closely offenders as well as the offenses they commit. Thus, where crime displacement occurs, a knowledge of the choice-structuring properties which the offenses share may permit more accurate identification of the subgroups of offenders involved; and this may well prove a more fruitful way of investigating the interface between offense and offender—and, in particular, issues relating to specialization and generalization (Cornish and Clarke, 1989)—than the more static and rigid offender typologies of traditional criminology.

Greater knowledge about all these matters would undoubtedly improve policy makers' ability to predict the likelihood and direction of displacement. But, as well as requiring more information about the way offenders perceive and utilize the choice-structuring properties of crimes, more needs to be known about the criminal opportunity structure within which the offender operates if a complete picture of the determinants of displacement is to be given (Cook, 1986b). At a macro level, more ecological research is required in order to explore the changes in opportunities and hence in crime rates, brought about by changes in routine activities, lifestyles, and commercial practices. The processes through which these changes in opportunities at the macro level take place also require elucidation.

Rational Choice Theory and Crime-Control Policy

The rational choice perspective was originally developed to provide policy makers with a useful framework to guide thinking about crime prevention and control. The present paper has attempted to develop certain aspects of the theory in the interests of answering critics of situational crime prevention who have implicitly assumed that the outcome of such efforts is simply to displace offending. A similar analysis, making use of the concept of choice-structuring properties, has also been attempted elsewhere to clarify aspects of the longstanding debate over whether offenders are generalists or specialists (Cornish and Clarke, 1989). Rational choice approaches have also proved useful in suggesting reasons for the limited effectiveness of rehabilitative efforts (Cornish, 1987) in emphasizing the need of deterrent policies to pay greater attention to offenders' perceptions of opportunities, risks, costs, and benefits (Bennett and Wright, 1984), and in identifying potentially adverse side effects of policies such as selective incapacitation (Cook, 1986a).

More generally, a rational choice perspective on offending can suggest, if not explanations, lines of enquiry to account for stability and change in criminal behavior. The importance of this for directing crime prevention policy and practice should not be underestimated. Even under the most apparently favorable of circumstances, Tremblay's (1986) study found that displacement was by no means inevitable: only 10 per cent of his "checkmen" switched their attentions to credit card bank frauds. Before dismissing this discrepancy as a crude exemplification of Zipf's (1949) Principle of Least Effort, it should be recognized that this low take-up may have resulted from the limited period for which this particular "window of vulnerability" was left open by the banks and the fact that, even as knowledge grew about this novel form of crime, so were the risks and effort involved in its commission rapidly escalating. Critics of situational crime prevention might consider this example for whatever the value of longer-term social prevention strategies that attack the "root" causes of crime, the constant innovation in criminal methods in response to the changing criminal opportunity structure demands similar vigilance and continued investment time and effort on the part of those engaged in crime control. It is hoped that the rational choice perspective can offer some assistance in this enterprise.

3

Causes of White-Collar Crime

Travis Hirschi and Michael Gottfredson

Now that white-collar crime is securely established as an important area of inquiry for criminology the costs and benefits of the idea can be more clearly assessed. In this paper we outline a general theory capable of organizing the facts about all forms of crime, including white-collar crime. Our thesis is that the usefulness of the distinction between white-collar crime and crime in general has been illegitimately generalized to areas where it is inapplicable and therefore inappropriate. The utility of crime-specific analyses for policy purposes (e.g., Cornish and Clarke, 1986a) is not evidence of the utility of the same distinctions for etiological or research purposes. That vandalism may be reduced by banning the sale of paint in aerosol cans does not mean that vandals and muggers are produced by different causes. The desire to control white-collar criminals should not be confused with the conclusion that they are products of unique causal processes. Our general theory of crime accounts for the frequency and distribution of all forms of crime, whether they be rape, vandalism, simple assault, or white-collar crime. Given the large literature assuming that white-collar crime poses unique theoretical problems, several conceptual issues must first be resolved.

Origins of the Concept of White-Collar Crime

Classical theory assumed that resort to force or *fraud* was an ever present potential in human affairs. Both force and fraud were seen as means of pursuing self-interest, and the distinction between the two was theoretically uninteresting. In contrast, positivists assumed that crime is

Edited and abridged from *Criminology*, Volume 25(4):949–74 (1987).

evidence of biological, psychological, or social pathology and therefore some special motive or compulsion was required to explain it. The major social source of such compulsion was low social class, poverty, or inequality. This explained the high rate of crime among the poor (as really the fault of the rich and powerful). Unfortunately for some political purposes, it also assumed that the poor really did have a high rate of crime compared to the rich and powerful, who were relatively crime-free. Still, invention of the concept of white-collar crime had two desirable consequences: it falsified poverty-pathology theory and it revealed the criminality of the privileged classes and their impunity to the law.

Those sociological theories that continued to accept the class-poverty-inequality model (e.g., Merton, 1938; Cloward and Ohlin, 1960; Blau and Blau, 1982) did so only by remaining silent on the white-collar crime issue. Those that accepted the idea of white-collar crime were forced to move either toward a general theory that denied "pathological" causes (e.g., differential association) or toward theories tailored to particular crimes or types of crime (e.g., Clinard and Quinney, 1973; Gibbons, 1973; Bloch and Geis, 1970).

The current popularity of the white-collar crime concept attests as much to its political attractiveness as to its scientific value (Geis and Goff, 1983; Braithwaite, 1985:1). We argue that the major impact of the idea of white-collar crime has been to complicate the positivistic conception of its dependent variable and to deny the results of positivistic research that does not attend to the idea that crime and its causes are somehow class-specific.

Existing Theory of White-Collar Crime

A major problem in studying white-collar crime is to determine the claims or assertions implicit in the concept. The term assumes that white-collar crimes are indeed crimes, that people of high social standing commit real crimes, that the crimes they commit differ from common crimes, that the causes of their lawbreaking differ from those affecting other people, and that official responses to white-collar crime differ from those to common crime. Also commonly encountered is the view that white-collar crime is more serious, dangerous, or detrimental than is ordinary crime (Sutherland, 1983; Will, 1987). The concept of "church crime" would permit the same conclusions. The crimes committed by church leaders are undoubtedly real or true crimes that differ from nonchurch crimes (i.e., theft of nontaxable contributions is only possible in a nonprofit organization); the reasons for their crimes may be particular to their culture or economic situation; and the legal system may respond more leniently or severely to church crime than to crime in other systems.

So what appears to be a straightforward or useful concept turns out to be a potential source of considerable complexity. If we did not know that "white-collar crime" arose as a reaction to the idea that crime is concentrated in the lower class, there would be nothing to distinguish it from other ways of reminding us that crime may be found in all groups, even in the low rate categories of its causes (e.g., intact-home crime; valedictorian crime; female crime; elderly crime; small-town crime). The question is: Does the concept of white-collar crime have virtues or uses that distinguish it from the countless alternative ways of classifying crimes by the characteristics of their perpetrators? This may be answered by considering each of the main assumptions.

Is White-Collar Crime Crime? This question could not arise in classical theory, which did not attend to the characteristics of the offender, to the form of the crime, or to the likelihood that the crime would be met with legal sanction. Since crimes were attempts to gain personal advantage by force or fraud, they could obviously be committed by the rich and powerful, they could certainly involve force or fraud, and they could clearly be committed without punishment by the state.

Positive criminology made the concept of crime problematic in all respects. Essentially, offenders were people unable to learn civilized behavior, or people compelled to misbehave by forces over which they had little control. As a result, the law and its punishments were themselves concepts or institutions at odds with scientific knowledge of human behavior.

In this sense, the concept of white-collar crime is again a reaction against positivism, an assertion that something must be wrong with a worldview that denies that intelligent, powerful people use force and fraud to secure their own ends.

The evidence clearly supports this element of white-collar theorizing. There is no good reason to restrict the notion of crime to the lower classes (*contra* Merton, 1938; Cloward and Ohlin, 1960; Blau and Blau, 1982). When it comes to the use of force and fraud, crime is possible at all social levels, and white-collar crime is clearly crime. In fact, we would suggest that any theory of crime that makes claim to generality should apply without difficulty to the crimes of the rich and powerful, committed in the course of an occupation, in which a position of power, influence, or trust is used for the purpose of individual or organizational gain (Reiss and Biderman, 1980:4).

Do Persons of High Standing Commit Crimes? The concept of white-collar crime is said to be valuable because it reminds us that actual crime is not restricted to the lower class. "This study has attempted to . . . present evidence that persons of the upper socioeconomic class commit many crimes . . . . [This objective] has been realized in that a sample of large corporations is found to have violated laws with great frequency" (Sutherland, 1983:264).

So white-collar crime does occur. Some doctors commit murder, and others cheat on Medicare (Geis, et al., 1987); some lawyers misuse funds entrusted to them; some business executives engage in bid-rigging; some labor union executives embezzle funds from pension plans; some manufacturers hazardously dispose of toxic chemicals contrary to law. White-collar crime is an empirical reality as well as a conceptual possibility, regardless of any distinction between people and organizations. Nor are motivational elements required to distinguish white-collar crime from other forms of crime. As with common crime, the white-collar offender clearly seeks personal benefit. This benefit may come directly to the offender or indirectly to the offender through membership in a group or organization. As with other crimes, miscalculation of benefits is not evidence that benefits were not sought. One need not introduce unit of analysis issues (e.g., do organizations commit crime?) to document offending by persons of high social standing.

Do White-Collar Crimes Differ from Common Crimes? In order to explore the differences thought to exist between white-collar and common crimes, it is necessary to examine a sample of definitions of white-collar crime and derivative or analogous concepts:

> White-collar violations are those violations of law to which penalties are attached that involve the use of a violator's position of significant power, influence, or trust in the legitimate economic or political institutional order for the purpose of illegal gain, or to commit an illegal act for personal or organizational gain. (Reiss and Biderman, 1980:4)

> An illegal act or series of illegal acts committed by nonphysical means and by concealment or guile, to obtain money or property, to avoid the payment or loss of money or property, or to obtain business or personal advantage. (Edelhertz, 1970, in Braithwaite, 1985:18)

According to Clinard and Quinney, "occupational crime consists of offenses committed by individuals for themselves in the course of their occupations and the offenses of employees against their employers." According to the same authors, corporate crime is defined as "the offenses committed by corporate officials for the corporation and the offenses of the corporation itself" (Clinard and Quinney, 1973:188).

Obviously, advocates of the concept of white-collar crime believe they have identified a significant distinction among types of crime and types of criminals. We shall assess the value of these distinctions by their usefulness in explaining, predicting, or controlling the behavior of offenders, victims, or officials of the criminal justice system. Otherwise, analysis and evaluation of such concepts would be difficult or impossible without such criteria.

How Do White-Collar Criminals Differ from Other Criminals? Arguably, the concept of white-collar crime takes a fresh view of the relation between crime and employment. It challenges the traditional assumption that unemployment is conducive to crime and that employment is conducive to noncrime (i.e., unemployment theory). The assumed relationship between unemployment and crime stresses motivation; that crime is a consequence of the deprivation resulting from relative poverty. In contrast, the assumption that employment is conducive to crime (employment theory or "occupation theory" (see Clinard and Quinney, 1973), stresses opportunity for crime, provided by on-the-job access to money and goods. Neither view examines the social status or other properties of the offender. Both suggest that different individuals will respond similarly to the stresses of unemployment and to the opportunities of employment.

Clearly, research on the impact of employment on crime does not require a distinction between ordinary or common criminals and white-collar criminals. Both views focus on the same criminal acts and differ only with regard to the direction of the predicted impact of a specific independent variable. This difference is consistent with our earlier characterization of "white-collar crime theory" as a reaction to "positivistic" (force or pressure) theory. While research favoring employment theory over unemployment theory would say something about the status of the independent variable, it could not demonstrate the need for a special category of criminal (the white-collar offender). Employment theory can be consistent with the evidence without requiring the notion that crime accompanying employment is the product of distinct causes.

In short, a finding that the employed are more likely to steal because of their employment no more justifies a unique theory of theft (white-collar crime) than a finding that the unemployed are more likely to steal justifies a theory focusing exclusively on the lower class (deprivation or strain theory).

Advocates of the white-collar crime concept sometimes restrict it to crimes committed by wealthy, high-status, or respectable people in positions of power or trust (Sutherland, 1983; see also Reiss and Biderman, 1980). Here the research question becomes: Where do we find an appropriate comparison group for white-collar criminals?

Those adopting this restrictive definition of white-collar criminals compare them with ordinary offenders and ignore people with low social status who commit white-collar offenses. This allows them to use the same terms to describe common criminals and offenders of high status. For example, Sutherland shows that the acts of white-collar criminals are "deliberate," that they often "recidivate," and that they are difficult to "rehabilitate." This comparison also allows concerns about high-status, white-collar crime statistics traditionally reserved for ordinary crime statistics. Thus, according to Sutherland and others, official statistics vastly underestimate the extent of the criminal activities of high-status white-collar offenders, just as they underestimate those of ordinary offenders (1983:227–28; Reiss and Biderman, 1980).

Comparing high-status, white-collar offenders with low-status, ordinary offenders loses a large segment of the criminal population, but it allows description of those of high status in terms usually reserved for those of low status (e.g., "White-collar criminals possess a pimp's mentality" [Bequai, 1987a]). It also allows the suggestion that the revealed rot at the top is only the tip of the iceberg. But it has little else of positive value. It forces a separate theory of offending by suggesting that the causes of criminal behavior among the rich and powerful are different from those among the poor and weak. Some other comparison would seem to be required.

One possibility is to compare offenders in high social location with nonoffenders in the same positions. This is analogous to comparing lower-class people who commit crimes with lower-class people who do not or comparing good students who commit delinquencies with good students who do not. Given that both groups share the locational attribute, that attribute cannot account for the difference in their behavior. Therefore, this comparison directs attention away from social location toward microlevel or individual-level attributes such as strain, opportunity, or pathology. Since the same microlevel attributes may account for differences between offenders and nonoffenders among good students and among lower-class people, we are led to question the unique contribution of the concept of white-collar crime to crime theory.

White-collar criminals are also distinguished from other criminals through the concept of corporate crime (Braithwaite, 1985; Ermann and Lundman, 1982). According to Braithwaite (1985:19), "corporate crime, as the core area of concern, is . . . a broad but reasonably homogeneous domain for coherent theorizing. While useful theories of white-collar crime have proved elusive, influential corporate or organizational crime theory is a possibility." However, the empirical data generated on corporate crime do not require this concept for their interpretation, nor has it proved useful in identifying an important type of crime that would otherwise be missed. Those who prefer the organization rather than the individual as a unit of study, drop this idea when they collect or interpret their own data. Thus, although Sutherland tabulated his crime data on firms (referring to some large portion of them as "habitual criminals") and ridiculed explanations of their behavior based on individual pathology, he continued to explain corporate crime with the theory of differential association, and he consistently equated the behavior of the corporation with the behavior of the people in positions of power within it (Cohen, Lindesmith et al., 1956; Geis and Meier, 1977:84). Braithwaite's own review of the research on company executives who violate the law reaches the conclusion that "it is top management attitudes, most particularly those of the chief executive, that determine the level of compliance with the law in a corporation. . . . Moreover, middle managers are frequently reported as squeezed by a choice between failing to achieve targets set by top management and attaining the targets illegally" (1985:17). It seems to us that these assertions take the corporation as a setting in which crimes may or may not occur, but do not treat the corporation as the criminal actor. Again, white-collar crime is no different from other crimes that occur in group or organizational settings where those in authority have more to say about what happens than those in subordinate positions—for example, governments, military units, university departments, and, for that matter, delinquent gangs.

It may be, then, that the discovery of white-collar criminals is important only in a context in which their existence is denied by theory or policy as it was in Sutherland's time, but not so today. Some other research comparison is therefore required. Perhaps the theoretical utility of the concept can be found in comparisons of crimes rather than criminals.

How Do White-Collar Crimes Differ from Other Crimes? This question can be approached in several ways. First, white-collar crimes can be defined as crimes that can only be committed by persons occupying positions of power and influence. This rules out crimes committed by both high- and low-status people. For example, murder of one's spouse and rape would not be considered white-collar crime, unless they are a consequence of the offender's occupational power and influence. In contrast: bank embezzlement can only be committed by employees of banks; insider trading can only by committed by stock brokers; Medicaid fraud can only be committed by those who bill their services to the program; only automobile manufacturers can build cars that fail to meet legal standards; income taxes can be evaded only by people who owe taxes.

This approach appears to identify a distinct class of crimes that *could* require a unique explanation. But what is the theoretical value in distinguishing a pharmacist's theft of drugs from a carpenter's theft of lumber? The white-collar crime concept tends to suggest that the pharmacist's theft is more important or serious than, or the product of different causes from, the carpenter's theft. It suggests that the doctor's fraud is more important (socially damaging?) or serious than the patient's, that the causes of one differ from the causes of the other, and so on. These suggestions really involve two, largely unrelated but often confused questions: (1) Are the causes of various offenses the same? (2) Are the offenses themselves equally serious? It is often assumed that the answer to the second question bears on the answer to the first, that more serious crimes must have causes different from (more powerful than?) those of less serious crimes. However, neither logic nor, as we shall see, the evidence support this assumption.

If distinguishing white-collar crimes from analogous blue-collar crimes is of little value, is there value in distinguishing *among* such white-collar crimes as Medicaid fraud, income tax evasion, insider trading, antitrust violations, bid-rigging, and consumer fraud? For purposes such as detection, prosecution, and crime control, distinctions among crimes are clearly useful (Cornish and Clarke, 1986a). But these purposes do not require offender differences across such crimes or unique theories of offending. Students of juvenile delinquency have found no utility in studying specialization in vandalism, arson, rape, or burglary. By extension, there is little reason to think that specialization in white-collar offenses will bear fruit. On the contrary, we shall show that a single theory applies to all types of white-collar offenses and to all other offenses.

The Connection between Crime Types and Types of Criminals. In explaining the connection between age and crime, we distinguished between crime as an event and criminality as a characteristic of people (Hirschi and Gottfredson, 1986). It made more sense to talk about types of crime than about types of criminals. Events have distinct sets of causes (e.g., autos are necessary for auto theft, access to other people's money is necessary for embezzlement, and so on). Also the evidence seems clear that offenders do just about everything, rather than specialize in any particular type of crime. Identifying offenders with offenses is therefore misleading. Robbers may have committed robbery, but they are more likely in the future to engage in theft than robbery, and only very slightly more likely than any other offender to rob again. This might also be true for embezzlement, fraud, and forgery. While embezzlement, fraud, and forgery are distinct events, and may therefore have distinct causes, there is no reason to think that offenders committing these crimes are causally distinct from other offenders. A general theory of criminality is therefore not logically precluded by white-collar crime any more than by robbery or any other specific type of crime. The assumption that white-collar criminals differ from other criminals is not supported by good evidence.

A General Theory of Crime

Starting from the distinction between crimes as events and criminality as a characteristic of people, we have been developing a general theory of crime designed to account for the distribution of all forms of criminal behavior (Hirschi and Gottfredson, 1986, 1987b; Gottfredson and Hirschi, 1987b). Whereas traditional positivistic theories begin by looking at offenders, we begin by looking at crime. We conclude that the properties of criminal events must be taken into account in any explanation. Features of criminal events are capable of falsifying traditional theories that derive their dependent variable from ordinary disciplinary perspectives. For example, crimes have in common features that make those engaging in any one of them extremely likely to engage in others as well. These common features are not money, success, or peer approval. They are therefore inconsistent with most theories of crime and must be identified by a valid theory of crime. Most theories of crime assume that offenders specialize; that they have careers in crime that progress, develop, or change over time; and that each type of crime has its own motives. These assumptions are contrary to the evidence.

Crime. Because the evidence suggests that the essential properties of crimes are not money, success, reduction of frustration, or peer approval and because versatility in offenders is an empirical fact, all crimes must share other common properties that make them appealing to potential offenders.

Such a concept of crime presupposes a concept of human nature. In our view, the concept of human nature that best organizes the data is that found in the classical assumption that human behavior is motivated by the self-interested pursuit of pleasure and the avoidance of pain. Crimes are events in which force or fraud are used to satisfy self-interest, where self-interest refers to the enhancement of pleasure and the avoidance of pain. Features of events that enhance their pleasure or minimize their pain will be implicated in their causation. To be maximally pleasurable, events should take place immediately; pleasure is therefore enhanced by the *rapidity* with which it is obtained. Force and fraud can often produce more rapid results than alternative means; they are therefore useful in the pursuit of self-interest. To be maximally pleasurable, events should be *certain* in outcome; force and fraud can provide more certain benefit than alternative means, particularly when the benefit sought is short-term and the long-term consequences of the act are of little concern. To be maximally pleasurable, events should require *minimal effort*; force and fraud can provide benefit with less effort than alternative means, especially when the benefit also has the properties of rapidity and certainty.

White-collar crimes satisfy these defining conditions. They provide relatively quick, relatively certain benefit, with minimal effort. Crimes, including white-collar crimes, therefore require no motivation or pressure that is not present in any other form of human behavior.

Since crimes involve goods, services, or victims, they have other constituent properties: they all require opportunity, and are thought to result in punishment of the offender if he or she is detected. Such properties cannot account for the general tendency of particular individuals to engage in crime, and they are therefore not central to a theory of criminality.

Criminality. Our conception of the essential features of *crime* provides the basis of a theory of *criminality*. Criminality is the tendency of individuals to pursue short-term gratification in the most direct way with little consideration for the long-term consequences of their acts. (Indicators of such a tendency include impulsivity, aggression, activity level, and lack of concern for the opinion of others.) People high on this tendency are relatively unable or unwilling to delay gratification; they are relatively indifferent to punishment and to the interests of others. As a consequence, they tend to be impulsive, active, and risk taking.

Research demonstrating consistency in behavior over substantial periods of time is consistent with this concept of criminality. For example, differences in the tendency toward aggression persist from childhood to adulthood (Eron, 1987; Olweus, 1979), as do differences in the tendency toward delinquency and crime (Loeber, 1982; Loeber and Dishion, 1983; McCord, 1979; Glueck and Glueck, 1968; West and Farrington, 1977).

Such tendencies do not lead ineluctably to crime, regardless of the setting. Crimes require physical opportunity and immunity from immediate punishment in addition to individual tendencies. Also, many noncriminal acts provide the benefits of crime and are therefore attractive to those with high levels of "criminality"—for example, drug, alcohol, and cigarette use, sex, divorce, job quitting, and fast cars. To complicate things further, these tendencies often affect the settings in which the individuals possessing them are located—for example, the amount of education they attain, the kind of job they have, whether they marry and stay married.

Application of the General Theory to White-Collar Crime. The characteristics described above have implications for the likelihood of criminal acts, but they also have implications for selection into the occupational structure. Ordinary occupations require people to be in a particular place at a particular time. They also require educational persistence, willingness and ability to defer to the interests of others, and attention to conventional appearance. These occupational requirements tend to be inconsistent with the traits comprising criminality. White-collar occupations therefore tend to demand characteristics inconsistent with high levels of criminality. Selection processes inherent to the high end of the occupational structure tend to recruit people with relatively low propensity to crime.

Our theory therefore predicts a relatively low rate of offending among white-collar workers, contrary to the now standard view (e.g., Reiman, 1979; Sutherland, 1983). The standard view is based on misleading statistics about the extent of white-collar offending. White-collar researchers often take *organizations* as the unit of analysis and do not adjust for their size and complexity when making comparisons with blue-collar *individuals*. Also, the reference period for the organization is often much longer than that applied to individuals (Sutherland, 1983). Consequently, the white-collar crime literature often compares the number of crimes committed by an organization with many thousands of employees over a period of many years with those committed by single individuals in a single year.

When comparable units (such as individuals with the same crime relevant characteristics, e.g., age, sex, ethnicity), comparable reference periods (e.g., one year), and comparable methods of measurement (e.g., self-reports or arrests) are employed, rates of crime among employed white-collar workers should be low compared to those of persons in less structured occupations with similar opportunities, and compared to those outside the occupational structure with similar opportunities.

Our distinction between people and events treats white-collar crimes as events occurring in an occupational setting, not as characteristics of people employed in those settings. Therefore, it makes problematic the connection between the people and the events and allows the possibility that this connection is less strong than the connection between people in other settings and the criminal events unique to those settings. Obviously, only white-collar workers can commit white-collar crimes, but this cannot be taken as evidence of their criminality unless (1) other people are given the opportunity to commit the same crimes in the same setting, or (2) other settings and crimes are construed, for purposes of comparison, to be equivalent to white-collar crime. The latter solution is the one adopted by the criminal law, and by most compilations of crime statistics.

In law and in crime statistics, embezzlement, fraud, and forgery are defined without reference to the occupational setting in which they occur. Consequently, it is possible to study the demographic distributions of white-collar crimes and compare them with the same distributions for other crimes. Our general theory predicts that differences in the demographic correlates across crimes should be nonexistent given similar opportunity structures. Data from the Uniform Crime Reports show similar *patterns* in: (1) the arrest rates for fraud and embezzlement by age; (2) the arrest rates of embezzlement of males and females and of whites and blacks/others; and (3) the age distribution of arrests for murder, embezzlement, and fraud. Moreover, when opportunity is taken into account, demographic differences in white-collar crime are the same as demographic differences in ordinary crime. (See Hirschi and Gottfredson, 1987a, for a full discussion of these data.)

Individual Differences and White-Collar Crime. Research and theory relating individual characteristics to involvement in crime are often ridiculed on the grounds that white-collar offenders have traits "opposite" to those said to cause crime:

> Quite obviously, the hypothesis that crime is due to personal and social pathologies does not apply to white-collar crimes, and if it does not explain these crimes such pathologies are not essential factors in crime in general. In contrast with such explanations the hypothesis of differential association and social disorganization may apply to white-collar crimes as well as to lower class crimes. (Sutherland, 1983:264)

Trait theorists are particularly vulnerable to this criticism, since most of the traits they believe are conducive to crime (e.g., aggressiveness, risk taking, activity level, mesomorphy, sociability) could also be said to be conducive to business success. The problems with this argument are threefold. (1) There is no empirical evidence that "traits" positively correlated with ordinary crime are negatively correlated with white-collar crime. (2) It denies that a single cause (or set of causes) may have differential manifestations such that an active person may be both more likely to succeed in business and to engage in criminal acts; an impulsive person may be both more likely to shoplift and to embezzle. (3) It confuses location in the business world with success in business. It assumes that white-collar criminals are successful at white-collar occupations. Although one must be in the white-collar world to be a white-collar offender, most white-collar workers do not enjoy high power, income, and prestige. However, this erroneous assumption leads to the expectation that the correlates of white-collar crime will be opposite to the correlates of ordinary crime. After all, it takes a while to be successful in the business world, and while this is happening one is growing older, a fact that must reverse the usual negative relation between age and crime; obviously, whites have an advantage over blacks in the white-collar world; therefore, here at least whites should have a higher rate of crime; obviously, intelligence is positively related to white-collar success and therefore should be positively related to white-collar crime. In all cases where data are available, they suggest otherwise.

Scholars continue to argue that the criminal justice system favors white-collar workers, that businesses protect them to maintain their own reputations, and that white-collar crimes are relatively easily concealed. However, the Bureau of Justice Statistics reports that, in 1983, the probability of incarceration for white-collar offenders was as high as that for violent offenders. Research shows that punishments for white-collar offenses are governed by the same criteria governing punishments for other crimes (Wheeler, et al., 1982).

The Value of White-Collar Crime for Crime Theory. The concept of white-collar crime is usually seen as incompatible with most theories of crime, particularly theories that focus on differences in the biology, psychology, or social position of offenders and nonoffenders. Other theories have gained considerable advantage from appearing to be peculiarly compatible with the concept. It is universally agreed that the more general a theory, the better, and theories that can encompass white-collar crime along with common crime must, it seems, be very general and therefore superior to theories that deal only with ordinary crime, or, worse, only with "juvenile delinquency." Indeed, the objection most frequently raised to explanatory efforts in criminology is typically phrased something like: "Yes, but what about white-collar crime?" We believe that distinctions among types of criminals confuse more than they clarify and that the general model we use here and, especially, elsewhere (Hirschi and Gottfredson, 1986, 1987b; Gottfredson and Hirschi, 1987b) accounts for all criminal behavior.

The theories gaining most from the white-collar crime concept are those focusing on learning, especially of cultural values, such as Sutherland's theory of differential association. Sutherland asserted that white-collar crime could only be understood as a consequence or natural extension of ordinary business values (1983:240–64; see also Cressey, 1986). Those socialized within the business world could come to define their criminal activities as required by the needs of profit making and as generally supported in the business community by "neutralizing verbalizations" (Cressey, 1986:200). Additionally, they could there find training in the techniques required to commit crimes of such complexity. Modern variants of this perspective seek to answer similar questions: "In what ways is society organized that it may encourage the very phenomenon it seeks to control?" (Vaughan, 1983:19).

The survival of such theories of crime is directly attributable to their apparent generality, to their apparent ability to account for phenomena beyond the reach of theories that focus on individual differences. Ironically, although these theories owe their current popularity and even survival to their connection to white-collar (or organizational) crime, they have not helped our understanding.

Consider the causal mechanisms used to understand crime in the cultural theory tradition. In this tradition, the individual learns that crime is condoned by the values of the organization or is required as a natural byproduct of its pursuit of profits. In some versions, the organization creates expectations of performance that may be met only by law violation (Braithwaite, 1985:17; Vaughan, 1983); in others, the techniques and rationalizations required for white-collar crime are simple extensions of routine business practices. In either case, criminal activity is seen as consistent with, rather than contrary to, the values of those engaging in it.

However, contrary to the expectations of these theories, white-collar offenses are relatively rare. If the white-collar workforce is actually socialized to the virtues of embezzlement, bid-rigging, and fraud, what accounts for the extraordinarily high level of law-abiding conduct among white-collar workers? It is easily shown that crime by partners or employees may increase the cost of doing business to the point that business is no longer profitable. The limits on white-collar crime set by requirements of profits and survival are rarely recognized by white-collar crime theorists. These limits have, however, been noted by students of "organized crime" (see Reuter, 1983).   Another difficulty for such theories is suggested by the routine finding that white-collar offenders tend to receive little support for their criminal activities from the organization or from other white-collar workers. Indeed, the evidence suggests that they are especially concerned with concealing their crimes from co-workers and management (Cressey, 1953; Vaughan, 1983; Lasley, 1987). The reasons for such concern are revealing: the victim of white-collar crime is typically the organization itself, not the general public. Since white-collar offenders share the general propensity of offenders to pursue self-interest, they naturally take advantage of the most readily available opportunities. By ascribing larger purposes to white-collar criminals, cultural theories tend to mispredict the nature of white-collar victimization.

The cultural theory of white-collar crime also mispredicts the correlates of the phenomena, suggesting that the longer the exposure to the business culture, the higher the level of criminal activity (contrary to the age distribution of white-collar crime), suggesting that opportunity itself is sufficient to overcome ordinary differences in the likelihood of criminal activity (contrary to the sex, race, and age differences referred to earlier), suggesting that white-collar crimes are so complicated that unusual training or skill is required for their performance (contrary to evidence showing that most white-collar crime involves such activities as the transfer of funds from one account to another, dumping barrels of chemicals in remote areas, or alteration of routine billing practices; see Vaughan, 1983), all within a context of belief that such practices are unlikely to be discovered. To say that such practices are consistent with the offender's profit motive (self-interest) is obviously true; to say that they are consistent with the generally accepted values of the business world is wrong.

Finally, these theories all fail as explanations of ordinary crime and delinquency (Kornhauser, 1978). The white-collar crime area thus falls prey to its own critique of criminological theories: the generally accepted white-collar crime theories cannot explain ordinary crime and are thus, by their own logic (Sutherland, 1983), incapable of explaining crime, whether white-collar or ordinary.

Our general theory of crime avoids these problems. It predicts variation in rates across social settings, with white-collar crime rates being relatively low, depending on the process of selection into the particular white-collar occupation. Our theory disagrees with traditional "white-collar" theory on the rate issue, and thus leads to a directly testable empirical question. Our theory is of course not bothered by the fact that people can pursue criminal activities without social support. On the contrary, it explicitly predicts lack of social support for most white-collar crimes because (1) they are contrary to general social norms, and (2) are against the interests of the organization itself. We therefore have a second empirical issue of direct theoretical relevance.

We earlier asserted that our general theory expects the properties of those committing crime to be similar regardless of the type of crime. Our theory therefore asserts that the distinction between crime in the street and crime in the suite is an *offense* rather than an *offender* distinction, that offenders in both cases are likely to share similar characteristics. We therefore have a third directly testable distinction between our general theory and the commonly accepted view of white-collar crime.

Our theory was constructed with common offenses and offenders in mind. It is meant to predict and explain ordinary crime, juvenile delinquency, drug abuse, serious crime, "organized" crime, status offending, as well as white-collar crime. Since our theory permits no propensity distinctions among types of offenses, it is perfectly general, and is once again directly contrary to cultural theories, with their view that crimes have unique, specific cultural motives.

Conclusion

It is time criminology recognized that the typological approach inherent in the concept of white-collar crime is a mistake. One of the causes of this mistake is found in the enduring tendency of those who study crime to subordinate the topic to the interests of their parent discipline. This tendency is particularly marked among sociologists, who see in white-collar crime an opportunity to save conceptual schemes that have not proved useful with ordinary offenders. It is also present among economists, who see in white-collar crime an opportunity to explicate once again the grand scheme of their discipline. Psychologists, comfortable with the idea of typologies, endlessly divide offenders into groups thought to be "relatively homogeneous" with respect to the meaning of their offenses. And quantitative analysts of all disciplinary persuasions see white-collar crime as one more opportunity to specify a formal model. All these disciplinary interests are served by acceptance of the received view of "white-collar offending." This essay questions the received view and reasserts the view that crime is a unitary phenomenon capable of explanation by a single theory, a theory that seeks first the features common to all crimes and deduces from them tendencies to criminality in the individual. It is then in position to outline the causes of such tendencies and to consider the differential manifestation of these tendencies. Such differential manifestation is of course a function of the opportunities available to people, of the circumstances in which they find themselves. To think otherwise is to confuse social location with social causation.

Biological and Psychological Theory

Introduction

In response to what they saw as the naive analysis of crime, classical policy's inability to control increasing rates of crime, and influenced by the growing role of science as a solution to control life's problems, nineteenth-century Italian anthropologist and psychiatrist Cesare Lombroso (1835–1909) and his student Enrico Ferri (1856–1928) founded a new approach called positivist criminology. Instead of focusing on the crime and the offender's choice about whether or not to commit it, this approach sought to discover what it was about criminals that caused them to commit offenses. Through detailed description of the characteristics of the cadavers of criminals, they claimed to have discovered what made these offenders different from nonoffenders. They believed this biological difference resulted from criminals being "atavistic," born as reversions to a more primitive evolutionary state. No matter that their subjects were exclusively convicted offenders, and disregarding the use of control groups to check whether there was any difference between offenders and nonoffenders, these founders of the biological perspective spawned the first "scientific" criminology. Although their ideas were later disproved, and even though they modified them to accept more multicausal factors, including social ones, to explain other classes of offender, the tradition diffused to the United States. It did so through the writing of criminal anthropologists, physical constitutional theorists, and later extended to degeneration or "feeblemindedness" ideas that linked delinquency to mental underdevelopment, before dispersing into a variety of diverse biologically rooted crime concepts where it remains today.

The history of the emigration of these ideas from Europe to the United States is colorfully illustrated in Nicole Hahn Rafter's contribution (chap. 4). Drawing on the original major works of U.S. criminal anthropologists in the period between 1881 to 1911, Rafter exposes their complete denial of free will among criminals, their blurring of criminals with other degenerate types, their lack of criminological knowledge, training, and professional uniformity, and their construction of criminal typologies under the assumption that if these emerged from empirical measurements of criminal bodies using scientific instruments, then the outcome must be science. Rafter argues that criminology's multi-disciplinary nature, permeable disciplinary boundaries, and diverse methodologies persist today in part because of the approach taken by these early theorists.

Since the early 1920s, although criminal anthropology has all but been abandoned, biological theories of causality have simmered on criminology's back burner, occasionally erupting with a flurry of new findings. These have included everything from chromosomes (XYY) to hormones as the culpable inner forces that allegedly cause some people to offend. However, the most prevalent biological theorists today focus on the more slippery notion of genetic forces, typically using studies of twins and adoptees to demonstrate genetic effects. As the article by Diane Fishbein (chap. 5) demonstrates, contemporary biological theorists have a more sophisticated argument, suggesting not only that genes interact with the environment to affect human behavior, but that even when they do so, they typically only account for a proportion of it. Fishbein assesses the contribution of biological "markers" in shaping the behavior of the most persistent or most "vulnerable" antisocial offenders. Rather than taking biological contribution alone, Fishbein considers this in combination with environmental and sociocultural conditions to provide us with a taste of the latest research integrating biology, psychology, and sociology toward a behavior-genetic approach to understanding serious crime.

Like the body, the mind has long been considered a source of abnormal behavior and has been subject to psychiatric and psychological analyses. Henry Maudsley (1835–1918) argued that crime was a release for pathological minds that prevented them going insane, while Isaac Ray (1807–81) believed that pathological urges drove some to commit crime. These early psychiatric explanations were founded on the assumptions that psychoses were biologically based. However, from this perspective it is not so much sick minds that cause crime but that certain psychological processes in any mind may produce criminal behavior. Psychological theories of crime explain abnormal behavior as the result of mind and thought processes that form during human development, particularly during the early years.

The development of psychological theory in relation to crime began with the idea of uncovering hidden unconscious forces within a person's mind. Although Sigmund Freud (1856–1939) is credited with founding this approach to crime, he wrote little on criminals, but his theory has been applied by others. Since Freud, psychology has taken divergent directions. It increasingly recognizes the role of environmental influences on learning, and that the human learning process involves complex creative interpretation and analysis of information. One direction, behavioral and situational learning theories, based on Pavlov and B. F. Skinner's theories of operant conditioning, was to see persons' present behavior based on accumulations of responses resulting from past learning. (We exemplify theories of crime based on this approach in a subsequent section of this reader.) Another direction, the trait-based perspective founded on the work of Gordon Allport (1937), sees human development as leading to distinctive personality types based upon learned traits. Trait-based personality theories differ from the psychoanalytic approach in that rather than seeing abnormal behavior as the result of unconscious causes, it is said to stem from abnormal or criminal personality traits. Traits "represent consistent characteristics of individuals that are relevant to a wide variety of behavioral domains" (Caspi et al., 1994:165). Allport (1937:48) defined personality as the dynamic organization of an individual's psychophysical systems of predispositions to the environment. One task of trait-based theory then is to measure these various, frequently occurring, traits to see how they are assembled differently in different people and with what effects. Trait-based personality takes the view that criminal behavior is a manifestation of an underlying trait-based problem within the individual.

In the example selected here, Avshalom Caspi, Terrie Moffitt, and their colleagues (chap. 6) report on their studies on the relation between personality traits and crime in two studies. In one study based in New Zealand, they studied eighteen-year-old males and females from an entire birth cohort. In a second study based in Pittsburgh they studied an ethnically diverse group of twelve- and thirteen-year-old boys. In both studies they gathered multiple and independent measures of personality and delinquent involvement. They report that the personality correlates of delinquency were "robust" in different nations, in different age cohorts, across gender, and across race: greater delinquent participation was associated with a personality configuration characterized by high Negative Emotionality and weak Constraint. They argue that when Negative Emotionality (the tendency to experience aversive affective states) is accompanied by weak Constraint (difficulty in impulse control), negative emotions may be translated more readily into antisocial acts.

4

Criminal Anthropology in the United States

Nicole Hahn Rafter

This chapter examines the U.S. experience with criminal anthropology in order to expose the roots of key debates within American criminology. I argue that by investigating the interplay between U.S. criminal anthropologists' professionalization of criminology and the kinds of information they produced, criminologists can better grasp criminology's difficulties in (1) establishing a clear-cut disciplinary identity; (2) defining its methods; and (3) distinguishing its role as a knowledge enterprise from its contributions to crime control.

This study covers criminal anthropology in the United States from 1881 to 1911. By 1911 leading theorists had rejected the doctrine of the criminal as a physically anomalous type (Parmelee, 1911) and begun to favor defective delinquency theory, which equated criminality with mental retardation (Fernald, 1909).

Terms and Method

The term *criminal anthropologists* refers to writers who held that the worst criminals ("born," "congenital," "incorrigible," or "instinctive") deviate from ethical and biological normality because they are atavisms, reversions to a more primitive evolutionary state. *Criminal anthropology in the United States* includes all writings endorsing this doctrine published in the United States through 1911. *U.S. criminal anthropology* includes those works authored by Americans. I use the term *professionalization of criminology* to describe criminal anthropologists' establishment of the field as a new scholarly specialty.

Edited and abridged from *Criminology*, Volume 30(4):525–45 (1992).

It is necessary to say a few words about *positivism*, which criminal anthropologists interpreted somewhat differently than we do today. Gottfredson and Hirschi (1987a:10) define positivism as "the scientific approach to the study of crime where science is characterized by methods, techniques, or rules of procedure rather than by substantive theory." Contemporary positivism is empirical, often but not necessarily quantitative, inductive, and grounded in "belief in an objective external reality" (Gottfredson and Hirschi, 1987a:19). Likewise criminal anthro-pologists emphasized direct observation and data collection, but unlike current positivists they also accepted folk wisdom, anecdotes from creative literature, and analogies between criminals and "lower" forms of life that would no longer be considered "empirical." When they dealt with the "born" criminal they equated positivism with the philosophy of materialism (or naturalism), according to which all phenomena can be explained in terms of physical laws, and they espoused an absolute determinism, denying any role whatsoever to free will.

I am not concerned here with documenting criminal anthropology's methodological sins and inaccuracies but with the ways in which as a discourse it laid the basis for some of criminology's ongoing debates.

The Diffusion of Criminal Anthropology in the United States

To follow the diffusion of criminal anthropology in the United States, one must distinguish among three groups of producers: (1) *"originators,"* Europeans who generated the theory in the first place; (2) *"channelers,"* those who initially gave Americans access to the originators' work; and (3) *"U.S. criminal anthropologists,"* the Americans who elaborated on the channelers' materials. Few U.S. criminal anthropologists had first-hand contact with the work of Cesare Lombroso, the founding originator, and few had expertise in social science. As a result, U.S. criminology began without a well-defined research agenda or sense of its disciplinary boundaries.

The Originators

The first work on criminal anthropology published in the United States, Moriz Benedikt's *Anatomical Studies upon Brains of Criminals* (1881), appeared before Lombroso's work was available. A Hungarian aware of Lombroso's studies in Italy, Benedikt was inspired to study the cranium and brain of criminals by Franz Joseph Gall, the founder of phrenology. Dissections led Benedikt to conclude that criminal brains deviate from the normal and that "criminals are to be viewed as an anthropological variety of their species" (Benedikt, 1881:157). This finding excited debate, especially among physicians (Fink, 1938:107–9), on the existence of an anatomically distinct criminal type. But Benedikt's book was too abstruse and clinical to have much impact on mainstream U.S. social scientists interested in the causes of crime, and the work became little more than a footnote.

In contrast, Lombroso exercised great influence, but for years Americans knew his work mainly through secondary sources. Both Arthur MacDonald's *Criminology* (1893) and August Drahms's *The Criminal* (1900) carried introductions by Lombroso. Subscribers to the journal *The Forum* could read Lombroso's "Criminal Anthropology: Its Origin and Application," an 1895 survey of the field. Portions of one of his major studies also appeared in English in 1895 as *The Female Offender* (Lombroso and Ferrero, 1895), just two years after its Italian publication, and by 1911 this book had been reprinted six times. However, Lombroso's key work, *L'Uomo Delinquente,* first appearing in Italian in 1876, was not published here until 1911 as *Criminal Man.* Even then it was a compilation by Lombroso's daughter (Lombroso-Ferrero, 1911). Lombroso's *Crime: Its Causes and Remedies* appeared in English the same year (Lombroso, 1911).

Thus Americans who could not read Lombroso in the original or French translation lacked direct access to his work until criminal anthropology's heyday had passed. Those who built on his research from a distance were often doubly derivative, dependent on both Lombroso's research and the channelers who gave them access to it.

The Channelers

Translators played an important role by determining which European works would reach U.S. audiences. Americans might never have heard of Benedikt, for example, had E. P. Fowler, a New York physician, not translated his *Anatomical Studies* from German. Henry P. Horton, who translated Lombroso's *Crime: Its Causes and Remedies* from French and German sources, also helped introduce Americans to Italian criminal anthropology.

European criminal anthropology further flowed to the United States through the work of the English eugenicist Havelock Ellis, author of *The Criminal* (1890), a book that relied primarily on Lombroso's work. By 1911 *The Criminal* was in its fourth edition and had gone through nine printings; it became the well into which many U.S. Lombrosians dipped for data on born criminals.

Other very early and brief American reports on Lombroso's research formed yet another channel for criminal anthropology. Psychologist Joseph Jastrow's (1886:20) article "A Theory of Criminality," uncritically outlined criminality as "a morbid phenomenon . . . a defect," deriving its information from a French review by Lombroso. A physician at New York's Bloomingdale Asylum, William Noyes, wrote a paper (1887) on "The Criminal Type," emphasizing the criminal's bad heredity and primitive nature; based on a French edition of *L'Uomo Delinquente*, it too was undilutedly Lombrosian.

It was a physician at New York's Elmira Reformatory, Hamilton Wey (1888, 1890), who introduced members of the National Prison Association to criminal anthropology. Citing Benedikt, the influential English hereditarian Francis Galton, and Ellis as well as Lombroso, Wey supplemented the theory of criminal anthropology with his own data gathered at Elmira. Wey's relatively critical attitude toward Lombroso and his transcending of European sources made him a transitional figure between the channelers and the U.S. criminal anthropologists.

U.S. Criminal Anthropologists

As Lombroso's theory spread, a third group of producers, U.S. elaborators of criminal anthropology, outnumbered the other two (see Table 1). MacDonald's *Criminology* (1893) was the first U.S. treatise to identify its subject as "criminology" and its author as a specialist in the area. MacDonald listed his credentials, claimed that his findings had scientific status, and dedicated his book to Lombroso, "the founder of criminology," who wrote its introduction. For these reasons, *Criminology's* 1893 appearance may be taken as the U.S. field's starting point. However, for some time to come the study of crime and criminals remained intertwined with investigations of other "degenerate" types.

The major American books on criminal anthropology addressed somewhat different audiences, but all were directed toward educated lay people, especially the growing body of social welfare workers. Henderson designed his *Introduction to the Study of the Dependent, Defective and Delinquent Classes* (1893) as a textbook for college students and welfare workers; Parsons's *Responsibility for Crime* (1909), originally a Columbia University dissertation, was also written for classroom use. Lydston intended *The Diseases of Society* "primarily for professional readers" but hoped it would do "a little missionary work" among "the reading public" as well (1904:9). Other works were written to inform—usually to alarm—the general public. None was aimed chiefly at scholars.

The major U.S. criminal anthropologists were all well-educated male

Table 1: Major U.S. Books on Criminal Anthropology
Published 1893–1911

Author	Title	First Date of Publication	Other Dates of U.S. Publication
MacDonald, A.	*Criminology*	1893	--
Boies, H.	*Prisoners and Paupers*	1893	--
Henderson, C. R.	*An Introduction to the Study of the Dependent, Defective and Delinquent Classes*	1893	1901 1908 1909
Talbot, E.	*Degeneracy*	1898	1904
Drahms, A.	*The Criminal: His Personnel and Environment*	1900	--
McKim, W. D.	*Heredity and Human Progress*	1900	1901
Boies, H.	*The Science of Penology*	1901	
Lydston, G. F.	*The Diseases of Society*	1904	1905 1906 1908
Parsons, P.	*Responsibility for Crime*	1909	--

professionals. They included social welfare workers (Boies, Drahms, and Henderson), educators (Henderson, Lydston, MacDonald, and Talbot), physicians (Lydston, McKim, and Talbot), and ministers (Drahms and Henderson; MacDonald, too, had studied theology). Most were professionally qualified across one or more specialties.

Eventually, this multiplicity of professional backgrounds affected the field of criminology negatively. Like Lombroso, who trained as a physician, the Americans came to criminology from the outside, as amateur specialists. This was inevitable. Like social science in general, criminology was still in its "formative period" (MacDonald, 1893:271). The field had no "inside," no training program (Kellor, 1901:5) that could give its practitioners a common set of skills or foster consensus on research goals. MacDonald's European studies had included some formal training in criminology, and four of the other authors had extensive contact with prisoners; but otherwise American advocates of the "new science" (Lombroso-Ferrero, 1911:5) had few qualifications other than an ability to digest their sources and speak knowledgeably. Although they presented masses of data, they did no experimental work (also see Garland, 1985:97). Thus, the field they founded initially had no clearly defined kernel of skills or even goals, other than to broadcast versions of criminal anthropology. Nor did they themselves have a uniform professional identity. The result was a discipline that lacked boundaries and continues into the present to overlap with others, such as psychology and sociology.

The Substance of U.S. Criminal Anthropology

At the time criminal anthropologists were writing, the primary experts on criminal matters were legal authorities and penologists. A tradition of positivist criminological research had been accumulating throughout the nineteenth century, provided by "alienists" who analyzed the connections between mental disorders and crime (e.g., Ray, 1838), phrenologists who investigated the organic causes of crime (e.g., Farnham, 1846; also see Davies, 1955:chap. 8; Savitz et al., 1977), and degenerationists, such as Richard Dugdale (1877), who associated criminal behavior with bad heredity. But these forerunners did not present their work as "criminology" nor themselves as "criminologists." Lombroso's followers had to stake out new professional territory, separate from jurisprudence and penology, over which criminologists would have authority (Abbott, 1988). To accomplish this they first claimed that their approach constituted an entirely new science and then they produced information on criminal types that confirmed that claim.

Criminal Anthropology as a Science

Echoing Lombroso, the Americans insisted that criminal anthropology had for the first time carried the study of crime across the divide between idle speculation and true science. Noyes (1887:32) heralded the advent of a "new science, which considers the criminal rather than the crime"; Drahms, calling crime a "social disease," claimed that "Criminology . . . reaches the dignity of a science by the same right of necessity that gives to the medical profession its place" (1900:xxi–xxii). They did not always label this science "criminology," however. They sometimes preferred to fold their emerging study of criminal man into better accepted sciences—"scientific sociology" (MacDonald, 1893:173), "the science of penology" (Boies, 1901), or the "scientific" investigation of degeneracy (Talbot, 1898:viii). But all considered their work "scientific," meaning that unlike those who had earlier included God and free will in the causational picture of crime, they would be materialists, examining only phenomena anchored in the natural world of matter.

Benedikt made his materialism explicit: "man thinks, feels, desires, and acts according to the anatomical construction and physiological development of his brain" (1881:vii). Wey observed, "Of criminologists there are, generally speaking, two schools, the theological or spiritualistic and the material or anthropological" (1890:275; also see Drahms, 1900:22). Lydston (1904:18) contrasted the work of "the sentimental, non-scientific moralist" and that of "the scientific criminologist," whose job was "to reduce the subject to a material, scientific, and, so far as possible, evolutionary basis." With such remarks, criminal anthropologists voiced their determination to uncover the physical determinants of crime.

Materialism led to an approach that relied exclusively on empirical methods, using direct observation instead of theory or metaphysics. They would report on measurements of criminals' bodies made with scientific equipment, such as calipers, the dynamometer, and the aesthesiometer; they would collect information on criminal jargon and tattoos, excerpt passages from confessions, and gather "proverbs expressing distrust of the criminal type" (Lombroso-Ferrero, 1911:50). All such data would be recorded dispassionately. "A large part of the most rigid science," said MacDonald in his *Criminology* (1893:17), "consists in simple and exact description, which should be given, of course, without regard to any views that one may consciously or unconsciously hold." Materialism also implied that criminal anthropologists would use induction to formulate natural laws. Like other scientists, they would build up to whatever theory the facts indicated.

Materialism led criminal anthropologists to their central assumption—that the body must mirror moral capacity. They took for granted a one-to-one correspondence between the criminal's physical being and ethical behavior. Criminals, wrote Boies (1893:265–66), are "the imperfect, knotty, knurly, worm-eaten, half-rotten fruit of the human race," their bodies illustrating "the truth of the reverse Latin adage, *'insana mens insano corpora'.*" Nature had made the investigator's task relatively simple: To detect born criminals, one needed only the appropriate apparatus. Degree of criminality could be determined by charting the offender's deformities.

The assumption that offenders literally embody their criminality led in turn to criminal anthropology's distinctive collapse of methods and findings. The doctrine's adherents believed that, just as moral worth could be directly read from the body, so too could the body be unmediatedly charted by their documents (also see Green, 1985; Sekula, 1986). Theoretical assumptions did not intervene in either case, for theirs were the methods of science.

The Born Criminal

At criminal anthropology's heart lay Lombroso's perception of "the congenital criminal as an anomaly, partly pathological and partly atavistic, a revival of the primitive savage" (Lombroso-Ferrero, 1911:xxii). All the major U.S. books reiterated this message. "Criminals," Talbot (1898:18) wrote,

> form a variety of the human family quite distinct from law-abiding men. A low type of physique indicating a deteriorated character gives a family likeness due to the fact that they form a community which retrogrades from generation to generation.

Most U.S. criminal anthropologists repeated Lombroso's descriptions of the born criminal's physical anomalies—his pointed head, heavy jaw, receding brow, scanty beard, long arms, and so on (I follow criminal anthropologists' own usage in referring to "the criminal" with masculine pronouns). They also adhered closely to Lombroso by enumerating the criminal's "psychical" anomalies—his laziness and frivolity, his use of argot and tendency to inscribe both his cell and his body with hieroglyphics (tattooing), his moral insensibility, and emotional instability. Seemingly the most scientific aspect of criminal anthropology, these were also its most sensational findings.

But several of the American authors expressed doubts about the born criminal's existence even while devoting entire chapters to his stigmata. Apparently unable to resist reporting Lombroso's galvanizing findings, they simultaneously qualified their reports, often without reconciling their enthusiasm for the "new science" with their uneasiness about it. For example, after filling many pages with such statements as "Flesch, out of 50 brains of criminals, did not find one without anomalies," MacDonald (1893:58, 65) confessed that little was known about the relation of "psychical" to organic peculiarities. Henderson (1893:113) lauded Lombroso while warning that his views "are by no means universally accepted as final." Lydston (1904:25–26) masked his ambivalence by mocking the "ultra-materialism" of "so-called criminal anthropologists" and aligning himself with the doctrine's true practitioners. But Drahms (1900) and Parsons (1909) completely failed to harmonize their misgivings about born-criminal theory with their desire to advance it. These criminologists lacked confidence in the scientific centerpiece of their doctrine. They endorsed a science that even to them seemed shaky.

Insofar as they deviated from Lombroso, these Americans did so not by rejecting his theory but by supplementing it, particularly by placing greater emphasis on the criminal's weak intelligence. In *Criminal Man,* Lombroso paid little attention to the criminal's mentality aside from stating that "*Intelligence* is feeble in some and exaggerated in others" (Lombroso-Ferrero, 1911:41 [emphasis in original]; also see Lombroso and Ferrero, 1895:170–71). Four of the eight U.S. criminal anthropologists, in contrast, carried Lombroso's implications to their logical conclusion by finding criminals intellectually as well as ethically weak, mentally as well as morally imbecilic. Talbot (1898:18), for example, drew on evolutionism to explain that "there is truly a brute brain within the man's, and when the latter stops short of its characteristic development, it is natural that it should manifest only its most primitive functions." Lydston (1904:946), noting that "a defective moral sense is most likely to be associated with defective development of the brain in general," concluded that it is "not surprising that the typic or born criminal should lack intelligence" (also see MacDonald, 1893:chap. 4; Drahms, 1900:72–75). The American concern with the criminal's poor intelligence formed the bridge between criminal anthropology and its successor, defective delinquency theory, which identified criminality with "feeble-mindedness."

The U.S. authors further supplemented Lombroso's work by thoroughly integrating criminal anthropology with degeneration theory. Degenerationism attributed the genesis of socially problematic groups—paupers and the insane and feeble-minded, as well as the criminalistic—to an inherited tendency toward organic devolution ("degeneracy," "depraved heredity," "innate viciousness," and other synonyms) (see Chamberlin and Gilman, 1985; Pick, 1989). Lombroso did not immediately realize that degeneration could explain the criminal's bad heredity; at first he relied on the notion of atavism (Parmelee, 1911:xxix; Wolfgang, 1972:247, 249). His American followers, writing later, made degeneration theory the basis for their hereditarianism. Aside from MacDonald, the U.S. authors emphasized that the born criminal was "of a degenerate line, and that if he have offspring some measure of his innate viciousness will be transmitted" (McKim, 1900:23).

American criminal anthropologists stressed the close connections among degenerate types; poverty, mental disease, and crime were but interchangeable symptoms of the underlying organic malaise. "The Degenerate Stock," Henderson (1893:114) explained, "has three main branches, organically united,—Dependents, Defectives and Delinquents. They are one blood." It followed that "vice, crime, and insanity may be regarded as merely different phases of degeneracy which so resemble one another that we are often at a loss when we would distinguish between them" (McKim, 1900:64). The term "criminal anthropology," Haller (1963:16) has pointed out, was "in a sense . . . a misnomer," for the doctrine "was concerned with the nature and causes of all classes of human defects." This was especially true of U.S. criminal anthropology. Wedded to degenerationism, the first American criminologists had no interest in defining the study of crime as a field apart from the study of other social problems.

Other Criminal Types

Lombroso eventually expanded his investigation to a range of criminal types, distinguishing between born criminals and "criminaloids," such as habitual criminals, who did not inherit but acquired the habit of offending; juridical criminals, who violated the law accidentally; and the handsome, sensitive criminal-by-passion, who was motivated by altruism (Lombroso-Ferrero, 1911:chap. 4). These were, in large part, etiological distinctions: Heredity alone determined the behavior of born criminals, whereas environmental and sociological factors increasingly shaped the criminality of higher offender types. Several of the American books included substantial material on the etiology of criminal types. The Americans' typologies, like that of Lombroso, ultimately implied a close correlation between degree of criminality and social class. The positivist approach began by promoting a theory heavy with class content.

The Americans' commentaries on criminal types fall along a continuum that starts with the very crude typification of Boies's *Prisoners and Paupers* (1893) and ends with the highly developed typology of Parsons's *Responsibility for Crime* (1909). *Prisoners and Paupers* did not relate the causes of degeneration to a subsequent discussion of degrees of criminality. Boies had not yet realized that he could explain differences among criminal types in terms of varying causes of crime (see Boies, 1901). His typology, moreover, was rudimentary, distinguishing between "born" or incorrigible" offenders, who had "inherited criminality" and constituted 40 per cent of the "criminal class," and "the victims of heteronomy [multiple factors], the subjects of evil associations and environment," who constituted the other 60 per cent (Boies, 1893:172–83, 184). Only the latter could be reformed. Boies vaguely indicated that incorrigibles could be identified by number of convictions and offense seriousness (1893:178, 185), but he mostly avoided the issue of how to distinguish the hereditary from the heteronomic criminal.

Drahms's *The Criminal* (1900) marks a chronological midpoint in criminal anthropologists' construction of criminal types differentiated by the causes of their offenses. Drahms recognized: (1) the *instinctive criminal* whose "biological, moral, and intellectual equipments are the results of hereditary entailment from prenatal sources" (1900:56); (2) the *habitual criminal* who "draws his inspirational forces from . . . environment rather than parental fountains" (1900:57); and (3) the "essentially social misdemeanant," whom Drahms labeled not a "criminal" but rather a *single offender*, "possibly as free from the antisocial taint as the average man" (1900:55). "He is a criminal because the law declares it" (1900:57).

Parsons's *Responsibility for Crime* (1909) culminated this typification process by identifying a plethora of criminal types. Parsons started with the most abnormal, the *insane criminal,* after which he described the *born criminal* ("His normal condition is abnormal . . . he is born to crime. It is his natural function" [1909:35]); the *habitual criminal* ("he is capable of something else, at least in one period of his life. The born criminal never is" [1909:36]); and the *professional criminal* ("frequently of a high order of intelligence,—often a college graduate. His profession becomes an art in which he sometimes becomes a master" [1909:37]). Of the next type, the *occasional criminal,* Parsons informed us that, "Here, for the first time environment plays an important part in the nature of the crime committed"; the occasional criminal, moreover, "frequently possesses a keen sense of remorse" and is "frequently a useful citizen" (1909:41). Parsons's typology ended with the *criminal by passion or accident,* who was characterized by a high "sense of duty" and "precise motive," unmarred by anomalies, and in need of neither cure nor punishment (1909:42–44).

Whereas Boies (1893) had trouble explaining how to differentiate among criminal types, Parsons (1909) used explicit criteria, including the frequency of physical and mental anomalies; degrees of reformability, intelligence, skill, and remorse; the extent to which environment influences behavior; and the offender's ability to exercise free will. These criteria, putatively derived from biology and then used to establish gradations within the criminal class, were in fact derived from social class and then attributed back to biology. Criminal anthropology had finally unraveled the implications latent in Boies's distinction between hereditary and heteronomic criminals, arriving at a hierarchy of criminal types that corresponded to the social class hierarchy. At the bottom of the scale was the born criminal, rough in appearance and manners, a foreigner or Negro (Boies, 1893:chaps. 6 and 7), uneducated, of poor background, a drinker. At the top stood Parsons's gentlemanly normal offender, anomaly-free, a product not of heredity but of environment, intelligent and skilled, conscience-stricken and reformable.

Criminal anthropologists' "upper" groups "made it possible to maintain a sharp separation, not just of degree, but of essence, between the motivation and character of the ordinary respectable citizen and that of the lower-class offender" (Zeman, 1981:390). This "essence" was what criminal anthropologists called "heredity." In the process of distinguishing among types of criminal bodies, they established a biological hierarchy in which worthiness was signified by class attributes.

The criminal anthropologists' biologism had two long-term effects: It gave positivism a bad name, and it slowed the development of sociological approaches to the study of crime. Positivism suffered no immediate harm by making its criminological debut through criminal anthropology, but its initial confirmation of class biases helped make it suspect to mid-twentieth-century criminologists, some of whom rejected any methods that seemed remotely positivistic (see Gottfredson and Hirschi, 1987a:9–10 and 14–17). Moreover, the biologistic and individualistic emphases of the criminal anthropologists, together with their wide-net degenerationism, attracted nonsociological specialists into criminology's domain. Even when they used a multifactorial approach, criminal anthropologists located "the causes of human conduct in the physiological and mental characteristics of the individual" (Parmelee, 1911:xii). This set the stage for the heavy involvement of psychologists, armed with intelligence tests, in the articulation and application of the next criminological theory, that of defective delinquency (e.g., Gould, 1981:chap. 5), and of physicians and psychiatrists in the subsequent theory of psychopathy. In the long run, criminal anthropology dampened the development of sociological approaches to crime and legitimated those associated with biology and psychology. This is one reason why, even today, criminology draws researchers from a variety of disciplines.

Criminal Anthropology and Eugenics

Advocating that punishments be tailored to fit the offender types they had identified, criminal anthropologists aimed at making justice as well as criminology a "science" based on the lawbreaker's biology (Parsons, 1909:194). Much as some Americans had gone beyond Lombroso in developing aspects of criminal anthropology, so too did some outdo the master in deriving from the doctrine social defense conclusions of the sort that became known as *eugenics*.

According to eugenics theory, a nation can save its stock from degeneration by preventing reproduction of the unfit (negative eugenics) while simultaneously encouraging the fit to produce more offspring (positive eugenics). Without using the term "eugenics," some U.S. criminal anthropologists joined those Americans who had been calling for eugenic measures since the 1870s (e.g., Lowell, 1879; see Haller, 1963; Rafter, 1992), employing such synonyms as "the selection of the fittest and the rejection of the unfit" (McKim, 1900:185).

In *Criminal Man* and *Crime: Its Causes and Remedies*, Lombroso argued merely for the individualization of consequences: "Punishments should vary according to the type of criminal" (Lombroso-Ferrero, 1911:185). Criminals of passion and political offenders should "never" be imprisoned. For criminaloids, probation and indeterminate sentencing were appropriate (Lombroso-Ferrero, 1911:186–87). Even habitual and born criminals may be improved under the indeterminate sentence; but those who continued to demonstrate incorrigibility should be kept in "perpetual isolation in a penal colony" or, in extreme cases, executed

(Lombroso-Ferrero, 1911:198, 208; also see Lombroso, 1911, Pt. III:chaps. 2 and 3). Lombroso made these last recommendations not to prevent reproduction but "to realise the supreme end—social safety" (Lombroso-Ferrero, 1911:216; Lombroso, 1912:59–60).

Like Lombroso, half of the major U.S. criminal anthropologists showed little or no interest in eugenics. The others, however, championed eugenic solutions. Two supported life sentences on the grounds that they would prevent criminals from breeding (Boies, 1893; Parsons, 1909). Several recommended marriage restriction. "The marriages of all criminals should be prohibited, but the utmost vigilance should be exercised to prevent the marriage of the instinctive" (Boies, 1901:239; also see Boies, 1893:280; Lydston, 1904:557–62; and Parsons. 1909:198–99). Some advised sterilization (Boies 1893, 1901; Lydston, 1904).

The most extreme eugenic solution came from McKim (1900), who objected to perpetual detention due to its costliness and to sterilization partly because it "could not be repeated" (1900:24). For "the *very* weak and the *very* vicious *who fall into the hands of the State,*" McKim proposed "a *gentle, painless death*" (1900:188; emphasis in original). Execution by "carbonic acid gas" is the "surest, the simplest, the kindest, and most humane means for preventing reproduction among those whom we deem unworthy of this high privilege" (1900:193, 188). Their disappearance would result in "a tremendous reduction in the amount of crime" (1900:255).

Although there was no necessary connection between criminal anthropology and eugenics, some of the major U.S. Lombrosians endorsed eugenic applications for their doctrine. In McKim's case in particular, advocacy of eugenic solutions was clearly the author's main purpose (1900:iii–v); Boies's two treatises and that of Lydston were also suffused with eugenic rationales. In these works, science became the servant of not just crime control but a highly charged ideology. Their authors treated criminology as a means to an end rather than a science of value in its own right. While most of today's criminologists would be appalled by such overt partisanship (not to mention eugenics theory itself), we remain divided over whether our field can or should even try to produce agenda-free information.

Conclusion

Beset by European critics, Lombroso took comfort in his "almost fanatical" U.S. following (Lombroso-Ferrero, 1911:xxi). American criminal anthropologists, although they established criminology as a specialized branch of inquiry, were less successful than other early U.S. social scientists (Ross, 1979, 1991) in conceptualizing their field. In part, this difficulty was a function of the way Lombroso's science was transplanted to the United States: Dependent on channelers, few American criminal anthropologists had immediate contact with Lombroso's work. Moreover, lacking the skills to conduct social scientific research themselves, they addressed the educated lay person, not scholars, and generated work that soon proved of little value. Even though they cannibalized one another's books, they had almost nothing in common professionally and never agreed on a disciplinary agenda independent of their doctrine. They did share common ground as positivists, but their version of positivism was so tightly tied to materialistic premises that it made even them uncomfortable. When they broke free of biological determinism to use a multifactor approach and develop typologies, they mainly produced guidelines for differential sentencing by social class.

Its origins in criminal anthropology account for some (though certainly not all) of criminology's subsequent problems in defining itself, specifying its methods, and reaching consensus on goals. True, the field's first members had to clear new professional terrain, apart from jurisprudence and penology, but they themselves were unclear about the nature of their authority and the type of training the next generation should receive. Moreover, as degenerationists, they were disinclined to demarcate the field's contours so as to exclude noncriminal groups. Their fondness for biologistic and individualistic explanations also kept criminology's perimeters fluid, making it a field into which specialists from other areas flowed. If one result has been cross-fertilization, ferment, and richness, another has been criminology's lack of disciplinary boundaries.

A closely related problem, lack of agreement on methods and on whether criminologists can or should try to qualify as scientists, is also rooted in criminal anthropology—in its unexamined methodological assumptions, its collapse of methods with findings, and its advocates' inability to define the nature (much less the practice) of their science. Absence of methodological unanimity, too, has contributed to criminology's fertility and flexibility. But it has also impeded the field's ability to build on past findings and has fostered methodological animosities over the value of positivism. The third problem, the continuing dispute over whether criminology's main goal should be to help control crime or to produce knowledge with no direct use-value, can also be traced to criminal anthropology—to some of its proponents' subordination of criminology to eugenics. As their overeagerness to turn criminology into an applied science demonstrates, criminology has from the start been characterized by this tension in goals. The study of criminal anthropology cannot settle these persistent issues, but it can help us put them in historical perspective and grasp the origins of our disciplinary cleavages.

5

Biological Perspectives in Criminology

Diana H. Fishbein

Consistent observations that a small percentage of offenders are responsible for a preponderance of serious crime (Hamparin et al., 1978; Moffitt et al., 1989; Wolfgang, 1972) suggest that this population is at high risk for repetitive antisocial behavior. Evidence shows that chronically violent criminals have an early history of crime and aggression (Loeber and Dishion, 1983; Moffitt et al., 1989). Findings that conduct disorder and delinquency precede drug abuse and related criminal behaviors (Fishbein, 1991) also support the suggestion that a subgroup of offenders is at high risk. The possibility that biological conditions play a role in the development of antisocial and criminal behavior in this "vulnerable" subgroup has spurred a search for biological markers (Mednick et al., 1987).

In the past, theories of the biological aspects of criminal behavior were flawed by a general lack of knowledge regarding the human brain and by serious methodological shortcomings (see, e.g., Glueck and Glueck, 1956; Goddard, 1921; Hooton, 1939a; Jacobs et al., 1965; Lombroso, 1918; Sheldon et al., 1949). Early "biological criminology" was eventually discredited for being unscientific, simplistic, and monocausal. However, since the 1970s biological aspects of criminal behavior have been investigated by behavioral scientists employing a multidisciplinary approach including: genetics, biochemistry, endocrinology, neuroscience, immunology, and psychophysiology.

My purpose here is threefold. First, I will summarize the main findings of biological research that are relevant for explanations of criminal behavior. Second, I will present an indicative model of the way

Edited and abridged from *Criminology*, Volume 28(1):27–72 (1990).

biological, behavioral, and sociological perspectives interrelate to explain crime and to address the central question: Given similar environmental and sociocultural experiences, why does only a subgroup engage in antisocial and sometimes violent behavior? Using such an integrationist approach, reliable biological aspects of criminal behavior may be incorporated into present theoretical frameworks in criminology to provide a comprehensive understanding of antisocial behavior. Finally, I raise some of the criminal justice implications of the integrationist perspective presented. Before summarizing the relevant research evidence it is important to clarify precisely what behavior is being explained.

Criminality versus Maladaptivity

The term *criminality* includes behaviors that do not necessarily offend all members of society, such as certain so-called victimless acts, and excludes behaviors that may be antisocial or illegal but that are not detected by the criminal justice system. *Maladaptivity* includes antisocial behaviors that are costly to citizens and to society. Such behaviors do not necessarily violate legal norms or come to official attention. Individuals who display maladaptive behavior have a high probability of being labeled delinquent or criminal, but being so labeled is not a sufficient criterion to be identified as maladaptive. For example, schizophrenics have abnormalities in brain structure and function that cause them to behave maladaptively; their behavior is poorly regulated, detrimental to their own well-being, and considered "deviant" by others. Nevertheless, they rarely manifest criminal tendencies. Similarly, individuals who have been diagnosed with antisocial personality disorder, a condition associated with several aberrant physiological traits (see Hare and Schalling, 1978; Howard, 1986; Yeudall et al., 1985), are more likely to violate legal norms given conducive social circumstances. Yet there are numerous examples of individuals with antisocial personality disorder who find legal avenues for their behavioral tendencies (such as competitive sports, high-risk activities, corporate life, and politics).

Criminal behavior is not exclusively maladaptive or dysfunctional; thus, biological theories are differentially relevant to various forms of criminality. Biological findings in behavioral research are of particular interest for the study and management of maladaptive behaviors. Here, then, I use the broader concept of maladaptive behaviors that may place an individual at risk for criminal stigmatization, in particular violent criminal behavior.

Selected Studies of the Biology of Maladaptive Behavior

Evolutionary Dictates

According to sociobiologists, human instinctual drives such as eating, reproduction, and defensive behavior, ensure our survival and are stable over time. The mechanisms for acting on these drives, however, especially the brain, continuously evolve to enhance our survival capabilities. With the advent of human consciousness, psychological forces and cultural values interact and sometimes compete with biological drives dictated by evolutionary trends (Thiessen, 1976). Thus, human behavior is a product of the profound and complex interaction of biological and social conditions. Due to the intricacy of this interaction and the elusiveness of evolutionary directions, the nature and outcome of this process are difficult to identify and to study.

Most behaviors reflect attempts to adapt to environmental conditions and, thus, can be studied in an evolutionary context. Aggression, for example, facilitates adaptions to the environment and is normally functional. However, aggressive behavior can become dysfunctional under "abnormal" conditions, particularly those associated with displays of extreme, overt aggression, because they are perceived as threats to survival. Electrical shock, loud noises, extreme heat, starvation, crowding, and other conditions elicit or exacerbate fighting behaviors in many primates, including humans (Carlson, 1977; Thiessen, 1976; Valzelli, 1981), partially explaining aggressive outbursts in prisons. Similar responses are elicited by stimulating areas of the brain responsible for the perception of painful stimuli, enabling the identification of neural mechanisms involved. The prevalence of abnormal conditions has increased with the breakdown of the family structure, community disorganization, disparity between public policy and biological needs, crowding, and other frequently cited characteristics of U.S. urbanization (Archer and Gartner, 1984:98–117; Larson, 1984:116–41). Investigation of how these deleterious conditions exacerbate antisocial behaviors may eventually lead to socioenvironmental programs to enhance, rather than detract from, adaptive capabilities.

Genetic Contributions

Behavior (criminal or otherwise) is not inherited; what is inherited is the way in which an individual responds to the environment. Inheritance provides an orientation, predisposition, or tendency to behave in a certain fashion. Also, genetic influences on human behavior are polygenic—no single gene effect can be identified for most behaviors. The bulk of genetic research on antisocial behavior indicates that traits predisposing to antisociality which may be inherited are behavioral, temperamental, and personality dispositions, and include irritability, proneness to anger, high activity levels, low arousal levels, dominance, mania, impulsivity, sensation-seeking, hyperemotionality, extraversion, depressed mood, and negative affect (Biederman et al., 1986; Cadoret et al., 1985; DeFries and Plomin, 1978; Ghodsian-Carpey and Baker, 1987; Plomin et al., 1990; Rushton et al., 1986). In the presence of a negative mood state, antisocial behavior more likely results under stressful conditions, when supported by social learning. Heritable intellectual deficits (Bouchard and McGue, 1981; Cattell, 1982) have also been shown to increase the risk for antisocial behavior. Individuals with several such traits report an increased familial incidence of similar behavioral problems and show differences in certain biochemical, neuropsychological, and physiological parameters (Biederman et al., 1986; Cadoret et al., 1975; DeFries and Plomin, 1978; Hare and Schalling, 1978; Plomin et al., 1990; Rushton et al., 1986; Tarter et al., 1985; Zuckerman, 1983).

Numerous studies have attempted to estimate the genetic contribution to the development of criminality, delinquency, aggression, and antisocial behavior using family, twin, adoption, and molecular genetic studies. Because it is difficult to isolate genetic factors from developmental events, cultural influences, early experiences, and housing conditions, research findings are not always straightforward (Mednick et al., 1987; Plomin et al., 1990; Walters and White, 1989; Wilson and Herrnstein, 1985).

FAMILY STUDIES

The family study identifies genetic influences on behavioral traits by evaluating similarities among family members. Cross-generational linkages have found personality and behavioral attributes related to criminal behavior, including temper outbursts (Mattes and Fink, 1987), sociopathy (Cloninger et al., 1975, 1978; Guze et al., 1967), delinquency (Robins et al., 1975; Rowe, 1986), hyperactivity and attention deficit disorder (Cantwell, 1979), conduct disorder, aggression, violence, and psychopathy (Bach-y-Rita et al., 1971; Stewart et al., 1980; Stewart and DeBlois, 1983; Stewart and Leone, 1978; Twito and Stewart, 1982).

Despite their frequent conclusion that genetic effects are largely responsible for criminal behavior, this method does not directly assess genetic contributions. Environmental influences on measures of behavior may be common to parents and offspring, and thus, researchers cannot account for large environmental correlations among relatives. Diet, environmental toxins, neighborhood conditions, and television-viewing habits are only some of the environmental factors that similarly influence family members. We may conclude only that the incidence of criminal and related behaviors appears to have a familial basis.

TWIN STUDIES

The classic twin design involves testing identical (monozygotic or MZ) and fraternal (dizygotic or DZ) twins. MZ twins share genetic material from the biological parents and are thus considered identical. DZ twins are approximately 50 per cent genetically alike, as are regular siblings. The extent to which MZ twins share a characteristic as compared to DZ twins provides evidence for a genetic influence. To the extent that there is still some degree of DZ resemblance after genetic influences have been accounted for, there is evidence for the influence of common family environment on the variable. For example, if a sample of MZ twins is 60 per cent similar for IQ and a matched sample of DZ twins is 25 per cent similar for IQ, one can conclude that IQ is largely a function of heredity.

Overall, twin studies provide strong evidence for a genetics-environment interaction showing that MZ twins were more alike in their antisocial activity than DZ twins (see Christiansen, 1977). Significant genetic effects have been found for both self-report and official rates of delinquent or criminal behavior (Rowe, 1983; Rowe and Osgood, 1984) and personality or temperamental traits related to criminal behavior, for example, aggression (Ghodsian-Carpey and Baker, 1987; Rowe, 1986; Rushton et al., 1986; Tellegen et al., 1988), although discrepant studies exist (Owen and Sines, 1970; Plomin et al., 1981; Plomin et al., 1988).

Twin studies commonly suffer from a number of unique method-ological weaknesses (Plomin et al., 1980). First, sampling techniques may favor the selection of MZ pairs that are similar in relevant behavioral traits, which may bias results. Second, MZ twins tend to share more similar environments than do DZ twins because of their similar appearance. Because environmental assessments are not commonly conducted, such similarities cannot be estimated to determine their relative influence. Yet there is evidence that physical and environmental similarities among MZ twins do not bias studies of personality (see DeFries and Plomin, 1978:480; Plomin and Daniels, 1987), which adds weight to the twin method. Third, only recently have researchers employed biochemical tests to verify the zygosity of the twins; prior studies may have underestimated genetic influence. Fourth, measurement errors may further increase the tendency to underestimate genetic influences. However, the twin method can only examine the level of genetic contribution over and above environmental influence. Thus, there is contamination from an unknown amount of environmental contribution.

Notwithstanding, twin studies do provide fairly consistent findings providing intriguing evidence for a genetic effect.

ADOPTION STUDIES

This method examines individuals who were raised from infancy by unrelated adoptive parents rather than biological relatives. To the extent that subjects resemble the biological relatives and not the nonbiological relatives, heredity is thought to play a contributory role. The adoption study method provides richer information about the relative contribution of heredity to behavioral traits and for genetics-environment interactions. Nevertheless, the method has some weaknesses (see Mednick et al., 1984; Plomin et al., 1990; Walters and White, 1989). Fourteen adoption studies indicate noteworthy genetic effects on criminal or delinquent behavior and related psychopathology, that is, psychopathy (see Raine, 1993). They suggest that the biological relatives of criminal or antisocial probands have a greater history of criminal convictions or antisocial behavior than the biological relatives of noncriminal control adoptees. In general, family environment, including social class, rearing styles, and parental attitudes, played a smaller role than did purported genetic effects.

Genetic influences on criminality may differ for those who are also alcoholic (Bohman et al., 1982). When the biological parents are both criminal and alcoholic, crimes of adoptees tend to be more violent. Cadoret et al. (1995) demonstrated the strong effect of a biological parent with both alcohol problems and antisocial personality on the eventual substance abuse and antisocial behavior of the adopted-away offspring. Antisocial personality in individuals with biological antisocial parents is first manifest in childhood and adolescence as a conduct disorder, followed by the early onset of substance use. Aggressivity, which was correlated with biological parent antisocial personality, was most predictive of drug abuse.

Adoption studies highlight the importance of gene-environment interactional models (Rowe and Osgood, 1984). Having a criminal adoptive parent most profoundly affects those with a genetic propensity for criminality (Mednick et al., 1984). Those who inherited certain antisocial personality and temperamental traits are more likely to manifest criminal behaviors in the presence of deleterious environmental conditions (e.g., criminal parents).

MOLECULAR GENETIC STUDIES

While family, twin, and adoption studies have been predominant in efforts to assess genetic contributions to antisocial behavior, they do not directly identify the actual biological features transmitted. Molecular genetic techniques are increasing our understanding of the causal links between genetics, brain function, temperament, and behavioral outcome. Investigators have isolated DNA from blood to identify specific genetic features that may be involved (Comings et al., 1994; Noble et al., 1993). Genetic defects in two neurotransmitters, dopamine and serotonin, have been identified in certain drug abusers and appear to play a role in forms of excessive and compulsive behaviors, including aggressivity, conduct disorder, obsessive-compulsive disorder, and post-traumatic stress disorder, all of which are associated with violence. The sensitivity of brain regions to both abusable drugs and aggressive behavior is a function of these neurotransmitters. Thus, the use of drugs and/or aggressivity may relieve or stimulate systems that are chronically imbalanced. Vulnerable individuals may attain a "neurological high" from both drug abuse and antisocial or violent behavior (Gove and Wilmoth, 1990).

Genetic studies of criminal behavior have been criticized (Mednick et al., 1987; Plomin et al., 1990; Rowe and Osgood, 1984; Walters and White, 1989; Wilson and Herrnstein, 1985) as highly abstract because "criminal behavior" is a legalistic label, not descriptive of actual behavior. Criminal behavior, as a single phenomenon, is far too variable and subject to individual and cultural judgments to be defined for reliable and valid investigation. Instead, research should be predicated on disaggregated behaviors that are reflective of actual acts that can be consistently and accurately measured and examined. Accordingly, genetic studies that focus on criminal behavior per se may be inherently flawed; as criminal behavior is heterogeneous, genetic effects may be more directly associated with particular traits that place individuals at risk for criminal labeling. Nevertheless, in spite of some attempts to overcome this (Mednick et al., 1984), categories are still often based on criminal offenses rather than behavioral constructs such as impressive-aggression, alcoholism, and psychopathy which can be more precisely identified (Plomin et al., 1990).

Also critical, particularly in genetic research, is the need to examine subjects who exhibit a history of repetitive violent behavior relative to those who do not. Most current studies include subjects who have committed only one or two violent offenses, without a history of violence. It is likely that many of those who exhibit only isolated displays of violence may do so only as a result of present circumstances rather than an inherent predisposition to chronic violent offending.

Biological Contributions

Genetic foundations for behavioral disorders are manifested in the resulting visible expression of a genetic trait called a phenotype. Although we can rarely trace a behavioral disorder to a specific gene, we can measure the manifestation of a genetic blueprint in nervous system features. Other biological traits associated with behavioral problems are not directly genetic in origin; they may be due to mutations in a genetic constitution, biochemical exposures, or a deleterious social environment. All of these conditions, from the genetic to the environmental, exert their influence on the nervous system and, thus, can be directly measured and manipulated. The following correlates of behavioral disorders illustrate selected ways in which genetic and environmental factors impact on the nervous system to alter behavior.

BIOCHEMICAL CORRELATES

A number of biochemical differences have been found between controls and individuals with psychopathy, antisocial personality, violent behavior, conduct disorder, and other behaviors associated with criminal behavior. These groups have been discriminated on the basis of levels of certain hormones, neurotransmitters, peptides, toxins, and metabolic processes (Brown et al., 1979; Davis et al., 1983; Eichelman and Thoa, 1972; Mednick et al., 1987; Rogeness et al., 1987; Roy et al., 1986; Valzelli, 1981; Virkkunen and Narvanen, 1987).

Current investigations of biochemical mechanisms of aggressiveness focus on the study of central neurotransmitter systems mentioned above. Animal and human studies, for example, indicate that serotonin globally inhibits behavioral responses to emotional stimuli and modulates aggression (Muhlbauer, 1985; Soubrie, 1986; van Praag et al., 1987). Several indicators of lower levels of serotonin activity in individuals characterized as violent or impulsive, in comparison with those who are not, have been reported (Brown et al., 1979; Fishbein et al., 1989a; Linnoila et al., 1983; Virkkunen et al., 1987, 1989). These studies indicate that serotonin functioning is altered in some types of human aggressiveness and violent suicidal behavior. Thus, a decrease in serotonin activity reduces inhibition in both brain mechanisms and behavior, resulting in increased aggressiveness or impulsivity.

Examination of neurotransmitters that interact with serotonin is necessary to provide a more complete understanding of the neural mechanisms involved. Dopamine (DA) and norepinephrine (NE) are excitatory transmitters that counterbalance the inhibiting influence of serotonin. In a sense, DA and DE operate as the "fuel" while serotonin provides the "brakes" for behavioral responses. An imbalance between the activity of these chemicals may lead to a psychiatric disorder, mood disturbance, or behavioral dysfunction. For example, low levels of NE are associated with clinical depression; many antidepressants work by raising

NE activity. High levels of DA are associated with certain mood disorders and behavioral agitation. The location of the imbalance within the brain determines the behavioral outcome. Alcohol can substantially contribute to antisocial behaviors because it lowers serotonin activity while raising dopamine levels.

Biological factors contributing to individual differences in temperament, arousal, or vulnerability to stress may be important in the etiology of female criminal behavior (Widom, 1978b). Socioenvironmental influences may differentially interact with biological sex differences to produce variations in male and female criminality (see Ellis and Ames, 1987). For example, in males, high levels of the sex hormone testosterone may influence aggressive behavior (Kreuz and Rose, 1971; Olweus et al., 1988; Rada et al., 1983; Schiavi et al., 1984), although discrepant studies exist (Coe and Levine, 1983). Because in utero exposure to various levels of sex hormone play a role in determining later sensitivity to sex hormone release, unusually high levels of exposure may increase sensitivity in adolescence. For example, exposure to abnormally high levels of testosterone in utero may precipitate a heightened response to the release of testosterone in puberty among affected males. As a result, testosterone levels in puberty may be normal, but the response may be exaggerated. A similar situation may theoretically be true for affected females, particularly those who are constitutionally masculinized, possibly resulting in increased risk for antisocial behavior. Masculine features such as abnormal hair growth, large musculature, low voice, irregular menses, fertility disorders, hyperaggressiveness, and other features reflecting sensitivity to male hormones (androgenization) can only develop as a result of prenatal exposure to sex hormone imbalances, steroid use (a testosterone derivative), or certain medical disorders (see Fishbein, 1992).

Premenstrual and postpartum periods have also been associated with elevated levels of aggressivity and irritability in some women. These phases of the cycle are marked by a hormonal upset which may trigger both physical and psychological impairments in a subgroup of women, for example, sharp changes in mood, depression, irritability, aggression, difficulty in concentration, and substance abuse (Haskett, 1987; Trunnell and Turner, 1988). A significant number of females imprisoned for aggressive criminal acts were found to have committed their crimes during the premenstrual phase, and female offenders were found to be more irritable and aggressive during this period (see Ginsburg and Carter, 1987 for review). Despite methodological shortcomings (see Harry and Balcer, 1987), there remains a general impression among investigators and clinicians that a small percentage of women appear to be vulnerable to cyclical hormonal changes which cause them to be more prone to anxiety and hostility (Carroll and Steiner, 1987; Clare, 1985).

Exposure to toxic trace elements is yet another factor that has been shown to interfere with brain function and behavior. Exposure to lead, for example, has a deleterious effect on brain function by damaging organ systems, impairing intellectual development, and subsequently interfering with the regulation of behavior. Sources of lead include our diet and environment (e.g., paint chips and house dust), and contamination among children may be serious and grossly underestimated (Bryce-Smith and Waldron, 1974; Moore and Fleischman, 1975). Resulting impairments may be manifested as learning disabilities and cognitive deficits (hyperactivity and attention deficit disorder), particularly in measures of school achievement, verbal and performance IQ, and mental dullness (see Benignus et al., 1981; Lester and Fishbein, 1987; Pihl and Parkes, 1977), all of which are risk factors for delinquency (Denno, 1988). Lead intoxication is significantly associated with violence (Pihl et al., 1982) and can substantially increase the risk for antisocial behavior (see Rimland and Larson, 1983).

PSYCHOPHYSIOLOGICAL CORRELATES

Psychophysiological variables are quantifiable indices of nervous system function, for example, heart rate, blood pressure, attention and arousal levels, skin conductance, brain waves. These measurable responses directly reflect emotional state. Studies have repeatedly found psychophysiological evidence for mental abnormality and central nervous system disturbances as putative markers for antisocial behavior. Psychopaths who are relatively unemotional, impulsive, immature, thrill-seeking, and "unconditionable" (Cleckley, 1964; Moffitt, 1983; Quay, 1965; Zuckerman, 1983), have also been characterized as having low levels of perceptible anxiety and physiological responses during stressful events (Hare and Schalling, 1978; House and Milligan, 1976; Syndulko et al., 1975; Venables, 1987; Yeudall et al., 1985). Psychopaths differ from nonpsychopathic controls in several physiological parameters, including: (a) electroencephalogram (EEG) differences, (b) cognitive and neuropsychological impairment, and (c) electrodermal, cardiovascular, and other nervous system measures (Raine, 1993). In particular, psychopathic individuals tend to show relatively slower wave activity in their EEG compared with controls, which may be related to differences in cognitive abilities (Fishbein et al., 1989b; Hare, 1970; Howard, 1984; Pincus and Tucker, 1974; Syndulko, 1978). Relatively high levels of EEG slowing in psychopathic subjects may reflect a maturational lag in brain function (Kiloh et al., 1972; Pontius and Ruttiger, 1976). Thus, individuals with EEG slowing who also demonstrate immature behavior and an inability to learn from experience may be developmentally delayed.

EEG slowing among some psychopaths is consistent with findings of hypoaroused autonomic function (ANS: a portion of the nervous system that regulates emotional state via certain bodily functions, e.g., heart rate, blood pressure, hormone release, and skin conductance) and other differences in psychophysiologic parameters mentioned above. When the ANS is underactive, the need for external stimulation is higher and more difficult to satisfy due to a lower level of internal stimulation. Consequently, psychopaths with low ANS activity tend to be more sensation-seeking (Blackburn, 1978; Quay, 1965; Wilson and Herrnstein, 1985) and prone to risky, dangerous, and perhaps criminal activity. This condition appears true for many children with hyperactivity, who require Ritalin, an amphetamine, to provide the internal stimulation required to physically relax in order to concentrate and respond to the environment appropriately. Thus, it is not surprising that significantly more psychopaths than nonpsychopaths were hyperactive as children (see Wilson and Herrnstein, 1985).

Stimulation of the ANS produces subjective feelings of anxiety. Individuals experience anxiety when the threat of a negative repercussion exists due to the learned association between the behavior and its likely consequence. Thus the brain initiates a release of hormones that stimulates a feeling of stress whenever we contemplate a behavior that we have been effectively conditioned to avoid. Individuals with a properly functioning nervous system become conditioned to avoid stressful situations given the learned contingencies discussed above. Most of us, for example, would experience psychological and physical discomfort at the thought of picking a pocket or burglarizing a convenience store. Thus, we make a rational choice based on a calculation of costs and benefits and deterrence is most likely achieved.

The learning and conditioning of behavior occur differentially among individuals given their neurological status. Theoretically, psychopaths do not sufficiently experience the discomfort of anxiety associated with a proscribed behavior due to an underactive ANS, and thus, are not easily conditioned or deterred (Hare and Schalling, 1978; Lykken, 1957). They make a rational choice based on the calculation that the benefits of the act (e.g., monetary gain) outweigh the costs (e.g., anxiety and detection). Accordingly, psychopaths encountered by the criminal justice system would be resistant to most deterrence programs.

PSYCHOPHARMACOLOGICAL INDUCEMENTS

Psychopharmacology is the study of drug effects on the brain and their psychological and behavioral consequences. Certain psychoactive drugs are reported to increase aggressive responses (Fishbein and Pease, 1996), for example, amphetamines, cocaine, alcohol, and phencyclidine (PCP). The actual expression of aggressive behavior depends on the dose, route of administration, genetic factors, set and setting, and type of aggression.

Several biological mechanisms have been proposed as explanations for alcohol-induced aggression: (1) pathological intoxication, sometimes involving psychomotor epilepsy or temporal lobe disturbance (Bach-y-Rita et al., 1970; Maletsky, 1976; Marinacci, 1963); (2) hypoglycemic reactions (low blood sugar; Cohen, 1980; Coid, 1979; Wallgren and Barry, 1970); and (3) alterations in neurotransmitter activity (Weingartner et al., 1983). Because most drinkers do not become aggressive, indications are that alcohol either changes the psychological state or the psychological state has an effect on the behavioral outcome of alcohol consumption. In the second scenario, alcohol would stimulate an existing psychiatric condition or psychological predisposition to aggress or misbehave (Pihl and Ross, 1987). For most individuals, behaviors under the influence of a psychoactive drug are not completely uncharacteristic or bizarre; drugs simply act as a trigger for underlying tendencies to be expressed. Because serotonin plays a modulating role in drinking behavior, individuals with low serotonin are more likely to drink to excess and also to exhibit aggressive behavior under the influence. Administration of drugs that elevate serotonin activity reduce the craving for alcohol and its consumption. Hence, alcohol does not appear to "cause" aggression, but rather permits its expression under specific circumstances and biological conditions.

Chronic use of PCP (phencyclidine) has been repeatedly associated with extreme violence to self and others (Aronow et al., 1980; Fauman and Fauman, 1980; Linder et al., 1981; Schuckit and Morrissey, 1978; Seigal, 1978; Smith and Wesson, 1980). According to some anecdotal reports, violent reactions appear to be an extension of PCP toxic psychosis, which affects some users (Fauman and Fauman, 1980).

PCP-related aggression may be due to influences on hormonal and neurotransmitter activity (Domino, 1978, 1980; Marrs-Simon et al., 1988). Also, neuropsychological impairments have been observed that minimally reflect a temporary organic brain syndrome (Cohen, 1977; Smith and Wesson, 1980), sometimes associated with aggressiveness. Studies of PCP users indicate that specific factors in the user's background, personality, and drug history are important determinants of the drug-related experience (Fauman and Fauman, 1980; McCardle and Fishbein, 1989). These observations suggest that the consequences of PCP use, independent of the drug's purity and varying strengths, are determined by a number of individual factors, including pharmacological, psychological, and situational.

"Vulnerability" studies suggest that certain personality types may be more at risk for drug abuse than others (Brook et al., 1985; Deykin et al., 1986; Kellam et al., 1980; McCardle and Fishbein, 1989). This does not mean, however, that these individuals will inevitably become drug abusers due to a natural predisposition. There is evidence for the substantial contribution of family support systems in the final determination of whether an individual with a vulnerable personality type will, in fact, abuse drugs (Tarter et al., 1985:346–47). Natural and acquired traits interact in a given environment and are inseparable in the evaluation of such a complex phenomenon as human behavior.

Integrating Biological Research into Criminological Theory

In considering how the above biological research findings can be integrated with other behavioral sciences into a comprehensive criminological explanation it is important to emphasize that, since the mid-1970s the old nature versus nurture dichotomy has been replaced. A consensus has emerged that the "truth" lies somewhere between "nature plus nurture" (see Plomin, 1989) and that outcomes depend upon the *interaction* between the two. As we have seen above, biological factors in interaction with certain environmental conditions result in antisocial behavior.

Second, most contemporary behavioral scientists have moved beyond the simple dichotomy between classicism's free will and the hereditarian ideas of determinism. Most accept a compromise on the forces behind human behavior referred to as *conditional free will* (see also Denno, 1988). Social behavior is contingent on numerous possible decisions from among which an individual may choose. Not all of those decisions are feasible. Choosing a course of action is limited by preset boundaries, which narrows the range of possibilities substantially. Decision-limiting factors include current circumstances and opportunities, learning experiences, physiological abilities, and genetic predispositions. Each one of these conditions collaborates internally (physically) and externally (environmentally) to produce a final action. The behavioral result is thus restricted to options available, yet it is "indeterminable" and cannot be precisely predicted. However, certain patterns of behavior are a common individual characteristic, and some patterns are more probable than others in a given situation in a given individual.

The principle of conditional free will postulates that individuals choose a course of action within a preset, yet changeable, range of possibilities and that, assuming the conditions are suitable for rational thought, we are accountable for our actions. Given "rational" thought processes, calculation of risks versus the benefits, and the ability to judge the realities that exist, the result is likely to be an adaptive response; the behavior will be beneficial for the individual and the surrounding environment.

This theory of conditional free will predicts that if one or more conditions to which the individual is exposed are disturbed or irregular, the individual is more likely to choose a disturbed or irregular course of action. Thus, the risk of such a response increases as a function of the number of deleterious conditions.

With these issues clarified, it is possible to envisage a theoretical framework for relating and integrating the research evidence from biological studies with the basic concepts from different behavioral science disciplines. The learning process is equally central to this integral framework.

While a full integration would require us to take into account all the various findings discussed earlier, for the present illustration we can look at a simple example of this process: the link between IQ or learning disabilities and delinquent/criminal behavior (see Critchley, 1968; Hirschi and Hindelang, 1977; McGee et al., 1986; McManus et al., 1985; Perlmutter, 1987; Poremba, 1975; Robins, 1966; Shonfeld et al., 1988; Wolff et al., 1982). Children with conduct disorders tend to have lower IQ scores than nondeviant controls (Huesmann et al., 1984; Kellam et al., 1975; Lewis et al., 1981; Robins, 1966). Probable conditions that may antedate both low IQ and conduct disorder are parental psychopathology, temperamental disturbances, neurological problems, genetic suscept-ibilities, and disadvantageous environmental influences (Shonfeld et al., 1988). With a learning-disabled or conduct-disordered child, the existence of one or more of these deleterious conditions will increase the likelihood of further adjustment problems. Over time, behavioral difficulties become compounded and, to some extent, reinforced once the child has established mechanisms to protect himself or herself and cope with his or her liabilities. Thus, maladaptive behavior is a function of a cumulative developmental process.

Although low IQ or a learning disability is not inherently criminogenic, in the absence of proper intervention the child may become frustrated attempting to pursue mainstream goals without the skills to achieve them (strain theory). Kandel et al. (1988) demonstrated that juveniles with high IQ who were otherwise at high risk for criminal involvement due to their family environments, resisted serious antisocial behavior. Students with a high IQ find school more rewarding and, consequently, bond more strongly to the conventional social order (social control theory). However, parents and school systems ill-equipped to deal with a child suffering from a learning disability, may indirectly contribute to delinquency by removing the child from the classroom, thereby alienating him or her from friends and inculcating the belief that the child is "different," possibly even inadequate (labeling theory). Self-esteem is likely to decline dramatically, and the child may learn that there are rewards to be gained from interacting with others who experience similar frustrations (subcultural theory). The child's behavior elicits a negative response from his or her environment, which leads to further reactions from the child (see Patterson et al., 1989). Consequently, the cycle of negatively interacting forces continues and the risk of becoming delinquent and eventually criminal is heightened. Once the individual attracts the attention of the criminal justice system, the problem is already significantly compounded (labeling theory).

The learning process as it contributes to behavior cannot be underestimated in this model because, fundamentally, both biological and social behaviors are learned. Biological traits and proclivities are reinforced or altered through social learning processes. Temperamental traits producing shyness or introversion (see Kagan et al., 1988; Plomin and Daniels, 1986) may be reinforced by external rewards or expectations or may be overcome by modeling. Thus, the actualization and longevity of this trait depend on environmental experiences or stressors, including hospitalization or family discord.

Humans are equipped with the innate biological capacity to learn as a product of their genetic blueprint, which is physically expressed in the structure of the brain. When an individual is exposed to a stimulus from the internal (biological) or external (social) environment, permanent changes occur in the neural structure and biochemical function of the brain, that is, "memory." Humans interrelate current experiences with information previously learned, and the future response to an equivalent stimulus may be different.

The learning process of comparing new information with memories to produce a response frequently results in "behavioral conditioning." There is an innate foundation for learning in our biological structure that sets contingencies for behavioral conditioning consistent with the premise of conditional free will. Consequently, behavioral sequences are neither programmed nor innate; they are acquired.

The two forms of behavioral conditioning, classical and instrumental, both directly involve biological mechanisms. Classical conditioning refers to the response elicited by a neutral stimulus that has been associated with the acquisition of a reward or the avoidance of harm; for example, viewing drug paraphernalia elicits craving for a drug.

When an individual is instrumental in causing a stimulus to occur, operant or instrumental conditioning is at work. The stimulus being elicited either satiates a drive or permits one to avoid a noxious result. For example, if we learn that stealing results in a reward, the behavior will continue; if we are consistently punished for such behavior, we are unlikely to repeat the action. Both forms of conditioning involve the same contingencies (biological dictates to avoid pain and seek pleasure, known as hedonism), which function to reinforce our behavior.

Certain behaviors are reinforced when the following conditions exist: (1) the behavior and the stimulus occur together in time and space (continuity), (2) repetition of the association strengthens the conditioned response, (3) the result either evokes pleasure or relieves pain, and (4) there is no interference from new experiences, to weaken or extinguish the response. The concept of deterrence is founded on these principles (see Moffitt, 1983).

In general, the criminal justice system relies on the association made between illegal behaviors and the application of a painful or punitive sanction, which generally involves the removal of certain freedoms and exposure to unpleasant living conditions (classical theory). The painful stimulus must be temporally associated with the behavior, consistently applied, and intense enough to prevent further such behaviors. According to the fourth condition listed above, the individual must not learn that the intrinsic reward properties of the behavior are greater or more consistent than the punishment. Finally, opportunities for preferred modes of behavior must be available. Due to the prevalence of low clearance rates, trial delays, inconsistently applied dispositions, legal loopholes, the learning of improper reward and punishment contingencies, and a lack of available legitimate opportunities, the criminal justice system and societal responses have been unable to meet the criteria set above for deterrence and prevention.

The experience of a painful consequence being associated with a behavior is encoded into memory, and when we calculate the consequences of performing that behavior in the future we are deterred by the possible negative response. The impetus for such behavioral change resides in our nervous system. We feel anxiety when the threat of a negative repercussion exists because of the learned association between the behavior and its likely consequence. Subjective feelings of anxiety are a result of unconscious autonomic nervous system responses, such as increased heart rate, blood pressure, and hormone release. Thus, the brain initiates a release of hormones that stimulates a subjective feeling of stress whenever we contemplate a behavior that we have been effectively conditioned to avoid. Individuals with a properly functioning nervous system are quite effectively conditioned to avoid stressful situations given the learned contingencies discussed above. But as we learned earlier with respect to psychopathy, learning and conditioning of behavior occur differentially among individuals given their neurological status.

In sum, social behavior is learned through the principles of conditioning, which are founded on biological and genetic dictates in accord with stimulus-response relationships. Social rewards remain secondary to biological rewards; our desire for money is social, but it is secondary to being a means for obtaining food and shelter. Thus, social behavior satisfies biological needs and drives by providing adaptive mechanisms for reproduction, mating, rearing, defense, and numerous other biological functions. Even though these strategies are fundamentally biological, how we behave to satisfy them relies heavily on learning.

Conclusion

Exactly how biological variables interact with social and psychological factors to produce human behavior generally and antisocial behavior specifically needs to be further researched. Since the mid-1970s most "multidisciplinary" studies have examined only a few isolated variables and have generally failed to evaluate dynamic interrelationships among biological and socioenvironmental conditions (see Denno, 1988; Wilson and Herrnstein, 1985). Only recently has there been a concerted effort to assess relative and interactive relationships, and advances in statistical and methodological techniques have facilitated that development.

While caution against the premature application of biological findings is clearly advised, insights from these behavioral sciences strongly indicate that a number of social programs will reduce biological vulnerabilities to antisocial behavior. Rather than some vague recognition that certain social conditions are deleterious to human functioning, we now have a better understanding of how such conditions influence biological systems to alter risk status. Child abuse, for example, heightens later risk for an antisocial outcome in the victim. Not all victims, however, become victimizers. What differentiates those more vulnerable from those seemingly "protected" from such adversity? While the answer to that question would enable society to identify vulnerable children and provide individualized interventions, even without an answer, global social changes need to be undertaken to protect children's rights. Such action is necessary not just for humanitarian reasons, but also to protect society from the victimizers we are creating. Also illustrative is the consistent finding that adverse and stressful environmental conditions lower serotonin levels, increasing impulsivity and impairing coping skills. Perhaps this observation partially explains the level of violence and drug abuse occurring in our inner cities, but it more directly speaks to the issue of why only a subgroup manifests these behaviors. Specifically, individuals with lower initial levels of serotonin activity may be more vulnerable to adversity than others who do not become antisocial under the same social circumstances. Once again, in either event, these findings highlight the centuries-old appeal to initiate and properly fund programs that provide social insulation from both the psychological and biological results of environmental stress.

Compelling evidence suggests that biological conditions have a profound impact on the adaptive, cognitive, and emotional state of the individual. Investigation of the discriminants for behavioral dysfunctions indicates that the impact of these factors is substantial. When a biological disadvantage is present due to genetic influences or when a physical trauma occurs during the developmental stages of childhood, the resultant deficit may be compounded over time and drastically interfere with behavioral functions throughout life. Such conditions appear to place an individual at high risk for persistent problematic behavior. Disturbances associated with poor environmental and social conditions coupled with impaired brain function may eventually be amenable to intervention. As it stands, the tendency in society is to ignore the developmental and emotional needs of children at risk until they are old enough to incarcerate. The unfortunate reality for those who come into contact with the courts by virtue of their dysfunction, however, is that the underlying causes of their disorder are inaccurately evaluated or simply left unattended. The capability to identify and predict the factors responsible for maladaptivity may eventually enable society to employ innovative methods of early detection, prevention, remediation, and evaluation.

Criminal justice policies must be based on well-founded theories and findings that survive scientific scrutiny. The application of scientific principles or findings to criminal justice programs that are well recognized and accepted by the discipline have more value than trial and error approaches in preventing or minimizing the onset of criminal behavior. Although biological techniques in the assessment of human behavior are still under the microscope and definitive answers have yet to surface, the foregoing description of biological foundations for behavior provides evidence of their applicability and value. By undertaking a collaborative strategy, we can implement more effective prevention and therapeutic programs and develop a legal system that reflects public consensus, meets human needs, and maintains an ethical and organized social structure.

6

Are Some People Crime-Prone? Replications of the Personality-Crime Relationship across Countries, Genders, Races, and Methods

Avshalom Caspi, Terrie E. Moffitt, Phil A. Silva, Magda Stouthamer-Loeber, Robert F. Krueger, and Pamela S. Schmutte

Are some people crime-prone? Is there a criminal personality? Psychologists and criminologists have long been intrigued by the connection between personality and crime. Here we report findings from two studies in which the strengths of both disciplines were employed to determine whether personality differences are linked to crime. We used a two-pronged approach: (1) we studied individuals in different developmental contexts; (2) we used multiple and independent measures of both their personality and criminal involvement. In New Zealand we studied eighteen-year-olds from an entire birth cohort and were able to make detailed comparisons between males and females. In the United States we studied an ethnically diverse group of twelve- and thirteen-year-old boys, enabling us to make detailed comparisons between blacks and whites. By studying different age cohorts in different nations, boys and girls, blacks and whites, and by collecting multiple and independent measures of behavior, we can ascertain with relative confidence the extent to which personality differences are linked to crime.

Personality and Crime

Personality psychologists have proposed numerous well-articulated theories linking personality to crime and other antisocial outcomes. Eysenck (1977) associates crime with extreme individual values on three personality factors: extroversion, neuroticism, and psychoticism. Zuckerman (1989) regards criminality as the hallmark of individuals

---

Edited and abridged from *Criminology*, Volume 32(2):163–95 (1994).

characterized by impulsivity, aggressiveness, and lack of social responsibility. Cloninger (1987), using his three-factor biosocial model of personality, suggests that persons high in novelty-seeking and low in harm avoidance and reward dependence are likely to be today's delinquents and tomorrow's violent antisocial adults. In addition, psychologists have proposed a link between antisocial behavior and theoretical physiological systems within the brain that are presumed to modulate impulse expression (Gray, 1977). Deficiencies in these neural systems have been suggested as the source of aggression in adults (Fowles, 1980; Gorenstein and Newman, 1980), and of conduct problems in children (Quay, 1986).

Many of these theories rely on trait-based personality models. In the past, the existence of traits was controversial (Mischel, 1968). Since the 1970s, however, researchers have amassed solid evidence documenting the cross-situational consistency (Epstein and O'Brien, 1985) and the longitudinal stability (Caspi and Bem, 1990) of traits, and psychology has witnessed a renaissance of the trait as an essential personality construct (Kenrick and Funder, 1988; Tellegen, 1991). Traits represent consistent characteristics of individuals that are relevant to a wide variety of behavioral domains, including criminality (see Eysenck, 1991).

Advances in personality theory and assessment, however, have had little influence on research conducted by criminologists (Gottfredson and Hirschi, 1990). Reviews of research on personality and crime appearing in mainstream criminology have identified numerous methodological problems with previous research (e.g., Schuessler and Cressey, 1950; Tennenbaum, 1977; Waldo and Dinitz, 1967), leading most criminologists to dismiss personality as a fruitless area of inquiry.

Methodological Problems in Linking Personality to Crime

Although some researchers are convinced that personality variables are essential to understanding crime (e.g., Eysenck and Gudjonsson, 1989), criminological reviews suggest that this belief is far from universal. Critics of empirical efforts to link personality to crime have pointed to problems in *measurement of personality*, *measurement of delinquency*, and *sampling*.

Measurement of Personality

In previous studies of personality and crime, the most commonly used personality instruments have been the Eysenck Personality Inventory (EPQ), the Minnesota Multiphasic Personality Inventory (MMPI), and the California Psychological Inventory (CPI) (Arbuthot et al., 1987; Wilson and Herrnstein, 1985). Among these instruments, the EPQ Psychoticism

(P) scale, the MMPI Psychopathic Deviate (Pd) scale, and the CPI Socialization (So) scale differentiate most clearly between criminal and noncriminal samples (Arbuthot et al., 1987; Eysenck and Gudjonsson, 1989). This is not surprising because each of these scales was constructed to detect criminal deviation. These scales are highly effective clinical tools for detecting criminals in an ostensibly normal population. Yet a theory based on observed correlations between delinquency and the P, Pd, or So scales may be tautological, limited to demonstrating that adolescents who are most delinquent are most similar to the definition of delinquency that was built psychometrically into the scales.

In our studies we used assessment instruments that were not designed to differentiate offenders from nonoffenders. Rather, we used assessment instruments that measure a comprehensive variety of personality traits designed to blanket the human personality. These instruments allowed us to identify a constellation of personality traits that might be linked to criminal involvement.

Previous studies of personality and delinquency also have been criticized for employing delinquency and personality questionnaires that included virtually identical items (Tennenbaum, 1977). In our studies we evaluate each personality item in terms of its potential semantic overlap with any actual illegal acts.

Measurement of Delinquency

In previous studies of personality and crime, the most commonly used delinquency measure was the subject's conviction record or presence in a correctional facility. A fundamental problem with official measures, however, is that "hidden criminals," offenders who commit crimes but are not caught, escape empirical attention and may slip into "control" samples (Schuessler and Cressey, 1950). Because only the tip of the deviance iceberg is reflected by official statistics (Hood and Sparks, 1970), many criminologists have turned to less strongly biased measures—specifically, self-reported delinquency questionnaires (Hindelang et al., 1979, 1981; Hirschi et al., 1980). Because both official records and self-report delinquency questionnaires have unique benefits and shortcomings, the use of the two measures in tandem is the most effective empirical strategy (Hirschi et al., 1980).

In our studies we have collected multiple and independent measures of delinquent behavior: police records of contact, court records of conviction, self-reports, and reports from independent informants, parents, and teachers. These multiple measures allowed us to identify robust personality correlates of crime that replicate across different measurement strategies.

Sampling

In previous studies of personality and crime, the most commonly used samples were drawn from incarcerated populations. These samples are not representative of offenders as a whole, only the subset of offenders who actually are caught and subsequently are sent to jail (Hood and Sparks, 1970; Klein, 1987). Moreover, adjudicated offenders may differ systematically from unadjudicated offenders; offenders who are white, middle class, or female may be overlooked inadvertently (e.g., Taylor and Watt, 1977). In addition, the offenders' personal characteristics may influence official responses to their aberrant behavior; for example, some offenders may have enough poise to talk their way out of an arrest. Finally, incarceration itself may contribute to personality aberrations (Schuessler and Cressey, 1950; Wilson and Herrnstein, 1985).

In our studies, we surveyed two different age cohorts whose members' level of involvement in illegal behaviors ranges from complete abstinence to a wide variety of delinquent violations. Therefore, our results are not limited to a selected minority of convicted adolescent offenders.

In the following, study 1 explores the personality-crime relationship in a birth cohort of eighteen-year-old males and females living in New Zealand. Study 2 attempts to replicate these findings among twelve- and thirteen-year-olds living in a large American city.

Study 1: Personality and Crime among Males and Females: Evidence from a New Zealand Birth Cohort

Study 1 explores the personality-crime relationship in a longitudinal epidemiological sample (Krueger et al., 1994) whose members have been studied since birth. At age eighteen they were administered an omnibus self-report personality inventory that assesses individual differences in several focal personality dimensions. In addition, we gathered information about their delinquency using multiple and independent data sources: self-reports, informant reports, and official records.

Method

Subjects

Subjects were adolescents involved in the Dunedin Multidisciplinary Health and Development Study. The cohort's history has been described by Silva (1990). The study is a longitudinal investigation of the health, development, and behavior of a cohort of consecutive births between April 1, 1972 and March 31, 1973, in Dunedin, New Zealand. Perinatal data were obtained; when the children were traced for follow-up at age three, 1,139 children were deemed eligible for inclusion in the longitudinal study by residence in the province. Of these, 1,037 (91 per cent) were assessed.

The sample has been reassessed with a battery of diverse psychological, medical, and sociological measures every two years since the children were three years old. Data were collected for 991 subjects at age five, 954 at age seven, 955 at age nine, 925 at age eleven, 850 at age thirteen, 976 at age fifteen, and 1,008 at age eighteen. With regard to social origins, the children's fathers are representative of the social class distribution in the general population of similar age in New Zealand. Members of the sample are predominantly of European ancestry (fewer than 7 per cent identify themselves as Maori or Polynesian).

Measurement of Personality

As part of the age-eighteen assessment, 862 subjects completed a modified version (Form NZ) of the Multidimensional Personality Questionnaire (MPQ; Tellegen, 1982). The MPQ is a self-report personality instrument designed to assess a broad range of individual differences in affective and behavioral style. The 177-item version of the MPQ (Form NZ) yields 10 different personality scales (Tellegen, 1982:78). These ten scales define three superfactors: Constraint, Negative Emotionality, and Positive Emotionality (Tellegen, 1985; Tellegen and Waller, in press). *Constraint* is a combination of the Traditionalism, Harm Avoidance, and Control scales. Individuals high on this factor tend to endorse conventional social norms, avoid thrills, and act in a cautious and restrained manner. *Negative Emotionality* is a combination of the Aggression, Alienation, and Stress Reaction scales. Individuals high on this dimension have a low general threshold for the experience of negative emotions such as fear, anxiety, and anger, and tend to break down under stress (Tellegen et al., 1988). *Positive Emotionality* is a combination of the Achievement, Social Potency, Well-Being, and Social Closeness scales. Individuals high on Positive Emotionality have a lower threshold for the experience of positive emotions and for positive engagement with their social and work environments, and tend to view life as essentially a pleasurable experience (Tellegen et al., 1988).

Measurement of Delinquency

Self-reports of delinquency were obtained for 930 subjects during individual interviews with the standardized instrument developed by Elliott and Huizinga (1989) for the National Youth Survey (Elliott et al., 1983). Self-report measures of delinquency have been shown to have strong psychometric properties (see Hirschi et al., 1980; Moffitt, 1989). The instrument used in our study is the most highly respected self-report assessment of antisocial behavior.

For this research we used two self-report variables: a "variety" scale and a scale of index offenses. The variety scale indicates how many of 43 different illegal acts the respondent committed at least once during the past twelve months.

To distinguish between serious crime and less serious crime, we also constructed a scale of index offenses. Nine percent of the sample members (62 males and 16 females) reported that they had committed multiple (two or more) index offenses during the past twelve months.

At the age-eighteen assessment, subjects were asked to nominate a friend or family member who knew them well, and to give us informed consent to send them a 41-item mail questionnaire. Of those who returned the questionnaire, 824 provided responses to four items that inquired about our subjects' antisocial behavior during the last twelve months: "problems with aggression, such as fighting or controlling anger," "doing things against the law, such as stealing or vandalism," "problems related to the use of alcohol," and "problems related to the use of marijuana or other drugs."

We obtained records of police contacts from ages ten through sixteen for 991 subjects from Youth Aid constables in police departments throughout New Zealand. "Police contacts" included all police actions that resulted in the filing of a standard incident form listing offenses which the officer knew had been committed by the juvenile. These records were unavailable for twelve subjects who had died, and for thirty four others who had moved outside New Zealand. Of the males in the sample, 18.8 per cent were known to the police as juvenile delinquents; the number of contacts between males and the police ranged from O to 18. Among the females, 9.8 per cent were known to the police as juvenile delinquents; the number of contacts between females and the police ranged from O to 12. The sample was representative of New Zealand juveniles as a whole in regard to the number of police contacts (Moffitt, 1989).

We obtained computerized records of 932 subjects' court convictions for nontraffic offenses at all courts in New Zealand and Australia by searching the central computer system of the New Zealand Police. The 22 participants who denied consent did not differ from the whole sample on self-reported delinquency at ages thirteen, fifteen, or eighteen. Of the males, 14.9 per cent had one conviction or more (range 0–68); for females, the comparable figure was 5.5 per cent (range 0–10).

To distinguish between one-time offenders and repeat offenders, we identified those who had two or more criminal convictions. Six percent of the sample members (45 males and 13 females) were repeat offenders.

To distinguish between court convictions for minor offenses (e.g., underage drinking) and more serious offenses, we identified sample members who had been convicted in adult court for a violent offense. Three percent of the sample members (21 males and 4 females) had been convicted of a violent offense (convictions for a violent offense constituted 26 per cent of all the convictions).

To be certain that all three measures of delinquency (self-reports, informant reports, and official records) were converging on the same phenomenon, we computed correlations between the delinquency measures separately for males and for females. Only the correlation between police contacts and informant reports on female delinquency was not significant.

Finally, we examined whether subjects who did complete the MPQ (compared to those who did not) differed in self-reported delinquency. Subjects who completed the MPQ did not differ significantly from nonrespondents in self-reported delinquency at age eighteen. Subjects who did not complete the MPQ at age eighteen, however, had reported more delinquent activity at age fifteen than those who completed the MPQ. This finding suggests that some very delinquent fifteen-year-olds were not available to complete the MPQ at age eighteen.

Results

To assess the relation between personality characteristics and delinquency, we computed correlations between the ten MPQ scales and measures of delinquency drawn from independent data sources.

For both males and females, self-reports of delinquency were associated positively with the MPQ scales Aggression, Alienation, Stress Reaction, and Social Potency, and negatively with the MPQ scales Traditionalism, Harm Avoidance, and Control.

We also asked independent informants about the delinquent acts committed by our subjects during the previous year, and found convergence between the personality correlates of the self-reports and the informant reports of delinquency. For boys, of the seven MPQ scales that correlated with self-reports of delinquency, four also correlated with informant reports about delinquency. Informant reports of delinquency were related positively to the MPQ scales Aggression and Alienation, and negatively to the scales Traditionalism and Control. For girls, five of the eight MPQ scales that correlated with self-reports of delinquency also correlated with informant reports about delinquency. Informant reports of delinquency were related positively to the MPQ scales Aggression, Alienation, and Stress Reaction, and negatively to the scales Traditionalism and Control.

Whereas self-reported and informant-reported data are closest to the subject's actual behavior, official data attest to the consequential nature of involvement in criminal behavior. Thus, the number of police contacts is an index of behavior serious enough to have warranted official intervention. A still more accurate detector of serious delinquency is the subject's conviction record. For boys, we found convergence between the personality correlates of self-, informant-, and official reports of delinquency. All four MPQ scales that correlated with both self-reports and informant reports of delinquency also correlated with official reports of delinquency. Official reports of delinquency were related positively to the MPQ scales Aggression and Alienation, and negatively to the scales Traditionalism and Control. For girls, three of the five MPQ scales that correlated with both self-reports and informant reports of delinquency also correlated with official reports: official reports of delinquency were related positively to Aggression and negatively to Traditionalism and Control.

Earlier we identified predictor-criterion overlap as a pervasive problem in research linking personality to delinquency. To ensure that our correlations did not suffer from this shortcoming, four psychologists independently judged all 177 MPQ items for content overlap with the domain of delinquent activity. Predictor-criterion overlap does not appear to be a significant problem in the present study of personality and delinquency.

To derive the personality correlates of delinquent behavior across the three independent data sources, we examined correlations between the MPQ's three higher-order factors and each measure of delinquent activity.

Among both males and females, Constraint and Negative Emotionality emerged as robust correlates of delinquent behavior across the three different data sources. *Positive emotionality* was not associated significantly with any measure of delinquent behavior. The correlations suggest that male and female delinquents exhibited convergent personality profiles characterized by impulsivity, danger seeking, a rejection of traditional values, aggressive attitudes, feelings of alienation, and an adversarial interpersonal attitude.

The overall MPQ personality profiles explained 25 per cent (girls) to 34 per cent (boys) of the variance in self-reported delinquency, 6 per cent (boys) to 11 per cent (girls) of the variance in informant-reported delinquency, and 3 per cent (girls) to 4 per cent (boys) of the variance in official delinquency records.

Criminologists would be persuaded more fully by evidence linking personality traits to crime if personality traits could be shown to relate to serious criminal behavior. To address this issue, we examined the higher-order personality scores of three groups of persons: (1) persons who self-reported having committed multiple (two or more) index offenses in the past year, (2) persons who were identified through court conviction records as repeat offenders, and (3) persons who had been convicted for a violent offense. We restricted this examination to males because relatively few females were involved in serious criminal acts, as defined above. Persons involved in serious criminal behavior scored significantly lower on MPQ Constraint and significantly higher on Negative Emotionality.

In sum, the results from our analyses of the personality correlates of serious crime are very similar to the results from our analyses of the personality correlates of other antisocial activities. Apparently the same personality traits are implicated in antisocial acts of varying severity.

Summary

The results have revealed robust personality correlates of delinquency. Among both males and females, three personality scales were correlated with all three independent sources of delinquency data (self-reports, informant reports, and official reports): delinquency was associated negatively with the MPQ scales Traditionalism and Control, and positively with Aggression. These results suggest that young men and women who engaged in delinquency preferred rebelliousness to conventionality, behaved impulsively rather than cautiously, and were likely to take advantage of others.

Two additional personality scales showed consistent patterns. Among males, all three data sources correlated with the MPQ scale Alienation, and two data sources correlated with the MPQ scale Stress Reaction; among females, two data sources correlated with both Alienation and Stress Reaction. These results suggest that young men and women who engaged in delinquency were also likely to feel betrayed and used by their friends and to become easily upset and irritable. At the higher-order factor level, greater delinquent participation was associated with a unique trait configuration: greater negative emotionality and less constraint.

These findings were not compromised by problems inherent in measuring delinquency; the personality correlates were robust across different methods of measuring delinquency. Moreover, the interpretation of these data was not compromised by predictor-criterion overlap because we eliminated any content overlap between the personality items and the delinquency measures. These findings, however, were observed in a single sample. We now turn to a replication of these findings in a different context.

Study 2: Personality and Crime among Blacks and Whites: Evidence from an American Metropolis

Study 1 reported on mostly white adolescents who live in a midsized city with little social decay in comparison with America's largest cities. It is possible that the racial or ecological composition of this sample may have distorted the relation between personality and crime. For example, relations between personality characteristics and crime may be attenuated among inner-city youths who experience many contextual pressures to engage in illegal behavior. Will negative emotionality and constraint predict delinquent behavior in individuals from different environments and during different developmental stages?

We address these issues in Study 2 by exploring the personality-crime relationship in a separate sample of American inner-city youths ages twelve and thirteen. At that age, caregivers provided extensive personality descriptions of the youths. In addition, we gathered information about the youths' delinquency using multiple and independent data sources: self-reports, teachers' reports, and parents' reports.

Method

Subjects

Subjects were participants in the Pittsburgh Youth Study (PYS), a longitudinal survey on the causes and correlates of early forms of delinquency. The sample was selected randomly from fourth-grade boys enrolled in public schools in Pittsburgh. An initial screening assessment of the sample took place in spring 1987 (N = 249) and spring 1988 (N = 619). The overall cooperation rate of the children and their caregivers was 85 per cent. At the screening, each boy, his main caregiver, and a teacher were interviewed with the appropriate form of the Child Behavior Checklist (Achenbach and Edelbrock, 1983), supplemented by additional items drawn from a delinquency inventory (Elliott et al., 1985), to identify boys at risk for delinquency and criminal behavior. The information provided by the three informants was combined into an overall risk index. Boys ranking in the top 33 per cent were retained in the study, together with a random half selected from the remainder of the sample. This procedure yielded a sample of 508 boys (half high-risk, half not at risk) to be followed in the study (for sample details, see Loeber et al., 1989).

The mean age for the fourth-grade boys was 10.2 at the time of the screening interview. After screening, the percentage of blacks was 53.5, compared with 53.9 per cent for the population of fourth-grade public school classrooms in Pittsburgh (race is distributed equally across risk status). Slightly fewer than half of the sample members (44.2 per cent) lived in households where the main caregiver had been separated, divorced, widowed, or never married; 40.6 per cent of the boys had a father in the home. High school had not been completed by 21.2 per cent of the mothers or acting mothers; at the other extreme, 5.5 per cent of the mothers had earned a college degree. For fathers or acting fathers living with the child, the corresponding figures were 9.4 per cent and 6.5 per cent.

During the summer of 1990, when the boys averaged between twelve and thirteen years old, they were invited to the University of Pittsburgh with a primary caregiver, for our testing session. We tested a total of 430 subjects. Attrition for this part of the PYS research program was slightly higher than for other parts because subjects were required to travel to the study laboratory to be tested under standardized conditions. (For all previous waves, the PYS conducted interviews in the subjects' homes.) We performed analyses to determine whether there were differences between the sample members we studied and those we were unable to study. The 430 studied boys were compared with the 78 boys not studied separately on risk status (low, high), race (white, nonwhite), and social background (Hollingshead SES score). We found no significant differences between the two groups on risk status. These analyses suggest that our findings are unlikely to be compromised by attrition bias.

Measurement of Personality

Because the MPQ is not appropriate for younger adolescents, we used a different personality assessment instrument to describe the personalities of the boys in Pittsburgh. The caregivers completed the "Common Language" version of the California Child Q-sort (CCQ), a language-simplified personality assessment procedure intended for use with lay observers (Caspi et al., 1992). The CCQ does not contain the same items as the MPQ. Nevertheless, the CCQ's item pool can be used to construct the three MPQ superfactors: Constraint, Negative Emotionality, and Positive Emotionality.

We used a "criterion-scoring" approach to assess individual differences in Constraint, Negative Emotionality, and Positive Emotionality. We asked three psychologists who have conducted extensive research with the MPQ to use the California Child Q-sort cards to describe three prototype adolescents, each one corresponding to each of the three MPQ personality dimensions: Constraint, Negative Emotionality, and Positive Emotionality. The agreement between the experts was good. Then we combined the psychologists' independent depictions into a composite profile for each personality dimension. In turn, we "scored" each Pittsburgh boy's Q-sort profile for each of the three personality dimensions by correlating it with the psychologists' criterion profiles.

Measurement of Delinquency

The Pittsburgh boys gave self-reports of their delinquency at ages twelve to thirteen during the Self-Report Delinquency interview (SRD), which is based on the National Youth Survey (Elliott et al., 1985). The data gathered with this instrument in the Pittsburgh study are highly reliable, as reported by Loeber et al. (1991).

As in previous reports about this sample, the PYS principal investigators classified the delinquent behaviors according to severity ratings developed by Wolfgang et al. (1985). These ratings place boys in one of six delinquency levels on the basis of the most serious offense committed in the last six months.

The Pittsburgh boys' teachers completed the Teacher Report Form (TRF); the boys' caregivers, usually mothers, completed the Parent Report Form (PRF). The teachers and caregivers completed these reports when the boys were twelve to thirteen years old.

To be certain that all three measures of delinquency (self-reports, informant reports, and official records) were converging on the same phenomenon, we computed correlations between the delinquency measures separately for black and white adolescents. All correlations were statistically significant.

Results

To assess the relation between personality characteristics and delinquency, we computed correlations between the CCQ measures of Constraint, Negative Emotionality, and Positive Emotionality with measures of delinquency drawn from the three independent data sources: self-reports, teachers' reports, and parents' reports.

Across all three data sources, Constraint and Negative Emotionality emerged as robust correlates of delinquency among both black and white adolescents. The positive correlations with Negative Emotionality suggested that delinquent adolescents were prone to respond to frustrating events with strong negative emotions, to feel stressed or harassed, and to approach interpersonal relationships with an adversarial attitude. The negative correlations with Constraint suggested that delinquent adolescents were likely to be impulsive, danger-seeking, and rejecting of conventional values. Positive emotionality was not associated robustly with delinquent behavior.

Discussion

Our studies revealed that individual differences in personality are correlated consistently with delinquency. Although we performed many analyses, the significant correlations were not scattered randomly across variables; rather, the same pattern of personality correlations was repeated consistently. We obtained these correlations in different countries, in different age cohorts, across gender, and across race. We also obtained these correlations when we measured delinquent involvement with self-reports, teachers' reports, parents' reports, informants' reports, and official records, and when we measured serious crime and less serious delinquency. Finally, we obtained these correlations when we measured personality both with self-reports and with parents' reports. The personality correlates of delinquency were robust: greater delinquent participation was associated with greater negative emotionality and less constraint.

Gottfredson and Hirschi (1990) have suggested that individual differences in "self-control" predispose some people to criminal behavior; this single stable individual difference is said to define a propensity or proneness to crime. Our findings both support this theory somewhat, and suggest that it is simplistic psychologically. Crime-proneness is defined not by a single tendency (such as self-control or impulsivity) but by multiple psychological components. Across different samples and methods, our studies of personality and crime suggest that crime-proneness is defined both by high negative emotionality and by low constraint.

How Might Negative Emotionality and Constraint Lead to Crime?

Negative emotionality is a tendency to experience aversive affective states such as anger, anxiety, and irritability (Watson and Clark, 1984). It is likely that individuals with chronically high levels of such negative emotions perceive interpersonal events differently than others. They may be predisposed to construe events in a biased way, perceiving threat in the acts of others and menace in the vicissitudes of everyday life.

This situation may be aggravated when negative emotionality is accompanied by weak constraint—that is, great difficulty in modulating impulses. In low-constraint individuals, negative emotions may be translated more readily into action. Such volatile individuals should be, in the vernacular of the Wild West, "quick on the draw." Theoretically, antisocial behavior should be likely among individuals who are high in negative emotionality and low in constraint.

What Are the Origins of Negative Emotionality and Constraint?

Our findings may be placed into a developmental context by considering theories about the environmental and biological origins of negative emotionality and constraint. The family environment has a pervasive influence on children's lives and personality development, particularly on the development of antisocial behavior (e.g., Patterson, 1982). Harsh, inconsistent disciplinary practices and a chaotic home environment have been shown to predict later aggression (Loeber and Stouthamer-Loeber, 1986). Living under the constant threat of emotional or physical harm makes negative affect more than simply a perceptual bias for these youths; negative affect is rooted in the realities of their everyday lives. Constraint also may be affected by family dynamics. For example, parental conflict has been found to predict children's scores on constraint at age eighteen (Vaughn et al., 1988). Thus, a personality configuration involving high levels of negative affect and low levels of constraint may develop when children grow and learn in a discordant family environment where parent-child interactions are harsh or inconsistent.

Negative affectivity and constraint also are considered to have specific neurobiological underpinnings. Recent research has pointed to a possible connection between the rate at which the brain expends its neurotransmitter substances and dimensions of personality (Cloninger, 1987). For example, abnormally low levels of a metabolite by-product from the neurotransmitter called serotonin have been found in the cerebrospinal fluid of prison inmates whose offense history is habitually violent and impulsive (Linnoila et al., 1983; Virkkunen et al., 1987). This finding has led theorists to outline the neural mechanisms by which low serotonin levels in the brain could simultaneously produce impulsivity and greater negative affectivity (Depue and Spoont, 1986; Spoont, 1992).

Theories linking personality traits to the primary neurotransmitters also may have important implications for research on the link between crime and genetics. Some adoption and twin studies have demonstrated a significant heritability for criminal behavior (see DiLalla and Gottesman, 1989; Mednick et al., 1986; Plomin et al., 1990), but these findings remain controversial in criminology (Walters and White, 1989). If future behavior genetic studies should document significant heritability for criminal behavior, how should we interpret this finding? Clearly, behavior itself cannot be inherited. Low serotonin levels, however, may be a heritable diathesis for a personality style involving high levels of negative affect and low levels of constraint, which generates in turn a vulnerability to criminal behavior. Indeed, negative affect and constraint themselves appear to be highly heritable; a study of twins reared together versus twins reared apart (Tellegen et al., 1988) found that more than 50 per cent of the observed variance in both Negative Emotionality and Constraint (assessed by the MPQ) could be attributed to genetic factors.

Personality and Crime: The Causal Question

The research reported in this article is cross-sectional; it cannot untangle the causal direction of the personality-crime relationship. For this purpose, we still must answer at least two questions.

   1. *Can negative emotionality and constraint measured prospectively in childhood predict which youths will take up delinquency when they enter adolescence?*

Longitudinal studies must address this question, but the answer is likely to be yes. In the New Zealand study we tested the continuity hypothesis that temperamental variations in early childhood predict personality differences in later life (Caspi et al., 1995; Caspi and Silva, 1995). In particular, we found that children who were "undercontrolled" at age three had elevated scores at age eighteen on MPQ Negative Emotionality and very low scores on MPQ Constraint (Caspi and Silva, 1995). At age three, undercontrolled children were described by the examiners as irritable, impulsive, and impersistent; they had difficulty sitting still, were rough and uncontrolled in their behavior, and were labile in their emotional responses. At age eighteen, the same children described themselves as reckless and careless; they enjoyed dangerous and exciting activities, and preferred rebelliousness to conformity. They also enjoyed causing discomfort to others; yet they felt mistreated, deceived, and betrayed by others. This is the very personality configuration that we have linked to delinquency in the present study.

   2. *Can negative emotionality and constraint measured during adolescence predict which adolescents will sustain adult crime careers and which will abandon delinquency for a conventional lifestyle?*

Longitudinal studies must address this question as well; here, too, the answer is likely to be yes. A recent study of individual differences in personality—as assessed by the MPQ—confirms the great extent to which individual differences are preserved throughout young adulthood. Across a ten-year period, from age twenty to age thirty, negative emotionality and constraint yielded cross-age correlations of .60 and .58 respectively (McGue et al., 1993). These correlations imply that individual differences are likely to be preserved throughout time and in diverse circumstances. In the absence of radical environmental change, individuals are unlikely to change their relative standing in the population: persons who respond with strong negative emotions to everyday events as children are likely to continue to do so throughout adulthood; persons who are impulsive as children are likely to remain so throughout adulthood. Insofar as these individual differences predispose persons toward antisocial behavior earlier in life, they may be linked to antisocial behavior later in life.

Ecology Theory

Introduction

Ecology theorists use an epidemiological emphasis to explain the differential distribution of rates of crime. While social ecologists consider certain conditions in the social and physical environment affecting the rate of crime, over the years there have been differing emphases within the ecological tradition. Tracing their roots to the works of the French statistician, Guerry (1833) and the Belgian mathematician Quetelet (1831), who first noted the nonuniform distribution of crime, social ecologists have integrated biological as well as geographical concepts into their theoretical formulations. Noting that crime varied consistently, the forerunners of contemporary social ecologists used simple correlation techniques to show associations between a host of variables such as conditions of poverty, demographics of the population, geographic locations, even seasonal changes and crime. They termed these associations "societal conditions" and considered them to be the cause of crime. In England Fletcher (1848) made associations between certain neighborhoods and crime. Mayhew's well-known work, *London Labour and the London Poor* (1861), described the criminal areas of London. These associations of poor physical/environmental conditions were later shown to exist in American cities as well, first in the work of Shaw and McKay (1942).

Early social ecologists applied the analogy of plant ecology to humans in their environment. Robert E. Park, Ernest Burgess and Roderick McKenzie (1925), for example, claimed that as in plant environments so also in human communities there is a struggle for scarce resources; just as plants of a more hardy variety replace other less adaptable plants, so in human environments one group replaces another in a sequence of change and dominance. This plant analogy seemed apt during the early part of the twentieth century since this was the time of the waves of European immigrants representing different ethnicities entering the United States and settling for the most part in the urban areas of the East and Midwest. Being new in the country, mostly poor, and not readily accepted, they tended to stay together in different neighborhoods or what Park called "natural areas," forming ethnic and racial enclaves. The city, at the time, became the focus of attention as a natural laboratory to study populations.

Major field studies were conducted in Chicago by those who became known as the Chicago sociologists or the Chicago school. Shaw and McKay were part of this group and their researches became the most widely known works, representing the early part of the social ecology tradition. Seeing the city as developing outward from a central business area in a series of concentric zones, Shaw and McKay studied the dispersion of crime and delinquency throughout the city. Their findings indicated that delinquency as well as other social ills were not equally distributed but rather tended to be concentrated in the zones closest to the center of the city and diminished in proportion to the distance from the center. These findings seriously questioned any individualistic explanation of crime. How could individual explanations account for some neighborhoods having high rates and others not or how could some areas remain crime-prone despite population changes? Although not all cities followed the Chicago pattern, spatial differentials in the rates of crime are now recognized as a universal phenomenon in all major cities of the world. In its extreme form social ecology can become environmental determinism because it denies human agency. Critics of the approach have used this, as well as the fact that it concentrates only on official definitions of crime, that it relies on official statistics as the measure of crime (Baldwin, 1979; Davidson, 1981; Nettler, 1984), that it cannot account for high crime rates in stable working-class communities (Bursik and Grasmick, 1993), and that it ignores the political economy (Davis, 1975), to indicate its limitations. Recent theorists have made revisions in the approach taking these criticisms into account and have become sensitive to political and economic influences in the creation of particular urban environments.

The first selection combines rational choice assumptions with those of ecology theory and has been called "routine activity theory." It argues that the victim plays an important role in the circumstances surrounding a criminal act. Identifying the environmental triggers that facilitate criminal action becomes a central issue for routine activities theorists. In particular, routine activities theory considers how everyday life brings together, at a particular place and moment of time, potential offenders, criminal targets, and the vulnerability of those targets. Vulnerability is particularly affected by the absence or presence of guardians. In the reading selected here, Marcus Felson (chap. 7), one of the founders of this perspective, demonstrates how city planners and managers can frustrate the flow of opportunistic offenders away from crime targets by manipulating the environment.

In contrast to the rational choice assumptions of routine activity theory, Rodney Stark's essay (chap. 8) contributes to an understanding of the persistence of crime in certain neighborhoods by developing a "kinds of places" explanation of crime in juxtaposition to the "kinds of peoples" explanation favored by biologists and psychologists. He classifies almost a century of previous ecological research on crime and deviance into a set of propositions as a first step toward a theory of deviant places.

The article by Robert J. Bursik, Jr. (chap. 9) tackles the problem of "social disorganization" raised by Shaw and McKay and the criticism it subsequently created. Bursik discusses recent attempts to address these criticisms.

As we shall see later, the ideas of social ecology, once thought to have been abandoned by criminologists, have through these writers taken on new life, and feature strongly in some versions of integrated theory (see chap. 29).

7

Routine Activities and Crime Prevention in the Developing Metropolis

Marcus Felson

The "routine activity approach to crime rate analysis" (Cohen and Felson, 1979) specifies three elements of crime: a likely offender, a suitable target, and the absence of a capable guardian against crime. The approach considers how everyday life assembles these three elements in space and time, and it shows that a proliferation of lightweight durable goods, and a dispersion of activities away from family and household, could account for the U.S. crime wave in the 1960s and 1970s. Indeed, modern society invites high crime rates by offering a multitude of illegal opportunities.

In the years since the routine activity approach was first presented, some criminologists have rediscovered how crime prevention can be accomplished through situational and environmental design (Clarke, 1983; Brantingham and Brantingham, 1984; Poyner, 1983). Others have explored how offenders move about in urban space and how they think about and respond to illegal opportunities (Cornish and Clarke, 1986a; Brantingham and Brantingham, 1981). The early work on defensible space (Newman, 1972) now takes on new significance.

This article first identifies the minimal elements of routine lawbreaking. It then discusses some important metropolitan trends which offer new opportunities to prevent crime, and finally it considers new metropolitan forms which alter everyday life, providing new crime prevention opportunities.

Crime Types and Requirements

There are at least four types of crime (Felson, 1983): (1) *exploitative* (or predatory) offenses require that at least one person wrongly take or

Edited and abridged from *Criminology*, Volume 25(4):911–31 (1987).

damage the person or property of another; (2) *mutualistic* offenses (such as gambling or prostitution) link two or more parties illegally acting in complementary roles; (3) *competitive* violations (such as fights) involve two parties illegally acting in the same role, usually a physical struggle against one another; and (4) *individualistic* offenses are lonely illegal acts (such as solo drug use or suicide).

Although the original routine activity approach applied only to exploitative offenses, its reasoning can be extended to all four types of lawbreaking. Each type usually requires that certain minimal elements converge in space and time. For example, a prostitute must meet john away from police and spouse. Predatory violations require the offender, target, and absent guardian.

A fourth element applies to exploitative violations, also playing a role in the other types of crime: the absence of an "intimate handler" (Felson, 1986b). Although some offenders may have no social bonds (hence are not subject to informal social control), other offenders are "handled," having a social bond to a parent or some other "intimate handler" who is able to "seize the handle" and impose informal social control. Unfortunately for crime victims, handled offenders can evade their intimate handlers, thus avoiding informal social control for many hours each day. This evasion links routine activities to informal social control. As Hirschi (1969) noted, social bonds prevent delinquent behavior; yet such prevention is difficult to accomplish by remote control. Indeed, informal social control is often carried out when youths (handled potential offenders) are within sight of their parents (intimate handlers). Felson and Gottfredson (1984) offer evidence of a major dispersion of adolescent activities away from parents and other adults, including strong declines in the probability of having family meals together, with dramatic increases in the tendency to stay out late with other teenagers.

In general, a potential offender must first shake loose from parent or handler, then find a target for crime unmonitored by a guardian. The next section examines offender routines relevant to seizing criminal opportunities.

Offender Routines

If offenders were well-informed, forward-looking, and unrelenting, crime prevention would be very tough indeed. The current article assumes the contrary.

Zipf's *Principle of Least Effort* (1950) states that people tend to find the shortest route, spend the least time, and seek the easiest means to accomplish something. Least effort means not wasting calories or time, not traveling forever to get someplace. Based on this principle it is possible to predict a good deal of human physical behavior from proximity and available routes. If offenders travel minimal distances and often carry out illegal activities while en route to other ones, then their routines will set the stage for the illegal opportunities which come their way. If the criminal seizes the most convenient and obvious target, using lazy reasoning and taking easy action, this leaves little to detect. Although crime victims normally expend no effort *aiming* to be victimized, their exposures to risk are also subject to calculation.

The Principle of Least Effort leads to the Principle of the Most Obvious. According to this second principle, people (including offenders) rely on ready information, including sense data. Thus, imperfect shoppers pick the best buy right under their nose, missing a better buy in small print in another aisle. They pick the best store on main street but miss a better store on side street. The reasoning criminal (Cornish and Clarke, 1986a) finds an interesting target on the route home from school, neglecting better targets nearby. The thief picks the flashiest car; the corner house; the shiniest bicycle. Even pains avoided are those most obvious and proximate: a slap in the face, a punch in the nose, a dirty look from a passerby who might summon the police.

This second principle leads to the quick risk corollary that offenders tend to expose themselves to risk for very little time over very little space. This makes the risk seem small because it is over in a flash. The child who drops a cookie on the floor picks it up immediately so that it still seems safe to eat. The driver who cuts in front of your car risks your life and his for but a moment. Each forbidden pleasure tempts a quick dart, puff, snort, or grab, a short detour from a safe route. Even a long visit to an illegal house can be covered with fast entry through the back door.

Systematic Accident

Yet risk takers sometimes lose. A burglar gets caught, a daredevil breaks a leg, a drug taker has an overdose, or someone going to work or out for fun becomes a victim of crime. Every exploitative crime or crime prevention implies that somebody failed. Either the offender succeeded at the victim's expense or vice versa. The study of crime is a study of accidents, wreaking havoc with simple choice models. This requires a general science of surprise, applying to both pleasant and unpleasant events, such as traffic accidents, stumbling on a pot of gold, or chance encounters of old friends (Bandura, 1982).

Routine activity analysis and human ecology in general offer such a science of surprise, since events which shock the victim can be collected and analyzed statistically and explained in terms of other activities. This leads to the principle of *systematic accident*: many surprises are structured via the physical world. Systematic accident applies both to the crime victim's shock and the offender's windfall.

How can sporadic events be systematic? Although the fox finds each hare one by one, the ecologist knows that the fox population varies with the hare population upon which it feeds. Similarly, the swelling population of video cassette recorders plus the recent upsurge in property offenses alerts us to connections. Criminal offenders disproportionately find victims in certain settings or high-risk occupations (Block et al., 1985). Similarly, a professional sports event sets the stage for nearby traffic jams and car break-ins. A convention supplies visitors to local art museums and massage parlors. Indeed, some of the principles of systematic accident are so general that they apply as well to volcanic eruptions as to criminal events (Felson, 1980, 1981). This is why criminology is partly a physical science, explaining how bodies move, how they mix, and how their mixtures produce reactions, even explosions not possible when they were separate.

By engineering bodily convergences, crime prevention can be effected. One of the most important principles for understanding such sociophysical processes is urbanization.

Urban Physical Structures

For traditional urban ecologists, the local urban community was the basic unit of daily interaction, except for the important daily trip to the workplace. The latter was contained in either the industrial zone or the central business district. People walked and used public transit, relying upon convenient community institutions. Neighborhoods covered far less area than today, and neighborhood schools and shops were much smaller and nearer. Delinquency clustered near the industrial zone. Although sometimes rampant, crime was usually contained.

In the past three decades, the automobile and truck have greatly dispersed metropolitan residence, work, schooling, shopping, and leisure. The dissipation of the central business district and the traditional industrial zone complicates urban ecology. Cars cross traditional community boundaries in a flash. The traditional notion of a city as a collection of communities is greatly strained when people can live here, work there, and shop yonder. Friends can visit one another after a short drive, not needing local community sustenance. Commuters no longer head toward the urban core, as industry and shopping disperse to suburbs and beyond.

Years after men gained automobility, women often remained housewives, keeping localism alive for a few extra decades. Subsequent increases in women's employment and automobility freed them from their own communities, which were no longer the unit of daily sustenance, save for children. Even the young are increasingly schooled and transported elsewhere. New suburbs adopt old communal names and facades for marketing purposes, easily fooling those too young to remember the pedestrian community. In light of these developments, a new ecology of crime is required for an age of automobility.

How can one describe a new physical entity which seems to have no boundaries? Many geographers have put mathematics to good use for describing metropolitan spatial behavior. Yet one still needs to know what replaced the "community." Does some other bounded entity mediate between the individual and the modern metropolis?

Jacobs (1961) hated the suburbanized metropolis, which widened streets for autos and narrowed sidewalks. By killing pedestrian traffic, American cities undermined community life. Jacobs anticipated the crime wave which followed. However, automobiles and roadways give people more choice, more nonlocal access, hence reducing the tyranny of the neighborhood. The modern metropolis provides new access to households, businesses, industries, schools, and places of leisure. People circulate over greater distances, gaining sustenance in a new way. In effect, the city as a collection of neighborhoods gives way to the metropolis as a collection of buildings, linked by automotive streets into a vast sociocirculatory system.

City streets are not new, but their function has changed. The world of pedestrians was a world of shortcuts. Pedestrians cut across yards and through alleys or public buildings, traversed streets, hopped over fences. The world of urban vehicles has different routines and routings. Drivers enter curbed, constructed channels, going from driveway to street to the next street to freeway to side street to parking lot. They walk only the route to and from their parked vehicle. The street is the core of the sociocirculatory system linking various buildings. People, equipment, and supplies move via streets from one building to another, often several miles away. Although we are accustomed to think of streets as "outside," they might as well be inside; flanked by curbs and buildings, they impair the freedom of the great outdoors. One's home or business is an appendage to the street.

Because this sociocirculatory system leads so far so quickly, internal community interaction declines, although net movement increases. One cannot rely upon "natural" community areas, on immediate proximity, as the basis for symbiosis. Families, friendships, and businesses use streets and automobiles to thrive, as people, equipment, and supplies circulate quickly. The Principle of Least Effort has new consequences when the only effort needed is stepping on the gas pedal.

Much of modern suburban North American housing was developed to look like a quiet, socially integrated neighborhood. After constructing streets and sewers, and selling off homes one by one, developers usually deeded the common areas to municipalities for future maintenance, or even helped to form governments to perform this function. Builders wanted profits, not a century of fixing sewers, filling potholes, and providing security. Dumping sociocirculatory costs and problems, including crime, onto the public system is a fundamental fact of urban life. Municipal governments generally agree to take over these burdens on condition that streets become public. Public access in an age of automobility opens suburbs to thousands of strangers while giving residents a vast range for shopping, work, and friendship.

Via the street, one finds friend, job, service; one draws sustenance from the larger environment. Via the street, offender finds victim (Beavon, 1985) and teenager evades parent. The street belongs to everyone, hence is supervised by no one, except for an occasional police officer who does not know who belongs there anyway. The very system that fosters easy movement and vast opportunity for good experiences also interferes with informal social control of youths and protection of person and property from intruders. And so the street system exposes people to serendipity and calamity.

Streets not only provide the means for drawing sustenance from an urban environment, but also constitute its organ of growth. In a world of pedestrians, homes may precede streets; but in a world of cars, streets precede or accompany the construction of homes, businesses, and even parks. Few North Americans will buy a home or business without adequate parking and street access at the outset. Few will patronize a business or a forest preserve lacking automotive convenience. Indeed, modern North American growth is connective growth, with streets extending outward from existing cities, allowing new units to append themselves. Each new unit must connect to the larger sociocirculatory system before it can come to life.

This pattern of sustenance and growth can be dubbed the Great Metropolitan Reef. Each home and business clings to this metroreef like coral, gaining sustenance from the street-flows of people, equipment, and supplies. The metroreef proliferates, organizing and sustaining daily life for a vast array of human activities. Young delinquents flow rather freely about the metroreef, drawing illegal sustenance readily from its rich stores and routine activities. Will the reef simply continue to grow or will the metropolis evolve into a new phase?

Metroreef to Metroquilt: The Role of Facilities

An important new urban form has emerged in recent decades. Business developers have begun to take care of sewers, sidewalks, streets, and security for a fee (Stenning and Shearing, 1980). An early example was the shopping center whose developers provided member businesses a package of many services: parking, security, utilities, and (they hoped) a crowd of big spenders.

A good word for such a setup is *facility*. Its Latin root is *facil* (meaning easy); the facility makes it easy for shoppers to shop and merchants to sell; for offices to get work done; for owners to have time to tend their own business; for people to park and feel safe.

The shopping center has been followed by other important types of facilities which are changing the urban landscape. Each development links several independent businesses or departments into a single territorial complex, offering facility management services. Examples include the condominium, the "smart" office building or office condominium, the "minimall," the industrial park, the mobile home park, the college or hospital campus, the school district campus, the private recreation facility, the public recreation facility. In general, these facilities attempt to draw all the benefits they can from the metroreef while trying to limit litter, crime, and extraneous traffic by privatizing internal traffic. Recent facilities developers are combining two or more activities, such as office space, hotels, homes, and apartments. Some include child care services. Although the apartment facility and feudal manor go back centuries, today's facility serves without necessarily providing a community. This noncommunal symbiosis is an innovative way to provide services and protection in a dispersed metropolis, representing an important shift in the organization of routine activities.

Many people prefer single family dwellings to condominiums, or stand-alone businesses to those which are part of a larger cluster. However, the metroreef is getting too large and crowded for the urban coral to cling singly. Facilities offer wholesale access to the metroreef, providing convenience while regulating the mutual impingements of people. Were suburban communities completely safe, spacious, and clean, facilities might not be necessary. If the reef still had plenty of convenient space for self-attachment, facilities would have no niche. But the proliferation and problems of the metroreef have reached a point where facilities attract customers.

Why are modern developers so inclined to take over so many municipal functions at their own expense? Sometimes, they are compelled to do so by local authorities. Sometimes, unprofitable services draw profitable customers. Sometimes, customers pay extra for special services.

Whatever the reason, one sees a growth of facilities in various parts of North America.

By taking on some new forms and increasing its share of the ecosystem, the facility can break the continuous extension of the metroreef. Today's metropolis mixes community, street, and facility. A majority of urban units continue to have their own direct hookup to the metroreef, while other facilities attach to the much larger metroreef. Yet urban specialists should begin to ponder whether the metropolis will become a collection of facilities rather than of communities!

How can facilities squeeze out the existing stand-alone units to transform the metroreef into something new? (1) Sometimes a university or hospital campus swallows up nearby housing like an amoeba digesting a food particle. They may bulldoze and rebuild, or simply convert the acquired property to their own uses, but the point is that facilities can spread. (2) Although facilities may begin at the edge of town, where land is vacant, the outward movement of industry and business may place them increasingly at the core rather than the periphery of daily productive activity. (3) Cities can quickly revitalize an old area by using their rights of eminent domain to clear the space before inviting facilities to reclaim and rebuild. (4) Sometimes stand-alone units band together to form a facility. For example, single-family dwellers might get together to hire security. Sometimes local law permits them to privatize streets, but this remains rare in the United States (Newman, 1975). (5) If facilities succeed in providing desirable services, stand-alone units may follow their lead, either by joining together and privatizing an area, by allowing the bulldozer in, or permitting existing facilities to gobble up surrounding turf in return for providing services.

Thus, one imagines a new metropolitan form: the Great Metropolitan Quilt, a patchwork of coterminous facilities intervening between homes, businesses, and the larger society. This metroquilt would divide urban space among a large set of corporations, whose facilities managers would be responsible for organizing everyday movements, including security.

This metroquilt would have a special sociocirculatory system, including two types of trips: those within facilities and those between facilities via boulevards and freeways. Within facilities, people would walk, drive, take elevators, escalators, and moving sidewalks. Between facilities, they would drive from the parking structure of the origin facility to that of the destination facility. All parking and walking would occur within a facility, unless a car breaks down. Public arteries would remain in the interstices, the last vestige of local government management responsibility. The evolution from metroreef to metroquilt would vastly alter the role of the police, as well as the ecological basis of lawbreaking.

A metropolitan "drift" seems evident. The city of the past was a collection of communities. Today's American metropolis approximates a metroreef, with vestiges of community. The metroquilt of the future may combine many facilities with a few remaining traces of community and metroreef.

All too little is known about crime production and prevention in existing facilities, but some inferences can be drawn from current spatial imbalances in crime distribution.

Imbalanced Crime Production and Occurrence

The metroreef moves offenders, targets, guardians, and handlers so quickly that it creates tremendous imbalances in crime risk. Some spots are very risky, letting offenders find ready targets. Worse, some spots appear to draw or assemble offenders and targets, while dumping the resulting offenses on the neighbors. For example, Roncek and Lobosco (1983) found that public high schools elevate the crime rates of nearby neighborhoods, presumably by assembling youths, who are likely to be offenders as well as victims. Brantingham and Brantingham (1982) show that local crime risk varies inversely with distance from McDonald's restaurants. Even though the restaurant itself may be safe, it draws those in prime offending and victim ages, producing high crime risk for nearby properties. On the other hand, being surrounded by intact couples tends to depress the crime risk at any point on the city map (Felson, 1985; Sampson, 1987b). Fewer streets leading directly to your home puts you less at risk of household victimization than many such streets (Beavon, 1985).

Detailed local analysis is the best way to learn how crime reaches people. However, large-area data sometimes help. For example, 441,561 property crimes were reported to police agencies in the state of Illinois in 1984. Sorting these by their type of location in the sociocirculatory system reveals that the residential category accounts for 22 per cent of these offenses. Retail and trade outlets account for almost 19 per cent. Public channels, vehicles, storage nodes, and gateways (including streets, parking facilities, yards, and driveways) host 45 per cent of all property crimes, as much as all residential and retail and trade categories combined.

Although industries may produce the bulk of goods stolen or damaged, very few property crimes are linked to their premises. They appear to pass most of this risk on to retail outlets, households, or places of public transit. Whatever liquor stores and bars do to lubricate property crime, they suffer relatively little. If offices, hospitals, and other services assemble some offenders and targets, the resulting crime may not be "charged" to their accounts. If schools are great producers of property crime, official Illinois data indicate that very little ends up being assigned to schools themselves. It appears that certain organizations suffer a fraction of the crime they probably "help" to produce, and are assigned little statistical credit for their "contribution" to crime production.

Uneven crime risk generates an uneven incentive to do something about it. For example, factories which produce lightweight durable goods suffer few thefts of what they produce. Thefts of electronic items occur mostly in transit, in retail, or in residential settings. The industrialist has little incentive to worry about the theft of his product from customers. Even cheap and simple crime prevention is generally neglected by the manufacturer because the incentive is absent. For example, each new electronic product could easily be encoded for the owner's exclusive use, removing the incentive for theft. Similarly, twenty four-hour automatic bank tellers may produce a vast amount of robbery and purse snatching, without impinging upon bankers, who save labor costs through automation.

Yet many facilities may successfully prevent crime from occurring *inside* their premises. As more transport channels, nodes, and gateways are incorporated within the walls of facilities, might one expect crime rate decreases?

A New Role for Facilities

A facility has a distinct crime prevention advantage over the average street: it can limit access and direct flows of people. Facilities can remove many routine activities from the public domain, giving a business or corporation a chance to make a profit selling safety to the public or enhancing security for its own employees or property.

Victims of street crime cannot ordinarily sue their city for negligence. However, victims of crime within private facilities are tempted to bring such lawsuits, compelling facility managers and their insurers to consider crime prevention.

If the metroreef gives way to the metroquilt, the facility would become the main organizational tool for crime prevention. That formal organizations take responsibility for large swaths of urban turf is encouraging for those interested in crime reduction. When the parking, paths, and trees are managed by a specific suable entity, the incentive for serious crime prevention emerges. Indeed, the shift from community to street to facility as the main unit of ecological organization implies a shift in crime prevention. When community is dominant, largely unaided informal social control reigns. When streets are dominant, crime control is largely charged to hit-or-miss public policing, diluted by suburban sprawl. When facilities become dominant, architects, security planners, and facilities managers become the central actors in the crime prevention process. The growth of facilities has special significance for the inequality of security. Today's metroreef probably enhances crime risk for everyone, but especially for those who live within range of many offenders. On the other hand, the modern sociocirculatory system makes it difficult to purchase true security, since some offenders can easily find their way to wealthy victims and have an incentive to do so. Nice neighborhoods are not necessarily very secure. On the other hand, a walled facility with a twenty four-hour doorkeeper can protect those able to pay for it. The growth of facilities may render security more a matter of supply and demand in the future than it is today (Birkbeck, 1985; Cooke, 1987).

Some facilities will undoubtedly protect themselves, not clients. For example, shopping centers sometimes patrol inside to protect their merchants, while neglecting the parking lot vulnerabilities after the customer has paid for the goods and left. Security vendors are often more interested in selling hardware than more intricate and comprehensive crime prevention. Facilities may offer what Waller (1979) calls a "security illusion," namely, conspicuous locks and alarms.

Private organizations cannot guarantee protection for their own property, much less anybody else's, simply by hiring guards. Large-scale organizations have difficulty monitoring their own employees, who can easily be tempted by "inside jobs." For this reason, those organizing crime prevention efforts need to think in terms of physical design and kinetic management. Facilities designers should attempt to divert flows of likely offenders away from likely targets, or else contain these flows within limited areas which are easily monitored. Facilities designers should also consider natural informal controls, working indirectly and inadvertently to control the flows of offenders and targets. Besides, what manager wants to pay wages when surveillance can be engineered almost for free?

Such criminokinetic analysis must be more sophisticated than posting rules and demanding compliance. If one designs products which seem to say "take me," yards which invite trespassing, and unsupervised areas which welcome intrusions, should one be surprised about what follows?

If the routines and routings of young people keep them systematically under informal supervision and away from interesting crime targets, youths will be less likely to commit crimes. Thus, crime control must take into account the natural flows of people and things and try to guide them so that offenders and targets seldom converge in the absence of handlers and guardians, respectively. Crime control efforts must bear in mind that offenders seek quick risks and follow obvious routes. Similarly, potential victims of crime can be guided and channeled in their daily movements so as to minimize their risk. Just as unseen traffic engineers do us all a good deed by designing streets and intersections to minimize citizen danger, so can architects, planners, and facilities managers quietly and unobtrusively help prevent crime victimization. Alternatively, poor planning and management delivers crime right to the doorstep and offers ready temptation to youths.

A number of important ideas about flow management are assembled by Poyner (1983): privatizing residential streets; limiting pedestrian access; separating residential from commercial uses; limiting access to the rear of houses; blocking access from open land; arranging apartment doors and windows carefully; allocating residential child density; dispersing market facilities; favoring pedestrian overpasses, not subways; keeping schools visible from buildings serving adults; keeping school buildings compact; encouraging resident caretakers in schools.

Brantingham and Brantingham (personal communication, 1987) report several ideas and experiences in crime prevention planning: segregating schools from self-service stores; channeling a youth hangout within view of an all-night taxistand; letting the recreation center caretaker live on the premises; building crime-impact planning into early design stages; in a high-rise building for the elderly, placing the recreation room on the first floor with direct view of the doors; regulating flows of adolescents by placement of fast food establishments and electronic arcades.

Wise (personal communication, 1987) adds other ideas: minimizing obstructions and using bright pastel paints to protect flows through parking structures; carefully positioning bank tellers, doors, and flows of customers to discourage robberies; localizing taverns to create informal social control; providing specific crime prevention training for facilities managers.

Clever policing in Palm Springs, California, prevented a recurrence of student holiday violence by turning all the lights green and directing the flow of automobiles right back out of town. Of course, police have less control over the metroreef than a facilities manager has over private property.

The largest sustained crime prevention research effort has been carried out by researchers connected with the British Home Office Research and Planning Unit (Clarke and Mayhew, 1980; Clarke, 1983; Hope, 1982). Among their ideas for situational prevention are timing the arrival of football buses so spectators have no time to get drunk; keeping school plants small; and paying attention to pub size, location, and age structure. The many crime prevention successes of these British researchers were accomplished only through dozens of attempts, some of which failed. Their work showed clearly that intuition, while a valuable resource, is not foolproof. Crime prevention through social engineering can progress only through sustained experimentation and detailed collection of existing experience.

Other ideas include designing public parks and parking lots in long strips to maximize visibility from those passing by, doing away with open-camp designs, and using telecommunications and computers to reduce the size of offices and to develop "scattered site" business practices. Facilities incorporating many young males will have special problems, but even these can be reduced in size and designed for maximal inadvertent adult surveillance. The United States' pattern of several thousand students per secondary school is especially suspect.

Facilities planning and management surely deserve consideration as a tool of future crime reduction. As the metroquilt grows, it may become the only tool available.

8

Deviant Places: A Theory of the Ecology of Crime

Rodney Stark

Norman Hayner, of the Chicago school of human ecology, noted that in the area of Seattle having by far the highest delinquency rate in 1934, "half the children are Italian." Hayner described the social and cultural shortcomings of these residents: "largely illiterate, unskilled workers of Sicilian origin. Fiestas, wine-drinking, raising of goats and gardens . . . are characteristic traits." The businesses in this neighborhood were declining and "a number of dilapidated vacant business buildings and frame apartment houses dot the main street," while the area has "the smallest percentage of homeowners and the greatest aggregation of dilapidated dwellings and rundown tenements in the city" (Hayner, 1942:361–63). Today this district remains the prime delinquency area. There are virtually no Italians living there. Instead, the neighborhood is the heart of the Seattle black community.

This is the point. How is it that neighborhoods can remain the site of high crime and deviance rates *despite a complete turnover in their populations?* If the Garfield district was tough *because* Italians lived there, why did it stay tough after they left? Why didn't the neighborhoods the Italians departed to become tough? Questions such as these force the perception that the composition of neighborhoods, in terms of characteristics of their populations, cannot provide an adequate explanation of variations in deviance rates. Instead, *there must be something about places as such that sustains crime.* This is *not* to claim that neighborhoods do not change in terms of their levels of crime and deviance. Of course they do, even in Chicago (Bursik and Webb, 1982). It also is clear that such changes in deviance levels often are accompanied by changes in the kinds of people who live there. The so-called gentrification of a former slum area would

---

Edited and abridged from *Criminology*, Volume 25(4):893–909 (1987).

be expected to reduce crime and deviance, just as the decline of a once nicer neighborhood into a slum would be expected to increase it. However, such changes involve much more than changes in the composition of the population. Great physical changes are involved too, and my argument is that these have effects of their own.

This article presents an integrated set of propositions that summarize and extend our understanding of ecological sources of deviant behavior. The aim is to revive a *sociology* of deviance as an alternative to the social psychological approaches that have dominated for thirty years. The focus is on the traits of places and groups rather than on the traits of individuals. I shall attempt to show that by adopting survey research as the *preferred* method, social scientists have lost touch with significant aspects of crime and delinquency. Poor neighborhoods disappeared, to be replaced by individual kids with various levels of family income, but no detectable environment. Moreover, the phenomena themselves became bloodless, sterile, and almost harmless; questionnaire studies cannot tap homicide, rape, assault, armed robbery, or even significant burglary and fraud—too few people are involved to turn up in significant numbers in feasible samples, assuming that such people turn up in samples at all. So delinquency, for example, which once had meant offenses serious enough for court referrals, soon meant taking $2 out of mom's purse, having "banged up something that did not belong to you," and having a fistfight. This transformation led repeatedly to the "discovery" that poverty is unrelated to delinquency (Tittle et al., 1978).

Yet, social scientists somehow still knew better than to stroll the streets at night in certain parts of town or even to park there. Despite the fact that countless surveys showed that kids from upper- and lower-income families scored the same on delinquency batteries, even social scientists knew that the parts of town that scared them were not upper-income neighborhoods. When examined with finesse, the research showed that class *does* matter—that serious offenses are very disproportionately committed by a virtual underclass (Hindelang et al., 1981).

So, against this backdrop, let us reconsider the human ecology approach to deviance. To begin, there are five aspects of urban neighborhoods which characterize high deviance areas of cities. No member of the Chicago school ever listed them, but these concepts permeate their whole literature (Park, Burgess et al., 1925; Faris and Dunham, 1939; Shaw and McKay, 1942). The essential factors are (1) density; (2) poverty; (3) mixed-use; (4) transience; and (5) dilapidation.

Each of the five will be used in specific propositions. However, in addition to these characteristics of places, the theory also will incorporate some specific *impacts* of the five on the moral order as *people respond to them*. Four responses will be assessed: (1) moral cynicism among residents; (2) increased opportunities for crime and deviance; (3) increased motivation to deviate; and (4) diminished social control.

Finally, the theory will sketch how these responses further *amplify* the volume of deviance through the following consequences: (1) by attracting deviant and crime-prone people and deviant and criminal activities to a neighborhood; (2) by driving out the least deviant; and (3) by further reductions in social control.

The remainder of this article weaves these elements into a set of integrated propositions, clarifying and documenting each as it proceeds.

Proposition 1: *The greater the density of a neighborhood, the greater the association between those most and least predisposed to deviance.*

There is a higher average level of interpersonal interaction in dense neighborhoods where individual traits have less influence on patterns of contact. Consider kids. In low-density, wealthy suburban neighborhoods active effort (a ride from a parent) is required for one twelve-year-old to see another. Here, kids and their parents can easily limit contact with bullies and those in disrepute. Not so in dense urban neighborhoods. The "bad" kids often live in the same building as the "good" ones, hang out close by, dominate the nearby playground, and are nearly unavoidable. Hence, peer groups in dense neighborhoods tend to be inclusive, and all young people living there face maximum peer pressure to deviate—as differential association theorists have long stressed.

Proposition 2: *The greater the density of a neighborhood, the higher the level of moral cynicism.*

Moral cynicism is the belief that people are much worse than they pretend to be. In dense neighborhoods it is much harder to keep up appearances; morally discreditable information about us is likely to leak.

Survey data suggest that upper-income couples may be about as likely as lower-income couples to have physical fights (Stark and McEvoy, 1970). But upper-income couples are much less likely to be *overheard* by neighbors when they have a fight. In dense neighborhoods, where people live in crowded, thin-walled apartments, neighbors hear. In these areas teenage peers, for example, are much more likely to know embarrassing things about one another's parents. This colors their perceptions about normality, and reduces their respect for conventional moral standards. People in dense neighborhoods serve as inferior role models for one another—the same people would *appear* to be more respectable in less dense neighborhoods.

Proposition 3: *To the extent that neighborhoods are dense and poor, homes will be crowded.*

This proposition serves as a necessary step to the next propositions on the effects of crowding.

Proposition 4: *Where homes are more crowded, there will be a greater tendency to congregate outside the home in places and circumstances that raise levels of temptation and opportunity to deviate.*

Crowded homes cause family members, especially teenagers, to stay away (Gove et al., 1979). Since crowded homes are largely located in mixed-use neighborhoods (see Proposition 9), when people stay away from home they tend to congregate in places conducive to deviance (stores, pool halls, street corners, cafés, taverns).

Proposition 5: *Where homes are more crowded, there will be lower levels of child supervision.*

Children from crowded homes tend to stay out of the home and their parents let them. Gove, Hughes, and Galle (1979) found strong empirical support for the link between crowding and less supervision of children.

Proposition 6: *Reduced levels of child supervision will result in poor school achievement, with a consequent reduction in stakes in conformity and an increase in deviant behavior.*

This is one of the most cited and strongly verified causal chains in the delinquency literature (Thrasher, 1927; Toby and Toby, 1961; Hirschi, 1969; Gold, 1970; Hindelang, 1973). Hirschi and Hindelang (1977:583) claim that "school variables" are among the most powerful predictors of delinquency. Toby's (1957) concept of "stakes in conformity" refers to things people risk losing by being detected in deviant actions. These may be things we already possess as well as things we can reasonably count on gaining in the future. An important aspect of the school variables is their potential for future rewards, rewards that may be sacrificed by deviance, but only for those whose school performance is promising.

Proposition 7: *Where homes are more crowded, there will be higher levels of conflict within families, weakening attachments and thereby stakes in conformity.*

Gove, Hughes, and Galle (1979) found a strong link between crowding and family conflict, confirming earlier research (Frazier, 1932:636). Here we also recognize that stakes in conformity are not merely material but include our attachments to others, which are among the most potent stakes in conformity. We risk our closest and most intimate relationships by behavior that violates others' expectations. People lacking such relationships do not risk their loss.

Proposition 8: *Where homes are crowded, members will be much less able to shield discreditable acts and information from one another, further increasing moral cynicism.*

As neighborhood density causes people to be less satisfactory neighborhood role models, density in the home causes moral cynicism. Crowding makes privacy more difficult. Kids see and hear parental fights and sexual relations, as was documented in 1846 by Buchanan observing the dense and crowded London slums (cited in Levin and Lindesmith, 1937:815). Granted that dense, poor, crowded areas in the city centers of North America are not nearly so wretched. But the link of "decency" and "shame" to lack of privacy retains its force.

Proposition 9: *Poor, dense neighborhoods tend to be mixed-use neighborhoods.*

"Mixed use" refers to urban areas where residential and commercial land use coexist, where homes, apartments, retail shops, and light industry are mixed together. Since much of the residential property in such areas is rental, typically there is less resistance to commercial use (landlords often welcome it because of the prospects of increased land values). The poorest, most dense urban neighborhoods often are adjacent to the commercial sections of cities, forming what the Chicago school called the "zone of transition" (to note the progressive encroachments of commercial uses into a previously residential area).

Proposition 10: *Mixed use increases familiarity with and easy access to places offering the opportunity for deviance.*

Consider kids in many suburbs. To undertake shoplifting they have to ask mom or dad for a ride. In purely residential neighborhoods there are fewer conventional opportunities for serious deviant behavior.

Proposition 11: *Mixed-use neighborhoods offer increased opportunity for congregating outside the home in places conducive to deviance.*

Suburbs lack places of potential moral marginality where people can congregate. But in dense, poor, mixed-use neighborhoods, when people leave the house they have all sorts of places to go, including the street corner. A frequent activity in such neighborhoods is "leaning." A bunch of guys will lean against the front of the corner store, the side of the pool hall, or up against the barber shop. In contrast, out in the suburbs young guys don't gather to lean against one another's houses, and since there is nowhere else for them to lean, whatever deviant leanings they might have go unexpressed. Nor is there in the suburbs, come winter, a close, *public* place to congregate indoors.

When people, especially young males, congregate and have nothing special to do, the incidence of their deviance is increased greatly (Hirschi, 1969). Most delinquency, and a lot of crime, is a social rather than a solitary act (Erickson, 1971).

Proposition 12: *Poor, dense, mixed-use neighborhoods have high transience rates.*

McKenzie (1926:145) wrote: "Slums are the most mobile . . . sections of a city. Their inhabitants come and go in continuous succession."

Proposition 13: *Transience weakens extrafamilial attachments.*

The greater the local population turnover, the more difficult it is for individuals or families to form and retain attachments.

Proposition 14: *Transience weakens voluntary organizations, thereby directly reducing both informal and formal sources of social control.*

Recent studies of population turnover and church membership rates show that such membership is dependent upon attachments, and suffers where transience rates reduce attachments (Wuthnow and Christiano, 1979; Stark et al., 1983; Welch, 1983; Stark and Bainbridge, 1985). Similarly, organizations such as PTA or even fraternal organizations suffer where transience is high. Where these organizations are weak, there are reduced community resources to launch local self-help efforts to confront problems such as truancy or burglary. Neighborhoods deficient in voluntary organizations also are less able to influence how external forces such as police, zoning boards, and the like act vis-á-vis the community (Park, 1952; Suttles, 1972; Lee et al., 1984; Guest, 1984b). Simcha-Fagan and Schwartz (1986) found that the association between transience and delinquency disappeared under controls for organizational participation. Transience *causes* low levels of participation, which in turn *cause* an increased rate of delinquency. That is, participation is an *intervening variable* or *linking mechanism* between transience and delinquency. When an intervening variable is controlled, the association between X and Y is reduced or vanishes.

Proposition 15: *Transience reduces levels of community surveillance.*

In areas abounding in newcomers, it is difficult to know when someone doesn't live in a building he or she is entering; in stable neighborhoods strangers are easily noticed and remembered.

Proposition 16: *Dense, poor, mixed-use, transient neighborhoods will also tend to be dilapidated.*

This is evident to anyone who visits these parts of cities. Housing is old and not maintained. Often these neighborhoods are very dirty and littered as a result of density, the predominance of renters, inferior public services, and a demoralized population (see Proposition 22).

Proposition 17: *Dilapidation is a social stigma for residents.*

Neighborhoods not only reflect the status of their residents, but confer status upon them. In Chicago, for example, strangers draw favorable inferences about someone who claims to reside in Forest Glen, Beverly, or Norwood Park. But they will be leery of those who admit to living on the Near South Side. Knowledge of other aspects of communities enters into these differential reactions, but simply driving through a neighborhood such as New York's South Bronx is vivid evidence that very few people would actually *want* to live there.

Proposition 18: *High rates of neighborhood deviance are a social stigma for residents.*

Neighborhoods abounding in crime and deviance stigmatize the moral standing of all residents. To discover that you are interacting with a person through whose neighborhood you would not drive is apt to influence subsequent interaction.

Proposition 19: *Living in stigmatized neighborhoods causes a reduction in an individual's stake in conformity.*

People living in slums see themselves as having less to risk by being detected in acts of deviance. Moreover, as suggested below in Propositions 25–28, the risks of being detected are lower in stigmatized neighborhoods.

Proposition 20: *The more successful and potentially best role models will flee stigmatized neighborhoods whenever possible.*

Since moving is widely perceived as easy, the stigma of living in particular neighborhoods is magnified. Even in the most disorderly neighborhoods, *most* residents observe the laws and norms. Usually they continue to live there simply because they can't afford better. Hence, as people become able to afford to escape, they do. The result is a process of selection whereby the worst role models predominate.

Proposition 21: *More successful and conventional people will resist moving into a stigmatized neighborhood.*

The same factors that pull the more successful and conventional out of stigmatized neighborhoods *push* against the probability that conventional people move into these neighborhoods. This means that only less successful and less conventional people move there.

Proposition 22: *Stigmatized neighborhoods will tend to be overpopulated by the most demoralized kinds of people.*

Here congregate the mentally ill (especially since the closure of mental hospitals), chronic alcoholics, the retarded, and others with limited capacities to cope (Faris and Dunham, 1939; Jones, 1934).

Proposition 23: *The larger the relative number of demoralized residents, the greater the number of available "victims."*

As mixed use provides targets of opportunity by placing commercial firms within easy reach of neighborhood residents, the demoralized serve as human targets of opportunity. Many muggers begin simply by searching the pockets of drunks passed out in doorways and alleys near their residence.

Proposition 24: *The larger the relative number of demoralized residents, the lower will be residents' perception of chances for success, and hence they will have lower perceived stakes in conformity.*

Bag ladies on the corner, drunks on the curbs, and schizophrenics in the doorways are not advertisements for the American Dream. They testify that people in this part of town are losers, going nowhere.

Proposition 25: *Stigmatized neighborhoods will suffer from more lenient law enforcement.*

Police tend to be reactive, to act upon complaints rather than seek out violations. People in stigmatized neighborhoods complain less often.

People in these neighborhoods frequently are much less willing to testify when the police do act—and the police soon lose interest in futile efforts to find evidence. In addition, it is primarily vice that the police tolerate in these neighborhoods, and they tend to accept the premise that vice will exist *somewhere*. Therefore, they tend to condone vice in neighborhoods from which they do not receive effective pressures to act against it (see Proposition 14). They may even believe that by having vice limited to a specific area they are better able to regulate it. Finally, the police frequently come to share the outside community's view of stigmatized neighborhoods—as filled with morally disreputable people, who deserve what they get.

Proposition 26: *More lenient law enforcement increases moral cynicism.*

Where people see laws violated with impunity, they tend to lose respect for conventional moral standards.

Proposition 27: *More lenient law enforcement increases the incidence of crime and deviance.*

As deterrence theory suggests, where the probabilities of being arrested and prosecuted for a crime are lower, the incidence of such crimes will be higher (Gibbs, 1975).

Proposition 28: *More lenient law enforcement draws people to a neighborhood on the basis of their involvement in crime and deviance.*

Reckless (1926:165) noted that areas of the city with "wholesome family and neighborhood life" will not tolerate "vice," but that "the decaying neighborhoods have very little resistance to the invasions of vice." Thus, stigmatized neighborhoods become the "soft spot" for drugs, prostitution, and gambling. These activities require public awareness about where to find them, for they depend on customers rather than victims. Vice can function only where it is, to some degree, condoned. As McKenzie (1926:146) said, the slum "becomes the hiding-place for many services that are forbidden by the mores but which cater to the wishes of residents scattered throughout the community."

Proposition 29: *When people are drawn to a neighborhood on the basis of their participation in crime and deviance, the visibility of such activities and the opportunity to engage in them increases.*

It has already been noted that vice must be relatively visible to outsiders in order to exist; to residents, it will be obvious. Even children not only will know *about* whores, pimps, and drug dealers, they will *recognize* them.

Proposition 30: *The higher the visibility of crime and deviance, the more it will appear to others that these activities are safe and rewarding.*

There is nothing like having a bunch of pimps and bookies flashing big wads of money and driving expensive cars to convince people in a neighborhood that crime pays. If young girls ask local hookers why they are doing it, they will reply with tales of expensive clothes and jewelry. Hence, in some neighborhoods, deviants serve as role models that encourage residents to become "streetwise." This is a form of "wisdom" about the relative costs and benefits of crime that increases the likelihood that a person will spend time in jail. The extensive recent literature on perceptions of risk and deterrence is pertinent here (Anderson, 1979; Jensen et al., 1978; Parker and Grasmick, 1979).

Conclusion

A common criticism of the ecological approach to crime and deviance has been that although many people live in bad slums, most do not become delinquents, criminals, alcoholics, or addicts. Of course not. For one thing, as Gans (1962), Suttles (1968), and others have recognized, bonds among human beings can endure amazing levels of stress and thus continue to sustain commitment to the moral order, even in the slums. Indeed, the larger culture seems able to instill high levels of aspiration in people even in the worst ecological settings. However, the fact that most slum residents aren't criminals is beside the point to claims by human ecologists that aspects of neighborhood structure can sustain high rates of crime and deviance. Such propositions do not imply that residence in such a neighborhood is either a necessary or a sufficient condition for deviant behavior. There is conformity in the slums and deviance in affluent suburbs. All that ecological propositions imply is a substantial correlation between variations in neighborhood character and variations in crime and deviance rates. What an ecological theory of crime is meant to achieve is an explanation of why crime and deviance are so heavily concentrated in certain areas, and to pose this explanation in terms that do not depend entirely (or even primarily) on *compositional* effects—that is, on answers in terms of "kinds of people."

To say that neighborhoods are high in crime because their residents are poor suggests that controls for poverty would expose the spuriousness of the ecological effects. In contrast, ecological theory would predict that the deviant behavior of the poor would vary as their ecology varied. For example, the theory would predict less deviance in poor families in situations where their neighborhood is less dense and more heterogeneous in terms of income, where their homes are less crowded and dilapidated, where the neighborhood is more fully residential, where the police are not permissive of vice, and where there is no undue concentration of the demoralized.

The aim here is not to dismiss "kinds of people" or compositional factors, but to restore the theoretical power that was lost when the field abandoned human ecology. As a demonstration of what can be regained, let us examine briefly the most serious and painful issue confronting contemporary American criminology—black crime.

The Chicago school's primary motivation was to refute "kinds of people" explanations of slum deviance based on Social Darwinism. They regarded it as their major achievement to have demonstrated that the real cause of slum deviance was social disorganization, not inferior genetic quality (Faris, 1967).

Today Social Darwinism has faded into insignificance, but the questions it addressed remain—especially with the decline of human ecology. For example, like the public at large, when American social scientists talk about poor central city neighborhoods, they mainly mean black neighborhoods. And since they are not comfortable with racist explanations, social scientists have been almost unwilling to discuss the question of why black crime rates are so high. Nearly everybody knows that in and of itself, poverty offers only a modest part of the answer. High black crime rates are, in large measure, the result of where they live.

For several years there has been comment on the strange fact that racial patterns in arrest and imprisonment seem far more equitable in the South than in the North and West. For example, the ratio of black prison inmates per 100,000 to white prison inmates per 100,000 reveals that South Carolina is the most equitable state (with a ratio of 3.2 blacks imprisoned to 1 white), closely followed by Tennessee, Georgia, North Carolina, Mississippi, and Alabama, while Minnesota (22 blacks to 1 white) is the least equitable, followed by Nebraska, Wisconsin, and Iowa. Black/white arrest ratios, calculated the same way, also show greater equity in the South while Minnesota, Utah, Missouri, Illinois, and Nebraska appear to be least equitable (Stark, 1986). It would be absurd to attribute these variations to racism. Although the South has changed immensely, it is not credible that cops and courts in Minnesota are far more prejudiced than those in South Carolina.

But what is true about the circumstance of Southern blacks is that they have a much more normal ecological distribution than do blacks outside the South. For example, only 9 per cent of blacks in South Carolina and 14 per cent in Mississippi live in the central core of cities larger than 100,000, but 80 per cent of blacks in Minnesota live in large city centers and 85 per cent of blacks in Nebraska live in the heart of Omaha. This means that large proportions of Southern blacks live in suburbs, small towns, and rural areas where they benefit from factors conducive to low crime rates. Conversely, blacks outside the South are heavily concentrated in areas where the probabilities of *anyone* committing a crime are high. Indeed, a measure of black center city concentration is correlated .49 with the black/white arrest ratio and accounts for much of the variation between the South and the rest of the nation (Stark, 1986).

"Kinds of people" explanations could not easily have led to this finding, although one might have conceived of "center city resident" as an individual trait. Even so, it is hard to see how such an individual trait would lead to explanations of why place of residence mattered. Surely it is more efficient and pertinent to see dilapidation, for example, as a trait of a building rather than as a trait of those who live in the building.

Is there any reason why social scientists must cling to individual traits as the *only* variables that count? Do I hear the phrase "ecological fallacy"? What fallacy? It turns out that examples of this dreaded problem are very hard to find, and usually turn out to be transparent examples of spuriousness—a problem to which *all* forms of nonexperimental research are vulnerable (Gove and Hughes, 1980; Stark, 1986; Lieberson, 1985).

Finally, it is not being suggested that we stop seeking and formulating "kinds of people" explanations. Age and sex, for example, have powerful effects on deviant behavior that are not rooted in ecology (Gove, 1985). What is suggested is that, although males will exceed females in terms of rates of crime and delinquency in all neighborhoods, males in certain neighborhoods will have much higher rates than will males in some other neighborhoods, and female behavior will fluctuate by neighborhood too. Or, to return to the insights on which sociology was founded, social structures are real and cannot be reduced to purely psychological phenomena. Thus, for example, we can be sure that an adult human male will behave somewhat differently if he is in an all-male group than if he is the only male in a group.

9

Social Disorganization and Theories of Crime and Delinquency: Problems and Prospects

Robert J. Bursik, Jr.

After a relatively brief period of prominence during the 1950s and 1960s, many criminologists came to view the concept of social disorganization developed by Shaw and McKay (Shaw et al., 1929; Shaw and McKay, 1942, 1969) as marginal to modern criminological thought. Arnold and Brungardt (1983:113), for example, dismissed its relevance to theories of crime causation since "it is not even a necessary condition of criminality, let alone a sufficient one." Similarly, Davidson (1981:89) argued that social disorganization "should be seen as a descriptive convenience rather than a model of criminogenic behavior." More recently Unnever (1987:845) stated that "Shaw and McKay's theory of social disorganization, which gave birth to this area of research, has been soundly dismissed."

The past few years, however, have seen several publications (e.g., Byrne and Sampson, 1986; Reiss and Tonry, 1986; Stark, 1987) indicating that the perspective continues to have important ramifications for modern criminology. This article examines two basic aspects of the revitalization of the social disorganization approach. First, five central criticisms of the social disorganization tradition are discussed, and recent attempts to address its theoretical and empirical problems are examined. Second, some successful extensions of the framework are reviewed.

The Social Disorganization Approach of Shaw and McKay

Shaw and McKay are primarily cited for their finding that the economic composition of local communities is negatively related to delinquency rates. There is an important difference between their documentation of

Edited and abridged from *Criminology*, Volume 26(4):519–51 (1988).

that negative association and their theoretical interpretation of the relationship. This has led to some basic misunderstandings of the social disorganization perspective. Shaw and McKay did *not* posit a direct relationship between economic status and rates of delinquency. Rather, areas characterized by economic deprivation tended to have high rates of population turnover and population heterogeneity. These assumptions are rooted in the human ecology model of Park and Burgess (1924) and Burgess (1925; see Bursik, 1986a, 1986b). Population turnover and population heterogeneity were assumed to increase the likelihood of social disorganization. This concept is very similar to Park and Burgess's (1924:766) formation of social control as the ability of a group to engage in self-regulation.

Social disorganization refers to the inability of local communities to realize the common values of their residents or solve commonly experienced problems (Kornhauser, 1978:63; Thomas and Znaniecki, 1920). Population turnover and heterogeneity are assumed to increase the likelihood of disorganization because: (1) institutions pertaining to internal control are difficult to establish when many residents are "uninterested in communities they hope to leave at the first opportunity" (Kornhauser, 1978:78); (2) primary relationships that result in informal structures of social control are less likely to develop when local networks are in a continual state of flux (see Berry and Kasarda, 1977); and (3) heterogeneity impedes communication and thus obstructs the quest to solve common problems and reach common goals (Kornhauser, 1978:75).

The causal link between social disorganization and neighborhood delinquency rates was not clearly explained by Shaw and McKay. The dynamics of social disorganization lead to variations across neighborhoods in the strength of residents' commitment to group standards. Thus, weak structures of formal and informal control decrease the costs associated with deviation within the group, making high rates of crime and delinquency more likely. Shaw and McKay's model of social disorganization is basically a group-level version of control theory and assumes very similar processes of internal and external sources of control (see Pfohl, 1985a).

Criticism I: The Disciplinary Shift in Emphasis

Macrosociological models, such as social disorganization, refer to properties of *groups*; that is, they assume that there are important community-level dynamics related to crime, that are not simple reifications of individual motivational processes. Some, however, dismiss the social disorganization perspective simply because its findings do not (and usually cannot) lead to predictions concerning individual behavior. Such criticisms are based on an inappropriate standard of evaluation (see McBride and McCoy, 1981). The traditional emphasis on group dynamics and organization has given way to a concern with the sources of individual motivation. This disciplinary trend had a devastating effect on the development of the social disorganization approach. Robinson (1950) questioned the problematic nature of ecological correlation, specifically of making individual-level inferences on the basis of aggregate data. "[T]he caution became, for many, a rigid taboo on the use of aggregated data" (Borgatta and Jackson, 1980:8).

Robinson's use of the term "ecological" was especially unfortunate given Park and Burgess's (1924) theory of human ecology. Many used Robinson's findings to conclude that ecological models of crime were fairly meaningless (Brantingham and Brantingham, 1981:17; Baldwin, 1979). This resulted in a shift in spatial research, from models emphasizing social disorganization to "opportunity models" of crime. The latter focus on the geographic distribution of targets of crime and the means of crime commission, the routine activities of people that may lead to an increased likelihood of crime and victimization, and the situations in which crime takes place (see, e.g., Brantingham and Brantingham, 1981; Cohen and Felson, 1979; Cohen et al., 1981; Harries, 1980; Messner and Tardiff, 1985; Pyle et al., 1974; Roncek, 1981). Even though such models often used aggregate data, the ensuing inferences had a very individualistic flavor.

The increased focus on individual motivation provided a balance to the previous overemphasis on group processes and resulted in important theoretical modifications and developments. The discipline has, however, overcompensated in that the group aspects of criminal behavior have almost ceased to be examined. Most became more social-psychological than sociological (see Erickson and Jensen, 1977; Johnstone, 1978).

Some criminologists have strongly resisted the reincorporation of group dynamics relating to social disorganization into models of crime and delinquency, even when the focus of an analysis is on the neighborhood. At best, many believe that such considerations should occupy a distinctly secondary position since "a test of the significance of area research requires study of individuals" (Nettler, 1984a:117). Group- and individual-level dynamics, however, are actually complementary components of a comprehensive theory of crime. This is well illustrated in Stark's (1987) propositions concerning the volume of crime based on community characteristics which converge with those developed by opportunity theorists, assuming individual motivational processes. Reiss (1986:7–8) argues that a full understanding of many criminological issues is only possible through a linkage between the two traditions. In sum, the group orientation of social disorganization is not in itself a valid basis for criticism.

Criticism II: The Assumption of Stable Ecological Structures

The concept of social disorganization is grounded in the human ecology theory of urban dynamics, in which notions of change and adaptation are central. Thus, the full set of dynamics that may lead to such disorganization can only be discerned when long-term processes of urban development are considered. Luckily, Shaw and McKay had access to a unique set of data that enabled them to analyze the relationship between ecological change and delinquency over a period of several decades. Without this, it would have been impossible for them to document the fact that local communities tend to retain their relatively delinquent character despite changing racial and ethnic compositions (see Stark, 1987). The compilation of such information over an extended period is extremely difficult and costly. With the exception of Schmid (1960a, 1960b), subsequent studies were forced to rely on cross-sectional data. Since it is impossible to study change in such a design, cross-sectional studies must assume that local communities are not undergoing a redefinition of their role in the ecological system, that is, the spatial distribution of crime and delinquency rates is relatively stable. Yet, as Schuerman and Kobrin (1983, 1986) have argued, the ecological stability assumed to exist by Shaw and McKay disappeared after World War II, when an acceleration in the rate of decentralization in urban areas significantly altered the character of urban change. The effects of such developments on the distribution of crime and delinquency are impossible to detect without longitudinal data. Thus, the cross-sectional models of social disorganization were grounded in a basic assumption of stability that was simply not justified by the historical evidence.

The reappearance of the social disorganization perspective has been accompanied by a renewed emphasis on the dynamics of urban change and the reflection of these dynamics in changing spatial distributions of crime and delinquency. Bursik (1984, 1986a; Bursik and Webb, 1982), for example, has shown that the ecological structure of Chicago was relatively stable between 1930 and 1940, but dramatic changes began to appear after 1940. The redefinition of the ecological position of Chicago's local neighborhoods was accompanied by significant changes in the relative levels of delinquency found in those areas. Bursik and Webb (1982) attribute this to changes in the dominant forms of population invasion and succession that characterized northern urban centers after World War II.

Schuerman and Kobrin (1983, 1986) have examined in detail the sequence of ecological changes involved in the transition of an area from a low-crime to high-crime neighborhood in Los Angeles. Changes in land-use patterns from predominantly owner-occupied dwellings to rental units led to changes in the population composition, population turnover, and socioeconomic composition of an area. The culmination of this process was a decrease in the prevailing controls in the area (i.e., an increase in social disorganization), which in turn increased the likelihood of crime and delinquency.

The changing role of communities within an ecological system has also been examined by Shannon and his associates (1982, 1984), who argue that there was little evidence of a significant relationship between the amount of change in the characteristics of an area and related changes in the local arrest rates of Racine, Wisconsin, between 1950 and 1970. The apparent incompatibility of their Racine findings with those for Chicago and Los Angeles highlights an important drawback of these data sets: they pertain to particular ecological units with sometimes unique social histories of development. Thus, the degree to which the findings from, say, Chicago can be generalized to other cities is unclear. However, the number of available longitudinal ecological data sets has been increasing; research has examined the relationship between ecological change and crime and delinquency rates in Cleveland and San Diego (Roncek, 1987a, 1987b) and Baltimore (Covington and Taylor, 1988; Taylor and Covington, 1987). As the number of cities for which such data are available increases, much more confidence can be placed in the inferences that can be made concerning the general dynamics of social disorganization.

Criticism III: The Measurement of Social Disorganization

OPERATIONALIZING SOCIAL DISORGANIZATION

Indicative of the confusion over Shaw and McKay's concept of social disorganization is the existence of four extended efforts to explain their assumptions (Finestone, 1976; Kobrin, 1971; Kornhauser, 1978; Short, 1969). Shaw and McKay were not always clear when differentiating the presumed outcome of social disorganization (i.e., increased rates of delinquency) from disorganization itself. This led some to equate social disorganization with the phenomena it was intended to explain. Thus, Lander (1954:10) concluded that the value of the social disorganization construct "is dubious in view of the fact that social disorganization itself has to be defined as a complex of a group of factors in which juvenile delinquency, crime, broken homes . . . and other sociopathological factors are included." Lander defined delinquency *as* social disorganization and focused on determining the other community characteristics that should be included with it.

The common confounding of cause and effect added confusion to the evaluation of Shaw and McKay's model. Yet, as Berry and Kasarda (1977:55–56) have noted, the ecological model of Park and Burgess (1924), which provided the intellectual context for the work of Shaw and McKay, was an early version of the systemic approach to local community structure, which considers a neighborhood to be a complex system of friendship and kinship networks and associational ties. Drawing from this, recent work has attempted to clarify the unique conceptual status of social disorganization by defining it in terms of the capacity of a neighborhood to regulate itself through formal and informal processes of social control. Such an operational definition has made it much easier to differentiate social disorganization from the ecological processes that make internal self-regulation problematic and from the rates of crime and delinquency that may result. (See also Albrecht, 1982; Finsterbusch, 1982; Freudenburg, 1984; or Wilkinson et al., 1982.)

This reformulation of social disorganization assumes that the breadth and strength of local networks directly affect the effectiveness of community self-regulation. The ability of local neighborhoods to supervise the behavior of their residents has been most fully developed in the work of Greenberg and her colleagues (1982a, 1982b, 1985), who identify three primary forms: (1) informal surveillance—the casual but active observation of neighborhood streets by individuals during daily activities; (2) movement-governing rules—avoidance of unsafe areas in or near the neighborhood or city; and (3) direct intervention—questioning strangers and neighborhood residents about suspicious activities which may include chastening adults and admonishing children for unacceptable behavior (1982b:147–48).

Sampson (1986, 1987a) has provided an excellent discussion of the causal dynamics of informal control mediating between general ecological change and delinquency. As he argues (1987a:102), rapid rates of population turnover and increases in structural density lead to a greater proportion of strangers in a neighborhood, who are less likely to intercede on behalf of local residents in crime-related situations (see Stark, 1987).

Informal processes of social control are the central elements of Sampson's (1987a) discussion of the supervisory capacity of local communities. Although he recognizes that rapid ecological change can decrease participation in local formal organizations (1986:26; Bursik, 1986a; Bursik and Webb, 1982), he argues that "they are in large part controlled by city, state and national networks of power" (1987a:102). Thus, although such institutions can have important effects on the prevention of delinquency, much of their effectiveness is determined by sources outside the local community.

There is no question that externally determined funding priorities and program requirements shape the role of local institutions as supervisory agencies in a community (Spergel and Korbelik, 1979:109). Yet the existence of certain types of formal local organizations is a direct reflection of a neighborhood's attempt to regulate itself. For example, local neighborhood associations with community crime prevention as a primary goal, have arisen in many areas. They provide a forum for discussing and evaluating such developments, thereby increasing the sensitivity of the residents to area crime risks (Greenberg et al., 1982b). Although empirical evidence is ambiguous due to methodological problems (Greenberg et al., 1985:chap. 9), there is growing evidence indicating that such programs do have a significant effect on crime rates.

The systemic formulation of social disorganization does not assume that networks of affiliation and association have solely a supervisory effect on local rates of crime and delinquency. To concentrate exclusively on this form of self-regulation would seriously distort the original argument of Shaw and McKay who were centrally concerned with the "effectiveness of socialization in preventing deviance" (Kornhauser, 1978:38). Shaw and McKay (1969:172) argued that children living in areas of low economic status "are exposed to a variety of contradictory standards and forms of behavior rather than to a relatively consistent and conventional pattern." This indicates the subcultural aspects of their model. They concluded that there exists in certain neighborhoods a "coherent system of values supporting delinquent acts" (1969:173). Kornhauser (1978) concluded that the cultural assumptions are not a necessary component of the social disorganization model. Rather they are more consistent with the control-theoretic assumptions of the general model focusing on variability in the effectiveness of local structures of conventional socialization. Current models of social disorganization have also downplayed the notion of subcultural variability and have emphasized the viability of the institutions of socialization embedded in the local networks of association and affiliation. Thus, the community self-regulation implicit in the notion of social disorganization reflects the socializing, rather than supervisory, capabilities of a neighborhood (see Janowitz, 1978:283–300).

Few criminologists would dispute the contention that the family represents one of the key socializing agencies in our society, and many studies have examined the relationship between the distribution of family structures and crime/delinquency rates within local communities (see Sampson, 1986). The educational system also has played an increasingly important role in the socialization of children in the United States and has been a central component of other macrosociological theories of delinquency (e.g., Cohen, 1955). Social disorganization models, however, have generally failed to consider the degree to which the socializing capabilities of local schools are a source of neighborhood self-regulation.

Schwartz (1987) suggests that failure to consider the role of educational institutions within the larger context of the neighborhood may seriously limit our understanding of the processes of internal self-regulation. He notes that in the area he studied local schools serve as "the cultural battleground of the community" (1987:50). In this neighborhood, ethnic traditions, religious faith, family patterns, and other community standards are "woven into the fabric of local institutions," primarily through the educational system. Yet, in a second neighborhood located in the same city, the local high school is characterized as generally disorganized and "is experienced in the classroom as having little connection with the larger society's goals and values" (1987:222). It is no coincidence that these two areas also have very different rates of juvenile delinquency; the second, for example, has a heavy concentration of gang activity.

Social disorganization models will not be fully specified until the role of educational institutions is integrated into the larger conceptualization of community self-regulation.

THE TRADITIONAL STUDY DESIGN

In addition to confusion surrounding the concept of social disorganization, the perspective has been characterized by a second major problem pertaining to the empirical deficiencies of research designs. Most studies have used the population of local community areas within a given urban context as the unit of analysis. Shaw and McKay, for example, analyzed the distribution of delinquency in one hundred and forty square-mile areas of Chicago. More often, census boundaries are used to demarcate the local community areas. Arrest and/or court referral records are then geographically aggregated and the corresponding rates are computed.

It is fairly easy to derive measures such as socioeconomic composition, population turnover, and population heterogeneity from published census materials. This is not the case for the concept of social disorganization itself, however, except to the extent that it is reflected in the distribution of family structures in a community (see Sampson, 1986). The collection of relevant data entails very intensive interviews, surveys, and/or fieldwork within each local neighborhood of the urban system. The logistic and economic problems in large metropolitan areas, which may have over a hundred locally recognized communities, are obvious. Thus, even the most recent studies of entire urban systems have been forced either to rely on very crude indicators of social disorganization or to concentrate on the relationship between ecological processes and crime/delinquency, assuming that this central unmeasured process intervened between the two (see Bursik, 1986b).

This has compounded confusion concerning the measurement and conceptualization of social disorganization (see Byrne and Sampson, 1986:13–17). It becomes hard to distinguish the various components of the Shaw and McKay model, and the social disorganization framework may therefore appear to implicitly assume that lower-class neighborhoods with a large proportion of black or foreign-born residents are disorganized. Yet this is definitely *not* an inherent assumption of the theory. Rather, the degree to which these ecological processes are associated with the ability of a community to regulate itself is an empirical question. This is especially clear in McKay's (1967:115) later work, in which he interpreted the decline in the delinquency rates of several black communities in Chicago as representing a movement toward institutional stability (see also Bursik, 1984, 1986b; Bursik and Webb, 1982; Schuerman and Kobrin, 1983, 1986).

The theoretical status of social disorganization also suffered subsequent to Lander's (1954) research. It was erroneously assumed that neighborhoods characterized by low socioeconomic status and high degrees of minority composition were, by definition, disorganized (see Pfohl, 1985a:167).

To date, the only feasible way to obtain relatively direct indicators of social disorganization has been to concentrate on a few communities. Kapsis (1976, 1978), for example, conducted an extensive series of interviews with adults, adolescents, and community leaders who resided in three neighborhoods in the Richmond-Oakland area of California. His results suggest that communities with broad networks of acquaintanceship and organizational activity have lower rates of delinquency, even when the racial and economic composition of the area would predict otherwise.

Overall, it has not been possible to collect appropriate data concerning social disorganization for all the neighborhoods in an ecological system, due to practical limitations. Unfortunately, a full test of the model on the scale of the traditional studies will be impossible without an enormous outlay of funds. Nevertheless, the results of these smaller-scale analyses are very supportive of the predictions made by the Shaw and McKay model.

Criticism IV: The Measurement of Crime and Delinquency

As early as 1936, Robison criticized the use of official records in the Shaw and McKay research, arguing that systematic biases existed in the juvenile justice system that gave rise to the differences among local community areas and that the "actual" distribution of delinquency would be more evenly dispersed throughout the city (see Gold, 1987). Shaw and McKay admitted the possibility that variations in delinquency may only reflect variations in the number of offenders that are apprehended, raising the question "Is there not just as much real delinquent behavior in areas of low rates as there is in areas of high rates?" (Shaw et al., 1929:199).

Studies of the validity and reliability of these data sources have concentrated on characteristics of individuals (such as class, race, and gender; see Elliott and Ageton, 1980; Hindelang et al., 1981) or changes in police organizational priorities (such as DeFleur, 1975; Peterson and Hagan, 1984) that may lead to differential handling by the justice system. Very few have examined the extent to which neighborhoods are a consideration in police and court decisions, although DeFleur's argument strongly suggests that such biases exist.

There are two important exceptions. Hagan et al. (1978) suggest that a significant degree of community-specific bias may exist within police departments. Not only did they find that police impressions concerning the distribution of delinquency among seventy two Canadian neighborhoods were more strongly related to the socioeconomic status and residential density of those areas than to the actual rates of citizen complaints to the police, but those impressions were more strongly associated with variation in the official delinquency rate than with the rate of complaints. The findings of Hagan et al. suggest that the official rates analyzed in traditional social disorganization research may represent a mixture of differentials in neighborhood behavior patterns, neighborhood propensities to report behavior, and neighborhood-specific police orientations.

In his analysis of police behavior in sixty neighborhoods under the jurisdiction of twenty four metropolitan police departments, Smith (1986) found that the probability of arrest is highest in areas of low socioeconomic status even after controls are imposed for the nature of the offense, characteristics of the suspect, and the dispositional preferences of the complainant. These findings highlight the potential error of assuming that the sole sources of variation in neighborhood delinquency rates are the factors implicated in the social disorganization model.

To date, the degree to which the relative distribution of neighborhood rates of crime and delinquency is an artifact of police decision-making practices has not been extensively examined due to the lack of data. The ideal situation would entail the collection of alternative indicators of neighborhood delinquency rates (based on self-reported measures or victimization data) to be used in conjunction with the official records as multiple indicators of this construct (see Austin, 1976).

The Kapsis and Simcha-Fagan and Schwartz research analyzed both official records and self-reported data and found patterns in accordance with those predicted by social disorganization. In addition, the victimization rates analyzed by Sampson (1985, 1986) also provide strong support for the viability of the perspective. Thus, although only a few studies have examined alternative indicators, evidence has been consistently presented that officially based distributions of neighborhood crime and delinquency rates are not primarily an artifact of police decision-making biases.

Criticism V: The Normative Assumptions of Social Disorganization

The definition of social disorganization as the inability of a local community to regulate itself in order to attain goals that are agreed to by the residents of that community, implies that the notion of consensus is central. The normative assumptions of the social disorganization framework appear to be insensitive to the realities of political and social life.

Janowitz (1976:9–10) argues that a normative approach to social control (i.e., community self-regulation) does not necessarily mean rigid control and social repression. Rather, nonconformity in an area can be tolerated as long as it does not interfere with the attainment of a commonly accepted goal. All that has to be demonstrated is that the residents of an area value an existence relatively free of crime.

Nevertheless, the social disorganization framework does not seem suitable for the study of all crimes. Research on the perceived seriousness of crime shows that, for many less serious offenses, a strong degree of consensus does not exist.

In addition, for certain extremely serious crimes the social disorganization model may not provide an especially powerful explanation. Schrager and Short (1980) compared the perceptions of seriousness for organizational crimes (such as manufacturing and selling drugs known to be harmful, selling contaminated food, overcharging for credit, selling unsafe cars, and price-fixing) and crimes more commonly analyzed in social disorganization models (such as homicide, burglary, robbery, and theft). They presented strong evidence that organizational and common crimes with the same type of social impact (either physical or economic) are rated very similarly (1980:25–26). Thus, since organizational offenses are considered to be as serious as the types of "street crime" discussed by Shaw and McKay, it might be reasonable to expect the social disorganization approach to provide a viable explanation of their distribution in neighborhoods.

Unfortunately, the social disorganization framework has not generally been applied to white-collar crime (Pfohl, 1985a). Thus, to some extent, the applicability of the perspective is still unknown. There are reasons to expect, however, that the framework as it has traditionally been used would not successfully predict rates of such crime. Janowitz (1967) and Suttles (1972) have described modern local neighborhoods as "communities of limited liability," that is, characterized by the partial and differential involvement of their residents. Street crime committed within the boundaries of an area presents an immediate threat to the members of that community and provides a focus on which the residents can unite. At times, as for example in the case of a price-gouging supermarket or landlord, white-collar crime might also generate enough perceived common threat to set the processes of self-regulation into action. On the other hand, white-collar crime committed by residents of the community but having no widespread impact on that community may not be subject to the same internal processes of social control.

The caveat concerning the traditional emphasis of the model reflects its ongoing concern with local community processes. If the notion of the "group" is expanded from the neighborhood to any collectivity with an interest in self-regulation, then white-collar crime might easily be explained within a similar framework. In this respect, the notion of the organization would supplant the notion of the community. It would then be possible to determine the extent to which high rates of employee turnover and employee heterogeneity affect the ability of the organization to regulate itself and, in turn, whether this ability is related to white-collar crime.

A much more subtle and problematic normative assumption is embedded in the Shaw and McKay model. Shaw and McKay at least implicitly assumed that the ecological distribution and movement of populations within an urban area reflect the "natural" market of housing demand; they did not discuss in any detail the degree to which population turnover, population heterogeneity, and social disorganization could in fact be manipulated by nonmarket mechanisms. As Finestone (1976) has shown, the primary thrust of Shaw and McKay's model gives the impression that the composition and internal organization of local communities are relatively independent of the broader political and economic dynamics of the city (see also Bursik, 1988a).

Skogan (1986:206–7) has highlighted four key factors with sources outside the local community that can affect neighborhood stability: disinvestment, demolition and construction, demagoguery (i.e., real estate panic peddlers and politicians), and deindustrialization. The effects of such processes by slumlords on the distribution of populations within Chicago have been documented (Hirsch, 1983).

Market manipulation has not been solely determined by private initiative. Large bureaucracies have arisen since World War II that "undoubtedly have important influences over the political processes in determining the allocation of land" (Guest, 1984a:293). One of the reasons for the increase of such bureaucracies is that with the rise of suburbanization and the resulting decline in the population of the central cities, local governments are finding themselves facing extreme fiscal strain (Clark, 1981). A common response has been the creation of zoning regulations that attempt to maximize the tax yield from the properties in an area and simultaneously minimize the public dollars necessary to service the community (Foley, 1973:111).

In addition, incentives have been offered to potential builders/developers that were not necessary in the past (Suttles, 1972:82–86). Current decisions to develop are not simply based on an economical use of land, but also on expectations concerning the future potential of adjacent property (1972:86). Because few developers or realtors are large enough to control such a large block of land and because many private firms are reluctant to risk a major investment in an area with a problematic future, the local government is forced to provide inducements, such as financing of construction, clearance and sale of land, and the establishment of standards for builders (1972:82).

Such developments external to the local community can have three kinds of effects on the relative distribution of crime and delinquency rates. First, they may directly affect those rates by providing inducements to high-risk populations to move into a specific neighborhood. The allocation of housing in the public rental sector of Great Britain had pronounced effects on the distribution of offenders (Bottoms and Wiles, 1986:103).

Second, these developments may indirectly affect the rates of crime and delinquency by accelerating (or decelerating) the degree of residential stability in a neighborhood. The construction of new public housing projects in Chicago between 1970 and 1980 was associated with increased rates of population turnover, which in turn were related to changes in local delinquency rates (Bursik, 1988a). Importantly, this relationship did not reflect the effect of changing racial compositions.

Third, Suttles (1972:35) has given the label of "defended community" to areas in which residents attempt to maintain a stable neighborhood identity in the context of changes that appear to be imposed on them by city planners, realtors, politicians, and industry. In such neighborhoods, gang activities are often seen as a protection of local residents from a perceived threat of invasion from "undesirable" residents of nearby communities. Thus, the increased level of internal organization of the community may in fact result in higher rates of crime and delinquency (Heitgerd and Bursik, 1987).

Thus, the traditional social disorganization model is conceptually incomplete. A full specification requires a perspective that includes the broader economic, historical, and political dynamics in which the development of local communities is embedded.

Such a development reflects the recent broad efforts in criminology to integrate apparently disparate theoretical orientations in an attempt to obtain a more complete understanding of a phenomenon (see Elliott et al., 1985; Liska et al., 1988). There is nothing wrong with the social disorganization framework in particular for having failed successfully to complete such an integration. Thus, the preceding arguments do not imply that the model should be rejected; rather its focus should simply be expanded.

New Extensions of Social Disorganization

The Neighborhood as a Context for Individual Behavior

Stark (1987) has presented a series of theoretically derived propositions that can easily form the basis of a research agenda aimed at understanding the effects of neighborhood contexts on motivational processes that may lead to the commission of a delinquent or criminal act. Unfortunately, since such study designs require extensive data, they are not yet common. Two basic approaches to the contextual-effects issue have emerged, however. The first integrates individual-level official records with aggregate statistics pertaining to the community or residence (see Bursik, 1983; Gottfredson and Taylor, 1983). Since the existence of such an individual record indicates that some official court or police action has taken place in response to that person's illegal behavior, these studies have primarily focused on the likelihood of recidivism within particular neighborhood contexts. Research indicates that the effect of juvenile court sanctions on recidivism is not consistent across communities: it differs according to the rate of crime in the area and the likelihood that illegal behavior in that community receives official handling by the police and courts (Bursik, 1983).

Gottfredson and Taylor (1983, 1986) present evidence that the neighborhood context not only has a significant effect on the likelihood of recidivism (1986:151–52), but it also has an additional effect through an interaction with individual characteristics. Those offenders with an extensive past history of criminal involvement, for example, were more likely to be rearrested if released from prison into socially disorganized neighborhoods.

The second solution to the design of such contextual analyses is not restricted to the use of official records in its characterization of the individual. Johnstone (1978) examined the degree to which the economic structure of a youth's community affects the relationship between family socioeconomic status and delinquency; he found that low-status youths tend to be more delinquent if their families live in relatively affluent communities rather than poor ones. Shannon (1982, 1984) collected longitudinal data from three birth cohorts and examined how neighborhood dynamics shaped the nature of individual careers in delinquency. Although he found a significant degree of variation in typical career patterns among different communities, those patterns were not consistently related to the structure and organization of the neighborhood.

Simcha-Fagan and Schwartz (1986) collected extensive information concerning the formal and informal networks of control within a set of neighborhoods in New York City. Not only do many of the various dimensions of the neighborhood context continue to have significant effects on the rate of delinquency after controlling for individual characteristics, but Simcha-Fagan and Schwartz also provide evidence of important indirect effects. To date, such contextual research has appeared only rarely in the literature.

Social Disorganization and Victimization

Reiss (1986) has argued that one of the clearest areas in which the individual and community traditions in criminology can be linked is in the area of victimology. At first glance, this may seem to be an unusual extension of social disorganization, which has focused on the group regulation of offending behavior. The formal and informal dynamics of social control, however, are very similar to the notion of guardianship developed by Felson and Cohen (1980) within their "routine activities" approach. If, as they argue, the spatial structure of a city partially determines the rate at which motivated offenders meet criminal opportunities, then the degree to which a local community is disorganized should be reflected in its ability to supervise the interaction of potential offenders and opportunities and, therefore, affect the rate of victimization. As Sampson (1985, 1986) argues, areas with high levels of organization are able to take note of or question strangers, watch over property, supervise youth activities, and intervene in local disturbances.

Unfortunately, although the theoretical connection is fairly straightforward, victimization data at the local community level are extremely limited. Studies distinguishing between all acts of victimization and those that occur within the boundaries of the local community are the ones most pertinent to the notion of community guardianship and social control (e.g., Smith and Jarjoura, 1988) and suggest that the predictions of social disorganization for burglary victimizations holds. However, for violent crimes the effect of residential mobility depends on the level of poverty in a neighborhood. Thus a community's capacity for social control "must be viewed in relation to other community characteristics that can facilitate criminal activity" (Smith and Jarjoura, 1988:46).

The social disorganization-based approaches of Sampson and Smith and Jarjoura represent important extensions of our understanding of victimization. In addition, such work has the exciting potential to integrate fully two perspectives (social disorganization and opportunity theories) that have been traditionally seen as competing, alternative explanations of the spatial distribution of crime and delinquency. The continuation of this work in the area of victimology will be an important component of future research in the area of social disorganization.

The Nonrecursive Aspects of the Social Disorganization Model

The research discussed in this article has generally focused on the extent to which rates of crime and delinquency depend on the ability of local communities to regulate themselves. It may be, however, that most models of social disorganization are substantively incomplete by failing to consider the degree to which rates of crime and delinquency may also affect a community's capacity for social control.

The rationale for the consideration of a reciprocal relationship between crime and social disorganization has been most thoroughly developed by Skogan (1986) in his discussion of neighborhood feedback loops. As Skogan argues, the level of crime in a neighborhood has a marked (although imperfect) effect on the fear of crime experienced by the residents of that area. High levels of fear, in turn, may result in: (1) physical and psychological withdrawal from community life; (2) weakening of the informal social control processes that inhibit crime and disorder; (3) a decline in the organizational life and mobilization capacity of the neighborhood; (4) deteriorating business conditions; (5) the importation and domestic production of delinquency and deviance; and (6) further dramatic changes in the composition of the population. In turn these conditions can increase the existing level of crime.

Such nonrecursive implications of the social disorganization model have not been completely ignored in the literature (e.g., Shannon, 1982). For example, Bursik (1986a) found that the rate of increase in the nonwhite population in Chicago's local communities between 1960 and 1970 was significantly related to simultaneous increases in the delinquency rate. The magnitude of the effect of racial change on delinquency change, however, was not nearly so great as that for the effect of changes in delinquency rates on concurrent changes in the racial composition of an area. Such findings suggest that a large part of the traditionally high association between race and crime may reflect processes of minority groups being stranded in high-crime communities from which they cannot afford to leave. Schuerman and Kobrin (1986) also provide evidence in support of the nonrecursive nature of the social disorganization model in their study of Los Angeles between 1950 and 1970, concluding that increases in the crime rate are followed by shifts (in turn) in local land use, population and socioeconomic composition, and normative structures.

Given the very few nonrecursive models that have examined the social disorganization perspective, such results should be accepted only tentatively. A great deal of work must be done concerning the identification of these models, appropriate methods of estimation, the selection of instrumental variables, and so forth. But they do represent the source of potentially important revisions of the social disorganization models in the future.

Conclusion

This article has addressed some serious criticisms that have been leveled at social disorganization models of crime and delinquency. The framework is currently undergoing a significant reformulation from that presented by Shaw and McKay and many problems remain to be resolved. Yet the findings that are emerging from this work are sufficiently relevant to the current issues facing criminology to ensure a revived appreciation of the model within the discipline.

Strain and Subcultural Theory

Introduction

Strain theory, also known as anomie theory, broadly incorporates both psychological and sociological elements in its explanation of crime. It has a lengthy history and has had considerable influence in criminological theory building. One may trace this school of thought to Emile Durkheim who spoke of "anomie" or a state of uncertainty being produced when cataclysmic events, such as depressions or sudden boom periods, upset the balance in society. As a result individuals no longer are provided the normative guidance that allows them to fit into the social whole. This condition may cause excessive rates of crime. Durkheim also saw in developing capitalism other conditions conducive to crime, in particular the stress on individual freedoms without the cultural guidelines of normative restraints. Durkheim deduced that such a state led to ever increasing desires that seem never sufficiently fulfilled, causing anomic strain.

The theorist most widely associated with the early development of classic strain theories and who modified Durkheim's conceptualization is Robert K. Merton (1938, 1957). While it has been elaborated and qualified, strain theory's core idea as developed by Merton remains that in egalitarian societies, where cultural goals are set as examples for everyone to achieve (e.g., monetary success) but where the legitimate means to reach these universal goals are not equally available to all, crime and deviance may be a natural response.

Others who followed in Merton's footsteps, such as Cohen (1955) and Cloward and Ohlin (1960), focused on gang delinquency in lower-class urban areas. In the Cloward and Ohlin version strain came about because of the perceived or actual inability to achieve the cultural goal of financial success. Cloward and Ohlin observed that while legitimate opportunities to achieve goals may not be available, illegitimate opportunities are also socially structured. Thus depending on the neighborhood opportunity structure, different types of gangs arise. Where legitimate and illegitimate opportunities are blocked, violence becomes the norm. These findings were later to be challenged as being too simple (Spergel, 1964) and greater elaboration followed, as represented by Hagedorn in this collection. Cohen, on the other hand, focused on the goal of middle-class status. Strain for him was measured in terms of the disjunction between aspirations and expectations for success. Delinquency resulted from a conscious rejection of universal middle-class standards felt not to be achievable and "turning them upside down."

While these versions of strain theory focus on people situated in the lower class with limited legitimate opportunities to reach the prescribed goals, it is not only those who cannot achieve these goals that are subject to this strain to deviate. Even those who are able to achieve the pre-scribed goals may be dissatisfied for they perceive that they should be accomplishing more. These include the affluent white-collar professional and corporate executive who perceive themselves as never making sufficient profit and who continually deviate to reach the never attainable level, a condition Durkheim called "overweening ambition." While there is a similarity between Durkheim and Merton, for the former peoples' desires were structurally induced, whereas for Merton culture created these desires.

As with all theories considered here, anomie or strain theory has not been without its critics. Chief among the critics concerns is that the theory is too deterministic by not allowing sufficient space for human agency and that there are other goals besides financial success that are of importance in shaping human striving, minimized by the theory. A recent anthology of essays reviews the development, maturation, and critique of the theory (Adler and Laufer, 1995).

Foremost in the modification and recent elaboration of strain theory is Robert Agnew (chap. 10) who argues in his essay that the general strain theory of crime and delinquency can overcome previous criticism. He provides a comparison between strain theory and other theories, describes the major types of strain and their adaptations, and discusses the factors that influence the choice, whether delinquent or legitimate.

John M. Hagedorn's (chap. 11) Milwaukee, Wisconsin, research on male adult gang members who are involved in drug sales, reveals that only a few could be considered "committed long-term participants" in the drug economy. He develops a typology which indicates that only one type has rejected conventional values totally. Others are in the drug subculture on an irregular basis. His findings indicate some similarities as well as significant differences from earlier subcultural research and have serious implications for contemporary drug enforcement policy.

10

Foundation for a General Strain Theory of Crime and Delinquency

Robert Agnew

After dominating deviance research in the 1960s, strain theory came under heavy attack in the 1970s (Bernard, 1984; Cole, 1975), with suggestions that it be abandoned (Hirschi, 1969; Kornhauser, 1978). The theory survived, but its influence diminished (see Agnew, 1985b; Bernard, 1984; Farnworth and Leiber, 1989). It now plays a very limited role in explanations of crime/delinquency, either being entirely excluded or assigned a small role (e.g., Elliott et al., 1985; Johnson, 1979; Massey and Krohn, 1986; Thornberry, 1987b; Tonry et al., 1991). Currently dominant are differential association/social learning theory and social control theory.

This article argues that strain theory has a central role to play in explanations of crime/delinquency, but that it has to be substantially revised to take account of the wealth of new research on stress in medical sociology and psychology, on equity justice in social psychology, and on aggression in psychology—particularly recent versions of frustration-aggression and social learning theory. Also important is recent research in such areas as the legitimation of stratification, the sociology of emotions, and the urban underclass. This paper draws on the above literatures, as well as the recent revisions in strain theory, to present the outlines of a general strain theory of crime/delinquency.

The theory focuses on the individual and his or her immediate social environment—although some macroimplications of the theory are also explored. This general theory is capable of overcoming the theoretical and empirical criticisms of previous strain theories and of complementing the crime/delinquency theories currently dominating the field.

The article is in three sections. In the first section, there is a brief discussion of the fundamental traits that distinguish strain theory from the

---

Edited and abridged from *Criminology*, Volume 30(1):47–87 (1992).

other two dominant theories of delinquency: social control and differential association/social learning theory. In the second section, the three major sources of strain are described. And in the final section, the major adaptations to strain are listed and the factors influencing the choice of delinquent versus nondelinquent adaptations are discussed.

Distinguishing Strain Theory from Control and Differential Association/ Social Learning Theories

Strain, social control, and differential association are all sociological theories: They explain delinquency in terms of an individual's social relationships. Strain theory is distinguished from social control and social learning theory in its specification of (1) the type of social relationship that leads to delinquency, and (2) the motivation for delinquency.

Strain theory focuses explicitly on *negative relationships with others* in which the individual is upset with the way he or she is treated. Strain theory has typically focused on relationships in which others prevent the individual from achieving positively valued goals, but also may include relationships in which others present the individual with noxious or negative stimuli (Agnew, 1985a).

Social control theory focuses on the *absence of significant relationships with conventional others and institutions.* Delinquency is most likely when (1) the adolescent is not attached to parents, school, or other institutions; (2) parents and others fail to monitor and effectively sanction deviance; (3) the adolescent's actual or anticipated investment in conventional society is minimal; and (4) the adolescent has not internalized conventional beliefs.

Social learning theory is distinguished from strain and control theory by its focus on *positive relationships with deviant others.* Delinquency results from association with others who (1) differentially reinforce the adolescent's delinquency, (2) model delinquent behavior, and/or (3) transmit delinquent values.

Strain theory argues that adolescents are *pressured into delinquency by the negative affective states—most notably anger and related emotions that often result from negative relationships* (see Kemper, 1978; Morgan and Heise, 1988). This negative affect creates pressure for corrective action and may lead adolescents to (1) use illegitimate channels of goal achievement, (2) attack or escape from the source of their adversity, and/or (3) manage their negative affect with illicit drugs.

Control theory denies that outside forces pressure the adolescent into delinquency. The absence of significant relationships with other individuals and groups *frees the adolescent to engage in delinquency.* The freed adolescent either drifts into delinquency or turns to delinquency in response to inner forces or situational inducements (Hirschi, 1969:31–34).

In differential association/social learning theory, the adolescent commits delinquent acts because group forces lead the adolescent to *view delinquency as a desirable or at least justifiable form of behavior* under certain circumstances.

Strain theory, then, is distinguished by its focus on negative relationships with others and its insistence that such relationships lead to delinquency through the negative affect—especially anger—that they sometimes engender. Both dimensions are necessary to differentiate strain theory from control and differential association/social learning theory, which sometimes examine negative relationships. Control theory, however, would argue that negative relationships lead to delinquency not because they cause negative affect, but because they lead to a reduction in social control. For example, parental physical abuse leads to delinquency because it reduces attachment to parents and the effectiveness of parents as socializing agents. Likewise, differential association/social learning theorists sometimes examine negative relationships but would argue that negative relationships such as those involving physically abusive parents lead to delinquency by providing models for imitation and by implicitly teaching the child that violence and other forms of deviance are acceptable behavior.

Thus, it is easy to see that strain theory complements the other major theories of delinquency. While these other theories focus on the absence of relationships or on positive relationships, strain theory is the only theory to focus explicitly on negative relationships. And while these other theories view delinquency as the result of drift or of desire, strain theory views it as the result of pressure.

The Major Types of Strain

Negative relationships with others are relationships in which others are not treating the individual as he or she would like to be treated. The classic strain theories of Merton (1938), Cohen (1955), and Cloward and Ohlin (1960) focus on only negative relationships in which others prevent the individual from achieving positively valued goals. They focus on the goal blockage experienced by lower-class individuals trying to achieve monetary success or middle-class status. Revisions in classic strain theory have argued that adolescents are also concerned about the achievement of more immediate goals such as good grades, popularity with the opposite sex, and doing well in athletics (Agnew, 1984; Elliott and Voss, 1974; Elliott et al., 1985; Empey, 1982; Greenberg, 1977; Quicker, 1974).

Strain has also been said to result from the inability to escape legally from painful situations (Agnew, 1985b).

A more complete classification of types of strain can be developed by taking into account the stress, equity/justice, and aggression literature. Three major types of strain are described—each referring to a different type of negative relationship with others. Other individuals may (1) prevent one from achieving positively valued goals, (2) remove or threaten to remove positively valued stimuli that one possesses, or (3) present or threaten to present one with noxious or negatively valued stimuli.

Strain as the Failure to Achieve Positively Valued Goals

Three subtypes of strain fall in this category. The first encompasses the classic strain theories of Merton (1938), Cohen (1955), and Cloward and Ohlin (1960), as well as modern strain theories focusing on immediate goal achievement. The other two subtypes are derived from the justice/equity literature.

DISJUNCTION BETWEEN ASPIRATIONS AND EXPECTATIONS/ ACTUAL ACHIEVEMENTS

The classic strain theories of Merton, Cohen, and Cloward and Ohlin argue that the cultural system encourages everyone to pursue the ideal goals of monetary success and/or middle-class status. Lower-class individuals, however, are often prevented from achieving such goals through legitimate channels. For example, adolescent strain is typically measured in terms of the disjunction between *aspirations* (or ideal goals) and *expectations* (or expected levels of goal achievement). These theories have been criticized for (1) being unable to explain the extensive nature of middle-class delinquency, (2) neglecting goals other than monetary success/middle-class status, (3) neglecting barriers to goal achievement other than social class, and (4) not fully specifying why only *some* strained individuals turn to delinquency (Agnew, 1986, 1991b; Clinard, 1964; Hirschi, 1969; Kornhauser, 1978; Liska, 1987; Bernard, 1984; Farnworth and Leiber, 1989). The most damaging criticism, however, stems from the limited empirical support provided by studies focusing on the disjunction between aspirations and expectations (Kornhauser, 1978; Bernard, 1984; Elliott et al., 1985; and Jensen, 1986).

Consequently, the above theories have been revised. The most popular revision argues that there is a youth subculture that emphasizes a variety of immediate goals whose achievement depends on factors besides social class: such as intelligence, personality, physical attract-iveness, and athletic ability. As a result, many middle-class individuals find that they lack the traits or skills necessary to achieve their goals through legitimate channels. This version of strain theory, however, continues to argue that strain stems from the inability to achieve certain ideal goals emphasized by the (sub)cultural system. As a consequence, strain continues to be measured in terms of the disjunction between *aspirations* and *actual achievements*. It should be noted that empirical support for this revised version of strain theory is also weak (Agnew, 1991b).

DISJUNCTION BETWEEN EXPECTATIONS AND ACTUAL ACHIEVEMENTS

Social-psychological research on justice focuses on the disjunction between *expectations* and *actual achievements* (rewards). It is commonly argued that such expectations are existentially based, deriving from the individual's past experience and/or from comparisons with referential (or generalized) others who are similar to the individual (Berger et al., 1972, 1983; Blau, 1964; Homans, 1961; Jasso and Rossi, 1977; Mickelson, 1990; Ross et al., 1971; Thibaut and Kelley, 1959). Much research has focused on income expectations, although the theories apply to expectations regarding all manner of positive stimuli. The justice literature argues that failure to achieve such expectations may lead to anger, resentment, rage, dis-satisfaction, disappointment, and unhappiness—all the emotions customarily associated with criminological versions of strain. Further, individuals are said to be strongly motivated to reduce the gap between expectations and achievements—with deviance as one possible option. The limited empirical research on deviance suggests that the expectations-achievement gap is related to anger/hostility (Ross et al., 1971).

This alternative conception of strain, neglected in criminology, has the potential to overcome some of the problems of current strain theories. First, one would expect the disjunction between expectations and actual achievements to be more emotionally distressing than that between aspirations and achievements. Aspirations, by definition, are *ideal* or utopian goals; the failure to achieve them may not be taken seriously. The failure to achieve expected goals, however, is likely to be taken seriously since such goals are rooted in reality—that of previous experience, or of witnessing similar others experience such goals. Second, this conception of strain assigns a central role to the social comparison process neglected in classic strain theory (Cohen, 1965). Social comparison plays a central role in the formation of individual goals (expectations in this case; see Suls, 1977).

DISJUNCTION BETWEEN JUST/FAIR OUTCOMES AND ACTUAL OUTCOMES

The above models of strain assume that individual goals focus on the achievement of specific outcomes. Individual goals, for example, focus on the achievement of a certain amount of money or a certain grade-point average. A third conception of strain, also derived from the justice/equity literature, claims that individuals do not necessarily enter into interactions with specific outcomes in mind. Rather, they enter into them expecting that certain distributive justice rules will be followed, rules specifying how resources should be allocated. The equity rule has received the most attention. An equitable relationship is one in which the outcome/input ratios of the actors involved in an exchange/allocation relationship are equivalent (see Adams, 1963, 1965; Cook and Hegtvedt, 1983; Walster et al., 1978). Outcomes encompass a broad range of positive and negative consequences, while inputs encompass the individual's positive and negative contributions to the exchange. Individuals in a relationship will compare the ratio of their outcomes and inputs to the ratio(s) of specific others in the relationship. If the ratios are equal to one another, they feel that the outcomes are fair or just. This is true even if the outcomes are low. If outcome/input ratios are not equal, actors will feel that the outcomes are unjust and they will experience distress. Such distress is especially likely when individuals feel they have been underrewarded rather than overrewarded (Hegtvedt, 1990).

The possible reactions to this distress include deviance (see Adams, 1963, 1965; Austin, 1977; Walster et al., 1973, 1978; Stephenson and White, 1968). Inequity may lead to delinquency for several reasons—all having to do with the restoration of equity. Individuals in inequitable relationships may engage in delinquency in order to (1) increase their outcomes (e.g., by theft); (2) lower their inputs (e.g., truancy from school); (3) lower the outcomes of others (e.g., vandalism, theft, assault); and/or (4) increase the inputs of others (e.g., by being incorrigible or disorderly). In highly inequitable situations, individuals may leave the field (e.g., run away from home) or force others to leave the field. There has not been any empirical research on the relationship between equity and delinquency, although much data suggest that inequity leads to anger and frustration. A few studies also suggest that insulting and vengeful behaviors may result from inequity (see Cook and Hegtvedt, 1991; Donnerstein and Hatfield, 1982; Hegtvedt, 1990; Mikula, 1986; Sprecher, 1986; Walster et al., 1973, 1978). One would then predict that those involved in unfair relations will be more likely to engage in current and future delinquency.

This conception of the strain literature builds on the existing strain literature in several ways. First, the strain literature assumes that individuals are pursuing some specific outcome, such as a certain amount of money or prestige. The equity literature points out that individuals do not necessarily enter into interactions with specific outcomes in mind, but rather with the expectation that a particular distributive justice rule will be followed. Their goal is that the interaction conform to the justice principle. This perspective, then, points to a new source of strain not considered in the criminology literature.

Second, the strain literature focuses largely on individual outcomes. Individuals are assumed to be pursuing a specific goal, and strain is the disjunction between the goal and the actual outcome. The equity literature suggests that the individual's inputs may also have to be considered. An equity theorist would argue that inputs will condition the individual's evaluation of outcomes. Such that those who view their inputs as limited will be more likely to accept limited outcomes as fair.

Third, the equity literature also highlights the social comparison process, stressing that one's evaluation of outcomes is at least partly a function of the outcomes (and inputs) of those with whom one is involved in exchange/allocation relations. A given outcome may be evaluated as fair or unfair depending on the outcomes (and inputs) of others in the exchange/allocation relation.

To complicate matters further, in addition to the three subtypes identified above one can list additional types of strain in this category such as the disjunction between "satisfying outcomes" and reality, between "deserved" outcomes and reality, and between "tolerance levels" or minimally acceptable outcomes and reality. No study has examined all of these types of goals, but taken as a whole the data do suggest that there are often differences among aspirations (ideal outcomes), expectations (expected outcomes), "satisfying" outcomes, "deserved" outcomes, fair or just outcomes, and tolerance levels (Della Fave, 1974; Della Fave and Klobus, 1976; Martin, 1986; Martin and Murray, 1983; Messick and Sentis, 1983; Shepelak and Alwin, 1986). Given these multiple sources of strain, one might ask which is the most relevant to the explanation of delinquency. Given the current state of research the most fruitful strategy may be to assume that all of the above sources are relevant. Alwin (1987), Austin (1977), Crosby and Gonzalez-Intal (1984), Hegtvedt (1991), Messick and Sentis (1983), and Tornblum (1977) all argue that people often employ a variety of standards to evaluate their situation. Strain theorists, then, might employ measures that tap all of the above types of strain. One would expect strain to be greatest when several standards were not being met, with perhaps greatest weight being given to expectations and just/fair outcomes.

The Removal of Positively Valued Stimuli from the Individual

The literature on aggression and stress suggests that strain may involve more than the pursuit of positively valued goals. Some researchers deemphasize the pursuit of positively valued goals, pointing out that the blockage of goal-seeking behavior is a relatively weak predictor of aggression, particularly when the goal has never been experienced before (Bandura, 1973; Zillman, 1979). Rather than looking at the pursuit of positively valued goals as a source of stress, the stress literature focuses on (1) events involving the loss of positively valued stimuli and (2) events involving the presentation of noxious or negative stimuli (see Pearlin, 1983). So, for example, one recent study of adolescent stress employs a life-events list that focuses on such items as the loss of a boyfriend/girlfriend, the death or serious illness of a friend, moving to a new school district, the divorce/separation of one's parents, suspension from school, and the presence of a variety of adverse conditions at work (see Williams and Uchiyama, 1989; Compas, 1987, and Compas and Phares, 1991).

Therefore, a second type of strain or negative relationship involves the actual or anticipated removal (loss) of positively valued stimuli from the individual. The actual or anticipated loss of positively valued stimuli may lead to delinquency as the individual tries to prevent the loss of the positive stimuli, retrieve the lost stimuli or obtain substitute stimuli, seek revenge against those responsible for the loss, or manage the negative affect caused by the loss by taking illicit drugs. While there are no data bearing directly on this type of strain, experimental data indicate that aggression often occurs when positive reinforcement previously administered to an individual is withheld or reduced (Bandura, 1973; Van Houten, 1983). And, as discussed below, inventories of stressful life events, which include the loss of positive stimuli, are related to delinquency.

The Presentation of Negative Stimuli

The stress and recent aggression literature also focuses on the actual or anticipated presentation of negative or noxious stimuli. Except for work on the inability of adolescents to escape legally from noxious stimuli (Agnew, 1985b), criminology has neglected this third source of strain. Much data, however, suggest that the presentation of noxious stimuli may lead to aggression and other negative outcomes, even when legal escape from such stimuli is possible (Bandura, 1973; Zillman, 1979). Noxious stimuli may lead to delinquency as the adolescent tries to (1) escape from or avoid negative stimuli; (2) terminate or alleviate negative stimuli; (3) seek revenge against the source of the negative stimuli or related targets, although the evidence on displaced aggression is somewhat mixed (see Berkowitz, 1982; Bernard, 1990; Van Houten, 1983; Zillman, 1979); and/or (4) manage the resultant negative affect by taking illicit drugs.

Delinquency/aggression has been linked to such noxious stimuli as child abuse and neglect (Rivera and Widom, 1990), criminal victimization (Lauritsen et al., 1991), physical punishment (Straus, 1991), negative relations with parents (Healy and Bronner, 1969), negative relations with peers (Short and Strodtbeck, 1965), adverse or negative school experience (Hawkins and Lishner, 1987), stressful life events (Gersten et al., 1974; Kaplan et al., 1983; Linsky and Straus, 1986; Mawson, 1987; Novy and Donohue, 1985; Vaux and Ruggiero, 1983), verbal threats and insults, physical pain, unpleasant odors, disgusting scenes, noise, heat, air pollution, personal space violations, and high density (see Anderson and Anderson, 1984; Bandura, 1973, 1983; Berkowitz, 1982, 1986; Mueller, 1983). Delinquency has been found to be related to negative relations at home and school through anger (Agnew, 1985b), and the relationship between negative stimuli and delinquency has been shown to be due to the *causal* effect of the negative stimuli on delinquency (see Agnew, 1989).

Certain of the negative stimuli listed above, such as physical pain, heat, noise, and pollution, may be experienced as noxious largely for biological reasons. Others may be experienced as noxious largely because of their association with unconditioned negative stimuli (see Berkowitz, 1982). Whatever the case, it is assumed that such stimuli are experienced as noxious regardless of individual goals.

The Links between Strain and Delinquency

Three sources of strain have been presented: strain as the actual or anticipated failure to achieve positively valued goals, strain as the actual or anticipated removal of positively valued stimuli, and strain as the actual or anticipated presentation of negative stimuli. While these types are theoretically distinct from one another, they may sometimes overlap in practice. So, for example, the insults of a teacher may be experienced as adverse because they (1) interfere with the adolescent's aspirations for academic success, (2) result in the violation of a distributive justice rule such as equity, and (3) are conditioned negative stimuli and so are experienced as noxious in and of themselves.

Each type of strain increases the likelihood that individuals will experience one or more of a range of negative emotions. Those emotions include disappointment, depression, fear, and anger. However, anger, the most critical emotional reaction, results when individuals blame their adversity on others. It is a key emotion because it increases the individual's level of felt injury, creates a desire for retaliation/revenge, energizes the individual for action, and lowers inhibitions, in part because individuals believe that others will feel their aggression is justified (see Averill, 1982; Berkowitz, 1982; Kemper, 1978; Kluegel and Smith, 1986:chap. 10; Zillman, 1979). Anger, then, affects the individual in several ways that are conducive to delinquency and is distinct from many of the other types of negative affect in this respect. Importantly, delinquency may still occur in response to other types of negative affect such as despair, although delinquency is less likely in such cases. The experience of negative affect, especially anger, typically creates a desire to take corrective steps, with delinquency being one possible response. Delinquency may be a method for alleviating strain, that is, for achieving positively valued goals, for protecting or retrieving positive stimuli, or for terminating or escaping from negative stimuli. Delinquency may be used to seek revenge; data suggest that vengeful behavior often occurs even when there is no possibility of eliminating the adversity that stimulated it (Berkowitz, 1982). And delinquency may occur as adolescents try to manage their negative affect through illicit drug use (see Newcomb and Harlow, 1986). General strain theory, then, has the potential to explain a broad range of delinquency, including theft, aggression, and drug use.

Each type of strain may create a *predisposition* for delinquency or function as a *situational event* that instigates a particular delinquent act. The strain theory presented in this article, then, is a theory of both "criminality" and "crime" (Hirschi and Gottfredson, 1986) or a theory of both "criminal involvement" and "criminal events" (Clarke and Cornish, 1985). Strain creates a predisposition for delinquency in those cases in which it is chronic or repetitive. Examples include a continuing gap between expectations and achievements and a continuing pattern of ridicule and insults from teachers. Adolescents subject to such strain are predisposed to delinquency because (1) nondelinquent strategies for coping with strain are likely to be taxed; (2) the threshold for adversity may be lowered by chronic strains (see Averill, 1982:289); (3) repeated or chronic strain may lead to a hostile attitude—a general dislike and suspicion of others and an associated tendency to respond in an aggressive manner (see Edmunds and Kendrick, 1980:21); and (4) chronic strains increase the likelihood that individuals will be high in negative affect/arousal at any given time (see Bandura, 1983; Bernard, 1990). A particular instance of strain may also function as the situational event that ignites a delinquent act, especially among adolescents predisposed to delinquency. Qualitative and survey data suggest that particular instances of delinquency are often instigated by one of the three types of strain listed above (see Agnew, 1990; Averill, 1982).

Adaptations to (Coping Strategies for) Strain

So far this article has focused on the type of strain that might promote delinquency. Virtually all strain theories, however, acknowledge that only *some* strained individuals turn to delinquency. Attempts to identify factors that determine whether one adapts to strain through delinquency have mainly concentrated on the adolescent's commitment to legitimate means and association with other strained/delinquent individuals (Agnew, 1991b).

In the following discussion, the major cognitive, emotional, and behavioral adaptions to strain are described. Then, those factors that influence whether one adapts to strain using delinquent or nondelinquent strategies are described. What follows is a typology of the major cognitive, emotional, and behavioral adaptations to strain, including delinquency.

Cognitive Coping Strategies

Individuals sometimes cognitively reinterpret objective stressors to minimize their subjective adversity. Three general strategies of cognitive coping may be summarized as: "It's not important," "It's not that bad," and "I deserve it." This typology represents a synthesis of the coping strategies described in the stress, equity, stratification, and victimization literatures (Adams, 1963, 1965; Agnew, 1985a; Agnew and Jones, 1988; Averill, 1982; Della Fave, 1980; Donnerstein and Hatfield, 1982; Pearlin and Schooler, 1978; Walster et al., 1973, 1978).

IGNORE/MINIMIZE THE IMPORTANCE OF ADVERSITY

The subjective impact of objective strain depends on the extent to which strain is related to the central goals, values, and/or identities of the individual. Individuals may avoid subjective strain "to the extent that they are able to keep the most strainful experiences within the least valued areas of their life" (Pearlin and Schooler, 1978:7). Individuals, therefore, may minimize the strain they experience by reducing the absolute and/or relative importance assigned to goals/values and identities (see Agnew, 1983; Thoits, 1991a).

Individuals may claim that a particular goal/value or identity (e.g., money or status), is unimportant in an absolute sense. This strategy is similar to Merton's adaptations of ritualism and retreatism (see Hyman,

1953). Individuals may also claim that a particular goal/value or identity (e.g., work) is unimportant relative to other goals/values or identities (e.g., family and leisure).

The strategy of minimizing strain by reducing the absolute and/or relative emphasis placed on goals/values and identities has not been extensively examined. Some evidence, however, suggests that it is commonly employed and may play a central role in accounting for the limited empirical support for strain theory. Research on goals suggests that people pursue a wide variety of different goals and that they tend to place the greatest absolute and relative emphasis on those goals they are best able to achieve (Agnew, 1983; McClelland, 1990; Rosenberg, 1979:265–69; Wylie, 1979).

MAXIMIZE POSITIVE OUTCOMES/MINIMIZE NEGATIVE OUTCOMES

In a second adaptation, individuals attempt to deny the existence of adversity by maximizing their positive outcomes and/or minimizing their negative ones. This may be done by lowering the standards used to evaluate outcomes or distorting one's estimate of current and/or expected outcomes.

Lowering one's standards basically involves lowering one's goals or raising one's threshold for negative stimuli (Suls, 1977). Such action makes one's current situation seem less adverse than it otherwise would be. Individuals may, for example, lower the amount of money they desire (though not necessarily lowering the importance attached to money). This strategy is related to Merton's adaptations of ritualism and retreatism. Some argue that poor individuals in the United States are not strained because they have lowered their success goals—bringing their aspirations in line with reality (Hyman, 1953). Data suggest that this adaptation is employed by some but not all lower-class individuals (Agnew, 1983, 1986; Agnew and Jones, 1988; see Cloward and Ohlin, 1960; Empey, 1956).

In addition, to lowering their standards, individuals may also cognitively distort their estimate of outcomes. Many individuals exaggerate their actual and expected levels of goal achievement (Agnew and Jones, 1988). Individuals with poor grades, for example, often report that they are doing well in school; those with little objective chance of attending college often report that they *expect* to attend college (see Wylie, 1979). In addition individuals may also minimize negative outcomes—claiming that their losses are small and their noxious experiences are mild.

Two common strategies to accomplish such distortions are "downward comparisons," and "compensatory benefits." In "downward comparisons" individuals claim that their situation is less worse or at least no worse than that of similar others (e.g., Brickman and Bulman, 1977; Gruder, 1977; Pearlin and Schooler, 1978; Suls, 1977) or that it is an improvement over their past. Individuals often deliberately make downward comparisons, especially when self-esteem is threatened (Gruder, 1977; Hegtvedt, 1991; Suls, 1977). In "compensatory benefits," individuals cast "about for some positive attribute or circumstance within a troublesome situation . . . the person is aided in ignoring that which is noxious by anchoring his attention to what he considers the more worthwhile and rewarding aspects of experience" (Pearlin and Schooler, 1978:67). Crime victims, for example, often argue that their victimization benefited them in certain ways, such as causing them to grow as a person (Agnew, 1985a).

ACCEPT RESPONSIBILITY FOR ADVERSITY

Third, individuals may minimize the subjective adversity of objective strain by convincing themselves that they deserve the adversity. There are several possible reasons why deserved strain is less adverse than undeserved strain. Undeserved strain may violate the equity principle, challenge one's "belief in a just world" (Lerner, 1977), and—if attributed to the malicious behavior of another—lead one to fear that it will be repeated. This may help explain why individuals who make internal attributions for adversity are less distressed than others (Kluegel and Smith, 1986; Mirowsky and Ross, 1990).

There are two basic strategies for convincing oneself that strain is deserved. First, individuals may cognitively minimize their positive inputs or maximize their negative inputs to a relationship. Inputs are conceived as contributions to the relationship and/or status characteristics believed to be relevant to the relationship (see Cook and Yamagishi, 1983). Second, individuals may maximize the positive inputs or minimize the negative inputs of others. Della Fave (1980) uses both these strategies to explain the legitimation of inequality in the United States. Those at the bottom of the stratification system are said to minimize their own traits and exaggerate the positive traits and contributions of those above them. They therefore come to accept their limited outcomes as just (also see Kluegel and Smith, 1986; Shepelak, 1987).

Behavioral Coping Strategies

There are two major types of behavioral coping: those that seek to minimize or eliminate the source of strain and those that seek to satisfy the need for revenge.

MAXIMIZING POSITIVE OUTCOMES/MINIMIZING NEGATIVE OUTCOMES

Behavioral coping may assume several forms, paralleling each of the major types of strain. Individuals may seek to achieve positively valued goals, protect or retrieve positively valued stimuli, or terminate or escape from negative stimuli. Their actions in these areas may involve conventional or delinquent behavior. Individuals seeking to escape from an adverse school environment, for example, may try to transfer to another school or they may illegally skip school. This adaptation encompasses Merton's adaptations of innovation and rebellion, as well as coping strategies described as "maximizing one's outcomes," "minimizing one's inputs," and "maximizing the other's inputs."

VENGEFUL BEHAVIOR

When adversity is blamed on others it creates a desire for revenge which can constitute a second method of behavioral coping. Vengeful behavior may also assume conventional or delinquent forms, although the potential for delinquency is obviously high. Such behavior may involve efforts to minimize the positive outcomes, increase the negative outcomes, and/or increase the inputs of others (as when adolescents cause teachers and parents to work harder through their incorrigible behavior).

Emotional Coping Strategies

Finally, individuals may cope by acting directly on the negative emotions that result from adversity. Rosenberg (1990), Thoits (1984, 1989, 1990, 1991b), and others list several strategies of emotional coping. They include the use of drugs such as stimulants and depressants, physical exercise and deep breathing techniques, meditation, bio-feedback and progressive relaxation, and the behavioral manipulation of expressive gestures through playacting or "expression work." In all these examples, the focus is on alleviating negative emotions rather than cognitively reinterpreting or behaviorally altering the situation that produced those emotions. Many of the strategies are beyond the reach of most adolescents (Compas et al., 1988), and data indicate that adolescents often employ illicit drugs to cope with life's strains (Labouvie, 1986a, 1986b; Newcomb and Harlow, 1986). Emotional coping is especially likely when behavioral and cognitive coping are unavailable or unsuccessful.

Note that individuals may employ more than one of the above coping strategies (see Folkman, 1991). Also, still other coping strategies, such as distraction, could have been listed. It is assumed, however, that the above strategies constitute the primary responses to strain.

Delinquent versus Nondelinquent Adaptations

Overall the above typology suggests that there are many ways to cope with strain—only some of which involve delinquency; data from stress literature suggest that individuals vary in the extent to which they use the different strategies (Compas et al., 1988; Menaghan, 1983; Pearlin and Schooler, 1978). This goes a long way toward explaining the weak support for strain theory. With certain limited exceptions, these strategies are not taken into account in tests of strain theory. If strain theory is to have any value it must be able to explain the selection of delinquent versus nondelinquent adaptations. The aggression literature is especially useful here. Adversity is said to produce a general state of arousal, which can facilitate a variety of behaviors. Whether this arousal results in aggression is said to be determined by a number of factors, (see Bandura, 1973, 1983; Berkowitz, 1978, 1982). Those factors affect the choice of coping, strategies by affecting (1) the constraints to nondelinquent and delinquent coping and (2) the disposition to engage in nondelinquent versus delinquent coping.

CONSTRAINTS

While there are many adaptations to objective strain, those adaptations are not equally available to everyone. Individuals are constrained in their choice of adaptation(s) by a variety of internal and external factors. Delinquency is more likely to occur where: (1) *initial goals/values/identities of the individual* are high in absolute and relative importance, and where the individual has few alternatives (see Agnew, 1986; Thoits, 1991a); (2) *individual coping resources,* including traits such as temperament, intelligence, creativity, problem-solving skills, interpersonal skills, self-efficacy, and self-esteem, increase the individual's sensitivity to objective strains and reduce his or her ability to engage in cognitive, emotional, and behavioral coping (Agnew, 1991a; Averill, 1982; Bernard, 1990; Compas, 1987; Edmunds and Kendrick, 1980; Slaby and Guerra, 1988; Tavris, 1984); (3) *conventional social support,* including informational support, instrumental support, and emotional support (Vaux, 1988; House, 1981) is weak or absent; and (4) where *constraints to delinquent coping* are high, the situational costs of delinquency and the benefits are low (Clarke and Cornish, 1985), the individual is high in social control (see Hirschi, 1969), and the individual lacks the "illegitimate means" necessary for many delinquent acts (see Agnew, 1991a).

MACROLEVEL VARIABLES

The larger social environment may also affect the probability of delinquent versus nondelinquent coping by affecting all of the above factors. First, the social environment may affect coping by influencing the importance attached to selected goals/values/identities. For example, there is a strong social and cultural emphasis on the goals of money/status among certain segments of the urban poor (Anderson, 1978; MacLeod, 1987; Sullivan, 1989). These individuals should face more difficulty in cognitively minimizing the importance of money and status.

Second, the larger social environment may affect the individual's sensitivity to particular strains by influencing beliefs regarding what is and is not adverse. The subculture of violence thesis, for example, is predicated on the assumption that young black males in urban slums are taught that a wide range of provocations and insults are highly adverse.

Third, the social environment may influence the individual's ability to minimize cognitively the severity of objective strain. Individuals in some environments are regularly provided with external information about their accomplishments and failings (see Faunce, 1989), and their attempts at cognitively distorting such information are quickly challenged. Such a situation may exist among many adolescents and among those who inhabit the very public "street-corner world" of the urban poor.

Fourth, certain social environments may make it difficult to engage in behavioral coping of a nondelinquent nature. Adolescents often find it difficult to escape legally from negative stimuli, especially those encountered in the school, family, and neighborhood (Agnew, 1985b). Also, adolescents often lack the resources to negotiate successfully with parents and teachers (although see Agnew, 1991a). Similar arguments might be made for the urban underclass.

The larger social environment, then, may affect individual coping in a variety of ways. Certain groups, such as adolescents and the urban underclass, may face special constraints that make nondelinquent coping more difficult. This may explain their higher rates of deviance.

FACTORS AFFECTING THE DISPOSITION TO DELINQUENCY

The selection of delinquent verses nondelinquent coping strategies is also dependent on the adolescent's disposition to engage in delinquent versus nondelinquent coping. This disposition is a function of (1) certain temperamental variables (see Tonry et al., 1991); (2) the prior learning history of the adolescent, particularly whether past delinquency was reinforced (Bandura, 1973; Berkowitz, 1982); (3) the adolescent's beliefs, particularly rules defining appropriate response to provocations (Bernard,

1990); and (4) the adolescent's attributions regarding the causes of his or her adversity. Adolescents who attribute their adversity to others are much more likely to become angry, and as argued earlier, that anger creates a strong predisposition to delinquency.

A key variable affecting several of the above factors is association with delinquent peers. Adolescents who associate with delinquent peers are more likely to be exposed to delinquent models and beliefs and to receive reinforcement for delinquency (see Akers, 1985).

The individual's disposition to delinquency may condition the impact of adversity on delinquency. It is important to note that continued experience with adversity may create a disposition for delinquency (Bernard, 1990; Cloward and Ohlin, 1960; Cohen, 1955; Elliott et al., 1979). Under certain conditions the experience of adversity may lead to beliefs favorable to delinquency, lead adolescents to join or form delinquent peer groups, and lead adolescents to blame others for their misfortune.

Researchers have failed to examine whether the effect of adversity on delinquency is conditioned by factors such as self-efficacy and association with delinquent peers. This is likely a major reason for the weak empirical support for strain theory.

Conclusion

Following Hirschi's (1979) advice, this article has focused on the refinement of a single theory rather than on theoretical integration. The general strain theory builds upon traditional strain theory in criminology by pointing to several new sources of strain. In particular, it focuses on three categories of strain or negative relationships with others: (1) the actual or anticipated failure to achieve positively valued goals; (2) the actual or anticipated removal of positively valued stimuli; and (3) the actual or anticipated presentation of negative stimuli. Most current strain theories in criminology only focus on strain as the failure to achieve positively valued goals, and even then the focus is only on the disjunction between aspirations and expectations/actual achievements. The disjunctions between expectations and achievements and just/fair outcomes and achievements are ignored. The general strain theory, then, significantly expands the focus of strain theory to include all types of negative relations between the individual and others.

Second, the general strain theory more precisely specifies the relationship between strain and delinquency, pointing out that strain is likely to have a cumulative effect on delinquency after a certain threshold level is reached.

Third, the general strain theory provides a more comprehensive account of the cognitive, behavioral, and emotional adaptations to strain and sheds light on the reasons why many strained individuals do not turn to delinquency, and it may prove useful in devising strategies to prevent and control delinquency.   Fourth, the general strain theory more fully describes those factors affecting the choice of delinquent versus nondelinquent adaptations. The failure to consider such factors is a fundamental reason for the weak empirical support for strain theory.

Most of the above modifications in strain theory were suggested by research in several areas outside traditional criminology, most notably the stress research in medical sociology and psychology, the equity/justice research in social psychology, and the aggression research in psychology. With certain exceptions, researchers in criminology have tended to cling to the early strain models and to ignore the developments in related fields. And while these early strain models contain much of value and have had a major influence on the general strain theory in this paper, they do not fully exploit the potential of strain theory.

At the same time, it is important to note that the general strain theory is not presented here as a fully developed alternative to earlier theories. First, the macroimplications of the theory were only briefly discussed. It would not be difficult to extend the general strain theory to the macro level, however; researchers could focus on (1) the social determinants of adversity (see Bernard, 1990), and (2) the social determinants of factors that condition the effect of adversity on delinquency. Second, the theory did not discuss the nonsocial determinants of strain, such as illness, which should be investigated. Third, the relationship between the general strain theory and other major theories of delinquency must be more fully explored since strain, for example, may lead to low social control and association with delinquent others. Further, variables from control and differential association theory may interact with one another in producing delinquency. Individuals with delinquent friends, for example, should be more likely to respond to strain with delinquency. The general strain theory, then, is presented as a foundation on which to build.

Strain theory is the only major theory to focus explicitly on negative relations with others and to argue that delinquency results from the negative affect caused by such relations. As such, it complements social control and differential association/social learning theory in a fundamental way. It is hoped that the general strain theory will revive interest in negative relations and cause criminologists to "bring the bad back in."

11

Homeboys, Dope Fiends, Legits, and New Jacks

John M. Hagedorn

What happens to gang members as they age? Do most gang members graduate from gangbanging to drug sales, as popular stereotypes might suggest? Is drug dealing so lucrative that adult gang members eschew work and become committed to the drug economy? Have changes in economic conditions produced underclass gangs so deviant and so detached from the labor market that the only effective policies are more police and more prisons?

Related to these questions, are male adult gang members basically similar kinds of people, or are gangs made up of different types? Might some gang members be more conventional, and others less so? What are the implications of this "continuum of conventionality" within drug-dealing gangs for public policy? Data from a Milwaukee study on gangs and drug dealing shed some light on these issues.

Gang Members, Drugs, and Work

An underlying question is whether the drug economy provides sufficient incentives to keep gang members away from legal work. If drug sales offer highly profitable opportunities for those taking the risks, we might expect many adult gang members to be committed firmly to the drug economy. If drug dealing entails many risks and produces few success stories, gang members might be expected to have a more variable relationship to illicit

---

Edited and abridged from *Criminology*, Volume 32(2):197–219 (1994).

drug sales. In that case we could look at variation within the gang to explain different behaviors.

The research literature contains few empirical studies on the pull of the drug economy away from licit work. Taylor (1990:120) asserts that "when drug distribution becomes the employer, $3.65 or $8.65 can't compare with drug business income." Jankowski (1991:101) found an "entrepreneurial spirit" to be the "driving force in the world view and behavior of gang members." This "entrepreneurial spirit" pushes gang members to make rational decisions to engage in drug sales. Skolnick (1990) and his students argue that gangs are centrally involved with profitable midlevel drug distribution, although this has been challenged (Klein and Maxson, 1993; Waldorf, 1993).

However, gang involvement in drug sales varies substantially (see Cummings and Monte, 1993; Huff, 1990) and not all gangs are involved with drug sales (Klein et al., 1991), a point often overlooked in discussions of an invariant gang/drug nexus. Among those who sell drugs, actual income varies. Earnings from drug dealing in two Manhattan neighborhoods ranged from about $1,000 to nearly $5,000 per month (Fagan, 1991). Although most drug sellers had little involvement with the formal economy, 25 per cent of Fagan's dealers also worked in conventional jobs, and most reported both illegal *and* legal income for each month. This suggests that incentives from drug sales were not always sufficient to make dealing a full-time job.

Similarly, in Washington, D.C., small dealers typically made about $300 per month and the typical big dealer $3,700, with an average of about $1,300 (MacCoun and Reuter, 1992:485). Illicit economic activities in Brooklyn are found to be a youthful enterprise, quickly outgrown when "real" jobs offered themselves (Sullivan, 1989). The seriousness of criminal activity varied with the intactness of networks providing access to legitimate work. Most of Williams's (1989) New York "cocaine kids" matured out of the drug business as they became young adults and their drug-dealing clique broke up. Padilla's (1992:162) "Diamonds" became "disillusioned" with the empty promises of street-level dealing and aspired to legitimate jobs.

These few studies suggest substantial variation in the degree and duration of gang involvement in drug dealing. The drug economy is not an unquestionably profitable opportunity for gang members; rather, its promise appears to be more ambiguous. If that conclusion is valid, research must examine both the actual amounts of money earned by adult gang drug dealers *and* variation within the gang to understand gang involvement in drug dealing. We have a few studies on how much money gang members make from selling drugs, but hardly any contemporary data on different types of gang members.

Variation within the Gang

Some research has portrayed gang members as relatively invariant. Miller (1958) viewed gang delinquents as representative of a lower-class cultural milieu; his six "focal concerns" are persistent and distinctive features of the entire American "lower class." Similarly, Jankowski (1991:26–28) said that male gang members were one-dimensional "tough nuts," defiant individuals with a rational "social Darwinist worldview" who displayed defiant individualism "more generally" than others people in low-income communities.

Other research, however, has suggested that gang members vary, particularly in their orientation toward conventionality. Whyte (1943) classified his Cornerville street corner men as either "college boys" or "corner boys," depending on their aspirations. Cloward and Ohlin (1960:95), applying Merton's (1957) earlier typology, categorized lower-class youths depending on their aspirations and "criteria for success." Many of their delinquents repudiated the legitimacy of conventional society and resorted to innovative solutions to attain success goals. Cloward and Ohlin took issue with Cohen (1955) and Matza (1964), whose delinquents were internally conflicted but, as a group, imputed legitimacy to the norms of the larger society.

Recent researchers also have found variation in conventionality within gangs. Klein (1971), echoing Thrasher (1927), differentiated between "core" and "fringe" members. In the same view, Taylor (1990:8–9) saw gang members as "corporates," "scavengers," "emulators," "auxiliaries," or "adjuncts," mainly on the basis of their distance from gang membership. Fagan (1990:206), like Matza and Cohen, found that "conventional values may coexist with deviant behaviors for gang delinquents and other inner city youth." MacLeod (1987:124) observed surprising variation between ethnic groups. The white "hallway hangers" believed "stagnation at the bottom of the occupational structure to be almost inevitable" and were rebellious delinquents, whereas the African American "brothers" reacted to similar conditions by aspiring to middle-class status.

Moore looked carefully at differentiation within gangs. She discovered both square and deviant career models among East Los Angeles gang members (Moore, 1978). In an impressive restudy (1991) she found that most adult gang members were working at conventional jobs, but those who had been active in the gang in recent years had more difficulty finding employment as job networks collapsed. Many of the veteran gang members had been addicted to heroin for years, but by the 1990s few were dealing drugs to support themselves. Moore found that both male and female Chicano gang members could be categorized as "tecatos," "cholos," or "squares," a typology similar to those suggested for the nongang poor by Anderson (1978, 1990) and also by Hannerz (1969).

If adult gang members vary in their orientation to conventionality, and if the drug economy itself offers only an ambiguous lure, jobs and other programs that strengthen "social capital" (Coleman, 1988) might be an effective means of integrating them into the community (see Sampson and Laub, 1993). On the other hand, if adult gang members are look-alike criminals who are dazzled by the prospect of vast profits in the drug trade, jobs and social programs would have little effect, and our present incarceration strategy may be appropriate.

This article provides quantitative and qualitative data on the conventional orientations of young adult gang members in Milwaukee. First I report on the licit work and illicit drug-dealing patterns of adult gang members. Then I offer a typology, drawn from Milwaukee data, that demonstrates a "continuum of conventionality" between core members of drug-dealing gangs. In conclusion, I discuss research and public policy consequences of the study.

Research Methods and Sources of Data

The interpretations presented here draw on observation and extensive fieldwork conducted over a number of years, from two funded interview studies, in 1987 and in 1992. During the early 1980s I directed the first gang diversion program in the city and became acquainted with many leaders and other founders of Milwaukee's gangs. I have maintained a privileged relationship with many of these individuals.

In the 1987 study, research staff interviewed 47 members of 19 Milwaukee male and female gangs (Hagedorn, 1988). These "founders" were the core gang members who were present when their gangs took names. Founders are likely to be representative of hardcore gang members, not of peripheral members or "wannabes." As time has passed, the gang founders' exploits have been passed down, and younger Milwaukee gang members have looked up to them as street "role models." Our research design does not enable us to conclude how fully our sample represents subsequent groups of adult gang members.

As part of our current study, we conducted lengthy audiotaped interviews with 101 founding members of 18 gangs in the city; 90 were male and 11 female. Sixty percent were African American, 37 per cent Latino, and 3 per cent white. Their median age was 26 years, with 75 per cent between 23 and 30. Twenty-three respondents also had been interviewed in the 1987 study; 78 were interviewed here for the first time. Members from two gangs interviewed in the earlier study could not be located. Each respondent was paid $50.

The interview picks up the lives of the founding members since 1987, when we conducted our original study, and asks them to recount their careers in the drug business to discuss their pursuit of conventional employment, and to reflect on their personal lives. The respondents also were asked to describe the current status of their fellow gang members. In the 1987 study, we collected rosters of all members of each gang whose founders we interviewed. In the current study, we asked each respondent to double-check the roster of his or her gang to make sure it was accurate. In both studies, we asked respondents to tell us whether the other members were still alive, had graduated from high school, were currently locked up, or were working. In the 1992 study, we also asked whether each of the founding members was selling or using dope (in our data "dope" means cocaine), had some other hustle, or was on the run, among other questions.

To understand more clearly the variation between and within the gangs, we interviewed nearly the entire rosters of three gangs and about half (64 of 152) of the original founding members from eight male gangs in three different types of neighborhoods. In each of these gangs, we interviewed some who still were involved with both the gang and the dope game and some who no longer were involved. This paper reports on data on all of the 90 males we interviewed and on their accounts of the present circumstances of 236 founders of 14 male gangs. The interviews in this most recent study were conducted in late 1992 and early 1993.

Findings: Drug Dealing and Work

As expected, gang members appeared to be working more in 1992-93 than five years earlier, but participation in the formal labor market remains quite low (See Table 1). These low levels of labor market participation apply to more than gang members. A recent Milwaukee study revealed that in 1990, 51 per cent of jobs held by *all* African American males aged 20 to 24, slightly younger than our study population, lasted less than six weeks. The average *annual* income in retail trade, where most subjects held jobs, was $2,023; for jobs in service, $1,697; in education, $3,084 (Rose et al., 1992). African American young adults as a whole (and probably nongang Latinos) clearly were not working regularly and were not earning a living wage.

Selling cocaine seems to have filled the employment void. In 1987 only a few gang members dealt drugs, mainly marijuana. Within African American gangs, at least, cocaine dealing was not prevalent. By 1992, however, cocaine had become a major factor in Milwaukee's informal economy, evolving into widespread curbside sales and numerous drug

**Table 1. 1992 Status of Male Gang Founders,
236 Founding Members of 14 Male Groups**

Predominant Activity/Status	African American	White	Latino	Total
Work: Part-time or Full-time	22.2	68.8	27.6	30.5%
Hustling: Nearly All Selling Cocaine	50.4	15.4	56.3	47.9%
Deceased	7.7	6.3	5.7	6.8%
Whereabouts Unknown	19.7	9.4	10.3	14.8%
Total N=100%	N=117	N=32	N=87	N=236

Note: Percentages may not equal 100 because of rounding.

houses (see Hamid, 1992). Of the 236 fellow gang founders, 72 per cent, reportedly had sold cocaine at some time in the five years prior to 1992-93. (Half of those no longer involved with the gang had sold cocaine within that period).

We collected detailed data on the length of involvement in the drug economy and the amount of money made by those we interviewed. We asked respondents how they had supported themselves in each month of the three years 1989-1991, and then asked how much money they made in both legal and illegal employment. For most respondents, selling cocaine was an on-again, off-again proposition. About half (35) of those who had sold cocaine sold in no more than 12 months out of the past 36; only 12 per cent (9) sold in more than 24 of the past 36 months. Latinos sold for slightly longer periods than African Americans, 17.7 months to 13.1 months.

When gang members did sell dope, they made widely varying amounts of money. About one-third of those who sold reported that they

**Table 2. Mean Monthly Income from Drug Dealing:
1989-91, 87 African American and Latino Respondents**

Average Monthly Income from Drug Sales	African American	Latino	Total
Never Sold	15.8	23.3	18.4%
Less than $1000 ($6 per hour)	28.1	30.0	28.7%
$1000 - $2000 ($7-$12 per hour)	28.1	6.7	20.7%
$2000 - $4000 ($13-$25 per hour)	25.3	33.3	28.7%
More than $10,000	1.8	6.7	3.4%
Total *N*=100%	*N*=57	*N*=30	*N*=87

Note: Three whites were excluded from the analysis. Percentages may not equal 100 because of rounding.

made no more than they would have earned if they worked for minimum wage. Another one-third made the equivalent of $13 to $25 an hour. Only 3 of the 73 sellers ever made "crazy money," or more than $10,000 per month, at any time during their drug-selling careers. Mean monthly income from drug sales was approximately $2,400, or about $15 per hour for full-time work. By contrast, mean monthly income for legal work was only $677; Latinos made more than African Americans ($797 per month to $604 per month). The *maximum* amount of money earned monthly by any gang member from legal income was $2,400, the *mean* for gang drug sales (see Table 2).

Qualitative data from our interviews support the view that for some respondents, the dope game does indeed live up to its stereotype. One dealer credibly reported income from his three drug houses at about $50,000 per month for several months in 1989. Another told how he felt about making "crazy money":

Yeah . . . one time my hands had turned green from all that money. I couldn't wash it off, man, I loved it. Oh man, look at this . . . just holding all that money in my hand turned my hands green from just counting all that money. Sometimes I'd sit back and just count it maybe three, four times, for the hell of it.

Even for big dealers, however, that money didn't last. Some "players" were "rolling" for several years, but most took a fall within a year or so. As with Padilla's (1992) Diamonds, disappointments with the drug trade seemed to exceed its promise for most gang members. Prison and jail time frequently interrupted their lives. More than three-quarters of all gang founders on our rosters had spent some time in jail in the five years under study, as had two -thirds of our respondents. Even so, our respondents had worked a mean of 14.5 months out of the last 36 in legitimate jobs, had worked 14.5 months selling dope, and had spent the remaining 7 months in jail. Twenty-five percent of our respondents had worked legitimate jobs at least 24 of the past 36 months.

Yet an anomaly confronted us as we analyzed our data on work. As might he expected, nine out of ten of those who were not working at the time of our interview had sold dope in the past three years. We also found, however, that three-quarters of those who *were* working in 1992 had sold dope as well within the previous five years. It may be that this latter group had sold cocaine, but had stopped. Alternatively, full-time employment may be nothing more than an income supplement or "front" for continuation in the drug game. Another interpretation is that working and selling drugs are both part of the difficult, topsy-turvy lives led by our respondents. Liebow's (1967:219) colorful description of the confused lives on Tally's Corner also fits our data: "Traffic is heavy in all directions. "

These vicissitudes became too complicated for us to track, so we "froze" the status of founders on our rosters at the time of the last and most reliable interview. Some of our founders seemed to be committed to the dope business and a few had "gone legit," but most of those we were trying to track appeared to be on an economic merry-go-round, with continual involvement in and out of the secondary labor market. Although their average income from drug sales far surpassed their income from legal employment, most Milwaukee male gang members apparently kept trying to find licit work.

To help explain this movement in and out of the formal labor market, we created a typology of adult gang members, using constant comparisons (Strauss, 1987). This categorization intends to account for the different orientations of gang members in an era of decreased legitimate economic opportunities and increased drug-related, illicit opportunities.

A Typology of Male Adult Gang Members

We developed four ideal types on a continuum of conventional behaviors and values: (1) those few who had gone *legit*, or had matured out of the gang; (2) *homeboys*, a majority of both African American and Latino adult gang members, who alternately worked conventional jobs and took various roles in drug sales; (3) *dope fiends*, who were addicted to cocaine and participated in the dope business as a way to maintain access to the drug; and (4) *new jacks*, who regarded the dope game as a career.

Some gang members, we found, moved over time between categories, some had characteristics of more than one category, and others straddled the boundaries (see Hannerz, 1969:57). Thus a few homeboys were in the process of becoming legit, many moved into and out of cocaine addiction, and others gave up and adopted a new jack orientation. Some new jacks returned to conventional life; others received long prison terms or became addicted to dope. Our categories are not discrete, but our typology seemed to fit the population of gang members we were researching. Our "member checks" (Lincoln and Guba, 1985:314–16) of the constructs with gang members validated these categories for male gang members.

Legits

Legits were those young men who had walked away from the gang. They were working or may have gone on to school. Legits had not been involved in the dope game for at least five years, if at all. They did not use cocaine heavily, though some may have done so in the past. Some had moved out of the old neighborhood; others, like our project staff, stayed to help out or "give back" to the community. These are prime examples of Whyte's "college boys" or Cloward and Ohlin's Type 1, oriented to economic gain and class mobility. In the following quote a young African American man who "went legit" and is now working and going to college reflects on major changes in his life.

> I had got into a relationship with my girl, that's one thing. I just knew I couldn't be out on the streets trying to hustle all the time. That's what changed me, I just got a sense of responsibility.

Today's underclass gangs appear to be fundamentally different from those in Thrasher's or Cloward and Ohlin's time, when most gang members "matured out" of the gang. Of the 236 Milwaukee male founders, only 12 (5.1 per cent) could be categorized as having matured out: that is, they were working full time *and* had not sold cocaine in the past five years. When these data are disaggregated by race, the reality of the situation becomes even clearer. We could verify only 2 of 117 African Americans and 1 of 87 Latino male gang founders who were currently working and had not sold dope in the past five years. One-third of the white members fell into this category.

Few African American and Latino gang founders were resigned to a life of crime, jail, and violence. After a period of rebellion and living the fast life, the majority of gang founders, or "homeboys," wanted to settle down and go legit, but the path proved to be very difficult.

Homeboys

Homeboys were the majority of all adult gang members. They were not firmly committed to the drug economy, especially after the early thrill of fast money and "easy women" wore off. They had reached an age, the mid-twenties, when criminal offenses normally decline (Gottfredson and Hirschi, 1990). Most of these men were unskilled, lacked education, and had largely negative experiences in the secondary labor market. Some homeboys were committed more strongly to the streets, others to a more conventional life. Most had used cocaine, some heavily at times, but their use was largely in conjunction with selling from a house or corner with their gang "homies." Most homeboys either were married or had a "steady" lady. They also had strong feelings of loyalty to fellow gang members.

Here, two different homeboys explain how they had changed, and how hard that change was:

> The things that we went through wasn't worth it, and I had a family, you know, and kids, and I had to think about them first, and the thing with the drug game was, that money was quick, easy, and fast, and it went like that, the more money you make the more popular you was. You know, as I see it now it wasn't worth it because the time that I done in penitentiaries I lost my sanity. To me it feels like I lost a part of my kids, because, you know, I know they still care, and they know I'm daddy, but I just lost out. Somebody else won and I lost.

> Mad. I'm a mad young man. I'm a poor young man. I'm a good person to my kids and stuff, and given the opportunity to have something nice and stop working for this petty-ass money I would try to change a lot of things. . . . I feel I'm the type of person that given the opportunity to try to have something legit, I will take it, but I'm not going to go by the slow way, taking no four or five years working

at no chicken job and trying to get up to a manager just to start making six, seven dollars. And then get fired when I come in high or drunk or something. Or miss a day or something because I got high and smoked weed, drinking beer, and the next day come in and get fired; then I'm back where I started from. So I'm just a cool person, and if I'm given the opportunity and if I can get a job making nine, ten dollars an hour, I'd let everything go; I'd just sit back and work my job and go home. That kind of money I can live with. But I'm not going to settle for no three, four dollars an hour, know what I'm saying?

Homeboys present a more confused theoretical picture than legits. Cloward and Ohlin's Type III delinquents were rebels, who had a "sense of injustice" or felt "unjust deprivation" at a failed system (1960:117). Their gang delinquency is a collective solution to the failure of institutional arrangements. They reject traditional societal norms; other, success-oriented illegitimate norms replace conventionality.

Others have questioned whether gang members' basic outlook actually rejects conventionality. Matza (1964) viewed delinquents' rationalizations of their conduct as evidence of techniques meant to "neutralize" deeply held conventional beliefs. Cohen (1955:129–137) regarded delinquency as a nonutilitarian "reaction formation" to middle-class standards, though middle-class morality lingers, repressed and unacknowledged. What appears to be gang "pathological" behavior, Cohen points out, is the result of the delinquent's striving to attain core values of "the American way of life." Short and Strodtbeck (1965), testing various gang theories, found that white and African American gang members, and lower- and middle-class youths, had similar conventional values.

Our homeboys are older versions of Cohen's and Matza's delinquents, and are even more similar to Short and Strodtbeck's study subjects. Milwaukee homeboys shared three basic characteristics: (1) they worked regularly at legitimate jobs, although they ventured into the drug economy when they believed it was necessary for survival; (2) they had very conventional aspirations—their core values centered on finding a secure place in the American way of life; and (3) they had some surprisingly conventional ethical beliefs about the immorality of drug dealing. To a man, they justified their own involvement in drug sales by very Matza-like techniques of "neutralization."

Homeboys are defined by their in-and-out involvement in the legal and illegal economies. Homeboys' work patterns thus differed both from those of legits, who worked solely legal jobs, and new jacks who considered dope dealing a career.

To which goal did homeboys aspire, being big-time dope dealers or holding a legitimate job? Rather than having any expectations of staying in the dope game, homeboys aspired to settling down, getting married, and living at least a watered-down version of the American dream. Like Padilla's (1992:157) Diamonds, they strongly desired to "go legit." Although they may have enjoyed the fast life for a while, it soon went stale. Listen to this homeboy, who lost his lady when he went to jail, reflect on his future.

> Five years from now? I want to have a steady job, I want to have been working that job for about five years, and just with a family somewhere. . .that's basically what I'm working on. I mean, this bullshit is over now, I'm twenty-five, I've played games long enough, it don't benefit nobody. If you fuck yourself away, all you gonna be is fucked, I see it now.

Others had more hopeful or wilder dreams, but a more sobering outlook on the future. The homeboy who said he wouldn't settle for three or four dollars an hour said that in five years he wants to be:

> Owning my own business. And rich. A billionaire. . .
> [realistically?] probably working at McDonald's. That's the truth.

Homeboys' aspirations were divided between finding a steady full-time job and setting up their own business. Their striving pertained less to being for or against "middle-class status" than to finding a practical, legitimate occupation that could support them (see Short and Strodtbeck, 1965). Many homeboys believed that using skills learned in selling drugs to set up a small business would give them a better chance at a decent life than trying to succeed as an employee.

Most important, homeboys "grew up" and were taking a realistic look at their life chances. This homeboy spoke for most when he reflected on recent major changes affecting his life:

> I don't know, maybe maturity. . . Just seeing life in a different perspective . . . realizing that from sixteen to twenty-three, man, just shot past. And just realizing that it did, shucks, just realizing how quick it zoomed past me. And it really just passed me up without really having any enjoyment of a teenager. And hell, before I know it I'm going to hit thirty or forty, and I ain't going to have nothing to stand on. I don't want that shit. Because I see a lot of brothers out here now, that's forty-three, forty-four and ain't got shit. They's still standing out on the corner trying to make a hustle. Doing this, no family, stable home and nothing. I don't want that shit. . . . I

don't give a fuck about getting rich or nothing, but I want a comfortable life, a decent woman, a family to come home to. I mean, everybody needs somebody to care for. This ain't where it's at.

Finally, homeboys were characterized by their ethical views about selling dope. As a group, they believed dope selling was "unmoral"— wrong, but necessary for survival. Homeboys' values were conventional, but in keeping with Matza's findings, they justified their conduct by neutralizing their violation of norms. Homeboys believed that economic necessity was the overriding reason why they could not live up to their values (see Liebow, 1967:214). They were the epitome of ambivalence, ardently believing that dope selling was both wrong and absolutely necessary. One longtime dealer expressed this contradiction:

[It's] very wrong. Why? because it's killing people. . . . It's also a money maker. . . . Once you get a [dollar] bill, once you look at, I say this a lot, once you look at those dead white men [presidents' pictures on currency], you care about nothing else. . . . Once you see those famous dead white men. That's it.

How do I feel? Well a lady will come in and sell all the food stamps, all of them. When they're sold, what are the kids gonna eat? They can't eat the dope cause she's gonna go smoke that up, or do whatever with it. And then you feel like "wrong." But then, in the back of your mind, man, you just got a hundred dollars worth of food stamps for thirty dollars worth of dope, and you can sell them at the store for seven dollars on ten, so you got seventy coming. So you get seventy dollars for thirty dollars. It is not wrong to do this. It is not wrong to do this!

Homeboys also refused to sell to pregnant women or to juveniles. Contrary to Jankowski's (1991:102) assertion that in gangs "there is no ethical code that regulates business ventures," Milwaukee homeboys had some strong moral feelings about how they carried out their business:

I won't sell to no little kids. And, ah, if he gonna get it, he gonna get it from someone else besides me. I won't sell to no pregnant woman. If she gonna kill her baby, I want to sleep not knowing that I had anything to do with it. Ah, for anybody else, hey, it's their life, you choose your life how you want.

Homeboys were young adults living on the edge. Like most Americans, they had relatively conservative views on social issues and wanted to settle down with a job, a wife, and children. But they were afraid they would never succeed, and that long stays in prison would close doors and lock them out of a conventional life. They did not want to continue to live on the streets, but they feared that hustling might be the only way to survive. Homeboys varied as well. Some were entrepreneurs or "players"; typically they were the "dopemen" who started a "dopehouse" where other gang members could work. Others worked only sporadically in dopehouses as a supplement to legitimate work or during unemployment. Finally, some, often cocaine users, worked most of the time at the dopehouse and only sporadically at legitimate jobs. Although homeboys also varied over time in their aspirations to conventionality, as a group they believed that the lack of jobs and prison time were testing their commitment to conventional values.

Dope Fiends

Dope fiends are gang members who are addicted to cocaine. Thirty-eight percent of all African American founders were using cocaine at the time of our interview, as were 55 per cent of Latinos and 53 per cent of whites. African Americans used cocaine at lower rates than whites, but went to jail twice as often. The main focus in a dope fiend's life is getting the drug. Asked what they regretted most about their life, dope fiends invariably said "drug use," whereas most homeboys said "dropping out of school."

Most Milwaukee gang dope fiends, or daily users of cocaine, smoked it as "rocks." More casual users, or reformed dope fiends, if they used cocaine at all, snorted it or sprinkled it on marijuana (called a "primo") to enhance the high. Injection was rare among African Americans but more common among Latinos. About one-quarter of those interviewed abstained totally from cocaine use.

Of 110 gang founders who were reported to be currently using cocaine, 37 per cent were reported to be using "heavily" (every day, in our data), 44 per cent "moderately" (several times per week), and 19 per cent "lightly" (sporadically). More than 70 per cent of all founders on our rosters who were not locked up were currently using cocaine to some extent. More than one-third of our male respondents considered themselves, at some time in their lives, to be "heavy" cocaine users.

More than one-quarter of our respondents had used cocaine for seven years or more, roughly the total amount of time cocaine has dominated the illegal drug market in Milwaukee. Latinos had used cocaine slightly longer than African Americans, an average of 75 months compared with 65. Cocaine use followed a steady pattern in our respondents' lives; most homeboys had used cocaine as part of their day-to-day life, especially while in the dope business.

Dope fiends were quite unlike Cloward and Ohlin's "double failures," gang members who used drugs as part of a "retreatist subculture." Milwaukee dope fiends participated regularly in conventional labor markets. Of the 110 founders who were reported as currently using cocaine, slightly more were working legitimate jobs than were not working. Most dope fiends worked at some time in their homies' dope houses or were fronted an ounce or an "eightball" (3.5 grams) of cocaine to sell. Unlike Anderson's "wineheads'" gang dope fiends were not predominantly "has-beens" and did not "lack the ability and motivation to hustle" (Anderson, 1978:96–97). Milwaukee cocaine users, like heroin users (Johnson et al., 1985; Moore, 1978; Preble and Casey, 1969), played an active role in the drug-selling business.

Rather than spending their income from drug dealing on family, clothes, or women, dope fiends smoked up their profits. Eventually many stole dope belonging to the boss or "dopeman" and got into trouble. At times their dope use made them so erratic that they were no longer trusted and were forced to leave the neighborhood. Often, however, the gang members who were selling took them back and fronted them cocaine to sell to put them back on their feet. Many had experienced problems from violating the cardinal rule, "Don't get high on your own supply," as in this typical story:

> . . . if you ain't the type that's a user, yeah, you'll make fabulous money but if you was the type that sells it and uses it and do it at the same time, you know, you get restless. Sometimes you get used to taking your own drugs. . . . I'll just use the profits and just do it . . . and then the next day if I get something again, I'd just take the money to pay up and keep the profits. . . You sell a couple of hundred and you do a hundred. That's how I was doing it.

Cocaine use was a regular part of the lives of most Milwaukee gang members engaged in the drug economy. More than half of our respondents had never attended a treatment program; more than half of those who had been in treatment went through court-ordered programs. Few of our respondents stopped use by going to a treatment program. Even heavy cocaine use was an "on-again, off-again" situation in which most gang members alternately quit by themselves and started use again (Waldorf et al., 1991).

Alcohol use among dope fiends and homeboys (particularly forty-ounce bottles of Olde English 800 ale) appears to be even more of a problem than cocaine use. Like homeboys, however, most dope fiends aspired to have a family, to hold a steady job, and to find some peace. The wild life of the dope game had played itself out; the main problem was how to quit using.

New Jacks

Whereas homeboys had a tentative relationship with conventional labor markets and held some strong moral beliefs, new jacks had chosen the dope game as a career. They were often loners, strong individualists like Jankowski's (1991) gang members, who cared little about group norms. Frequently they posed as the embodiment of media stereotypes. About one-quarter of our interview respondents could be described as new jacks: they had done nothing in the last thirty six months except hustle or spend time in jail.

In some ways, new jacks mirror the criminal subculture described by Cloward and Ohlin. If a criminal subculture is to develop, Cloward and Ohlin argued, opportunities to learn a criminal career must be present, and close ties to conventional markets or customers must exist. This situation distinguishes the criminal from the violent and the retreatist subcultures. The emergence of the cocaine economy and a large market for illegal drugs provided precisely such an opportunity structure for this generation of gang members. New jacks are those who took advantage of the opportunities, and who, at least for the present, have committed themselves to a career in the dope game:

> I love selling dope. I know there's other niggers out here love the money just like I do. And ain't no motherfucker gonna stop a nigger from selling dope . . . . I'd sell to my own mother if she had the money.

New jacks, like other gang cocaine dealers, lived up to media stereotypes of the "drug dealer" role and often were emulated by impressionable youths. Some new jacks were homeboys from Milwaukee's original neighborhood gangs, who had given up their conventional dreams; others were members of gangs that were formed solely for drug dealing (see Klein and Maxson, 1993). A founder of one new jack gang described the scene as his gang set up shop in Milwaukee. Note the strong mimicking of media stereotypes:

> . . . it was crime and drug problems before we even came into the scene. It was just controlled by somebody else. We just came on with a whole new attitude, outlook, at the whole situation. It's like, have

you ever seen the movie *New Jack City*, about the kid in New York? You see, they was already there. We just came out with a better idea, you know what I'm saying?

New jacks rejected the homeboys' moral outlook. Many were raised by families with long traditions of hustling or a generation of gang affiliations, and had few hopes of a conventional future. They are the voice of the desperate ghetto dweller, those who live in Taylor's (1990:36) "third culture" made up of "underclass and urban gang members who exhibit signs of moral erosion and anarchy" or propagators of Bourgois' (1990:631) "culture of terror." New jacks fit the media stereotype of all gang members, even though they represent fewer than 25 per cent of Milwaukee's adult gang members.

Discussion: Gangs, the Underclass, and Public Policy

Our study was conducted in one aging postindustrial city, with a population of 600,000. How much can be generalized from our findings can be determined only by researchers in other cities, looking at our categories and determining whether they are useful. Cloward and Ohlin's opportunity theory is a workable general theoretical framework, but more case studies are needed in order to recast their theory to reflect three decades of economic and social changes. We present our typology to encourage others to observe variation within and between gangs, and to assist in the creation of new taxonomies and new theory.

Our article raises several empirical questions for researchers: Are the behavior patterns of the founding gang members in our sample representative of adult gang members in other cities? In larger cities, are most gang members now new jacks who have long given up the hope of a conventional life, or are most still homeboys? Are there "homeboy" gangs and "new jack" gangs, following the "street gang/drug gang" notion of Klein and Maxson (1993)? If so, what distinguishes one from the other? Does gang members' orientation to conventionality vary by ethnicity or by region? How does it change over time? Can this typology help account for variation in rates of violence between gang members? Can female gang members be classified in the same way as males?

Our data also support the life course perspective of Sampson and Laub (1993:255), who ask whether present criminal justice policies "are producing unintended criminogenic effects." Milwaukee gang members are like the persistent, serious offenders in the Gluecks' data (Glueck and Glueck, 1950). The key to their future lies in building social capital that comes from steady employment and a supportive relationship, without the constant threat of incarceration (Sampson and Laub, 1993:162–68). Homeboys largely had a wife or a steady lady, were unhappily enduring "the silent, subtle humiliations" of the secondary labor market (Bourgois, 1990:629), and lived in dread of prison. Incarceration for drug charges undercut their efforts to find steady work and led them almost inevitably back to the drug economy.

Long and mandatory prison terms for use and intent to sell cocaine lump those who are committed to the drug economy with those who are using or are selling in order to survive. Our prisons are filled disproportionately with minority drug offenders (Blumstein, 1993) who, like our homeboys, in essence are being punished for the "crime" of not accepting poverty or of being addicted to cocaine. Our data suggest that jobs, more accessible drug treatment, alternative sentences, or even decriminalization of nonviolent drug offenses would be better approaches than the iron fist of the war on drugs (see Hagedorn, 1991; Reinarman and Levine, 1990; Spergel and Curry, 1990).

Finally, our typology raises ethical questions for researchers. Wilson (1987:8) called the underclass "collectively different" from the poor of the past, and many studies focus on underclass deviance. Our study found that some underclass gang members had embraced the drug economy and had forsaken conventionality, but we also found that the majority of adult gang members are still struggling to hold onto a conventional orientation to life.

Hannerz (1969:36) commented more than two decades ago that dichotomizing community residents into "respectables" and "disrespectables" "seems often to emerge from social science writing about poor black people or the lower classes in general." Social science that emphasizes differences within poor communities, without noting commonalities, is one-sided and often distorts and demonizes underclass life.

Our data emphasize that there is no Great Wall separating the underclass from the rest of the central-city poor and working class. Social research should not build one either. Researchers who describe violent and criminal gang actions without also addressing gang members' orientation to conventionality do a disservice to the public, to policy makers, and to social science.

Differential Association and Social Learning Theory

Introduction

Social learning theory assumes that humans commit crime as a result of learning and socialization experiences with significant others. Edwin Sutherland (1883–1950) founded this idea in criminology arguing that delinquents and criminals, including white-collar criminals, learn to commit crime just as noncriminals learn to behave conventionally, through socialization with significant others in primary groups (Sutherland, 1949). Sutherland called his theory "differential association" to describe how groups having criminal knowledge, skills, and practices could have an impact on nonoffenders in proportion to the extent to which they associated with them relative to associating with conventional groups. In such a context learning knowledge, skills, rationalizations, and justifications enable or facilitate rule-breaking activity by defining it as favorable and/or desirable.

Sutherland used these insights in his discussion of the development of professional type criminals such as professional thieves (see Sutherland, 1937). He advanced the idea that such types develop specific sets of norms and codes of conduct that they apply to themselves in their criminal activity. Later research on robbery and burglary tended to show that these specific rules no longer were viable in contemporary times.

John Rosecrance (chap. 12) objects to the notion that Sutherland's conceptualization of professional crime is excessively narrow, and no longer applies to modern criminal activity. Using qualitative data developed during an eighteen-month investigation he applies Sutherland's analysis to modern-day stoopers. These are persons who retrieve discarded winning racetrack tickets which they turn in for cash. Rosecrance argues that the stoopers' criminal behavior closely resembles Sutherland's characterization of professional crime. He describes the characteristics of stoopers using the five criteria of professionalism established by Sutherland: technical skills, status, consensus, differential association, and social organization. He argues that this analysis demonstrates that the Sutherland model remains viable and should not be relegated to the status of a historical footnote.

Sutherland's version of differential association is not the only kind of social learning theory. The "socially oriented" learning approach of Ronald Akers (Burgess and Akers, 1966; Akers, 1985), takes the view that social interaction in the social environment, particularly in subcultural groups, is a major source of behavioral reinforcement. Akers's argument draws on and expands the earlier differential association theory of Sutherland (Sutherland, 1939; Cressey, 1960b; Sutherland and Cressey, 1978), but also takes into account psychological ideas about behavioral learning based on Skinner's theory of operant conditioning (Skinner, 1953, 1971). Here humans are assumed to be rational responders to stimuli, avoiding pain and pursuing pleasure. As a result they are said to be considerably affected by the consequences of their behavior. They can be conditioned through the manipulation of rewards and punishments, which reinforce conventional action and punish antisocial conduct. Criminologically this idea was reflected in Jeffery's (1965) theory of differential reinforcement, which recognized the differences in people's reinforcement history and the different meaning stimuli have for them. However, it is Akers who has done the most to develop these combined sociological and psychological insights. In the reading we have selected here Akers reviews the arguments criticizing Sutherland's differential association theory as a "cultural deviance" theory, and goes on to examine how the critics continue to apply this same designation to his own social learning reformulation. Akers's article examines the basis and validity of this cultural deviance label and concludes that the usual attribution of cultural deviance assumptions and explanations to differential association/social learning theory is based on misinterpretations. He then offers a clarification of how cultural elements are incorporated into the theory. Readers are also encouraged to consult a reply to this article by Travis Hirschi (1994) in which he challenges Akers's position.

12

The Stooper: A Professional Thief in the Sutherland Manner

John Rosecrance

The professional criminal is traditionally defined as one who obtains a major portion of his or her income from illegal activity (Blumberg, 1981:46). Professional crime generally refers to nonviolent patterns of criminal behavior undertaken with skill and planning, the execution of which minimizes the possibility of apprehension (Inciardi, 1975:5). Sutherland was the seminal source of a systematic analysis of professional crime. In 1937, he advanced the concept of a behavior system to explain the existence of this form of criminal activity. Typically, members of such a system shared a distinct argot, an ideology of legitimation, normative expectations, a specialized activity, and a degree of technical expertise (Sutherland, 1937:197–216). Sutherland's model gained acceptance by many criminologists and police officials as an accurate representation of professional crime.

Since his pioneering work, there have been various criticisms of Sutherland's concept of professional crime. Criticisms have coalesced around three issues:(1) the existence of an established professional criminal organization, (2) the specialized character of professional crime, and (3) the contention that Sutherland's model is either too narrow or outdated. Lemert (1958) and Einstadter (1969), after investigating check forgers and armed robbers respectively, concluded that these offenders, who otherwise met the criteria of professional criminals, worked alone, were not part of a criminal system, and had not been tutored by other criminals. After conducting studies for a president's commission on crime, researchers (Gould et al., 1966) contended that professional thieves were not specialists but instead were generalists—that is, "hustlers" who sought available opportunities for illegal gain. Other criminologists (Shover, 1973;

Edited and abridged from *Criminology*, Volume 24(1):29–40 (1986).

Klein, 1974; Inciardi, 1974, 1975) have indicated that professional criminals are not reproducing themselves and their behavior systems are dying out:"Professional theft will continue to atrophy until its unique qualities become only references within the history of crime" (Inciardi, 1975:82). Walker (1981:171) has argued that Sutherland's model is unnecessarily narrow and can be applied accurately only to highly successful professionals who represent a criminal elite (e.g., class cannons or jewel thieves).

The research discussed here considers a group of contemporary thieves whose behavior patterns closely resemble the Sutherland model of professional crime. Following an analysis of this striking resemblance, the conclusion reached is that Sutherland's concept of professional crime is still applicable and can serve as a useful guide in depicting a modern criminal behavior system. The criminal group studied is that of racetrack stoopers. A stooper has been defined as "someone who looks through the litter of discarded [racetrack] tickets for a winner mistakenly thrown away" (Martinez, 1983:222). Although this group has been acknowledged by prior researchers (Scott, 1968; Maurer, 1974; Surface, 1976), their criminal activities have apparently never been delineated.

Those who frequent racetracks for the purpose of stooping are in violation of pandering laws. Stoopers are subject to both criminal prosecution and administrative banishment by track officials. They fit the general criteria of a sneak thief as one "who does not, at the outset of his crime, proclaim his intentions by some work or act; he is a thief who has the ability to remain unnoticed, blending with his environment while stealing in the proximity of his awake and active victims" (Inciardi, 1974:306).

This article describes the activities of professional stoopers and demonstrates how their behavior closely parallels the original Sutherland model of professional crime. In the case of the stooper, the major criticisms of Sutherland's concept have not lessened its applicability to a contemporary criminal behavior system. The accumulated data reveal that this group is reproducing itself, a finding that belies the contention that Sutherland's professional thief should be considered merely a historical reference (see also Chambliss, 1972).

Methodology

It is always difficult to collect data about professional criminals (Clinard and Quinney, 1967:429; Cressey, 1967:102; Letkemann, 1973:165–66; Abadinsky, 1983:4). By design, professional thieves are secretive and take elaborate steps to remain unobtrusive. This was certainly the case with stoopers who attempt to mingle with other race-goers in a chameleon-like deception. Professional stoopers have achieved virtual anonymity and conduct their business unnoticed by even longtime racing fans. I began investigating stoopers by first interviewing racetrack officials and security personnel. After learning how to identify stoopers, I observed their actions at racetracks in California, Louisiana, Maryland, and West Virginia. Because most stoopers refuse to discuss their activities, I was unable to interview any of them until I located a stooper in California who agreed to be an informant. This stooper introduced me to others and I was able to conduct interviews with eight stoopers in California. In Louisiana I developed a relationship with another informant and was able to interview five stoopers in that area. The stoopers who consented to be interviewed were all male, ranged in age from twenty to fifty five, and generally had minor criminal records. In interviewing the stoopers I asked questions such as: How did you get into stooping? Why do you remain a stooper? Can you support yourself by stooping? Do you follow the horses from track to track? Have you done time in jail? Do you know other stoopers? Do you work with other stoopers? What steps do you take to avoid detection? What do your family or friends think of your stooping?

During the study I was guided by the principles of grounded theory (Glaser and Strauss, 1967) and sought to develop analyses that were generated directly from the data gathered from the interviews with stoopers, racetrack officials, and personnel.

Findings

An analysis of the research data revealed that, in most respects, the behavior system of racetrack stoopers corresponds to that described by Sutherland in his classic work, *The Professional Thief* (1937). This finding will be clarified by describing their demonstrated behavior in terms of the five characteristics of professional crime outlined by Sutherland (1937: 198): (1) technical skill, (2) status, (3) consensus, (4) differential association, and (5) organization.

Technical Skills

In 1984 at racetracks in California, over three million dollars worth of winning tickets were not cashed. At one track alone (Belmont Park, New York) during a single racing season, tickets worth more than one and a half million dollars were not redeemed (Surface, 1976:183). In most states these unclaimed winnings subsequently revert to state treasuries. Racing patrons, who for various reasons lose their winning mutuel tickets, create a source of illegal income for stoopers. In the racing argot, live tickets (those that can be cashed) are there for the taking. However, actually finding and retrieving discarded winning tickets involves the application of skillful techniques.

The development and implementation of technical skills among stoopers closely resembles Sutherland's (1937:197) conception that "the professional thief has a complex of abilities and skills, just as do physicians, lawyers, or bricklayers." He indicated that these abilities were based upon cleverness and stealth, not upon strength or physical dexterity. Sutherland conceived of professionals as specialists who concentrated their talents in a particular form of criminal activity.

Professional stoopers are definitely specialists. They devote their efforts to finding winning tickets and rarely participate in other illegal endeavors. The time, commitment, and specialization involved in becoming a successful stooper precludes active participation in other illegal activities. The comment of a veteran stooper reflects this situation:

> I have to work so hard at stooping I just don't have time for other capers. Some guys I know are into stealing and fencing. I suppose I could get in on their action. But with busting my ass six days a week at the track I gotta pass. Besides, even though I know how to make it at the track, I don't know diddly shit about heavy-duty thieving.

The skills involved in stooping are not related to unusual physical abilities; moderate eyesight and normal mobility comprise the basic physical requirements.

The process of stooping is divided into four stages: (1) blending, (2) hunting, (3) identifying, and (4) cashing. During each of these stages the use of skillful techniques is required. Remaining unobtrusive while also looking for discarded tickets is the stooper's most basic skill. Stoopers often talk of the necessity of blending.

> You become part of the crowd—just like any other guy at the track. Security won't hassle you as long as you don't call attention to yourself. You're OK if you just act natural. First, last, and always you have to blend.

Stoopers are careful to dress like other racing fans. Those who "work" the grandstand, where blue-collar patrons congregate, dress in jeans or work clothes. Appropriately, stoopers who situate themselves in the clubhouse, where middle-class patrons are in the majority, wear jackets, dress slacks, and polished shoes. Most stoopers are not active gamblers. A stooper explained:"I haven't got the time to look at a Racing Form—too busy hustling tickets. Half the time I don't even know who's running." However, in order to blend they occasionally wager on races. "I throw away a few bucks every day just to look the part. I never saw a racing man who didn't bet some." Professional stoopers refrain from drinking or arguing while on the job to avoid "sticking out."

While remaining unnoticed is essential, the stooper must also develop an aptitude for finding discarded winning tickets. "Hunting" is a commonly used term to describe this search. Although stoopers maintain a continuing vigil, they usually do not begin a serious search until the middle of the racing day when a significant number of discarded tickets has accumulated. A stooper described this practice, "I can't bear down and go all out after each race. I'd get bummed out. I usually don't get serious until after the fifth race when the losers start to go home."

Certain kinds of race results and betting situations dictate an extensive search. Just after a disqualification (when the actual order of finish is changed) is considered by many stoopers to be an excellent time for locating cashable tickets. Although gamblers are always cautioned by the track announcer to "hold all tickets until the race is declared official," they often disregard this warning and throw their tickets away before the official winners are posted. Frequently, when bettors discover that a disqualification has made their seemingly worthless tickets winning ones, they are unable to locate the discarded ticket. Often the tickets have been picked up by an alert stooper who has blended into the crowd. Other situations that are conducive to mistakenly throwing away winning tickets occur when, for betting purposes, more than one horse is combined to form an entry (horses trained by the same person) or a field (more than twelve horses are entered in a single race). When such situations arise, stoopers must redouble their efforts in order to take advantage of a potential windfall.

If stoopers are to be successful, they must identify those mutuel tickets that can eventually be cashed. This must be accomplished quickly to avoid being noticed. A veteran stooper related, "Instant recall is required in this business. You can't linger over a ticket trying to remember whether it's live." Such identification necessitates that stoopers be able to recall a multitude of winning ticket numbers. They must remember numbers of the win, place, and show horses in each of nine races plus daily double, exacta, and quinella combinations. This form of mental acuity is often facilitated by development of a memory system. One stooper related that he used the childhood nursery rhyme, "One-two, buckle my shoe; three-four, shut the door" to remember the winning numbers. Others used color combinations or personally significant codes such as their age, social security number, and birthdate as recall keys.

Patience and persistence are important during the hunting and identification phases. Some days stoopers "come up empty," while other days tickets they locate result in payoffs between $2 and $20. On occasion, tickets worth over $100 or even $1,000 have been found. One of the informants indicated, "I find a lot of two-buck show tickets but every once in a while I make a big score. Those big ones are out there for the taking—keeps me coming back."

Once a live ticket has been retrieved, it must be redeemed at one of the cashier windows. Stoopers employ skillful techniques to achieve this end. Tickets with a low monetary value can be routinely cashed by presenting them at varied cashier locations. However, tickets that will result in large payoffs must be handled more circumspectly. Stoopers are aware that most security personnel and track officials know them on sight. Collecting a large payoff could attract unwanted attention and might cause the security department to more closely monitor their activities. In order to avoid notoriety, stoopers hire "beards" or accomplices to cash large-value tickets. These beards are usually "straight types" who are not regular track patrons. To the track cashier the beard appears as a solid citizen and is able to receive large payouts without incident.

Status

Accomplished stoopers, in common with Sutherland's professional thieves, have achieved status. This status is drawn from the attitudes of racetrack authorities, especially security personnel and other track insiders. Security personnel and local police assigned to the track expressed a grudging admiration for successful stoopers. Such respect works to their advantage. The observation of a security chief is illustrative.

> The pros are really something else. They don't even bend over until they spot a live ticket. Once they stoop you can bet they will come up with something good. These guys don't cause anyone any trouble and they go out of their way to avoid a hassle. They are real pros. I could bust 'em, but what's the point? As long as they keep out of everybody's way we don't bother them.

Others who work at the racetrack—for example, trainers, jockeys, grooms, and ticket sellers—also acknowledge the professional status of stoopers. A longtime horse trainer commented, "I don't know how those boys do it, but they sure can find live tickets. I guess it's because they're real professional about what they do."

At every racetrack there are people who attempt to find live tickets.

Most of these searchers are not professional in their manner or technique and are considered amateurs by track insiders. A popular method used by nonprofessional stoopers involves picking up all the tickets they can find and then openly culling through them. Some amateurs send their children around the grandstand area to scoop loose tickets into a bag. Children who engage in obvious ticket collection are less likely to arouse the ire of security forces than are adults. Other track bustouts will steal tickets from pockets, wallets, and purses, or take them directly from a winning bettor. One technique is grabbing and running with tickets taken from bar patrons who have waved them about while happily proclaiming, "I've got a winner." Security personnel report that many of these "snatch and grab" (Sutherland, 1937:201) thieves have tried stooping but did not have the skill or patience to be successful and instead have turned to more visible or violent criminal activities.

Professional stoopers, like other professional thieves, are "contemptuous of amateur thieves and have many epithets which they apply to amateurs" (Sutherland, 1937:200). They heap scorn and ridicule upon amateurs "who give stooping a bad name" and disdain methods deemed "unprofessional." Such perspectives can be illustrated by the statement of an accomplished stooper.

> Those assholes who run around the track with shopping bags while grabbing tickets off the floor are pathetic. They never find anything and security runs 'em off quick. The jokers who roll drunks or grab purses are just thugs and deserve to be put in the slammer. If I ever resort to those tactics I hope someone locks me up.

By most standards, stoopers are not financially successful. Because earnings fluctuate drastically, it is difficult to estimate their annual incomes. However, estimates among ten of the stoopers interviewed ranged from $6,000 to $20,000 per year. But most were quick to point out that "it's all tax free." An important source of status among stoopers is their independence and ability to operate outside the system. They frequently talked of the "uptight assholes" who lead a routine, structured life. Stoopers pride themselves on their ability to function without bureaucratic support.

> It's a heady feeling living without a safety net. There's no Blue Cross, dental plan, company retirement plan, sick days, or paid vacations to fall back on. On the other hand, there's no forms to fill out, supervisors to suck up to, or time clocks to punch. I don't work for wages. I can come and go as I want. I live by my wits alone. Sure beats being a scared little pencil pusher.

Consensus

Because of their common endeavor, as a group stoopers have developed similar attitudes and values. Shared feelings include rationalizations for their type of criminal activity as well as perspectives concerning their victims. Consensus among stoopers has fostered an informal but extant "code of helpfulness" (Sutherland, 1937:203).

Professional stoopers are able to rationalize much of their criminal activity by adhering to a prevailing societal attitude subsumed within the popular expression, "finders, keepers; losers, weepers." Such an attitude holds that careless persons should not expect to have their property returned by good samaritans. The responsibility to adequately safeguard one's personal property is a basic American tenet. Stoopers contend that by thoughtlessly throwing away winning tickets, racing patrons have forfeited their right to those tickets. They maintain that "If the sucker is not sufficiently smart enough to protect himself, his rights are gone" (Sutherland, 1937:173). This sentiment is shared by security personnel.

However, stoopers do not conceive of their activities as victimless crimes. They all have seen the frantic look of desperation on the faces of those searching for the discarded winning tickets that are already in the stooper's possession. Notwithstanding the victim's understandable anguish, there is a consensus among professionals that the victim's carelessness absolves the stooper of moral responsibility.

There is an implicit code among stoopers which stipulates that other professional stoopers should be treated with respect, protected from being apprehended, and given financial aid when needed. Adherence to this code, while not always absolute, does add to the consensual relationship among group members. Stoopers relate to one another in a generally friendly manner and are careful not to openly criticize each other. If stoopers are apprehended or detained, they do not attempt to curry favor from the authorities by "ratting on a buddy." Stoopers, in common with other racetrack types (Rosecrance, 1985:138), frequently lend each other money to mitigate their fluctuating financial fortunes. Stoopers are constrained to follow their code since their numbers are few and their professional reputations are at stake. As one explained:"I wouldn't screw other stoopers. It wouldn't be professional. Besides, I might need their help later on. The track's a small world."

Differential Association

Stoopers are separated from the larger society both by the racetrack milieu in which they operate and by their own specialized illegal activity.

This pattern of differential association tends to form social barriers which further accentuate the differences between them and nongroup members. They are often reluctant to discuss their stooping with those outside their social world, even with family members and close friends. Stoopers believe that "outsiders would never understand what we do." Frequently they tell their significant others that they are working at the track as cashiers, trainers, or even security workers. The stoopers' behavior system fits Sutherland's (1937:207) characterization that the "group defines its own membership." Only accomplished stoopers who act professionally are fully accepted into the inner world of this group. Those considered amateurs or part-timers must function on their own, without assistance from professional stoopers. Once accepted by other professionals, social contacts are generally contained within this group.

Although separated by differential association, stoopers are not totally isolated from the larger society. During their stooping efforts they must mingle and associate with the general population, even while planning to fleece them. Occasionally they need the assistance of those in conventional society—for example, beards, lawyers, and bail bondsmen. Stoopers, while engaged in an illegal endeavor, share many of society's basic values. They tend to be conservative, to strongly favor a capitalistic system, and to believe that hard work will ultimately be rewarded.

Social Organization

Even though stoopers are informally organized to help one another, they are not part of a larger criminal underworld. They do not have ties with either organized crime or large mobs, and typically do not associate or hang out with the general body of criminals. Consequently, they have little contact with traditional criminal organizations. In this respect, the stoopers' behavior patterns do not fit precisely the Sutherland model.

Stoopers prefer instead to consider themselves as a special breed of thief. Among themselves they cooperate and work together to increase their financial opportunities. The supply of discarded winning tickets is not inexhaustible, and most tracks cannot support more than four to six full-time stoopers. Professional stoopers divide the racetrack into work areas and then do not infringe on one another's territory.

The stoopers' pattern of tutelage closely resembles that described by Sutherland (1937:211-13). In most cases, stoopers have learned the business from an older and more accomplished professional. As tyros, they were introduced to the complex of skills that make up professional stooping by an already established thief. "In the course of this process a person who is not a professional may first become a neophyte and then a recognized professional thief" (Sutherland, 1937:212). Older, more established stoopers indicated that there was no shortage of potential recruits, and they could choose their apprentices carefully. One such professional said, "I don't know where these young guys come from, but every few months one comes around and wants to learn the business. Most of them I can't help but every once in a while I take a liking to a guy and show him the ropes."

Summary and Conclusions

This article has described and analyzed the criminal system of a little-known group of professional thieves. Accomplished racetrack stoopers are few in number, and their illegal activity does not represent a serious threat to society. For the most part, police are unaware of their existence, and knowledgeable security personnel have shown little interest in apprehending or prosecuting them. The victims, careless bettors, and the state treasuries that are entitled to the uncashed winnings have not demanded that action be taken to halt their loss. While stoopers are involved in illegal activity and their victims do incur financial loss, their interest to the criminology community rests upon the theoretical implications of the stoopers' empirically demonstrated behavior patterns, not the scope of their criminal activity.

Sutherland's (1937) original conceptualization of professional crime has been hailed as "an unforgettable moment for the disciplines of criminology, police science, and correctional administration," and has been said to have "made manifest the nature and complexity of a criminal career" (Inciardi, 1975:5). However, in the intervening years there has been a host of criticisms of Sutherland's definition of professional crime (Lemert, 1958; Gould et al., 1966; Einstadter, 1969; Jackson, 1969; Klein, 1974; Walker, 1981). Researchers have also contended that a rapidly changing, modern technology has rendered the Sutherland model obsolete (Shover, 1973; Inciardi, 1974, 1975; Wickman and Whitten, 1980). Sutherland's perspective of professional crime has been labeled traditional (Staats, 1977), and there is a suggestion that the professional thief may be "more the creation of journalism, romanticism, and commercialism than an empirically demonstrable social type" (Turk, 1969:15).

The research findings here demonstrate that the Sutherland model is still viable and that it has relevance to contemporary criminal activity. These findings lend support to Chambliss's (1972:168) contention that "professional theft is not about to become extinct." The ongoing behavior system of racetrack stoopers manifests the major characteristics of professional crime as delineated by Sutherland. A consideration of these characteristics has demonstrated that, with respect to this group, the major criticisms of Sutherland's concept of professional crime, discussed earlier, have not detracted from its applicability.

Professional stoopers employ a specialized complex of skills to perpetrate a unique form of criminal behavior. Although not financially successful by most standards, stoopers derive status from their professional manner, and in turn are contemptuous of amateur practitioners. Due to a common endeavor and the specialized nature of their activity, stoopers have developed a consensus which includes shared rationalization, attitudes toward victims, and an informal code of behavior. Through a process of differential association, stoopers are separated but not isolated from traditional society. While not belonging to a larger criminal network, stoopers are informally organized and tutelage is necessary to become part of that organization.

Professional crime as described by Sutherland should not be relegated to the status of a romanticized footnote. While modern technology may have drastically altered some forms of professional crime, in the case of racetrack stoopers it has not radically changed their behavior system. Contemporary stoopers go on plying their trade in much the same manner as their earlier counterparts. There is no evidence of a diminution of skills or that modern-day stoopers ignore the tenets of their code. Novice stoopers are being tutored, and there are many indications that stooping will provide a regular source of income for a determined cadre of skilled thieves. Racetrack patrons show no signs of becoming more careful, and a continuing supply of discarded live tickets seems assured. In this instance, a group of professional criminals continues to behave in the Sutherland manner.

13

Is Differential Association/Social Learning Cultural Deviance Theory?

Ronald L. Akers

Donald R. Cressey (1960a) reviewed the first thirty years of criticisms of Sutherland's differential association theory. He argued persuasively that many were simply "literary errors" or misinterpretation by the critics. For example, the theory was judged invalid because not everyone who came into contact with criminals became criminal. This misinterprets the theory's proposition that criminal behavior is learned through differential association (relative exposure to criminal and noncriminal patterns) not simply through any contact with law violators. Cressey clarified the major misconceptions of differential association theory, which have seldom been offered since.

Cressey, however, also recognized two major weaknesses of Sutherland's theory. First, his concept of "definitions" was imprecise. It did not give good guidance on how to operationalize the ratio or "excess of definitions" favorable to criminal behavior over those unfavorable to it. Second, Sutherland's theory left the learning process unspecified, providing no clue about what in particular would be included in "all the mechanisms that are involved in any other learning" (Sutherland, 1947:7). These two issues were addressed subsequently (Cressey, 1953; Short, 1960; Sykes and Matza, 1957) and in the social learning reformulation, originally called "differential association-reinforcement," theory (Akers, 1973, 1994; Burgess and Akers, 1966).

Cressey did not consider the major issue of differential association as a "cultural deviance" theory because this criticism did not emerge until the 1960s. Differential association theory was said to be the archetypical "cultural deviance" theory, to show that it made wrong assumptions about human behavior and the role of culture in deviant behavior. Matsueda

Edited and abridged from *Criminology*, Volume 34(2):229–47 (1996).

(1988: 290) believed this criticism "reduces his [Sutherland's] theory to a caricature." Similarly, Bernard objected to the way the cultural deviance label was applied to the original differential association and the social learning revision (Bernard and Snipes, 1995; Vold and Bernard, 1986: 227–29). Nevertheless, the shortcomings attributed to cultural deviance theory continue to be used as a critique not only of Sutherland's theory but also of Akers's social learning theory reformulation (Gottfredson and Hirschi, 1990).

Here I examine whether differential association/social learning can correctly be classified as cultural deviance theory. From this I shall conclude that the theory is not a "cultural deviance" theory. In the process, I clarify in what sense cultural elements are incorporated into the differential association/social learning explanation of crime and deviance.

The Cultural Deviance Critique

According to the cultural deviance critique, differential association/social learning theory rests on inherently untenable assumptions that "man has no nature, socialization is perfectly successful, and cultural variability is unlimited" (Kornhauser, 1978:34). These assumptions lead the theory into a dead end, where it cannot explain individual differences. It is doomed to apply *only* to those group differences in crime that rest on adherence to a criminal or deviant subculture opposed to conventional culture. The principal example of cultural deviance theory is said to be differential association/social learning theory.

This characterization of Sutherland's differential association theory apparently began with an unpublished paper by Ruth Kornhauser in 1963 which Hirschi (1969:3–15) refers to as "a truly devastating critique of theories of cultural deviance" (Hirschi, 1969:12). Later, Kornhauser (1978) referred to differential association as the quintessential "cultural deviance" theory and included in her analysis the social learning reformulation. Hirschi and Gottfredson (1979) then repeated the same criticism of the theory, as have Wilson and Herrnstein (1985) and more recently, Gottfredson and Hirschi (1990), in contrasting positivistic theories with their general self-control theory. Criticisms of differential association as a cultural deviance theory continue to repeat the assertions by Kornhauser and Hirschi (e.g., Messner and Rosenfeld, 1994), although Matsueda and Bernard's objections are sometimes noted (Shoham and Hoffman, 1991).

According to Kornhauser (1978:34), the theory's assumption that "socialization is perfectly successful" leads to the assumption that individuals are incapable of violating the cultural norms of any group to which they belong. The theory is said to rest on the assumption that everyone completely internalizes social norms and obeys them; belief in the norms of the group to which one belongs is sufficient alone to ensure behavioral conformity. Thus, if the cultures of these groups are deviant by the standards of conventional society, the individual members of the groups will automatically be deviant or criminal. Behavioral adherence to unconventional culture places one in direct violation of conventional norms. In Kornhauser's view, then, cultural deviance theory assumes that subscription to deviant values "requires" the individual to violate the norms of other groups if they are in conflict with one's own group norms. If the values of these other groups are incorporated into the law, the violations will be criminal. According to these assumptions imputed to cultural deviance theory, *individuals* cannot be deviant. Only the *cultures* or *subcultures* in which the criminal values are transmitted to the individuals can be deviant with regard to the culture of the larger society or with regard to groups sustaining different subcultures. The theory is incapable of explaining any deviation from the culture into which one is socialized or any behavior that is inconsistent with one's professed values. This criticism is reiterated by Hirschi (1969):

> A third set of theories [theories of cultural deviance] assumes that men are incapable of committing "deviant acts." A person may indeed commit acts deviant by the standards of, say, middle-class society, but he cannot commit acts deviant by his own standards. In other words, theorists from this school see deviant behavior as *conformity* to a set of standards not accepted by a larger (that is, more powerful) society. (1969:11)

> In simplest terms, cultural deviance theory assumes that cultures, not persons, are deviant. It assumes that in living up to the demands of his own culture, the person automatically comes into conflict with the law. (1969:229)

Vold's (1958) group conflict theory of crime comes close to the assumptions attributed to cultural deviance theory by hypothesizing that much crime results from individuals behaving as good members of their respective interest groups. But Vold does not rely on the concept of culture and does not assume that all persons in the group will support the group interest. Sellin's (1938) notions of culture conflict did not expressly state the assumptions Kornhauser attributed to cultural deviance theory. Shaw and McKay's (1942) notions of cultural transmission of delinquent values in urban areas, Miller's (1958) theory of lower-class culture, Wolfgang and Ferracuti's (1967) subcultural theory of violence, and theories of delinquent subcultures such as Cohen's (1955) and Cloward and Ohlin s (1960)—all have some elements of the assumptions imputed to cultural deviance theory (see Barlow and Ferdinand, 1992). Although Kornhauser refers to such theories she presents differential association/ social learning as the "pure" model of cultural deviance theory. Upon closer examination, however, it can be seen that this characterization is based on misinterpretations of the theory.

The Cultural Deviance Critique and Misinterpretations of Extreme Cases in Differential Association

Sutherland's differential association theory is explicitly designed to account for individual variations in criminal behavior, not differences in group rates of crime. Sutherland made an unequivocal distinction between differential association as a theory of *individual* behavior and differential social disorganization as a theory of *group* differences. To claim that differential association theory applies only to deviant cultures, and not at all to individual deviance, is to impute assumptions to the theory that are directly contradictory to its propositions and to distinctions expressly maintained by Sutherland (1947:5–6).

The theory posits that individual deviance comes from persons holding definitions favorable to norm-violation; acts that are shaped by relatively greater exposure to deviant than to conventional normative definitions. Thus, the extreme case in which an individual's deviance is based entirely on his or her having been socialized solely in, and having completely internalized the dictates of, a deviant subculture without contact with conventional society is consistent with differential association theory. But this is the extreme case and is not proposed as the only or even the typical case accounted for by the theory. The theory assumes neither that all (or even many) cases of deviance fall into this extreme category nor that everyone reared within the same subculture will conform perfectly to its norms. The theory does not propose that there is no possibility of violation of internal group norms by individuals. Thus, the defining characteristics attributed to "cultural deviance" by Kornhauser, Hirschi, and others apply to differential association theory only if one limits its scope to the most extreme cases within the purview of the theory. Similarly, nowhere does Sutherland state that his theory rests on the assumptions of perfect socialization and no possibility of within-group deviance by individuals. Further, there is nothing in Sutherland's statement of his theory that asserts that persons are incapable of violating the very group norms to which they express allegiance. Yet these are the assumptions that are listed by Kornhauser as the sine qua non of cultural deviance theory.

If the author of differential association theory does not state assumptions attributed to cultural deviance theory and, indeed, incorporates propositions in the theory that are contradictory to such assumptions, on what basis can the theory be characterized as the prime cultural deviance theory? It appears that the attribution of such assumptions is based on references to some of the theories mentioned above, rather than on an analysis of differential association theory itself. Hirschi (1969:11) quotes from a 1929 book by Shaw and others to substantiate his claim. Kornhauser (1978) neither analyzes nor discusses the nine propositions in differential association theory to support her position. Instead, she relies on interpretations of other passages from Sutherland, Cressey, Sellin, and others, in which culture conflict, social disorganization, and differential social organization, but not differential association, are discussed (Matsueda, 1988).

To support her contention that differential association theory rests entirely on the assumption of conflict between cultures and that one always obeys one's own group norms, Kornhauser (1978:37–38) quotes from remarks made by Sutherland in 1942 that he intended to illustrate culture conflict. She quotes Sutherland discussing how some members of the historically criminal tribes of India commit acts of violence and theft in obedience to tribal codes. This automatically brings them into conflict with the laws of the political state of India.

> This lack of homogeneity is illustrated . . . in the criminal tribes of India. Two cultures are in sharp conflict there. One is the tribal culture which prescribes certain types of assault on persons outside the tribe, in some cases with religious compulsions. The other is the legal culture as stated by the Indian . . . governments . . . . When members of the tribe commit crimes, they act in accordance with one code and in opposition to the other. According to my theory, the same principle or process exists in all criminal behavior . . . . (Sutherland, 1956:20, as quoted in Kornhauser, 1978:37–38)

Compare this with the full quotation from Sutherland (with the crucial phrases left out by Kornhauser indicated in italics):

> This lack of homogeneity is illustrated *in extreme form* in the criminal tribes of India. Two cultures are in sharp conflict there. One is the tribal culture which prescribes certain types of assault on persons outside the tribe, in some cases with religious compulsions. The other is the legal culture as stated by the Indian and provincial governments and made applicable to the criminal tribes . . . . When members of the tribe commit crimes, they act in accordance with one

code and in opposition to the other. According to my theory, the same principle or process exists in all criminal behavior, *although the conflict may not be widely organized or sharply defined as in the Indian tribe.* (Sutherland, 1956:20)

In this version Kornhauser deletes the key qualifying phrase that Sutherland used to introduce the point that it is "illustrated in *extreme form*" (Sutherland, 1956:20; emphasis added). Sutherland asserted here that the "principle" of culture conflict operates to some extent in all criminal behavior, but he qualified this, noting that it may not operate in the "sharply defined" or "organized" way given in the illustration. It is the general principle or process of relatively greater exposure to definitions favorable to crime that is operative in committing criminal behavior, not the specific way the process operates in this extreme case.

With the qualifying phrases omitted, the meaning of culture conflict is changed. The theory is also inaccurately represented because the quotation is taken out of context. Sutherland's reference to "my theory" in this quotation does not refer to differential association theory as found in his 1947 statement of the final version of the theory. Rather, Kornhauser is quoting from a 1942 Sutherland paper referring to the 1939 version of his theory. (See also Sutherland, 1973.) That version contained statements about culture conflict and differential association. Moreover, in this very paper Sutherland (1956:20–21) makes a clear distinction between culture conflict as a group principle and differential association as a principle of individual behavior.

Nevertheless, Kornhauser (1978:26) takes this example as demonstrating the "basic paradigm" of Sutherland's theory.

According to Sutherland, originator of the *pure cultural deviance* model, the *basic paradigm* of this approach is given by the fabled "criminal tribes of India," whose culture mandates crimes abhorred in the so-called legal culture. (emphasis added)

But it can be taken as such only by disregarding: the original date of the paper from which the paragraph was taken, Sutherland's qualifier that the example was an extreme case, his statement that the example illustrates but does not fully state the principle of culture conflict, and his distinction between culture conflict and differential association. It is inaccurate for Kornhauser to ignore Sutherland's own restrictions on the illustration and claim that it forms the basic assumption in his theory. Nor is there accuracy in Kornhauser's claim that the scope of the 1947 differential association theory is limited to the type of subcultural criminal behavior found in an anecdotal illustration published several years earlier.

Sutherland's theory does include cultural factors in its main proposition that individuals' norm-violating behavior is learned through their differential association with others supporting definitions favorable to criminal and deviant behavior. Differential association does not rest, however, on any of the main assumptions attributed to cultural deviance theory by the critics.

Kornhauser (1978) also misinterprets the proposition that differential association mediates sociodemographic variations in criminal behavior by hypothesizing that rules, norms, and role expectations differ by age, race, sex, class, and so on (Sutherland and Cressey, 1955). She believes Sutherland and Cressey are assuming a separate criminogenic culture or subculture to account for each of these differences. But their hypothesis is that one's location in the social system, as indicated by such characteristics as race, sex, and age, means that one will be differentially exposed to and learn definitions favorable and unfavorable to law violation (whatever the source of those definitions). Such a hypothesis does not require that each of these sociodemographic categories constitute an interacting group with a singular and distinctive culture into which, respectively, males, young people, or blacks are obediently enculturated. Cressey (1960a) made it clear that the conflict can come from normative variations and discontinuities in the same social system to which males and females, of all ages and all races are exposed, as well as from differences among subcultures.

Misinterpretation, Ambiguity, and Clarification of Definitions and Motivation for Criminal Behavior

The cultural deviance critique depicts the differential association process in criminal behavior as one in which internalization of definitions favorable to crime (1) "requires" the person to behave in violation of conventional norms, and (2) provides the "sole" motivation for behavior.

> Theories in the cultural deviance tradition suggest that in committing his acts the delinquent is living up to the norms of his culture. These theories *usually* suggest the existence of beliefs that *positively require* delinquent acts. (Hirschi, 1969:197; emphasis added)

> Internalized cultural values [according to differential association theory] provides the *sole* basis of motivation. . . . This view [Sutherland's] assumes first that there are *no other* determinants of human behavior than values. (Kornhauser, 1978:195–96; emphasis added)

Since cultural definitions are wholly determinative, and no other source of motivation is allowed to counteract them, all socialization is "perfectly successful," and all members of the group are rendered incapable of acting contrary to the deviant norms. Therefore, only the group's culture can be deviant; no member can deviate from the group's culture.

Neither Kornhauser nor Hirschi identify what specific statement(s) in differential association theory lead them to this interpretation. There is nothing in its theoretical statements that restricts the concept of definitions favorable to crime to norms that "positively require" deviant acts. Also, nowhere in the theory is it claimed that definitions are the only cause of crime. However, the theory is more vulnerable to this critique because of uncertainties as to exactly what Sutherland meant by "definitions" and the role they play in motivating law violations. The fourth statement of differential association theory refers to learning "techniques" and "the specific direction of motives, drives, rationalizations, and attitudes." The fifth hypothesizes that "the specific direction of motives and drives is learned *from* definitions of the legal codes as favorable or unfavorable" (Sutherland, 1947:6; emphasis added).

Sutherland's use of the terms "rationalizations" and "attitudes" along with "definitions" is straightforward; all are subsumed under the concept of definitions favorable and unfavorable to crime. Some confusion is introduced by his also listing in the same clause the direction of "motives" and "drives" without defining these terms. *Motives* ordinarily means anything that moves or induces a person to do something (or to refrain from doing something), and *drives* was often used in the literature during Sutherland's time to denote motivation based on strong internal pushes to satisfy emotional or innate needs. It could be that Sutherland wanted to stress that both criminal motivations and criminal acts are learned. But did he conceptualize "motives" and "drives" as alternative names for, or something very different from, "rationalizations" and "attitudes?" Why did he list them serially in the same sentence? Are motives and drives also subsumed, along with rationalizations and attitudes, under the concept of definitions? Are all the terms equivalent or are they separate and distinguishable factors in criminal behavior?

Sutherland does not explain his juxtaposition of these terms. In his fifth statement, he seems to view motives and drives not as independent variables, but as separate dependent variables "caused" by definitions or perhaps as intervening variables between learned definitions and criminal behavior. How can learned definitions of behavior as right or wrong motivate one to engage in the behavior or how can they constitute drives that produce behavior? Sutherland does not tell us. It is not clear how one's attitudes toward crime, by themselves, could provide the impetus or motivation to commit the criminal acts, especially when the balance of procriminal and anticriminal attitudes approaches unity, but also at all points on the balance scale.

In addition to these uncertainties part of this ambiguity is based on Sutherland's insertion of the proposition "from" in the fifth statement. It could be that Sutherland meant that one's own definitions are learned "from" exposure to others' definitions in the socialization process; once learned these definitions motivate the person to commit or refrain from law violations. In this sense of internalization of definitions, definitions favorable and unfavorable are attitudinal sets brought to a situation that make lawbreaking seem appropriate or inappropriate there. But does this mean that the cognitive set itself provides enough "motivation" to commit the acts? Does the theory propose that having a negative attitude toward a particular crime is all that is needed to deter it?

Perhaps Sutherland did not provide clear answers to these questions, but good answers, contrary to the cultural deviance interpretation, can be derived by placing the fourth and fifth statements in the proper context of the whole theory. One can extrapolate from the concept of definitions that strongly held beliefs may directly motivate crime in the sense that they direct what ought to be done or not done in certain situations. But committing a crime solely on the basis of adherence to a set of values or beliefs would be true only in extreme cases of highly ideologically motivated offenses or of intense group loyalty. Nowhere does Sutherland state that definitions favorable to crime and delinquency strongly require, compel, or motivate action in this sense. He does not state that definitions are the only source of motivation for behavior. His reference to "all" learning mechanisms elsewhere in the theory indicates that he did not conceptualize definitions as the sole causal stimuli. However, he did not delineate what these other motivating learning mechanisms were or how they relate to favorable/unfavorable definitions in motivating criminal acts.

Whatever confusion remained in Sutherland's original statements on this point, however, was rectified by the revised statements of social learning theory (Akers, 1973, 1994):

> For the most part, however, definitions favorable to crime and delinquency do not "require" or strongly motivate action . . . . Rather, they are conventional beliefs so weakly held that they provide no restraint or are positive or neutralizing attitudes that facilitate law violation in the right set of circumstances. (1994:98)

Social learning theory proposes that there are variations in the extent to which persons hold to deviant and prosocial definitions and that there are variations in the extent to which these beliefs and behavior are reinforced. These variations can develop within the same normative or cultural system. They do not require the existence or participation in an organized deviant subculture in direct conflict with the larger normative system of society.

Moreover, social learning theory (Akers, 1985; Burgess and Akers, 1966) proposes that the definitions themselves are learned through reinforcement contingencies operating in the socialization process, and they may function less as direct motivators than as facilitative or inhibitory "discriminative stimuli" or cues that signal that certain behavior is appropriate and likely to be rewarded, or inappropriate and likely to be punished. It is this anticipated reinforcement/punishment (based on direct or vicarious reinforcement in the past) that provides motivation for the behavior independently of whatever motivation to engage in or refrain from an act comes from the fact that it conforms to or violates one's beliefs or definitions. One may be willing to commit a crime in the sense of holding a favorable definition of the behavior, but one is less likely to act unless the situation also allows for the expectation of a payoff and low risk of punishment. The concept of instrumental learning in social learning theory, therefore, posits a precise role for definitions in motivation for crime that goes beyond Sutherland's notion that drives and motives are learned "from" definitions. Questions about social and nonsocial sources of variations in behavior beyond variations in definitions are answered by social learning theory.

Social learning theory proposes that reward/punishment contingencies shape both one's attitudes and overt behavioral repertoire over time and provides the motivation to engage or refrain from action at a given time and place. Consistent with the theory, one may violate group norms because of failures of socialization or because one has insufficiently learned the moral dictates of the group's norms. Embedded in the same general normative system may be both the prohibition of an act and definitions that justify the act (Sykes and Matza, 1957). Parents and other socializers may make inefficient or inconsistent use of rewards and punishments, with the unintended outcome of reinforcing behavior that is contrary to their own normative standards. They may fail as effective models (Patterson et al., 1975). Deviant models are available outside the family and other conventional socializing institutions, in the media, and among peers. One's own learned normative definitions may be violated because rewards for the behavior outweigh the normative inhibitions. One may refrain from law violation, despite having learned definitions favorable to violation, because he or she anticipates more cost than reward attached to the violation.

Social learning theory posits that, in addition to or counter to, a favorable attitude toward the criminal behavior one is motivated to engage in the behavior by the reward expected to be gained from it and is inhibited by the expected aversive consequences. Definitions are implicated in the reinforcement balance because part of the package of rewards and punishments is the congruence or discrepancy between one's beliefs and deeds. If the act is congruent with or allows one to demonstrate adherence to a certain norm or set of values, that may provide enough positive motivation to do it. If it is incongruent with one's beliefs, the attendant guilt and self-reproach will often be sufficiently aversive to deter commission of the act. But positive or negative attitudes are only part of the motivational package inducing or inhibiting behavior. Social learning theory proposes that the relative reinforcement from other known or anticipated rewards and costs motivates commission of the act even in the face of unwilling or negative attitudes. People may believe that it is wrong to lie, but lie anyway if it will get them off the hook when accused of a misdeed. That persons may be motivated to violate even those normative standards to which they subscribe is clearly explained by the balance of other social and nonsocial rewards and punishments attached to the behavior. Subscription to those normative standards is itself responsive to, and over time will be modified by, the rewarding or punishing consequences of the behavior to which they refer. Not only the overt behavior but also definitions favorable or unfavorable to it are affected by the positive and negative consequences of the initial acts. To the extent that they are more rewarded than alternative behavior, the favorable definitions attached to them will be strengthened and the unfavorable definitions will be weakened, and the more likely it is that the deviant behavior will be repeated under similar circumstances (see Akers, 1973:57).

The operation of other motivating factors beyond definitions that were implicit in Sutherland's reference to all the mechanisms of learning has been made explicit in social learning theory. The explanatory shortfall left by the ambiguity in Sutherland's statements regarding "motives" and cultural definitions as the "sole" factor in criminal behavior has been made up by social learning theory. One may reject the answer, but cannot deny that the theory provides an answer by stipulating that social and nonsocial reinforcement, modeling, discriminative stimuli, and other behavioral processes motivate behavior independently of, and in interaction with, the effect of cultural definitions. This incorporation of behavioral reinforcement and punishment (social and nonsocial) and other learning mechanisms into the equation plainly answers the question of how one can engage in behavior that is not congruent with one's own normative definitions. But Kornhauser (1978:198–99) rejects this answer and classifies social learning as a cultural deviance theory because the inclusion of nonsocial reinforcement into the social learning reformulation "certainly violates Sutherland's principle of cultural definitions as the sole causal stimuli." If the principle of definitions as the sole causal stimuli is crucial to cultural deviance theory as defined by Kornhauser and social learning propositions violate that principle, on what basis can the theory be called a cultural deviance theory?

Kornhauser's reasoning is circular. She begins by imputing to cultural deviance theory the assumption that cultural definitions are the sole cause of criminal behavior. Then she rejects any learning theory concept or proposition that would explicitly contradict the assumption precisely because it does not fit the imputed assumption with which she began. Thus, any theory can be classified as a cultural deviance theory whether or not it really includes the assumptions that define cultural deviance theory.

The fact that social learning theory contains such reinforcement processes is also misinterpreted by Kornhauser in other ways. For instance, although she clearly places differential association theory and social learning theory at the center of the cultural deviance theories, Kornhauser (1978:44) still maintains that *any* "cultural deviance theory denies that men ever violate norms out of considerations of reward and punishment." While this is true that Sutherland's theory does not refer to the impact of reward and punishment on individual behavior, it is precisely what social learning theory proposes. As noted above, Kornhauser dismisses the inclusion of nonsocial reinforcers in the theory as a way of providing noncultural motivation to crime because she believes it contradicts the assumption she ascribes to cultural deviance theory, that only cultural definitions can cause crime. Then, paradoxically, she claims that "since it is entirely possible for criminal behavior to be learned and maintained in the absence of social reinforcements," social learning theory is no more able than Sutherland's theory to explain individual deviant behavior (Kornhauser, 1978:199). Perhaps it is this reasoning that leads Kornhauser to view both theories as conforming to the assumptions she attributes to cultural deviance theory.

Clarification of Cultural Elements in the Concepts of Definitions and Differential Association

Culture is important in differential association/social learning theory. Cultural elements played a central role in differential association theory and remain, albeit less prominent, in social learning theory. Neither meets the criteria for a cultural deviancy theory ascribed to it by Kornhauser, Hirschi, and others. If the traditional cultural deviance critique is not accurate, what then is the proper way to describe the role of culture in the theory? The question has already been partially answered, but further clarification can be gained through a closer examination of the concepts of "culture," "definitions," and "differential association."

Culture is commonly defined as "transmitted and created content and patterns of values, ideas, and other symbolic-meaningful systems as factors in the shaping of human behavior" (Kroeber and Parsons, 1958:583). Social culture is conceptualized as conduct codes and "symbols and symbol-making" (Gilmore, 1992:409). This includes the values, norms, beliefs, moral evaluations, symbolic meanings, and normative orientations shared or professed by members of a social system (society, community, or subgroup). Values, beliefs, and norms are incorporated into differential association/social learning theory in the concepts of definitions and differential association.

The concept of definitions in the theory includes (1) group-shared definitions expressed or exhibited by others that are favorable or unfavorable to deviant or conforming behavior to which the individual is exposed through the family, peers, and other primary and secondary sources, and (2) the individual's own internalized or professed definitions/attitudes favorable or unfavorable to the behavior. The theory predicts that one's own definitions are positively correlated with others' definitions. But as I have shown above, it does not predict that the correlation will be perfect.

Since the general conventional culture in modern society is not uniform and there are conflicts and variations among subgroups in society, the individual is likely to be exposed to different, and perhaps conflicting, cultural definitions of specific acts as good or bad. The theory does not assume that one's own attitudes are a perfect replication of those cultural patterns or that exposure to them is the sole source of the individual's taking on and changing his or her definitions favorable or unfavorable to deviance. And, as shown above, once learned these definitions are not the sole motivation in the process whereby individuals come to the point of committing criminal and deviant acts.

The favorable and unfavorable definitions shared by others constitute the *normative or cultural dimension* of the process of differential association. But the concept of differential association also has a social *behavioral/interactional dimension* made up of the direct and indirect associations with others who are engaging in conforming or deviant behavior (see Akers, 1985, 1994). Sutherland (1947) viewed the former, the normative content of that which was shared through associations, as the key part of the process by which the individual acquires conforming or law-violating attitudes. His focus was on association with criminals and noncriminal "patterns," regardless of their source, rather than with criminal and noncriminals as different types of people (see Cressey, 1960). Thus he understated the causative role of the effects of social interaction with others. Nevertheless, Sutherland's (1947:6–7) statements about "all the mechanisms" of learning, communication of gestures as well as language in intimate groups, and modalities of "associations with criminal behavior and also associations with anti-criminal behavior" leave room in the theory for effects of differential association with persons and behavior beyond those coming only from exposure to cultural definitions.

Aside from some dismissive remarks about imitation, Sutherland did not address directly what those behavioral effects are, but social learning theory does. It proposes that the significance of primary groups comes not only from their role in exposing the individual to culturally transmitted and individually espoused definitions, but also from providing behavioral models to imitate and their mediation of social reinforcement for criminal or conforming behavior. This relates to the discussion of how persons may behave in violation of the tenets of their culture or subculture or even the very values they personally advocate. A child reared in a community that promulgates nonviolent values, living in a family that expresses nonviolent attitudes, may nonetheless come to engage in and justify violence as a result of witnessing abusive behavior in the home or being abused. Warr and Stafford (1991) raise the question of whether the impact of peers on one's behavior comes from "what they think or what they do." Social learning theory supplies the answer to this question: it is both. Peer influence comes from what peers think (or say) is right or wrong and from what they do, not only in the sense of committing or not committing delinquency, but also in the sense of modeling, reacting to, instructing, and supporting that behavior.

Conclusion

According to Kornhauser and others, differential association/social learning theory epitomizes "cultural deviance" theory. The main assumptions attributed to such a theory are that predeviant definitions are perfectly transmitted subcultural values held so strongly that they positively compel the person to violate the law. It is impossible for individuals to deviate from the culture or subculture to which they have been exposed. Thus there can only be deviant groups or cultures, not deviant individuals. There is no other individual or independent source of variations in these definitions beyond exposure to the culture of subgroups, and therefore, cultural definitions are the sole cause of criminal behavior.

Critics do not cite any part of Sutherland's 1947 theory to substantiate their ascription of these assumptions to differential association theory or to support their view that it is the purest form of what they call "cultural deviance theory." And one searches Sutherland's nine statements in vain to find anything explicit in them that would lead to the conclusion that they necessarily rely on these assumptions. The theory does not state that definitions favorable to deviance operate only by compelling norm violation, that it is impossible for individuals to violate the norms of groups with which they are in association, that there can only be deviant cultures, or that learned definitions constitute the only motivations to crime.

It may be that critics have attributed these cultural deviance assumptions to Sutherland's theory not because of what he specified in the theory, but because of something he wrote in his commentary on the theoretical propositions or comments he made elsewhere. For instance, Sutherland (1947:6) used a phrase in his commentary on the sixth statement of his theory that may imply that there is no individual variation in learning definitions—"any person inevitably assimilates the surrounding culture unless other patterns are in conflict." But this refers only to the general idea that what one learns depends on the extent to which he or she is exposed to only one set or to conflicting sets of values. It does not state that socialization is completely successful or that there is no individual variation in the assimilation of culture.

Perhaps the cultural deviance critique is based on the vagueness in Sutherland's stipulation of how definitions can provide the motivation for committing criminal acts. But again, the critics do not claim that their arguments rest on this ambiguity. And it is unlikely that this is the basis for their claim that the theory posits definitions as the only possible motivation for crime because they do not accept the social learning resolution of the ambiguity. Indeed, the critics do not make clear distinctions between Sutherland's theory and the behavioral reformulation of it. Thus, essentially the same cultural deviance assumptions are ascribed to social learning theory that are imputed to Sutherland's differential association theory. I have attempted to show here that this imputation is based on a misinterpretation of the original differential association theory and of social learning theory.

This conclusion does not forbid any reference to theory as cultural deviance if that simply means that an important role is given to cultural factors in explaining deviance. Sutherland's differential association theory would fit such a description, and although the cultural elements are less important to social learning theory, it too would fit. Thus, by objecting to the label of "cultural deviance," I do not mean that all references to cultural deviance elements in the theory are inapplicable. I do mean that if there is a class of cultural deviance theories as defined by Kornhauser, Hirschi, Gottfredson, and others, differential association/social learning theory does not belong in it.

Neutralization and
Social Control Theory

Introduction

In some ways neutralization theory is an extension and amplification of one aspect of social learning theory, but one that reintroduces an element of free will. Neutralization theory is found in the works of sociologist C. Wright Mills (1916–62) with his concept of "vocabularies of motive" (1940). It was applied to criminology by Sutherland's student Donald Cressey in his study of embezzlers (1953). Cressey showed how embezzlers consider their action in advance in relationship to whether they will likely be able to excuse or justify it afterward should they be subject to questioning. Cressey argued that the words and phrases embezzlers use, such as "borrowing" rather than stealing, are the most important component in the process that gets them into trouble (Cressey, 1970). Neutralization became fully developed by David Matza and Gresham Sykes in their criticism of the overly deterministic nature of subcultural theories of crime (Sykes and Matza, 1957; Matza and Sykes, 1961; Matza, 1964). Neutralization theory takes for granted that most people are socialized into conventional behavior. It assumes that what is learned are attitudes and devices, expressed in language and accounts, that temporarily free people from convention and conformity allowing them to commit crime without moral qualms. Crime can thus become a behavioral option for people when their commitment to conventional values and norms is neutralized by excuses and justifications that render them morally free, but not compelled to break rules.

In the first selection Michael Benson (chap. 14) reports on his study of convicted white-collar offenders which focuses specifically on the techniques that are used to deny their criminal intent. The strategies used to accomplish this end included the claim that their criminal behaviors are part of the everyday practices of their industry, that "everyone does it," that they result from overly aggressive prosecutions and are not "real" crime compared with the harm caused by street offenders. Finally, these accounts showed that competition and the need to survive, or unusual circumstances pressured them into such activity.

Critics of neutralization theory question how far lawbreakers are attached to convention in the first place, arguing that neutralization may be unnecessary. The selection by John Hamlin (chap. 15) draws on the body of knowledge concerning vocabularies of motives, to argue that motives in deviancy theory should not be viewed in such positivist/causal terms. Techniques of neutralization are motives which are more accurately utilized *after* behavior is committed and only when such behavior is called into question.

In an early version of social control theory, called *containment theory* (Reckless, 1950; Reckless et al., 1956; Carr, 1950) it was argued that the formation of positive or negative "self-concepts" in young people could affect their "inner controls" over their personal bio-psychological "pushes" and over universal environmental "pulls" toward rule-breaking behavior. However, Hirschi's (1969) version of social control through social bonding with conventional others has become the leading statement in the field.

Control theory according to Hirschi (1969) makes the reverse assumption to those made by both learning and neutralization theory. It assumes that most people are *already disposed* to nonconformity *unless* they receive protective socialization in the form of controls. Thus for control theorists what needs to be explained is not deviance and crime, but conformity. Social control theory argues that inadequate or ineffective external socialization can result in weak or absent internal controls over behavior. The theory is concerned with the ways in which relational ties between young people and adults result in some youth having respect for the values and norms of conventional adults while others do not. His version of the theory focuses on the idea that social controls are learned through particular kinds of bonding processes and that, were it not for these controls, we would all be lawbreakers. It implies that role modeling is important, especially of beliefs, values, and attitudes learned as a result of social bonds formed with conventional actors (e.g., parents, teachers, youth leaders) and conveyed through societal institutions.

L. Edward Wells and Joseph Rankin (chap. 16) review these different versions of social control theory and give special attention to the often neglected question of direct parental controls (including normative regulation, monitoring, and punishment) and their effects on delinquency. They argue that, rather than being simple, direct, and linear, the relationship between direct controls and delinquency is complex and sometimes contradictory.

14

Denying the Guilty Mind: Accounting for Involvement in a White-Collar Crime

Michael L. Benson

White-collar offenders are assumed to suffer subjectively as a result of the public humiliation of adjudication as criminals, but they are also assumed, paradoxically, to be able to maintain a noncriminal self-concept and to successfully deny the criminality of their actions (Conklin, 1977). The present study analyses the accounts given by a sample of convicted white-collar offenders, focusing specifically on identifying the patterns of techniques they use to deny their own criminality. The central research question is: How do convicted white-collar offenders account for their adjudication as criminals? Rather that attempting to understand this process, researchers have all too often morally condemned such offenders (Clinard and Yeager, 1978).

The continuing failure to confront and penetrate the rationalizations used by white-collar offenders and to get beyond a sympathetic view of the individual offender is considered by some one of the reasons for the continued widespread prevalence of white-collar crimes (Sutherland, 1949:222, 225; Geis, 1982:55–57; Meier and Geis, 1982:98). Others have argued that the leniency with which white-collar criminals are treated by the justice system derives in part from their ability to evoke sympathy from judges (Conklin, 1977).

These widely held beliefs about white-collar offenders, however, rely on anecdotal evidence about persons of extremely high status, convicted of particularly egregious offenses. Examples include former Vice President Agnew (Naughton et al., 1977) and the executives involved in the heavy electrical equipment antitrust case of 1961 (Geis, 1967). Celebrated cases are important as public morality plays about competing interests (Fisse and Braithwaite, 1983) but do not represent typical white-collar offenders.

Edited and abridged from *Criminology*, Volume 23(4):583–607 (1985).

Although it is assumed that white-collar offenders are able to maintain a noncriminal self-concept and avoid stigmatization as criminals, the subtle interactional processes whereby transformation of their personal and public identities is avoided, have been largely ignored (but see Rothman and Gandossy, 1982).

The major theme here is that accounting for involvement in white-collar offenses is intimately involved with the social organization of offenses. The accounts developed by white-collar offenders are delimited by the type of offense, its mechanics, and its organizational context. They are further structured in that they must be constructed so as to defeat the conditions required for a successful degradation ceremony.

The Study

This study is based on voluntary interviews conducted with a sample of thirty convicted white-collar male offenders supplemented by an examination of the files maintained on eighty white-collar offenders and by further interviews with federal probation officers, federal judges, Assistant U.S. Attorneys, and defense attorneys specializing in white-collar cases. The offenders interviewed were self-selected by responding to a letter sent by the researcher from the probation office. The sample is therefore nonrandom and the results must be viewed as provisional.

In the interviews no attempt was made to challenge the explanations or rationalizations given by offenders regarding their offenses. Rather, offenders were encouraged to talk of themselves and their feelings regarding the case and were allowed to focus on aspects they considered to be most important. This approach was followed because of the sensitive nature of the subject matter, the emotional trauma wrought by conviction, and the voluntary nature of the interviews. The goal of the study was not to determine the strength of the rationalizations, nor to bring about a "rehabilitative" awareness, but to determine how offenders account for their actions to themselves and to significant others.

The Offenders

White-collar offenders were considered to be those convicted of economic offenses committed through the use of indirection, fraud, or collusion (Shapiro, 1980). The offenses represented here include securities and exchange fraud, antitrust violations, embezzlement, false claims and statements, and tax violations. In terms of socioeconomic status, the sample ranges from a formerly successful international lawyer to a self-employed jewelry seller. For some, particularly licensed professionals and public sector employees, conviction was accompanied by job loss and other major lifestyle changes. For others, such as businessmen and private sector employees, conviction was not accompanied by collateral disabilities other than the expense and trauma of criminal justice processing (Benson, 1984).

Accounts

An account is either a justification or an excuse made to explain unanticipated or untoward behavior (Scott and Lyman, 1968). In a justification the actor admits responsibility for the act in question but denies its pejorative content. In an excuse the actor admits the act in question is wrong, but denies having full responsibility for it. Accounts are used to narrow the gap between expectation and behavior and to present the actor in a favorable light. They serve to clear the offender of guilt or blame. Related to justifications and excuses is the apology in which the individual admits violating a rule, accepts the validity of the rule, and expresses embarrassment and anger at himself or herself. An individual "splits [him or her]self into two parts, the part that is guilty of an offense and the part that disassociates itself from the delict and affirms a belief in the offended rule" (Goffman, 1972:113).

Accounts can be viewed either as impression management techniques used to exonerate the self and to avoid being labeled a criminal or as indicators of an offender's cognitive structure. The present study cannot demonstrate conclusively which of these is more accurate. Nonetheless, it should be recognized that offenders probably engage in a process of self-persuasion in defining their situations. Accounts intended to shore up their public identity may evolve into their view of themselves and their offense.

According to Sykes and Matza (1957), before committing offenses juvenile delinquents unwittingly use "techniques of neutralization" (accounts) that relieve them of the duty to behave according to norms. Studying neutralizations helps us to understand the individual and situational causes of crime. Whether white-collar offenders engage in a similar process before their offenses is not clear. Cressey's (1953) theory of embezzlement hinges on this assumption. Since white-collar offenders are strongly committed to the central normative structure, many go through elaborate neutralization processes prior to their offenses. The accounts developed afterward may describe the process employed by the offender. Thus the study of accounts provides a guide to microlevel analysis of the causal factors involved in a white-collar crime.

Accounts, however, are not foolproof guides to intentions (Nettler, 1982:15–17). It is important to distinguish between neutralizations that cause or allow an offense to be committed and accounts that are developed afterward to excuse or justify it. By definition, an account is a linguistic act performed before an audience, that is, "impression management" (Goffman, 1959).

In giving an account after an offense, an offender is not trying to identify reasons that allow the commission of an offense, but addressing an audience and attempting to explain that offense while at the same time demonstrating an essential lack of personal criminality. To accomplish this it is necessary to take personal actions to correspond with the class of actions that is implicitly acceptable to society. For this reason, accounts should not be thought of as solely individual inventions. Rather, they are invented by and in a historical and institutional context which delimits the range of superficially plausible justifications and excuses.

Corporate capitalism creates opportunities for particular forms of crime and makes plausible certain types of justifications and mitigations for engaging in crime. The diffusion of responsibility in corporations, for example, makes it plausible for an actor to either deny responsibility altogether or to partially excuse actions by claiming to have been working at the request of superiors. The widespread acceptance of such concepts as profit, growth, and free enterprise makes it plausible for an actor to argue that governmental regulations run counter to more basic societal values and goals. Criminal behavior can then be characterized as being in line with other higher laws of free enterprise (Denzin, 1977:919). More generally, at the core of capitalist economies is the idea that society benefits most through the individual competitive strivings of its members, as opposed to collective cooperation. This provides a moral environment which facilitates the rationalization of criminal behavior. Just "trying to get ahead" becomes an understandable and perhaps acceptable motive, even when it occasionally leads to behavior that violates the law. A similar defense (or motive) would not seem acceptable in societies that do not promote individual material success as a desirable goal.

The study of accounts, therefore, can reveal how history and social structure make possible certain characterizations of events. This creates a moral environment conducive to crime in two ways. First, convicted offenders can rationalize their behavior to themselves prior to engaging in crimes. Second, after the discovery of an offender's involvement in criminal activity, offenders may avoid the stigma of being labeled a criminal by proper accounting practices.

Accounts are important, therefore, for three reasons: (1) they shed light on neutralizations and vocabularies of motive and help us understand the causes of crime at the individual and situational level; (2) as impression management, they illuminate underlying assumptions about what constitutes culpable criminality versus acceptable illegalities; and (3) accounts may play an important and poorly understood role in the judicial process, potentially reducing sentencing severity (Rothman and Gandossy, 1982).

Denying the Guilty Mind

This chapter focuses on how offenders attempt to defeat the success of the adjudicatory "degradation ceremony" (Garfinkel, 1956) by denying their own criminality through the use of accounts. However, it is also necessary to consider the guilt and inner anguish felt by many white-collar offenders, even while denying they are criminals.

White-collar criminal prosecution focuses on *why* something was done, rather than *who* did it (Edelhertz, 1970:47). In white-collar crime cases, there is often relatively little disagreement as to what happened; the issue is criminal intent. If the prosecution is to proceed beyond investigation, the prosecutor must infer from the pattern of events that conscious criminal intent was present and believe that sufficient evidence exists to convince a jury. This can be difficult because of the way in which white-collar illegalities are integrated into ordinary occupational routines (Katz, 1979b:445–46). Thus, in conducting trials, grand jury hearings, or plea negotiations prosecutors spend much effort establishing that the defendant had the necessary criminal intent. By concentrating on the offender's motives, the prosecutor attacks the very essence of the white-collar offender's public and personal image as an upstanding member of the community. The offender is portrayed as someone with a guilty mind.

Not surprisingly, therefore, the most consistent and recurrent pattern in the interviews was denial of criminal intent, as opposed to the denial of any criminal behavior. Most offenders acknowledged that their behavior probably could be construed as falling within the conduct proscribed by statute, but they uniformly denied that their actions were motivated by a guilty mind. However, indictment, prosecution, and conviction provoke a variety of emotions among offenders.

The enormous reality of the offender's lived emotion (Denzin, 1984) in admitting guilt is illustrated by one offender:

> You know (the plea's) what really hurt. I didn't even know I had feet. I felt numb. My head was just floating. There was no feeling, except a state of suspended animation. . . . For a brief moment, I almost hesitated. I almost said not guilty. If I had been alone, I would have fought, but my family. . .

The traumatic nature of this moment lies, in part, in the offender's feeling that only one small part of his life is being considered. It does not typify his inner self, and to judge him solely on the basis of this one event seems an atrocious injustice to the offender.

For some the memory of the event is so painful that they want to obliterate it entirely:

I want quiet. I want to forget. I want to cut with the past.

I've already divorced myself from the problem. I don't even want to hear the names of certain people ever again. It brings me pain.

For others, rage seemed to be the dominant emotion.

I never really felt any embarrassment over the whole thing. I felt rage and it wasn't false or self-serving. It was really (something) to see this thing in action and recognize what the whole legal system has come to through its development, and the abuse of the grand jury system and the abuse of the indictment system.

Those whose cases were reported in the news media were embarrassed and/or embittered by the public exposure of their punishment and the stigmatization it brought.

The only one I am bitter at is the newspapers, as many people are. They are unfair because you can't get even. They can say things that are untrue. . . . They wrote an article on me that was so blasphemous, that was so horrible. They painted me as an insidious, miserable creature, wringing out the last penny.

Offenders whose cases were not reported in the media expressed relief at avoiding that embarrassment, sometimes saying that greater publicity would have been a worse sentence.

In court, defense lawyers present white-collar offenders as having suffered by virtue of the humiliation of public adjudication as criminals. Prosecutors, however, present them as cavalier individuals who arrogantly ignore the law and brush off its weak efforts to stigmatize them as criminals. Neither of these stereotypes is accurate. The subjective effects of conviction on white-collar offenders are varied and complex, as for all offenders. Further research on the emotional responses of offenders to conviction might reveal why some offenders stop their criminal behavior while others do not (Casper, 1978:80).

Offenders were nearly unanimous in denying their basic criminality through accounts justifying and excusing their crimes, as will be shown in the following analysis.

Antitrust Violators

Four of the offenders had been convicted of antitrust violations, all in the building and contracting industry. Four major themes characterized their accounts. First, antitrust offenders focused on the everyday character and historical continuity of their offenses. The offenders argued that they were merely following established and necessary industry practices: "It was a way of doing business," "part of the everyday. . . method of survival." These practices were presented as being necessary for the well-being of the industry as well as their own companies. Further, they claimed that cooperation among competitors was either allowed or actively promoted by the government in other industries and professions.

Second, offenders characterized their actions as blameless. They admitted talking to competitors and to submitting intentionally noncompetitive bids. However, they claimed this was done not for the purpose of rigging prices nor to make exorbitant profits, but as part of the everyday practices of the industry which required them to occasionally submit bids on projects they really did not want. To avoid the effort and expense of preparing full-fledged bids they would call a competitor to get a price to use.

> All you want to do is show a bid, so that in some cases it was for as small a reason as getting your deposit back on the plans and specs. So you just simply have no interest in getting the job and just call to see if you can find someone to give you a price to use, so that you didn't have to go through the expense of an entire bid preparation. Now that is looked on very unfavorably, and it is a technical violation, but it was strictly an opportunity to keep your name in front of a desired customer. Or you may find yourself in a situation where somebody is doing work for a customer, has done work for many, many years and is totally acceptable, totally fair. There is no problem. But suddenly they (the customer) get an idea that they ought to have a few tentative figures, and you're called in, and you are in a moral dilemma. There's really no reason for you to attempt to compete in that circumstance. And so there was a way to back out.

Managed in this way, an action that appears to be a straightforward and conscious violation of antitrust regulations becomes a harmless

business practice that happens to be a "technical violation." The offender
can then refer to personal history to verify the claim that they are law-
abiding. As one offender said, "Having been in the business for thirty-
three years, you don't just automatically become a criminal overnight."

Third, offenders were very critical of prosecutors who were accused
of being motivated solely by the opportunity for personal advancement
presented by winning a big case. Further, they were accused of employing
prosecution selectively and using tactics that allowed the most culpable
offenders to go free. The Department of Justice was painted as using
antitrust prosecutions for political purposes.

Finally, antitrust offenders compared their crimes to those of street
criminals: Antitrust crimes are not committed in one place and at one
time but are spatially and temporally diffuse and are intermingled with
legitimate behavior. In addition, unlike the victims of street crimes,
antitrust victims tend not to be identifiable individuals. These
characteristics are used by antitrust violators to contrast their own
behavior with that of common stereotypes of criminality. Real crimes are
pictured as discrete events that have beginnings and ends and involve
individuals who directly and purposely victimize others in a particular
place and time.

> It certainly wasn't a premeditated type of thing in our cases . . . . To
> me it's different . . . It wasn't like sitting down and planning I'm
> going to rob this bank type of thing . . . . It was just a common
> everyday way of doing business and surviving.

A consistent theme of all interviews was that the realities of the
business world made antitrust-like practices a necessity. Two sets of rules
seem to apply. There are legislatively determined rules (laws) which
govern how to conduct business affairs and there are higher rules based
on profit and survival, which define what it means to be in business in a
capitalistic society. These rules do not just regulate behavior; rather, they
constitute or create the behavior in question. If one is not trying to make
a profit or trying to keep one's business going, then one is not really "in
business." The former type of rule can be called regulative rules and the
latter, constitutive rules (Searle, 1969:33–41). In certain situations, one
may have to violate a regulative rule in order to conform to the
constitutive rule.

Trying to make a profit or survive in business is a constitutive rule
of capitalist economies. Laws governing profitmaking are regulative rules,
which can be subordinated to the rules of trying to survive and make a
profit. From the offender's point of view businesspersons in our society
are supposed to stay in business and make a profit. Thus, individuals who

violate society's laws or regulations in certain situations may conceive of themselves as acting more in accord with the central ethos of this society than if they had been strict observers of its law. An informal structure exists below the articulated legal structure, one which frequently supersedes the legal structure (see Denzin, 1977). The informal structure may define as moral and "legal" certain actions that the formal legal structure defines as immoral and "illegal."

Tax Violators

Six of those interviewed were income tax violators. Like antitrust violators, tax violators can rely upon the complexity of the tax laws and a historical tradition in which cheating on taxes is seen as not really criminal. Tax offenders claim "everybody cheats on their income tax" and present themselves as victims unlucky to have got caught. The widespread belief that tax cheating is endemic lends credence to the offender's claim to have been singled out and to be no more guilty than most people.

Tax offenders were more likely to have acted alone and were more prone to account for their offenses by referring to them as the product of either mistakes or special circumstances. Violations were presented as simple errors resulting from ignorance and/or poor record keeping. Any deliberate intention to steal from the government for personal benefit was denied.

> I didn't take the money. I have no bank account to show for all this money, where all this money is at that I was supposed to have. They never found the money, ever. There is no Swiss bank account, believe me.

> My records were strictly one big mess. That's all it was. If only I had an accountant, this wouldn't even've happened.

Other offenders justified their actions by admitting they were wrong while painting their motives as altruistic rather than criminal. Criminality was denied because they did not set out to deliberately cheat the government for personal gain. Like antitrust offenders, one tax violator distinguished between his own crime and the crimes of real criminals.

> I'm not a criminal. That is, I'm not a criminal from the standpoint of taking a gun and doing this and that. I'm a criminal from the standpoint of making a mistake, a serious mistake. . . . The thing that really got me involved in it is my feeling for the employees here,

256 Michael L. Benson

certain employees that are my right hand. In order to save them a certain amount of taxes and things like that, I'd extend money to them in cash, and the money came from these sources that I took it from. You know, cash sales and things of that nature, but practically all of it was turned over to the employees, because of my feeling for them.

None of the tax violators denied the legitimacy of the tax laws, nor did they claim that they cheated because the government is not representative of the people (Conklin, 1977:99). Rather, as a result of ignorance or for altruistic reasons, they made decisions which were criminal from a legal perspective. While they acknowledged technical criminality, they tried to show that they were not criminally motivated.

Financial Trust Violators

Four offenders were financial trust violators. Three were bank officers who embezzled or misapplied funds, and the fourth was a union official who embezzled from a union pension fund. These offenders were much more forthright about their crimes. They would not go so far as to say "I am a criminal," but they did say "What I did was wrong, was criminal, and I knew it was." Thus, the embezzlers were unusual in that they explicitly admitted responsibility for their crimes.

Unlike tax evasion or antitrust violations, embezzlement requires deliberate action by the offender and is committed for personal reasons. Embezzlement, therefore, cannot be accounted for by using the same techniques as used by tax violators or antitrust violators. It can only be explained by showing that extraordinary circumstances led to uncharacteristic behavior. Three of the offenders referred explicitly to extraordinary circumstances and presented the offense as an aberration in their life history. One said:

As a kid, I never even—you know kids will sometimes shoplift from the dime store—I never even did that. I had never stolen a thing in my life and that was what was so unbelievable about the whole thing, but there were some psychological and personal questions that I wasn't dealing with very well. I wasn't terribly happily married. I was married to a very strong-willed woman and it just wasn't working out.

A structural characteristic of embezzlement also helps the offender demonstrate an essential lack of criminality. Embezzlement is integrated into ordinary occupational routines. The illegal action does not stand out against the surrounding set of legal actions. Rather, there is a high degree of surface correspondence between legal and illegal behavior. To maintain this correspondence, the offender must exercise some restraint when committing the crime. The embezzler must be discrete in stealing; all of the money available cannot be taken without revealing the crime. Once exposed, the offender can point to this restraint as evidence of not being a real criminal. A comparison can be made with the more serious crimes that could have been committed.

> What I could have done if I had truly had a devious criminal mind and perhaps if I had been a little smarter—and I am not saying that with any degree of pride or any degree of modesty whatever, [as] it's being smarter in a bad, an evil way—I could have pulled this off on a grander scale and I might still be doing it.

Even though the offender forthrightly admits guilt, he distinguishes between himself and someone with a truly "devious criminal mind."

Contrary to Cressey's (1953:57–66) findings, none of the embezzlers claimed that their offenses were justified because they were underpaid or badly treated by their employers. Rather, attention was focused on the unusual circumstances and the offense's atypical character compared to the rest of the offender's life. This strategy is largely determined by the mechanics and organizational format of the offense. Embezzlement occurs within the organization but not for the organization. It cannot be committed accidentally or out of ignorance. It can be accounted for only by showing that the actor "was not himself" at the time of the offense or was operating under such extraordinary circumstances that embezzlement was an understandable response. This may explain why embezzlers tend to produce accounts that are viewed as more sufficient by the justice system than those produced by other offenders (Rothman and Gandossy, 1982). The only plausible option open to a convicted embezzler trying to explain his offense is to admit responsibility while justifying the action, an approach that apparently strikes a responsive chord with judges.

Fraud and False Statements

Ten offenders were convicted on a fraud or false statements charge. Unlike embezzlers, tax violators, or antitrust violators, these offenders were much more likely to deny committing any crime. Most claimed that they, personally, were innocent of any crime, although each admitted that fraud had occurred. Typically, they claimed to have been set up by associates and to have been wrongfully convicted. In this scapegoating strategy the offender attempts to paint himself as a victim by shifting the blame entirely to another party. Prosecutors were presented as being either ignorant or politically motivated.

The outright denial of any crime whatsoever is unusual. It may result from the nature of fraud. By definition, fraud involves a conscious attempt to mislead. While it is theoretically possible to accidentally violate the antitrust and tax laws, or to violate them for altruistic reasons, it is difficult to accidentally mislead someone for his or her own good. Furthermore, fraud is often an aggressively acquisitive crime. Offenders develop schemes to bilk others of money or property as an easy way to get rich. Stock swindles, fraudulent loan scams, and so on are often so large and complicated that they cannot be excused as foolish and desperate solutions to personal problems.

Furthermore, because fraud involves a deliberate attempt to mislead, the offender runs the risk of being shown to have a guilty mind, to possess the most essential element of modern conceptions of criminality: an intent to harm another. In this case the offender's inner self would be exposed as something other than presented, and all previous actions would be subject to reinterpretation. Thus defrauders are most prone to denying their crime. The cooperative and conspiratorial nature of many fraudulent schemes makes it possible to blame someone else and to present oneself as a scapegoat, claiming to have been duped by others:

> I figured I wasn't guilty, so it wouldn't be that hard to disprove it, until, as I say, I went to court and all of a sudden they start bringing in these guys out of the woodwork implicating me that I never saw. Lot of it could be proved that I never saw.

> Inwardly, I personally felt that the only crime that I committed was not telling on these guys. Not that I deliberately, intentionally committed a crime against the system. My only crime was that I should have had the guts to tell on these guys, what they were doing, rather than putting up with it and then trying to gradually get out of the system without hurting them or without them thinking I was going to snitch on them.

Of the three offenders who admitted committing crimes, two acted alone and the third acted with only one other person. Their accounts were similar to the others presented earlier and tended to focus on either the harmless nature of their violations or on the unusual circumstances that drove them to commit their crimes.

Discussion: Offenses, Accounts, and Degradation Ceremonies

The investigation, prosecution, and conviction of white-collar offenders involves a very undesirable status passage (Glaser and Strauss, 1971). The entire process is a long and drawn-out degradation ceremony with the prosecutor as the chief denouncer and the offender's family and friends as the chief witnesses. The offender is moved from the status of law-abiding citizen to that of convicted felon. Accounts are developed to defeat the process of identity transformation. They represent the offender's attempt to diminish the effect of legal transformation and to prevent its becoming a publicly validated label. The accounts developed by white-collar offenders take certain forms because they are: (1) required to defeat the success of the degradation ceremony, and (2) available, given the mechanics, history, and organizational context of the offenses.

From the data, three general patterns in accounting strategies can be identified depending on whether it is oriented toward the event (offense), the perpetrator (offender), or the denouncer (prosecutor). These are the subjects of accounts in that to be successful, a degradation ceremony requires each to be presented in a particular manner (Garfinkel, 1956). If an account giver can undermine the presentation of one or more element, then the effect of the degradation ceremony can be reduced.

Event

In order for a degradation ceremony to be successful, the event must be shown to be extraordinary, and obviously and unquestionably profane. Further, the event must indicate a pattern of behavior opposite of that expected of the normal citizen. When an account focuses on the event, therefore, the object is to remove the pejorative content from the behavior in question. Thus its similarity to accepted and routine practices must be emphasized. Alternatively, the account must portray the event as an aberration, not representative of typical behavior patterns.

Antitrust violators present the event as a normal, everyday practice. They are attempting to show that the offense is not "out of the ordinary" but normal, as is the offender. Similarly, tax violators also focus on the widespread incidence of tax violations. A practice that is widespread can hardly be considered extraordinary.

Antitrust offenders also refer to organizational loyalty and a complex business environment, tactics which have the effect of showing that the offense cannot be separated from its environment as an inherently and unquestionably profane event. It is presented in such a manner that its dialectical counterpart (Garfinkel, 1956) is not immediately obvious. In one sense, this attempted normalization has not succeeded as the offender has been convicted. But in a wider societal context, it may have succeeded. To the extent that white-collar offenders are not ostracized by family, friends, and business associates and can continue in their occupational careers, they have maintained their normalcy.

The embezzler faces a different problem when confronted with proof of the offense because it cannot be referred to as routine and/or of widespread prevalence. Rather, it must be shown to be an aberration from the offender's regular behavior patterns, a unique, one-time-only mistake.

Perpetrator

Perpetrators must be characterized similarly to events. Their true character must be revealed as extraordinary and unquestionably profane. They must be presented as all of one piece. The multifaceted and ambiguous nature of their personality must be denied and any sense of chance or accident made inconceivable. Thus, when the perpetrator is the subject of the account, the account giver must show that no matter how the event is eventually characterized, it is not indicative of true character. Account givers must separate themselves from their offense and emphasize its unique character. Above all, offenders must show that they are ordinary, understandable individuals. This strategy is plausibly used by tax violators and embezzlers.

> I'm sure you must have seen my background. I was in government service. I've had federal army service for thirty three years, and my record is not only excellent but outstanding in all these particular fields. . . . I think in all my years I made one mistake and this was the mistake I made.

If an offender can show that the offense was an aberration, regardless of whether it is the result of ignorance, confusion, or bad judgment, the criminal label can be avoided. Antitrust violators cannot really present their offenses as wholly uncharacteristic aberrations, but they can emphasize their confusion over what was really criminal and their ignorance of the law.

Embezzlers also focus on their role as perpetrators rather than attempting to justify their offenses. But, unlike tax violators, they forthrightly admit responsibility for their crimes. They have no option because the crime cannot be committed by accident or to help the organization. Thus, embezzlers are left with showing that they were not themselves when the offense was committed. Special circumstances or extraordinary pressures are referred to and the offense is claimed to be out of character, an aberration, a momentary lapse, or insignificant when compared to the embezzler's otherwise exemplary and impeccable moral career.

Embezzlers and other white-collar offenders must show that the offense is not part of a pattern. It must be presented as a one-time-only break from the real pattern of their life. The lack of a prior criminal record and a personal history of accomplishment greatly facilitates the typical white-collar offender's ability to establish this with a modicum of legitimacy.

There is some evidence that a white-collar offender's ability to show that the crime in question is an aberration in an otherwise impeccable life has a mitigating effect on societal reactions, and can result in reduced sentences from judges (Wheeler et al., 1982; Mann et al., 1980). The effect of impeccability on sanctions was independent and opposite to that of social status.

Denouncer

The denouncer must not seem to be personally involved in the case or display self-interest in the outcome, but must be seen as a representative of sacred values and claim to speak for them for the public good.

Antitrust offenders and those convicted of fraud were most prone to condemn their condemners. They claimed that the prosecutors assigned to their cases were motivated by personal interest rather than a desire to defend social or legal values, and that they were singled out for political or other reasons that had nothing to do with the harmfulness of their behavior.

The proactive nature of many white-collar investigations may undermine the denouncer's status as a personally disinterested public servant. Unlike street crimes, the prosecutor is often involved in the early stages of investigation for many white-collar offenses (Katz, 1979b). In their accounts, offenders present the prosecutor's active role in directing the investigation as evidence of a personal commitment to convict somebody for something. The practice of "focusing" on a particular industry or segment of the economy is recast by offenders as evidence that they, not the offense itself, have been the targets of the judicial system and thus that their behavior is not inherently contrary to unquestionable values. In addition, the checkered history of antitrust litigation, the waxing and waning of antitrust prosecutions with changes in presidential administrations and with the political fortunes of big business (Nader and Green, 1972), is available as an accounting resource.

Complete Denial

Complete denial of all wrongdoing was rare. Those convicted of fraud were more likely than the other offenders to completely deny committing any crime at all. This may result from the structure of the offense of fraud whose complex and conspiratorial nature undermines attempts to present it as a response to desperate circumstances. In defrauding another, an offender falsely pretends to be trustworthy. In addition, by means of deceit, others are induced to act contrary to their own best interests. In this sense fraud is a more aggressive crime than embezzlement. Once fraud is proven, it is difficult for the offender to admit a role in it and maintain a noncriminal identity. The only option is to deny involvement altogether, present oneself as a scapegoat, and shift the blame to another party.

Summary and Implications

This study of convicted white-collar offenders has examined their accounts of their crimes. Attention was given to the techniques used by offenders to deny their criminality and to maintain a legitimate persona. Accounts appear to be structured by the nature of the offense, its organizational format and history, and by the requirement that they undermine the conditions of successful degradation ceremonies. The most consistent and strongly emphasized theme was the denial of criminal intent.

In effect, offenders attempt to adjust the "normative lens" (Wheeler, 1984) through which society views their offenses. Although societal reaction to crimes and criminals varies, two elements of significance are (1) the seriousness of the offense, and (2) the blameworthiness of the offender. Any offender interested in avoiding a criminal label must minimize the blameworthiness and seriousness of his actions to a degree such that the label "criminal" will be regarded as inappropriate.

The presentability of an offense may play an important role in the decision to offend. For individuals interested in maintaining a noncriminal identity, offenses that can be made to appear less serious and less blameworthy will be more attractive than others. White-collar crimes are often structured or organizationally situated such that they are more malleable in this regard than traditional crimes.

The partial legitimacy of the outcomes of some white-collar crimes seems to play an important role in the offender's minimization of seriousness. Some antitrust offenses, tax violations, and false statements made to lending institutions may shore up a failing business or provide stability in employment. The congruence of legitimacy and illegitimacy that characterizes the commission of white-collar and corporate crimes (Clinard and Quinney, 1973) may be reproduced in the final products of those crimes and in the justifications presented by offenders.

The frequently expressed belief in widespread illegality fosters a callous attitude to criminal behavior (Denzin, 1977). This belief leads to the view that certain "normal" types of law violations are not really serious crimes. The belief in widespread illegality extends into society, which offenders seem to assume is at the mercy of rampant and unpunished street criminality. The lack of identifiable individual victims has been suggested as one of the reasons for the lack of societal concern with white-collar criminality. This characteristic of white-collar offenses may also be used by offenders before they commit their crimes to denying the harm.

The complexity of the laws and regulations governing the business world also relieves the offender's sense of blameworthiness. Crimes committed out of ignorance or inattention to detail are less offensive to the social conscience than those deliberately committed. Unlike common street crimes, it is possible to accidentally violate laws that govern businesses, the professions, and industry. The motives underlying such conduct cannot automatically be inferred from the conduct. An offense that would be considered blameworthy if committed knowingly may be excusable, or at least understandable, if committed out of ignorance. Complexity gives rise to an ambiguity in the connection between the act and its motive. This may allow offenders to persuade themselves and others that the motive was not really criminal, so the act was not really a crime.

Such a process may even work in advance of the crime when offenders maintain a concerted ignorance of the law or of the activities of subordinates. Individuals involved in organizational crimes are frequently aware that the crime may eventually come to light (Katz, 1979a). In spite of this possibility offenders may choose to participate, provided that they can construct anticipatory defenses that will allow them to eventually deny blameworthiness. Many features of corporate organization facilitate the building of these "metaphysical escapes" (Katz, 1979a). In other words, offenders may purposely attempt to structure crimes so that the connection between act and motive remains ambiguous and deniable.

Those who commit crimes outside an organizational context or who act against organizations (embezzlers) may attempt to reduce their blameworthiness by setting the crime within the context of an otherwise impeccable life. If a crime can be shown to be an aberration, then its importance as an indicator of the offender's true character is dramatically reduced. His or her personality can be shown to have both good and bad points with the good outnumbering the bad. The obvious inconsistency of the offender's conviction vis-à-vis the rest of his or her life may be handled by family, friends, and society by denying the implications of the offender's actions in order to maintain a consistent and favorable attitude (Geis, 1982:97).

As with the use of concerted ignorance, the process of setting the crime within a context of impeccability may be used by offenders prior to the illegal act as a neutralization technique. A lifetime of socially acceptable and desirable behavior in one arena is used to excuse an occasional indiscretion in another.

What needs to be determined is how effective these strategies are in helping the offender avoid stigmatization as a criminal—that is, avoid being thought of and treated like a criminal by others. If certain classes of offenders can commit crimes, be convicted, and yet still, through the use of appropriate accounting strategies, avoid being labeled as criminals, then one of the primary functions of the criminal law and the criminal justice system—the symbolic separation of the offender from the community—is negated. A moral environment is thereby perpetuated in which the symbolic consequences of criminal behavior for some offenders can largely be ignored.

15

The Misplaced Role of Rational Choice in Neutralization Theory

John E. Hamlin

In 1957 Gresham Sykes and David Matza made a small but lasting contribution to criminological theory. Their attempt to clarify one of Sutherland's propositions still commands the attention of criminologists in spite of weak empirical support. In his rendition of differential association theory Sutherland (Sutherland and Cressey, (1955] 1980) suggested that learning deviant behavior requires that technical knowledge be communicated and that justifications permitting the application of techniques must also be learned. A person must be exposed to "motives, drives, rationalizations, and attitudes" for violating norms (1980:180). If people know how to break the law (or other norms of conduct) but see the behavior as inappropriate, they will likely refrain from it. If they believe there are justifiable reasons for the transgression but do not have the knowledge to commit it, they will either not commit it, learn through trial and error, or bungle the job and suffer the consequences.

Sykes and Matza ([1957] 1980) described what delinquents learned as motives, drives, rationalizations, and attitudes as "techniques of neutralization," identifying five types: (1) denial of responsibility, (2) denial of injury, (3) denial of the victim, (4) condemnation of condemners, and (5) appeal to higher loyalties. These techniques of neutralization allow individuals to bridge the gap between legally defined appropriate and inappropriate behavior.

Neutralization's Place in Deviance Theory

Neutralization theory contributes to two broader traditions in deviance theory. The tradition stemming from Sutherland, called social learning

Edited and abridged from *Criminology*, Volume 26(3):425–38 (1988).

theory (Akers, 1977), implies that deviants, especially juvenile delinquents, must neutralize moral prescriptions *prior* to committing deviance. It is because the standards have been removed or qualified that deviance is possible (Frazier, 1976:59; Pelfrey, 1980:34; Pfohl, 1985a:249).

A second tradition, social control theory (Hirschi, 1969) also utilizes the assumptions of neutralization:

> The apparent methodological difficulty with this [denial of responsibility] and several other techniques of neutralization, both at the level of on-the-spot observation and in the analysis of survey data, is that they may appear only *after* the delinquent act(s) in question has been committed. They may thus be seen as after-the-fact rationalizations rather than before-the-fact neutralizations. The question boils down to this: Which came first, the delinquent act or the belief justifying it? (1969:207–8)

Hirschi states that it is logical that what was an after-the-fact rationalization in one instance may be a causal neutralization of delinquency in the next instance.

Neutralization's Place in Sociological Theory

Neutralization theory stems from the tradition of symbolic interactionism. In the 1940s and 1950s sociologists studied the relationship between linguistic expression and its object. Mills ([1940]1972) and later Gerth and Mills (1953) established the sociological understanding of motives as distinct from their meaning in psychology. Motives were expressed after the act and did not rise from some internal wellspring of human inspiration. Motives were socially established vocabularies, culturally learned and readily available, to be used as soon as the situation required rationalization. Scott and Lyman (1972) further distinguish the sociological meaning of motives from psychological meanings. They prefer to use the term "accounts" rather than motive and place these expressions at the end of social action, not causally prior to it.

The relationship between vocabularies of motives and techniques of neutralization is important for understanding the arguments presented here. The connection between actual techniques of neutralization and vocabularies of motives is as much methodological as it is theoretical. Techniques are the operationalization of vocabularies of motives. If a particular acceptable vocabulary is economic, then an appropriate neutralization technique surrounding a theft incident might involve such notions as "everybody cheats on their taxes." Figure 1 shows three levels

Figure 1. Relationship between Techniques of Neutralization and Vocabularies of Motives

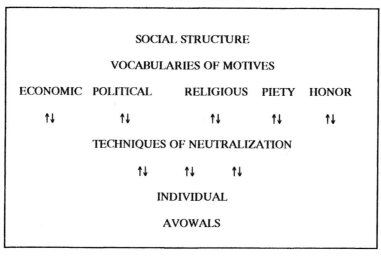

of conceptualization, from the individual level to the social structural level, with techniques of neutralization acting as a linking mechanism between avowals at the level of person and motives at the level of structure. In short, techniques are one set of linking mechanism connecting the individual to the structure of society.

Changes in the vocabularies of motive are unidirectional. The use of techniques and concrete individual statements will reinforce existing vocabularies or indicate movement from one set of motives to another, but actual changes in vocabularies result from historical-structural change.

Motives exist prior to most human action simply because they exist in the cultural structure. However, Sykes and Matza seem to imply that the motives come first and must necessarily imply rational action on the part of youths. This approach is much more psychological than sociological and is thus a source of many problems when testing neutralization theory. Sykes and Matza claim that according to Sutherland, motives come prior to the deviant act and sociologists have missed the theoretical point by not pursuing this assertion further. What Sutherland said was (Sutherland and Cressey, [1955] 1980:180): "In our American society these definitions are almost always mixed, with the consequence that we have culture conflict in relation to the legal codes." People learn alternative definitions of behavior as a result of diversity in society. This does not mean that an individual will consciously think of one definition rather than another prior to committing a particular act.

268   *John E. Hamlin*

Testing Neutralization

Validation of neutralization theory has met with continual difficulty. Minor (1980) addressed the problems associated with research in the area and noted that all the studies conducted to date fell short of any real standard of proof, supportive or not, of neutralization theory. Minor's (1980) endeavors to test Sykes and Matza's theory using 1973 data also fell short of supporting neutralization. Further research by Minor (1981) provided limited support but the sample was so methodologically inadequate that even this limited support must be seriously questioned.

Minor turns to various explanations to account for his findings. He rejects Hirschi's observation, itself consistent with sociological research on motives, that actions precede motives, not the other way around (Minor, 1981:310). Yet Minor neglects to consider that Sykes and Matza were theoretically wrong about techniques of neutralization. Conceptually, it is important to return to the theoretical component of neutralization theory, especially the assumptions on which it is constructed.

Neutralization Theory

Sykes and Matza (1980:210–11) created a fundamental problem when they made a commonsense assumption about motives preceding human actions.

> These justifications are commonly described as rationalizations. They are viewed as following deviant behavior and as protecting the individual from self-blame and the blame of others after the act. But there is also reason to believe that they precede deviant behavior and make deviant behavior possible. It is this possibility that Sutherland mentioned only in passing and that other writers have failed to exploit from the viewpoint of sociological theory. Disapproval flowing from internalized norms and conforming others in the social environment is neutralized, turned back or deflected in advance. Social controls that serve to check or inhibit deviant motivational patterns are rendered inoperative, and the individual is freed to engage in delinquency without serious damage to his self-image. In this sense, the delinquent both has his cake and eats it too, for he remains committed to the dominant normative system and yet so qualifies its imperatives that violations are "acceptable" if not "right."

Providing rationality to the delinquent act may be uncalled for. Reliance on causal relationships and instrumental thinking leads to the assumption that people have reasons for what they do. It is just as likely that a great deal of human behavior is nonrational. We provide rationality to the act after it has occurred. Sykes and Matza ignore their own insight that norms are only "qualified guides," not imperatives for social action. Behavior may be more controlled by structure and habit than by reason. Matza (1964) has stated that juveniles drift in and out of delinquent behavior, flirting with both delinquent and nondelinquent behavior indiscriminately. Why delinquent behavior has to be tied to neutralization in a causal sense can only be attributed to the positivism inherent in U.S. sociology and, perhaps, the perceived importance of instrumental reason in modern industrial societies.

Instrumental reason is only one of the many significant features contained in the structure of industrial societies. These societies are complex and highly differentiated, predicated on the subdividing of human activity into numerous processes, the creation of a social and technical division of labor, which often seems unrelated (Durkheim, [1897] 1951). One result of the division of labor is alienation (Marx, [1844] 1977). In an alienated society the process and product of our social relations appear as something completely unrelated to our everyday activity; no longer are we in command of the processes and structural arrangements that we as human beings set in motion. Through a process of objectification we produce a society that appears totally apart from our activities and energy (Berger and Luckmann, 1967). Orwell's (1949) conception of history—those that control the past control the future and those that control the present control the past—is vitally important. We create a conception about the rationality of human behavior that fits current social relationships, redefine the past in those terms, and then predict and orchestrate the future in that image. Rationality in an instrumental sense is not likely to direct the behavior of young people or adults. The assumption that moral constraints need to be circumvented prior to an act assumes that individuals are making choices about behavior prior to committing the act. As human beings become more controlled, human action as purposeful activity is negated. The world appears as Weber's iron cage (Mitzman, 1969:26) only surrounded with the illusion of free will and rational choice, as in Orwell's *1984*.

The Structural Existence of Vocabularies of Motives

The morality of any social action is represented by motives characteristic of the specific historical context. If motives are conceived of as reasons for, and/or causes of, social action, they should logically correspond to their referent. Motives, however, are at best mere reflections, or afterthoughts, of social action. It is only through their identity with a particular social action that meaning is given to them. For example, Anne Hutchinson's actions against the established religion and political leaders in Massachusetts Bay in the 1630s were cloaked in religious terminology and focused on the proper interpretation of the Bible (see Chambliss, 1976; Erickson, 1966). The inequality that women experienced could not be expressed in feminist terms. Anne's actions and corresponding motives fit the historical and social context in which she was embedded. Did Anne's expressed motives free her from the moral constraints of a patriarchal Puritan society? Or did she merely conduct her business until her behavior was questioned, which resulted in the necessity to justify her behavior?

The universal applicability of motives exists to the extent that they no longer have instance-specific meaning. They have become mere abstractions to be used in multiple situations. Motives seem to originate from individual subjects, yet they are commonly applied by diverse individuals. The fact that we commonly share meanings attributed to motives indicates that motives do not originate with individuals but, indeed, have a social life of their own. Motives that exist exclusively in social reality become privatized and individualized when we overlook their uniquely social character.

Historical and structural contexts provide us with motives, which in turn reflect our conception of morality and truth. Motives, reflecting human action, simultaneously create a tendency for historical and structural change. Thus, the structural condition of a given historical period provides us with motives to legitimate social action. When an individual is in the process of committing many acts, motives are virtually nonexistent. After the acts are committed, motives provide explanations and simultaneously legitimize those acts. Those motives may then become causes for further action (Hirschi, 1969). The historically structured conditions may provide us with the appropriate motives to be used, but because social structure continuously undergoes change, so will the motives. Either the motives change or they become functionally incompatible with social-structural conditions of life. Motives are substantially rational and only incidentally instrumentally rational. One contradiction of industrialized life is that rationality has come to be defined in instrumental terms; rationality is more brutally calculating and idiosyncratic, while conditions of life become more of an iron cage governed by substantive rationality, albeit faulty.

Motives appear and can be defined as genuinely personal when used by individual actors. We perceive the motives as truth (except when we suspect someone to be lying), that is, we assume the motive is the real cause (means) of action (goals) for the individual. This aspect of motives was disputed years ago by Durkheim in his study of suicide ([1897] 1951). We must constantly recognize that motives do not materialize out of thin air at the individual's discretion but are drawn from a structurally determined vocabulary of motives.

Motives are utilized and changed in the process of legitimating social action and have very little to do with the actual cause of the action. We generate the motive in response to a "question situation" and logically put the motive prior to the action. This prior sequencing is a fallacy. Motives are a product of social action. It is not until after a social action, or more precisely not until action needs to be legitimized, that motives are produced. In an alienated society motives are denied their structural characteristics and conceptually insulated from action on the macrolevel. They become reunited on an individual level through the "question situation." If social action was part of a rational society, motives would be incorporated in the action itself.

Motives mask the creative aspects of knowledge to the extent that they legitimize social action by reference to established and static conceptions of social organization. By conceiving of society as orderly, static, and harmonious, corresponding motives provide a picture of human activity as orderly. Human social action that is not defined as orderly is perceived as disruptive, and motives are used to justify the necessity for that disruption, simultaneously carrying the connotations that the universe will again be brought back into accordance with social statics. *Motives thus become a legitimation of the societal level for variations from the acceptable definition of reality without calling that reality into serious question.* At the individual level acceptable or unacceptable behavior makes very little difference, except to affirm or deny the validity of the vocabulary of motives being used.

If industrialized societies were relatively stable and orderly, there would logically be little need to profess motives, since motives arise in a "question" situation (Mills, 1972:395). The "question" pinpoints situations of dilemmas, crises, and conflicts. To the extent that individuals practice alternative paths in the process of becoming, conflicts and dilemmas arise, leading to "question situations," which in turn mandate resolution and the reestablishment of legitimate lines of action. Within short periods of history, ideological legitimation expressed through motives will not change dramatically unless conflicts are acute enough to bring about radical change in structure, for example, revolutions.

Vocabularies of motives related to major social categories, for example, economic, religious, or political, may serve as a barometer of diversity and change in all societies. Contradictions inherent in the political economy produce conflicts and dilemmas in society that mandate resolutions (Chambliss, 1979). In the process of resolving conflicts and dilemmas, verbalized motives present themselves in a clear and meaningful fashion. During the attempts at resolution, participants are forced to consider and examine the situation. They come up with a definition of the situation (Thomas, [1931] 1972). At this point existing motives can be called upon to supply a rational explanation of any situation involving action. According to Mills (1972:395), motives are needed because people

> live in immediate acts of experience and their attentions are directed outside themselves until acts are in some way frustrated. It is then that awareness of self and motive occur. The "question" is a lingual index of such conditions. The avowal and imputation of motives are features of such conversations as arise in "question" situations.

Certain situations or arenas of conflict necessitate a transference from one set of established motives to another, or in particular circumstances, the creation of a new set of motives (Mills, 1972:396). This may materialize as a result of renaming the situation (Strauss, [1959] 1972:382), or because the social structures have changed to the degree that traditional motives are unacceptable or the questioning agents are more powerful.

The immediate circumstances in which actors define the situation gives the appearance that participants pick and choose motives according to some set of intrinsic criteria. The vocabulary of motives, from which individual participants pick and choose, however, is structurally provided and cannot be taken for granted or understood outside its historical and structural context (Mills, 1972:400). Within any situation the number of verbalized motives will be large, yet are unlikely to stray outside the more general vocabularies of motives corresponding to ideological and material conditions. The vocabularies of motives include motives on the fringe of generally accepted motives. The use of, and reliance on, fringe motives is not likely unless conflicts are serious enough to mandate the need for marginal motives while still remaining in the realm of the generally accepted vocabulary of motives. If conflict reaches the point that qualitative changes are inevitable, new vocabularies of motives will be created to correspond to changing ideological and material conditions.

Not all situations, dilemmas, or conflicts are equally important. It becomes crucial to distinguish the elements at any given period in time having the greatest impact on shaping, directing, and creating history. Mills looked at people in power, those who control economic and political reality. Such people, institutions, and structures are instrumental in initially creating and sustaining vocabularies of motives (Mills, 1972:398).

Delinquency is often considered a minor conflict, although at times crime and delinquency are defined as a real threat to society. In the life of juveniles there exists a hierarchy of authority figures (adults) who can successfully label their behavior as wrong. Yet only at certain times do very powerful individuals and groups create the codes that other adults enforce against them.

Situations, dilemmas, and conflicts also involve varying degrees of changing vocabularies of motives. The more the potential for dramatic social or behavioral change, the higher the likelihood of a complete change in vocabularies of motives. The actual degree of change and direction of change depend on the nature of any conflict resolution. Nevertheless, vocabularies of motives that arise prior to resolution and at the outcome of the resolution process should result in an accurate indication of potential change. One must realize that motives change in the course of resolving conflicts. For example, the motives expressed by a juvenile on arrest are likely to change by the time of his or her court appearance, and change again during the adjudication process. As charges change, expressed motives necessarily change as a result of redefining the behavior that renders previously selected motives inadequate.

Sykes and Matza suggest that certain behaviors lend themselves to specific neutralization techniques. Minor's research found mixed results here. It is possible that the changing definitions of the behavior required a scramble for acceptable motives, because the behavior is not that static, nor directly connected to expressed motives.

The need to provide motives initially is one indication that change is occurring. Also, the types of accounts applied to social action are additional indications of change. For example, if justifications are given for a particular act or behavior, it is implied that the act or behavior had a positive value (Scott and Lyman, 1972:406). As the conflict situation becomes more serious accounts take on characteristics of excuses, as individuals begin to deny responsibility. The final indication of change would be a complete change in vocabularies of motives.

The importance of vocabularies of motives is to be found not so much in the social-psychological aspects of motives but rather in the historical-structural context in which those motives are created and manifest themselves (Mills, 1972:400). The task is to place vocabularies of motives within the dialectical process illuminating the degree and nature of change in society.

In a society that is characterized by contradictions and conflicts, the structure of society has a specific rationality. As a result of diversity in society, motives present themselves differently to individuals. What is rational to one person is a rationalization to another person (Mills, 1972:400). But it is just those disputes surrounding conflict situations, placed in their historical and structural context and perceived in a dialectical relationship, that lead to insightful social analysis. When social life is rational, human action will be rational and corresponding motives will be rational. As long as language reflects the expression of the act, behavior, or object, and neglects its essence, motives will always contain the tendency to be mere rationalization or ideology.

Neutralizing Cultural Norms—Again

Sykes and Matza's formulation of neutralization is different in form from Mills's vocabularies of motives or Scott and Lyman's formulation of accounts. Sykes and Matza operate in the realm of social psychology, while Mills is much more structural, even in his social psychology. Also, Sykes and Matza claim that neutralization takes place prior to the deviant action and hence allows it to happen by supplanting moral constraints. Individuals must perceive the reason why it is acceptable to violate norms in a situation in which they would usually abide by those norms. They neutralize the moral commitment.

Inasmuch as vocabularies of motives exist structurally, to say they precede an individual's action is to state the obvious. The real question is: Do techniques, drawn from existing motives, really suspend moral constraints for the actor prior to or after the action is committed? Mills is correct in saying that motives come into play after a "question situation." Thus, by extension, so will techniques of neutralization. Another important question yet to be answered is: Where do delinquents learn the techniques of neutralization? In what context are they learned? Clearly, techniques are not a subcultural set of motives different from those of the rest of society, rather they are operationalized motives. If human behavior is moment to moment, it is probable that behavior is only consciously considered after the fact. It may be the case that motives are learned as part of normal socialization for all youths, just learned in a different context. It is possible that actual statements (further operationalized motives) might reflect subcultural, class, gender, or ethnic differences.

Conclusion

Techniques of neutralization are valuable tools for analyzing delinquent behavior, but not as they affect the breakdown of moral constraints. Rather, techniques are important in neutralizing guilt after the "question situation." For many juveniles the actions they commit are not defined by them in moral terms until someone forces them to define their actions that way, or until someone else defines their actions for them. The guilt individuals will feel after being told that what they did was wrong or that they themselves are bad can be destructive of social identity. Justifications and excuses neutralize guilt and enable individuals to continue to feel good about themselves, at least at a functional level.

A more sophisticated analysis of just how people operationalize vocabularies of motives, how motives relate to social structure, how people come to accept motives as causal is awaited. Further research in this area may help sociologists bridge the gulf that exists between social-structural analysis and social-psychological analysis. Further research into the relationship between vocabularies of motives and techniques of neutralization would help overcome the tendency toward overrelativism and almost total reliance on social-psychological orientations to the almost complete neglect of structural models.

16

Social Control Theories of Delinquency: Direct Parental Controls

L. Edward Wells and Joseph H. Rankin

Social control theory seems to dominate the theoretical landscape in criminology, arguably being the most important theory in present-day criminology and criminal justice science. Certainly, it is the perspective most favored by the general public for thinking about the "problem of crime," as well as by politicians for generating new policies. Calls for new and better models to both explain and reduce crime typically rely on ideas of restraint, restriction, discipline, deterrence and discouragement, all of which are implicit in social control theory.

Beyond its broad appeal in popular and political commentary, social control theory pervades new theoretical development, and it features prominently in empirical research. Many new theoretical developments embody a version of social control, either by design or implicitly by content, not least because of their common assumptions about humans as rational beings. Social control-related theories include, for example: rational choice theory (Cornish and Clarke, 1986a), situational crime prevention and environmental design theories (Clarke, 1992, 1995), routine activities theory (Felson, 1986a, 1994), self-control theory (Gottfredson and Hirschi, 1990), control balance theory (Tittle, 1995), life-course development theory (Sampson and Laub, 1993), antisocial personality theories (Eysenck, 1996; Lykken, 1995), evolutionary psychology (Daly and Wilson, 1988), power-control theory (Hagan, 1989, 1991), and biosocial theories focusing on a variety of factors from neurological deficiencies (Raine, 1993) to IQ deficiencies (Herrnstein and Murray, 1994). Importantly, social control processes are also a prominent component in a number of "integrated theories" (e.g. Colvin and Pauly, 1983; Elliott et al., 1985; Thornberry, 1987; Braithwaite, 1989).

Edited and abridged from *Criminology*, Volume 26(2):263–85 (1988).

This ubiquity is perhaps not surprising, given that the concept of social control is so fundamental to the very idea of social science. Theorists from E. A. Ross (1901) to Jack Gibbs (1989) have maintained that sociology is essentially the study of social control, with Gibbs arguing specifically that social control is sociology's "central notion." Even some critical theorists have acknowledged that "disciplinary technology" is pervasive to social institutions and that, following Foucault (1977), social control is a central feature of both modern and postmodern social order (Henry, 1994).

What is the core idea that distinguishes social control theory from other explanations? The defining idea of social control theory is the *control premise*, which assumes that while human behavior can be viewed as a result of both motivations and restraints (or impulses and controls), it is theoretically more fruitful to focus on variations in restraints to explain orderly behavioral events. That is, *conformity* rather than crime is the issue to be explained (Hirschi, 1969), and it is to be explained through the exercise of social control. Crime and delinquency are seen as errors or failures of this control process. However, different versions of social control theory focus on various "modes of control" or control processes thought to have the greatest restrictive effects on behavior. Two versions of this theory, Hirschi's (1969) theory of the "social bond" and Nye's (1958) version of the control process, have been particularly important in attempts to explain juvenile delinquency.

Social Control Theories and Delinquency

Probably the most widely cited and tested theory of delinquency is Hirschi's (1969) "social bond" version of control theory, which depicts the family as the major source of attachment to the conventional social order. However, the emphasis on testing Hirschi's model has turned attention away from earlier and more inclusive conceptualizations of social control, such as Nye (1958). Recent considerations of control theory (e.g., Hirschi, 1983; Patterson, 1980; Wilson and Herrnstein, 1985) indicate that a more complete view of social control is necessary. The aim in this article is to consider the relation between delinquency and a somewhat forgotten concept in control theory—what Nye (1958) calls "direct controls."

A number of control perspectives explain delinquency (or more accurately, they explain conformity) by variations in juveniles' "ties" to the conventional social order (e.g., Briar and Piliavin, 1965; Hirschi, 1969; Nye, 1958; Reckless, 1967; Reiss, 1951). According to Hirschi's (1969) model, these ties (or "bonds") have four components: attachment, involvement, belief, and commitment. These components are positively related to conformity (and to each other) and are thought to have independent effects on delinquency. The two components most closely related conceptually to parental controls are attachment and involvement.

"Attachment" refers to the strength of one's ties to parents, peers, and school. The premise is that individuals who are not strongly attached to others are also insensitive to their opinions. Thus, they are not bound by others' norms and are free to deviate. Alternatively, those juveniles who closely identify with, and who are close to or have positive affect for, their parents are more likely to take their feelings and opinions into account when and if a delinquent act is contemplated. As such, attachment is essentially a social-psychological concept, involving the motivational value of social approval and imitation.

A juvenile may also be so "involved" in conventional activities that he or she could not even find the time for delinquent activities. The idea here is that if juveniles can be kept busy and "off the streets," then they will not have time to get into trouble. Almost by definition, a juvenile who is studying, playing baseball, or spending time with family in other conventional activities (e.g., picnics, vacations, watching television) is not violating the law.

Nye's (1958) depiction of control theory is more inclusive, identifying four types of social control: (1) direct control, based on the application (or threat) of punishments and rewards to gain compliance with conventional norms; (2) indirect control, primarily based on affectional attachment to or identification with conventional persons (especially parents); (3) internalized control, based on the development of autonomous patterns of conformity located in the individual personality, self-concept, or conscience; and (4) control over opportunities for conventional and deviant activities whereby compliance results from restricted choices or alternatives. Although direct restraints can take many forms (e.g., formal laws or informal customs) and can be imposed or enforced by a variety of individuals in different social roles (e.g., police, teachers, peers), Nye viewed the family as the closest and most important agency of direct control.

Hirschi's (1969) concepts of attachment and belief correspond conceptually to Nye's concepts of indirect and internalized controls, except that Hirschi locates the conscience in the bond to others rather than making it part of the individual personality. Hirschi's concept of involvement and Nye's concept of direct control have some conceptual overlap, but they clearly are not identical. Although the premise behind involvement is "time" ("idle hands are the devil's workshop"), direct controls are more concerned with the physical restriction and surveillance of behaviors. Increased involvement in conventional activities does tend to increase the accessibility of youthful behavior to monitoring and supervision by parents, but it includes other elements of control as well. The notion of involvement is conceptually more ambiguous and complex.

Both Nye and Hirschi argued that for adolescent children, the utility of direct monitoring and supervision by parents is probably limited, because youths in this age period are relatively autonomous from their parents and more involved in peer networks. Although Nye found an inverse relation between self-reported delinquency and several measures of parental monitoring, he suggested that its potential for control was limited: "Since there are many times when the child is outside the sphere of direct control, it cannot be effective by itself" (Nye, 1958:7). The implication is that the major impact of the family will be through other forms of control—principally, indirect ones.

Similarly, Hirschi argued that direct parental controls offer little effect in controlling delinquent behaviors beyond that already offered through attachments or indirect controls: "So-called "direct control" is not, except as a limiting case, of much substantive or theoretical importance. The important consideration is whether the parent is psychologically present when temptation to commit a crime occurs" (1969:88).

Research on Direct Controls

Early research supports the view that adolescent behaviors are generally not affected by direct parental controls. Items measuring the amount of time talking with parents, engaging in various activities with parents, and working around the house indicate the degree to which juveniles will be within the sphere of direct parental control. Such variables are inversely related to delinquency but uniformly weak and not statistically significant (e.g., Hirschi, 1969:88n17). Similarly, the correlations between various indicators of involvement (e.g., after-school jobs, sports activities, club memberships, hobbies, extracurricular school activities) and delinquent behavior reveal few statistically reliable relations (e.g., Hirschi, 1969; Rankin, 1977). Measures of adolescent freedom and autonomy (e.g., frequency of dating, number of evenings "out" per week, availability of a car, freedom to dress as desired) show similar patterns of association with delinquency.

Structural Variables

Other empirical evidence on direct control by parents relies on proxy variables, such as broken homes, mother's employment, and family size as substitute indicators of (the loss of) direct control. For instance, the literature on *broken homes* and delinquency is generally consistent with the views of Nye and Hirschi, based on the assumption that loss of one (or more) parents results in less direct control over adolescent behaviors. Recent reviews (e.g., Rankin, 1983; Rosen and Neilson, 1982; Wells and Rankin, 1985) suggest that, except for relatively trivial offenses (e.g., running away and truancy), the relation between broken homes and delinquency is negligible.

Despite the purportedly harmful consequences of *mother's employment* on delinquency, there is little evidence of such effects. Most studies have found little or no association (e.g., Reige, 1972; Roy, 1963), particularly when other family variables confounded with employment are controlled (Glueck and Glueck, 1957; Nye, 1958; Hirschi, 1969).

One consistent research finding is the positive association between *family size* and delinquency (see Hirschi, 1985). A variety of theoretical processes can be hypothesized to explain this relationship (see Loeber and Stouthamer-Loeber, 1986): (1) parents with larger families have more difficulty in disciplining and supervising their children (i.e., less "direct" control); (2) a greater economic strain is placed on parents with larger families, leading to a greater risk of poverty and overcrowding; (3) parents with larger families are more likely to delegate child rearing to older siblings, who may not have the requisite skills for such a task; and (4) larger families may increase the risk of exposure to a delinquent sibling. As with the "broken home" and "working mother" variables, however, the association between family size and delinquency is exceedingly small (Rosen, 1985).

In sum, although broken homes, working mothers, and large families have provided convenient ideological targets, their actual empirical impacts on delinquency appear negligible. The difficulty in generalizing from these findings, however, is that such variables involve structural conditions that are only inferentially and indeterminately tied to direct control. At best, they provide very crude indicators of the loss of direct parental control.

Recent Research

More recently, however, a few delinquency researchers appear to have "rediscovered" direct parental controls. In a study that assessed the relative explanatory power of key elements of four theories of delinquency, Smith and Paternoster (1987) included two measures of parental supervision ("How often do your parents know 'where you are'/'whom you are with' when you are away from home?") as reflective of social control theory's bond of family attachment. Cernkovich and

Giordano (1987) used a similar measure to assess the relative impact of various family elements on delinquency, and Hagan et al. (1985) examined comparable parental measures to test Hagan's "power-control" theory of delinquency.

These three studies all found statistically significant relations between direct parental controls and delinquency. Indeed, the effect of direct controls on delinquency was just as great as that of indirect controls or attachments (see Cernkovich and Giordano, 1987). This finding is somewhat unexpected, given our discussion of previous research. We suggest that there are at least three conceptually distinct aspects of direct parental controls.

A Reconceptualization

Conceptually, a fuller explication of the notion of direct control is required—what it includes and what its conceptual structure might be. Indeed, the conceptual and empirical distinction between direct and indirect parental controls is often confused and blurred (e.g., see Rosen, 1985; Wilson and Herrnstein, 1985). What we call "direct parental control" involves the instrumental control of children's behaviors through the use of rewards and punishments. It is "coercive" and mostly negative, aimed at inhibiting undesired responses. In this analysis, we use the term "discipline" to refer more specifically to the administration of punishment. Drawing upon developmental psychology (e.g., Patterson, 1980, 1982), we suggest that "direct parental control" actually has three basic components: normative regulation, monitoring, and punishment.

First, *normative regulation* refers to the process by which parents specify the rules, constraints, and criteria for their children's behavior. Parents may determine, for example, what activities children can engage in, who their friends are, how they dress, and so on. This part of "laying down the law" is an explicit specification of parental expectations and restrictions.

A second component of direct control is *monitoring* children's behaviors for compliance or noncompliance. This involves parents' surveillance or supervision of children's activities, such as checking to see if family rules are followed. Some parents simply do not make their children accountable for their behaviors. For example, parents may not supervise their children's recreational activities, inquire about their homework, enforce a regular bedtime hour, or care about their choice of friends (Nye, 1958). In short, parents may spend insufficient time interacting with and monitoring their children's behaviors, thereby making it easier for them to engage in delinquent behaviors.

The third component of direct parental control is discipline or *punishment*—applying negative (unwanted) sanctions to misbehavior and deviation. This involves the consequences administered by parents for rule violations. The last part of "laying down the law" seems to involve "picking up the rod."

One complication is that punishment is not a single, unitary variable, but rather reflects multiple component issues, such as severity, contingency, frequency, consistency, perceived fairness, and so on. Also, the term "punishment" has been used to denote a variety of disciplinary practices, including paddling and hitting, yelling and scolding, and the withdrawal of affection and privileges. As Walters and Grusec's (1977) review indicates, punishment as a social-scientific concept is a much more complex idea than ordinary usage of this term suggests.

Although the traditional child development literature consistently reports a positive relation between punishment and children's antisocial behaviors (see Patterson, 1980), the association is not strong. Loeber and Stouthamer-Loeber's (1986) review, for example, found only a very weak and often nonsignificant relation between physical punishment and children's aggression. Moreover, none of these studies analyzed "normal" (e.g., random) samples of children.

The relation (or lack of it) between punishment and delinquency also presents a problem in causal interpretation. Given that delinquent children commit punishable behavior more often than nondelinquents, the same rate of punishment would produce a higher absolute frequency of punishment for delinquents than for nondelinquents. In fact, the more frequent punishment of delinquents may actually reduce their rate of misconduct. Because their rate of misconduct is already high, however, it may appear that more frequent punishment actually causes more frequent delinquency. "Thus, measuring the amount of one reinforcer (e.g., physical punishment) without taking into account the other reinforcers at work (the context of reinforcement) can easily lead to erroneous conclusions" (Wilson and Herrnstein, 1985:228).

Which aspects of punishment are causally important? Patterson (1980, 1982) argues that it is not the frequency or the severity of punishment, but rather its *consistency* and *contingency* that affects the content of children's behaviors. Parents of misbehaving children lack the requisite skills to know how to punish effectively. Thus, punishment may occur (even frequently and vigorously), but it results in little control over misbehavior. Undoubtedly, there are additional conceptual distinctions that can be made. At present, there are few clear predictions regarding which distinct elements of "punishment" are likely to involve important differences in effect.

This review indicates that there is actually little "hard" empirical data regarding the impact of direct parental control over delinquency. Existing research is sketchy and based on a loose assortment of presumed measures of direct control. To some degree, this lack of systematic data is due to a deficiency in conceptual explication. Without a clear specification of the essential ideas, it is difficult to know what is a good measure; without good measures, it is difficult to collect informative data. Our aims in this analysis are expository and exploratory: to indicate conceptually what the relevant content of direct parental control variables might be and to consider what relationships they have with delinquency.

Direct Parental Controls and Delinquency

Based on this reconceptualization, we analyzed the Youth in Transition data (Bachman, 1970; Bachman et al., 1978) using responses Bachman gathered on a nationwide sample of boys who were in the tenth grade in 1966 during their sophomore and junior years in high school. Four variables selected to correspond closely to the dimensions of direct control of children by parents—regulation, monitoring, and punishment—were used to measure the multidimensional content of direct parental control. These variables were: (1) *regulation/restriction* (the degree to which parents decided their sons' friends and activities); (2) *strictness* (how strict respondents rated their parents to be); (3) *punishment contingency* (how frequently parents ignored rather than punished wrongdoing); and (4) *punitiveness* (how vigorously and frequently parents punished their sons, ranging from yelling to hitting). All of these measures are based on sons' (respondents') ratings of parental behavior when the respondents were high school sophomores. These measures of parental control correspond closely to measurements used in other studies of family discipline (see Cernkovich and Giordano, 1987; Johnson, 1979; Miller et al., 1986; Norland et al., 1979; Smith and Paternoster, 1987).

Six variables were used to measure involvement in juvenile delinquency. Four of these variables index specific types of delinquent activity: (1) *school delinquency* (reflecting serious misconduct at school and truancy); (2) *theft-vandalism* (reflecting property offenses, such as theft, trespassing, damaging property, setting fires); (3) *assault-threat* (reflecting offenses against persons, such as hitting, fighting, or strong-arming, carrying weapons); and (4) *trouble with parents* (reflecting "family delinquency," such as running away from home and physically fighting with parents). A fifth variable, *trouble with police*, involves asking whether the youth had gotten into trouble with the police or authorities (self-reported). The sixth variable measures *total delinquency*. All the delinquency items were measured using the survey administered at the end of the eleventh grade. The measurement of delinquent behaviors is temporally subsequent to the measurement of direct parental control variables.

First, we examined the form of the association between direct control and delinquency to determine whether the relationship is linear or nonlinear. For one measure of direct control (perceived strictness of parents), the association with delinquent behaviors is nonlinear. That is, medium levels of perceived parental strictness show the lowest levels of self-reported delinquency, but low and high strictness result in higher delinquency. The relationship with delinquency is generally linear for the three other types of direct parental controls, although the differences for regulation/restriction are rather weak for most forms of delinquency and inconsistent in direction. The two other control variables, representing components of punishment (contingency and punitiveness), both show appreciable and consistent associations with all forms of delinquent behavior. These patterns hold rather consistently across different indicators of delinquent activity. The one exception occurs for regulation/restriction, where the sign of the correlation changes for two forms of delinquency—trouble with parents (reflecting mainly running away behaviors) and assault/threat. These types of delinquency may reflect expressive, hostile, rebellious responses to parental attempts at regulation. Indeed, for fifteen-year olds (such as the respondents in our sample), strong parental control may be interpreted as an intrusion on their privacy and independence, thus prompting selective "acting out" forms of misbehavior rather than generalized delinquency. However, because the levels of correlation for regulation/restriction with delinquency are quite low, we must be cautious in their interpretation.

Two patterns are noteworthy. One is the direction of the relationship between punitiveness and delinquent behaviors, which is a positive association. More vigorous (frequent or severe) punishment is associated with higher levels of delinquency. This pattern persists even when prior levels of delinquency are controlled. The second pattern of interest is the nonlinear association between perceived parental strictness and delinquency—medium strictness results in the lowest levels of delinquency. These patterns indicate that the relation between direct controls and delinquency is variable (albeit in consistent ways). The effects of "more control" on curbing delinquency do not follow a simple and unitary pattern.

Our initial results suggest that the form of the relationship is dependent on which aspect of control is being examined. For some dimensions, the relation is nonlinear and cannot be estimated well by ordinary correlational procedures that assume linear relations between variables. For those variables that do have linear relationships with delinquency, the direction of the relation varies among different components of control.

A second question concerns the magnitude of the relationships between direct parental controls and delinquency. Are they large enough to be statistically reliable? Which variables have the greatest impact on delinquency? For three of the four control variables (i.e., strictness, punishment contingency, and punitiveness), the correlations are moderate and statistically significant. For regulation/restriction, correlations are not statistically reliable. Of the four measures of direct parental control, punitiveness is the most strongly and consistently related to delinquency. One indicator of delinquency (trouble with police) relates less consistently with all the direct control measures.

When all the measures of direct control are simultaneously examined, the combined (multiple) correlations with delinquent behavior are statistically significant but not especially large (see e.g., Johnson, 1979; Norland et al., 1979; Wiatrowski et al., 1981). When all direct control variables are included simultaneously, the same patterns of relationship hold.

In summary, our results indicate that direct controls by parents have as great an impact on delinquency as that of "indirect controls" or parental "attachments." Further, the results suggest that the form of the relation between direct controls and delinquency is not simple, direct, and linear. Depending on which specific component of direct control is examined, its relationship to delinquency may be either linear or nonlinear, positive or inverse (see Wells and Rankin, 1988 for a detailed discussion of the methods and findings).

Discussion

Our results indicate that measures of direct parental control relate in consistent ways to the occurrence of delinquent behavior. Thus, such variables should not be summarily dismissed as theoretically and empirically irrelevant, as suggested by earlier research. Indeed, despite Hirschi's (1985) apparent change of heart, parental "functioning" or "childrearing" variables are rarely highlighted in delinquency theory and research. Instead, "indirect controls" (Nye, 1958) or parental "attachments" (Hirschi, 1969) are viewed as the more critical variable in controlling delinquent behaviors. Our research suggests, however, that even when controlling statistically for the effects of "attachments," direct parental controls are significantly related to various measures of delinquency.

Direct controls by parents are at least as effective as measures of indirect controls or attachments (also see Cernkovich and Giordano, 1987).

Our results also indicate that the form of the relation between direct control and delinquency is not simple, direct, and linear. Conceptually, "direct control" over delinquent behavior is a complex, multidimensional set of processes in which distinct component dimensions of control operate in very different ways. In some cases, parental attempts to control children have a nonlinear relation to delinquency; either too much or too little control leads to greater frequency of delinquent behavior. In other cases, the relation is generally linear. The direction of such relationships is also variable, however. Some kinds of control increase delinquency, and other kinds inhibit it. Only one indicator of delinquency (trouble with police) relates less consistently with all the direct control measures. This variable may be more indicative of social circumstances and police reactions than it is of delinquent behavior. As a variable indicating an uncommon event, it also has rather restricted variance, which limits the size of its correlations.

Such conclusions are consistent with conclusions drawn in other areas of social and psychological research concerning the issue of social control. For instance, work in experimental and developmental psychology (e.g., Walters and Grusec, 1977) has modified earlier ideas about the supposed ineffectiveness of punishment as a way to shape behavior and learning. According to this research, punishment works, but its effects are not generally simple and linear; some punishment is often effective but more is not always better. Similarly, Miller et al. (1986) found a nonlinear relation between adolescents' perceptions of parental strictness/rules and adolescent sexual experience (intercourse). Sexual permissiveness was highest among adolescents who perceived their parents as not being strict at all and having few rules, lowest among those who perceived their parents as moderately strict, and intermediate among those who perceived their parents to be very strict and to have many rules. Rollins and Thomas (1979) reached a similar conclusion in their view of over 230 studies of parental control and support: very low and very high levels of parental control were least effective in obtaining desired behaviors from children. Loeber and Stouthamer-Loeber (1986) also concluded that both strict and punitive as well as lax and erratic disciplinary styles are related to child conduct problems (including delinquency). The conclusion in this literature is that after a generation or more of neglect (due more to ideological than empirical factors), new research is needed to detail what kinds of punishment work, under what conditions, and with what effects, as well as to elaborate the dimensional structure of punishment.

The situation in the sociology of delinquency is remarkably similar. Earlier dismissal of direct parental control was not grounded in a clear empirical demonstration of its lack of utility, but rather in an ideological preference for other forms of social control. At this point, researchers cannot say they know very much about the operation of direct social control; much of what is "known" is based on indirect evidence or borrowed from other fields of study (e.g., Hirschi, 1983; Wilson and Herrnstein, 1985). The comparative impact of direct versus indirect forms of control has yet to be elaborated or tested. Also unclear are the probable interdependencies between direct and indirect control that condition their effects. Subsequent research might explore, for instance, the hypothesized interaction (e.g., Hirschi, 1983) between direct parental control and attachment, where effective parental discipline is conditional on a strong parent-child bond. Our aim here has been to begin an examination in that direction and to suggest its utility to the sociology of delinquency.

Labeling and Social
Constructionist Theory

Introduction

The roots of labeling or interactionist theory may be traced to the social psychology of George Herbert Mead (1934) who pioneered the idea that the human self is a social construction built up in interaction with others. According to Mead, we become who we are in interaction with others and define ourselves in terms of others' definitions of us. We are not passive actors in this process but interact with others in terms of meanings derived from symbols, hence the term "symbolic interactionism" (Blumer, 1969). What type of interactions we have and who interacts with us therefore becomes important, for through these interactions and reactions we become constituted as social actors. Not all interactions are of equal importance; the greatest impact comes from those who have significant meaning and influence in the lives of the actors.

Interactionist theory found a niche in criminology chiefly through the ethnographic work of Howard Becker (1963) on jazz musicians and marijuana smokers, and the analysis by Edwin Lemert (1951, 1967) of differences in kinds of deviance. Becker argued that social deviants are created largely as a result of the negative reaction by agents of social control to some people's rule-breaking behavior. Through social reaction, actors are "labeled" as deviant types based on some aspects of their behavior; that is, they are defined or considered different because of the variation in their behavior in relation to some rule or law. In its simplest formulation, labeling/interaction theory asserts that it is the negative reaction by enforcement agents to some people's rule breaking that induces changes in the identity of the actor who then is transformed into a deviant or a criminal. Those labeled, when conventional routes are closed to them because of the label, often adopt the negative definitions of themselves and become "outsiders." In Lemert's terms people are transformed from participants in minor primary deviance to social identities committed to secondary deviance. Secondary deviance occurs when the societal response to primary deviance is such that the actor is prevented from functioning normally and resorts to deviant behavior. The interactions that bring about such social transformation take place in specific social settings whose context also must be taken into account in determining the final outcome of significant interactions. The work of Erving Goffman (1963) went a considerable way in enlightening us about not only the contexts and strategies of interaction, but also the damaging stigmatizing effects of the deviant label and the ways in which those labeled cope.

Exemplifying the importance of context in interaction, Gary Reed and Peter Yeager (chap. 17) in their critique of a general theory of crime, focus on white-collar crime and show how in the unique setting of the corporation certain acts considered criminal in other contexts are not defined and reacted to as such in certain corporations. Because this type of offending is "socially constructed in a broad institutional context that emphasizes profit making," it is not seen to be within the purview of criminality.

Very important in this process is how rules and laws are constructed and how they are enforced on others, since such enforcement carries with it the significant power of state authority. Richard Hollinger and Lonn Lanza-Kaduce (chap. 18) focus on yet another area, the process of criminalization itself. Their essay analyzes how, society's ever-increasing dependency on the computer, and its potential use as a tool in the performance of deviant and criminal acts, has led to new definitions of what is considered property and what is considered privacy. They also consider the major players and influences which are responsible for the new constructions of these definitions and thereby demonstrate the role of power in the creation of these definitions.

17

Organizational Offending and Neoclassical Criminology: Challenging the Reach of a General Theory of Crime

Gary E. Reed and Peter Cleary Yeager

Criminologists have used white-collar crime (1) to demonstrate the inadequacy of causal theories based on poverty, the disintegration of basic institutions, or personal pathologies, (2) to forward their own general theories, or (3) to develop specific theoretical arguments about the uniqueness of this sort of offending (Sutherland, 1949; Clinard and Quinney, 1973; Clinard and Yeager, 1980; Coleman, 1987; Stone, 1975; Vaughan, 1983). Recently, Gottfredson and Hirschi (1990; Hirschi and Gottfredson, 1987a, 1994) have used white-collar crime to argue the generality of their own theory and for the proposition that typologies of crime are unnecessary. While sympathetic with the quest for wide-ranging criminological theory, we do not believe that Gottfredson and Hirschi have delivered a general theory of crime. Here we critique the application of their general theory to organizational crime and deviancy, particularly corporate misdeeds. We argue that organizational wrongdoing has unique characteristics that require specific explanation. Many of these characteristics may be common to corporate lawbreaking and offending in other bureaucracies, such as those in government, health care, and higher education.

We first present a brief summary of Gottfredson and Hirschi's general theory and some recent critiques of their arguments. We then summarize and assess their application of the theory to white-collar offending. We question their characterization of this type of lawbreaking, and we argue that a more complex specification of motivation and opportunity is required for theorizing about its organizational variant.

Edited and abridged from *Criminology*, Volume 34(3):357–82 (1996).

The Revival of Classical Criminological Theory

Gottfredson and Hirschi revive and revise the arguments of classical criminology that human behavior is premised on individual calculations of the relative costs and benefits of action and that both criminal and noncriminal behavior result from the pursuit of self-interest (Gottfredson and Hirschi, 1990:5). They maintain that the classical emphasis on voluntary human action better fits the data on offending than positivistic accounts of external determinants of behavior. These overpredict crime since many who are in so-called criminogenic environments do not commit criminal offenses. Like classicists, the authors argue that when opportunity is afforded but restraints from proper socialization are absent, people are free to commit deviant acts. This contrasts with the positivist assumption that persons are compelled to commit deviant acts by forces beyond their control.

Gottfredson and Hirschi claim they are not merely resurrecting classical theory but are correcting its flaws and extending its scope. According to them, early classical theorists overemphasized the role of political (legal) sanctions in restraining deviants. They argue that legal penalties are often redundant because they overlap with sanctions rooted in moral and religious codes. Legal penalties are relatively ineffective against those likely to commit crimes. The authors incorporate family socialization into their account of crime, and extend the range of behavior to be explained by classical theorizing beyond acts that the state defines as criminal. For them, the relevant empirical terrain involves a much larger set of deviant acts and consequences of risky acts, including accidents, victimizations, truancies from home, school, and work, substance abuse, family problems, and disease (Gottfredson and Hirschi, 1990:xiv; Hirschi and Gottfredson, 1994).

Of Crime and Criminality

That such a broad array of deviancy might be encompassed by Gottfredson and Hirschi's theory derives from their specific conceptualization of crime as events and criminality as involving characteristics of individuals. The two concepts are tightly interdependent: Crimes are precisely the sort of events that are attractive to individuals possessed of criminality.

Gottfredson and Hirschi (1990) began their general theory by isolating the common properties of crimes as events. They sought a definition of crime, unfettered by disciplinary boundaries, that captured its essential features. They "defined crimes as acts of force or fraud undertaken in pursuit of self-interest" (1990, 15–16). The authors ignore the standard distinction between violent personal crimes and property crimes, employing the more general language of "force" and "fraud" (Grasmick et al., 1993:10). Force and fraud are attractive methods for criminals because they are seeking near-term gains realized with a minimum of effort and little concern for longer-term consequences (Hirschi and Gottfredson, 1987a:959).

Gottfredson and Hirschi (1990) deduce that the essence of criminality lies in individuals' low self-control. Criminals are unable or unwilling to delay gratification; they seek short-term pleasures and are relatively unconcerned with the long-term results of their behavior; and while they may use charm for gain, they are generally insensitive to the needs and suffering of others (Gottfredson and Hirschi, 1990:89–90). The authors assert that the link between low self-control and crime is probabilistic rather than deterministic (Gottfredson and Hirschi, 1990:91; Hirschi and Gottfredson, 1993, 1994:9). Under certain conditions, such as a lack of criminal opportunity, low self-control may lead to acts "analogous" to crime, like smoking, alcohol abuse, and other risky behaviors.

The authors argue that low self-control results from poor parenting in which the manifestations of weak self-control were not recognized and remedied at an early age. The consequence of failure—or success—in correcting low self-control during childhood is a stable level of self-control throughout life.

Relative to early socialization and self-control, Gottfredson and Hirschi (1990) deemphasize the importance of opportunity (see Grasmick et al., 1993:10–11). While opportunity is a necessary condition for low self-control to produce a criminal event, it is not tightly bound to criminality: "Crimes . . . all require opportunity . . . [but] properties [like opportunity] cannot account for the general tendency of particular individuals to engage in crime, and they are therefore not central to a theory of criminality" (Gottfredson and Hirschi, 1990:190). Opportunities influence the distribution of criminal events. Areas with accessible targets posing little risk of detection are more likely to be associated with crime than those with higher risk targets.

Gottfredson and Hirschi's work represents an impressive attempt to construct a parsimonious explanation of high generality, applicable to virtually all crimes and a host of behaviors beyond the purview of most criminological theorizing. The theory appears to capture the essence of crimes that concern criminology and public policy. It also rightly avoids overly deterministic explanations of crime. Moreover, the characterization of actors who assess their environments and deliberate the consequences of their actions fits empirical data on ethical and legal decision making in corporations (Yeager, 1995).

General Critiques of a General Theory

Gottfredson and Hirschi's provocative thesis has received considerable criminological attention. Keane et al. (1993) report a link between low self-control and driving under the influence. Arneklev et al. (1993) found mixed support for relationships between elements of low self-control and behaviors such as drinking and gambling. Grasmick et al. (1993) report that the interaction between (low) self-control and opportunity does help predict self-reported acts of force and fraud (see also Hirschi and Gottfredson, 1994).

Despite partial empirical confirmation, the theory has been challenged on logical and theoretical grounds. Scholars have criticized the theory's reliance on tautological relationships between such key variables as low self-control, criminality, and criminal behavior (Akers, 1991, 1994; Barlow, 1991; Meier, 1995). The role of opportunity is underdeveloped, but this may be more important than self-control as a predictor of crime (Barlow, 1991; Grasmick et al., 1993). One manifestation of criminality, "risk seeking," appears to contradict the low risk of detection characteristic of criminal opportunity, which should be relatively unattractive to many persons manifesting criminality (Grasmick et al., 1993:11). Yet Arneklev et al. (1993) found that the risk-seeking component of low self-control was the most successful predictor of a subset of behaviors analogous to crime. In addition, Barlow (1991) has criticized the theory's treatment of self-control as a stable construct throughout one's life. And critics have challenged that by emphasizing an individualistic notion of self-control, the theory neglects the role of criminogenic social milieus (Barlow, 1991; Sampson and Laub, 1993:7; Thornberry et al., 1993; Tittle, 1995). Such milieus are key to criminal motivation, a concept the theory also dismisses (Arneklev et al., 1993; Tittle, 1991, 1995; cf. Benson and Moore, 1992).

Gottfredson and Hirschi responded to these challenges by amplifying their position. They argue that the charge of tautology does no harm to their arguments (Hirschi and Gottfredson, 1993:52). They assert that the relationship between self-control and crime only appears to be tautological; there are independent indicators of low self-control: acts "analogous" to crime, such as alcohol abuse.

Hirschi and Gottfredson (1993:50) have argued that opportunities to commit crime are unlimited and that self-control and opportunity generally have independent effects on crime. But they also recognize that opportunities to commit some kinds of crime may be quite limited and that therefore self-control and opportunity may interact to produce specific crime patterns. For example, some white-collar crimes (e.g., bank embezzlement) require the sort of opportunity generally only experienced by persons with levels of self-control that are adequately high for achieving the requisite positions of trust in banks. But if this response enriches their conceptualization of the role of opportunity, it appears to do so at the expense of the logic and parsimony of their argument linking low self-control and crime.

In addition to this problem, we suggest that other key issues remain unresolved. First, we are not persuaded that their use of the concepts of self-interest and short-term versus long-term considerations is useful for their theory or for the explanation of organizational offending. We suggest that their neoclassical development of "motivation" does not lend itself well to the analysis of organizational violations of law (cf. Barlow, 1991; Benson and Moore, 1992; Tittle, 1991). Second, we agree that Gottfredson and Hirschi do not adequately develop the role of opportunity and its interactions with other features of criminal choices, such as motivation (Barlow, 1991; Grasmick et al., 1993). Opportunity plays a key role in the explanation of organizational offending and is dynamically intertwined with its motivational aspects. In contrast to Gottfredson and Hirschi's emphasis on early socialization, this points to the causal importance of criminogenic social milieus specific to this type of offending.

The General Theory and White-Collar Crime

In explaining white-collar crime, Gottfredson and Hirschi retain their definition of crime as the use of force or fraud in the perpetrator's self-interest. More important is their operational definition of white-collar crime as embezzlement, fraud, and forgery, which enables them to compare distributions in offending using Uniform Crime Report (UCR) data (Gottfredson and Hirschi, 1990:180-201; Hirschi and Gottfredson, 1987a:961–67). From these data, they draw several key conclusions in support of the argument that their general theory readily accounts for white-collar offending.

First, they assert that white-collar crime exhibits the same demographic distribution (e.g., race and age) as ordinary crime. They find that white-collar crimes bear the defining characteristics of all crime: "They provide relatively quick and relatively certain benefit with minimal effort. They *require no motivation or pressure that is not present in any other form of human behavior*" (Gottfredson and Hirschi, 1990:190; italics added).

Second, the authors argue that white-collar crime is relatively uncommon (e.g., Gottfredson and Hirschi, 1990:19, 191), explaining that business culture is hostile to white-collar crime, and selects out such traits of criminality as impulsiveness and aggression in favor of such traits as the ability to defer gratification and willingness to defer to the interests (and, by implication, the authority) of others, keys to conventional careers and bureaucratic functioning. Thus, their theory "explicitly predicts lack of social support for most white-collar crimes since (1) they are contrary to general social norms, and (2) are against the interests of the organization itself" (Hirschi and Gottfredson, 1987a:970).

Third, Gottfredson and Hirschi (1990:190) generalize to white-collar lawbreakers their argument that offenders do not specialize in types of crime. Like their "blue-collar" counterparts, they will act out criminal impulses when favorable opportunities arise for easy and immediate benefit.

Finally, these authors make two claims about the concept of corporate or organizational crime (as a subtype of white-collar crime): that data have not yet demonstrated that a special subcategory is needed for explanation, and that researchers who say the unit of study is the organization—rather than the individual—do not actually apply it, "do not treat the corporation as the criminal actor" in their interpretive efforts (Gottfredson and Hirschi, 1990:188).

Organizational Offending: Retying the Gordian Knot

There are three principal weaknesses in Gottfredson and Hirschi's argument as applied to lawbreaking by business organizations. These involve (1) defining and counting the phenomena of interest, (2) the nature of the interest that commonly underlies them, and (3) the role of opportunity in them. A satisfactory theory of organizational offending requires an adequate account of these matters and will look substantially different from Gottfredson and Hirschi's theory of crime.

Defining and Counting: The Role of Screens

In operationalizing their definition of crime in terms of embezzlement, fraud, and forgery, Gottfredson and Hirschi have incorporated conceptual and methodological screens that too narrowly constrain the phenomena of interest. Their definition identifies data whose demographic distributions most resemble those for conventional crimes and best fit their thesis. (See Steffensmeier, 1989; Hirschi and Gottfredson, 1989). For example, the UCR data on embezzlement include many such offenses as teenage cashiers taking money from registers (Steffensmeier, 1989). Similarly, fraud and forgery are commonly committed by poor individuals acting alone or in small groups. As Gottfredson and Hirschi suggest, these "white-collar" crimes are typically uncomplicated, requiring little skill or special motivation. Such acts lend themselves to an account emphasizing the undersocialized pursuit of short-term self-interest. So defined, however, they have less in common with many white-collar offenses, especially organizational offenses. This type of lawbreaking suggests the importance of such factors as organizational (sub)cultures and structures and the social construction of opportunities, matters left untheorized by Gottfredson and Hirschi.

The offenses we have in mind, organizational violations that are defined by the processes of administrative, civil, or criminal law, are not logically excluded by the definition of crime as the use of force or fraud for self-interested reasons. Indeed, most organizational violations involve either force, fraud, or both, whether perpetrated against customers, employees, citizens, competitors, or government. For example, the knowing marketing of unsafe products or maintenance of unsafe workplaces combines elements of fraud and force in victimizing consumers and workers, respectively. Victims are defrauded when they are not made aware of the unreasonable physical risks they face, and too commonly harmed, while employees may be effectively coerced into exposure to illegal workplace hazards by fear of job loss or other retribution. Price-fixing conspiracies, military contract fraud, tax fraud, securities fraud, and bank fraud clearly fit this conceptual definition of crime. So, too, do many environmental violations. Here, costs and risks are knowingly imposed upon the environment and citizens, fraudulent transfers that also often impose real physical harms.

Researchers have documented significant rates of such corporate offending, the high monetary and physical costs they collectively impose on victims, the forces that underlie them, and legal efforts at social control. Gottfredson and Hirschi's arguments must be examined against this evidence, most of which escapes the UCR data they have utilized.

That such offenses are numerous and quite costly is now a commonplace in criminological research. (See Baucus and Near, 1991; Clinard and Yeager, 1980; Clinard et al., 1979; Mokhiber, 1988; and Ross, 1992. Studies of antitrust offenses include those by Baker and Faulkner, 1993; Jamieson, 1994; Perez, 1978; Simpson, 1986, 1987; and Staw and Szwajkowski, 1975. Useful studies of financial fraud are Calavita and Pontell, 1991, 1994; Pontell and Calavita 1993; and Reichman, 1993. For pollution offenses, see, Adler and Lord, 1991; and Yeager, 1987, 1993.) This accumulated research on business lawbreaking demonstrates that lawbreaking by even powerful corporations occurs sufficiently frequently to be of substantial concern and that much of this offending readily fits the definition of crime as the use of force and fraud. And this research includes only those offenders that the government has officially labeled. While such legal processes always disproportionately select the simpler offenses because of their greater ease of detection and legal proof, this screening process operates with more force for organizational offenses than for the types of violations Gottfredson and Hirschi have targeted in their assessment of white-collar crime. And it does so for reasons entailed in the causal nexus of such offenses. The result is that organizational violations of law are both underrepresented and "undertheorized" in *A General Theory of Crime*.

Many studies report that business offenses are often highly complex, difficult to detect, and burdensome to prove in terms of specific responsibilities and mens rea (see Clinard and Yeager, 1980; Cullen et al., 1987; Shapiro, 1984; Stone, 1975). Mann (1985) shows how many complex white-collar offenses are screened out of the criminal justice system prior to the decision to charge (or arrest). Because of the great complexity of many tax and securities transactions, for example, and the ambiguity of relevant legal concepts (e.g., of fraud), defense counsel are often able to convince prosecutors to drop potential cases, because proving them is not feasible (see McBarnet, 1991; Reichman, 1992). Mann's work implies that many of these cases are dropped because facts and/or the law are rendered more complex in negotiations (prior to charging) between specialized defense counsel and government regulators. These negotiations provide advantages to white-collar crime defendants relative to more conventional criminal defendants. Moreover, the sort of high-priced expertise required to make technical legal and factual arguments favors screening out of enforcement the larger, resource-rich businesses. In relation to securities regulation, for example, "Small, pennystock firms may find themselves more likely to be classified as violators because they cannot 'authoritatively reinterpret (within limits) what the rules mean'" (Reichman, 1992:256, quoting Clegg, 1989).

Similarly, larger companies are more likely than smaller firms to negotiate reductions in water pollution controls (Yeager, 1987, 1993) and to have inspectors see their violations as "accidents" rather than as evidence of recalcitrance (Hawkins, 1983, 1984; cf. Shover et al., 1986). Able to afford expensive technical expertise, larger companies often convince regulators of their good faith efforts to comply. Meanwhile, smaller firms tend to face higher standards and more stringent enforcement. In this way law is negotiated rather than simply enforced.

Less subtle forms of corporate power also operate in regulatory decisions. Regulators often avoid full enforcement of the law, fearing that major firms may mount aggressive defenses and other legal challenges to the government's underfunded efforts. They also often fail to refer potential criminal cases for prosecution rather than lose enforcement credit to the prosecutorial authorities (Bequai, 1977b; California Department of Justice, 1988:69; Yeager, 1991). The results range from nonenforcement to deferred compliance agreements instead of harsher criminal and civil penalties.

In sum, not only is organizational offending substantially more diverse and widespread than Gottfredson and Hirschi suppose, but official criminal justice data on such offenses significantly distort the profile of offenses and offenders. Research shows that organizational offending does not mirror the demographic distribution of conventional offending. Although this research does not address the question of whether organizational offenders are generalists in crime, as Gottfredson and Hirschi argue, there is little to suggest that these lawbreakers commonly engage in offenses like embezzlement, drug use, assault, or general theft. As Wheeler (1992:109) noted, "Many white-collar offenders have led lives not only unmarked by prior trouble with the law, but characterized by positive contributions to family and community life. . . . [A number of those we studied] made a conscious though difficult decision to engage in illegality when they apparently hadn't done so before."

Finally, research has produced data that require specific white-collar crime concepts for their explanation, concepts lodged at the organizational and institutional levels of analysis. If this sort of white-collar crime is ordinary, it is ordinary only in the sense of neatly fitting into the routines of business management, thus appearing to be unremarkable.

The Structure and Culture of Motivation

Gottfredson and Hirschi's account deemphasizes motivation, arguing that crime is simply a product of low self-control of self-interest in the context of opportunities. They assume that self-interest is an unproblematic concept and that self-control is an evident and stable property of personalities. Neither assumption is adequate for the evidence on organizational lawbreaking.

An important weakness of the authors' neoclassical emphasis on the calculation of interests is its nonfalsifiable character. Gottfredson and Hirschi argue that if a person's calculations and subsequent actions produce an outcome that contradicts self-interest, this is not evidence contradicting the *pursuit* of self-interest. Rather, unfavorable outcomes may simply be evidence that the person is either not very good at interest calculations or not adept at connecting means to ends.

Taylor et al. (1973) argued that classical theory implies its theorists have special access to the criteria by which to judge an act's rationality. Indeed, Gottfredson and Hirschi (1990:184) imply that they have access to criteria by which to judge how a person's self-interest is best pursued, even if the individual is unable to apply these criteria or disagrees with them. Classical theorizing further begs the question of whether individuals have a singular self-interest or competing self-interests that need to be reconciled. Particularly in the context of large bureaucratic organizations, with their highly specialized divisions of labor and complex and differentiated responsibilities, individuals are likely to develop conflicting views of their own self-interests, as when business requirements contradict the conventions of ordinary morality learned early in one's socialization (e.g., in decisions to break laws to secure profits and jobs [Yeager, 1995]). In short, rather than being evident or given in the "human condition," interests are socially constructed perceptions that evolve in people's patterns of interaction and socialization.

Also problematic is Gottfredson and Hirschi's insistence that crime involves the pursuit of short-term at the expense of long-term gains. The vagueness of this distinction renders it virtually impossible to measure. It is not clear what counts as "short-term," nor who sets the standard for distinguishing short-term from long-term. And must an act, a choice, be directed at one or the other of these time frames rather than both?

Nor is this distinction helpful in distinguishing between organizational offending and standard business practices. Gottfredson and Hirschi imply that organizational lawbreaking is occasioned by short-term interests, whereas standard business practice is premised upon a longer, strategic view. However, while organizations sometimes commit offenses in the pursuit of interests such as quick profits, they also violate laws in order to realize financial health several years in the future (e.g., price-fixing conspiracies, contract fraud). In either case, the offenses are commonly motivated by the rational pursuit of legitimate goals rather than by the undersocialized, impulsive pursuit of immediate self-gratification.

Gottfredson and Hirschi's concept of self-control is similarly troubled. Along with the stability thesis, they assert that business organizations select managers and executives on self-control, screening out impulsive, undercontrolled personalities likely to commit acts of force or fraud. Given the evidence of these acts in organizations, they subsequently suggested that self-control is a continuous variable across individuals (Hirschi and Gottfredson, 1993:53; 1994:12). Thus, organizational offenders commit fewer offenses (and offense types) because they have more self-control than other criminals, but less self-control than their business peers.

This specific argument enlarges the problem of tautology since, given the organizational screen for self-control and the purported infrequency of crimes and analogous acts, the offense may be the only measure of self-control (see Akers, 1994:121–23; Tittle, 1995:58–59; and Arneklev et al., 1993).

In addition, because of the highly refined division of labor in complex organizations, organizational offenses can be committed only by specific role incumbents, whose acts and reasons cannot simply be compared with those of incumbents in other roles. Gottfredson and Hirschi therefore must argue either that a less self-controlled person found his or her way through substantial screens and into the relevant role "by accident" or that "unusual" processes selected him or her into the role. In the first case, theory stands silent in the face of "unexplained" variance; in the second case, theory must specify the apparently extraordinary selection mechanisms.

To theorize such offenses fully, therefore, requires attending to such factors as the structures of roles in organizations, and selection and socialization into role requirements, factors shaping aspects of motivation (i.e., perception of self-interest) and (perceived) opportunity.

Organizations and Managers

Research on corporations consistently suggests the routine nature of much offending and the forces in organization and culture that occasion it. Surveys of corporate officials indicate that unethical and illegal practices are common. Studies find that substantial majorities of executives agree that criminal antitrust violations and other unethical acts are rather common in business (Baumhart, 1961; Nader and Green, 1972; Silk and Vogel, 1976). Managers see superiors as pressuring them toward ethical and legal offenses. For example, in a *Harvard Business Review* survey on corporate ethics, half the sampled managers thought that their superiors frequently did not wish to know how results were obtained so long as the desired outcomes were achieved. Moreover, "Respondents frequently complained of superiors' pressure to support incorrect viewpoints, sign false documents, overlook superiors' wrongdoing, and do business with superiors' friends" (Brenner and Molander, 1977:60). Retired middle managers have reported that unethical and illegal acts were connected to the culture established by top management (Clinard, 1983). These managers further suggested that the nature of the ethical climate depended in part on the professional backgrounds of corporate leaders and their mode of recruitment. Respondents saw leaders with engineering backgrounds, and those recruited from among long-standing employees, as more likely to establish positive ethical climates than financial specialists and recruits from outside the firm, who focused more on bottom-line results (Clinard, 1983:136-37).

Superficially, these data appear consistent with Gottfredson and Hirschi's arguments connecting offending to the pursuit of short-term self-interest but, in fact, they underscore these arguments' inadequacy for organizational offending. Rather than describing undersocialized "bad apples" who occasionally defeat institutional and organizational selection mechanisms and rise to positions of authority within firms, Clinard's respondents point to highly structured patterns of socialization and selection embedded in fundamental processes of corporate capitalism. Combined with findings that tendencies toward unethical and illegal acts are common in corporations, these data indicate a necessary place for both socialization in the professions and processes of selection into organizational roles in theorizing such offenses.

Moreover, a substantial body of research indicates that corporate bureaucracies shape members' views in ways that affect the moral quality of their decision making (e.g., Jackall, 1988; Kram et al., 1989; Stone, 1975; Yeager, 1995). Jackall (1988:82–84) argues that these bureaucracies focus managers' attention on short-term results. They do so by evaluating managers' performances on the basis of such results, a process accentuated in an increasingly uncertain economic climate in which securities markets place a high premium on short-term gains, and one supported by the increased hiring of cadres of business school graduates professionally trained in the virtues of financial "wizardry" and bottom-line achievement. Moreover, he notes bureaucracy's tendency to convert moral issues into pragmatic ones as managers are routinely socialized to "a world where the etiquette of authority relationships and the necessity of protecting and covering for one's boss, one's network, and oneself supersede all other considerations and where nonaccountability for action is the norm" (Jackall, 1988:111). This tendency is founded upon the segmentation of roles, duties, and knowledge that characterizes bureaucratic structures (Jackall, 1988; Stone, 1975; Yeager, 1995). Indeed, the very strengths of rational hierarchy—efficient pursuit of goals through specialization in a complex division of labor, impartiality, and universalism—virtually assure conflicts between the obligations of managers and at least some requirements of conventional morality, often including those of the law. In corporate hierarchies, authority and goal setting are established in the upper ranks while responsibility for achieving goals is delegated downward and subdivided among functions, divisions, and departments. Combined with a "conspiracy of ignorance," in which top managers do not wish to hear of problems and lower-level managers do not wish to tell them (for fear of being labeled incompetent) (Jackall, 1988:20–21, 89–90, 122–23; Stone, 1975), decisions are routinely reached in a context of secrecy and plausible deniability in which everyone evades a sense of moral responsibility for wrongdoing (Clinard and Yeager, 1980; Yeager, 1995). The evasion only reinforces the potential for misdeeds when managers face obstacles to the achievement of corporate purposes.

Our own research in large companies underscores the ordinariness of corporate offending (Kram et al., 1989; Yeager, 1995; Yeager and Kram, 1995). Legal and moral violations are "built into" the goal orientations, structures, and processes of complex business organizations. Moreover, the findings clearly indicate the intricate structuring of moral interests in managerial behavior. They suggest that when corporate officials break the law, they commonly do not do so on the basis of naked self-interest or antipathy for legal and moral requirements. Instead, our interview data portray highly trained, properly ambitious, and conventionally socialized individuals who strain to manage ethical and legal dilemmas they regularly face and to find moral justification for delicts.

An illustrative case involves a middle manager who manipulated accounts and inventory data to inflate corporate profits in a manner that clearly violated standard accounting principles and federal law. Under pressure from superiors to improve annual profits during a bleak financial period, he falsified the profit statement despite his clear recognition that the action violated accounting controls and the law. This manager had originally strongly resisted the pressure from above, but ultimately carried out the act, admitting, "I had to compromise my *financial ethics*" (emphasis added). Later, in assessing the role of the superior who had pressured him to commit the offense despite his principled resistance, he said:

> What he did was not unethical. . . he made the best of a bad situation without having to sacrifice the company's progress. If we wouldn't have gotten the [profits increased this way] . . . we might have had to cut back on some things we didn't want to sacrifice, like our marketing budget, or on people. You know, I mean the alternatives to [the decision] were probably a lot uglier.

It was clear not only that this offender had originally resisted the pressure to violate the law, but also that he was engaged in a complex process of distancing himself from full moral responsibility for the offense. For example, while clearly seeing the action as wrong in isolation, he was able to contextualize the event in two ways. First, he interpreted his struggle with the act in terms of a violation of professional [financial] norms rather than as a more fundamental matter of personal or ordinary morality, that is, of lying to or cheating shareholders and potential investors. Second, he asserted that his superior's pressure served "higher" organizational purposes in the context of real market pressures. In this moral calculus, therefore, the manager interpreted his role as standing between the competing ethical requirements of the organization's needs and those of his profession, while bracketing any sense that his personal morality was at stake. This could be interpreted as little more than rationalization by someone who should have shown more moral courage. In Gottfredson and Hirschi's account, perhaps this individual is doing nothing more than maximizing his self-interest in the short-term with little regard for others; he is less self-controlled than his peers in this large company and in comparable firms.

But such an argument fails to capture adequately the realm of meaning that underlies this form of human action. We agree with Gottfredson and Hirschi that human behavior is generally intentional; we also agree that self-interest underlies most behavior. But in stark contrast to the predatory, conscience-free criminality their theory depicts, corporate lawbreaking commonly springs from normative requirements of the organization itself, as they are interpreted against business exigencies and compellingly communicated in authority relationships. Rather than simply rationalizing after the fact of impulsive behavior, corporate executives and managers often construct and negotiate justifications as they contemplate and take wayward action, justifications lodged in the normative orientations of legitimate business and its various constituencies, including shareholders and employees among others (cf. Benson, 1985). Such collective orientations vary historically and cross-sectionally (e.g., by industry, firm, region), but they are always fateful for managers' definitions of situations, including their situated interests. The evidence of the force of these orientations is found in the way the manager speaks of the "higher" purposes served by the misaccounting, and in the collective nature of the endeavor directed at group ends. It is also found in the manager's claims that the specific action has a normative status in the industry: A key factor in the manager's decision to commit the offense was that one of the leading firms in the industry is known to have engaged in the same behavior, and the outside auditors "overlooked" the action in both companies.

Other evidence also illustrates the normative status of lawbreaking in some companies and industries. This status is commonly indicated in the taken-for-granted orientation personnel exhibit toward the offending, and it is often communicated through reward and promotion systems. For example, a long-standing price-fixing conspiracy brought the federal indictment of twenty three carton manufacturing corporations and fifty of their executives in 1976 (Clinard and Yeager, 1980:61–65). According to the government,

> These defendants were not engaged in a short-term violation based on sudden market pressures; price-fixing was their way of doing business. The participants demonstrated a knowing, blatant disregard for anti-trust laws. One grand jury witness testified that during a six-year period he personally engaged in thousands of price-fixing transactions with competitors. . . . This illegal conduct was carried on in all parts of the country by all management levels in the billion-dollar folding-carton industry. (*U.S. v. Alton Box Board Company et al.*, Criminal Action No. 76 CR 199 [May 7, 1976]:10–11)

Socialization into the illegal practices was part of the normal process of induction into the managerial role. For example, one executive said that, "Each was introduced to price-fixing practices by his superiors. . . when he [achieved] price-fixing responsibility" (Clinard and Yeager, 1980:64-65; see Benson, 1985).

Finally, analysis of this case in the *Harvard Business Review* indicates that this criminal behavior was not only routine within and between these leading manufacturers, but also that it was importantly motivated by the companies' standard practices for rewarding managers. Clearly, such practices represent and communicate a firm's normative priorities:

> On top of any other influences, the personnel practices used in many companies seemed actually to encourage people to engage in price-fixing. In a number of the companies convicted, management almost exclusively appraised individual performance on the basis of profits and volume. . . . One sales manager explained that . . . "If it is known that the operating chief of your area wants business conducted in a certain way, it seems that is what really counts." (Sonnenfeld and Lawrence, 1978)

Taken together, these case study and fieldwork data highlight the importance of normative constructions and socialization in managers' decisions to violate laws. As in virtually all human action, self-interest is at work, as managers and executives seek success and/or to avoid failure (Coleman, 1987; Wheeler, 1992). But commonly these offenses appear not to be the product of undersocialized, relatively less restrained individuals looking only to their own near-term interests. Instead, they are the behaviors of men and women well socialized to standard corporate practices and expectations, who often exhibit strong loyalties to their firms and their specific work units, and who as a result find their own self-interest firmly married to corporate purposes and goals. To theorize such offenses adequately, therefore, it is necessary to include the processes of socialization and selection into what Coleman (1987) has referred to as a "culture of competition." That is, one must understand the socially constructed intentions that underlie action; one must fully understand motivation.

The Construction of Opportunity

The other factor in the basic crime equation is opportunity. In their general theory Gottfredson and Hirschi construe the role of opportunity narrowly, limiting it to its influence on the distribution of illegalities. Opportunities either exist in one's environment, or they do not. This misses the intersubjective construction of opportunities and its relationship to motivation.

Coleman (1987:424) has outlined this fuller conception, pointing to the reciprocal relation between motivation and opportunity:

> motivation and opportunity are often closely associated in a particular setting. Many of the rationalizations that are such an important part of the symbolic motivational structures are formulated in response to a particular set of structural opportunities and have little meaning in another context. And, by the same token, an opportunity requires a symbolic construction making that particular behavioral option psychologically available to individual actors, and that construction may also include potential rationalizations. Thus an individual may learn of both the opportunity for a particular offense and at least part of the motivation for committing it at the same time in the same setting.

It is not merely an intrapersonal process that renders opportunities psychologically available. Opportunity is socially constructed in persons' relationships with other group members experiencing—while creating—shared contexts. The structural and cultural features of social settings shape motivation and opportunity in distinctive ways and must therefore be specifically accounted for in theorizing crime.

One such unique feature in the lawbreaking of corporations involves the role of law. In this context, unlike for most conventional offending, the relation between legal regulation and the regulated is highly dynamic. Not only may perceptions of law increase (or decrease) the psychological availability of illegal acts, but the regulated parties may be actively involved in shaping both law and the regard with which it is viewed. As such processes occur, motivation and opportunity will be dynamically produced and reproduced.

As we earlier noted, the implementation and enforcement of law regulating business commonly give way to complex deliberations between corporate and government experts regarding the costs and benefits of various degrees of control and even the nature and degree of compliance. In environmental law, for example, industry's technical input on technologies and feasibility takes precedence over citizens' and public interest concerns with the broader ethical bases of regulation (e.g., environmental values) because of inequalities in political, monetary, and technical resources (Yeager, 1991, 1993, 1995; see also Hawkins, 1983, 1984; Lynxwiler et al., 1983; Shover et al., 1986). Thus, there is a shift in moral emphasis from the often passionately held values that motivated the original legislation to a "demoralized" focus on technical problems and solutions.

The key consequence is that this process reinforces business managers' perception that much regulatory law itself is morally neutral or ambivalent, which in turn strengthens the limited, utilitarian moral calculus that emphasizes the imperative of financial success over other social considerations. At stake, then, is negotiation over the essential legitimacy of law and, therefore, over the moral weight of lawbreaking. When regulatory compliance costs compete with the fundamental profit-making aims of industry in a corporate context in which law has been morally neutralized, the "moral opportunities" for lawbreaking expand as law's moral salience declines, and they expand in close connection with systems of motivation (see Benson, 1985).

It is in this sense, then, that opportunities are socially constructed rather than "naturally" given, as in the simple availability of goods to steal or gullible citizens to fleece.

Conclusions

Gottfredson and Hirschi applied their arguments to white-collar crime to demonstrate the generality of their theory and to strengthen their position that various crime types do not require specific explanations. They argued that white-collar offending is uncommon, simple in technique, similar in demographic distribution to street crimes, and condemned in business culture. We have disagreed with them on all these counts. In particular we have argued that their theory cannot adequately explain lawbreaking in corporate business when this type of offending is understood in its full dimensions.

Certainly some offenses inside corporations are condemned in the culture of business, such as embezzlement and crimes that readily expose the firm to steep financial and reputational losses. Just as certainly, some of these offenses are driven more by self-interest than by normative enterprise. But on the substantial evidence on corporate lawbreaking and bureaucratic culture, it is equally clear that Gottfredson and Hirschi's neoclassical account of the springs of criminality is inadequate for theorizing this key form of offending. Most important, they have neglected the extent to which reasons for offending—motivation—and the opportunities for doing so are socially constructed in a broad institutional context that emphasizes profit making and in organizational contexts that privilege success and survival. While Gottfredson and Hirschi (1990:213) write that "the idea of crime is incompatible with the pursuit of long-term cooperative relationships, and people who tend toward criminality are unlikely to be reliable, trustworthy, or cooperative," the data on much of the most costly offending in corporate business paint a quite different picture. In this evidence we often find committed employees breaking laws on behalf of purposes to which the work group is loyal and upon which they are dependent, and which have been rendered as morally superior to those inscribed in law.

In sum, the explanation for corporate lawbreaking goes well beyond the concept of self-interest and necessarily outstrips the idea that criminality simply lies in its undersocialized pursuit. To the contrary, one must understand how political, economic, and bureaucratic systems of action create notions of self-interest and merge them with the legitimate goals of those systems. And one must assess the conditions under which such socially constructed interests lead to socially harmful outcomes, including lawbreaking. Whatever one ultimately determines about these conditions, it is already clear that an argument centered on the naked pursuit of short-term self-interest explains too little and ignores too much.

18

The Process of Criminalization: The Case of Computer Crime Laws

Richard C. Hollinger and Lonn Lanza-Kaduce

During the past three decades computers have become an indispensable tool of our technologically dependent society. In the process they have been used to commit an assortment of unethical and deviant acts. Since 1978, when Florida and Arizona first passed specific laws against computer abuse (Scott, 1984:8.17), state and federal governments have legislated an entirely new body of substantive criminal law specifically designed to prevent computer-related criminality by computer users (BloomBecker, 1986; Soma et al., 1985). The rapid criminalization of computer abuse represents an exception to the gradual and reformist nature of typical law formation in common law jurisdictions.

In this article we analyze the process by which recent computer crime laws were formed, based on our interpretation of a series of legislative actions as documented in multiple sources. We begin by summarizing the nature of computer abuse. Then, we describe the criminalization process, specifically (1) the media's role in the definitional process, (2) interest groups and individuals advocating criminalization, and (3) the normative climate of public and computer-user opinion during enactment. We conclude with a discussion of the implications of our findings for theory and research on the study of criminal law formation.

Computers and the Criminal Law

Since the advent of the computer, there has been increasing concern regarding its inherent vulnerability to deviant and criminal behavior (McKnight, 1974). Computer criminality is generally classified as an

Edited and abridged from *Criminology*, Volume 26(1): 101–26 (1988).

"occupational" form of white-collar crime that benefits the perpetrator by victimizing an individual or organization and is usually committed during the course of one's occupational activity (Clinard and Quinney, 1973). Parker (1976:17–21) has delineated four distinct types of criminal behavior involving computers. In the first type, the computer is the direct "object" of the illegal act. Examples include physical abuse, sabotage, vandalism, or arson directed against computer "hardware." The second type involves the "symbolic" use of the computer and data processing output "to intimidate, deceive, or defraud victims." These offenses, such as the false invoice scam, rely partially on the perceived infallibility of computer-generated information. In the third type the computer is used as the "instrument" of the offense. Here, electronic data processing equipment is used for theft and trespassing in ways that previously required physically removing something or entering the premises of the victim.

Most of the above types of "computer crime" are not new forms of criminality and, as such, can usually be prosecuted under traditional theft, embezzlement, fraud, property, or privacy statutes (Nycum, 1976a; Parker, 1983:240). At least forty federal statutes could be applied directly to many computer-related violations (Nycum, 1976b). A number of legal scholars have argued that most examples of "computer abuse" (Parker, 1976:12) are neither unique forms of behavior nor crimes (Ingraham, 1980; Kling, 1980).

A fourth type of computer activity, however, concerns an entirely new class of intangible property, which can become the "subject" of criminality. This type presents virtually all the unique legal questions (Parker, 1976:19). In the new "paperless office," proprietary information stored electronically can be accessed, altered, stolen, and sabotaged without the perpetrators being physically present or resorting to the use of force. Thus, it is the intangible, electronic-impulse nature of computerized information that has caused the greatest concern in the legal community over possible loopholes in criminal law.

One of the most novel legal problems associated with computer crime involves whether the mere unauthorized access or electronic "browsing" in another user's computer files constitutes trespassing, theft, or some other form of criminal activity. The earliest enactment of computer crime legislation, Florida's 1978 Computer Crimes Act, defined *all* unauthorized access as a third-degree felony regardless of specific purpose. At first, subsequent state legislatures elected instead to adopt California's less punitive approach to browsing. The California statute criminalized unauthorized access to a computer file made under false pretenses, but excluded actions that were not "malicious" in nature (Scott, 1984:8.16–17). Interestingly, in response to a widely reported case of computer browsing by a student at the University of California, Los

Angeles in late 1983 (Hafner, 1983), the California legislature subsequently amended its computer crime statute to include nonmalicious, intentional, unauthorized access as a misdemeanor offense (BloomBecker, 1985). Virtually every state with computer crime legislation has now also incorporated this nonmalicious "illegal access" provision, typically as a misdemeanor (Soma et al., 1985).

Given the intangible nature of "electronic property" and the legal ambiguity surrounding malicious intent, we should not be surprised to find states amending extant criminal law to cover abuse by computer. A few states (e.g., Alabama, Alaska, Maine, Maryland, Massachusetts, and Ohio) initially responded to the objective or perceived realities of computer-related abuses within the extant legal framework by incorporating crimes committed by computer into existing theft, trade secrets, or trespass laws (see Soma et al., 1985). Most jurisdictions, however, adopted a very different tactic. They defined computer crime as a unique legal problem and thereby created separate computer crime chapters in their criminal codes.

The Criminalization Process

Our understanding of the criminalization process depends on the important legacy of case studies regarding laws on theft (Hall, 1952), vagrancy (Chambliss, 1964), juvenile law (Platt, 1969), alcohol prohibition (Gusfield, 1963), marijuana (Becker, 1963), opiate use (Lindesmith, 1967), and sexual psychopathy (Sutherland, 1950, 1951). Many theoretical and empirical issues, however, remain unresolved. Hagan's (1980) review of over forty case studies of mostly twentieth-century criminal law formation is one of the most thorough attempts to systematize findings across various criminal enactments.

Hagan emphasized that the media usually played a critical role in criminalization efforts, noting that extensive media attention accompanied most successful enactments. He also reported that, counter to common wisdom, economic elites and interest groups generally did not dominate the actual criminalization process. Instead, Hagan frequently credited moral reformers or entrepreneurs as being the causal agents behind enactments, observing that many of these crusaders converted their moral fervor into personal, professional, or occupational benefits. Finally, Hagan found that there was generally little polarized disagreement over criminal enactments (with the exception of alcohol prohibition). Given the importance of Hagan's review to the study of criminalization, his observations are used here as a framework for analyzing the criminalization of computer abuse.

Media Give and Take

The media have played both a direct and indirect role in the formation of computer law. To know about the nature and incidence of the computer crime phenomenon is to rely essentially on the media. Indeed, this is exactly what the best known expert on computer crime, Donn Parker, has done. He amassed a data base on all forms of computer "abuse" (Parker, 1976, 1983). Collecting information almost exclusively from newspaper clippings, Parker has documented over one thousand reported instances of abuse involving computers. Virtually all estimates reported in the media regarding the incidence of computer crime have been made from his data base (Parker, 1980b).

Although Parker has been careful to point out that no one can possibly know the true extent of computer crime and abuse, he concluded from his collection of news accounts in 1976 that "the growth in this file appears to be rapid and exponential" (Parker, 1976:25). Parker suggested that we are seeing only the "tip of the iceberg" because so many cases have been discovered purely by accident (U.S. Congress, Senate, 1978:57). Thus, the "actual" level of computer abuse must be substantially higher. Although Parker claims that the media have misconstrued or inaccurately reported his statements (Parker, 1980a:332), he and many other experts have regularly responded to reporters' requests for incidence estimates with merely educated guesses. For example, one computer crime expert guesstimated that "95% of all computer crime is never discovered" (Rutenberg, 1981). Unfortunately, many of these media-generated educated guesses are then reified as fact when these experts are quoted later by the press.

Among other "experts" there is disagreement over whether computer crime is reaching epidemic proportions. For example, Taber (1980) has critically examined Parker's data base and has concluded that the actual incidence of computer crime has been grossly exaggerated. He cites instances of Parker's misclassification and poor verification procedures. Taber claims that a number of the more prominently cited computer crimes have been found not to be crimes directly perpetrated by computer. He argues that Parker's heavy reliance on newspaper accounts without independent verification has allowed his data set to become contaminated with a number of apocryphal events. After specifically comparing Parker's computer crime data with the substantially lower levels of victimization reported in a U.S. General Accounting Office (1976) study, Taber concludes there is no doubt that some computer crimes occur, but he seriously questions the incidence estimates made by Parker, and repeated by the media. This critique has had some effect on estimates made earlier. Even Parker now regrets claiming that his data base is a representative sample of computer abuses (1983:25).

Although the actual incidence and degree of harm associated with computer crime are unknown, the number of feature articles appearing in the mass media increased dramatically throughout the late 1970s and early 1980s. Regardless of whether this increase is attributable more to heightened media attention than to actual behavior, these reports have had an impact on the perceived incidence of computer crime. In the absence of verifiable and reliable data, computer law enactments seemed to have been catalyzed by the perception of serious computer crime as presented in the popular media.

The direct effect of the media is best illustrated in the evolution of post-1983 federal and state computer crime legislation. Two media events, in particular, have had the most significant effect on recent criminalization efforts. The first was the discovery of the "414 hackers." The "414 (their hometown telephone area code) hackers" were young computer aficionados arrested in 1983 for using their home computers and telephone modems to obtain illegal access to approximately eighty notable computer installations (including the Sloan Kettering Memorial Cancer Institute, Security Pacific National Bank, and the Los Alamos National Laboratory) (*Newsweek*, 1983a). Except for some files that were accidentally damaged at Sloan, no material harm was done. The activities of the "414 hackers" could best be characterized as instances of computer browsing.

At approximately the same time, the country was captivated by *WarGames*, the movie in which a fictitious young computer genius gained control over the North American Air Defense (NORAD) Command in Wyoming and almost triggered a nuclear world war by accident. The screenplay of this movie was loosely based on real NORAD computer hardware and software failures that had occurred a number of years earlier (U.S. General Accounting Office, 1981); however, little else in the movie was even remotely plausible (see *Newsweek*, 1983b). Nevertheless, in 1983, the media began to fixate on the prospect of young computer hackers creating international mayhem from their bedrooms using home computers and telephone modems (e.g., *ABC News Nightline*, 1983).

In the fall of 1983, *Newsweek* (1983a, 1983b), *People* (1983a, 1983b), and *Time* (1983a, 1983b) all featured stories on these juvenile hackers and the perceived threat of computer crime. Virtually all the reports in the popular press during this period painted an alarming picture of highly vulnerable private and public computer installations. The combined dramatic effect of the "414" case and *WarGames* was illustrated in subsequent congressional hearings. In September 1983, Neal Patrick, one of the now infamous "414 hackers," was brought to Washington to testify regarding his unauthorized computer activities. Immediately before Patrick's testimony a segment from the movie *WarGames* was shown to the subcommittee as evidence "of what real hackers do" (U.S. Congress, House, 1983c).

These 1983 media events ensured that both the public and its elected representatives "knew" that computer crime was a major problem and that something had to be done quickly. This was the emotional climate in which about half the states and the federal government passed initial computer crime legislation. It also was during this period that most earlier computer crime statutes were amended to criminalize nonmalicious browsing. Even before the above incidents (and especially after), many articles and news reports about computer crime focused on two so-called facts. First, the media told us there was a whole generation of young hackers who were involved in epidemic levels of computer crime (e.g., *Business Week*, 1981; Shea, 1984). Second, many articles pointed out that the criminal justice system was ill-trained and almost legally powerless to respond to this new threat (e.g., *Minneapolis Star*, 1978; *Time*, 1982; *New York Times*, 1983).

An Interest Group Analysis and the Role of Reformers

Pluralistic accounts of law formation direct us to look for specific interest groups and moral reformers who might have been instrumental in bringing about computer crime legislation. Accounts like Gusfield's (1963) suggest that social movements may be at the base of criminalization. Although social movements can frequently rely on pressure groups (see Useem and Zald, 1982), no consistently active interest groups or identifiable social movements were behind efforts to criminalize computer abuse. The only organized group to mount an early lobbying effort for computer crime legislation was the American Society for Industrial Security (ASIS), a professional organization for private security professionals and the security industry. It is difficult, however, to separate the impact of ASIS from that of its counsel, August Bequai, whose role as reformer is discussed below.

An other organized special interest group that may have had some influence was the American Bar Association (ABA), but its impact was primarily on recent federal legislation. The ABA released a survey purporting to show significant business and government victimization from computer crime immediately prior to the vote in 1984 on the first federal law (*New York Times*, 1984b). The impact of the ABA was probably due more to its authoritativeness than to specific entrepreneurial efforts. The ABA does not appear to have played an important role in the formulation of earlier state computer crime legislation.

Although representatives of some economic and organized interest groups (e.g., data processing professional groups, equipment manufacturers, computing service companies, insurers, and computer consulting firms) testified before legislative committees, there is little evidence of their spearheading an intense lobbying effort on behalf of computer crime legislation. In fact, some computer manufacturing and services interests were conspicuous by their absence or tardiness (see Conroy, 1985, 1986).

The most visible legislative input from economic interest groups at the federal level occurred in response to Senate inquiries as it was considering an early computer crime bill. Inquiries were also sent to various law enforcement and legal agencies. The responses offered suggested provisions and language changes (U.S. Congress, Senate, 1978) and some minor wording changes were incorporated into the subsequent federal laws. Examples include the elimination of nonmalicious and petty offenses by setting a minimal jurisdictional amount of loss and the definition of "computer" to exclude the handheld calculator.

Individual reformers, rather than widespread grassroots social movements or economic interest groups, have been the principal forces behind the passage of computer crime legislation. However, these reformers have not been the "moral entrepreneurs" (Becker, 1963) of previous criminalization efforts. Instead, computer abuse "experts" and legislators have been the most influential in the legislative process.

Without doubt the single most important expert has been Donn Parker. His data base was instrumental in convincing legislators that an objective problem exists. For example, after Parker's invited special presentation to the joint Florida House and Senate, those bodies passed the Computer Crimes Act unanimously with only two definitional amendments. Parker has made similar presentations to numerous state and federal legislative committees during the past decade. In these formal presentations Parker provides legislators with a summary of his data to document the widespread prevalence and increasing incidence of computer crime and abuse (e.g., U.S. Congress, Senate, 1978:52-69; U.S. Congress, House, 1982:45–53, 1983a:23–31). From the separate states to the U.S. Congress, Parker has had a profound impact on the proliferation of legislation, and in the process he has earned a national reputation as the premier computer crime expert.

Another important reformer is author and attorney, August Bequai. Already an established expert on white-collar crime (Bequai, 1977a), he quickly developed expertise on the subject of computer crime (1978, 1983, 1987). Bequai was instrumental in efforts to enact both state and federal computer crime statutes, and he was one of the authors of the first piece of proposed federal legislation, the Federal Computer Systems Protection

Act (Taber, 1980:302). Additionally, in his role as counsel for the American Society for Industrial Security, Bequai was the acknowledged principal author of ASIS's prepared statement submitted in support of this bill in 1978. In this document Bequai argued that computer crime was dramatically increasing and that new federal legislation with "large fines and lengthy prison terms" would be required to stem the tide (U.S. Congress, Senate, 1978:113–20). In 1983 Bequai testified before Congress in support of the Small Business Computer Crime Prevention Act. In his formal remarks Bequai maintained that computer crime is rapidly outpacing the criminal justice system's ability to respond to the threat (U.S. Congress, House, 1983a:4–12). In his writings and public speeches, using largely anecdotal data, Bequai has continued to lobby both legislatures and the general public for a tougher response to the myriad of "dangers" presented by our recently computerized and cashless society.

In the political arena a number of legislators have played a key role in the formation of federal legislation against computer crime, principally former Senator Abraham Ribicoff, Senator Joseph Biden, and Representative Bill Nelson. Senator Ribicoff introduced a bill that would have made virtually all crimes committed by computer a federal offense. The earliest testimony was in the Senate Judiciary Subcommittee on Criminal Laws and Procedures, chaired by Senator Biden, who specifically requested industry comment on the proposed legislation (U S. Congress, Senate, 1978, 1980). In their testimony on this bill and a subsequently introduced legislative revision Parker and others generally agreed that a problem existed, but there was no consensus in the Senate that computer crime was a federal matter.

During the 97th and 98th Congresses, Representative Bill Nelson became the advocate of a federal computer crime statute. Having been the principal author of Florida's computer crime act, Nelson viewed computer crime as one of his areas of personal expertise, as evidenced by its prominent mention in his list of personal legislative accomplishments (Nelson, 1985). He soon sponsored several computer crime bills in the House (U.S. Congress, House, 1982, 1983b).

Until 1984 the primary impact of House and Senate testimony on federal computer crime legislation was to provide the states with model legislative wording (Sokolik, 1980). While state computer crime statutes were proliferating, however, legislative initiatives continued to be delayed in the Congress, due primarily to concerns about federal jurisdictional overreach and redundancy. Despite testimony supporting a federal statute, no House or Senate committee was convinced that computer crime should be subject to federal control.

Opposition to computer criminalization efforts has been relatively minor and largely related to federal legislation. The FBI, for example, initially expressed reservations about the jurisdictional scope of legislation that would make the FBI responsible for investigating all instances of computer crime (U.S. Congress, Senate, 1978:34). Colorado's Attorney General, J. D. MacFarlane, argued before a Senate committee that the issue of computer crime could better be handled at the state level (U.S. Congress, Senate, 1980:5–16). Further, in 1982 Milton Wessel, a lawyer and computer law instructor at Columbia University, testified that a federal computer crime statute was not necessary given the fact that the Florida statute had not been used since its enactment.

The first piece of federal legislation passed by both the House and Senate that addressed computer crime was incorporated into the Counterfeit Access Device and Computer Fraud and Abuse Act of 1984 (U.S. Congress, House, 1984). Much of the wording from Representative Nelson's proposed legislation was incorporated into this bill which primarily addressed credit card fraud and the abuse of credit information. Thus, the first federal computer crime bill was passed by attaching it to a related banking and finance bill (U.S. Public Law 98–473, 1984), a subject over which there is clear federal jurisdiction. In addition, federal jurisdiction was limited and petty cases were excluded by mandating a minimum dollar amount of $5,000. Due to its banking emphasis, the bill assigned most enforcement duties to the Treasury Department's Secret Service rather than to an already overburdened and somewhat reluctant FBI.

The most recent addition to federal computer crime law was passed in the waning days of the 99th Congress. The Computer Fraud and Abuse Act of 1986 provides additional penalties for fraud and related activities in connection with access devices and computers (U.S. Public Law 99–474, 1986). This legislation extends federal privacy protection to computerized information maintained by financial institutions and clarifies unauthorized access of computers used by the U.S. government. Three new offenses are defined: unauthorized computer access with the intent to defraud, malicious damage via unauthorized access, and trafficking in computer passwords with the intent to defraud (e.g., placing such information on computer bulletin boards). In sum, The Computer Fraud and Abuse Act tightened, extended, and clarified the earlier 1984 legislation.

The Normative Climate during Enactment

Based on the substantial media and legislative attention directed to computer crime, one would expect to find widespread public debate over the relative merits of criminalization. No significant organized opposition to criminalization was mounted, however. In fact, the minimal opposition that surfaced was primarily at the federal level, and some was raised for reasons other than normative disagreement. The absence of normative conflict or "segmented dissensus" (Rossi and Berk, 1985) over criminalization, however, does not mean there was a public consensus that demanded the criminalization of certain computer activities. Even in the wake of the movie *WarGames* and the "414 hackers" case, computer criminalization did not result from grassroots popular politics. In fact, before 1983, there is evidence that the public was rather ambivalent about reports of embezzlements and thefts via computers. A Roper poll found that computer crimes ranked eighth on a list of eleven concerns (Roper, 1982b). In 1982, 80 per cent of those polled favored laws to protect "privacy" interests in personal data stored in large computer files (Roper, 1982a). Legislative bodies did not begin to emphasize the privacy themes in computer crime enactments until relatively late in the process."

Another aspect of the normative climate surrounding computer crime concerns whether computer users consider the various types of prohibited computer activity to be acceptable or deviant. Are they likely to support or resist criminalization? In one study, two hundred undergraduates enrolled in upper-division computer science courses at a Midwestern university were anonymously surveyed during the fall of 1982 to determine their propensity toward involvement in crime by computer (Hollinger, 1984). Each respondent was presented with scenarios that depicted four types of computer abuse: computer as "object," "symbol," "instrument," and "subject" of crimes (based on Parker, 1976). Hollinger found a high degree of normative consensus among users for the first three types of computer deviance; 90 per cent of the respondents (in a state that at the time did not have a computer crime statute) indicated they would not engage in behaviors in which computers were the "object," "symbol," or "instrument" of crime. For the last type, computer as "subject" of the abuse, there was more ambivalence. Twenty-two percent of the respondents indicated that they "definitely" or "probably" would examine or modify confidential information stored in a computer account if they had the opportunity, and only 3 per cent said they definitely would not.

This receptivity to browsing and modifying electronically stored information seems to reflect the informally established subcultural norms and customs found among some dedicated computer users. The unauthorized access of computer accounts is often not perceived as being either deviant or criminal by computer aficionados (Markoff, 1982, 1983). Some users accept a subcultural "hacker ethic," which is based on the philosophical position that all data files placed on telephonically linked computers are essentially in the public domain and should be free and accessible to all (see Levy, 1984:26; see also McCaghy and Denisoff, 1973, who found a similar ethic justifying music piracy). Some pioneering users of computers argue that the free and unrestricted use of computers is a human "right" that in recent years has become far too constrained and limited. There is evidence that this "high tech norm" may actually predate the microcomputer revolution. For example, some of the famous "phone phreaks" of the 1970s (i.e., those in the "blue-box" free long distance telephone subculture) later combined their telephone fascination with the new computer technology (Landreth, 1985:28–34).

An increasing number of contemporary examples suggest that hacking may be explicitly or implicitly encouraged during the process of becoming computer literate. In the extremely competitive environment of computer science, system hacking is viewed by some instructors and peers as an indicator of excellence. Students of computer science sometimes dare each other to break into computer systems as a test of programming prowess (e.g., Harrer, 1985). Parker (1976, 1983:134–36) and others have expressed concern that computer training may be criminogenic in that computer pranksterism generally is not negatively sanctioned and is sometimes even encouraged (*New York Times*, 1984a; Parker, 1979:54).

Because computer science is a relatively new profession, professional or occupational norms are still developing (e.g., Parker, 1983:196–203). Only recently have there been efforts to institutionalize norms regarding the unacceptability of certain types of acts (Johnson, 1985). Professional associations are developing codes of ethics and model penal codes relating to computer crime and abuse (see Johnson and Snapper, 1985). Since computer crime legislation preceded active involvement by professional associations establishing occupational norms, computer crime laws were not the result of occupations attempting to regulate themselves (see Akers, 1968).

Discussion

Summarizing the criminalization process is relatively easy. Public opinion neither called for nor opposed the criminalization of computer abuse. There was very little direct pressure on legislators from any interest group—moral or economic. Nor were "moral entrepreneurs" zealously seeking to legislate morality. Instead, individual state and federal lawmakers took the initiative. "Computer crime" presented activist legislators with an ideal issue with which to maximize personal media exposure without offending any major constituency. To legitimize their campaign, the legislators enlisted technical experts on computer abuse, who also gained recognition for themselves and their work.

Both the experts and the legislators relied heavily on the media in their efforts to advance criminalization. Legislators would not have received so much publicity and the experts could not have assembled the supporting data were it not for extensive media coverage of computer abuse. Unlike the experts and activist legislators, however, the media did not play a direct advocacy role in criminalization. It was the media's reporting, and not their advocacy, that was most indispensable to the criminalization process.

The most plausible explanation for the initial coverage of computer abuse and the later attention to criminalization efforts, is that trained news professionals made an occupational judgment that the stories were newsworthy. There was no need for the news professionals to favor or oppose criminalization to make such a judgment. Given the division of labor in most news organizations, it is unlikely that the day-to-day tactical reporting decisions directly reflected a profit motive. However, once the coverage piqued public interest, the managers of all major competitors were bound to report the phenomenon to maintain their market positions.

The occupational and economic utility of criminalization activities to the legislators, experts, and media is obvious. Equally obvious is the deterrent threat embodied in the new computer crime provisions. Even more important, however, computer crime laws possess a significant symbolic component. The objective existence of the phenomenon notwithstanding, the criminalization of computer abuse was primarily symbolic in the sense that the laws communicated cultural normative messages about the use and abuse of the expanding computer technology. This form of symbolism is different from that documented by Gusfield (1963) in his case study of Prohibition, in that computer crime did not represent the dominance of one status group over another (see also Galliher and Cross, 1983). Rather, computer crime laws are symbolic in that they "educate," "moralize," or "socialize" (see Andeneas, 1971) computer users. Perhaps the clearest example of this consequence is the development of occupational codes of ethics by data management professional organizations *after* criminalization was virtually completed (Johnson, 1985; Johnson and Snapper, 1985).

The importance of symbolism in the criminalization process is suggested by the indispensable, but nonadvocacy, role played by the media. Indeed, Hagan (1980:623) observed, the media are the "linchpin" in the process of criminalization. As dealers in symbols (see Tuchman, 1978), the media convey the normative meanings around which consensus for criminalization develops.

This article is consistent with previous work that shows several ways in which the media influence perceptions about crime and criminal enactments. First, the media convey a sense of frequency about a phenomenon. "Where a certain degree . . . of deviance . . . is reached, society acts to control it by codifying mores" (Evan, 1980:556). The media directly and indirectly, through Parker's expertise, brought the extent of computer abuse to our attention; they helped discover a problem (see also Best and Horiuchi, 1985; Dickson, 1968; Downs, 1972; Pfohl, 1977; Schoenfeld et al., 1979). Moreover, as has been learned from research on crime waves (e.g., Ben-Yehuda, 1986; Fishman, 1978), the media contribute to public perceptions of a threat, regardless of their accuracy. As Alix (1978:vii) argues in his case study of ransom kidnapping law, the amount of media attention is more important for criminalization than is the objective frequency of the phenomenon.

A second dimension of the media's role is also highly symbolic. The media influence the social definition of the phenomenon (see, Swigert and Farrell, 1980; Berk et al., 1977). That a behavior occurs frequently or is frequently reported does not in itself warrant criminalization. The behavior must also hold some symbolic importance for the culture. In this regard Durkheim (1933) admonished that criminal definitions reflect a social need to punish and that they cannot be understood in purely utilitarian terms. When the media highlight and stress a phenomenon's symbolic themes, they help convey a sense of normative threat or moral gravity, which in turn stimulates criminalization efforts.

Although others, especially Alix (1978), have linked the media to a belief in deterrence, it is the symbolic rather than the empirical basis of the belief that is important for criminalization. The media presented computer abuse as a threat the law could help remedy. Since utility is a cultural value, it is not surprising that advocates of criminalization advanced deterrent rationales, especially when seeking favorable publicity. Nevertheless, it was the symbolic threat rather than the prospect of a successful remedy that motivated criminalization.

The catalyst for criminalization in over half the jurisdictions that enacted computer crime laws was the media's portrayal of the threat personal computers and modems presented to possessory information. The drama in the media also prompted other jurisdictions to amend their "browsing" statutes by eliminating the "malicious intent" requirement. Until computer technology was disseminated to the general public, computer abuse remained an internal matter between victimized organizations (which used mostly mainframe computers) and their own employees (e.g., Parker, 1976; Whiteside, 1978). Personal computers and modems externalized the phenomenon. Computer abuse posed a new threat to extant normative and institutional relations, especially given the subterranean "hacker ethic" among some of the most capable young users. It is instructive to note that this external threat was depicted as coming from our children—not malevolent enemies.

Although the emphasis here on symbolism is principally motivated by the facilitating role played by the media in the process of criminalization, some additional features of the criminalization of computer abuse reinforce the argument. Of particular note are (1) the timing of the criminalization, (2) the form the criminal law took, and (3) the resulting pattern of enforcement associated with computer crime laws.

Computers were introduced more than two decades before any formal attempts to criminalize computer abuse began with the congressional hearings in 1978. Even though Parker's (1976, 1983) media-generated data may be flawed, there is little doubt that he documented many instances of computer-related involvement in crime long before the first criminalization efforts. This lengthy delay, followed by preliminary legislative concern in 1978 and culminating in rapid criminalization after 1983, is significant. The timing of criminalization corresponds more closely to the public availability of personal computers and telephone modems than to the introduction of computerized data processing or abuse. Arguably, any need to deter abuse existed long before the enactment of computer crime statutes. In fact, the available data suggest that serious economic losses linked to computer abuse have been and continue to be attributed to current and former employees of the victimized organization rather than to interloping hackers with modems (see Parker, 1976, 1983; Taber, 1980). The temporal lag in the criminalization of computer abuse (not observed with the introduction of other technological changes), seriously challenges the extent to which computer crime laws can be understood purely as instruments of classical deterrence.

Because most computer abuse is simply a "high tech" version of other forms of crime or deviance (e.g., theft, sabotage, fraud) and is not legally unique (Ingraham, 1980), a number of other criminal and regulatory laws were on the books to deter most abuse before the enactment of specific computer crime statutes (Nycum, 1976a, 1976b; Taber, 1979). The primary legal uncertainties that existed before the criminalization movement centered on the intangible nature of electronically stored information. A few states chose to close the legal loopholes by minor definitional amendments to preexisting criminal laws. This approach was consistent with the modern trend in criminal codes to consolidate all theftlike offenses into a single chapter (see Samaha, 1987). Nevertheless, most states chose a different legal form. They enacted separate, more exhaustive (but not mutually exclusive) computer crime chapters for their criminal codes (Soma et al., 1985). These "stand-alone" computer crime chapters, which in many instances merely transformed existing criminal activity involving computers into "computer crime," have few obvious deterrent advantages. However, they do convey a clear symbolic message about the gravity of computer offenses that would not have been so prominent if accomplished through minor definitional amendments or judicial interpretation.

Chambliss and Seidman (1982:315), whose analysis anticipated the findings presented here better than other approaches, argue that one way to identify symbolism is to locate laws that are not utilized extensively to combat the problem they were supposed to address. If the primary function of the new computer crime statutes was to deter rampant abuse, one would expect the new laws to result in vigorous prosecutions. The number of prosecutions under the new computer crime laws, however, has been surprisingly low, especially when contrasted with the media-created images of rampant abuse by groups of hackers collaborating to share passwords to break into systems (see Pfuhl, 1987). From 1978 to 1986, fewer than two hundred criminal prosecutions were initiated nationally (BloomBecker, 1986). Under the nation's oldest statute, Florida's, fewer than a half-dozen prosecutions had been filed in its first five years (U.S. Congress, House, 1982:41–43, 1983b:31–80). At the same time, some of the most visible offenders (e.g., the "414 hackers"), who could have become the clearest examples for general deterrence, have been dealt with leniently. This meager enforcement pattern might undermine direct utilitarian strategies like deterrence, but it is consistent with the symbolic functions of law formation.

Computer abuse and symbolic computer crime laws also speak to the distribution of power in society. Recall, there is little evidence of either conflict among powerful groups or a power elite attempting to use law as its instrument of control. Conflict formulations, like that of Chambliss and Seidman (1982), deemphasize pluralistic and instrumentalist perspectives for understanding law. Rather, Chambliss and Seidman (1982:180) argue that changing social relations change law, and they emphasize the importance of rational-legal legitimacy and symbolic law for understanding the legal order. They posit that legislators have relative autonomy to act and that they will frequently enact symbolic measures to persuade both dissident factions of the powerful class and the general population of the "need" for order and stability. Legislative autonomy is reduced where more material and instrumental concerns prevail. Such an account is consistent with much of what has been reported here about computer crime. Within the constraints of electoral politics, the legislators seemed to be operating quite autonomously using experts to provide rational-legal justification for the law. Both the autonomy and rational-legal legitimacy are consistent with a symbolic interpretation.

In another conflict formulation, Hagan and his associates (Hagan and Parker, 1985; Hagan et al., 1985, 1987) have tried to integrate macro- and microlevels of analysis by stressing the importance of different structural relations of power for both criminal behavior and the social reaction to it. Following their lead, it can be argued that young people from white-collar families find themselves in a structural position wherein they have both the opportunity to use computers and modems and the encouragement to master the technology. This occurs in a social context in which there is little direct monitoring of computer use and, heretofore, few established norms. More abuse should be expected in such a structural circumstance. The cultural novelty of "computer delinquency" makes the behavior newsworthy. At the same time, legislators, who have been designated to safeguard such central cultural values as property and privacy, should be expected to react by clarifying norms. Therefore, it is not surprising that so much media and legislative attention was given to the browsing activities of youthful hackers, even though browsing had little economic impact. The negligible economic impact and the structural position of the hackers should also cause us to expect a lenient enforcement reaction when hackers are detected. The principal function of symbolic computer crime laws, given current power arrangements, is that they send clear cultural messages to youthful dissidents in the privileged classes about the importance of property and privacy interests without penalizing them. In this context it would appear that computer crime laws were passed, in part, to stigmatize hacking but not the hacker.

Implications for Future Research

The criminalization of computer abuse raises several important implications for future research and theorizing about the formation of laws. Indeed, the formation of laws may proceed differently for legal enactments that are not so symbolic as was computer abuse. Given the procedural constraints on enforcement, prosecution, adjudication, and sanctioning in the criminal justice system, criminal law is a relatively inefficient and cumbersome means for attaining concrete goals. Economic interests may more easily obtain their material goals through other types of law, and hence less symbolic issues may be more likely to give rise to civil enactments or *mala prohibita* regulatory controls. Thus, instances of noncriminal law formation may be associated with more conflict between and greater input from economic interests (see McCaghy and Denisoff, 1973). Research should explore whether and how formative processes vary by type of law—civil, criminal, and regulatory.

In some ways, the formation of computer crime laws seems to be atypical in that moral entrepreneurs (e.g., Becker, 1963), social movements (e.g., Platt, 1969; Tierney, 1982; Useem and Zald, 1982), status groups (e.g., Gusfield, 1963), and fear of "dangerous classes" (e.g., Adler, 1986) were not involved. Future research should sort out the circumstances under which the routes to criminalization involve different factors.

Finally, since the media seem central to the enactment process, their role should be more clearly delineated. This article has described a two-pronged role by the media in the case of computer crime—establishing a frequency threshold and advancing a social definition of threat—both of which helped consensus to emerge. That role was attributed to relatively autonomous professionals making occupational judgments that were later filtered by media managers. Future research should more specifically examine the accuracy of this interpretation. Perhaps, in most circumstances, the media are less autonomous and act more as a conduit of the opinion of the public, elite insiders, moral reformers, and/or economic interests. Because of the media's centrality to criminalization, their role should be carefully documented across instances of law formation.

New Directions: Critical Theory

Introduction

Many new and some not so new streams of social and philosophical thought contribute to the criminological enterprise thereby promising to revitalize and enrich the discipline. If separated these differing but in many ways complementary influences are critical theory, feminist theory, and postmodernist theory and include attempts at integrating these and earlier theories into a single entity. Critical theory covers a number of different approaches to the understanding of crime that focus on broader societal processes rooted in social conflict. While there are differences in emphasis among critical theorists, all tend to dismiss traditional individualistic exegesis of crime for failing to consider how the offenders are themselves oppressed by societal inequities. Moreover, critical theorists indicate that there is a selective focus on individualistic forms of crime as causing harm as though these operate independently of their social context and to the exclusion of corporate and organizational activity which can also be criminal. All critical approaches consider inequalities in the social structure as important causal attributes and see the abatement of crime only if there are fundamental changes in the social and political organization of society itself.

From Conflict Theory to State-Organized Crime

Conflict theory, based on the nineteenth-century ideas of Max Weber and Georg Simmel, assumes that there is more division in society than consensus and that through struggle and alliances some groups gain more power than others. Power is based on several dimensions, not just money and wealth, and may include political power, social power, and the prestige that comes from social position. Sociologists like Lewis Coser (1956) and Ralf Dahrendorf (1959) introduced the notion of conflict as

331

a central dynamic of social systems. Conflict sociologists showed that as a result of the asymmetry of power, some groups are more influential than others and use their influence to maintain their position. Conflict criminologists like George Vold (1958) and Austin Turk (1969) applied these ideas to law and crime showing that because of their dominance, powerful groups are able to shape the process that determines what is crime and who is the criminal.

Using an analysis of society based on the nineteenth-century writings of Karl Marx, some critical theorists, later known as radical criminologists, saw power as chiefly based on the control of economic resources. Marx and his colleague Friedrich Engels argued that all other dimensions such as honor and prestige were ultimately shaped by whether people were owners of wealth or whether they simply owned their labor which they sold to capitalists for wages. The first to apply these ideas to crime was Willem Bonger (1916), who saw capitalism as criminogenic, promoting an egoism, competition, and selfishness at the expense of altruism, sharing, and cooperation. For Bonger egoism fostered criminal thoughts because it severed ties to others. More recently, radical theorists such as Chambliss (1975b), Richard Quinney (1973), and Taylor et al., (1973) have argued that an adequate social theory must place crime in the context of a capitalist political economy. They suggest that not only is crime determined largely by the behavior of the powerful in that what is criminalized is what most threatens their position, but that the state operates on behalf of the economically powerful to protect their interests.

Some such as Greenberg (1981) and Young (1981) find the evidence for this "instrumental view" too narrow, believing instead that the state is more autonomous and that laws serve a more ideological role in protecting the general institution of capitalism, even if this means it has to act against some individual capitalists whose own behavior threatens the legitimacy of the system. However, the autonomy of the state can lead to it committing its own harms, which, because of its control over the definition of crime, are not criminalized.

In his article Dario Melossi (chap. 19) points out that critical approaches are under attack in the current era of right-wing political dominance and that there is an intellectual stagnation in the development of criminal policies. He considers this a theoretical problem that may be solved by critical theorists creating a grounded labeling theory that takes into account the vocabulary of motives of individual actors in collectivities.

Consistent with this perspective, Chambliss's essay (chap. 20) concentrates on analysis of crimes that are organized by the state itself. These are acts that are defined as crimes if carried out by ordinary citizens, but if carried out by state officials "in the pursuit of their job as representatives of the state" they are not considered such. Chambliss gives a studied review of state-sponsored crimes such as: piracy, smuggling of arms and narcotics, and murder and relates their explanation to a general theory of crime based on critical theory concepts.

An excellent example of the assertion of critical theorists that traditional explanations of crime tend to concentrate on what is generally known as "street crime" and thereby deemphasize the greater and more widespread damage to society done by corporate criminals, is the selection by Andrew Szasz (chap. 21). Directing his research on the disposal of hazardous waste, Szasz shows how under certain circumstances there is a blurring between what is legitimate and illegitimate business in efforts to maximize profits and minimize responsibility for violations of regulatory law.

19

Overcoming the Crisis in Critical Criminology: Toward a Grounded Labeling Theory

Dario Melossi

What some call a "new," "critical," "radical," or "Marxist" criminology has been described as being in a state of crisis (Inciardi, 1980). In a period seeing a sharp shift to the political right, these attacks are quite understandable. They correspond to the pendulum-like political movement which characterizes issues of law and order and crime and punishment (Melossi, 1985). But if the alleged crisis of critical criminology is more than a polemical ploy by political and academic adversaries, then its roots should be sought within critical criminology itself. I argue that there is indeed a crisis in critical criminology and that it derives from intellectual stasis and powerlessness vis-à-vis criminal policies increasingly inspired by right-wing ideological positions. Thus, the impasse is fundamentally theoretical, not political.

This theoretical crisis can be identified with the following question: Has critical criminology really gone beyond the labeling approach's earlier formulations? The beginning of these formulations can be found in developments coming from a Meadian social psychology. First presented by Tannenbaum (1938:19–20), the notion that societal reaction to primary deviation leads to a more socially significant "secondary deviation" was systematically developed by Lemert (1951) with reference to diverse phenomena such as physical disabilities, political and sexual deviance, crime, alcoholism, and mental illness. A concept of "active" social control, alternative to the homeostatic concept of social control developed by Parsons but very much in line with Mead's idea of social control ([1925] 1964), was identified by Lemert (1942) as producing deviance instead of eliminating it. It was this pristine conception which in the early 1960s was

Edited and abridged from *Criminology*, Volume 23(2):193–208 (1985).

developed into what came to be called the labeling perspective on deviance (Kitsuse, 1962; Kitsuse and Cicourel, 1963; Goffman, 1963; Scheff, 1963; Becker, 1963). Becker's was probably the most straightforward, programmatic, and popular formulation of the labeling perspective which had the honor of being singled out as the primary target of a stinging attack by Gouldner, which itself became "classical" and the paradigm of subsequent critical/radical/Marxist critiques of the labeling perspective (Gouldner, 1968).

Once upon a Time There Was a "New" Criminology

The Becker-Gouldner exchange loomed large in *The New Criminology* by Taylor, Walton, and Young (1973). This book played a pivotal role in making American sociology of deviance known to the world and in turning some of its formulations toward Marxism. Further, Taylor, Walton, and Young gave the sociology of deviance a twist which made it able to converge intellectually with a rising Marxist "critique of the law" which was developing elsewhere in Europe and was then reimported into the United States under a different, if somewhat similar, label.

The American sociology of deviance of the 1960s had its roots in two currents of thought. The most important was the Chicago school; the other complementary root was the American tradition in sociologically oriented jurisprudence. The Chicago school inspired Sutherland's rejection of the "multifactorial" explanations of criminal behavior. It also inspired his option for a social learning theory in which the actors' "vocabularies of motive" (Mills, 1940) represented the central exogenous variable (Mills, [1959] 1963). The step from a social learning theory of criminal behavior to a labeling theory of criminal identity constituted a rather logical progression. Indeed, both kinds of theory relied on that interactionist philosophy which represented the most interesting and lasting heritage of the Chicago school of sociology. The step could easily be taken by anyone who assumed a disenchanted or skeptical attitude toward the legal definition of crime and the activities of the agencies of social control. Such an attitude was readily available in the political climate of early 1960s America. In the sociology of deviance, it was reinforced by convergence with the realist tradition in jurisprudence. For example, when Chambliss wrote of criminologists turning in the early 1960s from observation of the behavior of "criminals" to that of police, judges, and politicians, and called this process the study of "law in action" (1978:14), he was expressing the thirty or forty-year-old punch line of the "legal realists," who were disenchanted skeptics regarding the law and its enforcers.

The 1960s cultural revolution furnished the newborn sociology of deviance with an extremely favorable developmental environment and also with a cross-cultural framework which allowed its diffusion from North America to Britain, western Europe and Latin America. The politicization of the deviance issue was bound to be more immediate and "natural" in a society where the divisions between everyday life, academia, and politics were not as sharply drawn as in the United States. Nevertheless, the politics of the early years of the British "National Deviance Conference" were similar to the original American inspiration. Thus, they showed more sensitivity to an "underdog" perspective than to a "working-class" one and tended to stress a certain anarchist skepticism rather than a positive political commitment (Cohen, 1974:25).

But with the onset of more radical and/or more Marxist political and intellectual positions toward the end of the 1960s and the early 1970s, both in the United States and western Europe, a critical/radical criminology developed. It began moving away from the parental figure of the labeling perspective and toward what was called a "Marxist theory of crime and punishment." This was to be the self-assigned task of *The New Criminology*: to settle the issue with the "old" criminology, especially with recent interactionist theories, and to open the door on the new, undiscovered continent of a Marxist or "materialist" theory of deviance. The book did not really present a *new* criminology. Its main contribution was a critique of existing or previous criminological theories. *The New Criminology* was designed to reestablish the genealogical links of criminology with the great traditions of sociological thought: "This book has attempted to provide an implicit account of the uneven history of criminology's relationship to the social sciences" (Taylor et al., 1973:268). This is what the book did well. But such a goal was a very "European" one, the product of a situation in which remnants of the old legalist and psychiatric traditions were still very strong within European criminology. This was not the case in the United States, where the hegemony of sociology over criminology had been firmly established by the early 1930s. If Taylor, Walton, and Young's work was successful in criticizing the criminological positions derived from the legalist and psychiatric presuppositions of the "Classical" and "Positive" schools, it was far less so with respect to sociological criminology.

This is particularly true where *The New Criminology* tried to come to terms with the interactionist positions, from Chicago to labeling theory. The critical style of the book did not take a "sociology of knowledge" approach: the review of individual schools of thought was conducted chronologically, and each school was critiqued from the standpoint of the school which followed it. The theories thus were not considered from the perspective of a new, contemporary, overarching theory. The social theory of deviance invoked in Taylor, Walton, and Young's conclusions was a program yet to be realized; therefore it could not represent the standpoint from which other theories could be observed. This procedure became rather problematic when Taylor, Walton, and Young dealt with the most recent criminological theories, the interactionist ones, because a chronologically later viewpoint from which to criticize them had not yet emerged in sociology. Furthermore, Taylor, Walton, and Young were trying to lay the foundations for a neo-Marxist theory of crime and punishment, but such a theory could only be a product of their critique, not its inspiration.

This is where Gouldner's 1968 article was lowered as a god by the neocriminological machine (Taylor et al., 1973:166–71). Taylor, Walton, and Young certified Gouldner's positions. Ever since, the standard "Marxist" critique of the labeling, interactionist, and ethnomethodological approaches has been mainly an amplification of Gouldner's criticism. Gouldner's and/or Taylor, Walton, and Young's critiques would be repeated in a number of European analyses (Werkentin et al., 1974; Pitch, 1975; Baratta, 1982).

Taylor, Walton, and Young enriched Gouldner's analysis. Still, the core of their criticism was represented by Gouldner's fortunate label of a "zookeeping" sociology whose proponents romantically stared at the deviant without really taking sides, theoretically or practically, for the liberation of the ones labeled deviants (Gouldner, 1968:106–11). Becker's sociology was seen as "zookeeping," as little more than a variation on the old middle-class correctionalist tune. The difference, according to Gouldner, was that the sociologists of deviance were not interested in "correcting" deviants; they wished to preserve them, in their fascinating diversity, in their ghettoes or "Indian Reservations."

Gouldner brilliantly observed a relationship between the ideas of the labeling theorists and the policies of a federal administration which, in the 1960s, was heavily committed to the practice and ideology of welfare. This analysis was not gratuitous, as some have claimed. In retrospect, it can be seen as very prescient in a society where the structural level of unemployment moved up to 7 per cent of the labor force. Just as the Chicago sociologists of the 1920s and 1930s had wanted to integrate deviants in the American values of work, family, and the political process, so too, according to Gouldner, the neo-Chicagoans of the 1960s demanded respect for deviants whose only place could be the ghetto, since integration—in an economy whose employment rates in the private sector were rapidly shrinking—was no longer possible (Melossi, 1980:321–56). If the ghetto could be a gilded ghetto of polite and even pleasant tolerance, so much the better: San Francisco became the symbol of a "civility" where crimes should not be considered as such because they were "victimless" and therefore were to be regarded merely as an expression of diversity from America's standard 1950s values (Becker, 1971).

Labeling, Ideology, and Practice

It can be argued that the most important aspect of labeling theory was its application of the interactionist model to the definition of deviance and crime. By noting that Becker had not paid any attention to the role of "institutions" and "power elites," Gouldner raised the crucial theoretical point but then let it slide (Gouldner, 1968:111). Taylor, Walton, and Young, however, criticized labeling theory for not having been able to identify the sociostructural conditioning of the "power to define" (1973:166-70). Whereas the former criticism seems unfair against a sociologist who had assigned such an important role to the concept of "moral entrepreneurship" (Becker, 1963:147-63), the latter criticism hits home. The question of the relation between the study of "micro-sociological" mechanisms at work in defining the situation and the study of "macro-sociological" determinants of the power to define, is crucial to critical criminology. It is around this question that a conjunction seems to become possible between the interactionist orientation of the sociology of deviance and the Marxist orientation toward which critical criminology has been moving. It is also in relation to this issue that we can try to understand whether critical criminology has actually been able to go beyond labeling theory.

Despite the insight of their sociology of knowledge, the criticisms of the labeling perspective *à la* Gouldner tended to reduce the contribution of this perspective to that of taking an underdog stance. As a way of framing the issue of the power to define, it is said that the labeling perspective expresses an "idealistic" stance because it centers its explanatory power in language. But in order to characterize as idealistic a theory centered in language, it is necessary to think of language as something which is passively received, as a non-act. Such a conception of language presupposes a theory that sees the mind as reflecting reality and translating it into ideas which then can be expressed in language.

Labeling theories are thus criticized because they only point to the study of "mere" linguistic constructs, the labels, failing to analyze the "outside world." Such a critical standpoint is predicated upon a dualist opposition of the I and the world, of thinking subject and thought world. Such dualism, however, had been the very target of the pragmatist philosophy which was at the roots of the interactionist perspective in sociology. Furthermore, a typical research program of this pragmatist-interactionist tradition has stressed investigating connections between social organization and linguistic constructs. Other traditions, such as Marxism, tend to give reductionist answers, treating associations between organizational variables as causal processes without paying much attention to the participants' accounts of why it is that they do what they do.

It is then to the discussion of interactionism's roots that we must return. Mead attempted to provide a description of human behavior that avoided the traditional Western intellectual dualism between an internal reflecting Mind and an external reflected World. He saw the symbolic system we usually call "mind" as the outcome of a communication process in which the selves of individuals are shaped through interaction within society. It is hard to conceive of a less "idealistically" oriented enterprise than this (see Joas, 1981:180; Joas, 1985; Habermas, 1981, 2:7–170).

According to Mead (1934:259), "The process of communication is one which is more universal than that of the universal religion or universal economic process in that it is one that serves them both." But "back even of the process of discourse must lie cooperative activity." For Mead, Thomas's "definition of the situation" was clearly and inextricably connected with cooperative social processes which preside over the production and reproduction of human life. The set of meanings we call language is a product of this overall process, which is in turn possible only through communication. From this perspective, to name or define something is never merely an "idealistic" procedure. It is a consequence of an act. In a typically pragmatist fashion, a name, definition, or label designates something which is the product of a successful conversation of gestures. Instead of drawing attention away from the world of practice, Mead obliges us to look into this world in order to find our "discourses."

Mead's theory was only a beginning. His scanty development of the role of the "generalized other," leaves what is probably the most properly sociological issue quite open. A more macro-sociological interpretation of Mead's theory is found in some of Mills's, early writings. Mills read Mead in a politically relevant way because of his critical appraisal of the pragmatists' experience (Mills, [1959], 1963) and his familiarity with Weber's work (Mills, 1963:442–443). The most crucial connections between language and social control had been spelled out by Mead (see 1934 and 1964), but Mills's important addition emphasized the plurality of "audiences" which compete for a successful definition of meanings: "The control of others is not usually direct but rather through manipulations of a field of objects" (Mills, 1963:445). These audiences respond to specific "vocabularies of motive" which are grounded in "sets of collective action" (Mills, 1963:433). They are treated as a plurality of reference groups by Shibutani (1962), who connected Mead's social psychology to Simmel's concept of social organization. According to this, individual discursive perspectives depend on the unique combination of social circles in which the person participates (Simmel, [1908] 1955).

Sutherland's "differential association theory" dealt with the emotional value of an interaction by specifying several "modalities of association," and his theory of "differential social organization" developed the idea of a plurality of generalized others (Sutherland, [1947] 1973b). In discussing the psychology of embezzlers and of so-called "compulsive crimes," Cressey related Sutherland's theory of differential association to Mills's vocabularies of motive (Cressey, 1953:93–138; 1954). A more general specification of the ways in which motivational orientations account for delinquent behavior was then given by Sykes and Matza (1957) in their discussion of "techniques of neutralization."

The theoretical problem contributing to the theoretical crisis in critical criminology is the same one implicit in the works of Gouldner and Taylor, Walton, and Young—the problem of the relation between the interactionist model described above and a Marxist model centered in the "ideology" concept. Mills pointed out that "Marxists have not translated their connective terms into sound and unambiguous psychological categories . . . . What is needed is a concept of mind which incorporates social processes as intrinsic to mental operations" (1963:425).

The "mentalistic assumption" that both Mead and Mills saw as a fatal flaw in most of the social psychologies of their times seems to be present in Marx's architectural metaphor of structure/superstructure (Marx and Engels, 1976:35-37; Marx, 1970). But in *Capital* the categories of political economy are not a mere reflection of reality. They are instead the language of a specific stage of such a given mode of production. Mills could see that "'the profit motive' of classical economics may be treated as an ideal-typical vocabulary of motives for delimited economic situations and behaviors" (Mills, 1963:445n). The limits of this language are determined by the set of collective action within which it is wed.

The critiques of ideology and of political economy in *Capital* are the language of a new set of collective action; in Marx's terms, industrial capitalism and the creation of a modern working class. The potential members of this class are the audience for that redefinition of discourse which is the practical work of both Marxism and of the organizations which are the vehicles of this new discourse. Such relations, between the sets of collective action and their discourses, between language and the practice within which language is shaped, can be pinned down empirically. They can be shown in the "hunger for new words" in the early attempts by the working class to organize. They can be shown in the reciprocal adjustments of working masses and intellectuals, class and organizations, followers and leaders. They can be shown in the substitution of a socialistic vocabulary for an earlier religious one during periods of intense social transformation.

Smith (1976) has argued that we must disentangle ourselves from the ambiguity in Marx. We can no longer deal with the relation between what people do and the forms of thought as a simple relation of reflection:

> That we cannot assume [such a simple relation] is itself a product of our social organization. The relation which mediates the two terms of the observable is in the complex organization of the media, of formal administrative process, of the "scientific" media of research methodologies, professional journals and the like. These bring into being a universe of facts, images, data, findings, models, etc., etc., which stand in for and are treated as reality . . . . The character of ideological practice . . . is more now than a reflection of reality. It is a form of reality in becoming a form of action as well as representing a reality beyond itself. It is produced by actual living individuals as an actual concrete activity. . . . The critique [of ideology] is . . . a sociological work in itself. (1976:53–54)

Smith sees the ambiguity in Marx deriving from the very development of the most advanced societies. According to her, there is a tension in Marx's concept of ideology. It is a mere "reflection of reality" in a society which is still at a low level of technical and administrative rationalization. Yet it is becoming fully "symbolic" because such rationalization is no longer left to the observers but instead is offered to them in the predetermined form in which scientific and legal agencies have shaped it.

Marx considered this latter process from the perspective of the work process, since this was for him the paradigmatic relationship between the knowing subject and reality. Thus Marx saw, especially in the *Grundrisse*, that the mediation of machines between labor and the product of labor was less and less the mediation of a tool, an extension of the workers' hands. Instead, the mediator was labor itself, intellectual labor incorporated into the machine as science. The *direct* relation between workers and the "reality" which is transformed in the work process is then lost. The relation is rather between workers and the highly formalized and symbolic language of science.

During the course of the twentieth century, this kind of evolution has concerned not only the work process but the whole reality which surrounds the observer. "News" is not events of which the observer is a direct witness. It is the product of communication media. Almost every aspect of social life is no longer known by direct experience, but through the official channels of the private and public agencies which are called upon to administer it—a fact which is particularly relevant for the study of crime and punishment.

The critique of ideology cannot possibly be seen, then, as the task of the enlightened theoretician. It is an empirical work, says Smith, "a sociological work in itself." It is the work of deconstructing the ways in which the meanings of events are fixed within the activities of scientific and administrative bureaucracies. This is why Smith can write

> We have the beginnings of this kind of work in the sociological tradition which stems from symbolic interactionism, particularly in the study of deviance where "labeling" theory has been a focus. More recently some of the work done in ethnomethodology, particularly that concerned with the procedures for constructing administrative records, makes the social construction of social facts its primary research focus (1976:54n).

Toward a Grounded Labeling Theory

To define the kind of sociological work done in studies about "labels" or about participants' accounts in organizations as "idealistic" would be tantamount to defining the very development of contemporary society as idealistic. A "Marxism" which would try to ignore this kind of research would either be interested in telling its story about the capitalism of one hundred and fifty years ago or would represent a variant of economism. By "economism" I mean a specification of a structuralist view that reifies connections between structural variables without questioning the motives and orientations of the actors involved (Maynard and Wilson, 1980). In the early critical criminological literature, such a process of reification consisted essentially in coupling an economic determination of criminal behavior with an acceptance of the legal syllogism which explains punishment with crime. Thus, criminal behavior was seen as individual responses to situations of economic deprivation, and punishment was conceived as the capitalist state's attempt at controlling and repressing such responses (Melossi, 1985).

But after Taylor, Walton, and Young's *The New Criminology*, and especially after their *Critical Criminology* (1975), the positions *anarchisant* which romanticized crime as a form of individual, prepolitical response to oppression, have been criticized very harshly within the ranks of critical criminologists themselves (Young, 1975; Platt, 1978; Baratta, 1982). This more skeptical and critical view of criminal behavior has brought about a positive reevaluation of the social control function. But in a situation where the societal processes of social control had not been sufficiently investigated theoretically—or had been investigated by that labeling theory that radical criminology pragmatically excluded—a reevaluation of social control has often meant nothing more than a cosmetic reappraisal of the traditional legal model. The critical and/or Marxist positions in criminology, pressed by political urgency, seem nowadays to be engaged in presenting a left-wing, no-nonsense rhetoric in opposition to the rhetoric of the right. The problem, I submit, is not on which side of the rhetoric we are on. The problem is to further the sociological investigation of the issues at stake and to bracket, for the moment, suggestions of criminal policy which are substantially based on an acceptance of the traditional juridical view.

Most of the contemporary liberal or radical attempts at playing the role of the advisor to a (hoped-for) Prince—including those of Platt (1982), Taylor (1981), Lea and Young (1984), and of most of the participants in a debate organized a few years ago by the Italian journal *La Questione Criminale* (1981)—seem to assume that by working with the traditional, but reformed, toolbox of lawmaking, policing, doing justice, and applying some sort of penal sanction, predictable effects on crime and deviance can actually be produced. In order to express this confidence, most of these attempts have, in the tradition of liberalism, taken it for granted that a sociological explanation of "crime," "deviance," and "punishment" already exists and that such explanation is grounded in the traditional modeling of the relationships between the economic conditions of a society, its crime rates, and its punishment rates. Such an explanation is sought, with minor adjustments, in the traditional utilitarian model: economic determinism plus legal syllogism (Melossi, 1985). In short, the classical, becomes neoclassical, the tale told by economics and the law.

One is caught by the doubt, therefore, that the Marxist critique of the labeling perspective, which marked the starting point of a critical criminology, did not constitute much of a step forward. Instead, this critique constituted a classical case of the baby being thrown out with the bathwater. By criticizing the lack of practical roots of the labeling approach, a critique which often overlooked the original practical dimension of Mead's formulations, the Marxist critique went back to an economistic perspective which saw social actors as utilitarian dopes. This constitutes a fundamental misunderstanding of Marxian theory, because Marx saw his theory as the theory of an agency, the working class, engaged in a practical critique of political economy (as the subtitle of *Capital* spells out). Such a noneconomistic reading of Marx's work, to which reference is made above, makes it compatible with contributions coming from other intellectual inspirations (see Smith, 1976; Maynard and Wilson, 1980; Melossi, 1985).

An economistic variety of Marxism ended up, like "bourgeois" sociology, overlooking the new perception of the "structural" relationships between crime, punishment, and the economy, a new perception that characterizes the interactionist perspective. The path designed by this theoretical perspective is the one that critical criminologists need to follow, given the present state of knowledge of criminal and punishing behavior. Critical criminologists do not need to engage in drafting new political platforms or new legal codes which are based on unchallenged theoretical assumptions. Their role is to challenge such assumptions. A criminology deserving of the label "critical" must produce a theory which is able to deconstruct the discourses of the right *and* the left on issues of crime and punishment. Thus, a much more convincing and thoroughgoing discussion of the "Is" of the law—that is, of the sociology of the law-must precede discussion of its "Ought"—that is, of legal engineering. In his intervention in the Italian debate mentioned above, Baratta correctly pleads for a "pause for reflection" which might enable us to start over again on the right foot (1981:377–85).

If, as Baratta writes, a critical criminology is characterized by the conjunction of a "dimension of the definition" and a "dimension of power" (1981:362–63), then what is needed is not a scholastic rejection of the tradition which links the beginnings of the Chicago school to contemporary interactionist theories. What is needed is a process of trial and error, within the practice of research, where concepts deriving from both the interactionist and the Marxist traditions are set free to play their role and to prove themselves or not.

In this encounter, the objective of critical criminology should be to ground the vocabularies of motive on crime and punishment in those sets of collective action within which they are situated (see Melossi, 1976; Melossi and Pavarini, 1979). This would amount to putting into practice what might be called a *grounded labeling theory*, that is, a theory of the social discourse about deviance and crime grounded within the social discourse about the economy and the polity. Such theory must have its roots in the principle that social action cannot be made intelligible if it is not set within the specific orientation of the actor, an orientation which can be seen as expressed linguistically in a "vocabulary of motives." This set of linguistic constructs is situated in a sociohistorical context and represents the mediation between society, or a social group, and the individual self.

For example, unemployment, crime, and punishment are often seen as "naturally" destined to move together in the same direction. But many note that the "economic man" of the textbooks on economics is not even a good ideal type for business. Is there any reason, then, why this ideal type should characterize people who happen somehow to break the criminal law? In fact, while unemployment and imprisonment rates seem to move together with great synchrony, crime does not. Economism, whether of a Marxist or bourgeois variety, has a hard time explaining this statistical evidence. What pass for explanations are some magic structuralist formulas about "the needs of capital" or the "need for social control," magic because they hypostatize collectivities' behavior in a way which is independent from the motivated actions of the actual personnel involved (Maynard and Wilson, 1980; Giddens, 1984). If these relationships are to persist, there must be something going on in the motivational constructs employed by the agents of social control—be these government executives, media people, legislators, police, judges, prison wardens, or probation and parole officers—which somehow links the state of the economy with their professional activities (Melossi, 1985).

Research along these lines would avoid falling back into the kind of skeptical approach which essentially declares a radical relativism and, by so doing, induces practical powerlessness, an approach for which labeling theory was often chastised. On the contrary, "grounded labeling theory" should be used to produce a convergence of the most relevant outcomes of the skeptical approach with the need for a materialist foundation which has been stressed by critical criminologists at least since the publication of *The New Criminology*. I believe this is the path which will contribute to lead "beyond labeling" and, at the same time, take critical criminology out of the theoretical quicksands where it now seems to be mired.

20

State-Organized Crime

William J. Chambliss

Twenty-five years ago I began researching the relationship between
organized crime, politics, and law enforcement in Seattle, Washington
(Chambliss, 1968, 1971, 1975a, 1975b, 1977, 1980, 1988a). I concentrated
on understanding the political, economic, and social relations of those
organizing and financing vice in the local area. It became clear that to
understand the larger picture I had to extend my research to the United
States and, eventually, to international connections between organized
criminal activities and political and economic forces. This quest led me to
research in Sweden (Block and Chambliss, 1981), Nigeria (Chambliss,
1975b), Thailand (Chambliss, 1977), and the Americas.

Interviews with people at all levels of criminal, political, and law
enforcement agencies provided the primary data base, supplemented with
data from official records, government reports, congressional hearings,
newspaper accounts, archives, and special reports. I also began a parallel
historical study of piracy and smuggling. In the process I came to realize
that I was studying the same thing in different time periods: Some of the
piracy of the sixteenth and seventeenth centuries was sociologically the
same as some of the organized criminal relations of today—both are
examples of state-organized crime (see Chambliss, 1988a).

At the root of the inquiry is the question of the relationship between
criminality, social structure, and political economy (Petras, 1977;
Schwendinger and Schwendinger, 1975; Tilly, 1985). In what follows, I (1)
describe the characteristics of state-organized crime that bind acts that are
unconnected by time and space but are connected sociologically, (2)
suggest a theoretical framework for understanding those relationships, and
(3) give specific examples of state-organized crime.

Edited and abridged from *Criminology*, Volume 27(2):183–208 (1989).

State-Organized Crime Defined

The most important type of criminality organized by the state consists of acts defined by law as criminal and committed by state officials in the pursuit of their job as representatives of the state. Examples include a state's complicity in piracy, smuggling, assassinations, criminal conspiracies, acting as an accessory before or after the fact, and violating laws that limit its activities—such as illegal spying on citizens, and illegally diverting funds (e.g., illegal campaign contributions, selling arms to countries prohibited by law, and supporting terrorist activities).

State-organized crime does not include criminal acts that benefit only individual officeholders, such as bribery or illegal police violence, unless these acts violate existing criminal law and are official policy.

Smuggling

Smuggling occurs when a government successfully corners the market on some commodity or when it seeks to keep a commodity from another nation from crossing its borders. Everything from sheep to people, wool to wine, gold to drugs, and even ideas, have been prohibited from either export of import. Whatever is prohibited is at the expense of one group, for the benefit of another. Thus, laws that prohibit the import or export of a commodity inevitably face a built-in resistance. Part of the population will want to either possess or to distribute the prohibited goods. At times, the state finds itself in the position of having its own interests served by violating precisely the same laws passed to prohibit the export or import of the goods it has defined as illegal.

Narcotics and the Vietnam War

During the eighth century, Turkish traders discovered a market for opium in Southeast Asia (Chambliss, 1977; McCoy, 1973). Portuguese traders later found a thriving business in opium trafficking conducted by small ships sailing between trading ports in the area. One of the prizes of Portuguese piracy was opium taken from local traders and exchanged for tea, spices, and pottery. Centuries later, when the French colonized Indochina, traffic in opium was a thriving business. The French joined drug traffickers and licensed opium dens throughout Indochina the profits from which supported 50 per cent of the cost of the French colonial government (McCoy, 1973:27).

When the Communists began threatening French rule in Indochina, the French government used opium profits to finance the war. It cooperated with hill tribes, who controlled opium production, to ensure their allegiance in the war against the Communists (McCoy, 1973).

Defeated in Vietnam, the French withdrew, to be replaced by the United States who inherited the dependence on opium profits and the cooperation of the hill tribes, who in turn depended on being allowed to continue growing and shipping opium. The CIA went a step further and provided the opium-growing feudal lords in Vietnam, Laos, Cambodia, and Thailand with transportation for their opium via Air America, the CIA airline in Vietnam.

Air America regularly transported bundles of opium from airstrips in Laos, Cambodia, and Burma to Saigon and Hong Kong (Chambliss, 1977:56). An American stationed at Long Cheng, the secret CIA military base in northern Laos during the war, observed:

> so long as the Meo leadership could keep their wards in the boondocks fighting and dying in the name of. . . some nebulous cause. . .the Meo leadership [was paid off] in the form of a cart-blanch to exploit U.S.-supplied airplanes and communication gear to the end of greatly streamlining the opium operations. (Chambliss, 1977:56)

This report was confirmed by Laotian Army General Ouane Rattikone, who told me in 1974 that he was the principal overseer of the shipment of opium out of the Golden Triangle via Air America. U.S. law did not permit the CIA or any of its agents to engage in the smuggling of opium.

After France withdrew from Vietnam and left the protection of democracy to the United States, the French intelligence service that preceded the CIA in managing opium smuggling in Asia continued to support part of its clandestine operations through drug trafficking (Kruger, 1980). Although shrouded in secrecy, there is very strong evidence that French intelligence agencies helped to organize the movement of opium through the Middle East (especially Morocco) after their revenue from opium from Southeast Asia was cut off.

In 1969 Michael Hand, a former Green Beret and one of the CIA agents stationed at Long Cheng when Air America was shipping opium, moved to Australia, ostensibly as a private citizen, where he entered into a business partnership with an Australian national, Frank Nugan. In 1976 they established the Nugan Hand Bank in Sydney (Commonwealth of New South Wales, 1982a, 1982b). The Nugan Hand Bank began as a storefront operation with minimal capital investment, but almost immediately boasted deposits of over $25 million. The rapid growth of the bank resulted from large deposits of secret funds made by narcotics and arms smugglers and large deposits from the CIA (Nihill, 1982).

In addition to the bank records that suggest the CIA was using the bank as a conduit for its funds, the bank's connection to the CIA and other U.S. intelligence agencies is evidenced by the people who formed the directors and principal officers of the bank, including the following:

- Admiral Earl F. Yates, president of the Nugan Hand Bank was, during the Vietnam War, chief of staff for strategic planning of U.S. forces in Asia and the Pacific.
- General Edwin F. Black, president of Nugan Hand's Hawaii branch, was commander of U.S. troops in Thailand during the Vietnam War and, after the war, assistant army chief of staff for the Pacific.
- General Erle Cocke, Jr., was head of the Nugan Hand Washington, D.C., office.
- George Farris worked in Nugan Hand's Hong Kong and Washington, D.C. offices. He was a military intelligence specialist who worked in a special forces training base in the Pacific.
- Bernie Houghton, Nugan Hand's representative in Saudi Arabia, was also a U.S. naval intelligence undercover agent.
- Thomas Clines, director of training in the CIA's clandestine service, was a London operative for Nugan Hand who helped in the takeover of a London-based bank and was stationed at Long Cheng with Michael Hand and Theodore S. Shackley during the Vietnam War.
- Dale Holmgreen, former flight service manager in Vietnam for Civil Air Transport, which became Air America, was on the board of directors of Nugan Hand and ran the bank's Taiwan office.
- Walter McDonald, an economist and former deputy director of CIA for economic research, was a specialist in petroleum, became a consultant to Nugan Hand, and served as head of its Annapolis, Maryland, branch.
- General Roy Manor, who ran the Nugan Hand Philippine office, was a Vietnam veteran who helped coordinate the aborted attempt to rescue the Iranian hostages, chief of staff for the U.S. Pacific command, and the U.S. government's liaison officer to Philippine President Ferdinand Marcos.

On the board of directors of the parent company formed by Michael Hand that preceded the Nugan Hand Bank were Grant Walters, Robert

Peterson, David M. Houton, and Spencer Smith, all of whom listed their address as c/o Air America, Army Post Office, San Francisco, California.

Also working through the Nugan Hand Bank was Edwin F. Wilson, a CIA agent involved in smuggling arms to the Middle East and later sentenced to prison by a U.S. court for smuggling illegal arms to Libya. Edwin Wilson's associate in Mideast arms shipments was Theodore Shackley, head of the Miami, Florida, CIA station. Shackley, along with Rafael "Chi Chi" Quintero, a Cuban-American, forged the plot to assassinate Fidel Castro by using organized-crime figures. In 1973, when William Colby was made director of Central Intelligence, Shackley replaced him as head of covert operations for the Far East; on his retirement from the CIA Colby became Nugan Hand's lawyer.

In the late 1970s the bank experienced financial difficulties, and Frank Nugan was found dead of a shotgun blast in his Mercedes Benz on a remote road outside Sydney. The official explanation was suicide, but some investigators suspected murder. Nugan's death created a major banking scandal and culminated in a government investigation. The investigation revealed that millions of dollars were unaccounted for in the bank's records and that the bank was serving as a money-laundering operation for narcotics smugglers and as a conduit through which the CIA was financing gun-smuggling and other illegal operations throughout the world. These operations included illegally smuggling arms to South Africa and the Middle East. There was also evidence that the CIA used the Nugan Hand Bank to pay for political campaigns that slandered politicians, including Australia's Prime Minister Witham (Kwitny, 1987).

Hand tried desperately to cover up the operations of the bank. Hundreds of documents were destroyed before investigators could get into the bank. Despite his efforts, the scandal mushroomed and eventually Hand was forced to flee Australia. He managed this, while under indictment for a rash of felonies, with the aid of a CIA official who flew to Australia with a false passport and accompanied him out of the country.

Thus, the evidence uncovered by government investigation in Australia linked high-level CIA officials to a bank in Sydney that was responsible for financing and laundering money for a significant part of the narcotics trafficking originating in Southeast Asia (Commonwealth of New South Wales, 1982b; Owen, 1983). It also linked the CIA to arms smuggling and illegal involvement in the democratic processes of a friendly nation. Other investigations reveal that the events in Australia were but part of a worldwide involvement in narcotics and arms smuggling by the CIA and French intelligence (Hougan, 1978; Kruger, 1980; Owen, 1983).

Arms Smuggling

One of the most important forms of state-organized crime is arms smuggling. To a significant extent, U.S. involvement in narcotics smuggling after the Vietnam War can be understood as a means of funding the purchase of military weapons for nations and insurgent groups that could not be funded legally through congressional allocations or for which U.S. law prohibited support (NARMIC, 1984).

In violation of U.S. law, members of the National Security Council (NSC), the Department of Defense, and the CIA carried out a plan to sell millions of dollars worth of arms to Iran and use profits to support the Contras in Nicaragua (U.S. Senate Hearings, 1986). The Boland amendment (1985) prohibited any U.S. official from directly or indirectly assisting the Contras. To circumvent the law, a group of intelligence and military officials established a "secret team" of U.S. operatives, including Lt. Colonel Oliver North, Theodore Shackley, Thomas Clines, and Maj. General Richard Secord (testimony before U.S. Senate, 1986). Shackley and Clines were CIA agents in Long Cheng; along with Michael Hand they ran the secret war in Laos, which was financed in part from profits from opium smuggling.

Senator Daniel Inouye of Hawaii claims that this "secret government within our government" waging war in Third World countries was part of the Reagan doctrine (*Guardian*, July 29, 1987). Whether President Reagan or then Vice-President Bush were aware of the operations has not been established. But overwhelming evidence in testimony before the Senate and from court documents demonstrates that this group of state officials oversaw and coordinated the distribution and sale of weapons to Iran and to the Contras in Nicaragua. These acts were in direct violation of the Illegal Arms Export Control Act, which made the sale of arms to Iran unlawful, and the Boland amendment, which made it a criminal act to supply the Contras with arms or funds.

The weapons sold to Iran were obtained by the CIA through the Pentagon. Secretary of Defense Caspar Weinberger ordered the transfer of weapons from Army stocks to the CIA without the knowledge of Congress four times in 1986. The arms were then transferred to middlemen, such as Iranian arms dealer Yaacov Nimrodi, exiled Iranian arms dealer Manucher Ghorbanifar, and Saudi Arabian businessman Adman Khashoggi. Weapons were also flown directly to the Contras, and funds from their sale were diverted to support Contra warfare. There is also considerable evidence that this "secret team," along with other military and CIA officials, cooperated with narcotics smuggling in Latin America in order to fund the Contras in Nicaragua.

In 1986, the Reagan administration admitted that Adolfo Chamorro's Contra group, which was supported by the CIA, was helping a Colombian drug trafficker transport drugs into the United States. Chamorro was arrested in April 1986 for his involvement (Potter and Bullington, 1987:54). Testimony in several trials of major drug traffickers in the past five years has revealed innumerable instances in which drugs were flown from Central America into the United States with the cooperation of military and CIA personnel. These reports have also been confirmed by military personnel and private citizens who testified that they saw drugs being loaded on planes in Central America and unloaded at military bases in the United States. Pilots who flew planes with arms to the Contras report returning with planes carrying drugs.

At the same time that the United States was illegally supplying the Nicaraguan Contras with arms purchased, at least in part, with profits from the sale of illegal drugs, the administration launched a campaign against the Sandinistas for their alleged involvement in drug trafficking. Twice in 1986, President Reagan accused the Sandinistas of smuggling drugs. Barry Seal, an informant and pilot for the Drug Enforcement Administration (DEA), was ordered by members of the CIA and DEA to photograph the Sandinistas loading a plane. During a televised speech in March 1986, Reagan showed the picture that Seal took and said that it showed Sandinista officials loading a plane with drugs for shipment to the United States. After the photo was displayed, Congress appropriated $100 million in aid for the Contras. Seal later admitted to reporters that the photograph he took was a plane being loaded with crates that did not contain drugs. He also told reporters that he was aware of the drug-smuggling activities of the Contra network and a Colombian cocaine syndicate. Seal was murdered in February 1987. Shortly after his murder, the DEA issued a "low key clarification" regarding the validity of the photograph, admitting that there was no evidence that the plane was being loaded with drugs.

Other testimony linking the CIA and U.S. military officials to complicity in drug trafficking includes the testimony of John Stockwell, a former high-ranking CIA official, who claims that drug smuggling and the CIA were essential components in the private campaign for the Contras. Corroboration for these assertions comes also from George Morales, one of the largest drug traffickers in South America, who testified that he was approached by the CIA in 1984 to fly weapons into Nicaragua. Morales claims that the CIA opened an airstrip in Costa Rica and gave the pilots information on how to avoid radar traps. According to Morales, he flew twenty shipments of weapons into Costa Rica in 1984 and 1985. In return, the CIA helped him to smuggle thousands of kilos of cocaine into the United States. Morales alone channeled $250,000 quarterly to Contra leader Adolfo Chamorro from his trafficking activity. A pilot for Morales, Gary Betzner, substantiated Morales's claims.

The destination of the flights by Morales and Betzner was a hidden airstrip on the ranch of John Hull. Hull, an admitted CIA agent, was a primary player in Oliver North's plan to aid the Contras. Hull's activities were closely monitored by Robert Owen, a key player in the Contra Supply network. Owen established the Institute for Democracy, Education, and Assistance, which raised money to buy arms for the Contras and which, in October 1985, was asked by Congress to distribute $50,000 in "humanitarian aid" to the Contras. Owen worked for Oliver North in coordinating illegal aid to the Contras and setting up the airstrip on Hull's ranch.

According to an article in the *Nation*, Oliver North's network of operatives and mercenaries had been linked to the largest drug cartel in South America since 1983. The DEA estimates that Colombian Jorge Ochoa Vasquez, the "kingpin" of the Medellin drug empire, is responsible for supplying 70 to 80 per cent of the cocaine that enters the United States every year. Ochoa was taken into custody by Spanish police in October 1984 when the United States requested his arrest. The embassy specified that Officer Cos-Gayon, who had trained with the DEA, should make the arrest. Other members of the Madrid Judicial Police were connected to the DEA and North's arms smuggling network. Ochoa's lawyers informed him that the United States would alter his extradition if he agreed to implicate the Sandinista government in drug trafficking. Ochoa refused and spent twenty months in jail before returning to Colombia. The Spanish courts ruled that the United States was trying to use Ochoa to discredit Nicaragua and released him. (*Nation*, September 5, 1987.)

There are other links between the United States government and the Medellin cartel. Jose Blandon, General Noriega's former chief advisor, claims that DEA operations protected the drug empire and that the DEA paid Noriega $4.7 million for his silence. Blandon also testified in Senate committee hearings that Panama's bases were used as training camps for the Contras in exchange for "economic" support from the United States. Finally, Blandon contends that the CIA gave Panamanian leaders intelligence documents about U.S. senators and aides; the CIA denies these charges (*Christian Science Monitor*, February 11, 1988:3).

Other evidence of the interrelationship between drug trafficking, the CIA, the NSC, and aid to the Contras includes the following:

- In January 1983, two Contra leaders in Costa Rica persuaded the Justice Department to return over $36,000 in drug profits to drug dealers Julio Zavala and Carlos Cabezas for aid to the Contras (Potter and Bullington, 1987:22).

- Michael Palmer, a Miami drug dealer, testified that the State Department's Nicaraguan humanitarian assistance office contracted with his company, Vortex Sales and Leasing, to take humanitarian aid to the Contras. Palmer claims he smuggled $40 million in marijuana to the United States between 1977 and 1985 (*Guardian*, March 20, 1988:3).

- During House and Senate hearings in 1986, it was revealed that a major DEA investigation of the Medellin drug cartel of Colombia, expected to culminate in the arrest of several leaders of the cartel, was compromised when someone in the White House leaked the story to the *Washington Times*, which published it on July 17, 1984. According to DEA Administrator John Lawn, the leak destroyed what was "probably one of the most significant operations in DEA history" (Sharkey, 1988:24).

- When Honduran General Jose Buseo, who was described by the Justice Department as an "international terrorist," was indicted for conspiring to murder the president of Honduras in a plot financed by profits from cocaine smuggling, Oliver North and officials from the Department of Defense and the CIA pressured the Justice Department to be lenient with General Buseo. In a memo disclosed by the Iran-Contra committee, North stated that if Buseo was not protected "he will break his longstanding silence about the Nic[araguan] resistance and other sensitive operations" (Sharkey, 1988:27).

Why Do Governments and Their Agencies Violate the Law?

Why would government officials from the NSC, the Defense Department, the State Department, and the CIA become involved in smuggling arms and narcotics, money laundering, assassinations, and be willing to commit other criminal activities in wholesale disregard of the law? The answer lies in the structural contradictions that inhere in nation-states (Chambliss, 1980).

As Weber, Marx, and Gramsci pointed out, no state can survive without establishing legitimacy. The law is a fundamental cornerstone in creating legitimacy and an illusion (at least) of social order. It claims universal principles that demand some behaviors and prohibit others. The protection of property and personal security are obligations assumed by states everywhere both as a means of legitimizing the state's franchise on violence and as a means of protecting commercial interests (Chambliss and Seidman, 1982).

The threat posed by smuggling to both personal security and property interests makes laws prohibiting smuggling essential. Under some circumstances, however, such laws contradict other interests of the state. This contradiction prepares the ground for state-organized crime as a solution to the conflicts and dilemmas posed by the simultaneous existence of contradictory "legitimate" goals.

The military-intelligence establishment in the United States is resolutely committed to fighting the spread of "communism" throughout the world. This mission has prevailed since the 1800s. Congress and the presidency are not consistent in their support for the money and policies thought by the frontline warriors to be necessary to accomplish their lofty goals. As a result, programs under way are sometimes undermined by a lack of funding and even by laws that prohibit their continuation (such as the passage of laws prohibiting support for the Contras). Officials of government agencies adversely affected by political changes are thus in a dilemma. If they comply with the legal limitations on their activities they sacrifice their mission. The dilemma is heightened by the anticipation of future policy changes that will reinstate their resources and their freedom. When that time comes, however, programs adversely affected will be difficult if not impossible to recreate.

A number of events that occurred between 1960 and 1980 left the military and the CIA with badly tarnished images. Those events and political changes underscored their vulnerability. The CIA lost considerable political clout with elected officials when its infamous planned "Bay of Pigs" invasion of Cuba was a complete disaster. The United States showed itself vulnerable to the resistance of a small nation. The CIA was blamed, even though it was President Kennedy's decision to go ahead with the plans that he inherited from the previous administration. Additionally, the complicity between it and International Telephone and Telegraph (ITT) to invade Chile and overthrow the Allende government was yet another scar (see below), as was the involvement of the CIA in narcotics smuggling in Vietnam.

These and other political realities led to a serious breach between Presidents Kennedy, Johnson, Nixon, and Carter and the CIA. During Nixon's tenure, one of the CIA's top men, James Angleton, referred to national security advisor, Henry Kissinger (who became secretary of state) as "objectively, a Soviet Agent" (Hougan, 1984:75). Another top agent of the CIA, James McCord (later implicated in Watergate) spoke for many of the top U.S. military and intelligence officers when he wrote: "I believed that the whole future of the nation was at stake" (1974:60). These views show the depth of feeling toward the dangers of political "interference" with what is generally accepted in the military-intelligence establishment as their mission (Goulden, 1984).

When Jimmy Carter was elected president, he appointed Admiral Stansfield Turner as director of Central Intelligence. At the outset, Turner made it clear that he and the president did not share the agency's view that they were conducting their mission properly (Goulden, 1984; Turner, 1985). Turner insisted on centralizing power and overseeing clandestine and covert operations. He met with a great deal of resistance and opposition from within the agency, but reduced the size of the covert operation section from 1,200 to 400 agents. Agency people still refer to this as the "Halloween massacre."

Old hands at the CIA believe zealously, protectively, that their work is essential for the salvation of humankind. With threats from both Republican and Democratic administrations, the agency sought alternative sources of revenue to carry out its mission. The alternative was already in place with the connections to the international narcotics traffic, arms smuggling, the existence of secret corporations incorporated in foreign countries (such as Panama), and the established links to banks for laundering money for covert operations.

State-Organized Assassinations and Murder

Assassination plots and political murders are usually associated with military dictatorships and European monarchies. The practice of assassination, however, is not limited to unique historical events but has become a tool of international politics that involves modern nation-states.

In the 1960s a French intelligence agency hired Christian David to assassinate the Moroccan leader Ben Barka (Hougan, 1978:204–7). David had connections to the DEA, the CIA, and international arms smugglers such as Robert Vesco.

In 1953 the CIA organized and supervised a coup d'etat in Iran that overthrew the democratically elected government of Mohammed Mossadegh, who had become unpopular with the United States when he nationalized foreign-owned oil companies. The CIA's coup replaced Mossadegh with Reza Shah Pahlavi, who denationalized the oil companies and, with CIA guidance, established one of the most vicious secret intelligence organizations in the world: SAVAK. In the years to follow, the Shah and CIA-trained agents of SAVAK murdered thousands of Iranians. They arrested almost 1,500 people monthly, most of whom were subjected to torture and punishments without trial. Not only were SAVAK agents trained by the CIA, but they were instructed in techniques of torture (Hersh, 1979:13).

In 1970 the CIA repeated the practice of overthrowing democratically elected governments unfavorable to U.S. investments. When

Salvador Allende was elected president of Chile, the CIA organized a coup that overthrew him, during which he was murdered, along with the head of the military, General Rene Schneider. Following Allende's overthrow, the CIA trained agents for the Chilean secret service (DINA). DINA set up a team of assassins who could "travel anywhere in the world . . . to carry out sanctions including assassinations" (Dinges and Landau, 1980:239). One of the assassinations carried out by DINA was the murder of Orlando Letellier, Allende's ambassador to the United States and his former minister of defense, by a car bomb on Embassy Row in Washington, D.C. (Dinges and Landau, 1982).

Other bloody coups planned, organized, and executed by U.S. agents include coups in Guatemala, Nicaragua, the Dominican Republic, and Vietnam. American involvement in those coups was never legally authorized. The murders, assassinations, and terrorist acts that accompany coups are criminal acts by law, both in the United States and in the country in which they take place.

More recent examples of murder and assassination for which government officials are responsible include the car bomb death of eighty people in Beirut, Lebanon, on May 8, 1985. The bomb was set by a Lebanese counterterrorist unit working with the CIA. Senator Daniel Moynihan has said that when he was vice president of the Senate Intelligence Committee, President Reagan ordered the CIA to form a small antiterrorist effort in the Mideast. Two sources said that the CIA was working with the group that planted the bomb to kill the Shiite leader Hussein Fadallah (*New York Times*, May 13, 1985).

A host of terrorist plans and activities connected with the attempt to overthrow the Nicaraguan government, including several murders and assassinations, were exposed in an affidavit filed by reporters Tony Avirgan and Martha Honey. They began investigating Contra activities after Avirgan was injured in an attempt on the life of Contra leader Eden Pastora. In 1986, Honey and Avirgan filed a complaint with the U.S. District Court in Miami charging John Hull, Robert Owen, Theodore Shackley, Thomas Clines, "Chi Chi" Quintero, Maj. General Richard Secord, and others working for the CIA in Central America with criminal conspiracy and the smuggling of cocaine to aid the Nicaraguan rebels.

A criminal conspiracy in which the CIA admits participating is the publication of a manual, *Psychological Operation in Guerrilla Warfare*, which was distributed to the people of Nicaragua. The manual describes how the people should proceed to commit murder, sabotage, vandalism, and violent acts in order to undermine the government. Encouraging or instigating such crimes is not only a violation of U.S. law, it was also prohibited by Reagan's executive order of 1981, which forbade any U.S. participation in foreign assassinations.

The CIA is not alone in hatching criminal conspiracies. The DEA organized a "Special Operations Group," which was responsible for working out plans to assassinate political and business leaders in foreign countries who were involved in drug trafficking. The head of this group was a former CIA agent, Lou Conein. George Crile wrote in the *Washington Post* (June 13, 1976; see also Hougan, 1978:132):

> When you get down to it, Conein was organizing an assassination program. He was frustrated by the big-time operators who were just too insulated to get to . . . . Meetings were held to decide whom to target and what method of assassination to employ.

It is a crime to conspire to commit murder. The official record, including testimony by participants in three conspiracies before the United States Congress and in court, make it abundantly clear that the crime of conspiring to commit murder is not infrequent in the intelligence agencies of the United States and other countries.

It is also a crime to cover up criminal acts, but there are innumerable examples of instances in which the CIA and the FBI conspired to interfere with the criminal prosecution of drug dealers, murderers, and assassins. In the death of Letellier, the FBI and the CIA refused to cooperate with the prosecution of the DINA agents who murdered him (Dinges and Landau, 1980:208–9). Those agencies were also involved in the cover-up of the criminal activities of a Cuban exile, Ricardo Morales. While an employee of the FBI and the CIA, Morales planted a bomb on an Air Cubana flight from Venezuela, killing seventy three people. The Miami police confirmed Morales's claim that he was acting under orders from the CIA (Lernoux, 1984:188). Morales, who was arrested for overseeing the shipment of ten tons of marijuana, admitted to being a CIA contract agent who conducted bombings, murders, and assassinations. He was killed in a bar after he made public his work with the CIA and the FBI.

Other State-Organized Crimes

Every agency of government is restricted by law in certain fundamental ways. Yet structural pressures exist that can push agencies to go beyond their legal limits. The CIA, for example, is not permitted to engage in domestic intelligence. Despite this, the CIA has opened and photographed the mail of over one million private citizens (Rockefeller Report, 1975:101–15), illegally entered people's homes, and conducted domestic surveillance through electronic devices (Parenti, 1983:170–71).

Agencies of government also cannot legally conduct experiments on human subjects that violate civil rights or endanger the lives of the subjects. But the CIA conducted experiments on unknowing subjects by hiring prostitutes to administer drugs to their clients. CIA-trained medical doctors and psychologists observed the effects of the drugs through a two-way mirror in expensive apartments furnished to the prostitutes by the CIA. At least one of the victims of these experiments died and others suffered considerable trauma (Anderson and Whitten, 1976; Crewdson and Thomas, 1977; Jacobs 1977a, 1977b).

The most flagrant violation of civil rights by federal agencies is the FBI's counterintelligence program (COINTELPRO). This program was designed to disrupt, harass, and discredit groups that the FBI decided were in some way "un-American." Such groups included the American Civil Liberties Union, antiwar movements, civil rights organizations, and a host of other legally constituted political groups whose views opposed some of the policies of the United States (Church Committee, 1976). With the exposure of COINTELPRO, the group was disbanded. There is evidence, however, that the illegal surveillance of U.S. citizens did not stop with the abolition of COINTELPRO, but continues (Klein, 1988).

Discussion

Elsewhere I have suggested a general theory to account for variations in types and frequency of crime (Chambliss, 1988a). That theory assumes that in every era political, economic, and social relations contain certain inherent *contradictions*, which produce *conflicts* and *dilemmas* that people struggle to resolve. The study of state-organized crime brings into sharp relief the necessity of understanding the role of contradictions in the formation and implementation of law.

Contradictions inherent in the formation of states create conditions under which there will be a tendency for state officials to violate the criminal law. State officials inherit from the past laws that were not of their making and that were the result of earlier efforts to resolve conflicts wrought by structural contradictions (Chambliss, 1980; Chambliss and Seidman, 1982). The inherited laws nonetheless represent the foundation on which the legitimacy of the state's authority depends. These laws also provide a basis for attempts by the state to control the acts of others and to justify the use of violence to that end.

Law is a two-edged sword; it creates one set of conflicts while it attempts to resolve another. The passage of a particular law or set of laws may resolve conflicts and enhance state control, but it also limits the legal activities of the state. State officials are thus often caught between conflicting demands as they find themselves constrained by laws that interfere with other goals demanded of them by their roles or their perception of what is in the interests of the state. There is a contradiction, then, between the legal prescriptions and the agreed goals of state agencies. Not everyone caught in this dilemma will opt for violating the law, but some will. Those who do are the perpetrators, but not the cause, of the persistence of state-organized crime.

When Spain and Portugal began exploiting the labor and natural resources of the Americas and Asia, other European nations realized the implications for their own power and sovereignty. France, England, and Holland were powerful nations, but not powerful enough at the time to challenge Spain and Portugal directly. The dilemma for those nations was how to share in the wealth and curtail the power of Spain and Portugal without going to war. A resolution to the dilemma was forged through cooperation with pirates. Cooperating with pirates, however, required violating their own laws as well as the laws of other countries. In this way, the states organized criminality for their own ends without undermining their claim to legitimacy or their ability to condemn and punish piracy committed against them.

It should be noted that some monarchs in the sixteenth and seventeenth centuries (e.g., James I of England) refused to cooperate with pirates, no matter how profitable. So, too, not all CIA or NSC personnel organize criminal activities in pursuit of state goals.

The impetus for the criminality of European states that engaged in piracy was the need to accumulate capital in the early stages of capitalist formation. State-organized criminality did not disappear, however, with the emergence of capitalism as the dominant economic system of the world. Rather, contemporary state-organized crime also has its roots in the ongoing need for capital accumulation of modern nation-states, whether the states be socialist, capitalist, or mixed economies.

Sociologically, the most important characteristics of state-organized crime in the modern world are at one with characteristics of state-organized crime in the early stages of capitalist development. Today, states organize smuggling, assassinations, covert operations, and conspiracies to criminally assault citizens, political activists, and political leaders perceived to be a threat. These acts are as criminal in the laws of the nations perpetrating them as were the acts of piracy in which European nations were complicitous.

At the most general level, the contradictions that are the force behind state-organized crime today are the same as those that were the impetus for piracy in sixteenth-century Europe. The accumulation of capital determines a nation's power, wealth, and survival today, as it did three hundred years ago. The state must provide a climate and a set of international relations that facilitate this accumulation if it is to succeed. State officials will be judged in accordance with their ability to create these conditions.

But contradictory ideologies and demands are the very essence of state formations. The laws of every nation-state inhibit officials from maximizing conditions conducive to capital accumulation at the same time that they facilitate the process. Laws prohibiting assassination and arms smuggling enable a government to control such acts when they are inimical to their interests. When such acts serve the interests of the state, however, then there are pressures that lead some officials to behave criminally. Speaking of the relationship between the NSC, the CIA, and drug trafficking, Senator John Kerry, as chairman of the U.S. Senate Foreign Relations Subcommittee on Terrorism, Narcotics and International Operations, pinpointed the dilemma when he said "stopping drug trafficking to the United States has been a secondary U.S. foreign policy objective. It has been sacrificed repeatedly for other political goals" (U.S. Senate Hearings, 1986). He might have added that engaging in drug trafficking and arms smuggling has been a price government agencies have been willing to pay "for other political goals."

These contradictions create conflicts between nation-states as well as internally among the branches of government. Today, we see nations such as Turkey, Bolivia, Colombia, Peru, Panama, and the Bahamas encouraging the export of illegal drugs while condemning them publicly. At the same time, other government agencies cooperate in the export and import of illegal arms and drugs to finance subversive and terrorist activities. Governments plot and carry out assassinations and illegal acts against their own citizens in order to "preserve democracy," while supporting the most undemocratic institutions imaginable. In the process, the contradictions that create the conflicts and dilemmas remain untouched and the process goes on indefinitely.

A U.S. Department of State report (1985) illustrates the logical outcome of the institutionalization of state-organized crime in the modern world. In this report the State Department offered to stop criminal acts against the Nicaraguan government in return for concessions from Nicaragua. Three hundred years earlier England, France, and Spain signed a treaty by which each agreed to suppress its piracy against the others in return for guarantees of economic and political sovereignty.

Conclusion

Although I have suggested some theoretical notions that appear promising, the more important goal is to raise the issue for further study.

The theoretical and empirical problems raised by advocating such study are, however, formidable. Data on contemporary examples of state-organized crime are difficult to obtain. The data I gathered depended on sources that must be used cautiously. Government hearings, court trials, interviews, newspaper accounts, and historical documents are replete with problems of validity and reliability and there is room for error in interpreting the findings. It will require considerable imagination and diligence for others to pursue research on this topic and add to the empirical base from which theoretical propositions can be tested and elaborated.

We need to explore different political, economic, and social systems in varying historical periods to discover why some forms of social organization are more likely to create state-organized crimes than others. We need to explore the possibility that some types of state agencies are more prone to engaging in criminality than others. It seems likely, for example, that state agencies whose activities can be hidden from scrutiny are more likely to engage in criminal acts than those whose record is public. This principle may also apply to whole nation-states: the more open the society, the less likely it is that state-organized crime will become institutionalized.

There are also important parallels between state-organized criminality and the criminality of police and law enforcement agencies generally. Local police departments that find it more useful to cooperate with criminal syndicates than to combat them are responding to their own particular contradictions, conflicts, and dilemmas (Chambliss, 1988b). An exploration of the theoretical implications of these similarities could yield some important findings.

The issue of state-organized crime raises again the question of how crime should be defined to be scientifically useful. For the purposes of this analysis, I have accepted the conventional criminological definition of crime as acts in violation of the criminal law. This definition has obvious limitations (see Schwendinger and Schwendinger, 1975), and the study of state-organized crime may facilitate the development of a more useful definition by underlining the interrelationship between crime and the legal process. At the very least, the study of state-organized crime reminds us that crime is a political phenomenon and must be analyzed accordingly.

21

Corporations, Organized Crime, and Hazardous Waste Disposal: Making a Criminogenic Regulatory Structure

Andrew Szasz

The generation of hazardous waste is a side effect of modern industrial production. Factories must cope daily with large accumulations of nonrecyclable chemical byproducts of production. The processing or disposal of these byproducts is a significant cost of production that the prudent owner or manager minimizes.

For years industrial hazardous waste was not legally distinguished from municipal garbage and other solid wastes. It was disposed of with ordinary garbage, at very low cost to the generator, mostly in coastal waters or in inadequate landfills. During the 1970s concern grew that improper disposal of hazardous waste was creating an environmental and public health burden of unknown but potentially massive scale. This concern finally moved some states and eventually the federal government to legislate new regulations. The centerpiece of this regulatory effort was the federal Resource Conservation and Recovery Act (RCRA) of 1976. On paper, RCRA mandated comprehensive mechanisms to guarantee the safe disposal of hazardous waste. It established standards and procedures for classifying substances as hazardous. It authorized the states to register corporate generators of hazardous waste and license hauling and disposal firms. It mandated the creation of a manifest system that would document the movement of hazardous waste "from cradle to grave," from the generator, through the hands of the transporter, to the shipment's final destination at a licensed disposal site.

By legally distinguishing hazardous waste from other wastes and by directing that such wastes be treated differently than municipal solid waste, the new regulations dramatically increased the demand for hazardous waste hauling and disposal services. Unhappily, state and

Edited and abridged from *Criminology*, Volume 24(1):1–27 (1986).

federal investigations have documented both that illegal waste disposal is widespread (U.S. General Accounting Office, 1985; U.S. House of Representatives, 1980) and that organized crime elements, traditionally active in garbage hauling and landfilling, have entered this burgeoning and potentially profitable new market (Block and Scarpitti, 1985; U.S. House of Representatives, 1980, 1981b). Although the extent of organized crime involvement in hazardous waste hauling and disposal is uncertain, its involvement is certain. Some corporations, it seems, discharge their regulatory obligations under RCRA by entering into direct contractual relationships with firms dominated by organized crime. This article analyzes the complex nature of this relationship between corporate generators of hazardous waste and elements of organized crime active in industrial waste disposal and does so by analyzing the formation and implementation of RCRA legislation.

This article relates to the literature that examines the relationship between legitimate and illicit enterprise and to the literature that examines criminogenic market structures. Researchers have challenged the distinction between legitimate business and organized crime. Schelling (1967), Smith and Alba (1979), Smith (1980), and Albanese (1982) all argue that organized crime is primarily a form of entrepreneurial activity and that its ethnic or conspiratorial nature is of secondary importance. The view that the underworld exploits legitimate business through extortion, racketeering, and so on (Drucker, 1981) is one-sided; rather, the relationship is one of mutually beneficial interdependence (Martens and Miller-Longfellow, 1982; Block and Chambliss, 1981; Block, 1982; Brady, 1983). Chambliss (1978:181–82) even argues that organized crime can exist only because the structure of the legitimate economy and its accompanying political organization make its emergence possible and even inevitable. Smith (1980) and Smith and Alba (1979) challenge the very distinction between business and organized crime and begin to dissolve that distinction in the common dynamic of a market economy. The study of organized crime participation in hazardous waste disposal presents an opportunity to once again examine this relationship between legitimate and illegitimate entrepreneurship.

The story of RCRA may also have links to the concept of criminogenic market processes. Studies have shown that the normal operating logic of an industry may force some sectors of that industry into illegal activity in order to survive (Farberman, 1975; Leonard and Weber, 1977; Denzin, 1977). Needleman and Needleman (1979) describe a second type of criminogenesis in which criminal activity is an unwelcome drain on business, but it is unavoidable. This is because the conditions that make it possible are necessary to the overall functioning of that industry and to change them would fundamentally affect the industry's business practice.

Needleman and Needleman discussed securities fraud as an example of what they call a "crime-facilitative," as opposed to a "crime-coercive," market sector. RCRA has not prevented illegal hazardous waste dumping; moreover, it has attracted organized crime to the industry. This suggests that the concept of criminogenesis may be fruitfully extended to regulatory processes.

Hazardous Waste as a Social Issue

The Environmental Protection Agency (EPA) defines waste products as "hazardous" if they are flammable, explosive, corrosive, or toxic. Major national industries, such as the petroleum, chemical, electronic, and pharmaceutical industries, generate copious amounts of hazardous waste. Although there is still great uncertainty about the exact effect of industrial hazardous waste on public health (Greenberg and Anderson, 1984: 84–105), improper management may result in explosions, fires, and other uncontrolled releases that pollute water resources, putting surrounding communities at risk and may cause problems ranging from skin irritation to increased incidence of cancer, lung disease, birth defects, and other serious illnesses.

It is difficult to know how much hazardous waste is generated and how much has accumulated. The generation and disposal of hazardous waste was unregulated until the late 1970s and no systematic data-gathering occurred until the passage of RCRA. Estimates have risen regularly as more sites are located and assessed. The EPA has estimated that there are 25,000 sites nationally that contain some hazardous waste. Of these, about 2,500 are priority sites judged to be imminently hazardous to public health. Research by the General Accounting Office (GAO) and the Office of Technology Assessment (OTA) suggests that there may be 378,000 total sites nationally, perhaps 10,000 of them requiring priority attention (Shabecoff, 1985).

The availability of data should have improved greatly following passage of RCRA. Generators of hazardous waste were now required to create written documentation—the manifest—of the amount and content of every shipment of hazardous waste signed over to outside haulers and disposers. This documentation is forwarded to state agencies following final disposition of each waste shipment. However, the actual quality of the data produced was compromised by several factors. First, there was little agreement, particularly between industry representatives and environmentalists, over what substances should be defined as hazardous (U.S. Environmental Protection Agency, 1976, 1979; U.S. House of Representatives, 1975, 1976; U.S. Senate, 1974, 1979). Second, firms generating less than one metric ton (2,200 lbs.) of hazardous waste per month are exempt from RCRA regulation (U.S. House of Representatives, 1983:56, 60). There are over four million privately owned industrial sites in the nation. The "small generator" exemption leaves all but a few tens of thousands of these sites out of RCRA's registration and manifest system. Third, some firms that generate significant amounts of hazardous waste have either failed to cooperate with EPA requests for data (Williams and Matheny, 1984:436–37) or have failed to identify themselves to the EPA as generators that can be regulated (U.S. General Accounting Office, 1985:14–20). Fourth, even those firms that appear to comply with reporting requirements may not be reporting accurately the types and quantities of hazardous waste they generate (U.S. GAO, 1985:20–23). Consequently, knowledge of the amount and content of current hazardous waste generation is still imprecise. Estimates, like those of hazardous waste accumulation, have been rising. In 1974, the EPA was estimating hazardous waste generation at 10 million metric tons per year (U.S. Senate, 1974:70). In 1980, the EPA estimate had risen to 40 million metric tons. In 1983, new research led the EPA to nearly quadruple its estimate to 150 million metric tons (Block and Scarpitti, 1985:46), while the OTA was estimating 250 million metric tons per year (U.S. House of Representatives, 1983:1; see Greenberg and Anderson, 1984).

Where does hazardous waste end up? In response to EPA inquiries in 1981, 16 per cent of generating firms reported treating their wastes completely on site and another 22 per cent reported treating part of their wastes on site. The remaining 62 per cent contracted with other parties to handle all of their wastes (Block and Scarpitti, 1985:48–49). Where do transported wastes actually end up? The exemptions and noncooperation cited above leave an unknown fraction of total hazardous waste movement out of the paperwork of the manifest system (U.S. GAO, 1985:3–4, 14–24). The manifests that are filed are poorly monitored and vulnerable to undetected falsification (Greenberg and Anderson, 1984:242; U.S. GAO, 1985:25–31; U.S. House of Representatives, 1980:140; 1981a:124). Consequently, this question also cannot be answered with great certainty. On the basis of poor and incomplete data, the OTA estimates that no more than 10 to 20 per cent of all hazardous waste is rendered harmless by incineration or by chemical or biological treatment. There are few facilities that can treat wastes in these ways and the price of treatment is much higher than the price of other means of disposal (U.S. House of Representatives, 1983:2, 56). The remaining 80 to 90 per cent is either landfilled or disposed of illegally. Only a small proportion of hazardous waste goes into landfills that have the site studies, proper containment practices, and continuous monitoring to be fully licensed by the EPA, since there are only about two hundred such landfills in the nation (Block and Scarpitti, 1985:49; U.S. House of Representatives, 1981b:187). Even these top landfills are only required by the EPA to keep wastes contained for thirty years (U.S. House of Representatives, 1983:2). Most hazardous waste goes to landfills that have only interim license to operate, landfills that are of much poorer quality and are likely to pollute the surrounding land and water within a few years.

Illegal hazardous waste dumping is even more likely to have adverse short-term environmental and public health consequences. The full extent of illegal hazardous waste disposal is not known. One study surveyed hazardous waste generators in forty one cities and estimated that one in seven generators had illegally disposed of some of their wastes during the preceding two years (U.S. GAO, 1985:10). A wide array of illegal disposal practices has been documented. Waste shipments may end up comingled with ordinary garbage. A 20-cubic yard "dumpster" full of dry garbage can be made to absorb up to sixty 55-gallon drums of liquid hazardous waste (U.S. House of Representatives, 1980:63) and then be deposited in unlicensed municipal landfills never designed to contain hazardous waste. Liquid hazardous waste may be released along a roadway. An 8,000-gallon truck can be emptied in eight minutes (U.S. House of Representatives, 1980:101). Shipments may simply be stockpiled at sites awaiting alleged transfer that never happens or at disposal facilities that have no real disposal capability (U.S. House of Representatives, 1980:10). Wastes may be drained into local city sewer systems, rivers, and oceans, or dumped in out-of-the-way rural spots (U.S. House of Representatives, 1980:93). Flammable hazardous waste may be commingled with fuel oil and sold as pure heating oil (U.S. House of Representatives, 1980:63–64) or sprayed on unsuspecting communities' roads for dust control (U.S. House of Representatives, 1980:151).

Organized Crime Participation in the Hazardous Waste Disposal Industry

Although organized crime activity likely accounts for only a fraction of the illegal dumping taking place in the United States (U.S. House of Representatives, 1980:87), organized crime was ideally suited to fully develop the methodology of illegal hazardous waste practices. In those parts of the nation where garbage hauling and landfilling was historically controlled by organized crime, their movement into the newly created hazardous waste market was logical. In New Jersey, for example, organized crime had controlled the garbage industry through ownership or control of garbage hauling firms, landfills, and through labor racketeering (U.S. House of Representatives, 1981b:1–45). The regulations governing hazardous waste would have had to have been carefully written and tenaciously enforced were organized crime to be kept from applying this highly developed infrastructure to the new market. In fact, the opposite happened and organized crime easily entered both the hauling and the disposal phases of the hazardous waste handling industry.

Hauling. Organized crime had dominated traditional garbage hauling in states like New York and New Jersey for decades. Once associates of organized crime owned a number of hauling firms in any geographical area, they established an organizational infrastructure that governed their relationships and ensured high profits. Threats and violence persuaded other firms to join that infrastructure and abide by its rules or to sell and get out. The keystone of this infrastructure was the concept of "property rights" or "respect." Municipal solid waste hauling contracts were illegally apportioned among haulers. Having a property right meant that a hauler held rights to continue picking up the contract at sites currently serviced without competition from others. Other firms would submit artificially high bids or would not bid at all when a contract came up for renewal, thereby assuring that the site stayed with the current contractor. This system of de facto territorial monopolies permitted noncompetitive pricing and made garbage hauling a very lucrative activity. Property rights were recognized and enforced by organized crime authorities. Conflicts were adjudicated in meetings of the Municipal Contractors Association (MCA). Decisions of the MCA were enforced by threats and, if necessary, violence (U.S. House of Representatives, 1981b:142). When the RCRA mandated the licensing of firms deemed fit to transport hazardous waste, mob-connected garbage haulers found it easy to acquire state permits and declare themselves to be hazardous waste haulers. They brought their traditional forms of social organization with them. Individual haulers holding established property rights assumed that they would transfer those property rights to the new type of waste (U.S. House of Representatives, 1980:22). They also met as a group to set up a Trade Waste Association modeled after the MCA to apportion and enforce property rights in the new market (U.S. House of Representatives, 1980:910; 1981b:112, 212).

Disposal. The manifest system requires that someone sign off on the manifest and declare the proper disposal of a waste shipment. This means that mob control over hauling is not enough: organized crime figures had to have ownership of, or at least influence over, final disposal sites (U.S. House of Representatives, 1980:30). This requirement did not prove to be a serious stumbling block since many landfills were already owned wholly or in part by organized crime figures, a legacy of past mob involvement in the garbage business. These sites readily accepted dubious shipments of hazardous waste thinly disguised as ordinary municipal waste (U.S.

House of Representatives, 1981b:228; 1981a). Landfill owners not directly associated with organized crime could be bribed to sign manifests for shipments never received or to accept hazardous waste that was manifested elsewhere (U.S. House of Representatives, 1980:70, 90). In addition, known organized crime figures started or seized control of a network of phony disposal and "treatment" facilities. Licensed by the state, these outfits could legally receive hazardous waste and sign off on the manifest. They would then either stockpile the waste (where it would sit until it exploded, burned, or otherwise came to the attention of authorities) or dump it along roadways, down municipal sewers, into the ocean, or elsewhere (Block and Scarpitti, 1985:145, 158, 298; U.S. House of Representatives, 1980:25). In the extreme, actual ownership of or access to disposal sites was unnecessary for those willing to file totally fanciful manifests. In one case, several major corporations signed over their wastes to an out-of-state facility subsequently shown to simply not exist (U.S. House of Representatives, 1980:70, 135).

Enabling Causes: Creating a Vulnerable Regulatory Structure

It is no surprise that, given the opportunity, organized crime quickly entered the newly created market for hazardous waste handling. They had equipment, organization, know-how, and the will to corrupt the manifest system. It was an attractive prospect. Both the potential size of the market and the potential profits were enormous. Even if they charged only a fraction of the true price of legitimate disposal, that price would be much higher than the price charged to move the same stuff when it was legally just garbage, but their operating expenses would stay the same (if they commingled hazardous waste with ordinary garbage) or decrease (if they simply dumped). Why organized crime would want to enter into a relationship with corporate generators when the opportunity presented itself needs no subtle unraveling. The more complex task is to determine what political and social-structural conditions made it possible for them to "colonize" the hazardous waste disposal industry.

Lax Implementation, and Incompetent and/or Corrupt Enforcement

Explanations of organized crime's presence in hazardous waste handling focused on lax implementation and improper enforcement. Congressional hearings produced dramatic evidence that, at least in New Jersey, the state where organized crime's intrusion into hazardous waste is most thoroughly documented, the major provisions of RCRA were poorly implemented and enforced. Interim hauling and disposal licenses were freely granted. The manifest system was not sufficiently monitored.

Interim Licensing. Congress had mandated an extended transition period during which both transporters and disposal firms would operate under temporary permits until an adequate national hazardous waste industry developed. Generators lobbied quite heavily on this point (U.S. EPA, 1976:238, 1979:153, 307; Gansberg, 1979) and Congress agreed to this provision because of the severe shortage of adequate hazardous waste facilities. American industry would have choked in its own accumulating wastes had it not been permitted to continue to use less-than-adequate means of disposal. A reasonable concession to economic realities, implementation of interim licensing was poorly managed. New Jersey issued hauling permits to any applicant who paid a nominal $50 fee (U.S. House of Representatives, 1980:14–15). Existing landfills and even totally bogus firms with no real disposal facilities found it equally easy to get interim disposal permits (U.S. House of Representatives, 1980:10).

Manifest Oversight. Once a license was obtained, lax supervision of the manifest system made illegal and unsafe disposal of hazardous waste a relatively straightforward, low-risk activity (U.S. House of Representatives, 1980:140). Congressional testimony revealed that until 1980 New Jersey did not have a single person assigned to monitor the manifests being filed in Trenton (U.S. House of Representatives, 1981a:124). (Inadequate monitoring meant that the manifest system was unable to detect illegal disposal anywhere in the United States [U.S. GAO, 1985:25–31].)

Evidence suggested that the relevant New Jersey agencies—the Interagency Hazardous Waste Strike Force, the Division of Criminal Justice, and the Division of Environmental Protection were incapable of producing effective enforcement even when tipped off to specific instances of hazardous waste dumping (U.S. House of Representatives, 1980:144–46; 1981a:110–24). Block and Scarpitti (1985) present other examples that appear to show corruption or ineptitude by state officials responsible for investigating and prosecuting illegal hazardous waste practices.

Lax implementation and enforcement undoubtedly played a big role in facilitating organized crime's entry into the hazardous waste disposal industry. There are, however, more fundamental conditioning factors that logically and temporally preceded these causes. RCRA is a regulatory structure ripe with potential for subversion. Why did Congress create a regulatory structure so vulnerable to lax enforcement? A review of RCRA's legislative history shows quite clearly that corporate generators moved decisively to shape the emerging federal intervention to their liking. They fought for and achieved a regulatory form that would demand of them the least real change and that would minimize their liability for potential violations of the new regulations.

Generators' Strategic Intervention in the Legislative Debate

Compared to the regulatory mechanism written into the final language of the RCRA, some potential alternative forms that were proposed and then rejected would have proved much less hospitable both to noncompliance and to the entry of organized crime. The federal government could have mandated specific treatment and disposal practices, or directed generators to treat all their wastes themselves, or legislated that generators retain full responsibility for their wastes even if they assign them to other parties for shipping and disposal. Generators, led by representatives of major oil and chemical corporations, explicitly and vigorously opposed any such language. They hammered away with striking unanimity at two key points: (1) the government should in no way interfere in firms' production decisions, and (2) generators should not be held responsible for the ultimate fate of their hazardous wastes.

Individual generators, such as DuPont, Union Carbide, Dow Chemical, Monsanto, Exxon, and B. F. Goodrich, as well as industry trade associations repeatedly warned Congress not to intervene in production processes nor to require generators to follow specific waste treatment practices. They stressed, instead, the value of free enterprise and competitive market forces in the treatment or disposal decision and argued that regulatory controls are more properly imposed at the stage of final disposition. As Dupont expressed it: "We are opposed to regulations expressing the kind and amount of processing and recycle of wastes [by the generator] (DuPont, U.S. EPA, 1976:72-73; see also E.I. DuPont de Nemours and Co., U.S. Senate, 1974:454; Stauffer, U.S. Senate, 1974:1,745; Union Carbide, U.S. Senate, 1974:1,748; Dow Chemical, U.S. Senate, 1974:1,478; American Petroleum Institute, U.S. EPA, 1976:1,406, 1,410; Manufacturing Chemists Association, U.S. EPA, 1976:565).

Generator unanimity was equally impressive on the second issue of responsibility. They were willing to have limited responsibility, to label their wastes, and make sure they contracted only with firms approved by state authorities, but they vehemently opposed the idea that generators should bear legal responsibility for their wastes from cradle to grave. They argued that responsibility should pass to the party in physical possession of the hazardous waste. Under such a system, only the hauler and disposer would need to be licensed and the government should not license generators. As Union Carbide said, "we consider permits for the generation of hazardous wastes to be unneeded, and could result in unnecessary restriction of manufacturing operations" (Union Carbide, U.S. Senate, 1974:464; see also DuPont, U.S. EPA, 1976:73–74; Monsanto, U.S. EPA, 1976:410–11; Manufacturing Chemists' Association, U.S. EPA, 1976:565; B. F. Goodrich, U.S. Senate, 1974:1,441; Dow Chemical, U.S. Senate, 1974:1478–9).

Generators also lobbied for the other provisions to their liking—a narrow definition of substances to be regulated as hazardous, flexible time frames for implementation, and less stringent rules for on-site disposal— but the two points above were at the heart of their legislative intervention. In the end, they didn't get everything they wanted. The government would make generators register with the EPA. On-site, generator self-disposal would be subject to the same rules governing off-site disposal firms. However, the overall forms of RCRA passed by Congress embodied both their major demands.

The Legacy of Generator Inattention and Inaction

The generators also contributed indirectly to the shaping of RCRA legislation through their historical lack of attention to proper hazardous waste disposal. The EPA estimated in 1974 that ocean dumping and improper landfilling cost about 5 per cent of the price of environmentally adequate disposal and it reported: "Given this permissive legislative climate, generators of waste are under little or no pressure to expend resources for adequate management of their hazardous wastes" (U.S. Senate, 1974:71). Lack of generator demand for adequate disposal facilities discouraged the inflow of investment capital, and an adequate waste disposal industry had failed to develop by the time RCRA legislation was being debated. Had legislators ignored this situation and required an immediate shift to proper disposal, a production crisis could have been triggered as wastes accumulated and firms found few legal outlets for them. Industrial spokespersons predicted dire consequences. In a representative statement, a Union Carbide spokesperson warned legislators: "Those wastes which are nonincinerable and have no commercial value must be disposed of. To deny opportunity for disposal would effectively eliminate much of the chemical process industry. Disposal in or on the land or disposal in the oceans are the only viable alternatives available" (U.S. Senate, 1974:461).

Neither individual officeholders nor whole governments stay in office long if they pass legislation which, regardless of reasons, brings to a halt industrial sectors central to the national economy. Congress had to be realistic and mandate years of transition during which hazardous waste would be hauled and disposed of by operators having only interim licenses. This reasonable concession to the reality of the situation, a legacy of generator inattention, created a loophole through which many less than qualified parties could legally participate as providers in the hazardous waste market.

Corporate Generators and Organized Crime: A Complex Relationship

The discussion of enabling causes leads from the surface explanation of lax implementation and enforcement back to the moment of creation of a regulatory structure ripe for subversion and subterfuge. Analysis of the formation of RCRA shows that the actions of corporate generators were principally responsible for the passage of such a vulnerable structure. This is the most basic aspect of the generator-organized crime relationship. Did corporate generators intend this outcome and what effect did it subsequently have upon them? How did Congress deal with these issues?

Congress Discusses the Role of Corporate Generators

Having thoroughly documented organized crime's presence in the hazardous waste industry, Congress could have explored the relationship between organized crime and legitimate corporate waste generators. For the most part, though, such inquiry was avoided. The subject came up only a few times and was not pursued. The following two scenarios were tentatively suggested.

Ignorance and "Good Faith." Then Congressman Gore suggested to Harold Kaufman, the former Duane Marine employee turned star witness, that perhaps companies used Kaufman's phony "disposal" firm knowingly as a front. In response, Kaufman articulated the theory of ignorance and good faith on behalf of generators.

> Mr. Gore: "You offered a front to companies that wanted to pretend they were disposing of toxic waste."
> Mr. Kaufman: "No, that wasn't true. That wasn't true."
> Gore: "Well, explain it to me in your own words."
> Kaufman: "You're blaming the companies; 99 percent of these companies in good faith thought that Duane Marine had the facility."
> Gore: "I see."
> Kaufman: "Because the State licensed us. We were the first ones licensed, Duane Marine. . . . these industrial people who in good faith wanted to follow the law, if they wanted to cheat, they wouldn't

have brought the stuff to us, because we were charging a lot of money." (U.S. House, 1980:10)

Kaufman, later: "Forget about the generator. Let's not blame the people that are really trying to follow the manifest. . . . these companies operate in good faith—otherwise they wouldn't have called the people [i.e., Duane Marine], they would have thrown it in the nearest dump." (U.S. House, 1980:16)

According to this scenario, managers and owners see the license, the state's seal of approval, and believe in good faith that the shipment of hazardous waste that they sign over will be properly disposed of by responsible operators. They do not know that their wastes end up stockpiled on an Atlantic Coast pier, poured down a municipal sewer, or burned, commingled with fuel oil, in a school furnace. They do not know they are dealing with organized crime. They are being cheated because they pay large amounts for treatment and disposal services that are not performed.

The issue of awareness cannot be decisively resolved without in-depth interviewing of corporate managers in charge of waste disposal contracting, but the preponderance of circumstantial evidence makes claims of ignorance appear unconvincing. Organized crime's control of garbage hauling and disposal had been known in New Jersey for decades. It had been the subject of numerous state hearings and investigations since 1958 (U.S. House of Representatives, 1981b:15–16, 36, 39). Organized crime's rapid entry into hazardous waste was so readily apparent that New Jersey established an Inter-Agency Hazardous Waste Strike Force to investigate and attack the problem in 1978, shortly after the new system of licensing and manifesting was begun. Management also knew that there were few adequate hazardous waste facilities available, yet the feared shortage of disposal sites never materialized.

Rather than ignorance and good faith, these facts suggest that rational industrial managers would have had ample reason to distrust the identity of their contractual partners. Had their suspicions been aroused, it would have been easy to hire investigators, as state and local officials had done, to follow some hazardous waste shipments and lay their doubts to rest (U.S. House of Representatives, 1980:20).

If managers and owners were ignorant, ignorance must either have been achieved through vigilant inattention or have been the fruit of a profound lack of interest. Indeed, generators may have good material reasons to desire to stay ignorant. In its comments on the GAO's draft report on illegal waste disposal, the EPA states that the "key reason" why generators do not notify officials when they suspect that a waste shipment may have gone astray is "the unwillingness of the generator to 'turn-in' its low-bid transporter. This is especially true for smaller volume generators who routinely have great difficulty finding transportation for their wastes" (U.S. GAO, 1985:62).

More to the point, the right of owners and managers to be ignorant is structured into the regulatory scheme of RCRA. The generator bears no obligation to know its contractual partner beyond assuring itself that the firm has been licensed, declared fit to handle hazardous waste by one of the states. Rather than attempt to argue what corporate actors know, do not know, could know, or should have known, one must remember that generators explicitly fought for RCRA language that entitled them to a state of ignorance.

Powerlessness. Kaufman and New Jersey Deputy Attorney General Madonna suggested a second theory that also tends to absolve the generator of responsibility. Even if the corporate generator knows that it is dealing with organized crime, the "property rights" system forces it into a passive, powerless position:

> Madonna: ". . . numerous customers of garbage or solid waste collectors who have attempted to secure alternative collectors, for whatever reason, have found that it is virtually impossible to obtain a different garbage man to pick up their garbage." (U.S. House of Representatives, 1981b:12)

> Congressman Marks: "If a disposer of chemical waste sought a different company to haul those wastes, could that person voluntarily change without there being a problem?"
> Kaufman: "Not to my knowledge has it ever happened, because you see, most of the haulers of toxic wastes that are in the garbage business respect the same thing in toxics as solid, so he has no choice. He has a man there and nobody will go in." (U.S. House of Representatives, 1980:22)

This claim of generator powerlessness is also undermined by the previous discussion of the generators' role in shaping RCRA legislation. Individual generators, especially smaller firms, may indeed find themselves unable to shop around among hazardous waste haulers once the property rights system had assigned their site to a specific hauler, but the discussion above suggests that one must look beyond individual firms to see how corporate power was exercised collectively. Industries that produce the bulk of hazardous waste—oil, chemicals, pharmaceuticals, electronics— exert tremendous political power nationally and especially in states like New Jersey, where these four industries account for 36 per cent of all industrial production (Governor's Commission, 1983:18). These lobbying powerhouses used their collective political power during legislative debate over the form of RCRA to create a structure that, subsequently, allowed the emergence of a "property rights" system that could impose its will on some individual generators. Claims of generator powerlessness cannot be accepted without profound qualification.

The details of corporate intervention during the formation of RCRA undermine any explanation absolving them of all responsibility, but generator actions do not, by themselves, convey the full complexity of the resultant relationship. Two issues remain: Why did the corporate generators do it? And what were the consequences for them?

The Question of Intent

The cohesiveness and unanimity of generator intervention to shape RCRA legislation certainly shows that they intended *something*. Nonetheless, no evidence was found in the research discussed here to support an argument that generators consciously intended to create a context for organized crime's entry into the industrial waste disposal business, or even that they understood that such an outcome was possible. Rather, it appears much more likely that they acted out of a general tendency to resist full social responsibility for the "externalities," the environmental and public health consequences, of industrial production, and that they did not much care what, if any, unintended consequences would follow.

Why were generators so vehement that Congress not force them either to change production techniques or to assume full legal responsibility for proper waste disposal? These actions find their meaning within the larger context of industrial response to the whole spectrum of environmental, so-called "social" regulations. Industrial groups active during the passage of RCRA have consistently opposed congressional passage of every piece of recent social regulation, intervened to weaken its form when passage seemed inevitable, and mobilized to limit its impact once it was implemented. They have done so with regard to the EPA, the Occupational Safety and Health Administration (OSHA), the Toxic Substances Control Act (TOSCA), the Superfund law (CERCLA), surface mining regulation, and right-to-know laws (see Szasz, 1982, 1984).

Policy committees composed of corporate leaders and elected officials often state that an intact environment and a healthy public are objectively in the long-run interest of the corporate sector. For example, the Governor's Commission on Science and Technology of the State of New Jersey (1983:18) has stated: "The safe disposal of hazardous and toxic substances is of enormous concern; if the problem is not solved, it will severely limit industrial growth." But this understanding is not reflected in the individual or the collective behavior of industrial firms. Regardless of objective or long-term interest, their behavior indicates that they do not wish to "internalize" the true cost of the undesirable side effects of modern industrial production.

There are always some owners and managers who advocate a more enlightened, long-range view of industrial interest in environmental matters. Nonetheless, historical and content analysis of past regulatory initiatives supports the view that the majority of industrial spokespersons vigorously oppose increases in government regulation of their health externalities (see Crenson, 1971; Williams and Matheny, 1984).

Both generator failure to pay for proper waste disposal before RCRA and their position during RCRA legislative debate are manifestations of this posture. In some areas of regulation, such as worker safety and health, successful corporate intervention may delay passage of legislation, weaken its form, and lessen its impact through ongoing resistance to full implementation. But regulation of hazardous waste was a unique case because of the specific history of organized crime's control of garbage. Because of this peculiar circumstance, corporate resistance to regulation not only had the usual intended effect of avoiding the full internalization of responsibility and cost, it also had the effect—apparently unintended—of opening the door to mob colonization of the regulation-mandated market.

Even Unintended Outcomes Have Payoffs

Generators mobilized when it became apparent that the political moment for regulation of hazardous waste had decisively arrived. There was sufficient public awareness, fear, and organized demand for the government to legislate. They perceived, though, that the onerousness of impending federal intervention would be minimized if they could ensure (1) that regulation would not interfere with production decisions, and (2) that they would not be fully liable for all possible costs associated with the ultimate fate of their wastes. A manifest-and-disposal-licensing structure was the generators' best-case damage control strategy. Undoubtedly, the greatest benefit would accrue to the generators from their successful move to veto potentially more interventionist forms of regulation. The victory would hold the new regulation's impact to manageable proportions. However, the unintended effect of their legislative efforts then provided several important secondary benefits on top of the main payoff of defeating stronger forms of federal intervention.

Noninterruption of Vital Service. Industrial waste accumulates every day. It has to be dealt with. With passage of RCRA, firms faced new uncertainties in coping with their hazardous waste. They worried that RCRA would uncover a fundamental shortage of legal off-site facilities at the same time that the new rules would require firms to upgrade their facilities if they wished to treat wastes themselves. Lax implementation of interim licensing allowed enough parties to enter the new market that potentially crisis-inducing bottlenecks of accumulating waste were avoided. This benefit accrued to industry as a whole and was of central importance in cushioning the potential adverse impact of the transition from an unregulated to a regulated situation.

Cost. The transition to regulation also threatened an immense cost shock. As noted, the EPA estimated in 1974 that firms were customarily paying no more than 5 per cent of the price of adequate treatment (U.S. Senate, 1974:71). If generators discharged their RCRA obligations by dealing with shady haulers and phony disposal firms, they would typically pay a higher price for disposal than they had before RCRA, but these charges could still be significantly less than the full price of adequate treatment. The congressional hearings uncovered several instances of such cost savings by generators (U.S. House of Representatives, 1980:189), but how often this benefit occurred was not fully explored.

Obfuscation of Origins. The final potential benefit follows from organized crime's facility at falsifying manifests. As hazardous waste travels through the maze of illegitimate haulers and disposers, it becomes impossible to trace its industrial origins or to locate its ultimate destination. Officials find that even if a waste shipment can be followed from the generator to a nondisposing "disposal" site, its ultimate resting place still cannot be identified with any certainty. Conversely, when improperly disposed wastes are found, it is nearly impossible to trace backward and identify their corporate origins (U.S. House of Representatives, 1981a:153, 158). The Superfund law, passed shortly after RCRA, provides that the original generators of abandoned wastes be identified and forced to pay for remedial cleanup. According to the OTA, remedial cleanup can cost ten to one hundred times the cost of initial proper disposal (U.S. House of Representatives, 1983:7). Therefore, a firm can expect to escape serious liabilities if manifest manipulation has successfully "orphaned" its wastes by obfuscating its origins.

Discussion: Corporations, Organized Crime, and Externalizing Criminogenesis

Recent work has challenged the clear distinction between legitimate and illegitimate business, between corporate and organized crime. Organized crime is described as entrepreneurial activity (Schelling, 1967; Smith, 1980; Smith and Alba, 1979; Albanese, 1982), and its most overtly deviant features—conspiracy, violence—are explained as organizational necessities for businesses that cannot turn to the legal structure to govern their internal relationships (Smith, 1980:375). Chambliss (1978:181) argues, furthermore, that it is "the logic of capitalism . . . [which makes] the emergence of crime networks inevitable." Others (Barnett, 1981) assert that the logic of capital constantly presses legitimate economic actors to violate socially defined limits of business conduct. Studies showing widespread illegal activity (including fraud, bribery, and price-fixing) by a majority of Fortune 500 corporations (Clinard et al., 1979; Clinard and Yeager, 1980; Etzioni, 1985) support the view that the most powerful and legitimate enterprises routinely engage in highly rationalized criminal activity. The logical endpoint of this argument is the radical view that the process of capital accumulation is itself organized crime in some larger sense of that term.

Challenging the commonsense distinction between business and organized crime has the merit of drawing attention to the definitional processes whereby society labels some economic acts legitimate and others deviant. But even if one agrees that this distinction is a product of social construction and is on some level ideological, one can say that the central dynamic disclosed in this article depends on continued social and legal acceptance of the reality of that definitional boundary. Widely accepted ideologies are more than pure illusion: they have important material consequences.

Exactly because there is a socially and legally recognized boundary between legitimate business and organized crime, ethically unacceptable activities that benefit legitimate businesses may happen without compromising their reputation because those acts are committed by and can be blamed on those whose social reputation is already sullied. Block and Chambliss's (1981) analysis of labor racketeering in trucking, restaurants, and the garment trades shows clearly that owners may gain great benefits, such as lower wages and labor peace, when labor unions are dominated by organized crime (see also Brady's 1983 study of arson).

Societal acceptance of a definitional boundary between legitimate business and organized crime makes possible a type of criminogenic process different from the two types of criminogenesis defined by Needleman and Needleman (1979). Crimes that are functional for a particular industry are committed by actors who are not only not of that industry but are of a totally different economic world, the "underworld." One may think of this process as parallel to the process of externalizing the economic costs of production and call it "externalizing criminogenesis."

What is externalized here is the legal liability and the social blame for those dirty little acts that quicken the wheels of commerce.

Analysis of the formation of hazardous waste disposal regulations captures such a criminogenic structure at the moment of its formation. In the mid-1970s, corporations faced the prospect of new legislation that would force them to bear the responsibility and cost of environmentally safe disposal of massive amounts of hazardous waste. They responded with a legislative campaign that effectively limited their liability. The regulatory structure they advocated would prove to be highly vulnerable to the commission of disposal crime, but these crimes would be committed by others, not by the generators themselves. Even if generators did not intend this outcome, they were well served by it because illegal disposal activity effectively slowed the pace of change and cushioned the shock of transition from an unregulated to an increasingly regulated context.

New Directions: Feminist Theory

Introduction

An important and all-encompassing challenge to existing theories of crime causation of every stripe is feminist theory, which is continuously evolving. Feminist theory most fundamentally is an attack on all theories because they are seen as formulated on taken-for-granted patriarchal assumptions of human behavior that are dismissive of the female voice and draw conclusions on masculine-based definitions of reality. Specific formulations of feminist theory take as their foci different aspects of criminological interest. Thus some feminist theorists attempt to explain the differences in male and female crime and have shown that these differences are not treated with any theoretical consistency. Others have concentrated on the exclusion of gender from theories about crime. Still others have analyzed specific forms of criminality such as white-collar crime in their research.

Following Daly and Chesney-Lind's (1988) influential article, feminist criminologists believe that it is necessary to take a more inclusive "worldview" perspective than offered by traditional criminology. In such a view feminism is a "social movement that encompasses assumptions and beliefs about the origins and consequences of gendered social organization as well as strategic directions and actions for social change" (Simpson, 1989:606). Feminists preferring this broader based "feminist-oriented" criminology (Caulfield and Wonders, 1994) attempt to understand and explain crime in general as part of the wider configuration of social arrangements. While women are presently the major proponents of this theoretical stance, its content and development are not restricted by gender and are not generally intended to exclude others employing a gender-aware analysis (e.g., Messerschmidt, 1986, 1993).

Feminist theory contains diverse strands and "competing conceptions of the origins and mechanisms of gender inequality/oppression, and divergent strategies for its eradication" that inform the different feminist criminologies (Simpson, 1989:606). Four major approaches have be identified as liberal, radical, Marxist, and socialist versions of feminism (Jaggar, 1983). *Liberal feminism* is concerned with gender discrimination as an issue of equal rights between men and women. It takes a noncritical stance on gender and seeks to end discrimination by institutional changes and legal reform, aimed at increasing women's opportunities (Hoffman-Bustamente, 1973; Adler, 1975; Simon, 1975; Edwards, 1990). *Radical feminism* sees the problem of gender inequality and the subordination of women to male power as a systemic problem of "patriarchy." Patriarchy is rooted in male aggression and male domination in the public and private domains, through the control of women's sexuality. Part of the radical agenda involves the liberation of women from male definitions of women's roles, and their "place" in male society, especially in relation to the nuclear family and child care (Simpson, 1989; Castro, 1990). *Marxist feminism* recognizes gender relations and patriarchal structure but sees these as rooted in class relations of production. Historically these class relations have created and used gender differences to control and subordinate women. As a result women are in weak positions of economic power, and like other minorities, are vulnerable to exploitation. Finally, *socialist feminism* "unites the primary concepts in radical and Marxist feminism to identify women's oppression as based in capitalist patriarchy" (Danner, 1991:52). Socialist feminism says that it is important to recognize *both* the technology and class relations used in the production of goods and services (Marxist) *and* the construction of gender categories in labor, child care, and domestic care (Radical), without prioritizing the one over the other, as the interrelated source of gender inequality and male domination over women (Eisenstein, 1979; Hartmann, 1979, 1981; Messerschmidt, 1986; Currie, 1989, 1991). The socialist feminist agenda believes that inequality and gender oppression can only be overcome by constructing a noncapitalist, nonpatriarchal society. Merely replacing or tinkering with parts of the system perpetuates the subordination of women in a different form.

In spite of their differences feminists share several core assumptions that they have contributed to criminology. Caulfield and Wonders (1994) have identified five of these "commonalities" as: gender, power, context, social process, and social change. They argue that gender, power, and social context shape human relations along gendered lines through a social process. They believe all feminists share a commitment to develop methods to understand this process and to change the way it currently operates.

Consistent with this new direction in feminism is the selection included here, Sally Simpson (chap. 22) addresses not only gender differences but social class and race as well in her examination of violence among women. She says that criminological research often targeted gender as an important discriminator of criminal participation and persistence. However, Simpson argues that such research often contrasts the criminality of males and females without taking into account key differences among female populations. In her essay she demonstrates how race and class combine to produce uniquely situated populations of females (e.g., "underclass" black females) who, when compared with their gender and racial counterparts, also appear to have unique patterns of criminality.

As Simpson integrates gender with class and racial dimensions of inequality, so the selection by Robbin Ogle, Daniel Maier-Katkin, and Thomas Bernard (chap. 23) seeks to integrate gender concerns with a variety of macro- and microdimensions of more traditional theories in order to explain homicidal behavior by women in a variety of settings. They argue that structural, social, and cultural conditions of modern societies generate strain for all women, which produces negative affect. They argue that women tend to internalize negative affect as guilt and hurt rather than externalize it as anger directed at a target. This, they say, results in a situation analogous to overcontrolled personality, and results in low overall rates of deviance punctuated by occasional instances of extreme violence. The conditions found in long-term abusive relationships and pre- or postpartum environments are more likely to produce this result, but their theory is not limited to explaining female homicide in these settings.

Each of these selections represents a move away from the early tendency of feminist theory to be isolated by showing how its concerns more directly permeate those of criminological theory.

22

Caste, Class, and Violent Crime: Explaining Difference in Female Offending

Sally S. Simpson

Class-oppressed men, whether they are white or black, have privileges afforded them as men in a sexist society. Similarly, class-oppressed whites, whether they are men or women, have privileges afforded them as whites in racist society. . . . Those who are poor, black and female have all the forces of classism, racism, and sexism bearing down on them. (Mantsios, 1988:66-67)

Violent criminality provokes an imagery that borders on caricature but one that is reinforced through official statistics and scholarly investigations. Serious street crime is a lower-class phenomenon (Elliott and Huizinga, 1983; Silberman, 1978; Wolfgang, 1958), disproportionately enacted by young (Greenberg, 1979), black (Hindelang, 1978; Tracy et al., 1990; Wolfgang et al., 1972), males (Hindelang, 1981; Tracy et al., 1991; Steffensmeier and Cobb, 1981). Studies and reports that support this portrait rely heavily on official arrest statistics, victimization surveys, and offender self-reports. With few exceptions, these data are not conducive to analyses of the often complex interactive effects of caste (gender and race) and class. Consequently, comparisons of violence within or between certain subgroups in the population, say lower-class white females versus lower-class black females, are typically neglected.

There has been intense debate among scholars regarding the "true" relationship between social class and crime (see Braithwaite, 1981; Fagan et al., 1986; Hindelang et al., 1981; Tittle et al., 1978; Tittle and Meier, 1990), but the relationship between gender and violence is more certain. The violent female offender is an anomaly—both in the United States and cross-culturally (Harris, 1977; Weiner and Wolfgang, 1985). Yet when

Edited and abridged from *Criminology*, Volume 29(1):115–35 (1991).

women are violent, their victims tend to be intimates (Bowker, 1981; Mann, 1987; Norland and Shover, 1977).

However, this truism conceals unique patterns and trends in female criminal violence. Specifically, if females are not as a group violent, what accounts for variations in rates of criminal violence among them—particularly between blacks and whites (Hindelang, 1981; Laub and McDermott, 1985; Tracy et al., 1991)? As will be demonstrated, black females, especially those in the "underclass," engage in what might be considered anomalous behavior for their gender (i.e., violent crimes) but not for their race (Lewis, 1977). Yet, given the high level of violence among black males, black female rates of violent crime are relatively low.

Black females appear to respond differently to conditions of poverty, racism, and patriarchy than their class, gender, and racial counterparts. Race and gender merge into an important case that deserves systematic inquiry (Hill and Crawford, 1990).

In this review, violent crime among underclass black females is taken as illustrative of vertical (power) and horizontal (affiliative) differences between blacks and whites, males and females, and social classes (Hagan and Palloni, 1986). The degree to which existing theory can accommodate these caste and class differences in violent crime is assessed. Three perspectives (neo-Marxian, power-control, and socialist-feminist theories of crime) are evaluated as to their sensitivity to intraracial and intragender variations in violent crime. The article is divided into: (1) a review of the empirical literature on gender and violent crime; (2) a critical review of theory; and (3) recommendations for theory modification, including cultural analysis.

The Violent Female Offender

Making an Empirical Case: Problems of Identification

Distinguishing violent crime rates among females of different social classes and races is a difficult empirical task. Many studies employ noncomplementary instruments and measures that preclude comparison, or often, one or more of the key demographic variables of class, gender, and race is missing (see, for example, Laub and McDermott, 1985; Laub, 1983; Brownfield, 1986). Even the exceptions (e.g., Ageton, 1983), test mostly for direct, not interactive, effects; or when variable interactions are calculated, racial and class rather than racial and gender effects are the focus (Elliott and Huizinga, 1983).

In some cases, attempts to compare findings across the same variable are problematic. As Brownfield (1986) and others (Tittle and Meier, 1990)

388   *Sally S. Simpson*

note, class may be calculated as relational (Colvin and Pauly, 1983; Hagan et al., 1985); common characteristics (Matza, 1966; Wilson, 1982); gradational (Elliott and Ageton, 1980; Hirschi, 1969; or social-ecological (Shaw and McKay, 1942). Race is typically dichotomized into white and black or the nonwhite category is broadened to include groups other than blacks (e.g., Hispanic and Asian). The only variable that seemingly defies this definitional drift is gender.

Patterns and Trends

RACE

Although speculative, piecing together "apparent" patterns and trends from Uniform Crime Reports (UCRs) and victimization and self-report data about violent female crime, yields intriguing and remarkably consistent, relationships. Black females have higher rates of homicide and aggravated assault than whites (Mann, 1987; McClain, 1982; Steffensmeier and Allen, 1988; Von Hentig, 1942). For certain types of personal crime victimizations, black female rates for both adults and juveniles are more similar to those for white males than those for white females (Hindelang, 1981; Laub and McDermott, 1985; Young, 1980).

Among juveniles, black females are consistently more involved in assaultive crimes than whites (Ageton, 1983). A cohort study (Tracy et al., 1991) found nonwhite female participation in UCR violent offenses to be 5.5 times that of white females. They are also more apt to be chronic offenders (see also Sheldon, 1987). The sole exception to the greater involvement of black females in violent crime is hitting parents. Here, white female participation exceeds that of blacks.

Black female participation in violent criminality does not compare with the high rates among their male counterparts; yet, "black women constitute well over half of all incarcerated women and are a higher proportion of all female offenders than are black men of all male offenders" (Lewis, 1981:69). Clearly, gender alone does not account for the variation in criminal violence. Race as constitutive of structural and/or cultural difference demands greater conceptual and empirical attention (Chilton and Datesman, 1987; Hill and Crawford, 1990). However, because of the difficulty of obtaining data on other women of color (e.g., Chicanas, Indians, Asians, other Hispanics) "race" is hereby operationalized as black and white. This is not to imply that black female experiences represent those of all women of color. Qualitative and historical studies (e.g., Campbell, 1984; Miller, 1986; Ross, 1988) show that different historical and cultural experiences of oppressed groups, intersecting with material conditions, influence the degree to which group members are apt to act criminally.

RACE AND CLASS

Of the variables most often related to violent crime, class position is important for both blacks and whites (Elliott and Ageton, 1980; Tracy et al., 1991), but underclass status for blacks may be essential. A number of researchers (Blau and Blau, 1982; Currie, 1985; Silberman, 1978; Wilson, 1987) assert that economic inequality—especially the increasing marginalization and social isolation of underclass blacks—is correlated with high levels of criminal violence.

Changes in divorce laws, occupational segregation coupled with low pay for women, and the rise of single-parent mothers (Goldberg and Kremen, 1987; Norris, 1984; Weitzman, 1985) have significantly lowered the objective class position of many women. Since the 1960s, the major increase in poverty has occurred among those living in households headed by a single-parent mother (Goldberg and Kremen, 1987). Of these women, one-third are black (Norris, 1984). One out of three white children and three out of four black children can expect to spend some of their childhood in a single-parent family (*New York Times*, April 29, 1983). As with the crime statistics, black women and children are overrepresented.

The majority of single-parent mothers work, but most work v ithin the pink-collar ghettos of clerical, service, and sales. Their average weekly earnings place them under the poverty level, which has earned them the title "the working poor" (Norris, 1984).

THE UNDERCLASS

The lower class, while disproportionately female and black, is relatively heterogeneous. Yet the bottom of the lower class is more racially homogeneous. Wilson (1982:157) characterizes this population as underclass: "In underclass families, unlike other families in the black communities, the head of the household is almost invariably a woman. The distinctive makeup of the underclass is also reflected by the very large number of adult males with no fixed address."

The underclass is poorly educated, unskilled, and chronically under- or unemployed (Lichter, 1988; Wilson, 1987). Its single-parent mothers (often teenagers) are typically welfare-dependent (Norris, 1984). The question of how an underclass is created and sustained is debatable. But whether its origins lie in large-scale, race-neutral structural change (Wilson, 1987) or in institutional racism (Duster, 1988; Lichter, 1988), its demographic characteristics are without refute. The face of the underclass is young and black; its geographical terrain is center-city urban.

Violence and the Underclass

Rates of violent crime vary significantly with the economic characteristics of communities. Some researchers suggest that violence is caused by relative economic deprivation, that is, by ascriptive inequality (Blau and Blau, 1982; Blau and Golden, 1984); others argue the violence is correlated with absolute poverty (Messner and Tardiff, 1986) or some interaction of class with race and urbanism (Blau and Blau, 1982; Laub, 1983; Wilson, 1987). Once again, causation is refutable but empirical patterns are more straightforward. Violent crime rates are highest in underclass communities—urban communities that are disproportionately black (Wilson, 1987).

In a study of underclass violence (Sampson, 1987c), "disrupted" families (female-headed households) are found to have increased juvenile and adult robbery offending for both blacks and whites, but they reveal a greater effect on black homicide rates. Although gender differences in the use of violence are not taken into account, Sampson suggests that underclass position, particularly labor marginality among black males and its accompanying economic marginalization, has profound negative consequences for black women with children.

Similarly, Matsueda and Heimer (1987) discover a positive relationship between broken homes and delinquency, an effect that is much stronger among blacks than whites. Moreover, black delinquency is more likely to be affected by "neighborhood trouble" than white. The authors conclude that "broad historical trends have led to different patterns of social organization among the urban underclass which influence rates of delinquency" (1987:837).

Given the significant impact of family structure on violent criminality among males, researchers must ask (1) whether this same pattern holds for females, and (2) what it is about single-parent families that contributes to such a relationship. Both are empirical questions but, because of the paucity of data, the answers are necessarily speculative.

Two types of family structure emerge from poverty: (1) extended domestic networks (Stack, 1974; Valentine, 1978), and (2) isolated single-parent units (Miller, 1986). The structure of one's family of origin may influence whether females become involved in criminal activity and in what types of illegality they may engage. Miller's (1986) study of deviant street networks in Milwaukee found poorer women, especially blacks, to be members of shifting households composed of kin, nonkin, and pseudokin.

The extensive and shifting domestic networks in which black females are found are closely associated with criminal recruitment. According to Miller (1986:67),

> Because of the severe limitations that poverty places upon the control exercised by parents and guardians, young women from poor families are more likely to be recruited to deviant networks than those from families that are better off. Moreover, because of the greater frequency of highly developed and far reaching domestic networks among poor blacks than among poor whites, black girls appear to be differentially recruited to the fast life of the street.

The fast life described by Miller heightens female exposure to all types of crime, especially property, but personal offenses as well (e.g., robbery and assault). Yet, because much violent crime is irrational and noninstrumental, exposure to criminal opportunities through deviant street networks may only partially explain the violent crime gap between black and white females. And given that both males and females participate in deviant networks and share similar class experiences, why is there not greater gender convergence in violent crime rates? Obviously, other elements are operative.

Feminists were among the first to call for greater sensitivity to class and racial differences among females, but feminist criminology has yet to produce a cohesive perspective that accounts for intragender racial differences in criminal offending (see, e.g., Messerschmidt, 1986). Similarly, most theories of crime are sensitive to class (see Meier, 1985), but not to gender and race. In this next section, three criminological perspectives are assessed with regard to their ability to account for gender, class, and racial differences in violent offending. The three theories are examined precisely because they tie illegality to class and/ or gender *oppression* and because feminist critics of androcentric criminological theory suggest that Marxian and control perspectives are more amenable to the "gender variable" (Leonard, 1982; Naffine, 1988).

Theoretical Considerations

Neo-Marxian Theory

Neo-Marxian explanations formulate the crime problem by examining the objective class position of workers. Depending on the type of employment and employer (e.g., skilled worker/monopoly capitalist versus unskilled worker/competitive capitalist), workers will be disciplined differently and develop different bonds to authority (Colvin and Pauly, 1983). Parents who experience alienative bonding to authority in coercive work situations reproduce those relations with their children. Alienative bonding in juveniles is reinforced through the educational system (through such practices as tracking) and peer relations. The alienated youths who emerge from this process are more apt to be violently delinquent than youths who experience other types of discipline and bonding (e.g., remunerative/calculative or symbolic/moral).

> The more coercive the control relations encountered in these various socialization contexts tend to be, the more negative or alienated will be the individual's ideological bond and the more likely is the individual to engage in serious, patterned delinquency. (Colvin and Pauly, 1983:515)

Therefore, children whose parents are least skilled and subject to coercive discipline at work are more likely to act out in criminally violent ways.

This theory adds conceptual precision to the class-violent delinquency relationship, but it fails to account for gender differences among juveniles whose parents are similarly located. Colvin and Pauly's theory has received mixed support for both males and females, especially the class-delinquency relationships (Messner and Krohn, 1990; Simpson and Elis, 1994). However, these findings may be due to questionable operation-alization of concepts such as Marxian class categories and serious patterned delinquency. Also, in the Messner and Krohn (1990) study, blacks are excluded from the analysis. Finally, if violence is highest among underclass populations who are increasingly isolated from the labor market (see Simpson and Elis, 1994), then the processes that are deemed essential to the production of violent crime (i.e., coercive disciplinary control and alienative bonding in the workplace) are not in place.

Power-Control Theory

Power-control theory (Hagan et al., 1985, 1987, 1988) builds on the idea that workplace-family power relations affect how parental discipline operates (mother or father as instrument of control) as well as which child is most apt to be disciplined by which parent (male or female as object of control). According to this theory, delinquency will be gendered only under certain class and familial structures. Patriarchal families (which reflect the unequal authority positions of parents in the workplace) produce greater rates of "common" delinquency by sons than daughters, because within the family males are socialized to have a greater taste for risk than females. In more egalitarian families (i.e., both parents share similar work positions or households are female headed), delinquency is not patterned (or as patterned) by gender. "As Mothers gain power relative to husbands, daughters gain freedom relative to sons" (Hagan et al., 1987:792). Ostensibly, under these conditions, females become more risk-prone and consequently more delinquent.

In framing power-control theory, Hagan and his associates (1979, 1985:1153–54) clearly limit their focus to "common" forms of delinquency. Yet power-control theory can be modified to account for class and gender differences in violent crime. Indeed, one permutation of power-control theory nestles the concept of power in the same neo-Marxian class categories that Colvin and Pauly (1983) theoretically link to "serious patterned delinquency." Additionally, the inclusion of personal assaults in Hagan et al.'s (1985, 1988) measure of common delinquency raises the question of whether all juvenile assaults are benign enough to be viewed as not serious, or "common."

Appropriate modifications of the theory should focus on how violence is related to freedom to deviate, an absence of controls, and/or socialized risk preferences. For example, Colvin and Pauly (1983) and Hagan and colleagues (1985) claim that discipline and control within the family reproduce workplace authority structures. Common delinquency is expected to be positively related to class position (because freedom to deviate is associated with upper-class socialization and power position), but violent offending should vary negatively with class. Alienative bonding coupled with coercive discipline in the workplace will produce inconsistent bonding to authority and high levels of frustration and alienation in families. Following the original logic of power-control theory, one would expect greater gender differences in violent offending in patriarchal than in nonpatriarchal families. Patriarchal power within the family supports and reinforces traditional gender role socialization (i.e., male as aggressive/female as passive). Gender differences in violent offending should decrease with class position, partially because of the dispro- portionate representation of "egalitarian" single-parent mothers among lower-class families, but also as a result of the deteriorating authority of male and female workers, which is reproduced in parental relations with children.

Risk preference is expanded to include (a) the functionality of risk, and (b) the perceived costs if one is caught. In employer classes, violence is apt to be dysfunctional for most males because it does not prepare them for careers nor, given the increased likelihood that this behavior is more apt to come to the attention of authorities than common delinquency, are the costs worth it. For upper-class females, violence is neither functional nor legitimate. And, considering that countertype criminality by females (i.e., masculine crime) may be more harshly viewed by authorities (Bernstein et al., 1977; Schur, 1984; Visher, 1983), the costs of violence for this population of females may be especially high. As one moves down the class ladder, however, definitions of violence and its legitimacy may change. Violence as a means of achieving desired ends—whether pecuniary or interpersonal (power and dominance)—is apt to be more commonplace and less gender-role defined.

Power-control theory has been relatively unsuccessful in subsequent empirical tests (Singer and Levine, 1988), perhaps because it fails to address how patriarchy varies across racial groups and social class lines. Male dominance and control do not necessarily operate similarly for black and white females, nor for racial groups across different classes (Simpson and Elis, 1995). The relationship between black women and black men is not "the same or necessarily analogous to that which white women have to white men . . . these relationships are patriarchal and oppressive . . . [but] their form can be very different" (Brittan and Maynard, 1984:64). Consequently, power-control theory may offer insights into class and gendered delinquency, but as currently conceived its insensitivity to race is a major weakness.

Socialist-Feminist Theory

Socialist-feminist approaches to crime, although also unable to link race and racism systematically with class and patriarchy, are at least concerned with such conceptual failures. Messerschmidt (1986:xi) acknowledges that "racial oppression is as important as class and gender oppression, [but] socialist feminism has not linked it systematically with patriarchy and capitalism." Even with these confessed flaws, socialist-feminist approaches provide helpful ways in which to think about class and gender differences in crime.

The strengths of socialist-feminism for this analysis are twofold. First, the criminality of males and females varies in frequency and type due to the gendered social organization of productive (class) and reproductive (family) spheres. Neither sphere is privileged over the other as a source of oppression; they are mutually reinforcing. Consequently, the economic base of capitalist society and its ideological superstructure (social institutions and culture) are seen as dynamic and dialectical. Second, personality and individual consciousness are seen to reflect the dominance/subordination relations found in production and reproduction (Messerschmidt, 1986:30–31).

Patriarchal capitalism creates two distinct groups: the powerful (males and capitalists) and the powerless (females and the working class). Opportunities to commit crime vary according to one's structural position. For the powerful, criminality is a means to maintain domination over the control of the powerless. Conversely, crimes by the powerless are interpreted as forms of resistance and accommodation to their structural position (Messerschmidt, 1986:42). From this perspective, the most costly and deleterious crimes are committed by capitalist males (e.g., corporate offenses). Lower-class and female crime reflects a powerless status, but because of gendered social organization (crime opportunities are distributed unequally and males are apt to resist while females accommodate their powerlessness), male and female criminality takes entirely different forms. Under patriarchal capitalism, powerless males commit violent street crime; powerless females engage mostly in nonviolent property and/or vice offending (primarily drugs and prostitution).

As noted earlier, one of the flaws of socialist-feminism is its neglect of how racial oppression and racism interact with other forms of oppression to produce distinct patterns of criminal offending. A related problem is its insensitivity to intragender variations in violent offending. To suggest that males are violent and females are not ignores the empirical reality of black female crime. In the next section, key concepts and theoretical insights from neo-Marxian, power-control, and socialist-feminist perspectives are used to address intraclass, gender, and racial differences in violent offending.

Toward Theoretical Inclusivity

Power

Class, gender, and race are best understood as intersecting systems of dominance and control. Power is ascribed and compliance determined by how these characteristics cluster across productive and reproductive spheres. Within the workplace, white females are less powerful than white males, but more powerful than black females. Bourgeois blacks are more powerful than lower-class blacks, but less powerful than bourgeois whites, and "white working class men are given at least a vicarious power over third-world peoples" (Silverstein, 1977:178).

In the family, it is less clear how class and race may affect gender relations. Although subsequently criticized by feminist scholars for ignoring the role of the gendered effects of the marriage contract (Johnson, 1988:251), Blood and Wolfe (1960) find greater middle-class attitudinal subscription to gender equality, but more equality in practice within working-class families (as measured by decision-making power). Because there is greater economic parity between black males and females than there is between whites (black female wage earnings are closer to those of black males than white female earnings are to those of white males) *(Wall Street Journal,* April 17, 1989), male's have less economic power within black families. At the bottom end of the class structure, black males are often unavailable for family participation due to violent death, drug addiction, prison, or unemployment (Wilson, 1982). Here, interpersonal male power is negated by absence, but replaced with the patriarchal state (e.g., through female interactions with Aid for Dependent Children, children's services, the criminal justice system, and so on).

The shared experience of racism also can affect the intrafamilial operation of patriarchy. Although black women recognize their own subordination to men, they keenly feel the racism that keeps black males "in their place." Racism changes the features of male privilege and dominance within the black family.

Control

In terms of control, ideology (constraining belief systems that reflect the interests of the powerful) and culture (the symbolic-expressive dimensions of human action) (Wuthnow, 1987) determine who gets controlled and how. In traditional working and upper-class families, control operates through patriarchal structures.

> Individuals are enmeshed in class and gender structures that organize the way people think about their circumstances and devise solutions to act upon them. Gender and class shape one's possibilities. The conditions individuals confront and the manner in which they choose to "handle" those conditions are socially regulated. Just as conforming behavior is socially regulated and intimately related to one's class/gender status, so is nonconforming behavior. (Messerschmidt, 1986:41)

Yet, membership in the underclass is disruptive of this process. For blacks, social controls within the family (i.e., parental bonding and learning of "gender-appropriate" behaviors) are attenuated across extensive domestic networks.

The disruption of intrafamilial patriarchal reproduction occurs within a system stratified by racial privilege and framed by race-conscious ideologies. Underclass position, because of alienation and the breakdown of traditional social control in the family, should produce higher crime rates for both black and white females compared with other classes, but blacks—because they have little invested in a racist system or less to gain through conformity with that system—should be more criminal than similarly positioned white women.

Collins (1986:519) offers an important insight as to why black males in the underclass have higher rates of crime than black females. She argues that being poor, black, and female offers "a clearer view of oppression than other groups who occupy contradictory positions vis-à-vis white male power." Black males can always attempt to negate their oppression through a "questionable appeal to manhood." The source of this appeal is ideological. Patriarchy provides males (white and black) with a "manhood" typescript (Harris, 1977). This typescript defines male-appropriate reactions to stress and frustration (i.e., they act out against others). The dominant "womanhood" typescript is just the opposite. Stress and anger are internalized into self-destructive behaviors like suicide, depression, and other types of mental illness (Piven and Cloward, 1979).

White women are more apt to be deterred from crime because of its perceived consequences (e.g., loss of status, negative labeling, and rejection by a system that benefits whites). They will take fewer risks because they have more to lose in a system that accords privilege to whites. Moreover, they can mitigate their powerlessness by "attaching" themselves to powerful white males in a patriarchal racist society. White women can use their sex and race to "realize personal gains from the system" (Hook, 1984:199). Thus, in a patriarchal power system, under the pretense of sharing power white females may be seduced into joining the oppressor (Lorde, 1988; also see Hook, 1984).

For the white poor, racist ideology provides a psychologically nonthreatening explanation for their poverty and a language of collective resentment. MacLeod's (1987) study of working- lower-class boys describes how white boys believe blacks and the wealthy are favored at school and in employment. In a system in which failure is attributable to individual weakness and white skin confers greater value than black skin, it makes sense that white males and females do not reject the system but blame others' privileges for their failures. Psychologically, they cannot afford to do so. Moreover, family structure among impoverished whites is more likely either to be nuclear or isolated, single-parent units (Miller, 1986; Wilson, 1987). These structures are less conducive to breakdowns in patriarchal control, and violent crime opportunities are fewer than in the extended and integrative domestic networks of underclass blacks.

Power and hierarchy determined by class, patriarchy, and race cannot be separated from horizontal relations of affiliation and solidarity (Hagan and Palloni, 1986). These relations are reciprocal and reinforcing. As structural conditions increasingly preclude mobility for the bottom of the surplus population, cultural redefinitions and adjustments may influence perceptions of, and beliefs about, the emergence and appropriateness of violence (Wilson, 1987).

Although power-control, neo-Marxian, and socialist-feminist perspectives link micro and macro factors to crime, none sufficiently develops the cultural processes that drive interpretation and social action. Most culturally attentive criminological theories (e.g., Cloward and Ohlin, 1960; Miller, 1958; Wolfgang and Ferracuti, 1967) are primarily concerned with male criminality. Consequently, they fail to explain how culture either restricts or patterns female criminality (Leonard, 1982). They also tend to employ a narrow and static definition of culture—a system of norms, beliefs, and values that impose on individual actions. This conception divorces cultural production from its situated context and tends to see culture as a distinct and imposing force.

Yet "culture is not composed of static, discrete traits moved from one locale to another. It is constantly changing and transformed, as new forms are created out of old ones" (Mulling, 1986:13). To understand the unique positioning of black women between two dominant groups in society (Lewis, 1977:343), it makes sense to discern how their material conditions affect the way culture is created, interpreted, and reproduced, as well as culture's relation to power and hierarchy.

Collins (1986:524) calls attention to an essential relationship between structural/material conditions, black women's subjective consciousness, and social action:

> Oppressive structures create patterns of choices which are perceived in varying ways by black women. Depending on their consciousness of themselves and their relationship to these choices, black women may or may not develop black-female spheres of influence where they develop and validate what will be appropriate . . . sanctioned responses.

Although Collins is interested in explaining how black females mobilize politically, criminal behavior can be seen as emerging from similar cultural processes. Class is an oppressive structure for both black and white females, but black women's experiences of their material circumstances and their perceptions of self and choice vary qualitatively from those of whites.

The lives of black women and children are "stitched with violence and hatred . . . [and] violence weaves through the daily tissues of . . . living" (Lorde, 1988:355). Living daily with the fact of violence leads to an incorporation of it into one's experiential self. Men, women, and children have to come to terms with, make sense of, and respond to violence as it penetrates their lives. As violence is added to the realm of appropriate and sanctioned responses to oppressive material conditions, it gains a sort of cultural legitimacy. But not for all. The observed gender differences in the way violence is interpreted and incorporated into one's behavioral repertoire emerge from the contradictory cultural tendencies of caste (i.e., female = nonviolent, black = violent) (Lewis, 1981). Black females, given their dedication to keeping home and community together (Joseph, 1981) are more apt than black males to delegitimate violence. However, given their racial oppression and differential experience of patriarchy in the family, black females are perhaps less apt to delegitimate violence than their white counterparts.

Summary and Conclusions

Criminologists have been mistaken to ignore important variations in criminal behavior among females. The simplistic assertion that males are violent and females are not misses the complexity and texture of women's lives. A review of the empirical literature on violence reveals the confounding effects of gender, race, and class. Although their combined influences are difficult to tease out, a firm understanding of how they interact is fundamental for a more inclusive and elegant criminological theory. Neo-Marxian, power-control, and socialist-feminist perspectives offer some help in this regard.

Before criminologists launch into a major revision of current theory, however, further research is clearly necessary. Until large-scale quantitative designs can readily and meaningfully sort out differences in crime rates, and qualitative research can offer subjective accounts of how violence is interpreted and understood by different subpopulations of interest, criminological theory will continue to be only vaguely relevant to the real world.

23

A Theory of Homicidal Behavior among Women

Robbin S. Ogle, Daniel Maier-Katkin, and Thomas J. Bernard

Men commit much more crime than women. But homicides by women have more consistent characteristics and circumstances than those committed by men (Browne, 1987; Browne and Williams, 1993; Bunch et al., 1983; d'Orban, 1990; Gelles and Cornell, 1985; Goetting, 1987; Jurik and Winn, 1990; Martin, 1981; Walker, 1989). About 80 per cent of homicides by women involve killing intimates (Browne and Williams, 1993; Bunch et al., 1983; d'Orban, 1990; Edwards, 1984; Goetting, 1988; Mann, 1990; Wolfgang, 1958), especially in long-term abusive relationships (Browne, 1987; Goetting, 1987) and in pre- or postpartum periods (d'Orban, 1979; Hamilton, 1989; Maier-Katkin and Ogle, 1993; Stern and Kruckman, 1983). These homicides generally occur in the home (Goetting, 1987; Mann, 1990; Wolfgang, 1958) and are spontaneous (Goetting, 1987). The women tend to be socially conforming, see themselves in traditional sex roles, and be under extreme life pressures, including depression (Bunch et al., 1983; Piven and Cloward, 1979; Totman, 1978; Widom, 1978b; Zimring et al., 1983). However, mental illness seems unimportant in the killings (d'Orban, 1990; Resnick, 1970; Scott, 1973; Totman, 1978). The same pattern tends to be replicated with female mass and serial killers (Segrave, 1992), and does not differ significantly by race (Bunch et al., 1983; Mann, 1990) despite the significant racial differences in crimes known to police and in arrest rates of females for homicide (Sommers and Basking, 1992; see Simpson, 1991; and Daly, 1993, on the interaction of race, class and gender).

Most theory and research in criminology focus on explaining criminal behavior by men, and explanations of criminal behavior by women have been adapted from the male-oriented findings (Laberge, 1991; Leonard,

Edited and abridged from *Criminology*, Volume 33(2):173–93 (1995).

1982; Smart, 1976). But consistency in the pattern of homicides by women, and differences from the patterns of homicides by men, suggests the need for a separate theoretical explanation of female homicidal behavior.

Prior theories of female criminality have limited use in explaining female homicidal behavior. First, because most theories focus on less serious criminality, homicide is the least discussed type of female crime (Simpson, 1991). Second, many theories attribute crime to individual female pathology and ignore the social structural context in which such behavior occurs (Bowker, 1978; Leonard, 1982; Smart, 1976). Third, some theories associate female crime and violence with women's liberation (e.g., Adler, 1975; Hagan et al., 1985, 1987), but studies indicate that female offenders tend to be more traditional in their lifestyles and beliefs about sex roles than the average woman (Bunch et al., 1983; Giordano and Cernkovich, 1979; Widom, 1979). Fourth, some theories (e.g., Jurik and Winn, 1990) explain violence by women in one setting without explaining violence in others (Mann, 1990; Simpson, 1991). Fifth, some theories blur the line between scientific explanation and legal defense. For example, "battered women's syndrome" can be part of the legal justification of self-defense for killing an abusive partner, while "postpartum psychosis" can be part of the legal excuse of temporary insanity for killing an infant. Sixth, theories like battered women's syndrome and postpartum depression are very different and largely incompatible explanations of homicidal behaviors by women, yet there are some similarities between women who have killed abusive spouses and women who have killed infants.

This article addresses the limits of prior theories by incorporating individual, situational, and structural variables, including the tendency for offenders to be traditional women, in a single explanation of violence by women in different settings.

An Overview of the New Theory

Concepts from three theories of criminal behavior are used to develop a new theory of female homicide. Agnew (1992) argues that the removal of positively valued stimuli and/or the presentation of negative stimuli result in "negative affect" and the adoption of "coping mechanisms" for avoiding this affect. Blockage of these coping mechanisms may generate deviant responses. Megargee (1966, 1973) argues that when an "overcontrolled personality" overcomes its high level of inhibition, an explosion of aggression occurs at a level "beyond the rational requirements of the situation." Bernard (1990, 1993) argues that chronic high arousal among the "truly disadvantaged" results in unfocused explosions of angry aggression against visible and vulnerable targets. These concepts are incorporated in an explanation for female homicide by interpreting them in the structural context of women's experiences in contemporary societies.

Feminist literature (de Beauvoir, 1952; Delphy and Leonard, 1992; Friedan, 1983; hooks, 1984; MacKinnon, 1987, 1989) argues that, because of social and cultural conditions in contemporary society, women frequently experience the removal of positively valued stimuli and/or the presentation of negative stimuli. This results in widespread negative affect among women, with high levels of chronic stress and attempts to develop coping mechanisms.

According to Agnew's (1992) General Strain Theory, a group's level of deviance depends on its members' level of stress, constraints from legal and illegal coping strategies, and members' disposition to delinquency and crime. Agnew does not necessarily predict high rates of violence among women, despite their high levels of stress. The reason is that women generally are socialized not to express or even experience anger (Bernardez-Bonesatti, 1978; Lerner, 1980). Anger necessarily includes external attributions of blame for the negative affect (Averill, 1982; Daly and Wilson, 1988:254–58). But women tend to interpret negative affect in ways that include internal attributions of blame, such as disappointment, depression, and despair. These internal attributions rule out coping mechanisms that address the external world in the attempt to reduce the negative affect. While this increases stress, it also decreases the tendency to adapt deviant responses to it. This results in a situation analogous to what Megargee (1966, 1973) described as overcontrolled personality. Most violent offenders are probably "undercontrolled" and act out their impulses without restraint. Some violent offenders, however, have very severe restrictions on their impulses, particularly the expression of anger. These offenders generally engage in almost no violence over long periods despite extremely high stress levels, but then occasionally and randomly erupt in extreme violence.

Since Agnew's theory suggests that women experience very high levels of stress combined with very high levels of controls, Megargee's theory would seem to predict low rates of violence for women, punctuated by very infrequent and almost random instances of extreme violence. This is much closer to the pattern of homicidal violence found among women.

In addition, the situations in which women kill frequently, including long-term abusive relationships and the immediate pre- or postpartum environment, are associated with high levels of chronic physiological arousal. Bernard (1990, 1993) argues that a large and well-established body of research predicts that biologically and psychologically normal people who experience such chronic arousal tend to direct violence against visible and vulnerable targets in their immediate environments. He uses this research to explain the high rates of violent behavior among the truly disadvantaged—extremely poor minority group members residing in inner cities. We make a comparable argument here for women experiencing these situational variables in their immediate relational environment.

"Baseline" Stress and Negative Affect in the Lives of Women

A central element of feminist thought is that women experience a significant degree of stress due to the structural, social, and cultural conditions of contemporary society. Women's stress actually may be higher than men's (Al-Issa, 1982; Hill and Crawford, 1990; Wethington et al., 1987), but at minimum women experience at least as high a level of stress as men.

The current psychological and psychiatric literature indicates that adult women are under a great deal of stress (Cutrona, 1984; Daly and Chesney-Lind, 1988; Dean and Lin, 1977; Eckenrode and Gore, 1981; Wethington et al., 1987). This points to the intensity of role socialization, role intersection and conflict, social/familial support, structural inequities and conditions of society, and individual coping techniques that frequently result in despair and depression.

Concrete examples of stresses in women's lives can be found in many aspects of social life. For example, women occupy jobs that have less status and salary, offer fewer opportunities for development of skills, and limit opportunities for professional advancement, economic success, and personal satisfaction. The inadequacies provide incentives for women to become dependent on men as "head of household" or to accept dependency on the welfare state for themselves and their children (Delphy and Leonard, 1992; Friedan, 1983). Additionally, their access to higher education and the legal process frequently are limited (Aisenberg and Harrington, 1988; Delphy and Leonard, 1992; Frug, 1983; Rich, 1979).

But such stresses do not reveal the more profound sources of "oppressive" stress in women's lives. Perhaps most significant is the internalization of ideas that devalue femaleness. Cultural messages imply that males are rational, moral, mature, independent, and assertive whereas females are irrational, immoral, emotional, dependent, and submissive (Delphy and Leonard, 1992; Edwards, 1981; Frug, 1983; Kessler and McKenna, 1978; Lowe and Hubbard, 1990; MacKinnon, 1987, 1989; Martin, 1981; Oberman, 1992). Such images are communicated in many forms and contexts from an early age, with children's movies and television shows, and persist over the life span through school and work. Women tend to internalize these messages into their own self-concepts.

This general cultural view of women is based on what Simone de Beauvoir (1952) characterized as the "otherness" of women. She argued that in the grammar of social life, men are always the subjects and women the objects in the male-centric universe: "(Woman) is defined and differentiated with reference to man, not he with reference to her. . . . He is the Subject, he is the absolute. . . . She is the Other" (1952:267; see also Cain, 1990).

This cultural message is so pervasive that women tend to incorporate it into their own self-concepts. Such "objectification" may then generate a need to take on the appearance prescribed by male fantasy, which may cause or intensify dissatisfaction with the physical self. The consequence of internalizing self-image on the basis of appearance rather than the substance of character (especially when the standard of appearance is unrealistic) is low self-esteem, which then generates low self-confidence and negative affect.

The general cultural view of women's otherness is especially prominent in sexual and reproductive roles. Legal and cultural restrictions exist on access to birth control, abortion, and prenatal care, and laws directed at the control of female sexuality and reproduction continue to develop (Delphy and Leonard, 1992; Lowe and Hubbard, 1990; Moyer, 1992; Oberman, 1992). These laws, and the ideology from which they derive, establish the social identity of women in reproductive and sexual roles and are at the core of a distinction between good girls and bad girls (MacKinnon, 1989; Moyer, 1992). Young single women receive mixed messages indicating that both participation and nonparticipation in sexual behavior is deviant. One effect of this is to promote marriage as the institution within which this dissonance can be resolved. Marriage is also the only way to confer "legitimacy" on children. Thus, the social status of a woman and of her children depends on the legality of her relationship to a man. But satisfactory marital relations are not available to all women (again the significance of race and class variation), so that some women can only experience parenthood if they are willing to violate social norms and suffer the consequences for that violation (Wilson, 1987).

Even the one social role that is highly honored and reserved exclusively for women—motherhood within the context of marriage—may generate stress (Cutrona, 1984; Hobbs, 1965; Wandersman et al., 1980). Achieving the status of "good mother" requires willingness to make great sacrifices, special "inherent knowledge," and nurturing ability bordering on the saintly. This status often is seen as the only fulfillment of womanhood, so that failures to achieve it may generate great negative affect.

The requirements of employment outside the home can interfere with attempts to achieve this status. In 1992, women represented 48 per cent of the U.S. labor force (U.S. Bureau of the Census, 1992). The burdens of motherhood may be undertaken as part of a sixteen- or eighteen-hour day and such roles frequently conflict (Aneshensel and Pearlin, 1987); failure to achieve an ideal of motherhood may be used to discredit the achievements of a woman in the workplace. A similar penalty is not applied to men when they fail to achieve an ideal of fatherhood.

Even with many recent changes in families, the burdens of raising children still fall primarily on women. They are the ones who are most penalized by the limited availability of child care services and the lack of resources committed to securing child-support payments. The result is the predominance of mothers and children—particularly minority mothers and children—in the ranks of the poor (U.S. Bureau of the Census, 1988; National Center for Children in Poverty, 1987).

While this is not an exhaustive list of the sources of stress in the lives of women, our point is that stresses in the structural and social domains of employment, marriage and personal relationships, motherhood, and the legal regulation of sexuality and reproduction, combined with more general stresses derived from the cultural devaluation of femaleness, are conducive to the development of negative affect in women. This line of argument leads to the following propositions:

1. Stress is higher for women, on average, than for men.
2. Women with lower social status experience higher stress, on average, than women with higher social status.

Blockage of Women's Coping Mechanisms

Early strain theories (Cloward and Ohlin, 1960; Cohen, 1955; Merton, 1938) focused on the relationship between blocked "goal achievement" and deviant behavior. Agnew (1992) added a new focus on the relationship between the "blockage of pain avoidance" and deviant behavior. Agnew argued that "the inability to escape legally" (1992:58) from negative stimuli results in negative affect, such as fear, despair, disappointment, depression, and anger. This leads to the adoption of coping mechanisms to alleviate the stress and manage the negative affect.

We argued above that there are important differences between men and women concerning the sources of stress and negative affect in their lives. Here, we argue that there are important differences between men and women in the coping techniques typically used to deal with negative affect and in the blockage of those techniques. Agnew considers coping techniques for a broad range of negative affects because he attempts to explain a broad range of deviant behavior, but we focus on coping techniques related to anger because it is the negative affect most directly linked to aggression and violence (Averill, 1982).

Women generally view themselves as part of a collective of relationships around them and evaluate their self-worth based on the value and success of these relationships. But anger involves alienation from those very relationships. Lerner (1980:145) argues that "the expression of legitimate anger and protest is more than a statement of dignity and self-respect; it is also a statement that one will risk standing alone even in the face of disapproval or the potential loss of love from others." For women, "standing alone" is particularly difficult because the collective of relationships in which they are involved is an essential element of self-concept, and anxiety about separation from significant others may threaten their sense of self-worth.

Lerner (1980) and Bernardez-Bonesatti (1978) assert that few women achieve the level of autonomy necessary to separate their sense of self-worth from the relationships in their life. Women who do so are able to experience and express anger when appropriate, but they must be prepared to face criticism that they are "shrill," "bossy," or "bitchy" for behaving in a way that might be considered "tough," "strong," or "assertive" if done by a man (Spelman and Minow, 1992).

Women with lower levels of autonomy often react to these same situations by striving to preserve relationships. The coping mechanism adopted involves cognitive reinterpretation, which delegitimizes the anger and recasts it as guilt (characterized by a sense of failure) or hurt (characterized by sadness) (Bernardez-Bonesatti, 1978; Lerner, 1980). This generally works through a culturally induced process of self-doubt (Lerner, 1980). This process begins with a series of questions about the anger: Is it legitimate? Am I really the aggrieved party? How will others view this reaction from me? Will I destroy a significant relationship if I become angry? These questions precipitate fear that the risks associated with being angry are too great to be tolerated. The cascading negative affect can include elements of anger, fear, guilt, hurt, self-doubt, and anxiety about the possibilities of separation and retaliation. This combines with the "baseline" negative affect, described above as experienced generally by women in contemporary societies, at which point the whole coping mechanism can break down.

This process may be interpreted by others as unreasonable or even irrational, particularly if the situation ultimately culminates in some form of aggression when the coping mechanism breaks down. In general, however, reinterpretations of anger into hurt or guilt are in compliance with the cultural message that women are weak, incapable of defending themselves, and willing to suffer. Therefore, it is also consistent with the woman's self-concept when she has internalized this cultural message. This argument leads to two more propositions:

3. Women, on average, have more blockages of coping mechanisms for dealing with anger than men.
4. Women with lower social status, on average, have more blockages of their coping mechanisms for dealing with anger than women with higher social status.

Overcontrolled Personality

Most criminological literature (e.g., Nettler, 1984b) describes homicidal offenders as undercontrolled personalities who respond too readily with aggression. Megargee (1966, 1973) identified overcontrolled personalties as a second category of violent offenders. These individuals ordinarily manage negative affect through a variety of coping mechanisms that involve cognitive reinterpretation or withdrawal, and they exhibit powerful inhibitions to the expression of anger, so they engage in much less violence and aggression overall than others. But on the infrequent occasions when their inhibitions are overcome, they erupt in a display of uncontrolled aggression that is very extreme and violent. Megargee's theory has been widely tested with generally supportive results, but mainly with populations of men (Blackburn, 1968, 1971, 1986; Holland and Holt, 1975; Lane and Kling, 1979; Lang et al., 1987; McGurk and McGurk, 1979; Walters et al., 1982).

One study on women by Widom (1978a) found that about one-fourth of female offenders awaiting trial had the characteristics of an overcontrolled personality and that they had the fewest prior convictions. However, the study included only sixty six subjects and did not focus on those who had committed homicide. Widom noted that, despite its apparent utility, the concept of overcontrolled personality had been neglected in the literature of female criminality. An extension of Megargee's theory to violent female offenders seems appropriate since women exhibit similar inhibitions on the expression of anger and similar behavior patterns with respect to the expression of aggression. Additionally, this phenomenon is not just a matter of individual adjustment; it receives strong reinforcement in structural and cultural institutions.

We assert that women are more "controlled" than men, particularly with respect to their experience and expression of anger. This is consistent with their generally low crime rate, which is the effect of the high controls predicted by control theories (e.g., Gottfredson and Hirschi, 1990; Hirschi,

1969). But it is also consistent with the opposite effect of producing overcontrolled personalities that, when overwhelmed, may produce the most extreme forms of violence, particularly homicide. This "overcontrol" is centered in women's tendency to respond with guilt and hurt to situations in which men tend to respond with anger. In these situations women experience the high level of inhibition that is central to the development of what Megargee (1966, 1973) characterized as overcontrolled personality. This leads us to a fifth proposition:

5.   Women are more likely to develop overcontrolled personalities than men.

Situational Stresses

Relying on biological and psychological research on the connection between physiological arousal, anger, and aggression, Bernard (1990) proposes a purely social theory to explain the high rate of violence among the poorest minority group residents of inner cities. This research leads to the prediction that people with normal biological and psychological characteristics would respond with high levels of violence to the social circumstances commonly experienced by this group. This is a purely social theory because variation in the rates of violence is explained solely by variation in social circumstances. Thus, the theory does not hypothesize any variation in biological or psychological characteristics, such as low autonomic nervous system functioning (Mednick, 1977) or low self-control (Gottfredson and Hirschi, 1990), although it does not deny that such variation might occur and might be related to violence.

Bernard identifies three factors: urban location, low social position, and discrimination as sources of chronic, high physiological arousal. A fourth factor—social isolation—concentrates the effects of the other factors and limits the availability of "targets" against whom the resulting aggression can be directed. These four factors are relevant to the explanation of inner-city violence, but analogous arguments can be made about the sources of chronic, high physiological arousal among women who are experiencing abusive relationships and pre- or postpartum environments. These two situational settings are not the only ones where women experience conditions culminating in homicide, but we discus them here because of their frequent association with female homicide.

Urban location is associated with increased physiological arousal because of (1) the physical difficulties of dealing with the environment (e.g., traffic) and the chronic assault on the senses caused by crowding, noise, and pollution, and (2) the loss of personal space and quiet time for rest and recuperation from the rigors of daily life. Similarly, abusive relationships and postpartum environments often entail a fairly wide range of the physical difficulties that increase physiological arousal as the woman struggles to cope with them.

A marked reduction of personal space is an inevitable consequence of the postpartum environment. Even under the best of circumstances, the new mother loses her ability to create a zone of privacy or separateness. In addition, abusive relationships (with or without physical battering) generally involve severe restrictions on personal space and freedom of movement. Both these circumstances would be expected to be associated with chronic, high physiological arousal and, thus, with an increased probability of angry aggression.

Low social position is associated with increased physiological arousal because it entails limited financial resources. People with such limited resources must live with a variety of aggravations, annoyances, and inconveniences that others would use their resources to avoid, resolve, or eliminate. The essence of being poor is that you live in difficult and stressful circumstances.

Women in long-term abusive relationships and in postpartum environments are distributed throughout the class structure, so they do not have fewer financial resources, on average, than other women. However, abusive relationships typically include tight controls on access to financial resources, even for those quite wealthy. Abused women frequently have limited financial resources. In addition, the birth of a child often is associated with severe financial strains due to a host of new expenses and restrictions on the ability to earn income (Belsky and Kelly, 1994). For most people, the period around the birth of their children is the poorest of their lives. Postpartum women often have limited financial resources. Finally, by far the largest group of poor people in the United States at present are women and their children (U.S. Bureau of the Census, 1988; National Center for Children in Poverty, 1987). This indicates that there is some direct relationship between these circumstances and limitations on financial resources (see Simpson, 1991; Daly, 1993).

Discrimination increases physiological arousal because it entails being the target of intentional harms, threats, and insults, as well as deliberate blocking of goal-directed activities (Allport, 1954:51-65). Because of the social context in which discrimination exists, the target usually is unable to prevent these actions from occurring or to retaliate against them. The result is chronic, high physiological arousal.

The baseline stress experienced generally by women in contemporary society can be attributed to discrimination based on institutionalized sexism. Beyond that, abusers typically use all the elements of discrimination within the abusive relationship, including intentional harms, threats, and insults, as well as the deliberate blocking of goal-directed activities. That is because the goals of abuse and discrimination are identical: to achieve, maintain, and manifest power over the target.

In addition, postpartum women may experience discrimination, couched in cultural terms of what is best for the child. Issues surrounding pregnancy and the care of young children, for example, may complicate a woman's relationship to the workplace, particularly for nonprofessional women. Employers who strongly adhere to the cultural standards of "good mother" may deliberately penalize female employees who they believe are failing to live up to this standard. Like other targets of discrimination, female employees often lack the power to prevent discrimination or to retaliate, and so would be left with residual chronic, high physiological arousal.

Social isolation in Bernard's (1990) theory plays two roles. The first relates to the formation of a "subculture of angry aggression." Chronically aroused people tend to believe that it is appropriate to become angry in more rather than fewer situations (constitutive rules of anger) and that it is legitimate to respond with higher rather than lower levels of violence and aggression (regulative rules of anger). Social isolation of a chronically aroused group means that interpersonal communication is largely restricted to other people who independently generate similar rules about anger out of their own socially structured experience. These people then legitimize each other's rules by understanding, acceptance, and approval. These broad and severe rules for anger, although structurally generated, become subcultural.

Women in abusive relationships and postpartum environments generally are isolated; not socially isolated in a group that has interpersonal communications among its own members but cut off from communication with others. This limits the opportunity for structurally generated rules about anger to become subcultural. Nevertheless, some level of subcultural approval for these homicides seems to be generated through media representations of battered women's syndrome and postpartum depression as defenses in cases of criminal homicide. There is some social support for the view that these killings are legitimate, appropriate, or at least excusable responses within the context of these situations.

Social isolation in Bernard's theory plays a second role: It limits the choice of the target for the angry aggression. For the "truly disadvantaged," the sources of chronic physiological arousal are largely invisible and invulnerable. For example, broad historical, economic, and social conditions are invisible in the sense that the aroused person may not really perceive them at all, while politicians, employers, and landlords are often invulnerable in that they can make retaliation too costly to be practical. Under these conditions, aroused people tend to transfer blame to visible and vulnerable targets in the immediate environment and retaliate against them (e.g., kick the dog, yell at the kids, slap the wife around). Physiologically, this reduces arousal (and therefore is reinforcing) even if these targets had no role in generating the arousal to begin with. This explains why so much angry aggression among the truly disadvantaged is directed at other truly disadvantaged people.

For women in abusive relationships and postpartum environments, the immediate sources of arousal may be readily visible—the abusive partner and the new baby—so that angry aggression is likely to be directed at these targets. The new baby is quite vulnerable, except that other adults can retaliate on the baby's behalf if they learn that the mother was aggressive toward it. The abusive partner is only rarely vulnerable, such as when she or he is asleep. One could certainly argue that there may be broader sources of arousal—for example, the relative lack of societal support for child care and child rearing, or the failure of criminal justice agencies to protect abused women adequately—but these would be invisible and invulnerable and thus not practical targets for retaliation and arousal reduction. In other situations in which women might experience these same variables, the act of striking out at the most visible and vulnerable target might involve other family members or possibly even those present in the work environment if it is perceived as presenting these variables.

Megargee (1973:137) points out that overcontrolled personalities do not progressively learn "socially acceptable or more moderate methods for expressing aggression." This observation seems particularly appropriate for women in these situations. They have little or no prior history of aggressive behavior and therefore have little experience in the expression of anger. Women simply are not socialized to understand expectations about appropriate levels of aggression and anger or in the use of physical aggression. In Bernard's terms, they have never developed "regulative rules" for anger.

"Regulative rules" imply the possibility that anger can be controlled and directed in appropriate ways, but this requires experience and learning. Men, for whom the experience and expression of anger are culturally approved, are more likely to establish personal rules for regulating anger and aggression. These rules have considerable variability—indeed, it is precisely their variation among the truly disadvantaged that Bernard was seeking to explain. Women are less likely to have regulative rules because of culturally generated restrictions on the experience of anger. They may have no regulative rules for the expression of anger precisely because they have only one constitutive rule for the experience of anger: Anger is always inappropriate and always forbidden. When these women finally experience anger, they are likely to express it in uncontrolled and unregulated ways. For example, women in long-term abusive relationships or postpartum environments are affected by chronic "baseline" stress (as experienced by all women) and also by the intense peaks of stress brought on by their particular situations. If these high levels of stress overwhelm their traditional coping mechanisms of converting anger into hurt and guilt, these overcontrolled women will come face-to-face with the experience of intense anger amounting to rage.

For these women, the experience of such anger implies that all the rules already have been broken. Under these circumstances, the regulation of their expressions of anger is unlikely. Since women spend a significant amount of time at home, this environment may be the most common place where the situational variables appear and homicidal behavior results. However, it is not necessarily the only place. This argument leads us to three more propositions:

6.   Women, on average, are less likely than men to have developed regulative rules for the experience and expression of anger.
7.   Women experiencing peaks of stress are more likely than men to explode, with episodes of extreme uncontrolled violence.
8.   Targets of this violence are most likely to be those in the immediate environment, whether or not those targets represent the actual source of stress.

Conclusion

Most theoretical explanations of women's homicidal behavior have concerned killing abusive partners. They have relied heavily on the immediate characteristics of abusive relationships to explain the killings. However, in addition to killing abusive partners, women also kill nonabusive partners, children, and other adults in their lives. In this article, we have attempted to explain women's homicidal behavior in all the settings in which it might occur.

In addition, because most women kill intimates, most previous explanations have tended to incorporate the woman's relationship to the victim into the explanation itself. Thus, there has been one type of explanation for killing spouses and another for killing children. There also has been some tendency for these theories to blur the line between scientific explanation and legal defense, so that the theories themselves provide the basis for exoneration in court—for example, battered women's syndrome and postpartum psychosis. In contrast, we have attempted to present a single, empirically adequate theoretical explanation for various types of homicide by women, and have ignored whether this explanation can form the legal basis for the court handling of these cases.

This theory is similar to Agnew's (1992) general strain theory, but it incorporates different sources of negative affect, different techniques for coping with that affect, and different limitations on those coping techniques, based on institutionalized conditions in the lives of women. It is similar to Megargee's (1966, 1973) theory of overcontrolled personality, but it proposes that this is a general, culturally supported, and institutionalized phenomenon among women even though it may be uncommon among men. Finally, it is similar to Bernard's (1990, 1993) theory of angry aggression among the truly disadvantaged, but the structural sources of chronic arousal are reinterpreted as situational variables related to various settings involving a group (women) that has developed little in the way of regulative rules for aggression.

This theory provides a number of empirically testable propositions at the aggregate level: the low overall rate of homicide by women, the high rate of intimates among the victims of homicides by women, and the distribution of homicides by women among racial and class groups. At the individual level, however, as with earlier theories, prediction would be considerably more difficult. Megargee's theory is considered to be empirically supported, but it includes a degree of randomness that makes individual-level prediction difficult (Blackburn, 1993). Individual-level prediction within Agnew's (1992) theory requires consideration of a variety of dispositional variables, and similar variables would have to be considered in this theory for prediction at the individual level. Finally, Bernard's (1990, 1993) theory was intended to assert aggregate-level predictions about rates of violence among the truly disadvantaged, not to predict which of the disadvantaged would be more likely to engage in violence.

New Directions: Postmodernist and Constitutive Theory

Introduction

The most recent critical approach in criminology is the current emphasis on postmodernist exposition in the study of crime. Of all the critical approaches we have briefly described, the application of postmodern thought to criminology, if followed in its ultimate logic, would have the most transforming consequences for the contemporary state of the discipline. Postmodernist theory challenges all traditional assumptions in social science in general and criminology in particular. It is a complex theory with underpinnings in French and German intellectual thought and has a "radically interdisciplinary character" (Rosenau, 1992). There is no single version of postmodernist theory, however, there are some assumptions about which there is general agreement.

Thus, postmodernists reject disciplinary boundaries and all global views. For postmodernists there are no eternal truths; indeed, any truth claims are subject to challenge and deconstruction. The emphasis is on what postmodernists term alternative discourse and meaning. Positivism is rejected in favor of subjectivistic accounts. There is no such thing as certainty, rather uncertainty is the order of the day. In its extreme form, no explanation of a phenomenon is superior to any other, a belief which, in the view of some, leads to nihilism. On the other hand, this is not the path criminologists have taken.

Criminologists writing in this framework accept the need to challenge traditional constructs of explanation and methodological purity by deconstructing accepted discourse. However, unlike the theoretical extremists, the postmodernist scholars who term their theory *constitutive criminology* wish also to *reconstruct* this discourse along lines seen to better reflect the human condition, but always subject to change. They see this being accomplished through what they call "replacement discourse," a way of talking about crime, harm, and social justice that invests energy in displacing the negative discourse which feeds structures of oppression.

The selection by Martin Schwartz and David Friedrichs (chap. 24) explores the broad themes of postmodern thought as they relate to criminology. They identify some of the principal themes associated with postmodern thought, the reasons for the current interest in it, and its potential relevance for criminology. They point out that there are many postmodernisms, but draw particularly on models from literary and linguistic analysis. Violence is used as a concrete example to explore these issues. Through this Schwartz and Friedrichs show how postmodern analysis can create "a greater sensitivity to the 'intertextuality' of different forms of violence." Intertextuality refers to the process whereby attitudes and taken-for-granted philosophies expressed in one context can affect behavior in another. For example, Schwartz and Friedrichs raise the question of how corporatism and patriarchy are related to corporate violence and how male attitudes toward women in the corporate sphere relate to domestic violence.

The constitutive version of the postmodern approach is exemplified here in the article (chap. 25) by Stuart Henry and Dragan Milovanovic, who are constructing a new direction for criminology. They assert that crime can only be reduced if people change their way of talking and thinking about crime, that is, change the discourse of crime. This does not come easily, but as Henry and Milovanovic argue, current policies for dealing with crime and ways of reacting toward crime "reproduce" in endless fashion the structures of dominance and crime itself. The authors aim high and seek to establish a new constitutive criminology whose policy seeks to encourage criminologists among others to cease investing in constructing the existing structures of power and oppression and to begin investing through replacement discourse in new, less harmful structures.

The third selection here is illustrative of the constitutive approach in that it shows how penal policy emerges and is transformed through discursive construction. Though not identifying themselves as constitutive theorists, and even less as postmodernists, Malcolm Feeley and Jonathan Simon (chap. 26) show how during the 1980s and 1990s the United States saw the emergence of a "new penology" driven by the discourse of risk. Feeley and Simon direct their attention to new strategies being used in correctional ideology. They show that a new discourse has emerged which is transforming the entire penal process. They are mindful of three areas of transformation: the greater emphasis on risk, the correctional system's shift in emphasis from rehabilitation to control, and the use of techniques to target offenders as aggregates or types rather than as individuals. These authors illustrate very well the negative structural outcomes that can follow if the potential to invest in more positive languages of possibility is ignored.

24

Postmodern Thought and Criminological Discontent: New Metaphors for Understanding Violence

Martin D. Schwartz and David O. Friedrichs

Frustration with the past and anxiety about the future have recently spawned a prodigious outburst of social science commentary characterized as postmodern (e.g., Bauman, 1991; Crook et al., 1992; Doherty et al., 1992; Rosenau, 1992; B. Smart, 1993; Turner, 1990; Woodiwiss, 1990). Yet criminology generally has been unaffected by postmodern theory and even critical criminologists increasingly aware of postmodernism have not incorporated it into their writings (Matthews and Young, 1992). In this article we explore some of the tensions and intersections between postmodernism and criminology. We pay special attention to the implications of postmodernist thought for formulating responses to violence.

Although we argue that postmodern thought has relevance for criminology generally, it is linked most closely to critical criminology, which arose in the late 1980s as the principal successor to a disparate tradition known as radical criminology (Inciardi, 1980; Lynch and Groves, 1989). Critical criminology is an umbrella term for a series of evolving, emerging perspectives such as feminism, left realism, and peacemaking (Schwartz, 1989), or a metaphor that allows an alternative discourse (Thomas and O'Maolchatha, 1989). Critical criminology claims that it is impossible to separate values from research, and advances a progressive agenda favoring underprivileged peoples. Of the various perspectives that make up critical criminology, however, postmodern thought is the least developed and least understood.

Acknowledging many of the criticisms of postmodernist theory, including the suggestion that much of what has been published is only a

Edited and abridged from *Criminology*, Volume 32(2):221–46 (1994).

pretentious intellectual fad, we argue that postmodernist theory offers criminology: (1) a method that can reveal how knowledge is constituted, can uncover pretensions and contradictions of traditional scholarship and can provide an alternative to linear analysis; (2) a highlighting of the significance of language and signs in the realm of crime and criminal justice; and (3) a source of metaphors and concepts (e.g., "hyperreality") that capture elements of an emerging reality, and the new context and set of conditions in which crime occurs.

The Postmodernist Conceptual Challenge

According to many, we have entered a postmodern world and need to change our social analyses toward a postmodern perspective. Unfortunately, there seems to be an almost infinite number of postmodern perspectives. It may well be a fundamental contradiction to attempt any coherent definition of postmodernism if indeed it can be characterized only as a somewhat loose collection of themes and tendencies (Dews, 1987) or as amorphous and politically volatile (Huyssen, 1986). But for helpful explications of this rapidly growing field, see Rosenau (1992) and Sarup (1989).

The term *postmodern* is commonly used to refer to: (1) a specific historical period representing a fundamental break with modernity, (2) post-1960 movements in the fine arts and architecture, (3) a collection of contemporary social theories associated most closely with French writers such as Baudrillard and Lyotard (Dowd, 1991; Haldane, 1992; B. Smart, 1993), and (4) alternatives to a general linear model of social relations, such as chaos theory (Baker, 1993; Young, 1992). All these dimensions are related but are hardly synonymous.

In this article we are concerned with interpretations of contemporary society and social theories inspired by French writers including not only Baudrillard and Lyotard, but also Derrida, DeLeuze, Foucault, Barthes, Lacan, Bataille, Kristeva, and others. We will try to identify some common themes inspired by these theorists which have some relevance to criminology. Later we will focus on a few authors who have brought these themes into criminology and sociolegal thought.

The French sociologist Baudrillard, who, in spite of his dissociation from the term postmodernism, has generally been considered one of the most important postmodern theorists, argues that new technologies have become the guiding forces which shape the world. A number of major breaks have been made from the modern to the postmodern: from representation to simulation, from reproduction to replication, from sex to genetic engineering, and from mind to artificial intelligence (Haraway,

1990). Whereas modernity is based on a belief that people can control objects, nature, and each other, Baudrillard finds that objects now have more and more control over us.

For those who can grope their way through the fog of a semiotic theory based on Saussure, Baudrillard (1983) argues further that commodities in a consumer society acquire use values so that we consume them for their *signs* and statements rather than for the exchange value of their utility. When the simulations constructed for us by technology (mostly television) conceal that the real no longer exists, when we cannot tell the difference between simulations and reality, we have entered *hyperreality*. Our primary experience now is to live and respond to simulations (Glassner, 1992). Accordingly, Willis (1991:162) asserts, "We have no way to experience or conceptualize relationships between people except as these are defined by the exchange of commodities."

The postmodern critique challenges the system of values and priorities that sustain contemporary life. It contends that modernity is no longer liberating, but rather has become a force for subjugation, oppression, and repression; this contention applies to social science itself, which is a product of modernity (Graham, 1992). Postmodernists are disillusioned with liberal notions of progress and radical expectations of emancipation (Kellner, 1990).

Certainly there are points in favor of this argument. The forces of modernism (e.g., industrialism) have extended and amplified the scope of violence in the world. Even worse, according to postmodernists, the major form of response to this violence is through rational organizations (e.g., the court system and regulatory bureaucracies), with great reliance on specialists and experts. Such a response, say postmodernists, simply reproduces domination in perhaps new but no less pernicious forms.

Criminology has long concerned itself with accurately representing the "truth" about violence, but postmodernist thought challenges any attempt to develop "totalizing" theories that reveal the fundamental "truth" about violence and "explain" it (Currie and Kline, 1991). Truth claims are a "form of terrorism," modern truth is "fragmentary, discontinuous, and changing," theory "conceals, distorts and obfuscates," and human experience must be understood in terms of inconsistencies and contradictions (Rosenau, 1992:78–82). Not only can concepts such as "violence against women" never be understood "coherently," we should not even attempt such an understanding.

Rather, postmodern thought tends to reverse the approach taken by criminology: violence is regarded as a form of "representation" (Armstrong and Tennenhouse, 1989). From a postmodern perspective, language is used in different historical contexts to "represent" very different acts as violent; thus representation itself is a form of violence because of its capacity to empower some and to cast others into subjugation. A challenge for postmodern analysis is to "deconstruct" a modernist rhetoric in which ruling ideas increasingly have become a form of violence in their own right (Michalowski, 1993).

Both Foucault and Derrida have promoted the notion of a rhetoric of violence, or "the violence of the letter." Foucault's (1977) proposition that criminology is a discourse/practice which in some sense creates the category of criminality, can be extended to the notion of all violence as a product of discourse: "From . . . an order of language which speaks violence—names certain behaviors as violent, but not others, and constructs objects and subjects of violence, and hence violence as a social fact—it is easy to slide into the reverse notion of a language which, itself, produces violence" (de Lauretis, 1989:240). The purpose of the postmodernist endeavor is to explore how images and meanings pertaining to such violence are constituted, giving privilege to the experience and perspective of the victimized over the victimizers, and attending to the marginal rather than the "representative" cases. Sociological and criminological scholarship, in the postmodernist view, has failed to provide us with a penetrating understanding of how ordinary people experience a postmodern world dominated increasingly by a media-generated "virtual" reality (Denzin, 1986; Pfohl, 1992). The guiding premise here is that a postmodernist approach enables us to comprehend at a more appropriate level our knowledge of a dynamic and complex human environment. It looks to different layers of "texts" (everything in life can be considered a text in postmodernist thought, including people, events, or even writings), which are interrelated with each other as the locus of social reality, and discounts the notion of some separate "factual" reality.

Postmodernism addresses some of the enduring fundamental questions—on such matters as causality, determinism, egalitarianism, humanism, liberal democracy, necessity, objectivity and subjectivity, responsibility, rationality, and truth—and rejects most if not all of the conventional epistemological assumptions pertaining to these questions.

Further, one of the most important aspects of postmodernism in the social sciences is an attack on all aspects of positivism. Postmodernism calls on empirically oriented social scientists to be reflexive and to confront "the ways in which their own analytical and literary practices encode and conceal value positions that need to be brought to light" (Agger, 1991:121). Conventional positivist sociology is regarded as fundamentally biased, and as engaged in a distorted misrepresentation of social reality.

Much of the postmodernist critique simply reiterates a number of existing critiques. Yet it often goes further, taking the critique to its most extreme form. An example of the difference begins with Mills's *The*

Sociological Imagination (1959). Here Mills uses the term *postmodern* and attacks the emergence of a new form of militarily guided economic rationality. Denzin (1990), however, argues that Mills *imposes* his interpretation on ordinary people, viewing them as "the other," whose lives could be described and explained objectively. Such a virtuoso reading of a social text by a theorist, according to Denzin (1990:13), no longer works in late capitalist, postmodern society because there is no longer a fixed reality that can be mapped by a theory or a method: "Our theoretical signifiers have lost their signified referents. They now refer to other texts, which in turn refer to yet others . . . ."

Similarly, although postmodernist interpretations continue along the social constructionist path, the difference lies in the tremendous distance traveled. Social constructionist critiques of science, for example, tend to ascribe intentions to those engaged in the practice of science. Woolgar and Pawluch (1985) demonstrate some of the conundrums that arise in relativist (e.g., definitional) approaches to social problems; these approaches, perhaps inevitably, incorporate some objectivist presuppositions or assumptions. Yet Hazelrigg (1986) showed that Woolgar and Pawluch hardly escape the problem of nonobjective interpretation, of which they accuse social constructionists. The important difference is that social constructionist critiques of science tend to ascribe intentions to those engaged in the practice of science, whereas the postmodern critique does not necessarily make such ascriptions. Pfohl (1985b:230), responding to Woolgar and Pawluch's criticism of his study of child abuse on precisely these grounds, contends:

> The aim of my work was not *constructive*—to uncover the true story of child abuse and to show how this truth was obscured at earlier points in history. Rather, it was *deconstructive*—to displace the truth of a dominant story about the humanitarian march of therapeutic intervention.

Thus if both social constructionism and postmodern thought embrace a relativistic approach to the interpretation of social phenomena, the latter takes this relativism a step further, focusing not on how meaning is constructed and imposed, but rather, as Pfohl (1985b:230) suggests, on the "ceaseless repetition of an indeterminant act of differentiation between colliding practices." In this view *all* knowledge, including that of the social observer, is indeterminant and artifactual.

Unfortunately the problem still remains: whether the discourse now being recommended advances our understanding of real people's suffering, or whether it is a form of rhetoric that is becoming increasingly irrelevant (Tong, 1989). Rosenau (1992:111) points out: "Critics argue that debate over issues such as the existence of an independent reality are of interest only to postmodernists (and other intellectuals) who, insulated from reality, never personally experience the violence, terror, and degradation prevalent in modern society." Here in a nutshell is one of the strongest reservations about the postmodernist enterprise—also leveled at critical and Marxist criminologies (see Boehringer et al., 1983)—one with potent relevance to our concern with violence.

The Postmodernist Semantic Challenge

Postmodernist thought is focused intensely on the central role of language in human experience; it is somewhat infamous for its own tendency to invoke a specialized jargon, to invent and discard terms, and to "play" with words (Rosenau, 1992). This may sensitize us to the importance of language in creating our understanding of violence in all its many guises. Not only can the power of the word be exposed as creating domination; in addition, one means of resistance for those who are oppressed is to recapture the meaning of words (Freire, 1970) or at least to bring "into awareness suppressed, alternate meanings which are subversive to the established order" (Currie and Kline, 1991:15). The problem is that these arguments have not been convincing to many students of violence (to say nothing of its victims). Those who do not agree with postmodernists tend to locate their core experience outside the realm of language, and to find that "word games" tend to trivialize or diminish their view of the nature of violence. Even those postmodernists who are not playing "games" may, at times, be accused of substituting an increasingly abstract study of language for a focus on what modernists might call empirical reality. Palmer (1990:199), for example, asserts: "Much writing that appears under the designer label of poststructuralism/postmodernism is, quite bluntly, *crap*, a kind of academic wordplaying with no possible link to anything but the pseudo-intellectualized ghettoes of the most self-promotionally avant-garde enclaves of that bastion of protectionism, the University."

Beyond the issue of wordplay, however, remains the problem of postmodernist prose. There is no virtue, postmodernists argue, in catering to the lowest common denominator in understanding. The following are among the arguments in favor of a dense and abstruse postmodernist style; (1) it is more responsive to the complexity of what is being addressed, or (2) it is a worthy enterprise to be deliberately playful because this enables readers to assume the central and appropriate role of making their own sense of the writing. The idea of the latter is to release the subject from the prison of language, to provide the opportunity to construct or read the text differently as a method of discovery. Thus the question: Is postmodernist work gratuitously obscure, incoherent, and undisciplined? Alternatively, is the obstacle the fact that the rest of us are unable to liberate ourselves from the constraints of interpreting the world in the familiar idiom of rational, contemporary social science? If we reoriented ourselves, would we find modes and styles of understanding that are ultimately more valid and more revealing in a changing, endlessly complex world?

The dilemma is not that it is impossible to decipher what Lacan or Derrida are saying. Rather, it is the difficulty of imagining how a body of work will ever attain broad influence when the "style" of writing—in the work of postmodernism's major figures (Derrida, Lacan, Lyotard, Baudrillard) and those directly influenced by them—is so dense and so obscure that it is largely inaccessible to all but the exceptionally dedicated or the masochistic (Michalowski, 1993), and ultimately to the "inner circle" of self-identified students of this body of work (Ritzer, 1990). Although feminist postmodernism can be regarded as a different field, these criticisms apply there as well. Tong (1989:231) recently noted the complaint that "postmodernist feminists apparently delight in their opacity, viewing clarity as one of the seven deadly sins of the phallologocentric order."

All this raises some basic questions about the nature of intellectual influence and intellectual elitism. A paradox is involved in the postmodernist insistence on not "privileging" the voices of the powerful over the voices of the powerless (including the victims of violence), but then writing and speaking in a form and style largely inaccessible to the powerless as well as to most of those in a position to act on their behalf. At the same time, the decision by some postmodernists (e.g., Baudrillard, not Foucault) to focus on the mundane (e.g., shopping malls) also may raise questions about their relevance for criminologists, who tend to favor topics such as conflict and violence. The focus by some key postmodernists on surfaces, imagery, and the mundane rather than on violence and suffering can be viewed as representing a highly privileged position. In a world filled with extraordinary starvation and bloodshed on a mass scale, and with malnutrition and terrible suffering on the individual scale, finding the superficial images portrayed in suburban shopping malls to be the most relevant objects of study is a powerful statement. This is not to say that these objects are not worthy of study; the question is whether one claims that they are the most important objects of study.

Despite our reservations about such stylistic obfuscation, we are open to the argument that the substance of postmodernist themes can be separated from the style in which they are originally formulated (undoubtedly this possibility is not universally acceptable). Here we will attempt some small conceptualization of this sort.

Postmodernist Possibilities for Understanding Violence

Postmodernism promotes a greater sensitivity to the "intertextuality" of different forms of violence. This key term refers to the idea that there is a complex and infinite set of interwoven relationships, "an endless conversation between the texts with no prospect of ever arriving at or being halted at an agreed point" (Bauman, 1990:42). Absolute intertextuality assumes that everything is related to everything else. Because postmodernists already have rejected the concept of "truth" waiting to be discovered, the concept of intertextuality redefines knowledge generally not as inquiry, but rather as "conversation" (Graham, 1992).

This is where some fruitful cross-fertilization can take place at the margins of both criminology and postmodernism. Here it is possible to raise questions about connections between (for example) corporate violence and violence against women (Messerschmidt, 1993). There has been little investigation of the interaction between corporatism and patriarchism in generating the "texts" of both types of violence. One can ask, however, how male attitudes in the corporate context and in regard to women are related, and whether victimization by corporate violence affects domestic violence. Some recent scholarship (e.g., DeKeseredy and Hinch, 1991; Gerber and Weeks, 1992) suggests ways corporations engage in domestic violence against women. "Institutionalized" sexual harassment, on the other hand, may be conceived of as a form of violence against women in a corporate context.

Still, postmodernism refutes any "necessary" reading of the "texts" on violence. It raises the possibility that criminologists impose "truths" on readers in inherently authoritarian ways. It also at least suggests—very controversially—that the pain and suffering associated with violence reside principally in the domination of a particular meaning of such violence. Do policies intended to challenge and "punish" violence "reproduce" the structures of dominance? Do they lead to the diffusion of violence in new forms? Stanley Fish (1989), one of the most prominent theorists of postmodernism, argues that there is no difference between being forced into an act by a gunman and being forced by law.

Indeed, some of this dispute concerns which approach is more elitist. Earlier we discussed whether the *language* of postmodernism fostered elitism. Here we debate whether it is elitist to presume that we, as researchers and theoreticians, can explain something of how the world operates. Are we imposing our categories of explanation on the oppressed peoples of the world with our analyses, silencing their voices in favor of our own? Certainly it is not hard to find examples of this within criminology. Just as one example (not chosen because it is the most problematic), when we label sex trade workers as oppressed, do we simply add another layer to their oppression by labeling them as helpless women when they might not view themselves as such (Assiter, 1993; Bell, 1987; Jenness, 1993; McClintock, 1993)? At the same time, the postmodern tendency toward nihilism in denying the legitimacy of all categories (racism, sexism, classism, rape, robbery) can be viewed, despite denials, as providing a justification for a lack of political action (Matthews and Young, 1992; Schwartz, 1989). Throughout all this discussion, the question endures: What should be the primary mission of scholars and academics?

A key point is that postmodernism suggests it is more liberating to empower "victims" (an imposed category?) of violence (an imposed category?) to reconstitute the meaning of the violence they experience than to impose on them a critical interpretation (e.g., "knowledge," "truth," "social policy") of this violence (Lather, 1991; Rosenau, 1992). Exposing the ultimate subjectivity of truth is regarded as intrinsically desirable. Of course, critical and progressive sociological and criminological analysis traditionally has championed the oppressed, including at least some classes of victims. The postmodernist criticism, however, is that progressive analysis presumes to speak for the oppressed rather than allowing the oppressed to speak for themselves. Denzin's (1990:4) attack on Mills is that "nowhere in the pages of his work(s) do these little people and their personal troubles speak. Mills speaks for them; or he quotes others who have written about them." At the same time, it is possible that the postmodern approach—which includes the rejection of all metanarratives—is vulnerable to the similar claim that it is removed even farther from the reality experienced by ordinary people than is Mills's allegedly patronizing approach.

Postmodern Theorists

Criminology may be the social science discipline least affected by postmodernism, although postmodernist thought has been far more conspicuous in the related field of sociolegal scholarship.

Meanwhile, the few criminologists who have embraced postmodern thought have taken quite different approaches. Dragan Milovanovic is the most energetic promoter of this perspective directly within criminology (e.g., 1986, 1988b, 1989, 1991, 1992a). Stuart Henry and Dragan Milovanovic (1991) have developed a "constitutive criminology" to integrate elements of postmodernist thought with a more traditional criminological project. They are concerned especially with highlighting the role of ideology, discursive practices, symbols, and sense data in the production of meaning in the realm of crime. We must understand, in their view, how those who engage in crime, who seek to control it, and who study it "co-produce" its meaning. Henry and Milovanovic argue (1993:12): "Crime then is the power to deny others. It is the ultimate form of reification in which those subject to the power of another suffer the pain of being denied their own humanity, the power to make a difference."

Others have attempted to apply a semiotic analysis to criminological phenomena. Peter Manning (1988), for example, finds concepts generated from semiotics useful in his analysis of the handling of 911 calls, with special emphasis on the coding of calls and the transmission of their meaning. For Manning (1991), critical semiotics has many potential applications in criminology for the study of signs that are commodified and circulated within the justice system; distorted communication is an important consequence.

Stephen Pfohl offers a different, authentically heretical, approach to the creation of a postmodernist criminology. He would have us abandon not only conventional methodology but also conventional modes of communication among scholars. According to Pfohl, an emerging postmodernist era calls for new, multimedia modes of communication and for the juxtaposition of direct observation, literary allusions, textual analysis, epiphanies, parenthetical observations, visual images, transcriptions of dialogue, and so forth (Pfohl, 1993; Pfohl and Gordon, 1986). For Pfohl, the objective of criminology should be to produce a "different knowledge" that exposes the nature of subjectivity and marginalization in a postmodern (or ultramodern) social environment where power and knowledge generate new forms of violence.

Law and society scholars thus far have been more attentive to postmodernist concerns than have criminologists. Language, signs, and discourse generally play a central role in the legal realm, and some scholars view postmodernist analysis as especially appropriate. Rosemary Coombe (1989), for example, draws on postmodernist thought in her effort to develop a theory of practice that integrates structuralist with subjectivist strands of critical legal theory. She is concerned primarily with exploring how "practices reproduce and change symbolic systems of power and domination and how these same systems construct the agents who realize and transform them" (1989:121). Other sociolegal scholars who have been inspired by postmodernist work include Susan Silbey and colleagues (Ewick and Silbey, 1992; Silbey and Sarat, 1988), who have explored how localized discourses have contributed to general institutional production and to the multiple and contingent character of legal consciousness. Jonathan Simon and colleagues (Feeley and Simon, 1992; Simon, 1988, 1993a, 1993b) have examined the emergence of postmodern modes of social control and penal practice, with a shift from individuals to categories, from society to subdivisions, and from normalization to prevention.

Perhaps the best known sociolegal scholar to adopt an appreciative attitude toward postmodern theorists' insights is Alan Hunt (1990, 1991, 1992, 1993), although at the same time he argues that this critique goes too far. Hunt regards as valuable the postmodernist challenge to the rationalist legacy of the Enlightenment in legal and criminological scholarship, but also considers it one-dimensional and overstated. He views the postmodernist critique of political metanarratives as provocative but ultimately insensitive to the dependence of local politics on larger institutional arrangements, as well as vulnerable to nihilism.

Postmodernism and the Social Policy Dilemma

Our central concern in this section is with the implications of postmodernism for social policy: Does postmodern thought have anything to contribute to some of the current debates among criminologists on state intervention in response to various forms of violence?

Assuming we agree that violence exists, the major social policy question is what to do about it. As we have seen, postmodernism asks criminologists to consider whether various calls for the fundamental transformation of social policies, and of the structures that create oppression, present illusions as to what can be accomplished, or ultimately reproduce an unequal distribution of power.

It is difficult to see whether this question inherently represents the left or supports the status quo (Agger, 1991). At least one strand of postmodernism has sunk so deeply into its epistemological relativism that it denies the legitimacy of any political view because any such views necessarily imply a foundational basis (Rosenau, 1992). Radical postmodernists who hold this view may urge withdrawal from political participation on the grounds that the struggle for social change is meaningless and that individual human beings are powerless to influence government and society (Jacoby, 1987; Palmer, 1990).

This withdrawal is not frustrating to the person sitting in a rustic but luxurious lodge on a $2,500 five-day New Age retreat, or at a $375 entrepreneurial seminar on Post-Feminist Male Parenting. The survivors of violence, however, and the frontline workers who deal with these survivors, have found it very easy for the past two decades to feel that criminologists, in the evocative Texas phrase, are "all hat and no cattle." These workers and survivors understandably may regard some postmodern thought as an effete mockery of their efforts and their suffering. Certainly some postmodernist theorists have a strong political agenda, as contradictory as this sounds (e.g., Lather, 1991). As Malcolm Bradbury (1988:4) points out, however, earlier theorists were strong on plight and anguish, but altogether too much postmodernism, "in keeping with the times, is clean absurdism or cool philosophy; it is laid back, requires no weighty black gear, and goes very well with Perrier water and skiing."

Three Concrete Examples

Responding to Violence against Women

The problem of whether to attempt reform by engaging the state has been debated most heavily within feminist theory, especially in relation to battered women. Many feminists and criminologists, for example, believe that it is essential for the state to intervene with men who commit violence against women by arresting and sentencing them to long prison terms (e.g., Box-Grainger, 1986; Edwards, 1989; Gregory, 1986). Here is the dilemma: Many feminists have argued that to work with the criminal justice system is to risk being coopted by it (C. Smart, 1989), but some believe that the risk of not using the state is more serious than the risk of using it (Dobash and Dobash, 1992). Feminists are actually using it; unlike other countries, the United States battered women's movement has succeeded in changing the practice of the criminal justice system. U.S. police departments have moved to a proarrest or mandatory arrest policy, and a broad variety of other changes such as protection orders, streamlined prosecution, and increased use of jail are being implemented widely (Hirschel et al., 1992), even though there is little or no "objective" evidence that these policies will have the desired effect (Sherman, 1992).

On the other hand, many feminist theorists have argued for an emancipatory agenda that incorporates postmodernist thought with a praxis (e.g., Lather, 1991). This agenda would include allowing women to define what is best for themselves, the ways in which they want help, and what they think will help them. Such an empowering of women may have some theoretical advantages, but at times (such as in battering) it may simultaneously be fairly meaningless. This position may assume a degree of agency that battered women lack when they are living in frightful circumstances with all their energies focused on getting out alive and protecting their children (Horley, 1991). It is admirable to be antihegemonic, but we may need to take some time out from congratulating ourselves to wonder how much responsibility we are placing on women in crisis to solve their own problems.

Thus there is a dilemma in assessing the value of postmodern analysis. Postmodern thought at least can help us appreciate both the limitations and the dangers involved in state intervention. This appreciation, however, provides an unsatisfactory basis for attending to the extraordinary vulnerability and powerlessness of many abused women. We are persuaded much more strongly by Dobash and Dobash (1992), who argue that an appreciation of these dangers mainly should be put to use in a modernist project to improve the interventionist role of the state in relation to women's struggles.

Responding to Corporate Crime

The question of how to respond to corporate violence presents criminologists with some conundrums. Our understanding of violence has an important political component, and violence has implicit and explicit political consequences (Friedrichs, 1981). Corporate violence—for example, polluting the environment, dangerous working conditions, unsafe products—is primarily a consequence (with the specific harm unintended) of efforts to enhance corporate profit making; yet it may be far more pervasive and more harmful than conventional forms of violence (Friedrichs, 1996). The purely radical strain of critical criminology obviously views corporate violence as an absolutely inevitable feature of a modern capitalist society, which cannot be obliterated or even diminished significantly without a revolutionary, structural transformation of the political economy (Lynch and Groves, 1989). Furthermore, the state is viewed as an important source of violence, and is connected closely with corporations in some of the most substantial forms of violence. In this view, state-based reform efforts directed at corporate violence are regarded largely as a means of enhancing the legitimacy of the political economy without substantially reducing corporate violence.

Most criminologists, however, concede that revolution is hardly imminent. Even most critical criminologists do not regard revolution as the necessary solution to oppressive social conditions. As a parallel to the feminist response, some criminologists favor strong state intervention against corporate violence (e.g., Pearce and Tombs, 1992; Snider, 1990); others favor alternative tactics that avoid reliance on the state and emphasize community-rooted solutions (e.g., Pepinsky and Jesilow, 1984). All camps, however, are likely to be united in skepticism toward a postmodern perspective that at least implicitly grants the victims of corporate violence—citizens, workers, and customers—the prerogative of assigning it their own meaning. The problem of "agency" may be even more difficult in this area than with battered women because initially victims of corporate violence may not even be aware of their victimization.

Some unfulfilled promise for future collaboration at the margins of

432   *Schwartz and Friedrichs*

criminology and postmodernism would seem to exist in the development of many new forms of crime, or "technocrimes" (Bequai, 1987b), which are emerging in the "age of information." These crimes involve computers, telecommunications, and other aspects of high technology. The analyses of postmodern approaches to the understanding of crimes that occur in a symbolic universe, and often in the realm of the "hyperreal," would seem to have some potential for criminology.

Analyzing "Street" Crime

Conventional forms of criminal violence are viewed widely today as becoming more pervasive and more vicious, with ever younger juveniles involved. Perhaps because of the considerable frustration with the limitations of mainstream approaches to understanding such violence, the publication of Jack Katz's (1988) highly original study attracted much attention. Although Katz does not consciously adopt a postmodernist perspective, his approach has distinctive postmodernist elements. Specifically, he draws on the Nietzschean notion of a need to create ourselves within the chaotic void of contemporary existence, and repudiates a positivist approach to science in favor of a reading of multiple "texts." He directs special attention to the centrality of language and symbolism while challenging conventional boundaries between crime and resistance (Ferrell, 1992). Katz takes seriously the texts of popular culture; finally, his approach is at least implicitly consistent with the postmodernist skepticism toward rational policy-making responses to crime. Altogether Katz's approach to understanding conventional criminal violence, with an emphasis on foreground as opposed to background factors, is quite consistent with some basic premises of the postmodern approach, and demonstrates how postmodern ideas could influence criminological theorizing.

Although both Katz and postmodern writers have been criticized severely for neglecting or dismissing background factors relevant to understanding crime, they counterbalance excessively structuralist explanations by attending to the way causes of crime are "constructed" or "constituted" by an individual adapting to an unstable, complex social environment. For example, Katz (1991:416) observes that reducing the availability of guns might reduce the number of fatalities from crimes of passion,

> [b]ut guns remain symbols that are embraced with uniquely profound passions in America. The key research question about guns and American violence is not how much or whether removing guns will

reduce crime, but why guns have acquired such strong moral and sensual meanings in the United States.

Conclusion: Postmodernism and Policy

Here we have concerned ourselves partially with the concrete example of violence as an important criminological concern. Drawing insights from postmodernist thought to contribute to the development of policy responses to violence is a difficult proposition. The more extreme version of postmodernism questions the possibility of changing society; it compels us to consider whether the commonplace calls for reform (e.g., regulating and controlling corporations) are a self-indulgent fantasy and illusion, and largely meaningless. This is not the call, more familiar in Marxist literature (e.g., Collins, 1982; Lynch and Groves, 1989), to ignore reform in favor of revolution; if anything, the postmodernist skepticism applies even more fully to calls for revolutionary transformation (e.g., Fish, 1989). We can only engage in personal, local efforts of "resistance." Postmodernism also challenges faith in "expertise" and rational organizations, and calls for a shift of focus to the ordinary, "local," daily experience of violence rather than its broad and large-scale dimensions. Postmodernism challenges tendencies to produce categories, and at least implicitly rejects conflating very different forms or dimensions of violence in order to advance broad propositions.

Thus postmodernism does not provide any practical guidance on policy (Dews, 1987; Matthews and Young, 1992). At most it offers a basis for exposing possible pretenses and illusions in the pursuit of a just policy. This theorizing can be defended as deeply political in that it destroys hegemonic discourses and creates a space to construct a new politics (Michalowski, 1993). Further, at least one major strand of postmodernist thought seems to promote the empowerment of victims, enabling them to engage more fully in a process of reconstituting the meaning of violence. Yet at the same time, others seem to echo the romantic early days of radical criminology in regarding terrorism, violence, and insurrection as laudatory efforts to deny legitimacy to the state (Rosenau, 1992). The victims of terrorism, one presumes, are not the ones who are empowered here. Overall, an approach that argues against direct action in favor of semantic groundwork opens itself, at the least, to criticism as idealistic and as utterly insensitive to the direct, concrete experience and needs of victims and survivors. According to Matthews and Young (1992:13) it ultimately becomes "a conservative stance, which is unable to offer any directions for social change."

Still, Baudrillard is correct in many ways about the effect of media imagery. Indeed, for close to thirty years it has been a standard and central theme of criminology that the public's attitude toward crime is shaped by the media. Baudrillard, however, has failed to analyze the idea that the media are a battleground which need not be won automatically by the forces of corporate capitalism. Perhaps the most potent critique of Baudrillard is that his theory depends on a stronger break with modernity than in fact has occurred; he "confuses *tendencies* of contemporary society with a *finalized state* of affairs" (Best, 1989:48).

There are important implications to the argument that society today might be described more accurately as being in a state of modernity while showing signs or tendencies in the direction that Baudrillard describes. This means that although it is possible to create a hyperreality to which most people react, it is also possible (although very difficult) to create a counter-hyperreality. Loseke (1992), for example, describes in detail the process by which women in the battered women's movement have created the image of the "battered woman." This image actually may fit the lived realities of few of the women who show up at the doors of shelter houses, but it dovetails into other U.S. ideologies that we use to choose which victims should be denied or awarded aid. In other words, just as we have constructed the concept of "battered woman" as a wife and mother severely abused, morally pure, and not complicit in her plight, grassroots claims makers rooted firmly in the project of modernity are able to create other definitions and realities. Postmodernists have claimed that this can be done only outside modernity.

Beyond the fact that we are not living in the seamless and completed postmodern society described by Baudrillard, in many ways the current condition of postmodernism *depends* on modernity for its vitality; the attack on modernity is the primary project of postmodernist theory. At the same time, the essential justification of modernity—the opposition to the forces of feudalism—is long dead. Thus Ferraris (1992:25) argues that modernity similarly needs postmodernism: "What could Habermas write without Derrida?"

Postmodernism serves to remind modernity of the reason for modernity's existence. It is not to serve progress in the sense of carrying the technical hyperreality of the postmodern world ever faster and ever closer. It is not to extend domination. The reminder delivered by postmodernism is that "progress" and domination are exactly the ends now being served by modern solutions. The key point of modernity is that it believes in human agency and reason: that we can, through our will and our hard work, change society for the better. Postmodernism has reminded modernity that too often it has failed in this task (Freire and Giroux, 1989); even if it has not failed, "the truth is that a [modernist criminology] has never been fully implemented" (Matthews and Young, 1992).

The various criticisms of postmodernist thought, especially as applied to criminological concerns, inevitably raise the question, "Why bother with it at all?" We have been persuaded that exposure to this literature is worthwhile and stimulating. First, it sensitizes us to certain ephemeral, fragmentary, and chaotic emergent tendencies in contemporary society, although we need not accept the claim that contemporary society as a whole is more postmodern than modern. Second, it exposes some of the pretenses of both mainstream and critical forms of criminological analysis, although we need not embrace deconstructive analysis in its totality. Finally, it provides us with some striking concepts (e.g., hyperreality), metaphors, and analytical tools (e.g., semiotics), which at least potentially enable us to achieve a richer understanding of contemporary social and criminological phenomena, although we need not adopt these concepts, metaphors, and analytical tools uncritically.

The task for criminology is to renew a sense of urgency that we can change the direction of the world, and to energize people into working toward that goal. It is impossible in a short article to specify all the directions in which we would move to accomplish this goal, but we must read Baudrillard as the parable Charles Dickens found in the Ghost of Christmas Future. If we ignore the postmodernists' warning, our future may be the seamless technological hyperreality that Baudrillard describes.

25

Constitutive Criminology: The Maturation of Critical Theory

Stuart Henry and Dragan Milovanovic

Critical criminology has recently seen the delineation of several new and competing perspectives (Schwartz, 1989; Thomas and O'Maochatha, 1989; MacLean and Milovanovic, 1997). These include left realist criminology, socialist-feminist criminology, peacemaking criminology, and poststructuralist/postmodernist criminology. Each is witnessing internal critique, while variously engaging the others. Here we draw on social constructionism, left realism, socialist-feminism, and poststructuralism, social and critical legal theory, constitutive theory, and discourse analysis. Our aim is to examine reflexively the paradigmatic umbrella under which these saplings of critical growth can gain strength. We term this umbrella *constitutive criminology* (Henry, 1989a). We address core themes toward the establishment of the necessary and logically ordered elements of a constitutive criminology: (1) the codetermination of crime and human subjects through crime control ideology and how this can reproduce and transform; (2) discursive practices as the medium for the structuring of crime and its control institutions; (3) symbolic violence as the hidden ideological dimension of legal domination; and (4) the use, by control agencies, of sense data to construct meaning which both claims space and displaces the intersubjective construction of meaning and through this, sustains control institutions as relatively autonomous structures.

The Codetermination of Crime as Ideology

A core theme of constitutive criminology is its rejection of reductionism. Advocates decline the seduction that either human agents, through choice

Edited and abridged from *Criminology*, Volume 29(2):293–315 (1991).

or predisposition, or structural arrangements at both the institutional and societal levels, have priority in shaping crime, victims, and control. Rather, following Giddens, they see social structure and its constituent control institutions as the emerging outcome of human interaction that both constrains and enables criminal action, and recognize that these structures are thereby simultaneously shaped by the crime and crime control talk that is part of their reproduction. Constitutive criminology is not an exercise in polemics, in which human agency is separated from the structures that it makes (Coombe, 1989:70).

The Making of Human Subjects: Transpraxis

Constitutive criminology is concerned with identifying the ways in which the interrelationships between human agents (subjects) constitute crime, victims, and control as realities. Simultaneously, it is concerned with how these emergent realities themselves constitute human agents. It follows from this that the current notion of *praxis* needs to be replaced. If praxis is taken to be purposive social activity born of human agents' consciousness of their world, mediated through the social groups to which they belong, then this must be supplanted by the richer notion of *transpraxis*. Transpraxis assumes that critical opposition must be aware of the reconstitutive effects—the reproductions of relations of production—in the very attempts to neutralize or challenge them. In the process of negation (opposition), relations of production are often reconstituted along with the human subjects that are their supports. But often neglected is that with affirmation (support), relations of production are also *deconstructed*, along with those same human subjects. Thus, the very dynamic of praxis reveals the tenuous nature of the ideological structure on which it is based. Critical theorists have been particularly myopic as to the potential for change afforded by this insight.

Labeling theory tried to cover some of this ground, particularly in its notions of role engulfment and deviancy amplification. But labeling separated meaning from the agents generating it. It posited a dualism between agency and structure rather than a duality (Giddens, 1984). Ignored was any sense of an interconnected whole. Although early symbolic interactionism elaborated the ways that the human actor became that which the audience constructed, it said little about the way audiences—their imageries, symbolic repertoire, and *verstehen*—are constructed, constituted, and undermined by historically situated human agents in the context of a historically specific political economy. The construction process tacitly acknowledged and uncritically accepted that the power relationship flowed one way, monolithically and asymmetrically. While those who were officially designated deviant actively participated in their own identity transformation, little construction was done of the control agents, by themselves. Actors designated as deviant or criminal, ultimately became passive acceptors of audiences' degradation and fulfillers of their prophecies. Audiences made victims. But little was said of the making of audiences during their attempt to construct labels for others; absent was the dialectic of control. Coombe (1989:117) notes that one of the most promising areas of research suggested by such an approach is "consideration of the ways in which legal discourse and practice actively participate in the making of human subjects and thus reproduce social relations of power." The danger here, however, is to reify human subjects by giving priority to their discourse, as though this somehow operated independently of those using it. Even more problematic is losing sight of the potential for transformation inherent in the reproduction process, since it is in the remaking of subjects through the ideology of control that they are revealed as vulnerable to unmaking.

Constitutive criminology, then, recognizes human agents' power to undermine the structures that confront them and asserts that agents both use and are used in the generation of knowledge and truth about what they do. Agents' ability to undermine and invert structures of control, to episodically render them edifices of subordination, is one of the major missing dimensions of conventional and critical criminology.

Occasional glimpses of the dual nature of this process are exposed in examples of prisoners' power over prison guards through trade in contraband, of police committing or facilitating the commission of property crime, and of the police provocation of the very riots they are supposed to prevent (see Jefferson, 1990). The notion of "confinement by consent" found in accounts of the inmate turned jailhouse lawyer, who inadvertently maintains legitimation and conventional understandings of capitalist legality (Milovanovic, 1988a; Milovanovic and Thomas, 1989), is as constitutive of the hegemony of overarching capitalist relations as is the workplace trade unionist defending employee disciplinary cases in settings of private justice (Henry, 1983). Both are also undermining of that which had previously been constructed. Or consider how some inmates in their "secondary adjustments" internalized and verbalized psychiatric jargon as a way of leveling hierarchical power relations (Goffman, 1961); while negating, they also affirmed, implicitly or explicitly, the very hierarchical structures that they attempted to neutralize. Similarly, we see the activist lawyer attempting to politicize a trial as making use of the constraining categories and legal discourse which are the very supports of the ideology of the rule of law (Bannister and Milovanovic, 1990). Indeed, Marx (1852:115) recognized this duality facing practitioners of radical change. For Marx the crucial issue for revolutionary change was whether the concepts of the past could be used selectively to enable the liberation of the future. Until the spirit of revolutionary change could be captured and used without reference to the past, automatically and spontaneously, it was but a bourgeois revolution, short-lived, soon reaching its climax. A vivid illustration of this process is found in accounts of the way oppositional collectives, cooperatives, and communes, whose commitment is to an alternative socialist order, typically resort to capitalist control forms and state law in their ironic attempts to defend their own internal order, thereby reproducing the very structures that undermine and overwhelm them (Henry, 1985, 1988b, 1989b). Similarly, in the polemic between Nietzsche and Hegel would-be reformers often react and negate rather than act and affirm positive values (Milovanovic, 1992b). Transpraxis, an oppositional agenda, actively negates and produces affirmatively, new values. Socialism, for example, as envisioned by Marx, is a transitional phase to the "higher forms." Here there still exists a predominant reactive and negative orientation and this still reconstitutes the very *forms* of domination found in capitalism, be it now by the victorious proletariat. The state apparatus becomes but an instrument of the victorious proletariat to be used to repress the former repressors, and thus the cycle react-negate-reconstitute is perpetuated.

Two Sides of Transpraxis

These contradictions are not temporary aberrations of the structure of control but fundamental pillars of its constitution. In Bourdieu's (1977) terms they are instances of the way that the discourse of control in society is in harmony, even when in apparent opposition. This dialectic of control must be addressed. That criminologists and practitioners ignore it is part of the constitutive silence that sustains crime and control as objectlike entities. A transpraxis must envision oppositional practices themselves as inadvertently reaffirming instruments of hierarchy and control.

Transpraxis should not, however, ignore the reverse side of this dialectic of control. The affirmative reproduction of social control by human purposeful action also undermines that which is being constituted. For example, it has been shown that when state agencies seek to control economic relations that fall outside national tax accounting, they label such activity with derogatory terminology and attribute to it motives carrying negative connotations (Henry, 1988a). Terms such as "black," "hidden," "underground," "shadow," "secret," "subterranean," and "submerged" are used to describe this kind of economic activity in order to suggest that the economic relations of those working "off the books" are perpetuated by nefarious creatures of the night, who are interested unilaterally in pecuniary rewards incommensurate with effort, who are dishonest, and cannot be trusted. While such attempts at control may initially dissuade some from participation, they also show many of those who participate, and others who subsequently do so, that these accounts are inaccurate descriptions of the meaning of their relations. Those whose actual experience of irregular work is enjoyable, communal, and socially nutritious, stand in contrast to the cut-throat black market dealing that control-labeling suggests.

Another well-documented example of the same process occurs in drug education with the discredit that can be brought on the "moral, clean living" messages found in the shock talk of health educators. When directed at young people whose actual experimentation and peer knowledge reveals that drug use produces neither instant addiction, necessary escalation, nor death, the effects can be counterproductive.

Thus the more state agencies elaborate their control talk, and the more people experience the different reality of relations subject to control, the more contempt accrues to the controllers and their control institutions. As a result, people begin to question other distinctions, such as those between theft and the legitimate acquisition of property, between honesty and dishonesty, between street crime and white-collar crime, and between hard and soft drugs. Such questioning, stemming from the attempts of control institutions to control, actually undermines that which the controls were designed to protect: the existing relations of production and the moral and social order.

We now turn to three additional foci (discursive practices, symbolic violence, and sense data and meaning construction) that are integral to the process of codetermination, as seen by constitutive criminology.

Discursive Practices as the Medium of Codetermination

A central issue in constitutive criminology is the role of human agents' discursive practices. The use of particular ways of talking, as in "control talk" (Cohen, 1985), "organizational talk" (Manning, 1988), or "law talk" (Milovanovic, 1986; 1988a; 1992b; Milovanovic and Thomas, 1989; Thomas, 1988) both reflects and constitutes narratives that provide the continuity to reproduce social structures of crime and its control, in time and space. As Knorr-Cetina and Cicourel (1981) have argued, human agents transform events that they see or experience as microevents into summary representations, or mind patterns, by relying on routine practices through which they convince themselves of having achieved the appropriate representation of those events; these are then objectified in coherent narrative constructions (see also Cressey, 1953; and Schwendinger and Schwendinger's, 1985:128–60). The well-documented media synthesis of harmful incidents into crime waves, allies with the "synoptic process," whereby disparate patterns of regulation are synthesized into formalized law (Fitzpatrick, 1988). But no clearer example exists than the very categorization of the diversity of human conflicts and transgressions into "crime," or the multitude of variously motivated acts of personal injury into "violent crime" or types of violent crime, such as when various disputes between family members are described under the unifying term "domestic violence" or "spouse abuse."

In the constitutive criminological vision, social structures are the categories used to classify the events that they allegedly represent. As such they are strengthened by routine construction in everyday life and by activity organized in relation to them, as though they were concrete entities. The principal means through which social structures are constituted is language use and the discursive practice of making conceptual distinctions through the play of differences (Derrida, 1973; 1981; Lacan, 1977).

At the organizational level of analysis, the complexity of the human condition is given a static, decontextualized meaning to enable controllers to better negotiate routine cases (Cicourel, 1968; Manning, 1988; Sudnow, 1965; Thomas, 1988). Discourse, indeed, is the "disciplinary mechanism" by which "docile bodies" are created and "bodies of utility" stabilized (Foucault, 1977).

At the societal level of analysis, capital logic and the integrally related processes of rationalization are constitutive of categories that capture essential relations, albeit oftentimes in fetishistic forms. Not the least are rhetorical structures, figurative expressions, and verbal mannerisms that are used as primary signifiers of meaning. Consider, for example, those signifiers used to give material form to capital logic (e.g., commodities, market forces, producers and consumers, the juridic subject), to technological imageries (e.g., "she's a dynamo," "coiled for action"), and to the phallocentric order itself in which male signifiers occupy a privileged position (e.g., the power "to penetrate," as opposed to the weakness of "seduction"). Hence, at the levels of intersubjective communication, organizational processing, and capital logic, discursive practices are given anchorings, a "pinning down" (Lacan, 1977; Manning, 1988; Milovanovic, 1992b). Thus, discursive practices produce texts (narrative constructions), imaginary constructions, that anchor signifiers to particular signifieds, producing a particular image claiming to be the reality. These texts become the semiotic coordinates of action, which agents recursively use, thereby providing a reconstruction of the original form.

Once social structures are constituted as summary representations, their ongoing existence depends upon their continued and often unwitting reconstruction in everyday discourse, a discourse replete with tacit understandings whose basis lies outside the realm of intrinsic intersubjective communication and intersubjectively established meaning. Core meaning constructs are typically preconstructed elsewhere as part of our common "stock of knowledge" (Schutz, 1967; Manning, 1988). Agents in organizational settings tend to reduce feedback which represents contaminating and disruptive "noise." The fluidity of organizational processing in criminal justice contexts is seen to demand a high degree of rationality and formalism, which is both the product and the effect of crime control practices. In part this is due to the increasing complexity in the social formation demanding more abstract categorization that encompasses more and more variants—a "surplus of possibilities" (Luhmann, 1985)—but producing, in the process, symbolizations that are steps removed from the "real" (i.e., concrete reality). For example, process justice is held to require equality of treatment which is claimed to be enabled by general rules of procedure that reduce people to like individuals, decontextualized of their different cosmologies of meaning, and substituted by a universal individual intent tied to units of material reward. In order to sustain abstractly constructed distinctions, these representations are made applicable to events, in spite of the contradictory evidence that comes from renewed microinteraction. Contradictory evidence and potential disruptions are engendered by the internal transfer of messages, a basis of instability that is best negotiated by framing it in already understood narrative constructs (Goffman, 1974; 1981; Manning, 1988; Thomas, 1988).

It is often not enough, however, to repeat distinctions in order that such representations be sustained as apparent realities. Part of the reality-constituting process involves the routine investment of faith and interest in distinctions; fighting over them, manipulating them, and above all defending them (Knorr-Cetina and Cicourel, 1981). These morality plays often take place in symbolic form in publicized trials, political and business scandals, "moral panics," and other boundary-policing structures. In more subtle forms, they take place by the use of prevailing discursive practices, even in the use of the oppositional form. As Foucault (1977) reminded us, oppositional discourse is as constitutive of existing reality as is supportive discourse, since each addresses and thereby reproduces the prevailing distinctions while disputing their content rather than deconstructing them or discrediting them through the construction of a new, replacement discourse. For example, Selva and Bohm (1987) have emphasized that an oppositional legal discourse which utilizes the existing structure of legal discourse may prove more productive and liberating than a replacement discourse. But this downplays the significance of the constitutive effects of "liberating" practices in law. A graphic example of this process is the oppositional reaction to school by adolescent working-class kids. While they "resist" and reject the system that rejects them, it is this very reaction that subsequently consigns them to the bottom of the hierarchy they despise (Willis, 1977).

Organizing action to defend representations—framed and objectified in narrative texts—is one of the principal means of both defending and conferring object-like reality on them, providing life, form, energy, sustenance, and a high degree of permanence. The institutions of capitalist legality (involving formal police, courts, and prisons) represent the visible manifestation of human agents organized to defend the overarching social form of capitalist society from internal deconstruction. Capital logic is a ubiquitous rationalizing form; the greater the investment that is made in it, the more difficult it is to sustain that which it is not. This is not to imply conspiracy but to specify formal function, for while defending the wider totality, agents and agencies also compete to defend their own integrity within the framework of capital logic (Jessop, 1982). Compare, for example, the mobilization of opposition to racism and sexism that manifested itself, within the legal frame, in the form of "affirmative action" programs, formal equality doctrines, and "comparable worth" legislation. The latter two essentially maintain capital logic—subjects are still measured by some external standard of equality, and are still compared to an abstract criterion that is constitutive of capitalistic social relations. Consider, also, Daly and Chesney-Lind's (1988) insightful analysis advocating a socialist-feminist perspective and critiquing "first-wave feminism," which often advertently or inadvertently (1) situated itself in legal discourse with its reliance on notions of formal "justice" and "equality," and hence celebrated the fetishistic notion of the juridic subject, (2) used male standards as the criteria of correctness and an ideal end, (3) laid the groundwork for greater and more pervasive forms of state and informal control in women's lives, and (4) grasped too quickly the get-tough approach, rejuvenating deterrence and retributivist theory.

Alternatively, human agents can be envisioned as unique with a multiplicity of needs, drives, desires, and abilities, and as intersubjectively constituted. Any subsuming of these qualities to some "equal" measure must be read as an imposition, a reification by submission to macroconstituted forms of capital logic, an idealization of relations constitutive of the capitalist mode of production. Affirmative action, indeed, is the more radical program insofar as the use of substantive rational criteria militates against universalism, and points to a recognition of built-in biases of the sociopolitical and legal order. The imagery of affirmative action is system destabilizing, and it is now evident that the sociopolitical order is coming around to recognizing this (e.g., the mobilization of the ideology of "reverse discrimination"). Socialist-feminism, however, is on the cutting edge in redirecting our analysis of hierarchical and exploitative relations often objectified in seemingly value-neutral criteria and standards.

From the perspective of constitutive criminology, then, control institutions are the relations among human agents acting to police the conceptual distinctions among discursively constructed social structures. These relations are mediated by the availability, through intersubjective relations, of a sedimented, differentiated symbolic system, a repository of value-laden signs that are politically anchored. Once constituted, these relations, expressed in symbolic form, themselves become structures, and, as agencies and institutions, appear to have relative autonomy. In turn, they too are policed by further "private" or internal relations of control. Thus, signifying chains, narrative constructions, objectified bits and pieces of everyday activity float within specific discourses within which distinctive, discursive subject-positions exist, that structure what can be framed, thought, and said. Tacit understanding is rooted in these subterranean semiotic systems that continuously receive support through their use (Manning, 1988).

Symbolic Violence as Ideological Domination

According to Bourdieu (1977:192), "symbolic violence" is a form of domination which is exerted through the very medium in which it is disguised. It is the "gentle, invisible form of violence, which is never recognized as such, and is not so much undergone as chosen, the violence of credit, confidence, obligation, personal loyalty, hospitality, gifts, gratitude, piety. . . ." But criminologists have forgotten this dimension of domination. The silence of the present and the celebration of that aspect that is likened to law, constitute the forms of control that appear as reality. Suppressed by silence, this pervasive domination is itself frozen in the past as "custom" (the informal law of nonindustrial societies), "prelaw," the "law" of multiplex relations (Black, 1976, 1989), as if multiplex relations can exist without simplex relations or simplex without multiplex! But, insofar as we accept that these relations exist independently, we are actively, though unreflexively, creating and maintaining the illusion that is the reality of law. The omission of informal nonstate social control from consideration as part of criminal justice is how criminal justice is constituted. Buying into dominant definitions of what counts as law, crime, policing, and justice by excluding rules, deviance, informal social control, and private justice, is part of the way these concepts, as entities, are made and remade as realities. Take as an example again, a constitutive view of law (Fitzpatrick, 1984; Harrington and Merry, 1988;

Hunt, 1987; Klare, 1979). Rather than treating law as an autonomous field of inquiry linked only by external relations to the rest of society, or investigating the way "law" and "society" as concrete entities "influence" or "affect" each other, as is done in nonconstitutive approaches, constitutive criminology takes law as its subject of inquiry. But as Hunt (1987) and Harrington and Yngvesson (1990) have argued, constitutive theory pursues the study of law by exploring the interrelations "between legal relations and other social relations":

> To speak of the constitutive dimension of ideology is to examine legal ideology as a form of power that also creates a particular kind of world, specifically, a liberal-legal world constituted as separate spheres of "law" and "community," with practice" or "process" located uneasily between the two. In such a world actors impose ideologies or persuade others to take them on as "voluntary." (Harrington and Yngvesson, 1990:143)

From the constitutive perspective, the "juridic subject" (i.e., the reasonable man/woman in law), for example, can only be understood in its inherent dualistic relation of being both a constitutive element and a recursive outcome of capital logic. As Henry (1983) argues, with such an approach one begins to see the possibility of transcending the view that law is either a product of structure or the outcome of interaction. One begins to see how informal social control is not so much an alternative form of law but a necessary part of the ideological process whereby the crystallized, formalized, objectlike qualities of law are created and sustained in an ongoing manner, albeit within a different arena. Thus, constitutive criminology directs attention to the way law, crime, and criminal justice are conceptualized and implied as objective realities having real consequences, consequences attributed to their claim.

Seen in this way, institutions of law are the organized acting out of discursively produced "control thoughts," whose very action reflects on the reality of that which they are organized to defend. There are parallels with John Brigham's (1987) research on social movements in which the social movement was found to be integral with the law that it used, such that "[l]egal forms are evident in the language, purposes, and strategies of movement activity as practice" (1987:306). As such, legal forms and their control institutions are rooted in control discourse and in their own parent social structures and cannot be divorced from them, but nor can the structures exist without their control forms since each implies the other.

No better example of symbolic violence exists than in the new "fighting crime" rhetoric. In a microcosmic form, policing in the 1980s has produced the new "maximum-security society" (Marx, 1988; Weiss, 1987).

Here, we see an increasing emphasis by control agents on developing dossiers in computerized form; an increasing use of predictive and actuarial instruments that focus on producing statements about persons in particular created categories (see Feeley and Simon, 1992); and an obsession with finding the "predisposed" criminal. This rhetoric has led to an extreme manipulation of the environment, with the continued acceptance by the courts, to induce the very criminality which is of the controller's own creation. It is concluded that the resultant new transparent society has seen the erosion of traditional notions of privacy such that even the citizenry has been recruited to monitor others as well as themselves for deviance or deviant tendencies (Marx, 1988:219).

At the same time, however, the constitutive nature of the dialectic of control is as apparent in its oppositional form. When Gary Marx and others oppose the affront of privacy, they actually take part in perpetuating the elaboration of privatized relations of production, since they unwittingly defend this bastion of capitalist society while discrediting and displacing notions of commonality. Indeed, it is ironic that in seeking to defend people against the invasion of their lives by control agents, critical criminologists have acceded to supporting the ideological protection of privacy while being silent about the theft of that which was traditionally held in common. Protecting privacy is nothing less than ideological legitimation for the theft of the common from the community (Einstadter, 1989; 1992).

Sense Data and Meaning Construction

All this leads to a recognition of the high premium on collecting, filtering, categorizing, and disseminating increasingly complex information framed in coherent narrative constructions (Jackson, 1988; Manning, 1988; Thomas, 1988). The process of constructing meaning intersubjectively is increasingly being both abdicated and usurped by agents of organizations who use these constructions as the criteria by which to further survey, control, and act on subjects, particularly those predicted to be in high-risk categories in the existing social arrangements. Simultaneously, these constructions are inadvertently given ideological support through oppositional attacks on the autonomation of social control instruments. Oppositional attacks by some critical theorists and reformers take as given many of the concepts, presuppositions, or working hypotheses of these same agents of control, thereby in the end reproducing the self-perpetuating machine. We are reminded of how escape from reproduction is constrained, even in the most radical perspectives, by the actions of others who read criticism as simply more of the same. Thus, for example, booksellers categorize works like Cohen's *Against Criminology* (1988), in the section of their bookstore dealing with criminology, and publishers reject proposals that they are unable to fit into the needs of a preexisting market. Indeed, there is some danger that the "left realist" criminological perspective has this tendency to reproduction, as has been recognized in the private soul-searching of various of its advocates. The challenge for a transpraxis here is substantial. How does one build an alternative "framing" of narrative texts to the exclusion of system-sustaining elements (e.g., imageries, signifier-signified anchorings, and so on)?

Institutions of social control are framed within the mediating effects of symbolic systems. Symbolic systems are constituted by sign systems which make use of the dyad signifiers—acoustic images, psychic imprints, or simply expressions—and the signified—the concept referred to, the content. Organizational agents, including control agents, must produce stable meaning in the very process of controlling deviance. Hence, human agents' semiotic work stabilizes the endless drift of signifieds under those signifiers, giving a particular meaning that is formal, rational, and logical, and producing a stable and static semiotic grid which henceforth anchors the multiplicity of forces in movement (Milovanovic, 1992b). Meaning construction based on "purposive rational action," as opposed to shared intersubjectively constituted meaning (Habermas, 1984, 1987), increasingly underlies the constitutive process within the semiotic grid-producing narrative coherence. This becomes the narrative structure (text) that conveys images of deviant behavior and simultaneously produces agents that are its supports. Those who, in their nonreflexive practices, oppose images of deviance, more often than not inadvertently affirm the reality of their existence. Organizational imperatives, which reflect human agents' deference to concepts of rationalization and capital logic, rely on the signifying practices of those agents. The agents in turn rely on a tacit understanding in constructing meaning (Manning, 1988).

The outcome of this constitutive work is the organizational supports, deviant cases, correctors, and rebels who unwittingly purify these structural distinctions in their critical attack on its assumed operating principles. Oppositional narratives (texts), for example, are most often replete with the very core imageries, metaphors, and signifiers that are the supports of a hierarchical and dominating apparatus. By activating system-supportive imageries and then attempting to react and negate them does not in itself produce alternative imageries of what could be. The "at best"—react and negate—turns often to be "at worst," for canceling a negation by a negation in the Hegelian sense does not produce transcendence. At best it produces, instead, destruction at one level, but a reconfirmation of system-generated elements at another.

Social control agents both produce and sustain deviant categories, and they tacitly frame coherent narratives of "what happened," hence objectifying primordial sense data. These objectifications increasingly become the anchoring points for everyday constructions by those in the social formation who sustain the organizationally framed narrative. Routine investment by them time and energy makes this constitutive process recursive and self-referential, cyclically generating a more refined and purified version of the substance of their actions, as object.

To refer to control institutions as relatively autonomous, then, is not to say that they are separate from the wider social structure, since they are part of its constitution. It is to say, rather, that recursivity reinforces conventional notions, giving permanence and stability to them. Nor do control institutions support the wider structure simply because that is their assigned social function. Such a vision is rabidly reifying because it ignores the integral role of human agency in this process. Rather, as Fitzpatrick (1984) has argued, control institutions support the relations of reproduction within the totality of society because they *are* some of those relations of reproduction. As we have argued elsewhere (Henry, 1985, 1987; Milovanovic, 1992b), these constitutive relations do not exist independently of human agents who repeatedly bring them into being.

Likewise, the "internal" relations that monitor control institutions *are* some of the relations of the control institutions that they police. A police agency would not be what it was without the relations that police it, informal or otherwise, and those relations would not be what they are without the action of human agents. As a result, any examination of control institutions that ignores the internal relations that police them, or that ignores human agents' recursive action, produces a partial account that itself becomes part of the constitutive discourse that sustains their reproduction. Concomitantly, any challenging practices used by agents not sensitive to the reconstitutive effects of their very practices, further reproduce, elaborate, and stabilize the existent structural arrangements. Thus, although relations of control are most visible in their institutional form, this should not lead us to neglect their pervasive presence in informal and alternative modes of control, or even in Foucault's (1977) sense of a dispersed disciplinary technology pervasive throughout our society. Nor should it lead one to gloss over the human agent's renditions and intersubjective creative work that daily makes these relations into organizations and structures. So what is to be done? As implied in our preceding argument, there are a number of ways that a constitutive approach to criminology can be transformative. In the concluding section we suggest one direction that this might take, but a more elaborate treatment must await further analysis (see Henry and Milovanovic, 1996).

Conclusion

In short, then, constitutive criminology in the tradition of dialectical theory is the framework for us to reconnect crime and its control to the society from which it is conceptually and institutionally constructed by human agents. Through it criminologists are able to recognize, as a fundamental assumption, that crime is both *in* and *of* society. Our position calls for abandoning the futile search for causes of crime since this simply elaborates the distinctions that maintain crime as a separate reality while failing to address how it is that crime is constituted as a part of society. We are concerned, instead, with the ways in which we actively coproduce that which they take to be crime. As a signifier, this perspective directs attention to the way that crime is constituted as an expansive and permeating mode of discourse, a continuously growing script—a text, narrative—whose writers are human agents, obsessed with that which we produce, amazed that *it* is produced, denying that *it* is created by us, claiming that *it* grows independently before us, but yet worshiping the very alienating, hierarchical creations that are our own. A direct consequence of such an approach is that any "rehabilitation" from crime requires that criminologists and practitioners deconstruct crime as a separate entity, cease recording it, stop dramatizing it, withdraw energy from it, deny its status as an independent entity. Through this vision we are suggesting that criminologists write a new script, a replacement discourse that connects us and our product back to the whole of which we are a part (see Henry, 1994; Henry and Milovanovic, 1994, 1996). "Control talk" (Cohen, 1985), "organizational talk" (Manning, 1988), "law talk" (Milovanovic, 1986; 1992b; Thomas, 1988) and "actuarial talk" or the language of probability and risk (see Feeley and Simon, 1992), must be replaced by a reflexive discourse which allows for change, chance, being, becoming, multiplicity, irony, and must reflect a sensitivity to the nuances of being human. Criminologists must explore "alternative logics" in criminology, as Nelken (1994) calls them. We must cease to invest in the myth that human agents are either individuals with free choices driven by a utilitarian calculus, or are biologically and psychologically programmed. Instead our knowledge shows that human agents are inextricably social beings. It is the total social script of human history that is the medium of birth for our differences and it is these differences that continuously but cumulatively shape humanity's total script.

Control concepts, such as the juridic subject and hierarchically organized dualisms—rational/irrational, subject/object, actor/action, center/periphery, agent/structure—which privilege the former term over the latter, and other logocentric, reconstitutive discursive practices, must give way to an "affirmative action" of discursive practices that privileges the interconnectedness, the interrelatedness, of phenomena in the social formation rather than any privileged hierarchical division. One of the few criminological scholars to recognize the importance of developing an agenda of replacement discourse is Gregg Barak (1988, 1993, 1994) with his "newsmaking criminology." He says (Barak, 1991:5) that "in the post-modern era, social problems such as homelessness, sexual assault, or drug abuse are politically constructed, ideologically articulated, and media produced events." He advocates that criminologists become credible spokespeople and that they make criminological news and participate in the popular construction of images of crime and crime control, that is, produce crime themes, "as a means of bringing about social change and social justice" (Barak, 1988:585; see also, Barak and Bohm, 1989; Barak, 1994, 1996).

Constitutive criminology, then, is a step toward the deconstruction of crime, a peacemaking movement (Pepinsky and Quinney, 1991) toward an alternative vision of what is and what might be. Transpraxis must be the guide for those challenging hierarchical structures of domination. Anything less advertently or inadvertently contributes to hegemonic practices that sustain human agents' subordination to that which we construct.

Accepting this does not mean that we are blind to the human suffering that is the reality of crime for those who are its victims (see Schwartz and Friedrichs, 1994). Indeed, their suffering is not aided by the public celebration of their pain, nor by the glorification, sensationalization, and vilification of their offenders. Constitutive criminology is also peaceful criminology. It recognizes the harm and suffering and seeks to examine how criminology might reduce it by transforming the totality of which it is a part. It does not imagine that some structural transformation will eventually rescue society from the harm of murder, rape, and corporate fraud. Rather, it seeks to affirm those aspects of our intersubjective experience that are capable, if invoked by us, of displacing the excess crime that comes from our giving in to those investing energy into its continuity. Of course it is true, as Durkheim observed, that even in a society of saints there will be sinners, but the task of constitutive criminology is to suck life from their discursive enterprise.

26

The New Penology: Notes on the Emerging Strategy of Corrections and Its Implications

Malcolm M. Feeley and Jonathan Simon

It is often observed that penal ideology and practice became more conservative during the 1970s and 1980s. This shift is only part of a deeper change in conception—discourse, objectives, and techniques—in the penal process. These shifts have multiple and independent origins and are not reducible to any one reigning idea (e.g., getting tough on criminals). Despite their different origins, the elements of this emerging new conception have coalesced to form a new strategic formation in the penal field, which we call the *new penology*. By *strategy* we do not mean a conscious and coherent agenda employed by a determinate set of penal agents. Rather, the loose set of interconnected developments that we call the new penology increasingly shapes the way the power to punish is exercised. Foucault's (1978:94) notion that power is both "intentional and nonsubjective" suggests we not deny that people have deliberate strategies but that the overall configuration created by multiple strategies is itself "strategic" without being deliberate (Foucault, 1982:225).

The transformations we call the new penology involve shifts in three distinct areas:

1. The emergence of new discourses: In particular, the language of probability and risk increasingly replaces earlier discourses of clinical diagnosis and retributive judgment. There has been a shift from focusing on the individual, beyond even managing behavior (Cohen, 1985; Wilkins, 1973) to managing segments of the "population."

2. The formation of new objectives for the system are in some sense newly "systemic," such as the efficient control of internal

Edited and abridged from *Criminology*, Volume 30(4):449–74 (1992).

system processes in place of the traditional objectives of rehabilitation and crime control. The sense that any external social referent is intended is becoming attenuated.

3.   The deployment of new techniques targeting offenders as an aggregate in place of traditional techniques for individualizing or creating equity.

The new penology has served a significant function in locking together some of the external factors impinging on the criminal justice system and in determining the prevailing responses of the system. Nothing seems as defining as the massive increase in the level of incarceration since the 1970s. Conventional understanding links rise to demographic changes, social changes (like increased drug use), improvement in the efficiency of law enforcement, and increases in the punitiveness of sentencing systems. More can be accomplished with models that allow for the contingent interaction of all these factors (Zimring and Hawkins, 1991:157). A shortfall of this approach, however, is that it holds constant the nature of the penal enterprise while varying external pressures and internal policy shifts. Our analysis of the new penology emphasizes more holistic features of the current penal formation.

The new penology is found among criminal justice practitioners and the research community as a communicative process, a system of discourse having "a life of its own." However, it has certainly not (yet) emerged as a hegemonic strategy for crime and crime policy. For instance, it contrasts in many respects with the "tough on crime" rhetoric in the political arena. Political themes get translated into the administrative practice of agencies like corrections and police. The problem (for the administrator at least) is whether they translate into anything that can provide a viable handle on the agency's tasks. Even the seemingly coherent command of legislatures and governors to "lock 'em up" leaves much unsaid about how to do it with existing resource allocations. The new penology has helped fill that gap even as it competes with crime control and other options as a master narrative for the system.

Unlike the "old" penology which concentrates on individuals as the unit of analysis, the new penology is markedly less concerned with responsibility, fault, moral sensibility, diagnosis, or intervention and treatment of the individual offender. Rather, it is concerned with techniques to identify, classify, and manage groupings sorted by dangerousness. The task is managerial, not transformative (Cohen, 1985; Garland and Young, 1983; Messinger, 1969; Messinger and Berecochea, 1990; Reichman, 1986; Wilkins, 1973). It seeks to *regulate* levels of deviance, not intervene or respond to individual deviants or social malformations.

Although the new penology is much more than "discourse," its language helps reveal this shift most strikingly. It does not speak of impaired individuals in need of treatment or of morally irresponsible persons who need to be held accountable for their actions. Rather, it considers the criminal justice *system*, and it pursues systemic rationality and efficiency. It seeks to sort and classify, to separate the less from the more dangerous, and to deploy control strategies rationally. The tools for this enterprise include "indicators," prediction tables, population projections. Individualized diagnosis and response is displaced by aggregate classification systems for purposes of surveillance, confinement, and control (Gordon, 1991).

Distinguishing Features of the New Penology

What we call the new penology is not a theory of crime or criminology but a focus on certain problems and a shared way of framing issues. This strategic formation of knowledge and power offers managers of the system a more or less coherent picture of the challenges they face and the kinds of solutions that are most likely to work. While we cannot reduce it to a set of principles, we can point to some of its most salient features.

The New Discourse

A central feature of the new discourse is the replacement of a moral or clinical description of the individual with an actuarial language of probabilistic calculations and statistical distributions applied to populations. Although social utility analysis or actuarial thinking is commonplace enough in modern life—it frames policy considerations of all sorts—in recent years this mode of thinking has gained ascendancy in legal discourse, a system of reasoning that traditionally has employed the language of morality and been focused on individuals (Simon, 1988). For instance, this new mode of reasoning is found increasingly in tort law, where traditional fault and negligence standards—which require a focus on the individual and are based upon notions of individual responsibility—have given way to strict liability and no-fault. These new doctrines rest upon actuarial ways of thinking about how to "manage" accidents and public safety. They employ the language of social utility and management, not individual responsibility (Simon, 1987; Steiner, 1987).

Although crime policy, criminal procedure, and criminal sanctioning have been influenced by such social utility analysis, there is no body of commentary on the criminal law that is equivalent to the body of social utility analysis for tort law doctrine. Nor has strict liability in the criminal law achieved anything like the acceptance of related no-fault principles in tort law.

However, there has been a rising trend in the penal system to target categories and subpopulations rather than individuals (Bottoms, 1983; Cohen, 1985; Mathieson, 1983; Reichman, 1986). This partly reflects actuarial forms of representation that promote quantification as a way of visualizing populations. The advance of statistical methods permits the formulation of concepts and strategies that allow direct relations between penal strategy and the population. Earlier generations used statistics to map the responses of normatively defined groups to punishment; today one talks of "high-rate offenders," "career criminals," and other categories defined by the distribution itself. Rather than simply extending the capacity of the system to rehabilitate or control crime, actuarial classification has come increasingly to define the correctional enterprise itself.

The importance of actuarial language in the system is evident to observers. Its significance, however, is often lost in the more spectacular shift in emphasis from rehabilitation to crime control. No doubt, a new and more punitive attitude toward the proper role of punishment has emerged in recent years, and it is manifest in a shift in the language of statutes, internal procedures, and academic scholarship. Yet looking across the past several decades, it appears that the pendulum-like swings of penal attitude moved independently of the actuarial language that has steadily crept into the discourse.

The discourse of the new penology is not simply one of greater quantification; it is also characterized by an emphasis on the systemic and on formal rationality. While the history of systems theory and operations research has yet to be written, their progression from business administration to the military and, in the 1960s, to domestic public policy, must be counted as among the most significant of current intellectual trends. The great government reports of the late 1960s, like *The Challenge of Crime in a Free Society*, combined the rehabilitative ideal with a new enthusiasm for actuarial representation, and helped make the phrase "criminal justice system" a part of everyday reality for the operatives and students of criminal law and policy.

Some identified this change early and understood that it was distinct from the concurrent rightward shift in penal thinking toward a "managerial" perspective with a focus on tighter administrative control through the gathering and distribution of statistical information about prison functioning (Jacobs, 1977).

The New Objectives

The new penology is neither about punishing nor about rehabilitating individuals. It is about identifying and managing unruly groups. It is concerned with the rationality not of individual behavior or even community organization, but of managerial processes. Its goal is not to eliminate crime but to make it tolerable through systemic coordination.

One measure of the shift away from trying to normalize offenders and toward trying to manage them is seen in the declining significance of recidivism. Under the old penology, recidivism was a nearly universal criterion for assessing success or failure of penal programs. Under the new penology, the word recidivism seems to be used less often, precisely because it carries a normative connotation that reintegrating offenders into the community is the major objective. High rates of parolees being returned to prison once indicated program failure; now they are offered as evidence of efficiency and effectiveness of parole as a control apparatus. This is especially true for intensive parole and probation supervision programs. Initially conceived as a way to reintegrate offenders into the community through a close interpersonal relationship, intensive supervision is now considered an enhanced monitoring technique whose ability to detect high rates of technical violations indicates its success, not failure.

It is possible that recidivism is dropping out of the vocabulary as an adjustment to harsh realities and as a way of avoiding charges of institutional failure. However, in shifting to emphasize the virtues of return as an indication of *effective* control, the new penology reshapes one's understanding of the functions of the penal sanction. By emphasizing correctional programs in terms of aggregate control and system management rather than individual success and failure, the new penology lowers one's expectations about the criminal sanction. These redefined objectives are reinforced by the new discourses discussed above, which take deviance as a given, mute aspirations for individual reformation, and seek to classify, sort, and manage dangerous groups efficiently.

The waning of concern over recidivism reveals fundamental changes in the very penal processes that recidivism once was used to evaluate. For example, although parole and probation have long been justified as a means of reintegrating offenders into the community (President's Commission, 1967:165), increasingly they are being perceived as cost-effective ways of imposing long-term management on the dangerous. Instead of treating revocation of parole and probation as a mechanism to short-circuit the supervision process when the risks to public safety become unacceptable, the system now treats revocation as a cost-effective way to police and sanction a chronically troublesome population. In such an operation, recidivism is either irrelevant or, as suggested above, is stood on its head and transformed into an indicator of success in a new form of law enforcement.

The importance that recidivism once had in evaluating the performance of corrections is now being taken up by measures of system functioning. Heydebrand and Seron (1990) have noted a tendency in courts and other social agencies toward decoupling performance evaluation from external social objectives. Instead of social norms like the elimination of crime, reintegration into the community, or public safety, institutions begin to measure their own outputs as indicators of performance. Thus, courts may look at docket flow. Similarly, parole agencies may shift evaluations of performance to, say, the time elapsed between arrests and due process hearings (Heydebrand and Seron, 1990:190–94; Lipsky, 1980:4–53).

Such technocratic rationalization tends to insulate institutions from the messy, hard-to-control demands of the social world. By limiting their exposure to indicators that they can control, managers ensure that their problems will have solutions. No doubt this tendency in the new penology is, in part, a response to the acceleration of demands for rationality and accountability in punishment coming from the courts and legislatures during the 1970s (Jacobs, 1977). It also reflects the lowered expectations for the penal system that result from failures to accomplish more ambitious promises of the past. Yet in the end, the inclination of the system to measure its success against its own production processes helps lock the system into a mode of operation that
has only an attenuated connection with the social purposes of punishment. In the long term it becomes more difficult to evaluate an institution critically if there are no references to substantive social ends.

The new objectives also inevitably permeate through the courts into thinking about rights. The new penology replaces consideration of fault with predictions of dangerousness and safety management and, in so doing, modifies traditional individual-oriented doctrines of criminal procedure.

New Techniques

These altered, lowered expectations manifest themselves in the development of more cost-effective forms of custody and control and in new technologies to identify and classify risk. Among them are low frills, no-service custodial centers; various forms of electronic monitoring systems that impose a form of custody without walls; and new statistical techniques for assessing risk and predicting dangerousness. These new forms of control are not anchored in aspirations to rehabilitate, reintegrate, retrain, or provide employment, but are justified in more blunt terms: variable detention depending upon risk assessment.

Perhaps the clearest example of the new penology's method is incapacitation, which has become the predominant utilitarian model of punishment (Greenwood, 1982; Moore et al., 1984). Incapacitation promises to reduce the social effects of crime by rearranging the distribution of offenders in society. Incapacitation theory holds that the prison can detain offenders for a time and thus delay their resumption of criminal activity. Moreover, if such delays are sustained for enough time and for enough offenders, significant aggregate effects in crime can take place although individual destinies are only marginally altered.

These aggregate effects can be further intensified, in some accounts, by a strategy of selective incapacitation. This approach proposes a sentencing scheme in which lengths of sentence depend not upon the nature of the criminal offense or upon an assessment of the character of the offender, but upon risk profiles. Its objectives are to identify high-risk offenders and to maintain long-term control over them while investing in shorter terms and less intrusive control over lower-risk offenders.

The New Penology in Perspective

The correctional practices emerging from the shifts we have identified above present a kind of "custodial continuum." But unlike the "correctional continuum" discussed in the 1960s, this new custodial continuum does not design penal measures for the particular needs of the individual or the community. Rather, it sorts individuals into groups according to the degree of control warranted by their risk profiles.

At one extreme the prison provides maximum security at a high cost for those who pose the greatest risks, and at the other, probation provides low-cost surveillance for low-risk offenders. In between stretches a growing range of intermediate supervisory and surveillance techniques. The management concerns of the new penology—in contrast to the transformative concerns of the old—are displayed especially clearly in justifications for various new intermediate sanctions.

What we call the new penology is only beginning to take coherent shape. Although most of what we have stressed as its central elements—statistical prediction, concern with groups, strategies of management—have a long history in penology, in recent years they have come to the fore, and their functions have coalesced and expanded to form a new strategic approach. Discussing the new penology in terms of discourse, objective, and technique risks a certain repetitiveness. Indeed, all three are closely linked, and while none can be assigned priority as the cause of the others, each entails and facilitates the others.

Thus, one can speak of normalizing individuals, but when the emphasis is on separating people into distinct and independent categories the idea of the "normal" itself becomes obscured if not irrelevant. If the "norm" can no longer function as a relevant criterion of success for the organizations of criminal justice, it is not surprising that evaluation turns to indicators of internal system performance. The focus of the system on the efficiency of its own outputs, in turn, places a premium on those methods (e.g., risk screening, sorting, and monitoring) that fit wholly within the bureaucratic capacities of the apparatus.

But the same story can be told in a different order. The steady bureaucratization of the correctional apparatus during the 1950s and 1960s shifted the target from individuals, who did not fit easily into centralized administration, to categories or classes, which do. But once the focus is on categories of offenders rather than individuals, methods naturally shift toward mechanisms of appraising and arranging groups rather than intervening in the lives of individuals. In the end the search for causal order is at least premature.

New Functions and Traditional Forms

It is best to conceive of the new penology as an interpretive net that can help reveal some directions the future may take. Below we reexamine three of the major features of the contemporary penal landscape: (1) the expansion of the penal sanction, (2) the rise of drug testing, and (3) innovation within the criminal process, and relate them to our thesis.

The Expansion of Penal Sanctions

During the past decade the number of people covered by penal sanctions has expanded significantly. Because of its high costs, the growth of prison populations has drawn the greatest attention, but probation and parole have increased at a proportionate or faster rate. The importance of these other sanctions goes beyond their ability to stretch penal resources; they expand and redistribute the use of imprisonment. Probation and parole violations now constitute a major source of prison inmates, and negotiations over probation revocation are replacing plea bargaining as modes of disposition (Greenspan, 1988; Messinger and Berecochea, 1990).

Many probation and parole revocations are triggered by events, like failing a drug test, that are driven by parole procedures themselves (Simon, 1990; Zimring and Hawkins, 1991). The increased flow of probationers and parolees into prisons is expanding the prison population and changing the nature of the prison. Increasingly, prisons are short-term holding pens for violators deemed too dangerous to remain on the streets. To the extent the prison is organized to receive such people, its correctional mission is replaced by a management function, a warehouse for the highest-risk classes of offenders.

From the perspective of the new penology, the growth of community corrections in the shadow of imprisonment is not surprising. The new penology does not regard prison as a special institution capable of making a difference in the lives of individuals who pass through it. Rather, it functions as but one of several custodial options. The actuarial logic of the new penology dictates an expansion of the continuum of control for more efficient risk management. For example, the various California prisons are today differentiated largely by the level of security they maintain and, thus, what level risk inmate they can receive. Twenty years ago, in contrast, they were differentiated by specialized functions.

Thus, community-based sanctions can be understood in terms of risk management rather than rehabilitative or correctional aspirations. Rather than instruments for reintegrating offenders into the community, they function as mechanisms to maintain control, often through frequent drug testing, over low-risk offenders for whom the more secure forms of custody are judged too expensive or unnecessary.

The new penology's technique of aggregation has been incorporated in a number of sentencing reforms. Minnesota and the U.S. Sentencing Commission have made population an explicit concern. As Alschuler (1991:951) has shown, although these guidelines have been defended as a step toward providing equal justice, in fact they are based upon "rough aggregations and statistical averages," which mask significant differences among offenders and offenses. The guidelines movement marks "a changed attitude toward sentencing—one that looks to collections of cases and to social harm rather than to individual offenders and punishments they deserve . . . [and rather than] the circumstances of their cases."

Drugs and Punishment

Drug use and its detection and control have become central concerns of the penal system with increasingly tough laws directed against users and traffickers, well-publicized data that suggest that a majority of arrestees are drug users, and an increasing proportion of drug offenders sent to prison.

The emphasis on drugs marks a continuity with the past thirty years of correctional history. Drug treatment and drug testing were hallmarks of the rehabilitative model in the 1950s and 1960s. The recent upsurge of concern with drugs may be attributed to the hardening of social attitudes toward drug use (especially in marked contrast to the tolerant 1970s), the introduction of virulent new drug products like crack cocaine, and the disintegrating social conditions of the urban poor.

Without dismissing the relevance of these continuities and explanations for change, it is important to note that there are distinctive changes in the role of drugs in the current system that reflect the logic of the new penology. In place of the traditional emphasis on treatment and eradication, today's practices track drug use as a kind of risk indicator. The widespread evidence of drug use in the offending population (Maguire and Flanagan, 1990:459) leads not to new theories of crime causation but to more efficient ways of identifying those at highest risk of offending. From the perspective of the new penology, drug use is not so much a measure of individual acts of deviance as it is a mechanism for classifying the offender within a risk group.

Thus, one finds in the correctional system today a much greater emphasis on drug testing than on drug treatment. This may reflect the normal kinds of gaps in policy as well as difficulty in treating relatively new forms of drug abuse. Yet, testing serves functions in the new penology even in the absence of a treatment option. By marking the distribution of risk within the offender population under surveillance, testing makes possible greater coordination of scarce penal resources.

Testing also fills the gap left by the decline of traditional intervention strategies. If nothing else, testing provides parole (and probably probation) agents a means to document compliance with their own internal performance requirements. It provides both an occasion for requiring the parolee to show up in the parole office and a purpose for meeting. The results of tests have become a network of fact and explanation for use in a decision-making process that requires accountability but provides little substantive basis for distinguishing among offenders.

Innovation

Our description may seem to imply the onset of a reactive age in which penal managers strive to manage populations of marginal citizens with no concomitant effort toward integration into mainstream society. This may seem hard to square with the myriad new and innovative technologies introduced over the past decade. Indeed the media, which for years have portrayed the correctional system as a failure, have recently enthusiastically reported on these innovations: boot camps, electronic surveillance, high security "campuses" for drug users, house arrest, intensive parole and probation, and drug treatment programs.

Although some of the new proposals are presented in terms of the "old penology" and emphasize individuals, normalization, and rehabilitation, it is difficult to know how these innovations will turn out. Historically, reforms evolve in ways quite different from the aims of their proponents (Foucault, 1977; Rothman, 1971). Thus, we wonder if these most recent innovations won't be recast in the terms we have outlined since many are compatible with the imperatives of the new penology: managing a permanently dangerous population while maintaining the system at a minimum cost.

One of the current innovations most in vogue with the press and politicians are correctional "boot camps." These are minimum security custodial facilities, usually for youthful first offenders, designed on the model of a training center for military personnel, complete with barracks, physical exercise, and tough drill sergeants. Boot camps are portrayed as providing discipline and pride to young offenders brought up in the unrestrained culture of poverty (as though physical fitness could fill the gap left by the weakening of families, schools, neighborhoods, and other social organizations in the inner city).

The camps borrow explicitly from a military model of discipline, which has influenced penality from at least the eighteenth century (see Rothman, 1971:105–8). The image of inmates smartly dressed in uniforms performing drills and calisthenics may appeal to long-standing ideals of order in post-Enlightenment culture. But in its proposed application to corrections, the military model is even less appropriate now than when it was rejected in the nineteenth century; indeed, today's boot camps are more a simulation of discipline than the real thing.

The military model was superseded by one modeled on factory discipline. Inmates were controlled by making them work at hard industrial labor (Ignatieff, 1978; Rothman, 1971). It was assumed that forced labor would inculcate the discipline required of factory laborers in the offenders so that they might earn their keep while in custody and join the ranks of the usefully employed when released. One can argue that this model was not fully achieved nor did it work very well, but at least it was coherent. The model of discipline through labor suited our capitalist democracy in a way the model of a militarized citizenry did not. The boot camp, like so much else in our increasingly anachronistic culture, is a signifier without a signified.

The 1980s decline of employment opportunities among the populations of urban poor most at risk for involvement in conventional crime left the applicability of industrial discipline in doubt. But the substitution of the boot camp for vocational training is even less plausible. Even if the typical ninety-day regime of training envisioned by boot camp proponents is effective in reorienting its subjects, at best it can only produce soldiers without a company to join. Indeed, the grim vision of the effect of boot camp is that it will be effective for those who will subsequently put their lessons of discipline and organization to use in street gangs and drug distribution networks. We suspect that the camps will be little more than holding pens for managing a short-term, midrange risk population.

Drug testing and electronic monitors being tried in experimental "intensive supervision" and "house arrest" programs are justified in rehabilitative terms, but both sorts of programs lack a foundation in today's social and economic realities. The drug treatment programs in the 1960s encompassed a regime of coercive treatment—"inpatient" custody in secured settings followed by community supervision and reintegration—which had enduring effects for at least some of the participants (Anglin et al., 1990). Today's proposals are similar, but it is questionable whether they can be effective without long-term treatment facilities, community-based follow-up, and prospects for viable conventional lifestyles and employment opportunities. In the meantime it is obvious that they can also serve the imperative of reducing the costs of correctional jurisdiction while maintaining some check on the offender population.

We anticipate that drug treatment and rehabilitation will become increasingly attractive as the cost of long-term custody increases. However, given the emergence of the management concerns of the new penology, we question whether these innovations will embrace the long-term perspective of earlier successful treatment programs, and we suspect that they will emerge as control processes for managing and recycling selected risk populations. If so, these new programs will further extend the capacity of the new penology. The undeniable attractiveness of innovations like boot camps, house arrest, and secure drug "centers," is their promise to provide secure custody in a more flexible format at less cost than traditional correctional facilities. Indeed, some of them are envisioned as private contract facilities that can be expanded or reduced with relative ease. Despite the lingering language of rehabilitation and reintegration, programs generated under the new penology can best be understood in terms of managing costs and controlling dangerous populations rather than social or personal transformation.

Social Bases of the New Penology

We are not arguing that shifts in the way the penal enterprise is understood and discussed inexorably determine how the system will take shape. What actually emerges in corrections over the near and distant future will depend on how this understanding itself is shaped by the pressures of demographic, economic, and political factors. Still, such factors rarely operate as pure forces. They are filtered through and expressed in terms in which the problems are understood. Thus, the strategic field that we call the new penology itself will help shape the future.

The New Discourse of Crime

Like the old penology, traditional "sociological" criminology has focused on the relationship between individuals and communities. Its central concerns have been the causes and correlates of delinquent and criminal behavior, and it has sought to develop intervention strategies designed to correct delinquents and decrease the likelihood of deviant behavior. Thus, it has focused on the family and the workplace as important influences of socialization and control.

The new penology has an affinity with a new "actuarial" criminology, which eschews traditional criminological concerns. Instead of training in sociology or social work, increasingly the new criminologists are trained in operations research and systems analysis. This new approach is not a criminology at all, but an applied branch of systems theory. This shift in training and orientation has been accompanied by a shift in interest. A concern with successful intervention strategies, the province of the former, is replaced by models designed to optimize public safety through the management of aggregates, which is the province of the latter.

In one important sense this new criminology is simply a consequence of steady improvements in the quantitative rigor with which crime is studied. The amassing of a statistical picture of crime and the criminal justice system has improved researchers' ability to speak realistically about the distribution of crimes and the fairness of procedures. But, we submit, it has also contributed to a shift, a reconceptualization, in the way crime is understood as a social problem. The new techniques and the new language have facilitated reconceptualization of the way issues are framed and policies pursued. Sociological criminology saw crime as a relationship between the individual and the normative expectations of his or her community (Bennett, 1981). Policies premised on this perspective addressed problems of reintegration, including the mismatch between individual motivation, normative orientation, and social opportunity structures. In contrast, actuarial criminology highlights the interaction of criminal justice institutions and specific segments of the population. Policy discussions framed in its terms emphasize the management of high-risk groups and make less salient the qualities of individual delinquents and their communities.

In actuarial criminology the numbers generate the subject (e.g., the high-rate offender of incapacitation research). Criminals are no longer the organizing referent (or logos) of criminology. Instead, criminology has become a subfield of a generalized public policy analysis discourse. This new criminal knowledge aims at rationalizing the operation of the systems that manage criminals, not dealing with criminality. The same techniques that can be used to improve the circulation of baggage in airports or delivery of food to troops can be used to improve the penal system's efficiency.

The Discourse of Poverty and the "Underclass"

The new penology may also be seen as responsive to the emergence of a new understanding of poverty in America. Although the term "dangerous classes" was part of early-nineteenth-century penal discourse in England, reflecting a management rather than an individualized approach to crime, the term *underclass* is used today to characterize that segment of society viewed as permanently excluded from social mobility and economic integration. The term is used to refer to a largely black and Hispanic population living in concentrated zones of poverty in central cities, separated physically and institutionally from the suburban locus of mainstream social and economic life in America.

In contrast to groups whose members are deemed employable, even though temporarily unemployed, the underclass is understood as a permanently marginal population, without literacy, without skills, and without hope; a self-perpetuating and pathological segment of society that is not integratable into the larger whole, even as a reserve labor pool (Wilson, 1987). So conceived, the underclass is also a dangerous class, not only for what any particular member may or may not do, but more generally for collective potential misbehavior. It is treated as a high-risk group that must be managed to protect society. Indeed, it is this managerial task that provides one of the most powerful sources for the imperative of preventive management in the new penology.

Reintegration and rehabilitation inevitably imply a norm against which deviant subjects are evaluated. As Allen (1981) perceived, rehabilitation as a project can only survive if public confidence in the viability and appropriateness of such norms endures. Allen viewed the decline of the rehabilitative ideal as a result of the cultural revolts of the 1960s, which undermined the capacity of the American middle classes to justify their norms and the imposition of those norms on others. It is this decline in social will, rather than empirical evidence of the failure of penal programs to rehabilitate, that doomed the rehabilitative ideal for Allen.

The emergence of the new penology in the 1980s reflects the influence of a more despairing view of poverty and the prospects for achieving equality. Rehabilitating offenders, or any kind of reintegration strategy, can only make sense if the larger community from which offenders come is viewed as sharing a common normative universe with the communities of the middle classes—especially those values and expectations derived from the labor market. The concept of an underclass, with its connotation of a permanent marginality for whole portions of the population, has rendered the old penology incoherent and laid the groundwork for a strategic field that emphasizes low-cost management of a permanent offender population.

The connection between the new penality and the (re)emergent term *underclass* also is illustrated by recent studies of American jails. Irwin (1985) entitled his book, *The Jail: Managing the Underclass in American Society.* His thesis is that "prisoners in jails share two essential characteristics: detachment and disrepute" (1985:2). For Irwin, the function of jail is to manage the underclass, which he reports is also referred to as "rabble," "disorganized," "disorderly," and the "lowest class of people."

The high rates of those released without charges filed, the turnstile-like frequency with which some people reappear, and the pathological characteristics of a high proportion of the inmates, lead many to agree with Irwin that the jail is best understood as a social management instrument rather than an institution for effecting the purported aims of the criminal process.

Social management, not individualized justice, is also emphasized in other discussions of the criminal process. Longtime public defender James M. Doyle (1992) offers the metaphors "colonial," "White Man's burden," and "Third World," in an essay drawing parallels between the careers of criminal justice officials and colonial administrators. Doyle parallels the corrupting influence of the White Man's effort to "manage" Third World natives with those of the criminal justice professionals' effort to handle cases. He concludes, "we have paid too much attention to the superficial exotic charms by which the reports of the colonial and criminal justice White Man entertain us, too little to the darker strains they also share" (1922:126).

Whether one prefers Irwin's notion of underclass or Doyle's "colonial" and "third world" metaphors, both resonate with our notion of the new penology. They vividly explain who is being managed and why. But in providing an explanation of these relationships, there is a danger that the terms will reify the problem, that they will suggest the problem is inevitable and permanent. Indeed, it is this belief, we maintain, that has contributed to the lowered expectations of the new penology—away from an aspiration to affect individual lives through rehabilitative and transformative efforts and toward the more "realistic" task of monitoring and managing intractable groups.

The hardening of poverty in contemporary America reinforces this view. When combined with a pessimistic analysis implied by the term *underclass*, the structural barriers that maintain the large islands of third world misery in America's major cities can lead to the conclusion that such conditions are inevitable and impervious to social policy intervention. This, in turn, can push corrections ever further toward a self-understanding based on the imperative of herding a specific population that cannot be disaggregated and transformed but only maintained—a kind of waste management function (in 1989 then-Californian Governor Deukmejian proposed to use prison inmates to process toxic waste). As the Los Angeles riots demonstrated, however, this kind of reversion is likely to be fatal to a democratic civil order.

Conclusion

Our discussion has proceeded as if the new penology has contributed to the recent rise in prison populations. Although we believe that it has, we also acknowledge that the new penology is both cause and effect of the increases. We recognize that those conditions we referred to at the outset as "external" have placed pressures on criminal justice institutions that, in turn, have caused them to adapt in a host of ways. Our purpose, however, has been to show just how thorough this adaptation has been. It has led to a significant reconceptualization of penology, a shift that institution-alizes those adaptive behaviors. It embraces the new forms that have arisen as a result of this adaptation. As such, the new language, the new conceptualization, ensures that these new forms will persist independently of the pressures. They appear to be permanent features of the criminal justice system.

New Directions: Integrated Theory

Introduction

Given the existence of various approaches in criminological theory the question has often arisen as to the possibility of a synthesis integrating these differing conceptual emphases into a grand theory that explains crime in all its complexities. The history of criminology is in many ways a history of both polarization and integration; new theories are built by using older concepts in new directions rather than creating total paradigmatic replacement. However, in recent years grand attempts have been made at integrating, not just one or two theories, but many. Is such a comprehensive, all-encompassing, integrated theory possible? Some criminologists have felt that those parts of theories that have empirical support ought to be combined into a single coherent theoretical model and the rest abandoned. However, as we have pointed out elsewhere (Einstadter and Henry, 1995), while seductive, such a stance has many pitfalls, not the least of which is the fact that theories are never discrete entities. Theories always combine a range of concepts current in a particular historical period. Therefore, to an extent all theories have a measure of synthesis at their base. Moreover, theories are never totally exclusive and recognize that there is no single linear causal nexus. On the contrary, theories must allow for intervening variables or processes which form the causal chain with the particular variables under consideration.

In his article Terence Thornberry (chap. 27) criticizes the limitations of contemporary theories of delinquency which tend to rely on uni-directional causal structures that represent delinquency in a static rather than dynamic fashion, do not examine developmental progressions, and inadequately link processual concepts to the person's position in the social structure. Thornberry points out that even when theories integrate a number of different propositions to explain delinquency, they fail to take into account "developmental patterns to explain the initiation, maintenance, and desistance of delinquency." In contrast, Thornberry's article develops an interactional theory of delinquency that addresses each of these issues. He views delinquency as resulting from the freedom afforded by the weakening of the person's bonds to conventional society and from an interactional setting in which delinquent behavior is learned and reinforced. He sees the control, learning, and delinquency variables as reciprocally interrelated, mutually affecting one another over the person's life-time. Thus, delinquency is viewed as part of a larger causal network, affected by social factors but also affecting the development of those social factors over time.

John Laub and Robert Sampson's article (chap. 28) examines conceptual issues relating to continuity and change in crime over the life course. Building on past efforts, they first distinguish self-selection from a cumulative developmental process whereby delinquent behavior attenuates adult social bonds (e.g, labor force attachment, marital cohesion). They then conceptualize various types of change and argue that social capital and "turning points" are crucial to understanding processes of change in the adult life course. They argue that while adult crime is clearly connected to childhood behavior, their data suggest that both incremental and abrupt change are structured by changes in adult social bonds. Finally, they conclude by considering the implications for future research on subjective contingencies, opportunity structures, and chance encounters as potential turning points for change, especially as these interact with race, class location, and historical context.

Going a step further in the integration process, Bryan Vila (chap. 29) sets an ambitious project for himself in attempting to develop a general integrated theory of crime by extending the evolutionary ecological approach used in the explanation of property crime to all criminal behavior. Vila demonstrates how consistent empirical findings and insights from the many disciplines that study crime may be integrated into a single comprehensive theoretical framework. At the microlevel, he explains how individual criminal behavior is influenced, but not determined, by systematic interactions between factors at the ecological, individual, and societal levels over the life course. At the macrolevel, he explains the evolution of population-level characteristics, such as the frequency and type of crime and crime control, as the cumulative result of the behaviors of individuals and their interactions with one another and the environment. If the proposed relationships between domains of variables can be refined, argues Vila, it appears possible to develop a truly general theory of criminal behavior.

27

Toward an Interactional Theory of Delinquency

Terence P. Thornberry

Of the variety of sociological theories developed to explain delinquent behavior, of primary importance are: social control theory (Hirschi, 1969), social learning theory (Akers, 1977), and integrated models (Elliott et al., 1979, 1985).

Control theory argues that delinquency emerges whenever the social and cultural constraints over human conduct are substantially attenuated. This theory assumes that we would all be deviant if only we dared (Hirschi, 1969). In contrast, learning theory assumes no natural impulse toward delinquency. Indeed, delinquent behavior must be learned through the same processes and mechanisms as conforming behavior. Because of their different assumptions, control and learning models give causal priority to somewhat different concepts. Integrated models capitalize on the complementary approaches by melding together propositions from these and other theories (e.g., strain) to explain delinquent behavior.

Although such approaches have substantially informed our understanding of the causes of delinquency, they and other contemporary theories suffer from three fundamental limitations. First, they rely on unidirectional causal structures. These ignore the reciprocal effects in which delinquent behavior is viewed as part of a more general social nexus, affected by, but also affecting, other social factors. Second, current theories tend not to be developmental, specifying causal models for only a narrow age range, usually mid-adolescence. They fail to capitalize on developmental patterns to explain the initiation, maintenance, and desistance of delinquency. Finally, contemporary theories tend to assume uniform causal effects throughout the social structure. By ignoring the person's structural position, they fail to provide an understanding of the

---

Edited and abridged from *Criminology*, Volume 25(4):863–91 (1987).

sources of initial variation in both delinquency and its presumed causes. In combination, these limitations have resulted in narrowly conceived, incomplete theories which provide misleading models of delinquency causation.

The present article develops a dynamic interactional theory of delinquency that addresses and attempts to respond to each of these limitations, in particular the issue of recursive versus reciprocal causal structures.

Origins, Assumptions and Organization

The basic premise of the model proposed here is that human behavior occurs in social interaction and can therefore best be explained by models that focus on interactive processes. It argues that adolescents interact with other people and institutions and that behavioral outcomes are formed through that interactive process. For example, adolescent delinquent behavior is formed in part by how the adolescent and parent(s) *interact* over time, not simply by the child's perceived *level* of attachment to parents. Moreover, since it is an interactive system, the behaviors of others—for example, parents and school officials—are influenced both by each other and by the adolescent, including his or her delinquent behavior. If this view is correct, then interactional effects have to be modeled explicitly if we are to understand the social and psychological processes involved with initiation into delinquency, the maintenance of such behavior, and its eventual reduction.

Interactional theory develops from the same intellectual tradition as the theories mentioned above, especially the Durkheimian tradition of social control. It asserts that the fundamental cause of delinquency lies in the weakening of social constraints over the conduct of the individual. However, it does not assume that the attenuation of controls leads directly to delinquency. The weakening of controls simply allows for a much wider array of behavior, including continued conventional action, failure as indicated by school dropout and sporadic employment histories, alcoholism, mental illness, delinquent and criminal careers, or some combination of these outcomes. For the freedom resulting from weakened bonds to be channeled into delinquency, especially serious prolonged delinquency, an interactive setting in which delinquency is learned, performed, and reinforced is required. This view is similar to Cullen's (1984) structuring perspective which draws attention to the indeterminacy of deviant behavior.

Although heavily influenced by control and learning theories, and to a lesser extent by strain and culture conflict theories, this model is less about theoretical integration than about theoretical elaboration (Thornberry, 1987a). Basic control theory is elaborated, using available theoretical perspectives and empirical findings, to provide a more accurate and logically consistent model of the causes of delinquency.

The paper begins by identifying the central concepts to be included in the model. Next, the underlying theoretical structure of the proposed model is examined and the rationale for moving from unidirectional to reciprocal causal models is developed. The reciprocal model is then extended to include a developmental perspective, examining the theoretical saliency of different variables at different developmental stages. Finally, the influence of the person's position in the social structure is explored. The last issue is concerned with sources of initial variation in the causal variables. Although it is logically prior to the others, it is discussed last so that the reciprocal relationships among the concepts can be more fully developed.

Theoretical Concepts

Given these basic premises, an interactional model must respond to (1) how traditional social constraints over behavior are weakened, and (2) once weakened, how the resulting freedom is channeled into delinquent patterns. To address these issues, an initial version of an interactional model is presented, focusing on the interrelationships among: attachment to parents, commitment to school, belief in conventional values, associations with delinquent peers, adopting delinquent values, and engaging in delinquent behavior. These concepts form the core of the model since they are central to social-psychological theories of delinquency and have been shown repeatedly to be strongly related to subsequent delinquent behavior (see Elliott et al., 1985).

The first three concepts (derived from social control theory) represent the primary mechanisms by which adolescents are bonded to conventional middle-class society (Hirschi, 1969). When these elements of the bond are weakened, behavioral freedom increases considerably. For that freedom to lead to delinquent behavior, however, delinquency-reinforcing interactive settings are required. In the model, those settings are represented by two concepts (derived from social learning theory): (1) associations with delinquent peers, and (2) the formation of delinquent values.

For the present purposes each of these concepts is defined quite broadly. Attachment to parents includes the affective relationship between parent and child, communication patterns, parenting skills such as monitoring and discipline, and parent-child conflict. Commitment to school refers to the stake in conformity the adolescent has developed and includes such factors as success in school, perceived importance of education, attachment to teachers, and involvement in school activities. Belief in conventional values represents the granting of legitimacy to such middle-class values as education, personal industry, financial success, deferral of gratification, and so on.

Three delinquency variables are included. Association with delinquent peers includes the level of attachment to peers, the delinquent behavior and values of peers, and their reinforcing reactions to the adolescent's own delinquent or conforming behavior. It is a continuous measure that can vary from groups that are heavily delinquent to those that are almost entirely nondelinquent. Delinquent values refer to the granting of legitimacy to delinquent activities as acceptable modes of behavior as well as a general willingness to violate the law to achieve other ends.

Delinquent behavior, the primary outcome variable, refers to acts that place the youth at risk for adjudication; it ranges from status offenses to serious violent activities. Since the present model is an interactional one, designed not only to explain delinquency but to explain the effects of delinquency on other variables, particular attention is paid to prolonged involvement in serious delinquency.

Theoretical Structure

Figure 1 describes the typical way variables are represented in predominately recursive theories of delinquency (Johnson, 1979; Weis and Sederstrom, 1981; Elliott et al., 1985). In these models all the variables are temporally ordered; earlier ones affect later ones, but there is no provision for feedback or reciprocal causal paths. The unidirectional specification can be illustrated by examining the relationship between attachment to parents and associations with delinquent peers. According to the model, attachment to parents reduces the extent to which the child associates with delinquent peers, an assertion consistent with both observation and empirical research (Poole and Regoli, 1979). Yet, by implication, the model also states that associations with delinquent peers *exert no causal influence* on the extent to which the child is attached to parents. If peer associations were thought to influence attachment to parents, then this effect would have to be specified and estimated but such effects are excluded by design.

In addition, the conventional recursive model treats delinquency entirely as an outcome of a social process rather than as integral to it. Such models assert that various social factors cause delinquent behavior

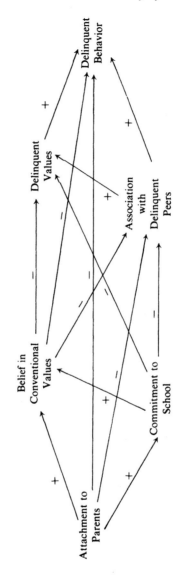

Figure 1
A Typical Recursive Causal Model of Delinquency

but ignore the possibility that delinquency and its presumed causes are part of a reciprocal causal structure, mutually influencing one another over the person's life span. For example, these models state that associations with delinquent peers increase the likelihood of delinquent conduct, an obviously reasonable assertion, but ignore the possibility that delinquent conduct affects the likelihood and intensity of associations with delinquent peers.

It should be noted that there is nothing inherently incorrect with recursive models; if the causal processes are unidirectional, recursive models offer a correct specification. It is only when the causal processes are reciprocal that unidirectional models lead to specification problems and to incorrect interpretations of causal effects. Indeed, the evidence suggests that unidirectional models are inadequate and that reciprocal models are required to understand the causes of delinquency.

Empirical Findings

Thornberry and Christenson (1984) estimated a reciprocal causal structure for unemployment and criminal involvement, measured at the individual level, for a sample of young adult males. They found that unidirectional models, either from unemployment to crime or from crime to unemployment, were inadequate to model the causal process since each of these variables has significant effects on the other (1984:408).

Liska and Reed (1985) studied the relationship among three control theory variables, attachment to parents, success in school, and delinquency. Although their results differed somewhat for blacks and whites, these variables appear to be embedded in a reciprocal causal loop. Overall, "the analysis suggests that parental attachment affects delinquency, that delinquency affects school attachment, and that school attachment affects parental attachment" (Liska and Reed, 1985:556–57).

Finally, Burkett and Warren's (1987) study of variables relating to self-reported marijuana use suggests that religious commitment and belief affect marijuana use indirectly, through association with delinquent peers, and that these variables are reciprocally related over time. Marijuana use increases associations with delinquent peers, and associations with delinquent peers reduce religious commitments. In addition, marijuana use at one time significantly affects both religious commitment and beliefs at later times and "this, in turn, contributes to deeper involvement with marijuana-using peers and subsequent continued use in response to direct peer pressure" (1987:123).

In spite of using different data sets, variables, and analytic techniques, each of these studies provides empirical support for the improved power of reciprocal causal models to explain the social settings in which delinquent behavior emerges and develops.

These findings also suggest that previous tests of delinquency theories based on recursive causal structures are incomplete, misleading, and inadequate to describe the actual processes in which delinquency is embedded.

Model Specification

A causal model allowing for reciprocal relationships among the six concepts of interest—attachment to parents, commitment to school, belief in conventional values, association with delinquent peers, delinquent values, and delinquent behavior—is presented in Figure 2. This model refers to the period of early adolescence, from about ages eleven to thirteen, when delinquent careers are beginning, but prior to the period at which delinquency reaches its apex in terms of seriousness and frequency.

The specification of causal effects begins by examining delinquent peers, delinquent values, and delinquent behavior, concepts at the heart of social learning theories of delinquency. For now we focus on the reciprocal nature of the relationships, ignoring until later variations in the strength of the relationships.

Traditional social learning theory specifies a causal order among these variables in which delinquent associations affect delinquent values and, in turn, both produce delinquent behavior (Akers et al., 1979; Matsueda, 1982). Yet, for each of the dyadic relationships involving these variables, other theoretical perspectives and much empirical evidence suggest the appropriateness of reversing this causal order. For example, social learning theory proposes that associating with delinquents, or more precisely, with people who hold and reinforce delinquent values, increases the chances of delinquent behavior (Akers, 1977). Yet the Gluecks (1950) challenged this specification. Arguing that "birds of a feather flock together," the Gluecks propose that youths who are delinquent seek out and associate with others who share those tendencies. Thus, rather than being a cause of delinquency, associations are the result of delinquents seeking out and associating with like-minded peers.

An attempt to resolve the somewhat tedious argument over the temporal priority of associations and behavior is less productive theoretically than capitalizing on the interactive nature of human behavior and treating the relationship as reciprocal. People often take on the behavioral repertoire of their associates but, at the same time, they often seek out associates who share their behavioral interests. Individuals clearly

Figure 2

A Reciprocal Model of Delinquent Involvement at Early Adolescence[a]

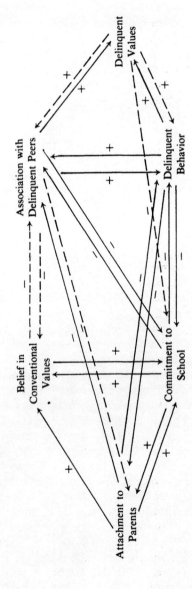

[a] Solid lines represent stronger effects; dashed lines represent weaker effects.

behave this way in conventional settings, and there is no reason to assume that they behave differently with regard to deviant activities such as delinquency.

Similar arguments can be made for the other relationships among the delinquency variables. Most recent theories, following social learning theory, posit that delinquent associations lead to the formation of delinquent values. Subcultural theories, however, especially those deriving from a cultural deviance perspective (Miller, 1958), suggest that values precede the formation of peer groups. Indeed, it is the socialization of adolescents into "lower-class culture" and its value system that leads them to the initial association with delinquent peers. This specification can also be derived from a social control perspective (Weis and Sederstrom, 1981; Burkett and Warren, 1987).

Finally, the link between delinquent values and delinquent behavior restates the social-psychological question of the relationship between attitudes and behavior. Do attitudes form behavior patterns or does behavior lead to attitude formation? Social psychological research, especially in cognitive psychology and balance models (e.g., Festinger, 1957; Brehm and Cohen, 1962), points to the reciprocal nature of this relationship. It suggests that people indeed behave in a manner consistent with their attitudes, but also that behavior is one of the most persuasive forces in the formation and maintenance of attitudes.

Such a view is consistent with both Hindelang's (1974:382) findings and with recent deterrence research which demonstrates that the "experiential effect," in which behavior affects attitudes, is much stronger than the deterrent effect, in which attitudes affect behavior (Paternoster et al., 1982, 1983).

Although each of these relationships appears to be reciprocal, the strengths of the associations are not equal during early adolescence (see Figure 2). Adolescent beliefs that delinquent conduct is acceptable and positively valued may be emerging, but such beliefs are not fully articulated for eleven- to thirteen-year-olds. Because of their emerging quality, they are viewed as more effect than cause, produced by delinquent behavior and associations with delinquent peers. As these values emerge, however, they have feedback effects, albeit relatively weak ones at these ages, on behavior and associations.

Summary. When attention is focused on the interrelationships among associations with delinquent peers, delinquent values, and delinquent behavior, it appears that they are reciprocally related. Human behavior is far more complex than a simple recursive one in which a temporal order can be imposed on interactional variables. Interactional theory sees these three concepts as embedded in a causal loop, each reinforcing the others over time. Regardless of where the individual enters the loop, delinquency increases associations with delinquent peers and delinquent values; delinquent values increase delinquent behavior and associations with delinquent peers; and associations with delinquent peers increases delinquent behavior and delinquent values.

Social Control Effects

As indicated, the premise of interactional theory is that the fundamental cause of delinquency is the attenuation of social controls over the person's conduct. Whenever bonds to the conventional world are substantially weakened, the individual is freed from moral constraints and is at risk for a wide array of deviant activities, including delinquency. The primary mechanisms that bind adolescents to the conventional world are attachment to parents, commitment to school, and belief in conventional values.

During the early adolescent years, the family is the most salient arena for social interaction and involvement. As a result, attachment to parents has a stronger influence on a youth's life than at later stages of development. Attachment to parents (or parent surrogates) is predicted to affect four other variables. Since youths who are attached to their parents are sensitive to their wishes (Hirschi, 1969:16–19) and, since parents are almost universally supportive of the conventional world, these children are likely to be strongly committed to school and to espouse conventional values. In addition, youths who are attached to their parents and are sensitive to their wishes are unlikely to associate with delinquent peers or to engage in delinquent behavior.

In brief, parental influence is seen as central to controlling the behavior of youths at these relatively early ages. Parents who have a strong affective bond with their children are likely to lead their children toward conventional actions and beliefs and away from delinquent friends and actions.

However, attachment to parents is not an immutable trait impervious to the effects of other variables. Indeed, associating with delinquent peers, lack of commitment to school or failure at school, and engaging in delinquency are so contradictory to parental expectations that they tend to diminish the level of attachment between parent and child. As a consequence, such adolescent behavior is likely to jeopardize the affective bond with parents, precisely because these behaviors suggest that the "person does not care about the wishes and expectations of other people" (Hirschi, 1969:18).

Belief in conventional values is involved in two different causal loops. First, it strongly affects commitment to school and in turn is affected by commitment to school. This loop posits a behavioral and attitudinal consistency in the conventional realm. Second, a weaker loop is posited between belief in conventional values and associations with delinquent peers. Youths who do not grant legitimacy to conventional values are more apt to associate with delinquent friends who share those views, and those friendships are likely to attenuate further their beliefs in conventional values (see Burkett and Warren, 1987). Finally, youths who believe in conventional values are seen as somewhat less likely to engage in delinquent behavior.

Although belief in conventional values plays some role in the genesis of delinquency, its impact is not particularly strong. For example, it is not affected by delinquent behavior, nor is it related to delinquent values. This is primarily because belief in conventional values appears to be quite invariant; regardless of class of origin or delinquency status, for example, most people strongly assert conventional values (Short and Strodtbeck, 1965). Nevertheless, these beliefs do exert some influence in the model, especially with respect to reinforcing commitment to school.

Finally, the impact of commitment to school is considered. This variable is involved in reciprocal loops with both the other bonding variables. Youngsters who are attached to their parents are likely to be committed to and succeed in school, and that success is likely to reinforce the close ties to their parents. Similarly, youths who believe in conventional values are likely to be committed to school, the primary arena in which they can act in accordance with those values, and, in turn, success in that arena is likely to reinforce the beliefs.

In addition to its relationships with the other control variables, commitment to school also has direct effects on two delinquency variables. Students who are committed to succeeding in school are unlikely to associate with delinquents or to engage in substantial amounts of serious, repetitive delinquent behavior. These youths have built up a stake in conformity and should be unwilling to jeopardize that investment by either engaging in delinquent behavior or by associating with those who do.

Low commitment to school is not seen as leading directly to the formation of delinquent values, however. Its primary effect on delinquent values is indirect, via associations with delinquent peers and delinquent behavior (Conger, 1980:137). While school failure may lead to a reduced commitment to conventional values, it does not follow that it directly increases the acceptance of values that support delinquency.

Commitment to school, however, is affected by each of the delinquency variables in the model. Youths who accept values that are consistent with delinquent behavior, who associate with other delinquents, and who also engage in delinquent behavior are unlikely candidates to maintain an active commitment to school and the conventional world that school symbolizes.

Summary. Attachment to parents, commitment to school, and belief in conventional values reduce delinquency by cementing the person to conventional institutions and people. When these elements of the bond to conventional society are strong, delinquency is unlikely, but when they are weak the individual is placed at much greater risk for delinquency. From an interactional perspective, two additional qualities of these concepts are evident.

First, attachment to parents, commitment to school, and belief in conventional values are not static, invariant attributes of the person. Rather they interact with one another during the developmental process. For some youths the levels of attachment, commitment, and belief increase as these elements reinforce one another, while for other youths the interlocking nature of these relationships suggests that a greater and greater attenuation of the bond will develop over time.

Second, the bonding variables appear to be reciprocally linked to delinquency, exerting a causal impact on associations with delinquent peers and delinquent behavior; they are also causally affected by these variables. As both the youth's delinquent conduct and associations with delinquent peers increase, the bond to the conventional world is further weakened. Thus, while the weakening of the bond to conventional society may be an initial cause of delinquency, delinquency eventually becomes its own indirect cause precisely because of its ability to weaken further the person's bonds to family, school, and conventional beliefs.

Support for Reciprocal Structures

The reciprocal model is logically consistent with, and is a logical extension of, the approaches of many other theoretical models (e.g., Hirschi, 1969; Akers, 1977; Elliott et al., 1979, 1985; Weis and Sederstrom, 1981; and Snyder and Patterson, 1986). Also, as discussed earlier, recent panel studies estimating reciprocal effects produce consistent support for this perspective; each suggest that there are substantial feedback effects involving delinquency and its presumed causes.

Further, using the National Youth Survey, Huizinga and Elliott (1986) report a number of significant reciprocal effects. Although they did not observe feedback effects from delinquent behavior to the conventional bonding variables posited by interactional theory, they do report reciprocal effects among the elements of the bond. They also report that delinquent behavior and associations with delinquent peers are mutually reinforcing (Huizinga and Elliott, 1986:12). Finally, they report that exposure to delinquent friends has significant feedback effects on a wide range of variables, including "internal deviant bonds, perceived sanctions, normlessness, prosocial aspirations, and involvement in prosocial roles" (Huizinga and Elliott, 1986:14).

Fourth, many studies have found that delinquent behavior (including drug use) measured at one time has significant effects on the presumed "causes" of delinquency measured at a later time. Among the variables found to be affected by prior delinquency are educational and occupational attainment (Bachman et al., 1978; Kandel and Logan, 1984); dropping out of high school (Elliott and Voss, 1974; Bachman et al., 1978; Polk et al., 1981; Thornberry et al., 1985); unemployment (Bachman et al., 1978; Thornberry and Christenson, 1984); attachment to parents (Paternoster et al., 1983); commitment to school (Paternoster et al., 1983; Liska and Reed, 1985; Agnew, 1985c); and belief in conventional values (Hindelang, 1974; Paternoster et al., 1983; Agnew, 1985c). These empirical findings are quite consistent with a reciprocal interactive theory of delinquent behavior.

Developmental Extensions

In addition to the unidirectional causal structure of delinquency theories, they also suffer from a tendency to provide a cross-sectional picture of the factors associated with delinquency at one age, but do not provide a rationale for understanding how delinquent behavior develops over time. The present section offers a developmental extension of the basic model.

Middle Adolescence

Middle adolescence is the period of fifteen to sixteen years of age during which youths show the highest rates of delinquency involvement (see Figure 3) and is the reference period for most theories of delinquency. Since the models for the early and middle adolescent periods have essentially the same structure and causal relationships (Figures 2 and 3), discussion focuses on the differences between them.

Perhaps the most important difference concerns attachment to parents, which is involved in relatively few strong relationships. By this point in the life cycle, the most salient variables involved in the production of delinquency are likely to be external to the home, associated with the youth's activities in school and peer networks. This specification is consistent with empirical results for subjects in this age range (Johnson, 1979:105; Schoenberg, 1975, quoted in Johnson).

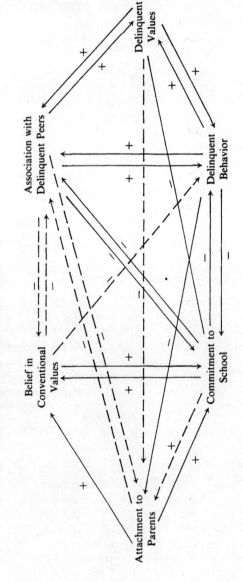

Figure 3

A Reciprocal Model of Delinquent Involvement at Middle Adolescence[a]

[a]   Solid lines represent stronger effects; dashed lines represent weaker effects.

Attachment to parents continues to be relevant in enhancing commitment to school and belief in conventional values, and in preventing associations with delinquent peers. However, the overall strength of parental effects is weaker than at earlier ages when the salience of the family was greater.

The second major change concerns the increased causal importance of delinquent values. At mid-adolescence, when delinquency is at its apex, these values are more fully articulated and have stronger effects on other variables. First, delinquent values are seen as major reinforcers of both delinquent associations and delinquent behavior. In general, espousing values supportive of delinquency tends to increase the potency of this causal loop. Second, since delinquent values are antithetical to the conventional settings of school and family, youths who espouse them are less likely to be committed to school and attached to parents. Consistent with the reduced saliency of family at these ages, the feedback effect to school is seen as stronger than the feedback effect to parents.

The other concepts in the model play the same role at these ages as they did at earlier ones. Thus, the major change from early to middle adolescence is that family declines in relative importance while the adolescent's own world of school and peers takes on increasing significance. While these changes occur, the overall structure of the theory involving mutually reinforcing interactive variables remains constant.

Later Adolescence

Finally, the causes of delinquency (now technically crime) during the transition from adolescence to adulthood, about ages eighteen to twenty, can be examined (Figure 4). Two new variables have been added to reflect the changing life circumstances at this stage of development. The more important of these is commitment to conventional activities which includes employment, attending college, and military service. Along with the transition to work, there is a parallel transition from the family of origin to one's own family. Although this transition does not peak until the early twenties, for many its influence is beginning at this stage. Included in this concept are marriage, and plans for marriage and for childrearing. Theoretically these new variables largely replace attachment to parents and commitment to school; they represent the major sources of bonds to conventional society for young adults.

Both attachment to parents and commitment to school remain but as exogenous variables. Attachment to parents has only a minor effect on commitment to school, and commitment to school is proposed to affect

Figure 4
A Reciprocal Model of Delinquent Involvement at Later Adolescence[a]

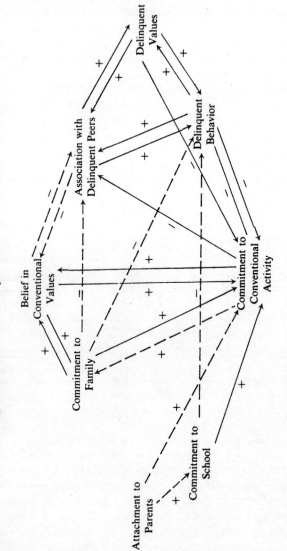

[a] Solid lines represent stronger effects; dashed lines represent weaker effects.

only commitment to conventional activities and, more weakly, delinquent behavior.

The other three variables—association with delinquent peers, delinquent values, and delinquent behavior—are still hypothesized to be embedded in an amplifying causal loop. This loop is most likely to occur among adolescents who, at earlier ages, were freed from the controlling influence of parents and school. Moreover, delinquent peers, delinquent values, and delinquent behavior further alienate the youth from parents and diminish commitment to school. Once this spiral begins, the probability of sustained delinquency increases.

If this situation continued uninterrupted it would yield ever increasing rates of crime as the subjects matured. Such an outcome is inconsistent with the evidence on desistance during this age period (Wolfgang et al., 1987). Rates of delinquency and crime begin to subside by the late teenage years, a phenomenon often attributed to "maturational reform." Such an explanation, however, is tautological since it claims that crime stops when adolescents get older, because they get older. It is also uninformative since the concept of maturational reform is theoretically undefined.

A developmental approach, however, offers an explanation for desistance. As the developmental process unfolds, life circumstances change, developmental milestones are met (or, for some, missed), new social roles are created, and new networks of attachments and commitments emerge. The effects of these changes enter the process model to explain new and often dramatically different behavioral patterns. In the present model, these changes are represented by commitment to conventional activity and commitment to family.

Commitment to conventional activity is influenced by a number of variables, including earlier attachment to parents, commitment to school, and belief in conventional values. And once the transition to work is made, tremendous opportunities are afforded for new and different effects in the delinquency model. Becoming committed to conventional activities —work, college, military service, and so on—reduces the likelihood of delinquent behavior and associations with delinquent peers because it builds up a stake in conformity that is antithetical to delinquency. Because of the increased saliency of commitment to conventional activities, the reinforcing loop is now set in motion to *reduce* rather than increase delinquent and criminal involvement.

The variable of commitment to family, at this stage only emerging, has similar, but weaker effects. Nevertheless, commitment to family is proposed to reduce both delinquent associations and delinquent values and to increase commitment to conventional activity. In general, as the individual takes on the responsibilities of family, the bond to conventional society increases, placing additional constraints on behavior and precluding further delinquency. These changes do not occur in all cases, however, nor should they be expected to since many delinquents continue on to careers in adult crime (Wolfgang et al., 1987).

The continuation of criminal careers can also be explained by the nature of the reciprocal effects. In general, extensive involvement in delinquency at earlier ages feeds back upon and weakens attachment to parents and commitment to school (see Figures 2 and 3). These variables, as well as involvement in delinquency itself, weaken later commitment to family and to conventional activities (Figure 4). Thus, these new variables, commitment to conventional activities and to family, are affected by the person's situation at earlier stages and do not "automatically" alter the probability of continued criminal involvement. If the initial bonds are extremely weak, the chances of new bonding variables being established to break the cycle toward criminal careers are low and it is likely that criminal behavior will continue.

Behavioral Trajectories

The way reciprocal effects and developmental changes are interwoven in the interactional model can be clarified by the concept of behavioral trajectories. For some youth a behavioral trajectory is established that predicts increasing involvement in delinquency and crime. The initially weak bonds in early adolescence between some youths, their parents, school, and conventional values, lead to high delinquency involvement. The high delinquency involvement further weakens the conventional bonds, and in combination both these effects make it extremely difficult to reestablish bonds to conventional society at later ages. As a result, all the factors tend to reinforce one another over time to produce an extremely high probability of continued deviance.

Alternatively, one can imagine many young adolescents who, initially, are strongly attached to their parents, highly committed to school, and believe in conventional values. The theoretical model predicts that this high level of bonding buffers them from the world of delinquency. Moreover, the reciprocal character of this loop establishes a behavioral trajectory that tends toward increasing conformity. Their initial strong conventional bonds reduce the chances of involvement in delinquency and thereby increase the chances of commitment to conventional activities and the like at later ages.

Thus, we can conceive of adolescents with differing and diverging behavioral trajectories. In one trajectory, social bonds become progressively weaker and delinquent behavior progressively more likely, while in the other commitment to conformity becomes progressively stronger and delinquent behavior progressively less likely.

Of course, if there are these extremes, there are also intermediate cases whose eventual outcome is much more in doubt. For example, some youths have a relatively high level of attachment to parents but low commitment to school (or vice versa). These adolescents are more likely candidates for delinquency involvement than are youths with both high attachment and commitment. But should delinquent involvement occur, its feedback effect on bonding is less certain. While delinquency may further reduce the already weak commitment to school, strong attachment to parents may serve as a buffer to offset some of the negative feedback. Such a situation allows for varied patterns of interactive effects as the developmental process unfolds. Moreover, the prediction of the eventual outcome for such youths awaits more direct empirical evidence establishing the relative strength of these competing effects.

The concept of behavioral trajectories raises the important theoretical issue that the initial values of process variables play a central role in the entire process since they set the basic path of the behavioral trajectories. Therefore, it is theoretically important to account for their initial variation. By way of illustration the role of one such variable, position in the social structure, is explored.

Structural Effects

Structural variables, including race, class, gender, and community of residence, refer to the person's location in the structure of social roles and statuses. How they are incorporated in the interactional model is illustrated here by examining social class. Although social class is often measured continuously, a categorical approach using: (1) the lower class, (2) the working lower class, and (3) the middle class, is more consistent with the present model. The lower class comprises those chronically or sporadically unemployed, who receive welfare, and subsist at or below the poverty level; some have called them the "underclass" (Johnson, 1979). The working lower class comprises those with more stable work patterns, training for semiskilled jobs, and incomes that allow for some economic stability. For these families, however, the hold on even a marginal level of occupational and economic security is always tenuous. Finally, the middle class refers to all families above these lower-levels. Middle-class families have achieved some degree of economic success and stability and can reasonably expect to remain at that level or improve their standing over time.

The way social class of origin affects the interactional variables and the behavioral trajectories can be demonstrated by comparing the life expectancies of children from lower and middle-class families. Compared to children from a middle-class background, those from a lower-class background are more apt to have (1) disrupted family processes and environments (Conger et al., 1984; Wahler, 1980); (2) poorer preparation for school (Cloward and Ohlin, 1960); (3) belief structures influenced by the traditions of the American lower class (Miller, 1958; Anderson, 1976); and (4) greater exposure to neighborhoods with high rates of crime (Shaw and McKay, 1942; Braithwaite, 1981). The direction of all these effects is such that we would expect children from lower-class families to be *initially* less bonded to conventional society and more exposed to delinquent values, friends, and behaviors.

As one moves toward the working lower class, both the likelihood and the potency of the above factors decrease. As a result, the initial values of the interactional variables improve but, because of the tenuous nature of economic and social stability for these families, both the bonding variables and the delinquency variables are still apt to lead to considerable amounts of delinquent conduct. Finally, youths from middle-class families, having greater stability and economic security, are likely to start with a stronger family structure, greater stakes in conformity, and higher chances of success, and these factors are likely to reduce the likelihood of initial delinquent involvement.

In brief, the initial values of the interactional variables are systematically related to the social class of origin. Moreover, since these variables are reciprocally related, it follows logically that social class is systematically related to the behavioral trajectories described above. Youngsters from the lowest classes have the highest probability of moving forward on a trajectory of increasing delinquency (Wolfgang et al., 1987).

In contrast, the expected trajectory of middle-class youths suggests that they will move toward an essentially conforming lifestyle in which their stakes in conformity increase and increasingly preclude serious and prolonged involvement in delinquency. Finally, because the initial values of the interactional variables are mixed and indecisive for children from lower working-class homes, their behavioral trajectories are much more volatile and the outcome much less certain.

Summary: Interactional theory asserts that both the initial values of the process variables and their development over time are systematically related to the social class of origin. Moreover, parallel arguments can be made for other structural variables, such as race, ethnicity, gender, and the social disorganization of the neighborhood. Like class of origin, these variables are systematically related to variables such as commitment to school and involvement in delinquent behavior, and as a group, they set the stage on which the reciprocal effects develop across the life cycle.

Conclusion

The present article has developed an interactional theory of delinquent behavior. Unlike traditional theories of delinquency, interactional theory does not view delinquency merely as an outcome or consequence of a social process but as an active part of the developmental process, interacting with other social factors over time to determine a person's ultimate behavioral repertoire.

Initial impetus toward delinquency comes from a weakening of the person's bond to convention, represented during adolescence by attachment to parents, commitment to school, and belief in conventional values. When these three links to conformity are attenuated, there is a substantially increased potential for delinquent behavior. For this freedom to be converted to delinquency, especially prolonged serious delinquency, a social setting in which delinquency is learned and reinforced is required. This is represented by associations with delinquent peers and delinquent values. These two variables, along with delinquent behavior itself, form a mutually reinforcing causal loop that leads toward increasing delinquency involvement over time.

Moreover, this interactive process develops over the life cycle, and the saliency of the theoretical concepts varies with age. During early adolescence, the family is the most influential factor in bonding the youth to conventional society and reducing delinquency. As the youth matures and moves through middle adolescence, friends, school, and youth culture become the dominant influences over behavior. Entering adulthood, commitment to conventional activities and to family offer a number of new avenues to reshape the person's bond to society and involvement with delinquency.

Finally, interactional theory posits that these process variables are systematically related to the person's position in the social structure. Class, minority-group status, gender, and the social disorganization of the neighborhood of residence all affect the initial values of the interactive variables as well as the behavioral trajectories. Youths from the most socially disadvantaged backgrounds begin the process least bonded to conventional society and most exposed to the world of delinquency. Furthermore, the reciprocal nature of the process increases the chances that they will continue on to a career of serious criminal involvement. In contrast, youths from middle-class families enter a trajectory which is strongly oriented toward conformity and away from delinquency.

But regardless of the initial starting points or the eventual outcome, the essential point of interactional theory is that the causal process is a dynamic one that develops over the person's lifetime. And delinquent behavior is a vital part of that process; it is clearly affected by, but it also affects, the bonding and learning variables that have always played a prominent role in sociological explanations of delinquency.

Epilogue

The version of interactional theory presented here is an initial statement of this perspective and does not represent a complete model of all the factors that are associated with delinquency. For example, the role of other structural variables, especially race and gender, which are so strongly correlated with delinquency, has to be fully explicated to better understand the sources of both the delinquency and bonding variables. Similarly, greater attention needs to be paid to the influence of early childhood behaviors and family processes since it is increasingly clear that delinquency is part of a progressive sequence that begins at much earlier ages (Patterson and Dishion, 1985; Loeber and Stouthamer-Loeber, 1986). In addition, other process variables similar to those incorporated in Figures 2 through 4 need to be considered. For example, the general issue of gang membership and co-offending should be examined in an interactional setting, as should concepts such as self-concept and self-efficacy. Finally, developmental stages have been represented here by rough age categories, and they require more careful and precise definition in terms of physical maturation and psychological growth.

28

Turning Points in the Life Course: Why Change Matters to the Study of Crime

John H. Laub and Robert J. Sampson

Criminological attention has recently been redirected to the importance of childhood. Gottfredson and Hirschi (1990) argue that effective child rearing in the early formative years produces high self-control, which is a stable phenomenon inhibiting crime throughout the life course. Wilson and Herrnstein (1985) consider constitutional differences (e.g., impulsiveness and temperament) in interaction with familial factors (see also Grasmick et al., 1993; Nagin and Paternoster, 1991). These works build on Sheldon and Eleanor Glueck's (see Glueck and Glueck, 1950, 1968) classic longitudinal study of five hundred delinquents and five hundred nondelinquents. Their primary thesis was that childhood temperament and family socialization matter most, and thus the "past is prologue" (Glueck and Glueck, 1968:167). However, profound questions can be raised regarding the childhood-stability argument. Are differences in child rearing and temperament all we need to understand patterns of adult crime? Are childhood differences in antisocial behavior invariably stable? Why does continuity in deviant behavior exist? What about individual change, salient life events, and turning points in adulthood?

Challenged by these questions, we have examined crime and deviance in childhood, adolescence, and adulthood, aware of both continuity *and* change over the life course. We synthesized and integrated the criminological literature on childhood antisocial behavior, adolescent delinquency, and adult crime with theory and research on the life course (Sampson and Laub, 1992). By rethinking longitudinal research findings, we developed an age-graded theory of informal social control to explain crime and deviance over the life span. We then tested this theory on the Gluecks' longitudinal data set (Sampson and Laub, 1993).

Edited and abridged from *Criminology*, Volume 31(3):301–25 (1993).

Here, we examine the conceptual issues relating to continuity and change in antisocial behavior over the life course. We highlight the distinction between self-selection and cumulative continuity and then unite the ideas of state dependence (Nagin and Paternoster, 1991) and cumulative continuity (Caspi and Moffitt, 1993a; Moffitt, 1993) in delineating a developmental, sequential model of crime across the life course. We explicate the relevance of the adult life course and various meanings of change. Our thesis is that social capital and turning points are important concepts in understanding processes of change in the adult life course. We illustrate these concepts using qualitative life-history data drawn from the Gluecks' study. We aim to challenge theories of crime which "presuppose a developmental determinism in which childhood experiences set the course of later development" (Bandura, 1982:747). To set the stage, we briefly highlight the theoretical framework on change from our recent study (Sampson and Laub, 1993).

An Age-Graded Theory of Informal Social Control

The central idea of social control theory—that crime and deviance are more likely when an individual's bond to society is weak or broken—is an organizing principle in our theory of social bonding over the life course. The life course has been defined as "pathways through the age differentiated life span" (Elder, 1985:17), the "sequence of culturally defined age-graded roles and social transitions that are enacted over time" (Caspi et al., 1990:15). Two central concepts underlie the analysis of life-course dynamics. A *trajectory* is a pathway or line of development over the life span, such as work life, parenthood, and criminal behavior. Trajectories refer to long-term patterns of behavior and are marked by a sequence of transitions. *Transitions* are marked by life events (e.g., first job or first marriage) that are embedded in trajectories and evolve over shorter time spans (Elder, 1985:31–32; Sampson and Laub, 1992).

Following Elder (1975, 1985), we differentiate the life course of individuals on the basis of age and argue that the important institutions of both formal and informal social control vary across the life span. However, we emphasize the role of age-graded, *informal* social control as reflected in the structure of interpersonal bonds linking members of society to one another and to wider social institutions (e.g., work, family, school). Informal social controls "emerge as by-products of role relationships established for other purposes and are components of role reciprocities" (Kornhauser, 1978:24).

Our theoretical framework follows a developmental strategy that views causality as "best represented by a developmental network of causal factors" in which dependent variables become independent variables over time (Loeber and LeBlanc, 1990:433; Patterson et al., 1989). Moreover, developmental criminology recognizes both continuity and within-individual changes over time, focusing on "life transitions and developmental covariates . . . which may mediate the developmental course of offending" (Loeber and LeBlanc, 1990:451). This is referred to as a "stepping-stone approach" whereby factors are time ordered by age and assessed with respect to outcome variables (Farrington, 1986).

Interactional theory (Thornberry, 1987b) also embraces a developmental approach arguing that causal influences are reciprocal over the life course and that delinquency may contribute to the weakening of social bonds over time. Thornberry's perspective is also consistent with a person-centered approach to development (Magnusson and Bergman, 1988:47). By focusing on "persons" rather than "variables" and examining individual life histories over time, this strategy offers insight into the social processes of intraindividual developmental change in criminal behavior over the life course.

Our "sociogenic" developmental theory first focuses on the mediating role of informal family and school social bonds in explaining childhood and adolescent delinquency (Sampson and Laub, 1993:chaps. 4–5). The second building block incorporates the subsequent continuity in childhood and adolescent antisocial behavior that extends throughout adulthood across a variety of life's domains (e.g., crime, alcohol abuse, divorce, unemployment).

Since we believe that salient life events and social ties in adulthood can somewhat counteract the trajectories of early child development, a third and major thesis of our work is that social bonds in adulthood, especially attachment to the labor force and cohesive marriage (or cohabitation), explain criminal behavior regardless of prior differences in criminal propensity. We contend that pathways to both crime and conformity are modified by key institutions of social control in the transition to adulthood (e.g., employment, military service, and marriage).

We emphasize the quality or strength of social ties in these transitions more than the occurrence or timing of discrete life events (Loeber and LeBlanc, 1990:430–32). For example, close emotional ties and mutual investment increase the social bond between individuals and should reduce criminal behavior (Shover, 1985:94). Employment coupled with job stability, commitment to work, and mutual ties binding workers and employers should increase social control and reduce criminal behavior.

In short, our theory attempts to unite continuity and change within the context of a sociological understanding of crime in the life course. A major concept in our framework is the dynamic process whereby the interlocking nature of trajectories and transitions generates turning points or a change in life course (Elder, 1985:32). Adaptation to life events is crucial because the same event or transition followed by different adaptations can lead to different trajectories (Elder, 1985:35). Despite the connection between childhood events and experiences in adulthood, turning points can modify life trajectories—they can "redirect paths." For some, turning points are abrupt—radical "turnarounds" or changes in life history that separate the past from the future (Elder et al., 1991:215). For most, however, turning points are "part of a process over time" and not "a dramatic lasting change that takes place at any one time" (Pickles and Rutter, 1991:134; Clausen, 1990; McAdam, 1989:745; Rutter, 1989a, 1989b). The process-oriented nature of turning points leads us to focus on incremental change embedded in informal social controls.

We analyzed the natural histories of two groups of boys that differed dramatically in childhood antisocial behavior and delinquency that were followed into adulthood. We reconstructed and examined the life histories originally gathered by Glueck and Glueck (1950, 1968) of five hundred delinquents and five hundred control subjects matched on age, IQ, ethnicity, and neighborhood deprivation (see Sampson and Laub, 1993).

Distinguishing Self-Selection from Cumulative Continuity

Some argue that individual differences combine with self-selection to account for patterns of behavior across the life course. They claim that individuals with an early propensity to crime (e.g., low self-control) determined mainly by family socialization and individual differences (e.g., impulsiveness) systematically sort themselves throughout adulthood into states consistent with this latent trait. For example, Gottfredson and Hirschi (1990:164–67) argue that delinquent and impulsive youths will choose deviant spouses, unstable jobs, and continue their delinquent ways in adulthood. If true, the adult life course is merely a setting within which predetermined lives are played out.

In one sense this self-selection thesis was supported in the Gluecks' study. Adolescent delinquents and nondelinquents displayed significant behavioral consistency well into adulthood. Delinquency and other forms of antisocial conduct in childhood were related not only to adult crime, but also to troublesome behaviors across a variety of adult domains (e.g., absent without leave in the military, economic dependence, marital discord). This continuity persisted despite matching delinquents and controls case-by-case on age, intelligence, neighborhood, and ethnicity.

The self-selection hypothesis, however, leads to a more fundamental methodological implication—correlations among adult behaviors (e.g., job instability and crime) are completely spurious and should disappear once controls are introduced for prior individual-level differences in criminal propensity or low self-control (Gottfredson and Hirschi, 1990:154–68). We believe the data do not support this spuriousness hypothesis. Our quantitative analyses revealed independent effects of marital attachment and job stability on adult crime which were consistent for a wide variety of outcome measures, control variables (e.g., childhood and adolescent antisocial behavior; individual-difference constructs, such as IQ, self-control, mesomorphy, and personality), and analytic techniques—including methods that account for persistent unobserved heterogeneity in criminal propensity (Nagin and Paternoster, 1991; Rutter et al., 1990).

Our theory incorporates the causal role of prior delinquency in facilitating adult crime by integrating the concept of *state dependence* (Nagin and Paternoster, 1991) with that of *cumulative continuity* (Moffitt, 1993). In our developmental model, delinquent behavior has a systematic, attenuating effect on the social and institutional bonds linking adults to society (e.g., labor force attachment, marital cohesion). The idea of cumulative continuity posits that delinquency incrementally mortgages the future by generating negative consequences for the life chances of stigmatized and institutionalized youths. For example, arrest and incarceration may spark failure in school, unemployment, and weak community bonds, in turn increasing adult crime (Tittle, 1988:80). Serious delinquency in particular leads to the "knifing off" (Caspi and Moffitt, 1993a; Moffitt, 1993) of future opportunities such that participants have fewer options for a conventional life. The cumulative continuity of disadvantage is thus not only a result of stable individual differences in criminal propensity, but a dynamic process whereby childhood antisocial behavior and adolescent delinquency foster adult crime through the severance of adult social bonds. In this view, weak social bonding is a mediating and, hence, causal sequential link in a chain of adversity between childhood delinquency and adult criminal behavior.

The thesis of cumulative continuity was supported in our quantitative analyses. Job stability and marital attachment in adulthood were significantly related to changes in adult crime—the stronger the adult ties to work and family, the less crime and deviance among delinquents and controls. Moreover, social bonds to employment were directly influenced by state sanctions—incarceration as a juvenile and as a young adult had a negative effect on later job stability, which in turn was negatively related to continued involvement in crime over the life course. Although we found little direct effect of incarceration on subsequent criminality, the indirect "criminogenic" effects through job stability were substantively important (see also Nagin and Waldfogel, 1992).

Our synthesis of cumulative continuity and state dependence recasts in a structural and developmental framework the original contention of labeling theory—that official reactions to primary deviance (e.g., arrest) may create problems of adjustment (e.g., unemployment) that foster additional crime in the form of secondary deviance (Becker, 1963; Lemert, 1951; Tittle, 1988). Hagan and Palloni (1990) suggested that continuity in delinquent behavior may result from a structural imputation process that begins early in childhood (see also Tittle, 1988:78–81). They show that this process may even extend across generations, thereby explaining the effects of parental conviction on sons' delinquency regardless of family background and propensity to crime.

Cumulative Disadvantage and Structural Background

Hagan's (1991) research further suggests that the deleterious effect of adolescent deviance on adult stratification outcomes is greatest among lower-class boys, especially as mediated by police contacts. Middle-class boys who escaped the negative consequences of official labeling did not suffer impairment in adult occupational outcomes as a result of their adolescent delinquency. Avoiding the snares of arrest and institutionalization provided opportunities for prosocial attachments among middle-class youths to take firm hold in adulthood. Jessor et al. (1991) show that for middle-class youths, delinquency is not a major handicap with respect to adult outcomes. These studies suggest that the concepts of knifing off and cumulative continuity are most salient in explaining the structurally constrained life chances of the disadvantaged urban poor.

In short, there is evidence that cumulative disadvantage, state dependence, and location in the class structure may interact. Among those in advantaged positions that provide continuity in social resources over time, nondelinquents and delinquents alike are presumably not just more motivated, but better able structurally to establish binding ties to conventional lines of adult activity. If nothing else, incumbency in prosocial middle-class roles provides advantages in maintaining the status quo and counteracting negative life events (e.g., last hired, first fired). Race, class, and crime pervade the consciousness of American society more generally and employers in particular, an is especially reflected through discrimination in hiring (Kirschenman and Neckerman, 1991). We therefore merge the state dependence thesis that historical time matters with a concern for structural location. The context of where and how long one has been in prior states is crucial to understanding later adult development.

Self-Selection Reconsidered

Our theoretical conceptualization of cumulative continuity and the causal role of the adult life course does not negate the potential direct or unmediated effect of self-selection through individual differences. By distinguishing self-selection from cumulative continuity, we incorporate the independent effects of early delinquency (or individual propensity) and the dimensions of adult social bonding on adult crime. This distinction is consistent with recent research on homophily—deviant individuals selecting deviant marriage or cohabitation partners in social choices across the life course (Kandel et al., 1990; Caspi et al., 1990). Nevertheless, social causation emerges as a crucial factor even in the face of such social selection. Kandel et al. (1990:221) state, "Although individual choices are made, in part, as a function of the individual's prior attributes, values, and personality characteristics, involvement in the new relationship has further effects and influences on that individual" (see also Rutter et al., 1990).

The emergence of significant social causation in tandem with homophily (or self-selection) undermines the theoretical individualism that pervades social scientific thought. We believe that an overemphasis on self-selection in social science stems from a

> broadly perpetuated fiction in modern society. . . that society consists of a set of independent individuals, each of whom acts to achieve goals that are independently arrived at, and that the functioning of the social system consists of the combinations of the actions of independent individuals. (Coleman, 1990:300)

Rather, social interdependence arises from the fact that actors have social investments in events and relationships that are partially under the control of other actors. Hence, the interdependent web of relations characteristic of social collectivities ensures the operation of constraints and opportunities in shaping behavior, notwithstanding individual intentions.

Why Change Still Matters

Whatever its source, a focus on stability is insufficient for understanding crime in the adult life course. First, the stability of antisocial behavior is difficult to reliably predict (Loeber and Stouthamer-Loeber, 1987; Farrington and Tarling, 1985). This reinforces the futility of an invariant or deterministic conception of human development (Jessor et al., 1991; Sampson and Laub, 1992).

Second, measures of stability refer to the consistency of between-individual differences over time and consequently rely on an aggregate picture of relative standing. The heterogeneity of individual behaviors over time are not measured and, hence, stability coefficients do not capture within-individual change (Huesmann et al., 1984:1131).

Life is dynamic; change is clearly possible. Yet the theoretical conceptualization of change has been surprisingly neglected (see Farrington, 1988; Sampson and Laub, 1992).

Social Capital and Turning Points

We think of change along a continuum and investigate the underlying processes that enable people to change the course of their lives. We believe this may be accomplished by viewing the life course as a probabilistic linkage or chain of events (Rutter et al., 1990) and by unraveling the mechanisms that operate at key turning points (e.g., when a risk trajectory is recast to a more adaptive path [Rutter, 1987:329]).

Of the different definitions of change, most interesting are: (1) "deep" change or "real" change—e.g., a high-rate offender who suddenly desists and becomes a productive citizen (Caspi and Moffitt, 1993a); and (2) "modified" change—e.g. a high-rate offender who begins to commit fewer crimes than expected (based on age and prior criminal propensity) because his or her trajectory has been modified. Both types of change are enhanced when changing roles and environments lead to social investment or *social capital* (Coleman, 1988, 1990; Nagin and Paternoster, 1992) in institutional relationships (e.g., family, work, community). As Coleman (1990:302) argues, the distinguishing feature of social capital lies in the structure of interpersonal relations and institutional linkages. Social capital is created when these relations change in ways that facilitate action: "social capital is productive, making possible the achievements of certain ends that in its absence would not be possible" (Coleman, 1988:98). By contrast, physical capital is wholly tangible, being embodied in observable material form (1990:304), and human capital is embodied in the skills and knowledge acquired by an individual. Social capital is even less tangible, for it is embodied in the relations among persons (1990:304). A core idea, then, is that independent of the forms of physical and human capital available to individuals (e.g., income, occupational skill), social capital is a central factor in facilitating effective ties that bind a person to societal institutions.

Linking Coleman's notion of social capital to social control theory, we have argued that the lack of social capital or investment is one of the primary features of weak social bonds (Sampson and Laub, 1993; see also

Coleman, 1990:307; Nagin and Paternoster, 1992). The theoretical task is to identify the characteristics of social relations that facilitate the social capital available to individuals, families, employers, and other social actors. One of the most important factors is the closure (i.e., "connectedness") of networks among actors in a social system (Coleman, 1990:318–20). In a system involving employers and employees, for example, relations characterized by an extensive set of obligations, expectations, and interdependent social networks are better able to facilitate social control than are jobs characterized by purely utilitarian objectives and nonoverlapping social networks. Similarly, the mere presence of a relationship (e.g., marriage) among adults is not sufficient to produce social capital, and hence the idea of social capital goes beyond simple structural notions of role change (i.e., married versus not married) to capture the idea of embeddedness.

We maintain that adult social ties are important insofar as they create interdependent systems of obligation and restraint that impose significant costs for translating criminal propensities into action. Adults will be inhibited from committing crime to the extent that over time they accumulate social capital in their work and family lives, regardless of delinquent background. By contrast, those subject to weak systems of interdependency (see also Braithwaite, 1989) and informal social control as an adult (e.g., weak attachment to the labor force or noncohesive marriage) are freer to commit deviance—even if nondelinquent as a youth. This dual premise enables us to explain desistance from crime as well as late onset, and it is consistent with Jessor et al.'s (1991:160) argument that change is "as much an outcome of the person's embeddedness in a socially organized and structured context of age-related roles, expectations, demands, and opportunities as it is of internal dispositions and intentions."

We also emphasize the reciprocal nature of social capital invested by employers and spouses. For example, employers often take chances in hiring workers, hoping that their investment will pay off. Similarly, a prospective marriage partner may be aware of a potential spouse's deviant background but may nonetheless invest his or her future in that person. This investment by the employer or spouse may in turn trigger a return investment in social capital by the employee or other spouse. The key theoretical point is that social capital and interdependency are reciprocal and embedded in the social ties that exist between individuals and social institutions.

Sullivan's (1989) research on gangs in New York provides insight into racial, ethnic, and community differences in the influence of social capital on transitions to work. As they entered young adulthood, the men in the low-income white neighborhood secured better-quality jobs than men in

African American or Hispanic neighborhoods. Whites were also better able to hold onto these jobs, in part because of their familiarity with the "discipline of the workplace" gained through personal networks and intergenerational ties (1989:100–105). Networks with the adult community thus differentiated the chances of white youths' escaping environmental adversity from those of their minority counterparts. In a similar vein, Anderson (1990) points to the importance of racial differences in intergenerational ties and the salience of those ties in facilitating employment among young males as they enter adulthood. These ethnographies underscore variations by race, ethnicity, and structural context in social capital and its role in promoting successful transitions to young adulthood (see also Short, 1990).

Thus, because individual-difference constructs and childhood antisocial behavior are independent of adult social capital and structural context, another key aspect of our theory is the partially *exogenous* nature of the adult life course. This suggests that turning points can redirect behavioral trajectories in the transition to adulthood. We strongly contend that behavioral changes do occur and that adult life-course patterns are not solely the result of childhood socialization (Bandura, 1982).

A Person-Based, Life-History Approach to Change

Our research includes an intensive qualitative analysis of the life-history records for a subset of men from the Gluecks' study (see Sampson and Laub, 1993:chap. 9). We adopt a "person oriented" strategy that allows us to explore "patterns or configurations of relevant person characteristics in a developmental perspective" (Magnusson and Bergman, 1990:101). This enables investigation of person-environment interactions, sequences of action, and individual change over time (see Abbott, 1992; Cairns, 1986; Magnusson and Bergman, 1988:47).

Consistent with our goal of integrating quantitative and qualitative methods, we used quantitative results to identify cases for in-depth qualitative analysis. For example, based on the finding that job stability was an important predictor of desistance from crime, we selected cases that displayed high job stability in combination with no arrest experiences as an adult. Similarly, we selected cases exhibiting low job stability and arrest experiences as an adult. When there was a sufficient number of cases we randomly selected them for in-depth analysis. We used a similar selection procedure for marital attachment. In total, we reconstructed and examined seventy life histories from the delinquent sample (see Sampson and Laub, 1993).

Integrating divergent sources of life-history data (e.g., narratives, interviews), our qualitative analysis was consistent with the hypothesis that the major turning points in the life course for men that refrained from crime and deviance in adulthood were stable employment and good marriages. As an illustration of our thesis, consider the case history of a subject we call Charlie.

Although Charlie had no official arrests during adulthood (ages seventeen to thirty two), this pattern sharply contrasted with his criminal experiences in childhood and adolescence. As a juvenile, Charlie had ten arrests, (primarily larcenies and burglaries). His first arrest occurred at age eight. He was incarcerated three times (first at age eleven), and spent a total of thirty months confined in reform schools.

At eighteen, Charlie joined the U.S. Maritime Service. He was employed by the same shipping line for two and a half years, working the eastern seaboard from Canada to Cuba. Once every three months, he returned home. Charlie gave virtually all his earnings to his mother to bank for him. His parole officer speculated that Charlie joined the merchant service to remove himself from detrimental neighborhood influences that were leading him to delinquency and crime. During this same period (ages eighteen to twenty), Charlie began a relationship with a woman whom he would marry. Although classmates together in high school, they began "an active courtship via letters" while Charlie was in the merchant service.

Married at age twenty one, Charlie was living with his wife in East Boston at age twenty five. He was devoted to his wife, and the couple appeared especially united in their mutual desire to advance economically. Their goal was to build their own home. Charlie appreciated his wife's cooperation and her enduring help and desire to advance economically. Accounting for why he reformed, Charlie explained, "I'm married, older, and settled down now."

Charlie's life did not change very much at his age thirty two interview. He was living with his wife and two children in a suburb near Boston. Charlie appeared happy and was especially devoted to his two children. In his spare time, he worked on home improvement. Throughout the period of age twenty five to thirty two, Charlie worked at one job and had recently been promoted to foreman. He had been a machine operator at the factory where he now acted as the foreman. From interviewer notes, Charlie was described as an industrious worker with no problems on the job whatsoever.

We selected other cases for qualitative analyses that demonstrated a change in social bonds (a general measure combining job stability and marital attachment) from age twenty five to thirty two. Our analysis revealed evidence of both incremental and abrupt change. Incremental change usually occurred over a period of time in the context of an ongoing relationship or institutional affiliation (e.g., marriage); abrupt change was linked to a single event (e.g., entering the military).

We also examined the investment processes involved in social capital formation through the development of strong marital ties. Marital investment is a reciprocal process between husbands and wives that, if successful, encourages desistance from crime because of the strength of social relations built up in the family. (See Laub and Sampson, 1993, for detailed illustrations).

Another set of cases we examined pointed to the military as a "settling influence" or turning point in the life course (see also Elder, 1986; Sampson and Laub, 1996). Given the available information in the Gluecks' case files, it is hard to uncover exactly what it was about the military experience that facilitated a change in behavior. Also, our finding of a positive influence is somewhat surprising, given our results on the continuity of antisocial behavior from adolescence into adult domains, including misconduct in the military (see Sampson and Laub, 1993:chap. 6). However, it is not inconsistent that the military can function to turn some men's lives around even as it disrupts other men's lives (Elder, 1986) or that it provides yet another setting for some men to continue their criminal and deviant behavior (Gottfredson and Hirschi, 1990:165).

We also examined a subset of men who experienced a significant decline in social bonding from ages twenty five to thirty two. In these cases it was difficult to detect clear turning points, but nevertheless certain patterns did emerge. For some men, a decline in job stability was due to changes in the labor market. Not surprisingly, layoffs, seasonal work, and factory closings all contributed to the weakening of ties to work. Clearly, macrolevel transformations of the economy bear on individual lives.

For several other cases the following scenario emerged. The subject married young, and often the marriage was forced due to pregnancy. Although prior to marriage there was some evidence of excessive drinking by the subject, the subject's wife claimed that he had matured into his familial responsibilities, and initially the couple got along well. Work was typically seasonal (e.g., construction work) and weather-dependent. But as the men became older (and while one would normally expect an increasing "conformity" or settling down), ties to marriage and work unraveled. There were separations, followed by reconciliations, followed by further separations. There was often evidence of physical abuse and nonsupport of children. The subject's wife objected to his drinking and was not pleased by the financial uncertainty of seasonal work. The subject resented what he perceived to be "overprotectiveness" on the part of his wife and claimed she "nagged" him. Often the subject's drinking continued to be a problem, exacerbated in part by the fact that in certain jobs drinking seemed to be tolerated or even encouraged (Vaillant,

1983:96–97). As a result, crime and deviance became more pronounced due to the severing of social ties to work and family.

Implications for Future Research

As Clausen (1990) argues, the idea of turning points is an important concept in the study of lives. Turning points are closely linked to role transitions, and conceptually, they are helpful in understanding change in human behavior over the life course. We adapted this perspective to explore turning points in the lives of a sample of disadvantaged, persistent adolescent delinquents. Some positive turning points in the course of their lives were cohesive marriage, meaningful work, and serving in the military. Clear negative turning points were prolonged incarceration, heavy drinking, and subsequent job instability during the transition to young adulthood.

Having established that change does in fact occur, the key research question for the future becomes: Why do some individuals change while others do not? Learning more about turning points—especially in the transition from adolescence to adulthood—is critical for understanding the development of social capital and the facilitation of change in life trajectories. For example, what predicts strong marital attachment in adulthood? How do troubled youths achieve job stability and a strong commitment to work as adults? Is military service an effective vehicle for reshaping the life course of disadvantaged youths? What roles do structural factors and historical context play in determining strong bonds to family and work? More generally, how does one explain differential change among individuals?

Although these questions are complex and form the basis of our current work, we advance some tentative hypotheses. One is simply that there is an element of luck, randomness, or chance operating throughout the course of life (Bandura, 1982). A more explicit theorizing of the roles of chance, "adventitious happenings" (Rutter, 1989b:33) or what Short and Strodtbeck (1965) many years ago called "aleatory" elements, may help to capture dynamic etiological processes.

The confluence of objective and subjective contingencies is also important in understanding the change process. In all likelihood, transitions involving structural role change, like marriage and employment, do not have the same meaning for everyone (Rutter, 1989a:20). Structural role changes only provide the possibility for change to occur—its realization is mediated by individual contingencies. Hence, there is a need to conceptualize and measure objective and subjective elements of turning points.

Macro-opportunity structures for marriage and the labor market also play central roles. Research on work and occupations shows that employment outcomes have as much to do with structural features of the labor market (e.g., vacancy chains, segmentation of the labor market, ethnic enclaves) as it does with individual predispositions to work (Rosenbaum, 1984; Rosenfeld, 1992). Similarly, network and exchange theory emphasize the importance of role multiplexity and interdependence that combine with other structural features of collective life to introduce numerous avenues for positive and negative change (Cook and Whitmeyer, 1992). The channeling of prior differences and the tendency toward cumulation of advantage and disadvantage in employment (e.g., increasing inequality over time) are so general that they have been referred to as the "Matthew effect" (Dannefer, 1987:216). Labor market research thus motivates a deeper appreciation of contextual forces and opportunity structures in shaping the life transitions of young adults.

Relatedly, variations in criminal propensity (e.g., low self-control) are incomplete as an explanation of adult crime because the latter's realization is dependent on criminal opportunity (e.g., lack of guardianship or surveillance; suitable targets). Ties to work and family in adulthood restrict many criminal opportunities and thus reduce the probability that criminal propensities will be translated into action. Some turning points in life may also reflect changes in the availability or profitability of criminal strategies (see Cohen and Machalek, 1988). We further recognize that some turning points may provide the opportunity for exposure to criminal and deviant peer networks. Moreover, it is possible that as social ties to criminal and deviant networks become stronger over time, one is less likely to abandon them.

Cumulative continuity and processes of change are likely to interact with race and structural location (Hagan, 1991; Jessor et al., 1991). There is increasing evidence that the probability of adolescent risks becoming transmuted into adverse adult circumstances is greatest among those in disadvantaged racial and economic positions. Research is needed to specify the dependence of trajectories on structural location.

Turning points and developmental change are bounded by historical context as well. The men in the Gluecks' study grew to young adulthood in a period of expanding economic opportunities during the 1950s and 1960s. They could take advantage of numerous opportunities offered by the G. I. Bill. Prospects for current cohorts may not be as promising as a result of changes in the industrial base of America (Wilson, 1987), the increase in global competition, and a decline in expectations for upward social mobility. Good jobs are harder to find and keep today than in previous decades. Moreover, the military may not be the vehicle out of poverty in the 1990s as it was during the 1940s and 1950s (Sampson and

Laub, 1996; Elder, 1986). Consistent with the life-course perspective, we thus stress the importance of conceptualizing and measuring secular change at the macrosocial level, especially through explicit cohort comparisons (see Ryder, 1965). We believe a central topic for future research is the interaction of turning points with the varying structural locations and historical contexts within which individuals make the transition to young adulthood.

Conclusion

Our dynamic conceptualization of social capital and informal social control at once incorporates stability and change in criminal behavior. Change is central to our model because we propose that variations in adult crime unexplained by childhood behavior are directly related to the strength of adult social bonds. Yet we incorporate the link between childhood and adult outcomes, positing a cumulative developmental process wherein delinquent behavior attenuates the social and institutional bonds linking adults to society (e.g., labor force attachment, marital cohesion). As such, we theorize that adult social bonds not only have important effects on adult crime in and of themselves, but help to explain the probabilistic links in the chain connecting early childhood differences and later adult crime.

The point is that adult life course matters, regardless of how one gets there. We do not deny the reality of self-selection or that persons may sometimes "create" their own environment. But once in place, those environments take on a history of their own in a way that invalidates a pure spuriousness or self-selection argument. Moreover, the self-selection view of the world is, in our opinion, much too deterministic and neglects the role of state sanctions, chance, luck, structural location, historical context, and opportunity structure in shaping the life course.

In sum, by redirecting attention to the significance of both pathways and turning points in the life course, we are optimistic about the possibilities for a new research agenda that has the potential to unify heretofore divergent conceptions of stability and change in human development. Future research is needed to examine these possibilities, especially the relative importance of stability and change throughout lives in varying contexts.

29

A General Paradigm for Understanding Criminal Behavior: Extending Evolutionary Ecological Theory

Bryan Vila

This article presents a paradigm for developing and extending Cohen and Machalek's (1988) evolutionary ecological theory of expropriative crime to encompass all criminal behavior. The evolutionary ecological approach uses the same techniques and theoretical concepts to study human behavior that behavioral ecologists use to study other organisms. It also gives special consideration to the unique properties of cultural traits used extensively by humans to adapt. The paradigm treats crime as a cultural trait whose frequency and type can evolve over time in response to such phenomena as interactions between people's routine patterns of activity, the availability and distribution of resources, modes of production, child-rearing practices, competition, and cooperation. Applying the theory enables us to integrate ecological factors that determine the opportunities for crime, microlevel factors influencing an individual's propensity to commit a criminal act at a particular point in time, and macrolevel factors influencing individual development in society over time.

Synthesizing these levels of analysis, it possible to simultaneously consider how individual variation in motivation for crime and propensities to act on that motivation in the presence of an opportunity are acquired over the life course, how opportunities for crime arise, and how all these factors evolve over time as a result of individual and group behavior. The result of this synthesis is an emphatically nondeterministic paradigm that treats human behavior as the outcome of systematic processes that are dynamic, complex, and self-reinforcing: that is, they involve ongoing interactions between many interconnected components, and the action of one component in the system affects subsequent actions of other components. This point draws attention to the importance of

Edited and abridged from *Criminology*, Volume 32(3):311–59 (1994).

intergenerational early life course, and strategic dynamics. The paradigm proposed here links crime control directly with a number of public health, educational, and child care problems. It identifies appropriate time scales for the application of different kinds of crime control strategies and for their anticipated results. Also, it requires answers to important questions before we can develop feasible long-term crime control strategies: (1) What are the limitations of strategies for reducing criminal opportunities? (2) How does individual criminality develop? (3) What strategies offer the greatest promise for reducing the probability that people will develop and retain strategic styles emphasizing criminality?

Correlates, Causes, and Policy

Much research indicates that serious crime is correlated highly with youthfulness and male gender, and that early involvement in crime predicts subsequent chronic involvement. Similarly, poverty, inequality, dysfunctional and disrupted families, inadequate socialization, and the presence of criminal opportunities seem to be important correlates of crime (e.g., Blau and Schwartz, 1984; Gottfredson and Hirschi, 1990; Land et al., 1990, 1991; Reiss and Roth, 1993; Sampson and Laub, 1993; Tonry et al., 1991). These general findings seem likely to endure, although criminologists continue to debate their relative causal importance and their interrelationships. This debate obscures issues regarding the appropriate causal scope and scale for understanding and controlling crime: that is, which variables interacting in what ways should be considered, and at what levels of analysis (Short, 1985). As a result, no satisfactory unified theoretical framework has yet been developed (Elder, 1992:1126–28; Sullivan, 1992; Tittle, 1985).

This article presents a paradigm for the systematic and complete organization of information and empirically supported theoretical insights from the many disciplines that study crime. From such a general paradigm we may establish a unified framework to guide research and policy that goes beyond the fragmented, short-sighted, and ineffective approaches that presently reinforce perceptions of crime as an intractable problem.

General Theories

Partial Theories

Although a number of "general" theories of crime have been proposed, no single perspective has been able to integrate causal factors across important ecological (environmental and situational), microlevel (intrinsic to the individual), and macrolevel (social structural and economic) domains to explain the full scope of criminal behavior. For example, Wilson and Herrnstein (1985) provide an exhaustive review of microlevel biopsychological factors associated with the development of criminal propensities by individuals, but largely ignore macrolevel factors such as social structure, cultural beliefs, and the role of ecological interactions. Gottfredson and Hirschi (1990) attend more to ecological and macrolevel factors associated with the development of self-control, but deny that biological factors have any causal importance. Young (1994:102–16) considers interactions between ecological, macrolevel, and microlevel factors but fails to specify the systematic relationships that link them. Braithwaite (1989, 1992) links micro- and macrolevel factors and processes with the ecological organization of communities, but fails to consider how these relations evolve over time or how individuals' propensities develop over the life course. Pearson and Weiner (1985) recommend a dynamic process-oriented approach to understanding how interactions between ecological, micro-, and macrolevel factors affect social learning and rational behavior in individuals, but they neglect the reciprocal influence of these individuals on the evolution of macrolevel factors and on ecological and biological changes. Others (e.g., Agnew, 1992; Elliott et al., 1979) lay a foundation for understanding how individuals' propensities develop over the life course in response to micro- and macrolevel factors, but ignore biological and ecological factors that influence criminal behavior.

Sampson and his colleagues address nearly all the salient relationships. For example, Sampson and Laub (1993) describe how macrolevel factors influence individuals over the life course via systematic links to family relations and the institutions of school and work. Sampson and Groves (1989; also see Sampson, 1988, 1991) identify how these factors are affected by the ecological organization of communities. These scholars, however, avoid discussing the role of biological factors and do not account for the evolution of macrolevel factors over time (see also Thornberry et al., 1994). Similarly, Farrington (1986) explains crime as the product of a chain of processes involving biological, microlevel, and ecological factors that influence what is desired, which strategies are selected to obtain desiderata, and what situational and opportunity factors affect decision making. He does not, however, deal with the evolution of macrolevel and ecological factors.

Developmental psychologists have focused more broadly on the etiology of antisocial behavior. For example, Moffitt (1993) and Patterson and his colleagues (Patterson et al., 1989, 1992) take into account generational and life span issues as well as demographic, micro-, and macrolevel factors. Yet they ignore the roles played by criminal opportunities and by factors associated with the evolution of criminal behaviors and social responses to crime. All these factors must be understood together before we can explain, predict, or adequately control crime.

The paradigm presented below is fundamentally different from earlier ones. Each of the perspectives mentioned thus far has attempted to show how analysis of variables within a favored domain, or associated with a particular construct or set of constructs, could be used to explain all or most aspects of criminal behavior. Each of these perspectives understandably has tended to be largely congruent with its authors' academic disciplines—disciplines whose boundaries exist in our minds and institutions, but not in reality. The paradigm suggested here similarly has its roots in the "interdiscipline" of evolutionary ecology, but it uses a problem-oriented, rather than a discipline-oriented, approach to understanding criminal behavior. For example, this approach does not ask, "How can one reconcile or integrate 'strain,' 'control,' 'labeling,' 'social learning,' and . . . *theories*?" (e.g., Pearson and Weiner, 1985). Instead it asks, "What relationships and processes tend to be fundamentally important for understanding changes over time in the resource-acquisition and -retention behaviors of any social organism?" This question focuses attention on the dynamic interactions between causal factors and domains rather than on competition between theories.

An Extension of Cohen and Machalek's General Theory

The paradigm presented here attempts to extend and modify Cohen and Machalek's (1988) evolutionary ecological general theory of expropriative crime to account for all forms of criminal behavior. It shows how their theory can be applied to all crimes, changes their original framework to acknowledge the motivational aspects of criminal opportunities, and identifies three fundamentally different types of counterstrategies to crime. Cohen and Machalek's theory explains only crimes in which material or symbolic resources are expropriated. Here I extend their theory to encompass any crime requiring intent by proposing that all crimes involve the use of force, fraud, or stealth and by focusing on the *primary* type of resource a crime is intended to acquire. Many crimes provide offenders with multiple types of resources. For example, armed robbery often is attractive as a source of material and hedonistic resources; it can provide money, power, and excitement (Katz, 1988; Letkemann, 1973). This assumes that obtaining one of these resources is of primary importance to an offender, whether consciously or unconsciously.

As Table 1 demonstrates, an arguably exhaustive categorization of crime requires only four types. Modifying Cohen and Machalek's theory in this way allows it to be applied to all crime and increases its generality with little loss of parsimony. It also enhances the utility of the theory for research and policy analysis by focusing attention on fundamental attributes of criminal behaviors rather than on political-legal definitions of acts as crimes; an emphasis that has confounded much past research (Sampson and Laub, 1993:252; Gottfredson and Hirschi, 1990:256).

Causal Scope

Criminal behavior is the product of a systematic process involving complex interactions between ecological, microlevel, and macrolevel factors that occur over the life course. From conception onward, the cognitive, affective, and physical attributes that people develop are influenced strongly by (1) their personal behavior and physical processes; (2) interactions with other people, groups, and institutions; and (3) interactions with the physical environment. Initially it is convenient to consider ecological, microlevel, and macrolevel factors separately. However, interactions between these types of factors are so extensive and so synergistic that a holistic understanding of crime demands that they be viewed as parts of a system rather than as distinct categories (see Haskell, 1940; Vila, 1990).

Ecological factors involve interactions between individuals, their activities in a physical environment, and their interactions with the physical environment. They include elements associated with the physical environment that can affect how people develop physically and emotionally over their lives, such as pollution, crowding, geography/topography, and recreational opportunities. For example, lead pollution from old paint or lead water pipes in a tenement may impair a child's development (e.g., Fishbein, 1990:48–49). Overcrowding may increase hostility (Baum and Paulus, 1987) or may affect the immediate fear or well-being that individuals feel from moment to moment in different physical surroundings such as hot, crowded subways, grid-locked freeways, dark, lonely parking lots, or serene parks. The environment also may influence the places where opportunities for crime occur by channeling people's movement and activities (e.g., Brantingham and Brantingham, 1981; Cohen and Felson, 1979). Ecological effects on opportunities for crime are especially important because a crime can occur only if a motivated offender and a suitable target (i.e., victim, property, or—to extend Cohen and Felson's definition of targets—illicit substance or behavior) converge in the absence of effective guardianship (someone or something capable of preventing the crime).

Table 1. Types of Crimes

Type	Example	Primary Resource Sought and Method Used
Expropriative	Theft Fraud Embezzlement	To obtain material resources such as property from another person without his/her knowing and/or willing cooperation
Expressive	Sexual assault Nonexpropriative assault Illicit drug use	To obtain hedonistic resources that increase pleasurable feelings or decrease unpleasant feelings
Economic	Narcotics trafficking Prostitution Gambling	To obtain monetary resources through profitable illegal cooperative activities
Political	Terrorism Election Fraud	To obtain political resources by using a wide variety of tactics

Macrolevel factors deal with systematic interactions between social groups. They include social structure and the variety and heterogeneity of various racial, ethnic, cultural, and productive groups as well as their behaviors, beliefs, rules, and economic relations. They encompass the group characteristics salient for understanding a particular problem, the relative distribution of the population among groups, and the flows of information, resources, and people between groups, considered by ecologists to be the conceptual dimensions of diversity (see Begon et al., 1986:700–813; O'Neill et al., 1986; Pielou, 1975). For example, macro-level factors relevant to understanding the level of economic crime (e.g., narcotics trafficking, prostitution, gambling) among different groups in a population might include differences in group beliefs about the morality of these behaviors, relative group size, migration between groups, language differences, and the strength, complexity, and direction of economic flows (see also Black, 1993).

Microlevel factors focus on how an individual becomes motivated to commit a crime where motivation results from a process in which a goal is formulated, costs and benefits are consciously or unconsciously assessed, and internal constraints are applied. The assessment of costs and benefits may be degraded by impulsivity (Dickman, 1990:95). When motivation is sufficiently strong and when an opportunity is present, a criminal act may be attempted. The relative importance of each component of this process may vary among individuals, across time, and situations. An individual's propensity to commit a criminal act at any point in time is a probabilistic function of both motivation and opportunity (Wilson and Herrnstein, 1985:531–35; Braithwaite, 1992; Clarke and Felson, 1993; Katz, 1988). Some may be motivated to actively exploit criminal opportunities offering extremely small rewards; others commit crimes only when they are presented with enormously rewarding opportunities and a small chance of being caught; still others are unlikely to commit crimes regardless of rewards. Moreover, some may be motivated by disadvantage, whereas others are motivated by elevated skills and status that provide access to lucrative, low-risk criminal opportunities (Braithwaite, 1992; Cohen and Machalek, 1988:495; Benson and Moore, 1992).

In addition to opportunity effects, an individual's motivation at a particular point in time results from interactions over the life course between biological, sociocultural, and developmental factors. Biological factors include physical size, strength, swiftness, and the excitability/reactivity of nervous and organ systems (e.g., Fishbein, 1990). Sociocultural factors influence the behavioral strategies and the personal beliefs, values, needs, and desires an individual acquires over the life course. Culturally acquired traits affect which behavioral strategies one learns how to apply (Sutherland, 1939), influence how one perceives the costs and benefits of a particular course of action (Becker, 1968), produce "strain" due to disjunctions between culturally learned desires and perceived legitimate opportunities (Merton, 1938), and influence the strength of internal "controls" against crime (Hirschi, 1969). Development is the sequential time-dependent change in individual behavior and capacity that results from reciprocal interactions between sociocultural and biological factors in an environment (Featherman and Lerner, 1985).

Although macrolevel and ecological factors are necessary for explaining and predicting crime, microlevel factors always intervene between them and a criminal act. Even though group interactions often are important in many kinds of crime (e.g., Geis, 1993), individual behavior always precedes a crime.

Interaction Effects

The paradigm presented here predicts that attempts to understand or control crime will tend to be confounded by interaction effects if they do not consider systematic links between ecological, microlevel, and macrolevel factors. Strong synergistic effects may arise because of repeated and/or multiple systematic interactions over time (e.g., see

Featherman and Lerner, 1985:662–66). For example, ecological factors that expose people to greater danger appear to be associated with microlevel increases in aggressiveness and/or fear (e.g., Perkins et al., 1993). As the number of more aggressive and/or more fearful people in a population increases, more draconian laws might be passed or productive relations might become more constrained. In turn, these macrolevel changes might lead more people to limit the geographic scope of their routine productive and recreational activities. This ecological change might tend to diminish interactions between people from different socioeconomic and ethnic groups, thus heightening suspicion and fear, and reducing cultural barriers to aggression. Over time a vicious spiral of increasing aggression, fear, and social disintegration could magnify the destructive potential of any single factor or set of factors.

Crime as Strategy

The concept that people are strategists is essential for an integrated understanding of crime (Cohen and Machalek, 1988; Vila and Cohen, 1993). Individuals or groups employ strategies to achieve desired ends, whether or not those ends are intended and consciously recognized. *Behavioral strategies* are decision-making rules that specify what to do in different situations (Axelrod, 1984:14). Which strategies people employ depends variably on both internal and external factors. The strategy a person selects may be the result of conscious attempts to calculate costs and benefits (e.g., Clarke and Cornish, 1985) as well as of socialization, habits, temperament, or instincts (e.g., Axelrod, 1984:14; Simon, 1990). Because of these social, habitual, temperamental, or instinctive effects, people need not be viewed as consistently attempting to maximize rewards. Although this approach does not preclude rational strategizing, it acknowledges that strategies often are acquired via "normal processes of socialization and social learning, and that people commonly acquire and execute . . . strategies *without any conscious awareness* of the expected costs and benefits that may derive from [them]" (Cohen and Machalek, 1994:21). Additionally, factors may influence individuals to acquire specific strategies because they are psychologically "comfortable" and/or compatible with other strategies in their repertoire, rather than because they are perceived to be optimal.

People tend to develop suites of behavioral strategies that are compatible and often synergistic. These suites tend to have identifiable *strategic styles* that characterize a person's general approach to acquiring symbolic, material, or cognitive/affective resources. Unlike specific *strategies*, acquired and modified or discarded throughout the life course, strategic styles are less mutable. Although these styles need not become fixed (e.g., see Sampson and Laub, 1993), they tend to become less plastic with age and experience. People generally exhibit a preferred style for dealing with problems by middle childhood (Dishion et al., 1991; Mann, 1973; Mischel et al., 1989; Patterson et al., 1989:329–31; Ramsey et al., 1990). The evidence for this consistency is particularly strong for aggressive and antisocial behaviors (Eron, 1987; Huesmann et al., 1984; White et al., 1990; Moffitt, 1993:679–85).

The development of stylistic consistency is reinforced by underlying dispositional differences, internal psychodynamics, social interactions, and functionality. *Dispositional differences*, "the 'familiar,' 'automatic,' 'default' behaviors in the individual's repertoire" (Caspi and Moffitt, 1993a:250), may reinforce the development of strategic styles because they are more or less compatible with particular kinds of strategies. Caspi and Moffitt (1993a, 1993c) argue that underlying dispositional differences tend especially to be reinforced when individuals find themselves under pressure in ambiguous novel situations.

Internal psychodynamics also reinforce the development of strategic styles because people need to maintain some degree of consistency between self-image and behavior in order to avoid cognitive dissonance (e.g., Aronson, 1980; Bem, 1967; Festinger, 1957).

Social interactions reinforce the development of stylistic consistency as people gravitate toward groups whose members employ, reward, and model a particular strategic style (e.g., Douglas, 1978; Thompson et al., 1990). For example, children employing coercive rather than cooperative strategies often are excluded by more conventional peers and gravitate toward groups whose members' behaviors are more similar to their own (Dishion et al., 1991:172; Thornberry et al., 1994).

Functionality also encourages the development of stylistic consistency because some strategies are compatible while others are not. For example, one major contemporary strategic style characterizes hierarchists such as bureaucrats, who use suites of strategies emphasizing formal rules and collective action. By contrast, entrepreneurs employ a very different but equally successful style emphasizing individual action and innovation.

Populations and subgroups within populations also may show evidence of coherent strategic styles. For example, the mix of strategic styles found in different birth cohorts may be influenced substantially by differences between the social environments they experience (Easterlin, 1987; Elder, 1992:1123-26; Ryder, 1965; Strauss and Howe, 1991). Stylistic differences at the population level may be even so fundamental as to constitute categorically distinct worldviews (Douglas, 1978; Thompson et al., 1990) or political and economic systems.

Criminality as a Property of Individual Strategic Style

Criminality describes the extent to which a person's strategic style emphasizes the use of force, fraud (Gottfredson and Hirschi, 1990:314), or stealth to obtain valued resources. It is characterized by self-centeredness, indifference to others, and low self-control or impulsivity (e.g., Gottfredson and Hirschi, 1990:89–90). Impulsivity is viewed as a necessary, but not sufficient, condition for criminality (Eysenck and Gudjonsson, 1989:55–89; Farrington, 1987; Robins and Ratcliff, 1979; White et al., 1994). Impulsive individuals tend to find criminality attractive because it can provide immediate gratification through relatively easy or simple strategies. These strategies are risky and thrilling, and require little skill or planning. They also often result in pain or discomfort for victims and offer few or meager long-term benefits to users because, if discovered, they can interfere with careers, family, and friendships. Although there appears to be substantial convergence between criminality and impulsivity, it is unclear how complex crimes requiring substantial forethought may be considered impulsive.

It is important to differentiate between crime and criminality. Criminality is an attribute common to all criminal behaviors, but only acts defined as such by political and legal systems are *crimes*. Although many theorists have asserted that models of criminal behavior must be specific to particular forms of crime and attend to tactical differences between, say, fraud, burglary, assault, or rape (e.g., Clarke and Cornish, 1985), the present paradigm focuses on strategic commonalities. Indeed, Gottfredson and Hirschi (1990:256) assert that most contemporary criminological research is flawed because it fails to distinguish between criminality and illegal criminal acts, allowing the state rather than the scientist to define the dependent variable (also see Sampson and Laub, 1993:252). Research that confuses these concepts is confounded because it treats different types of crimes as unique behaviors. In contrast, this paradigm treats them as highly situation-specific manifestations of an underlying strategic style favoring behaviors that are impulsive, self-centered, or harmful to others—many of which may not be considered criminal.

As Gottfredson and Hirschi argue, this means that the "within-person causes of truancy are the same as the within-person causes of drug use, aggravated assault, and auto accidents" (1990:256). Suicide, a leading source of mortality for adolescents and young adults, also seems often to be characterized by an impulsive unwillingness to discount short-term anguish in favor of longer-term goals (see Apter et al., 1993; Fishbein et al., 1992; Paul, 1990; Plutchik and van Praag, 1989). This conception of crime explains the wide variety of criminal activity, the fact that individuals tend not to specialize in one type of crime, and the simplicity and immediacy of benefits associated with criminal behavior (Gottfredson and Hirschi, 1990). It also is consistent with the general stability of individual criminality over long periods. Insofar as the "aging out of crime" phenomenon associated with middle adulthood is not confounded by differences between "adolescence-limited" and "life-course-persistent" antisocial behavior (see Cohen and Vila, 1996:144–47; Moffitt, 1993), it generally appears to be characterized by a shift toward fewer *illegal* behaviors rather than by changing behavioral style (e.g., Aronson, 1976, 1980; Blumstein et al., 1988; McCord, 1991; Mischel et al., 1989; Nagin and Paternoster, 1991; Wolfgang et al., 1972).

Although crimes that are carefully planned and patiently executed account for an extremely small proportion of all *reported* crimes, they might appear to threaten the generality of this paradigm. Privileged perpetrators such as Charles Keating and Ivan Boesky, who carefully planned and executed their crimes over long periods, certainly appear to have been self-centered and indifferent to the suffering of others. But were they more similar to "street" criminals on the dimension of impulsiveness than to peers who had similar opportunities for illicit gains? Wheeler (1992) offers some insight into this important empirical question. He characterizes the motivation of white-collar criminals, especially those involved in large-scale endeavors, as arising largely from greed, a tendency to seek risks, and/or strong aversion to failure. This constellation of terms is arguably congruent with self-centeredness, indifference to the suffering of others, and impulsiveness. Striking examples of these attributes are described in Calavita and Pontell's (1990, 1991, 1993) analysis of fraud in the thrift and insurance industries and in Jesilow et al.'s (1993:132–46) analysis of Medicaid fraud.

Critical Quagmires and Population-Level Strategic Styles

Power and privilege can provide especially attractive opportunities for expressing criminality, whether in the form of behaviors that are defined as crimes or those that are not. Crime in the suites often is more difficult to detect than crime in the streets, vast resources can purchase superb legal protection, and penalties arguably tend to be minimal when compared with criminal gains or the damage incurred by society. Sometimes, too, powerful individuals or groups can avoid having their expressions of criminality defined legally as crimes. Focusing on *criminality* rather than on political-legal definitions allows analysis of the causes of criminal behavior to finesse the perplexing problem of why some acts are defined as crimes, while similar, possibly more damaging, acts are not (e.g., Abadinsky, 1993:135). This question is important and central to conflict theories and critical theories of crime (e.g., Greenberg, 1981; Quinney, 1970; Sellin, 1938; Turk, 1969). Yet because conflict and critical theories focus on systematically deeper power relations between competing interest groups, they seldom provide feasible policy alternatives (Nettler, 1984a:202–3) and tend to reinforce perceptions of crime as an unsolvable problem.

Emphasizing individual-level characteristics does not necessarily place critical and conflict concerns outside the domain of this paradigm. Rather it underscores the importance of the effects of power relations on individuals over the course of their lives and on groups of individuals from generation to generation (see Wilson, 1987). Moreover, like individuals, populations and groups may be more or less impulsive, prone to use force rather than persuasion, and indifferent to the needs and suffering of outsiders. This point is important. For example, of the three categories of counterstrategies for controlling crime that I present later, the United States has emphasized aggressive strategies that provide immediate gratification to the public (see Pepinsky, 1991; Quinney and Wildeman, 1991) rather than more nurturant long-range approaches. Thus criminality might characterize styles of strategies at the population as well as the individual level. The potential importance of this insight emerges when one considers how reciprocal interactions between individuals and groups lead to the evolution of culture at the population level.

Evolutionary and Ecological Interactions

Culture as a Basis for Evolution

The paradigm recommends an evolutionary ecological approach (Cohen and Machalek, 1988) to identify what factors interacting in which ways appear to have the greatest influence on criminal behavior. This approach is *evolutionary* in the sense that the characteristics and relative frequency of behavioral strategies evolve over time via the differential transmission of cultural information between individuals in a population. Researchers from many disciplines have argued that because natural selection may operate on both genetic and nongenetic informational media, evolutionary reasoning is appropriate for the study of culture—as long as media-specific differences in evolutionary mechanisms and processes are taken into account (e.g., Anderson et al., 1988; Boyd and Richerson, 1985, 1992; Calvin, 1990; Cavalli-Sforza and Feldman, 1981; Cohen and Machalek, 1988:491; Dawkins, 1980; Holland, 1992; Lumsden and Wilson, 1981).

Both culture and genes are a means of conveying *information*. Genes code information via the arrangement of molecules in a chain; that information is transmitted, primarily by sexual reproduction, from one generation to the next (i.e., parents to child). Our biological selves, which are structured according to genetic instructions, code cultural information in a variety of forms such as spoken and written language, visual media, and memory. Thus cultural information can be transmitted readily from parent to child, from child to parent, between friends or strangers, and across many generations. Cultural traits such as criminal strategies may be "inherited" through social learning. More successful traits are more likely to be transmitted and hence to become more common over time (Vila and Cohen, 1993).

Ecology and Evolution

As is the case with evolution in purely biological acultural systems, cultural evolution results from ecological interactions over time between the members of a population and between individuals and environmental factors. These interactions create an opportunity structure in human populations in which the dimensions of resource niches are influenced strongly by social factors. Individuals acquire resources from a particular niche by employing behavioral strategies such as production, cooperation, violence, fraud, or stealth. Their success at acquiring resources from that niche depends on factors such as access, the amount of competition encountered, and compatibility between their strategies or attributes and the niche (Elder, 1992:1125; Cohen and Machalek, 1994).

Debunking Determinism

Theories that acknowledge a role for biological factors in influencing human behavior—or even use the terms *evolution* or Darwinian—often are discounted out of hand by social scientists as deterministic or irrelevant because they are incompatible with human free agency. Moreover, it often is claimed, that even if biology plays a role it does not provide information about how to deal with social problems because biological characteristics are immutable. Worse still is the possibility that any acceptance of a role for biological factors opens the door to the horrors of eugenics and racism. These misconceptions are clearly inconsistent with contemporary biology and the paradigm presented here.

Biological findings can be used for racist or eugenic ends only if we allow perpetuation of the ignorance that underpins these arguments. Individuals acquire traits over the life course in a systematic process involving biological, sociocultural, and developmental factors. Although development is a lifelong process, early circumstances, events, and characteristics such as strategic style tend to become self-reinforcing. Sampson and Laub refer to this tendency for consistency as a "trajectory" (1993:8) that may be changed at critical turning points. This conception of strategic style is strikingly similar to the way bifurcation diagrams portray the behavior of chaotic systems (see Eubank and Farmer, 1990: 107). Chaos theory suggests that biological, sociocultural, and developmental factors may influence—*but not determine*—behavior because the systematic processes underlying criminal behavior are complex, dynamic, and self-reinforcing. A key reason for the effective unpredictability of these and similar nonlinear systems is their extreme sensitivity to initial conditions. Even the smallest changes in initial conditions can be amplified into very large changes in long-term behavior (Eubank and Farmer, 1990:75–77; Hilborn, 1994:39–41; Ruelle, 1991:26–35).

It is well established that *biological* growth and development from the moment of conception are influenced profoundly by social factors such as health care, environmental pollutants, and the foods and drugs we ingest (Fishbein, 1990). If these links are ignored, an entire range of options for dealing with crime is lost. Researchers emphasize repeatedly that complex interactions between many different genes influence behavior, often in subtle ways and that there is no gene for crime (see Fishbein, 1990; Gould, 1981; Morell, 1993; Plomin, 1989; Wilson and Herrnstein, 1985).

The concept of "culling" or "weeding out" different groups from a human population is absurd and scurrilous. As Fairchild notes, "'[R]ace' is a proxy for a host of longstanding historical and environmental variables" (1991:112). So-called "racial" groups in U.S. society are largely a fiction (Harrison et al., 1988:322–33). A great deal of genetic variation exists *within* any sizable racial or ethnic group, but the variation *between* these groups for the large numbers of genes associated with behavior is exceedingly small (Boyd and Richerson, 1985:56, 157–71). These small differences continue to diminish with the increasingly free flow of people and genes throughout the world. No one who understands this could consider racially or ethnically based eugenics. Application of eugenics principles at the individual level is similarly ill-advised. Genetic diversity plays a vital role (see Black, 1992) in ensuring our ability to adapt to a rapidly changing and unpredictable environment.

The Life Cycle

One must apply a *generational timescale* in order to holistically understand the causes of individual criminal behavior. Early life experiences appear likely to have an especially strong influence on the development of criminality because individuals acquire traits sequentially. The traits we possess at any juncture are the result of the cumulative cognitive, affective, physical, and social effects of a sequence of events that began at conception. As a result of these events, individuals acquire a strategic style over the course of their lives. Some individuals develop *criminality*, a style that emphasizes the use of force, fraud, or stealth to obtain resources and is characterized by self-centeredness, indifference to the suffering and needs of others, and low self-control. Of the range of developmental factors, two especially important ones are whether an environment helps or hinders a child's attempt to cope with his or her temperamental propensities and parents' ability to cope with or redirect the behaviors of a difficult child (e.g., Caspi et al., 1987; Olson et al., 1990).

Systematic relations between children and adult caregivers can have important effects on development. Because these relations are dynamic and can be self-reinforcing, interactions between a child's behavior and parental and family environmental factors can have cumulative effects on one another over time (Bell and Harper, 1977; Lytton, 1990). As Werner and Smith (1992) note, children are placed at increasing risk of becoming involved in crime by factors such as economic hardships, living in high-crime neighborhoods, serious caregiving deficits, and family disruption. These risks, however, appear to be buffered by factors such as an easy temperament, scholastic competence, educated mothers, and the presence of grandparents or older siblings who serve as alternative caregivers. The relative importance of risk and protective factors varies according to life stage, gender, and social environment (Featherman and Lerner, 1985:664).

Demographic stressors such as poverty, lack of education, and high-crime neighborhood, as well as family stressors such as unemployment, marital conflict, and divorce, all tend to influence development by disrupting family management practices (Sampson and Laub, 1993:83). Growing up in a disrupted or dysfunctional family is associated strongly with a child's antisocial behavior, of which crime is one type.

Generational timescales are needed to understand criminal behavior because poor family management, antisocial behaviors, and susceptibility to stressors often are transmitted from grandparents to parents to children (Huesmann et al., 1984; Patterson et al., 1989). The intergenerational transmission of risk factors may have important policy implications.

Which traits are acquired depends on interactions between genes, social and individual learning, and environmental factors during development. For example, parents may transmit genes that—in conjunction with pre-, peri-, and postnatal experiences—cause offspring to develop nervous and organ systems which make them much more difficult and irritable. This affects the probability that they will bond properly with a parent, especially if that parent is under extreme stress from economic, social, or personal factors. Thus, children of poor parents beset by economic difficulties may be vulnerable to this dynamic, as may children of wealthy parents whose extreme focus on social and career concerns leads them to nurture their children irregularly (e.g., Binder et al., 1988:444–47). Moffitt (1993:682; 1994) describes in detail the ways in which emergence of antisocial behaviors may be associated with interactions between problem children and problem parents in adverse rearing contexts. The parent/child bond affects how strongly a child values parental approval: weakly bonded children tend to be much more impulsive and difficult to control. This situation can initiate a vicious cycle in which a child receives less affection and nurturance because of misbehavior and therefore seeks less and less to please. Over time, the child develops his or her strategic style in a setting where rewards often are unpredictable as parents struggle with alternating resentment and desire to nurture. Because the child perceives rewards as undependable, he or she learns to grasp immediately opportunities for short-term gratification rather than to defer them for future rewards. In this setting, a child also is less likely to acquire conventional moral beliefs. In addition, the risk of physical and emotional child abuse—which further tend to fuel this vicious spiral toward criminality—may be greater (see Widom, 1989, 1992; Zingraff et al., 1992).

More impulsive children tend to do less well in school. Poor school performance strongly influences future life chances and thus affects how much stake the children develop in conventional society. It also increases the likelihood that they will associate with deviant peers and will learn criminal behavioral strategies from them. Both these factors increase the likelihood of engaging in serious and frequent delinquency (Hirschi, 1969). Engaging in delinquency further can diminish conventional opportunities and weaken beliefs about the moral validity of specific laws, thus reinforcing criminality. This trajectory will tend to continue into adulthood until and unless it is altered. Sampson and Laub cite fundamental shifts in family relations and in work as the most important sources of potential change (1993:248; also see Caspi and Moffitt, 1993a). Unless the trajectory is deflected, this cycle of crime causation will tend to continue when people with high criminality become parents or role models. Thus, at the population level, this process can have an important effect on the evolution of the frequency, distribution, and character of crime.

Integrating Micro- with Macrolevel Causes

A Paradigm of Crime Causation

An integrated paradigm of criminal behavior emerges when we consider how individual microlevel factors interact over time with ecological and macrolevel factors to influence the evolution of criminal behaviors in a population. People acquire attributes such as knowledge, skills, attitudes, beliefs, and strategic styles over the life course via interactions between biological, sociocultural, and developmental factors. These attributes affect their "resource holding potential" and "resource valuation" (Cohen and Machalek, 1988; Parker, 1974)—that is, their ability to obtain resources at a particular point in time and the way they value those resources. Thus, an individual's motivation to commit a crime is determined by these factors *plus the motivational effects of a tempting opportunity* (see Clarke and Felson, 1993). If motivation is sufficiently high and if an opportunity exists, a crime can occur. Resource holding potential and resource valuation tend to vary substantially over the life course.

Moffitt's (1993) taxonomy of antisocial behavior provides an example of this dynamic. She proposes different causes for adolescence-limited and life-course-persistent antisocial behavior. According to her theory, adolescence-limited delinquency and antisocial behavior peak when resource holding potential is lowest, and resource valuation tends to be most consistent with those types of behaviors. Compared with older people, adolescents in contemporary industrial societies tend to be impoverished in the skills, status, and knowledge required to gain through conventional means the adult resources they value. At the same time, they tend to be less constrained by conventional attachments, and to place greater value on thrills, prestige, and immediate gratification. Moffitt argues that this situation causes most normal adolescents to engage in at least some delinquent behavior. As relatively normal youths gain age, experience, and education, their resource holding potential tends to increase; so do conventional opportunities and attachments. This process is consistent with their pattern of desistance from crime. In contrast, Moffitt contends that

> the life-course-persistent type [of antisocial behavior] has its origins in neuro-psychological problems that assume measurable influence when difficult children interact with criminogenic home environments. Beginning in childhood, discipline problems and academic failures accumulate increasing momentum, cutting off opportunities to practice prosocial behavior. As time passes, recovery is precluded by maladaptive individual dispositions and narrowing

life options, and delinquents are channeled into antisocial adult lifestyles. (1993:694–95)

Thus life-course-persistent offenders tend not to desist from crime in early adulthood because their resource holding potential deficit is not age-dependent, as is that of adolescence-limited delinquents.

The Evolution of Crime

When crimes occur, they tend to provoke counterstrategies (defensive responses). Over time, these ecological interactions cause individual and group responses to evolve. For example, higher crime rates often lead to more rigorous protective measures, which may cause crime rates to decline. In turn, barriers to crime may be relaxed as individuals and communities channel limited resources away from crime to deal with more pressing problems. Then, as crime rates decline, decreased vigilance and protective measures may make crime an easier and less risky behavioral strategy. Thus, as fewer individuals are attracted to crime, the potential rewards will tend to increase. Eventually, because of individual-level variation in resource holding potential and resource valuation, *someone* in the population will find the rewards of a criminal strategy attractive enough to employ it. These dynamics—and the tendency of defensive counterstrategies to initiate a vicious cycle by provoking counter-counterstrategies from offenders—suggest that crime probably always will exist at some level in society (Bueno de Mesquita and Cohen, 1995; Cohen and Machalek, 1988, 1994; Vila and Cohen, 1993). Understanding the different ways in which counterstrategies address the causes of crime is the key to making criminological research relevant to public policy.

Counterstrategic Options

The paradigm offered here suggests that countervailing evolutionary forces affect the frequency and prevalence of crime. The frequency of crime or of other expressions of criminality is fostered by coevolutionary dynamics and by the tendency of frequency-dependent payoffs and risks to make rare criminal strategies more attractive. Some crime always will exist. The *amount* of crime, however, can be changed to some extent by counterstrategic forces that tend to make crime less attractive.

Traditional crime control strategies that emphasize use of the criminal justice system have largely failed to reduce serious crime. From 1971 to 1990, total constant dollar expenditures for federal, state, and local criminal justice system activities rose 88 per cent, and imprisonment rates tripled (Maguire et al., 1993: Table 1.1, Fig. 6.4; U. S. Bureau of the Census, 1993: Table 755), becoming higher than in any other industrialized nation (Pease and Hukkila, 1990; UNAFEI, 1990). Yet rates of serious index crimes reported to the police increased by 40 per cent, violent crimes by 85 per cent, and more common property crimes by 35 per cent (Maguire et al., 1993: Table 3.122).

Although the direct physical, material, mental, and emotional injuries sustained by victims of crime are serious, the indirect damage to society is perhaps even more tragic. The responses of individuals and social control agents to crime often threaten personal freedoms, amplify mistrust and prejudice, and generally degrade social cohesion (Axelrod, 1984, 1986; Sampson and Groves, 1989; Shaw and McKay, 1969; Sugden, 1986; Vila and Cohen, 1993).

In the past, most crime control proposals ignored the simple fact that criminality is influenced strongly by early life experiences because of the cumulative, sequential nature of development. Usually we have employed counterstrategies that attempted to either reduce opportunities for crime or deter it. One type of control approach uses *protection or avoidance strategies* that attempt to reduce criminal opportunities by changing people's routine activities or by incapacitating convicted offenders via incarceration or electronic monitoring devices (Reiss and Roth, 1993:325). They also may increase guardianship by hardening targets, instituting neighborhood watch programs, and increasing the numbers or the effectiveness of police. *Deterrence strategies* attempt to diminish motivation for crime by increasing the perceived certainty, severity, or celerity of penalties. "Nonpunitive" deterrence approaches also advocate raising the costs of crime, but they emphasize increasing an individual's stake in conventional activities rather than punishing misbehavior (see Wilson and Herrnstein, 1985). A third possible approach employs *nurturant strategies*, that seldom have been included on crime control agendas. They attempt to forestall development of criminality by improving early life experiences and channeling child and adolescent development.

The long-term effectiveness of *protection and avoidance strategies* is limited. The evolutionary dynamics indicate that protection strategies tend to stimulate "arms races" reminiscent of predator-prey coevolution. Over time, for example, criminals adapt to better locks by learning to overcome them, to antitheft auto alarms by hijacking cars in traffic rather than while parked, to changes in people's routine activities by moving to areas with more potential targets (but see Barr and Pease, 1990). Protection strategies obviously always will be necessary in spite of their long-term limitations because of the opportunistic nature of much crime. This paradigm suggests that these strategies need to be able to evolve quickly in response to changes in criminal strategies because of the potentially rapid nature of cultural evolution. The effects of opportunity-reducing strategies such as incapacitation through incarceration are unclear, however, and may be confounded by the fact that younger offenders—who are least likely to be incarcerated—often committed most crimes (see Reiss and Roth, 1993:292–94). Moreover, incarceration is expensive and perhaps often counterproductive. Sampson and Laub (1993:9) assert that incarceration indirectly *causes* crime by disrupting families and ruining employment prospects (but see LeBlanc and Frechette, 1989:191–93 for a discussion of the effectiveness of incarceration as an intervention for some chronic juvenile offenders). Newer alternatives such as incapacitation of convicted offenders by electronic monitoring in their homes are cheaper than incarceration and may have fewer undesirable side effects.

Conventional deterrence strategies also are problematic. There is little evidence that, in a free society, they can be effective beyond some minimal threshold for controlling most crimes (Fisher and Nagin, 1978; Gibbs and Firebaugh, 1990; Reiss and Roth, 1993:292; Wilson and Herrnstein, 1985:397–99). One novel deterrence approach suggested recently by the National Research Council's Panel on the Understanding and Control of Violent Behavior might be more effective. It would attempt, through treatment and pharmacological intervention, to improve alcohol and psychoactive drug users' ability to calculate costs and benefits (Reiss and Roth, 1993:332–34).

Nonpunitive deterrence strategies that attempt to increase adolescents' and adults' stake in conventional life show promise for correcting life trajectories. Sampson and Laub's (1993) rigorous reanalysis of data from the Glueck Archive suggests that the best way to encourage most adult offenders to desist from crime is to increase their social capital by improving employment opportunities and family ties. Because improvement in employment opportunities appears to diminish the risk of offending, it is ironic that the United States, in comparison with most other industrialized nations, has largely ignored the occupational training needs of noncollege graduates, who make up more than 80 per cent of the U.S. adults over age twenty five. The National Center on Education and the Economy notes that "America may have the worst school-to-work transition system of any advanced industrial country" (Havemann, 1993:A1). Evidence also exists to show that military service among young men may help to compensate for the criminogenic effects of earlier risk factors because it provides an opportunity to repair educational and vocational deficits (Elder, 1986; Werner and Smith, 1992). The paradigm proposed here, however, suggests that nonpunitive deterrence strategies still may provide less potential crime control leverage than nurturant strategies. Because criminality has its roots in the early life course, changing adults' strategic styles generally is more difficult than influencing children's development. To paraphrase Alexander Pope ([1734] 1961), it is easier to bend a twig than a mature oak.

It should be possible to reduce the concentration of criminality in a population by improving early life experiences and channeling child and adolescent development. For example, nurturant strategies might attempt to (1) ensure that all women and children have access to high-quality prenatal, postnatal, and childhood health care; (2) educate as many people as possible about the basics of parenting and family management (e.g., Bank et al., 1987); (3) help people prevent unwanted pregnancies; (4) make help available for children who have been sexually, physically, and emotionally abused—and for their families; and (5) make available extended maternity leaves and high-quality child care for working parents. Nurturant strategies, however, such as educational, health care, and child care programs that address the roots of criminality early in the life course, seldom have been employed for crime control. Also, the results of educational and public health programs that attempted to improve early life course factors often have been equivocal or disappointing (e.g., Haskins, 1989; Marris and Rein, 1973; Moynihan, 1969; Short, 1975). In fact, substantial increases in crime have accompanied what some observers would argue are enormous improvements during the past one hundred years in, for example, access to health care, public education about family management, and provision of counseling for abuse victims. How might this apparent inconsistency be explained?

Despite substantial improvements in these areas at the national level, their distribution undeniably has been uneven. Furthermore, increases in reported crime rates have been most dramatic during the last forty years. Much of the increase in crime during this period appears to have been associated with such factors as fluctuations in demographic and business cycles (e.g., Cohen and Land, 1987; Easterlin, 1987; Hirschi and Gottfredson, 1983), and changes in people's routine activities (Cohen and Felson, 1979). Increased urbanization, social disorganization, and geographical concentration of those who are most deprived, as well as population growth, also appear to be very important (Land et al., 1991; Wilson, 1987; also see Sampson and Laub, 1993:64–98).

Time-lag effects may have confounded past attempts to *measure* the impact of nurturant strategies on crime rates. For example, previous empirical efforts to identify relationships between crime and social structural/economic variables (e.g., income inequality, poverty, and unemployment) by using aggregate data focused primarily on contemporaneous rather than lagged effects. The proposed importance of life-course thinking and intergenerational effects suggests that results of educational, health care, and child care programs implemented today should begin to be seen in about fifteen years—when today's newborns enter the fifteen- to twenty nine-year-old age group, which is most at risk for criminal behavior. Even then, according to the paradigm, change probably would be gradual; the population-level concentration of criminality would continue to decline as each generation of more fully nurtured people became parents themselves. This means that change associated with nurturant strategies might require three or four generations.

It is unclear whether the apparent failure of past nurturant programs (e.g., Cloward and Ohlin, 1960) reflects their lack of utility, faulty implementation, or a failure to pursue them *persistently* over generations. It also is possible that the effects of these programs have yet to be measured. Substantial payoffs could be realized if it were possible to successfully implement programs such as these over the long term. Strong evidence suggests that the five to seven per cent of male adolescents and young adults who are persistent chronic offenders are responsible for roughly fifty per cent of all reported crimes (Wolfgang et al., 1972:88–94; Tracy et al., 1990:82–92; Farrington et al., 1986:50–52). Moffitt (1993) asserts that antisocial behavior in this group is most likely to be the result of early life course factors.

Conclusions

The paradigm presented here demonstrates how an extended and modified version of Cohen and Machalek's (1988) general evolutionary ecological theory of expropriative crime could provide the basis for a truly general theory of criminal behavior and how that theory could provide consistent policy guidance. This paradigm is the first to describe holistically how ecological, microlevel, and macrolevel factors associated with criminal behavior interact and evolve over time, and how they influence individual development over the life course and across generations. If the proposed relationships and effects are supported by research, a single theoretical framework could explain how individuals acquire behavioral strategies such as crime and how they are motivated differentially to employ those strategies by variation in individual resource holding potential, resource valuation, strategic style, and opportunity. Thus we obtain a holistic perspective on human behavior by applying the same well-established techniques and concepts that have unified our understanding of complex organic systems in the biological sciences —while giving special consideration to the unique properties of culture. The paradigm allows us to view crime as a cultural trait whose frequency and type evolves over time as a result of dynamic interactions between individual and group behavior in a physical environment. An appreciation of the indeterminability of these processes encourages us to consider ways to guide the evolution of culture in desirable directions.

The paradigm indicates that crime control strategies should take evolutionary and ecological dynamics into account. These dynamics suggest that protection/avoidance and conventional deterrence strategies for crime control always will be necessary, but will tend to have limited effectiveness in a free society. Nonpunitive deterrence strategies that attempt to improve adults' social capital show promise, but they offer limited crime control leverage because the fundamental behavioral styles that individuals develop early in life are difficult to change. Strategies that address the childhood roots of crime over several generations appear to be very promising from a theoretical standpoint, but past efforts in this direction generally were disappointing. This paradigm emphasizes the importance of determining the reasons for their apparent failure and suggests several possible new avenues of research (see Vila, 1997a, 1997b).

The explanation of criminal behavior provided here suggests that *how* we approach crime-control may be almost as important as *what* we do. I argue that crime will be a persistent and evolving problem, but that it need not be viewed as intractable to control. To succeed, long-term strategies must adapt to constant change. Past attempts to fix fundamental social problems often may have failed because they attempted to "engineer" change. Engineering implies building a carefully fitted mechanism to solve a problem; this approach assumes that the problem is predictable. Humans now, however, are experiencing more rapid, more sustained, and more pervasive change than during any other period in history. Engineered social programs develop an enormous inertia over time. As they accumulate political, bureaucratic, and economic constituencies, they tend increasingly to become less efficient and more difficult to change. Effective long-term crime-control strategies must be able to evolve efficiently in response to rapidly changing needs and new knowledge.

However unattainable they may seem now, nurturant crime-control strategies are practically and philosophically appealing because they are proactive and emphasize developing restraint systems *within* individuals rather than increasing governmental control. They also have broader implications. If crime-control strategies were to focus on controlling the development and expression of criminality instead of controlling specific criminal acts, it might be possible to address the common source of *an entire set* of dysfunctional behaviors: crime, drug abuse, accidents, and perhaps even suicide. Also, we might do so in a way that builds human capital and improves social cohesiveness. Ironically, some think it naive to consider employing nurturant crime-control strategies which, according to this paradigm, will take generations to bear fruit. We routinely plan cities, highways, and military weapons systems twenty years or more into the future. Twenty-five years ago Richard Nixon became the first of six successive presidents to declare "war" on crime. It is time to *evolve* the culture of our society and to become less impulsive, less dependent on coercion, and more sensitive to the needs and suffering of others.

References

Abadinsky, Howard. 1983. *The Criminal Elite*. Westport, Conn.: Greenwood.
————. 1993. *Drug Abuse: An Introduction*. 2d ed. Chicago: Nelson Hall.
Abbott, Andrew. 1988. *The System of Professions*. Chicago: University of Chicago Press.
————. 1992. From causes to events: Notes on narrative positivism. *Sociological Methods and Research* 20:428–55.
ABC News Nightline. 1983. WarGames scenario: Could it really happen? July 8.
Abel, Richard. 1982. *The Politics of Informal Justice*. 2 vols. New York: Academic Press.
Abrahamsen, David. 1944. *Crime and the Human Mind*. New York: Columbia University Press.
Achenbach, Thomas M., and Craig S. Edelbrock. 1983. *Manual for the Child Behavior Checklist and Revised Child Behavior Profile*. Burlington: University of Vermont Department of Psychiatry.
Adams, J. Stacy. 1963. Toward an understanding of inequity. *Journal of Abnormal and Social Psychology* 67:422–36.
————. 1965. Inequity in social exchange. In Leonard Berkowitz (ed.), *Advances in Experimental Social Psychology*. New York: Academic Press.
Adler, Freda. 1975. *Sisters in Crime: The Rise of the New Female Criminal*. New York: McGraw-Hill.
Adler, Freda and William S. Laufer (eds.). 1995. *The Legacy of Anomie Theory. Advances in Criminological Theory*. Vol 6. New Brunswick, N.J.: Transaction Publishers.
Adler, Jeffrey, 1986. Vagging the demons and scoundrels: Vagrancy and the growth of St. Louis, 1830–1861. *Journal of Urban History* 13:3–30.
Adler, Robert W., and Charles Lord. 1991. Environmental crimes: Raising the stakes. *George Washington Law Review* 59:781–61.
Ageton, Suzanne S. 1983. The dynamics of female delinquency, 1976–1980. *Criminology* 21:555–84.
Agger, Ben. 1991. Critical theory, post-structuralism, postmodernism: Their sociological relevance. In W. Richard Scott and Judith Blake (eds.), *Annual Review of Sociology*. Palo Alto, Calif.: Annual Reviews.
Agnew, Robert. 1983. Social class and success goals: An examination of relative and absolute aspirations. *Sociological Quarterly* 24:435–52.
————. 1984. Goal achievement and delinquency. *Sociology and Social Research* 68:435–51.

————. 1985a. Neutralizing the impact of crime. *Criminal Justice and Behavior* 12:221–39.

————. 1985b. A revised strain theory of delinquency. *Social Forces* 64:151–67.

————. 1985c. Social control theory and delinquency: A longitudinal test. *Criminology* 23:47–62.

————. 1986. Challenging strain theory: An examination of goals and goal-blockage. Paper presented at the annual meeting of the American Society of Criminology, Atlanta.

————. 1989. A longitudinal test of the revised strain theory. *Journal of Quantitative Criminology* 5:373–87.

————. 1990. The origins of delinquent events: An examination of offender accounts. *Journal of Research in Crime and Delinquency* 27:267–94.

————. 1991a. Adolescent resources and delinquency. *Criminology* 28:535–66.

————. 1991b. Strain and subcultural crime theory. In Joseph Sheley (ed.), *Criminology: A Contemporary Handbook*. Belmont, Calif.: Wadsworth.

————. 1992. Foundation for a general strain theory of crime and delinquency. *Criminology* 30:47–88.

Agnew, Robert, and Diane Jones. 1988. Adapting to deprivation: An examination of inflated educational expectations. *Sociological Quarterly* 29:315–37.

Aichhorn, August. 1935. *Wayward Youth.* New York: Viking.

Aisenberg, Nadya, and Mona Harrington. 1988. Rules of the game. In Nadya Aisenberg and Mona Harrington (eds.), *Women of Academe: Outsiders in the Sacred Grove*. Amherst: University of Massachusetts Press.

Akers, Ronald L. 1968. The professional association and the legal regulation of practice. *Law and Society Review* 2:463–82.

————. 1973. 1977. 1985. *Deviant Behavior: A Social Learning Approach*. Belmont, Calif.: Wadsworth.

————. 1991. Self-control as a general theory of crime. *Journal of Quantitative Criminology* 7:201–11.

————. 1994. 1997. *Criminological Theories: Introduction and Evaluation*. Los Angeles: Roxbury Publishing Company.

Akers, Ronald L., Marvin D. Krohn, Lonn Lanza-Kaduce, and Marcia Radosevich. 1979. Social learning theory and deviant behavior. *American Sociological Review* 44:635–55.

Al-Issa, Ihsan. 1982. Gender and adult psychopathology. In Ihsan Al-Issa (ed.), *Gender and Psychopathology*. New York: Academic Press.

Albanese, Jay S. 1982. What Lockheed and La Cosa Nostra have in common: The effect of ideology on criminal justice policy. *Crime and Delinquency* 28:211–32.

Albrecht, Stan L. 1982. Commentary. *Pacific Sociological Review* 25:297–304.

Alix, Ernest K. 1978. *Ransom Kidnapping in America: 1887–1974*. Carbondale: Southern Illinois University Press.

Allen, Francis. 1981. *The Decline of the Rehabilitative Idea*. New Haven: Yale University Press.

Allport, Gordon W. 1937. *Personality: A Psychological Explanation*. New York: Holt.

————. 1954. *The Nature of Prejudice*. Reading, Mass.: Addison-Wesley.

Alschuler, Albert. 1991. The failure of sentencing guidelines: A plea for less aggregation. *University of Chicago Law Review* 58:901–51.

Alwin, Duane F. 1987. Distributive justice and satisfaction with material well-being. *American Sociological Review* 52:83–95.

Andenaes, Johannes. 1971. The moral or educative influence of criminal law. *Journal of Social Issues* 24:17–31.

Anderson, Craig A., and Dona C. Anderson. 1984. Ambient temperature and violent crime: Tests of the linear and curvilinear hypotheses. *Journal of Personality and Social Psychology* 46:91–97

Anderson, Elijah. 1976. 1978. *A Place on the Corner*. Chicago: University of Chicago Press.

———. 1990. *Streetwise: Race, Class, and Change in an Urban Community*. Chicago: University of Chicago Press.

Anderson, Jack, and Lee Whitten. 1976. The CIA's "sex squad." *Washington Post*, June 22:B13.

Anderson, L. S. 1979. The deterrent effect of criminal sanctions: Reviewing the evidence. In Paul J. Brantingham and Jack M. Kress (eds.), *Structure, Law and Power*. Beverly Hills, Calif.: Sage.

Anderson, Philip W., Kenneth J. Arrow, and David Pines (eds.). 1988. *The Economy as an Evolving Complex System*. Redwood City: Addison-Wesley.

Aneshensel, Carol S., and Leonard I. Pearlin. 1987. Structural contexts of sex differences in stress. In Rosalind Barnett, Lois Biener, and Grace K. Baruch (eds.), *Gender and Stress*. New York: Free Press.

Anglin, Douglas, George Speckhart, and Elizabeth Piper Deschenes. 1990. *Examining the Effects of Narcotics Addiction*. Los Angeles: UCLA Neuropsychiatric Institute, Drug Abuse Research Group.

Apter, A., R. Plutchik, and H. M. van Praag. 1993. Anxiety, impulsivity and depressed mood in relation to suicidal and violent behavior. *Acta Psychiatrica Scandinavica* 87:1–5.

Arbuthot, Jack, Donald A. Gordon, and Gregory J. Jurkovic. 1987. Personality. In Herbert C. Quay (ed.), *Handbook of Juvenile Delinquency*. New York: John Wiley & Sons.

Archer, D., and R. Gartner. 1984. *Violence and Crime in Cross-National Perspective*. New Haven: Yale University Press.

Armstrong, Nancy, and Leonard Tennenhouse, (eds.). 1989. *The Violence of Representation: Literature and the History of Violence*. London: Routledge.

Arneklev, Bruce J., Harold G. Grasmick, Charles R. Tittle, and Robert J. Bursik, Jr. 1993. Low self-control and imprudent behavior. *Journal of Quantitative Criminology* 9:225–47.

Arnold, William R., and Terrance M. Brungardt. 1983. *Juvenile Misconduct and Delinquency*. Boston: Houghton Mifflin.

Aronow, R., J. N. Miceli, and A. K. Done. 1980. A therapeutic approach to the acutely overdosed patient. *Journal of Psychedelic Drugs* 12:259–68.

Aronson, Elliot. 1976. *The Social Animal*. San Francisco: Freeman.

———. 1980. Persuasion via self-justification. In Leon Festinger (ed.), *Retrospections on Social Psychology*. New York: Oxford University Press.

Assiter, Alison. 1993. Essentially sex: A new look. In Alison Assiter and Avedon Carol (eds.), *Bad Girls and Dirty Pictures: The Challenge to Reclaim Feminism*. London: Pluto.

Austin, Roy L. 1976. Comment on DeFleur. *American Sociological Review* 41:893–96.

Austin, William. 1977. Equity theory and social comparison processes. In Jerry M. Suls and Richard L. Miller (eds.), *Social Comparison Processes*. New York: Hemisphere.

Averill, James R. 1982. *Anger and Aggression*. New York: Springer-Verlag.

Axelrod, Robert. 1984. *The Evolution of Cooperation*. New York: Basic Books.

———. 1986. An evolutionary approach to norms. *American Political Science Review* 80:1095–1111.

Bach-y-Rita, G., J. R. Lion, and F. R. Ervin. 1970. Pathological intoxication. Clinical and electroencephalographic studies. *American Journal of Psychiatry* 127:698–703.

Bach-y-Rita, G., J. R. Lion, C. E. Climent, and F. R. Ervin. 1971. Episodic dyscontrol: A study of 130 violent patients. *American Journal of Psychiatry* 127:1473–78.

Bachman, Jerald. 1970. *Youth in Transition*. Vol. II: *The Impact of Family Background and Intelligence on Tenth-Grade Boys*. Ann Arbor: Institute for Social Research.

Bachman, Jerald G., Patrick M. O'Malley, and John Johnston. 1978. *Youth in Transition: Adolescence to Adulthood—Change and Stability in the Lives of Young Men*. Ann Arbor: Institute for Social Research.

Bacon, Francis. 1632. *The Essayes or Counsels Civill and Morall, of Francis Lo[rd] Verulam*. London: John Haviland.

Baker, Keith Michael. 1975. *Condorcet: From Natural Philosophy to Social Mathematics*. Chicago: University of Chicago Press.

Baker, Patrick. 1993. Chaos, order, and sociological theory. *Sociological Inquiry* 63:123–49.

Baker, Wayne E., and Robert R. Faulkner. 1993. The social organization of conspiracy in the heavy electrical equipment industry. *American Sociological Review* 58:837–60.

Baldwin, John. 1979. Ecological and areal studies in Great Britain and the United States. In Norval Morris and Michael Tonry (eds.), *Crime and Justice: An Annual Review of Research* Vol. 1. Chicago: University of Chicago Press.

Bandura, Albert. 1973. *Aggression: A Social Learning Analysis*. Englewood Cliffs, N.J.: Prentice-Hall.

———. 1977. *Social Learning Theory*. Englewood Cliffs, N.J.: Prentice-Hall.

———. 1982. The psychology of chance encounters and life paths. *American Psychologist* 37:747–55.

———. 1983. Psychological mechanisms of aggression. In Russell G. Geen and Edward I. Donnerstein (eds.), *Aggression: Theoretical and Empirical Reviews*. Vol. 2. New York: Academic Press.

Bank, Lew, Gerald R. Patterson, and John B. Reid. 1987. Delinquency prevention through training parents in family management. *Behavior Analyst* 10:75–82.

Bannister, Shelley, and Dragan Milovanovic. 1990. The necessity defense, substantive justice and oppositional linguistic praxis. *International Journal of the Sociology of Law* 18:179–98.

Barak, Gregg. 1988. Newsmaking criminology: Reflections on the media, intellectuals, and crime. *Justice Quarterly* 5:565–87.

———. 1991. Homelessness and the case for community-based initiatives: The emergence of a model shelter as a short term response to the deepening crisis in housing. In Harold Pepinsky and Richard Quinney (eds.), *Criminology as Peacemaking*. Bloomington: Indiana University Press.

———. 1993. Media, crime, and justice: A case for constitutive criminology. *Humanity and Society* 17:271–96.

———. 1998. *Integrating Criminologies*. Boston: Allyn & Bacon.

——— (ed.). 1994. *Media, Process and the Social Construction of Crime: Studies in Newsmaking Criminology*. New York: Garland Publishing.

——— (ed.). 1996. *Representing O.J.: Murder, Criminal Justice and Mass Culture*. New York: Harrow and Heston.

Barak, Gregg and Bob Bohm. 1989. The crimes of the homeless or the crime of homelessness. *Contemporary Crises* 13:275–88.

Baratta, Alasandro. 1981. Criminologia critica e riforma penale. Osservazioni conclusive sul dibattito Il codice Rocco cinquant'anni dopo' e risposta a Marinucci. *La Questione Criminale* 7:349–89.

———. 1982. *Ciminologia critica e criticia del diritto penale*. Bologna: Il mulino.

Barlow, Hugh D. 1991. Explaining crimes and analogous acts, or the unrestrained will grab at pleasure whenever they can. *Journal of Criminal Law & Criminology* 82:229–42.

Barlow, Hugh D., and Theodore N. Ferdinand. 1992. *Understanding Delinquency*. New York: Harper Collins.

Barnett, Harold C. 1981. Corporate capitalism, corporate crime. *Crime and Delinquency* 27:4–23.

Barr, Robert, and Ken Pease. 1990. Crime placement, displacement, and deflection. In

Michael Tonry and Norval Morris (eds.), *Crime and Justice: A Review of Research.* Vol. 12. Chicago: University of Chicago Press.

Baucus, Melissa S., and Janet P. Near. 1991. Can illegal corporate behavior be predicted? An event history analysis. *Academy of Management Journal* 34:9–36.

Baudrillard, Jean. 1983. *In the Shadow of the Silent Majorities.* New York: Semiotext(e).

Baum, Andrew, and Paul B. Paulus. 1987. Crowding. In Daniel Stokols and Ira Altman (eds.), *Handbook of Environmental Psychology.* New York: John Wiley & Sons.

Bauman, Zygmunt. 1990. Philosophical affinities of postmodern sociology. *Sociological Review* 38:411–41.

———. 1991. *Intimations of Postmodernity.* New York: Routledge.

Baumhart, Raymond C. 1961. How ethical are businessmen? *Harvard Business Review* 39:6–12, 16, 19, 156–76.

Beattie, J. M. 1986. *Crime and the Courts in England 1550–1800.* Princeton: Princeton University Press.

Beavon, Daniel J. 1985. Crime and the environmental opportunity structures: The influence of street networks on the patterning of property offenses. Paper presented at the annual meeting of the American Society of Criminology, San Diego.

Beccaria, Cesare. 1762a. *Del disordine e de'rimedi delle monete nello stato di Milano nell'anno 1762.* In Sergio Romagnoli (ed.), *Cesare Beccaria: Opere.* 1958. Vol. 1. Florence: Sansoni.

———. 1762b. Tentativo analitico su i contrabbandi. In Sergio Romagnoli (ed.), *Cesare Beccaria: Opere.* 1958. Vol. 1. Florence: Sansoni.

———. 1764. *On Crimes and Punishments.* Trans. David Young. 1986. Indianapolis: Hackett.

———. 1765. Frammento sullo stile. In Sergio Romagnoli (ed.), *Cesare Beccaria: Opere.* 1958. Vol. 1. Florence: Sansoni.

———. 1766. Ad Andre Morellet, le 26 janvier. In Sergio Romagnoli (ed.), *Cesare Beccaria: Opere.* 1958. Vol. 2. Florence: Sansoni.

———. 1770. Ricercne intorno alla natura cello stile. In Luigi Firpo (ed.), *Cesare Beccaria: Opere.* 1984. Vol. 2. Milan: Mediobanca.

———. 1792. Voto per la riforma del sistema criminale nella Lombardia Austriaca riguargante la pena di morte. In Sergio Romagnoli (ed.), *Cesare Beccaria: Opere.* 1958. Vol. 2. Florence: Sansoni.

Becker, Gary S. 1968. Crime and punishment: An economic approach. *Journal of Political Economy* 76:169–217.

Becker, Howard. S. 1963. 1966. 1973. *Outsiders: Studies in the Sociology of Deviance.* New York: Free Press.

———. 1971. *Culture and Civility in San Francisco.* Chicago: Aldine.

Begon, Michael, John L. Harper, and Colin R. Townsend. 1986. *Ecology: Individuals, Populations, and Communities.* Sunderland, Mass.: Sinauer.

Beirne, Piers. 1987a. Adolphe Quetelet and the origins of positivist criminology. *American Journal of Sociology* 92:1140–69.

———. 1987b. Between classicism and positivism: Crime and penality in the writings of Gabriel Tarde. *Criminology* 25:785-19.

———. 1988. Heredity versus environment: A reconsideration of Charles Goring's *The English Convict* (1913). *British Journal of Criminology* 28:315–39.

Beirne, Piers and Alan Hunt. 1990. Lenin, crime, and penal politics, 1917–1924. In Piers Beirne (ed.), *Revolution in Law: Contributions to Soviet Legal Theory, 1917–1938.* Armonk, N.Y.: M. E. Sharpe.

Bell, Laurie. 1987. *Good Girls, Bad Girls: Sex Trade Workers and Feminists Face to Face.* Toronto: Women's Press.

Bell, Richard Q., and Lawrence V. Harper. 1977. *Child Effects on Adults.* Hillsdale, N.J.: Lawrence Erlbaum.

Belsky, Jay, and John Kelly. 1994. *The Transition to Parenthood.* New York: Delacorte.

Bem, Daryl J. 1967. Self-Perception: An alternative interpretation of cognitive dissonance phenomena. *Psychological Review* 74:183–200.

Ben-Yehuda, Nachman. 1986. The sociology of moral panic: Toward a new synthesis. *Sociological Quarterly* 27:495–513.

Benedikt, Moriz. 1881. *Anatomical Studies upon Brains of Criminals*. New York: William Wood & Company.

Benignus, V. A., D. A. Otto, K. E. Muller, and K. J. Seiple. 1981. Effects of age and body lead burden on CNS function in young children. 11: EEG spectra. *Electroencephalography and Clinical Neurophysiology* 52:240–48.

Bennett, James. 1981. *Oral History and Delinquency: The Rhetoric of Criminology*. Chicago: University of Chicago Press.

Bennett, Trevor. 1986. A decision-making approach to opioid addiction. In Derek B. Cornish and Ronald V. Clarke (eds.), *The Reasoning Criminal*. New York: Springer-Verlag.

Bennett, Trevor, and Richard Wright. 1984. *Burglars on Burglary*. Aldershot, Hants, U.K.: Gower.

Benson, Michael L. 1984. The fall from grace: Loss of occupational status among white-collar offenders. *Criminology* 22:573–93.

———. 1985. Denying the guilty mind: Accounting for involvement in a white-collar crime. *Criminology* 23:583–607.

Benson, Michael L., and Elizabeth Moore. 1992. Are white-collar and common offenders the same? An empirical and theoretical critique of a recently proposed general theory of crime. *Journal of Research in Crime and Delinquency* 29:251–72.

Bentham, Jeremy. 1776. 1988. *A Fragment on Government*. New York: Cambridge University Press.

Bequai, August. 1977a. *White Collar Crime*. Lexington, Mass.: Lexington Books.

———. 1977b. White-collar plea bargaining. *Trial Magazine* (July):38-41.

———. 1978. *Computer Crime*. Lexington, Mass.: Lexington Books.

———. 1983. *How to Prevent Computer Crime: A Guide for Managers*. New York: John Wiley & Sons.

———. 1987a. Justice department sends warning to white-collar criminals. *Arizona Daily Star*, March 15:F3.

———. 1987b. *Technocrimes*. Lexington, Mass.: Lexington Books.

Berger, Joseph, M. Hamit Fisck, Robert Z. Norman, and David G. Wagner. 1983. The formation of reward expectations in status situations. In David M. Messick and Karen S. Cook (eds.), *Equity Theory: Psychological and Sociological Perspectives*. New York: Praeger.

Berger, Joseph, Morris Zelditch, Jr., Bo Anderson, and Bernard Cohen. 1972. Structural aspects of distributive justice: A status value formulation. In Joseph Berger, Morris Zelditch, Jr., and Bo Anderson (eds.), *Sociological Theories in Progress*. New York: Houghton Mifflin.

Berger, Peter L., and Thomas Luckmann. 1967. *The Social Construction of Reality*. New York: Doubleday.

Berk, Richard, Harold Brackman, and Selma Lesser. 1977. *A Measure of Justice: An Empirical Study of Changes in the California Penal Code, 1955–1971*. New York: Academic Press.

Berkowitz, Leonard. 1978. Whatever happened to the frustration-aggression hypothesis? *American Behavioral Scientist* 21:691–708.

———. 1982. Aversive conditions as stimuli to aggression. In Leonard Berkowitz (ed.), *Advances in Experimental Social Psychology*. Vol. 15. New York: Academic Press.

———. 1986. *A Survey of Social Psychology*. New York: Holt, Rinehart & Winston.

Bernard, Thomas J. 1984. Control criticisms of strain theories: An assessment of theoretical and empirical adequacy. *Journal of Research in Crime and Delinquency* 21:353–72.

————. 1990. Angry aggression among the "truly disadvantaged." *Criminology* 28:73–96.

————. 1993. The intent to harm: Angry aggression as a form of violent crime. In Anna Wilson, *Homicide: The Victim/Offender Relationship*. Cincinnati, Ohio: Anderson.

Bernard, Thomas J., and Jeffrey B. Snipes. 1996. Theoretical integration in criminology. In Michael Tonry (ed.), *Crime and Justice: An Annual Review of Research*. Vol. 20. Chicago: University of Chicago Press.

Bernardez-Bonesatti, Teresa. 1978. Women and anger: Conflicts with aggression in contemporary women. *Journal of American Medical Women's Association* 33:215–19.

Bernstein, Ilene, Edward Kick, Jan Leung, and Barbara Schultz. 1977. Charge reduction: An intermediary stage in the process of labeling criminal defendants. *Social Forces* 56:362–84.

Berry, Brian J. L., and John D. Kasarda. 1977. *Contemporary Urban Ecology*. New York: Macmillan.

Best, Joel, and Gerald T. Horiuchi. 1985. The razor blade in the apple: The social construction of urban legends. *Social Problems* 32:488–99.

Best, S. 1989. The commodification of reality and the reality of commodification: Jean Baudrillard and postmodernism. *Current Perspectives in Social Theory* 9:23–51.

Biederman, J., K. Munir, D. Knee, W. Habelow, M. Armentano, S. Autor, S. K. Hoge, and C. Waternaux. 1986. A family study of patients with attention deficit disorder and normal controls. *Journal of Psychiatric Research* 20:263–74.

Binder, Arnold, Gilbert Geis, and Dickson Bruce. 1988. *Juvenile Delinquency: Historical, Cultural, Legal Perspectives*. New York: Macmillan.

Birkbeck, Christopher. 1985. The concept of opportunities for crime: Its definition and theoretical consequences. Unpublished manuscript. Merida, Venezuela: Universidad de Los Andes, Centro de Investigaciones Penales y Criminologicas.

Black, Donald J. 1976. *The Behavior of Law*. New York: Academic Press.

————. 1989. *Sociological Justice*. New York: Oxford University Press.

————. 1993. *The Social Structure of Right and Wrong*. San Diego: Academic Press.

Black, Francis L. 1992. Why did they die? *Science* December 11: 1739–40.

Blackburn, Ronald. 1968. The scores of Eysenck's criterion groups on some MMPI scales related to emotionality and extraversion. *British Journal of Social and Clinical Psychology* 7:31–33.

————. 1971. Personality types among abnormal homicides. *British Journal of Criminology* 11:14–31.

————. 1978. Psychopathy, arousal and the need for stimulation. In R. D. Hare and D. Schalling (eds.), *Psychopathic Behaviour: Approaches to Research*. Chichester, U.K.: John Wiley & Sons.

————. 1986. Patterns of personality deviation among violent offenders. *British Journal of Criminology* 26:254–69.

————. 1993. *The Psychology of Criminal Conduct*. New York: John Wiley & Sons.

Blackstone, Sir William. 1769. 1783. 1978. *Commentaries on the Laws of England*. 4 vols. London: Garland Publishing.

Blau, Peter. 1964. *Exchange and Power in Social Life*. New York: John Wiley & Sons.

Blau, Peter M., and Judith R. Blau. 1982. The cost of inequality: Metropolitan structure and violent crime. *American Sociological Review* 47:114–29.

Blau, Peter M., and Reid M. Golden. 1984. Metropolitan structure and criminal violence. Paper presented at the annual meeting of the American Sociological Association, San Antonio, Texas.

Blau, Peter M., and Joseph E. Schwartz. 1984. *Cross-Cutting Social Circles: Testing a Macrostructural Theory of Intergroup Relations*. Orlando: Academic Press.

Bledstein, Burton J. 1976. *The Culture of Professionalism*. New York: W. W. Norton.

Block, Alan A. 1982. "On the Waterfront" revisited: The criminology of waterfront organized crime. *Contemporary Crisis* 6:373–96.

Bloch, Herbert, and Gilbert Geis. 1970. *Man, Crime, and Society*. New York: Random House.

Block, Alan A., and William J. Chambliss. 1981. *Organizing Crime*. New York: Elsevier.

Block, Alan A., and Frank R. Scarpitti. 1985. *Poisoning for Profit: The Mafia and Toxic Waste in America*. New York: William Morrow.

Block, Richard, Marcus Felson, and Carolyn R. Block. 1985. Crime victimization rates for incumbents of 246 occupations. *Sociology and Social Research* 69:442–51.

Blood, Robert O., and Donald M. Wolfe. 1960. *Husbands and Wives: The Dynamics of Married Living*. Glencoe, N.Y.: Free Press.

BloomBecker, Jay. 1985. Computer crime update: The view as we exit 1984. *Western New England Law Review* 7:627–49.

———. 1986. *Computer Crime Law Reporter: 1986 Update*. Los Angeles: National Center for Computer Crime Data.

Blumberg, Abraham S. 1981. Typologies of criminal behavior. In Abraham Blumberg (ed.), *Current Perspectives on Criminal Behavior*. New York: Alfred A. Knopf.

Blumer, Herbert. 1969. *Symbolic Interactionism: Perspective and Method*. Englewood Cliffs, N.J.: Prentice-Hall.

Blumstein, Alfred. 1993. Making rationality relevant. *Criminology* 31:1–16.

Blumstein, Alfred J., Jacqueline Cohen, and David P. Farrington. 1988. Criminal career research: Its value for criminology. *Criminology* 26:57-74.

Blumstein, Alfred J., Jacqueline Cohen, Jeffrey A. Roth, and Christy A. Visher (eds.). 1986. *Criminal Careers and "Career Criminals."* Washington, D.C.: National Academy Press.

Boehringer, Gill, Dave Brown, Brendan Edgeworth, Russell Hogg, and Ian Ramsey. 1983. "Law and Order" for progressives? An Australian response. *Crime and Social Justice* 19:2–12.

Bohm, Robert, and Keith N. Haley. 1996. *Introduction to Criminal Justice*. New York: Glencoe/McGraw-Hill.

Bohman, M., C. R. Cloninger, S. Sigvardsson, and A.-L. von Knorring. 1982. Predisposition to petty criminality in Swedish adoptees: 1. Genetic and environmental heterogeneity. *Archives of General Psychiatry* 41:872–78.

Boies, Henry M. 1893. *Prisoners and Paupers*. New York: G. P. Putnam's Sons.

———. 1901. *The Science of Penology: The Defence of Society Against Crime*. New York: G.P. Putnam's Sons.

Bonger, Willem. 1916. *Criminality and Economic Conditions*. Boston: Little Brown.

Borgatta, Edgar F., and David J. Jackson. 1980. Aggregate data analysis: An overview. In Edgar F. Borgatta and David J. Jackson (eds.), *Aggregate Data: Analysis and Interpretation*. Beverly Hills, Calif.: Sage.

Bottoms, A. E. 1983. Neglected features of contemporary penal systems. In David Garland and Peter Young (eds.), *The Power to Punish*. London: Heinemann.

Bottoms, Anthony E., and Paul Wiles. 1986. Housing tenure and residential community crime careers in Britain. In Albert J. Reiss, Jr. and Michael Tonry (eds.), *Communities and Crime*. Chicago: University of Chicago Press.

Bouchard, T. J., Jr., and M. McGue. 1981. Familial studies of intelligence: A review. *Science* 212:1055–59.

Bourdieu, Pierre. 1977. *Outline of a Theory of Practice*. Cambridge: Cambridge University Press.

Bourgois, Phillippe. 1990. In search of Horatio Alger: Culture and ideology in the crack economy. *Contemporary Drug Problems* 16:619–49.

Bowker, Lee H. 1978. *Women, Crime, and the Criminal Justice System*. Lexington, Mass.: D. C. Heath.

———. 1981. *Women and Crime in America*. New York: Macmillan.

Box-Grainger, Jill. 1986. Sentencing rapists. In Roger Matthews and Jock Young (eds.), *Confronting Crime*. Beverly Hills, Calif.: Sage.

Boyd, Robert and Peter J. Richerson. 1985. *Culture and the Evolutionary Process.* Chicago: University of Chicago Press.

———. 1992. How microevolutionary processes give rise to history. In Matthew H. Nitecki and Doris V. Nitecki (eds.), *History and Evolution.* Albany: SUNY Press.

Bradbury, Malcolm. 1988. *My Strange Quest for Mensonge.* London: Penguin.

Brady, James. 1983. Arson, urban economy and organized crime: The case of Boston. *Social Problems* 31:1–27.

Braithwaite, John. 1981. The myth of social class and criminality reconsidered. *American Sociological Review* 46:36–57.

———. 1985. White-collar crime. *Annual Review of Sociology* 11:1–25.

———. 1989. *Crime, Shame and Reintegration.* Cambridge: Cambridge University Press.

———. 1992. Poverty, power, and white collar crime: Sutherland and the paradoxes of criminological theory. In Kip Schlegel and David Weisburd (eds.), *White Collar Crime Reconsidered.* Boston: Northeastern University Press.

Brantingham, Paul J., and Patricia L. Brantingham. 1981. *Environmental Criminology.* Beverly Hills, Calif.: Sage.

———. 1982. Mobility, notoriety and crime: A study in crime patterns of urban nodal points. *Journal of Environmental Systems* 11:89–99.

———. 1984. *Patterns of Crime.* New York: Macmillan.

———. 1987. Personal communication with Marcus Felson.

Brehm, J. W., and Arthur R. Cohen. 1962. *Explorations in Cognitive Dissonance.* New York: John Wiley & Sons.

Brenner, Steven N., and Earl A. Molander. 1977. Is the ethics of business changing? *Harvard Business Review* 55:59–70.

Briar, Scott, and Irving Piliavin. 1965. Delinquency, situational inducements, and commitments to conformity. *Social Problems* 13:35–45.

Brickman, Philip, and Ronnie Janoff Bulman. 1977. Pleasure and pain in social comparison. In Jerry M. Suls and Richard L. Miller (eds.), *Social Comparison Processes.* New York: Hemisphere.

Brigham, John. 1987. Right, rage and remedy: Forms of law in political discourse. *Studies in American Political Development* 2:303-16.

Brittan, Arthur, and Mary Maynard. 1984. *Sexism, Racism, and Oppression.* Oxford: Basil Blackwell.

Brook, J. S., S. Gordon, and M. Whiteman. 1985. Stability of personality during adolescence and its relationship to stage of drug use. *Genetic, Social and General Psychology Monographs* 111:317–30.

Brown, G. L., F. K. Goodwin, J. C. Ballenger, P. F. Goyer, and L. F. Major. 1979. Aggression in humans correlates with cerebrospinal fluid amine metabolites. *Psychiatry Research* 1:131–39.

Browne, Angela. 1987. *When Battered Women Kill.* New York: Macmillan, Free Press.

Browne, Angela, and Kirk R. Williams. 1993. Gender, intimacy, and lethal violence: Trends from 1976 through 1987. *Gender and Society* 7:78–98.

Brownfield, David. 1986. Social class and violent behavior. *Criminology* 24:421–38.

Bryce-Smith, D., and H. A. Waldron. 1974. Lead, behavior, and criminality. *Ecologist* 4:367-77.

Bueno de Mesquita, Bruce, and Lawrence E. Cohen. 1995. Self-interest, equity, and crime control: A game-theoretic analysis of criminal decision making. *Criminology* 33:483–518.

Bunch, Barbara, J., Linda A. Foley, and Susana P. Urbina. 1983. The psychology of violent female offenders: A sex-role perspective. *Prison Journal* 63:66–79.

Burgess, Ernest W. 1925. The growth of the city. In Robert E. Park, Ernest W. Burgess, and Roderick D. McKenzie (eds.), *The City.* Chicago: University of Chicago Press.

Burgess, Robert L., and Ronald L. Akers. 1966. A differential association-reinforcement theory of criminal behavior. *Social Problems* 14:128–47.

Burkett, Steven R., and Bruce O. Warren. 1987. Religiosity, peer influence, and adolescent marijuana use: A panel study of underlying causal structures. *Criminology* 25:109–31.

Bursik, Robert J., Jr. 1983. Community context and the deterrent effect of sanctions. In Gordon P. Whitaker and Charles D. Phillips (eds.), *Evaluating Performance of Criminal Justice Agencies*. Beverly Hills, Calif.: Sage.

———. 1984. Urban dynamics and ecological studies of delinquency. *Social Forces* 63:393–413.

———. 1986a. Delinquency rates as sources of ecological change. In James M. Byrne and Robert J. Sampson (eds.), *The Social Ecology of Crime*. New York: Springer-Verlag.

———. 1986b. Ecological stability and the dynamics of delinquency. In Albert J. Reiss, Jr. and Michael Tonry (eds.), *Communities and Crime*. Chicago: University of Chicago Press.

———. 1988a. Political decision-making and ecological models of delinquency: Conflict and consensus. In Allen E. Liska, Marvin Krohn, and Steven Messner (eds.), *Theoretical Integration in the Study of Deviance and Crime: Problems and Prospects*. Albany: SUNY Press.

———. 1988b. "Social disorganization and theories of crime and delinquency: Problems and prospects." *Criminology* 26:519–51.

Bursik, Robert J. Jr., and Harold G. Grasmick. 1993. *Neighborhoods and Crime: The Dimensions of Effective Community Control*. New York: Lexington Books.

Bursik, Robert J., Jr., and Jim Webb. 1982. Community change and patterns of delinquency. *American Journal of Sociology* 88:24–42.

Business Week. 1981. The spreading danger of computer crime, April 20, 86-92.

Byrne, James M., and Robert J. Sampson (eds.). 1986. *The Social Ecology of Crime*. New York: Springer-Verlag.

Cadoret, R. J., L. Cunningham, R. Loftus, and J. Edwards. 1975. Studies of adoptees from psychiatrically disturbed biologic parents. 11. Temperament, hyperactive, antisocial and developmental variables. *Journal of Pediatrics* 87:301–6.

Cadoret, R. J., T. W. O'Gorman, E. Troughton, and E. Heywood. 1985. Alcoholism and antisocial personality: Interrelationships, genetic and environmental factors. *Archives of General Psychiatry* 42:161–67.

Cadoret, R. J., W. R. Yates, E. Troughton, G. Woodworth, M. Stewart. 1995. Adoption study demonstrating two genetic pathways to drug abuse. *Archives of General Psychiatry* 52:42–52.

Cain, Maureen. 1990. Toward transgression: New directions in feminist criminology. *International Journal of the Sociology of Law* 18:1–18.

Cairns, Robert B. 1986. Phenomena lost: Issues in the study of development. In Jaan Valsiner (ed.), *The Individual Subject and Scientific Psychology*. New York: Plenum.

Calavita, Kitty and Henry N. Pontell. 1990. "Heads I win, tails you lose": Deregulation, crime and crisis in the savings and loan industry. *Crime and Delinquency* 36:309–41.

———. 1991. "Other People's Money" revisited: Collective embezzlement in the savings and loan and insurance industries. *Social Problems* 38:94–112.

———. 1993. Savings and loan fraud as organized crime: Toward a conceptual typology of corporate illegality. *Criminology* 31:519–48.

———. 1994. The state and white-collar crime: Saving the savings and loans. *Law & Society Review* 28:297–324.

California Department of Justice. 1988. Statement of Richard E. Drooyan, Chief Assistant U.S. Attorney, Los Angeles. In *Proceedings of Symposium 87: White Collar/Institutional Crime—Its Measurement and Analysis*. Sacramento: California Department of Justice, Bureau of Criminal Statistics and Special Services.

Calvin, William H. 1990. *The Cerebral Symphony*. New York: Bantam.

Campbell, Anne. 1984. *The Girls in the Gang*. New York: Basil Blackwell.

Campbell, Anne and John J. Gibbs. 1986. *Violent Transactions*. Oxford: Basil Blackwell.

Cantwell, D. P. 1979. Minimal brain dysfunction in adults: Evidence from studies of psychiatric illness in the families of hyperactive children. In L. Bellak (ed.), *Psychiatric Aspects of Minimal Brain Dysfunction in Adults*. New York: Grune and Stratton.

Carlson, N. R. 1977. *Physiology of Behavior*. Boston: Allyn & Bacon.

Carr, Lowell J. 1950. *Delinquency Control*. New York: Harper & Row.

Carroll, B. J., and M. Steiner. 1987. The psychobiology of premenstrual dysphoria: The role of prolactin. *Psychoneuroendocrinology* 3:171–80

Casper, Jonathan D. 1978. *Criminal Courts: The Defendant's Perspective*. Washington, D.C.: U.S. Department of Justice.

Caspi, Avshalom, and Daryl J. Bem. 1990. Personality continuity and change across the life course. In Lawrence A. Pervin (ed.), *Handbook of Personality: Theory and Research*. New York: Guilford.

Caspi, Avshalom, and Terrie E. Moffitt. 1993a. The continuity of maladaptive behavior: From description to understanding in the study of antisocial behavior. In Dante Cicchetti and Donald Cohen (eds.), *Manual of Developmental Psychopathology*. New York: John Wiley & Sons.

———. 1993b. Paradox regained. *Psychological Inquiry* 4:313–21.

———. 1993c. When do individual differences matter? A paradoxical theory of personality coherence. *Psychological Inquiry* 4:247–71. Caspi, Avshalom, and Phil A. Silva. 1995. Temperamental qualities at age 3 predict personality traits in young adulthood: Longitudinal evidence from a birth cohort. *Child Development* 66:486–98.

Caspi, Avshalom, Glen H. Elder, Jr., and Daryl J. Bem. 1987. Moving against the world: Life-course patterns of explosive children. *Developmental Psychology* 23:308–13.

Caspi, Avshalom, Glen H. Elder, Jr., and Ellen S. Herbener. 1990. Childhood personality and the prediction of life-course patterns. In Lee Robins and Michael Rutter (eds.), *Straight and Devious Pathways from Childhood to Adulthood*. New York: Cambridge University Press.

Caspi, Avshalom, Bill Henry, Rob McGee, Terrie E. Moffitt, and Phil A. Silva. 1995. Temperamental origins of child and adolescent behavior problems: From age 3 to age 15. *Child Development* 66:55–58.

Caspi, Avshalom, Terrie E. Moffitt, Phil A. Silva, Magda Stouthamer-Loeber, Robert F. Krueger, and Pamela S. Schmutte. 1994. Are some people crime-prone? Replications of the personality-crime relationship across countries, genders, races, and methods. *Criminology* 32:163–95.

Caspi, Avshalom, Jack Block, Jeanne H. Block, Brett Klopp, Donald Lynam, Terrie E. Moffitt, and Magda Stouthamer-Loeber. 1992. A "common language" version of the California Child Q-set for personality assessment. *Psychological Assessment* 4:512–23.

Castro, Ginette. 1990. *American Feminism—A Contemporary History*. Trans. Elizabeth Loverde-Bagwell. New York: New York University Press.

Cattell, R. B. 1982. *The Inheritance of Personality and Ability: Research Methods and Findings*. New York: Academic Press.

Caulfield, Susan, and Nancy Wonders. 1994. Gender and justice: Feminist contributions to criminology. In Gregg Barak (ed.), *Varieties of Criminology: Readings from a Dynamic Discipline*. Westport, Conn.: Praeger.

Cavalli-Sforza, Luigi L., and Marcus W. Feldman. 1981. *Cultural Transmission and Evolution: A Quantitative Approach*. Princeton: Princeton University Press.

Cernkovich, Stephen, and Peggy Giordano. 1987. Family relationships and delinquency. *Criminology* 25:295–321.

Chadwick, Owen. 1981. The Italian Enlightenment. In R. Potter and M. Teich (eds.), *The Enlightenment in National Context*. New York: Cambridge University Press.

Chaiken, Jan M., Michael W. Lawless, and Keith Stevenson. 1974. *Impact of Police Activity on Crime: Robberies on the New York City Subway System.* Report No. R1424-N.Y.C. Santa Monica, Calif.: Rand Corporation.

Chamberlin, J. Edward, and Sander L. Gilman (eds.). 1985. *Degeneration: The Dark Side of Progress.* New York: Columbia University Press.

Chambliss, William J. 1964. A sociological analysis of the law of vagrancy. *Social Problems* 11:67–77.

———. 1968. The tolerance policy: An invitation to organized crime. Seattle, October:23–31.

———. 1971. Vice, corruption, bureaucracy and power. *Wisconsin Law Review* 4:1150–73.

———. 1972. *Box Man: A Professional Thief's Journal.* New York: Harper Torchbooks.

———. 1975a. On the paucity of original research on organized crime: A footnote to Galliher and Cain. *The American Sociologist* 10:36–39.

———. 1975b. Toward a political economy of crime. *Theory and Society* 2:149–70.

———. 1976. Functional and conflict theories of crime: The heritage of Emile Durkheim and Karl Marx. In William L. Chambliss and Milton Mankoff (eds.), *Whose Law? What Order? A Conflict Approach to Criminology.* New York: John Wiley & Sons.

———. 1977. Markets, profits, labor and smack. *Contemporary Crises* 1:53–57.

———. 1979. Contradictions and conflicts in law creation. *Research in Law and Sociology* 2:3–27.

———. 1980. On lawmaking. *British Journal of Law and Society* 6:149–72.

———. 1988a. *Exploring Criminology.* New York: Macmillan.

———. 1978. 1988b. *On the Take: From Petty Crooks to Presidents.* Bloomington: Indiana University Press.

Chambliss, William J., and Robert B. Seidman. 1971. 1982. *Law, Order and Power.* Reading Mass.: Addison-Wesley.

Chesney-Lind, Meda. 1989. Girl's crime and woman's place: Toward a feminist model of female delinquency. *Crime and Delinquency* 35:5–29.

Chilton, Roland and Susan K. Datesman. 1987. Gender, race, and crime: An analysis of urban arrest trends, 1960–1980. *Gender and Society* 1:152–71.

Christiansen, K. O. 1977. A preliminary study of criminality among twins. In S. A. Mednick and K. O. Christiansen (eds.), *Biosocial Bases of Criminal Behavior.* New York: Gardner Press.

Church Committee. 1976. *Intelligence Activities and the Rights of Americans.* Washington, D.C.: Government Printing Office.

Cicourel, Aaron. 1968. *The Social Organization of Juvenile Justice.* New York: John Wiley & Sons.

Clare, A. W. 1985. Hormones, behaviour and the menstrual cycle. *Journal of Psychosomatic Research* 29:225–33.

Clark, Terry N. 1981. Fiscal strain and American cities: Six basic processes. In K. Newton (ed.), *Urban Political Economy.* New York: St. Martin's Press.

Clarke, Ronald V. 1983. Situational crime prevention: Its theoretical basis and practical scope. In Michael Tonry and Norval Morris (eds.), *Crime and Justice: An Annual Review of Research* Vol. 4. Chicago: University of Chicago Press.

———. 1995. Situational crime prevention. In Michael Tonry and David P. Farrington (eds.), *Building a Safer Society: Strategic Approaches to Crime Prevention.* Chicago: University of Chicago Press.

Clarke, Ronald V., and Derek B. Cornish. 1985. Modeling offenders' decisions: A framework for research and policy. In Michael Tonry and Norval Morris (eds.), *Crime and Justice: An Annual Review of Research.* Vol. 6. Chicago: University of Chicago Press.

Clarke, Ronald V., and Pat Mayhew. 1988. The British gas suicide story and its criminological implications. In Michael Tonry and Norval Morris (eds.), *Crime and Justice: An Annual Review of Research*. Vol. 10. Chicago: University of Chicago Press.

Clarke, Ronald V. (ed.). 1992. *Situational Crime Prevention: Successful Case Studies*. New York: Harrow and Heston.

Clarke, Ronald V., and Marcus Felson (eds.). 1993. *Routine Activity and Rational Choice*. New Brunswick, N.J.: Transaction Publishers.

Clarke, Ronald, and Pat Mayhew (eds.). 1980. *Designing Out Crime*. London: HMSO.

Clausen, John. 1990. Turning point as a life course concept: Meaning and measurement. Paper presented at the annual meeting of the American Sociological Association, Washington, D.C.

Cleckley, H. 1964. *The Mask of Sanity*. 4th ed. St. Louis: Mosby.

Clegg, Stewart. 1989. *Frameworks of Power*. Newbury Park, Calif.: Sage.

Clinard, Marshall B. 1964. *Anomie and Deviant Behavior*. New York: Free Press.

———. 1983. *Corporate Ethics and Crime: The Role of Middle Management*. Beverly Hills, Calif.: Sage.

Clinard, Marshall B., and Richard Quinney. 1967. 1973. *Criminal Behavior Systems: A Typology*. New York: Holt, Rinehart & Winston.

———. 1973. Corporate criminal behavior. In Marshall B. Clinard and Richard Quinney, *Criminal Behavior Systems: A Typology*. Rev. ed. New York: Holt, Rinehart & Winston.

Clinard, Marshall B., and Peter C. Yeager. 1978. Corporate crime: Issues in research. *Criminology* 16:255–72.

———. 1980. *Corporate Crime*. New York: Free Press.

Clinard, Marshall B., Peter C. Yeager, Jeanne M. Brissette, David Petrashek, and Elizabeth Harries. 1979. *Illegal Corporate Behavior*. Washington, D.C.: U.S. Government Printing Office.

Cloninger, C. Robert. 1987. A systematic method for clinical description and classification of personality variants. *Archives of General Psychiatry* 44:573–88.

Cloninger, C. Robert, T. Reich, and S. B. Guze. 1975. The multifactorial model of disease transmission: 11. Sex differences in the familial transmission of sociopathy (antisocial personality). *British Journal of Psychiatry* 127:11–22.

Cloninger, C. Robert, K. O. Christiansen, T. Reich, and I.I. Gottesman. 1978. Implications of sex differences in the prevalences of antisocial personality, alcoholism, and criminality for familial transmission. *Archives of General Psychiatry* 35:941–51.

Cloward, Richard A., and Lloyd E. Ohlin. 1961. *Delinquency and Opportunity—A Theory of Delinquent Gangs*. New York: Free Press.

Coe, C. L., and S. Levine. 1983. Biology of aggression. *Bulletin of the American Academy of Psychiatry Law* 11:131–48.

Cohen, Albert K. 1955. *Delinquent Boys: The Culture of the Gang*. Glencoe, Ill: Free Press.

———. 1965. The sociology of the deviant act: Anomie theory and beyond. *American Sociological Review* 30:5–14.

Cohen, Albert K., Alfred Lindesmith, and Karl Schuessler. 1956. *The Sutherland Papers*. Bloomington: Indiana University Press.

Cohen, Lawrence E., and Marcus Felson. 1979. Social change and crime rate trends: A routine activity approach. *American Sociological Review* 44:588–608.

Cohen, Lawrence E., and Kenneth C. Land. 1987. Age structure and crime: Symmetry versus asymmetry and the projection of crime rates through the 1990s. *American Sociological Review* 52:170–83.

Cohen, Lawrence and Richard Machalek. 1988. A general theory of expropriative crime: An evolutionary ecological approach. *American Journal of Sociology* 94:465–501.

———. 1994. The normalcy of crime: From Durkheim to evolutionary ecology. *Rationality and Society* 6:286–308.

Cohen, Lawrence E., and Bryan J. Vila. 1996. Self-control and social control: An exposition of the Gottfredson-Hirschi/Sampson-Laub debate.*Studies on Crime and Crime Prevention* 5:125–50.

Cohen, Lawrence E., James R. Kluegel, and Kenneth C. Land. 1981. Social inequality and predatory criminal victimization: An exposition and test of a formal theory. *American Sociological Review* 46:505–24.

Cohen, S. 1977. Angel dust. *Journal of the American Medical Association* 238:515–16.

———. 1980. Alcoholic hypoglycemia. *Drug Abuse and Alcoholism Newsletter* 9:14.

Cohen, Stanley. 1974. Criminology and the sociology of deviance in Britain. In Paul Rock and Mary McIntosh (eds.), *Deviance and Social Control*. London: Tavistock.

———. 1985. *Visions of Social Control: Crime, Punishment and Classification*. Oxford: Polity Press.

———. 1988. *Against Criminology*. New Brunswick, N.J.: Transaction Publishers.

Cohen, Stanley and Jock Young. 1980. *The Manufacture of News*. London: Constable.

Coid, J. 1979. Mania a potu: A critical review of pathological intoxication. *Psychological Medicine* 9:709–19.

Cole, Stephen. 1975. The growth of scientific knowledge: Theories of deviance as a case study. In Lewis A. Coser (ed.), *The Idea of Social Structure: Papers in Honor of Robert K. Merton*. New York: Harcourt Brace and Jovanovich.

Coleman, James S. 1988. Social capital in the creation of human capital. *American Journal of Sociology* 94:S95–120.

———. 1990. *Foundations of Social Theory*. Cambridge, Mass.: Harvard University Press.

Coleman, James W. 1987. Toward an integrated theory of white-collar crime. *American Journal of Sociology* 93:406–39.

Collins, Hugh. 1982. *Marxism and Law*. Oxford: Clarendon Press.

Collins, Patricia Hill. 1986. Learning from the outsider within: The sociological significance of black feminist thought. *Social Problems* 33:514–32.

Colvin, Mark, and John Pauly. 1983. A critique of criminology: Toward an integrated structural-Marxist theory of delinquency production.*American Journal of Sociology* 89:513–51.

Comings, D. E., D. Muhleman, C. Ahn, R. Gysin, and S. Glanagan. 1994. The dopamine D@ receptor gene: A genetic risk factor in substance abuse. *Drug and Alcohol Dependence* 34:175–80.

Commonwealth of New South Wales. 1982a. *New South Wales Joint Task Force on Drug Trafficking. Federal Parliament Report*. Sydney: Government of New South Wales.

———. 1982b. *Preliminary Report of the Royal Commission to Investigate the Nugan Hand Bank Failure. Federal Parliament Report*. Sydney: Government of New South Wales.

Compas, Bruce E. 1987. Coping with stress during childhood and adolescence. *Psychological Bulletin* 101:393–403.

Compas, Bruce E., and Vicky Phares. 1991. Stress during childhood and adolescence: Sources of risk and vulnerability. In E. M. Cummings, A. L. Greene, and K. H. Karraker (eds.), *Life-Span Developmental Psychology: Perspectives on Stress and Coping*. Hillsdale, N.J.: Lawrence Erlbaum.

Compas, Bruce E., Vanessa L. Malcarne, and Karen M. Fondacaro. 1988. Coping with stressful events in older children and young adolescents.*Journal of Consulting and Clinical Psychology* 56:405–11.

Condillac, Etienne Bonnot, Abbé de. 1754. A Treatise on the Sensations. In *Philosophical Writings of Etienne Bonnot, Abbé de Condillac*. Trans. Franklin Philip and Harlan Lane. 1982. Hillsdale, N.J.: Lawrence Erlbaum.

Condorcet, Marie-Jean-Antoine Nicolas Caritat. 1795. *Tableau historique des progrès de l'esprit humain*. 1990. Paris: G. Steinheil.

Conger, Rand D. 1980. Juvenile delinquency: Behavior restraint or behavior facilitation? In Travis Hirschi and Michael Gottfredson (eds.), *Understanding Crime*. Beverly Hills, Calif.: Sage.

Conger, Rand D., John A. McCarty, Raymond K. Wang, Benjamin B. Lahey, and Joseph P. Kroop. 1984. Perception of child, child-rearing values, and emotional distress as mediating links between environmental stressors and observed maternal behavior. *Child Development* 55:2234–47.

Conklin, John E. 1977. *Illegal But Not Criminal: Business Crime in America*. Englewood Cliffs, N.J.: Prentice-Hall.

Conroy, Cathryn. 1985. Computer crime law drafted. *Online Today*, June:8.

———. 1986. States cool toward computer crime laws. *Online Today*, November:14.

Cook, Karen S., and Karen A. Hegtvedt. 1983. Distributive justice, equity, and equality. *Annual Review of Sociology* 9:217–41.

———. 1991. Empirical evidence of the sense of justice. In Margaret Gruter, Roger D. Masters, and Michael T. McGuire (eds.), *The Sense of Justice: An Inquiry into the Biological Foundations of Law*. New York: Greenwood Press.

Cook, Karen, and Joseph Whitmeyer. 1992. Two approaches to social structure: Exchange theory and network analysis. *Annual Review of Sociology* 18:109–27.

Cook, Karen S., and Toshio Yamagishi. 1983. Social determinants of equity judgments: The problem of multidimensional input. In David M. Messick and Karen S. Cook (eds.), *Equity Theory: Psychological and Sociological Perspectives*. New York: Praeger.

Cook, Philip J. 1986a. Criminal incapacitation effects considered in an adaptive choice framework. In Derek B. Cornish and Ronald V. Clarke (eds.), *The Reasoning Criminal*. New York: Springer-Verlag.

———. 1986b. The demand and supply of criminal opportunities. In Michael Tonry and Norval Morris (eds.). *Crime and Justice: An Annual Review of Research*. Vol. 7. Chicago: University of Chicago Press.

———. 1987. *The Demand and Supply of Criminal Opportunities. Crime and Justice: An Annual Review of Research*. Vol. 7. Chicago: University of Chicago Press.

Coombe, Rosemary J. 1989. Room for manoeuver: Toward a theory of practice in critical legal studies. *Law and Social Inquiry* 14:69–121.

Cornish, Derek B. 1978. *Gambling: A Review of the Literature*. Home Office Research Study, No. 42. London: HMSO.

———. 1987. Evaluating residential treatment for delinquents: A cautionary tale. In Klaus Hurrelmann and Franz-Xaver Kaufmann (eds.), *Limits and Potentials of Social Intervention*. Berlin/New York: Walter de Gruyter.

Cornish, Derek B., and Ronald V. Clarke. 1986a. *The Reasoning Criminal: Rational Choice Perspectives on Offending*. New York: Springer-Verlag.

———. 1986b. Situational prevention, displacement of crime and rational choice theory. In Kevin Heal and Gloria Laycock (eds.), *Situational Crime Prevention: From Theory into Practice*. London: HMSO.

———. 1987. "Understanding Crime Displacement: An Application of Rational Choice Theory." *Criminology* 25:933–47.

———. 1989. Crime specialisation, crime displacement and rational choice theory. In H. Wegener, F. Losel, and J. Haish (eds.), *Criminal Behavior and the Justice System: Psychological Perspectives*. New York: Springer-Verlag.

Coser, Lewis. 1956. *The Functions of Social Conflict*. New York: Macmillan.

Covington, Jeanette, and Ralph B. Taylor. 1988. Neighborhood revitalization and property crime. Paper presented at the annual meeting of the American Sociological Association, Atlanta.

Crenson, Matthew A. 1971. *The Un-Politics of Air Pollution: A Study of Non-Decisionmaking in the Cities*. Baltimore: Johns Hopkins University Press.

Cressey, Donald R. 1953. *Other People's Money*. Glencoe, Ill.: Free Press.

———. 1954. The differential association theory and compulsive crimes. *The Journal of Criminal Law, Criminology and Police Science* 45:29–40.

———. 1960a. Epidemiology and individual conduct: A case from criminology. *Pacific Sociological Review* 3:47–58.

————. 1960b. The theory of differential association: An introduction. *Social Problems* 8:2–6.

————. 1967. Methodological problems in the study of organized crime as a social problem. *Annals of American Academy of Political and Social Sciences* 374:98–120.

————. 1970. The respectable criminal. In James Short (ed.), *Modern Criminals*. New York: Transaction, Aldine.

————. 1986. Why managers commit fraud. *Australian and New Zealand Journal of Criminology* 19:195–209.

Crewdson, John M., and Jo Thomas. 1977. Abuses in testing of drugs by CIA to be panel focus. *New York Times*, September 20.

Critchley, E. M. R. 1968. Reading retardation, dyslexia, and delinquency. *British Journal of Psychiatry* 115:1537–47.

Crook, Stephen, Jan Pakulski, and Malcolm Waters. 1992. *Postmodernization: Change in Advanced Society*. London: Sage.

Crosby, Faye, and A. Miren Gonzales-Intal. 1984. Relative deprivation and equity theories: Felt injustice and the undeserved benefits of others. In Robert Folger (ed.), *The Sense of Injustice: Social Psychological Perspectives*. New York: Plenum.

Cullen, Francis T. 1984. *Rethinking Crime and Deviance Theory: The Emergence of a Structuring Tradition*. Totowa, N.J.: Rowman and Allanheld.

Cullen, Francis T., William J. Maakestad, and Gray Cavender. 1987. *Corporate Crime under Attack: The Ford Pinto Case and Beyond*. Cincinnati, Ohio: Anderson.

Cummings, Scott, and Daniel J. Monte. 1993. *Gangs*. Albany: SUNY Press.

Currie, Dawn H. 1989. Women and the state: A statement on feminist theory. *The Critical Criminologist* 1:4–5.

————. 1991. Challenging privilege: Feminist struggles in the canadian context. *The Critical Criminologist* 3:1–2, 10–13.

Currie, Dawn H., and Marlee Kline. 1991. Challenging privilege: Women, knowledge and feminist struggles. *Journal of Human Justice* 2:1–36.

Currie, Elliott. 1985. *Confronting Crime*. New York: Pantheon.

Cutrona, Carolyn E. 1984. Social support and stress in the transition to parenthood. *Journal of Abnormal Psychology* 91:378–90.

d'Orban, P. T. 1979. Women who kill their children. *British Journal of Psychiatry* 134:560.

————. 1990. Female homicide. *Irish Journal of Psychological Medicine* 7:64–70.

Dahrendorf, Ralf. 1959. *Class and Class Conflict in an Industrial Society*. London: Routledge & Kegan Paul.

Daly, Kathleen. 1990. Reflections on feminist legal thought. *Social Justice*, 17:7–24.

————. 1992. Women's pathways to felony court: feminist theories of lawbreaking and problems of representation. *Review of Law and Women's Studies* 2:1–42.

————. 1993. Class-race-gender: Sloganeering in search of meaning. *Social Justice* 20:56–71.

————. 1994. *Gender, Crime and Punishment*. New Haven, Conn.: Yale University Press.

Daly, Kathleen, and Meda Chesney-Lind. 1988. Feminism and criminology. *Justice Quarterly* 5:497–38.

Daly, Martin and Margo Wilson. 1988. *Homicide*. Hawthorne, N.Y.: Aldine de Gruyter.

Dannefer, Dale. 1987. Aging as intracohort differentiation: Accentuation, the Matthew effect, and the life course. *Sociological Forum* 2:211–36.

Danner, Mona J. E. 1991. Socialist feminism: A brief introduction. In Brian D. MacLean and Dragan Milovanovic (eds.), *New Directions in Critical Criminology*. Vancouver: Collective Press.

Danzig, Richard. 1973. Towards the creation of a complementary decentralizes system of criminal justice. *Stanford Law Review* 26: 1–54.

Darnton, Robert. 1979. *The Business of Enlightenment: A Publishing History of the Encyclopedie, 1775–1800*. Cambridge, Mass.: Harvard University Press.

————. 1982. *The Literary Underground of the Old Regime*. Cambridge, Mass.: Harvard University Press.
Davidson, R. Norman. 1981. *Crime and Environment*. New York: St. Martin's Press.
Davies, John D. 1955. *Phrenology: Fad and Science*. New Haven: Yale University Press.
Davis, B. A., P. H. Yu, A. A. Boulton, J. S. Wormith, and D. Addington. 1983. Correlative relationship between biochemical activity and aggressive behavior. *Progress in Neuro-Psychopharmacology and Biological Psychiatry* 7:529–35.
Davis, Nanette J. 1975. *Sociological Constructions of Deviance: Perspectives and Issues in the Field*. Dubuque, Iowa: Wm. C. Brown Company.
Dawkins, Richard. 1980. Good strategy or evolutionarily stable strategy? In George W. Barlow and James Silverberg (eds.), *Sociobiology: Beyond Nature/Nurture*. Boulder, Colo.: Westview.
de Beauvoir, Simone. 1952. *The Second Sex*. New York: Random House.
de La Croix, Robert. 1962. *John Paul Jones*. London: Frederik Muller.
Dean, Alfred, and Nan Lin. 1977. The stress buffering role of social support: Problems and prospects for systematic investigation. *Journal of Nervous and Mental Disease* 165:403–17.
DeFleur, Lois B. 1975. Biasing influence on drug arrest records: Implications for deviance research. *American Sociological Review* 40:225–33.
DeFries, J. C., and R. Plomin. 1978. Behavioral genetics. *Annual Reviews in Psychology* 29:473–515.
DeKeseredy, Walter S., and Ronald Hinch. 1991. *Woman Abuse: Sociological Perspectives*. Toronto: Thompson.
Della Fave, L. Richard. 1974. Success values: Are they universal or class-differentiated? *American Journal of Sociology* 80:153–69.
————. 1980. The meek shall not inherit the earth: Self-evaluations and the legitimacy of stratification. *American Sociological Review* 45:955–71.
Della Fave, L. Richard, and Patricia Klobus. 1976. Success values and the value stretch: A biracial comparison. *Sociological Quarterly* 17:491–502.
Delphy, Christine, and Diana Leonard. 1992. *Familiar Exploitation*. Cambridge, Mass.: Polity Press.
DeLucia, Robert C., and Thomas J. Doyle. 1994. *Career Planning and Criminal Justice*. Cincinnati, Ohio: Anderson.
Demsky, L. S. 1984. The use of Depo-Provera in the treatment of sex offenders. *Journal of Legal Medicine* 5:295–322.
Denno, D. W. 1988. Human biology and criminal responsibility: Free will or free ride? *University of Pennsylvania Law Review* 137:615–71.
Denzin, Norman K. 1977. Notes on the criminogenic hypothesis: A case study of the American liquor industry. *American Sociological Review* 42:905–20.
————. 1984. *On Understanding Emotion*. San Francisco: Jossey-Bass.
————. 1986. Postmodern social theory. *Sociological Theory* 4: 194–204.
————. 1990. Presidential address on the sociological imagination revisited. *Sociological Quarterly* 31:1–22.
Depue, R. A., and M. R. Spoont. 1986. Conceptualizing a serotonin trait: A behavioral dimension of constraint. *Annals of the New York Academy of Sciences* 487:47–62.
Derrida, Jacques. 1973. *Speech and Phenomena*. Evanston, Ill.: Northwestern University Press.
————. 1981. *Positions*. Chicago: University of Chicago Press.
Dews, Peter. 1987. *Logic of Disintegration: Poststructuralist Thought and the Claims of Critical Theory*. New York: Verso.
Deykin, E. Y., J. C. Levy, and V. Wells. 1986. Adolescent depression, alcohol and drug abuse. *American Journal of Public Health* 76:178–82.
Dickman, Scott J. 1990. Functional and dysfunctional impulsivity: Personality and cognitive correlates. *Journal of Personality and Social Psychology* 58:95–102.

Dickson, Donald T. 1968. Bureaucracy and morality: An organizational perspective on a moral crusade. *Social Problems* 16:143–156.

DiLalla, Elizabeth F., and Irving I. Gottesman. 1989. Heterogeneity of causes for delinquency and criminality: Lifespan perspectives. *Development and Psychopathology* 1:339–49.

Dinges, John, and Saul Landau. 1980. *Assassination on Embassy Row*. New York: McGraw-Hill.

———. 1982. Fine CIA's link to Chile's plot. *Nation*, June 12:712–13.

Dishion, Thomas J., Gerald R. Patterson, M. Stoolmiller, and M. L. Skinner. 1991. Family, school, and behavioral antecedents to early adolescent involvement with antisocial peers. *Developmental Psychology* 27:172–80.

Dobash, R. Emerson, and Russell P. Dobash. 1992. *Women, Violence and Social Change*. London: Routledge.

Doherty, Joe, Elspeth Graham, and Mo Malek. 1992. *Postmodernism and the Social Sciences*. New York: St. Martin's Press.

Domino, E. F. 1978. Neurobiology of phencyclidine—An update. In R.C. Peterson and R.C. Stillman (eds.), *Phencyclidine (PCP) Abuse: An Appraisal. NIDA Research Monograph 21*. Rockville, Md.: National Institute on Drug Abuse.

———. 1980. History and pharmacology of PCP and PCP-related analogs. *Journal of Psychedelic Drugs* 12:223–27.

Donnerstein, Edward, and Elaine Hatfield. 1982. Aggression and equity. In Jerald Greenberg and Ronald L. Cohen (eds.), *Equity and Justice in Social Behavior*. New York: Academic Press.

Douglas, Mary. 1978. *Cultural Bias*. London: Royal Anthropological Institute of Great Britain and Ireland.

Dowd, James J. 1991. Social psychology in a postmodern age: A discipline without a subject. *American Sociologist* 22:188–209.

Downs, Anthony. 1972. Up and down with ecology—the issue attention cycle. *Public Interest* 28:38–50.

Doyle, James M. 1992. "It's the Third World down there!" The colonialist vocation and American criminal justice. *Harvard Civil Rights-Civil Liberties Law Review* 27:71–126.

Drahms, August. 1900. 1971. *The Criminal: His Personnel and Environment—A Scientific Study, with an Introduction by Cesare Lombroso*. Montclair, N.J.: Patterson Smith.

Drucker, Peter F. 1981. What is business ethics? *The Public Interest* 63:18–36.

Dugdale, Richard L. 1877. *"The Jukes": A Study in Crime, Pauperism, Disease and Heredity*; also *Further Studies of Criminals*. New York: G. P. Putnam's Sons.

Durkheim, Emile. [1895]. 1933. *The Division of Labor in Society*. New York: Macmillan.

———. [1897] 1951. *Suicide*. Trans. S. A. Solovay and J. H. Mueller. Glencoe, N.Y.: Free Press.

Duster, Troy. 1988. From structural analysis to public policy. A review of William J. Wilson's *The Truly Disadvantaged*. *Contemporary Sociology* 17:287–90.

Easterlin, Richard A. 1987. *Birth and Fortune*. Chicago: University of Chicago Press.

Eckenrode, John, and Susan Gore. 1981. Stressful life events and social supports: The significance of context. In Benjamin H. Gottlieb (ed.), *Social Networks and Social Support*. Beverly Hills, Calif.: Sage.

Edelhertz, Herbert. 1970. *The Nature, Impact, and Prosecution of White Collar Crime*. Washington, D.C.: U.S. Government Printing Office.

Edmunds, G., and D. C. Kendrick. 1980. *The Measurement of Human Aggressiveness*. New York: John Wiley & Sons.

Edwards, Susan. 1981. *Female Sexuality and the Law*. Oxford: Martin Robertson.

———. 1984. *Women on Trial*. New Hampshire: Manchester University Press.

———. 1989. *Policing "Domestic" Violence: Women, the Law and the State*. London: Sage.

———. 1990. Violence against women: Feminism and the law. In Loraine Gelsthorpe

References 551

and Allison Morris (eds.), *Feminist Perspectives in Criminology*. Milton Keynes: Open University Press.

Eichelman, B. S., and N. B. Thoa. 1972. The aggressive monoamines. *Biological Psychiatry* 6:143–63.

Einstadter, Werner J. 1969. The social organization of armed robbery. *Social Problems* 17:64–83.

———. Asymmetries of Control: Technologies of Surveillance in the Theft of Privacy. Paper Presented to Society for the Study of Social Problems, San Francisco.

———. 1992. Asymmetries of control: Surveillance, intrusion, and the corporate theft of privacy. *Justice Quarterly*, 9:285–98.

Einstadter, Werner, and Stuart Henry. 1995. *Criminological Theory: An Analysis of Its Underlying Assumptions*. Fort Worth, Tex.: Harcourt Brace.

Eisenstein, Zillah. 1979. *Capitalist Patriarchy and the Case for Socialist Feminism*. New York: Monthly Review Press.

Elder, Glen H., Jr. 1975. Age differentiation and the life course. *Annual Review of Sociology* 1:165–90.

———. 1985. Perspectives on the life course. In Glen H. Elder, Jr. (ed.), *Life Course Dynamics*. Ithaca, N.Y.: Cornell University Press.

———. 1986. Military times and turning points in men's lives. *Developmental Psychology* 22:233–45.

———. 1992. Life course. In Edgar F. Borgatta and Marie L. Borgatta (eds.), *Encyclopedia of Sociology*. Vol. 3. New York: Macmillan.

Elder, Glen H., Jr., Cynthia Gimbel, and Rachel Ivie. 1991. Turning points in life: The case of military service and war. *Military Psychology* 3:215-31.

Elliott, Delbert S., and Suzanne S. Ageton. 1980. Reconciling race and class differences in self-report and official estimates of delinquency. *American Sociological Review* 45:95–110.

Elliott, Delbert S., and David Huizinga. 1983. Social class and delinquent behavior in a national youth panel. *Criminology* 21:149–77.

———. 1989. Improving self-reported measures of delinquency. In Malcolm W. Klein (ed.), *Cross-National Research in Self-Reported Crime and Delinquency*. Dordrecht: Kluwer.

Elliott, Delbert, and Harwin Voss. 1974. *Delinquency and Dropout*. Lexington, Mass.: Lexington Books.

Elliott, Delbert S., Suzanne S. Ageton, and Rachelle. J. Canter. 1979. An integrated theoretical perspective on delinquent behavior. *Journal of Research in Crime and Delinquency* 16:3–27.

Elliott, Delbert, David Huizinga, and Suzanne Ageton. 1985. *Explaining Delinquency and Drug Use*. Beverly Hills, Calif.: Sage.

Elliott, Delbert S., Suzanne S. Ageton, David Huizinga, Brian A. Knowles, and Rachelle J. Canter. 1983. *The Prevalence and Incidence of Delinquent Behavior: 1976–1980*. Boulder, Colo.: Behavioral Research Institute.

Ellis, Havelock. 1890. *The Criminal*. London: Walter Scott.

Ellis, L., and M. A. Ames. 1987. Neurohormonal functioning and sexual orientation: A theory of homosexuality-heterosexuality. *Psychological Bulletin* 101:233–58.

Empey, LaMar. 1956. Social class and occupational aspiration: A comparison of absolute and relative measurement. *American Sociological Review* 21:703–9.

———. 1982. *American Delinquency: Its Meaning and Construction*. Homewood, Ill.: Dorsey.

Epstein, Seymour, and Edward J. O'Brien. 1985. The person-situation debate in historical and current perspective. *Psychological Bulletin* 98:513–37.

Erickson, Kai T. 1966. *Wayward Puritans: A Study in the Sociology of Deviance*. New York: Wilcox.

Erickson, Maynard L. 1971. The group context of delinquent behavior. *Social Problems* 19:114–29.

Erickson, Maynard L., and Gary F. Jensen. 1977. Delinquency is still group behavior: Toward revitalizing the group premise in the sociology of deviance. *Journal of Criminal Law and Criminology* 68:388-95.

Ermann, M. David, and Richard Lundman. 1982. *Corporate and Governmental Deviance: Problems of Organizational Behavior in Contemporary Society.* 2d ed. New York: Oxford University Press.

Eron, Leonard D. 1987. The development of aggressive behavior from the perspective of a developing behaviorism. *American Psychologist* 42:435-42.

Etzioni, Amitai. 1985. Shady corporate practices. *New York Times.* November 15.

Eubank, Stephen, and Doyne Farmer. 1990. An introduction to chaos and prediction. In Erica Jen (ed.), *1989 Lectures in Complex Systems: Santa Fe Institute Studies in the Sciences of Complexity, Lecture Vol. 2.* Redwood City: Addison-Wesley.

Evan, William. 1980. Law as an instrument of social change. In William Evan (ed.), *The Sociology of Law.* New York: Free Press.

Ewick, Patricia, and Susan Silbey. 1992. Conformity, contestation and resistance: An account of legal consciousness. *New England Law Review* 26:731-49.

Eysenck, Hans J. 1964. 1977. *Crime and Personality.* London: Routledge & Kegan Paul.

Eysenck, Hans J. 1991. Dimensions of personality: 16, 5, or 3?—Criteria for a taxonomic paradigm. *Personality and Individual Differences* 8:773-790.

———. 1996. Personality theory and the problem of criminality. In J. Muncie, E. McLaughlin, and M. Langan (ed.), *Criminological Perspectives.* London: Sage.

Eysenck, Hans J., and Gisli H. Gudjonsson. 1989. *The Causes and Cures of Criminality.* New York: Plenum.

Fagan, Jeffrey. 1990. Social processes of delinquency and drug use among urban gangs. In C. Ronald Huff (ed.), *Gangs in America.* Newbury Park, Calif.: Sage.

———. 1991. Drug selling and licit income in distressed neighborhoods: the economic lives of street-level drug users and dealers. In Adele V. Harrell and George E. Peterson (eds.), *Drugs, Crime, and Social Isolation.* Washington, D.C.: Urban Institute Press.

Fagan, Jeffery, Elizabeth Piper, and Melinda Moore. 1986. Violent delinquents and urban youths. *Criminology* 24:439-71.

Fairchild, Halford H. 1991. Scientific racism: The cloak of objectivity. *Journal of Social Issues* 47:101-15.

Farberman, Harvey A. 1975. A crimogenic market structure: The automobile industry. *Sociological Quarterly* 16:438-57.

Faris, Robert E. L. 1967. *Chicago Sociology, 1920-1932.* San Francisco: Chandler.

Faris, Robert E. L., and Warren Dunham. 1939. *Mental Disorder in Urban Areas.* Chicago: University of Chicago Press.

Farnham, E. W. 1846. "Introductory preface" to M. B. Sampson, *Rationale of Crime.* New York: D. Appleton & Company.

Farnworth, Margaret and Michael J. Leiber. 1989. Strain theory revisited: Economic goals, educational means, and delinquency. *American Sociological Review* 54:263-74.

Farrington, David P. 1986. Stepping stones to adult criminal careers. In Dan Olweus, Jack Block, and Marian Radke-Yarrow (eds.), *Development of Antisocial and Prosocial Behaviour: Research, Theories, and Issues.* New York: Academic Press.

———. 1987. Early precursors of frequent offending. In James Q. Wilson and Glenn C. Loury (eds.), *From Children to Citizens.* Vol. 3: *Families, Schools, and Delinquency Prevention.* New York: Springer-Verlag.

———. 1988. Studying changes within individuals: The causes of offending. In Michael Rutter (ed.), *Studies of Psychosocial Risk: The Power of Longitudinal Data.* New York: Cambridge University Press.

Farrington, David P., and Roger Tarling. 1985. *Prediction in Criminology.* Albany: SUNY Press.

Farrington, David P., Lloyd E. Ohlin, and James Q. Wilson. 1986. *Understanding and Controlling Crime: Toward a New Research Strategy*. New York: Springer-Verlag.

Fauman, M. A., and B. J. Fauman. 1980. Chronic Phencyclidine (PCP) abuse: A psychiatric perspective. *Journal of Psychedelic Drugs* 12:307–14.

Faunce, William A. 1989. Occupational status-assignment systems: The effect of status on self-esteem. *American Journal of Sociology* 95:378–400.

Featherman, David L., and Richard M. Lerner. 1985. Ontogenesis and sociogenesis: Problematics for theory and research about development and socialization across the lifespan. *American Sociological Review* 50:659–76.

Feeley, Malcolm, and Jonathan Simon. 1992. The new penology: Notes on the emerging strategy of corrections and its implications. *Criminology* 30:449–74.

Feeney, Floyd. 1986. Robbers as decision-makers. In Derek B. Cornish and Ronald V. Clarke (eds.), *The Reasoning Criminal*. New York: Springer-Verlag.

Felson, Marcus. 1980. Human chronography. *Sociology and Social Research* 65:1–9.

———. 1981. Social accounts based on map, clock and calendar. In Thomas Juster and Kenneth Land (eds.), *Social Accounting Systems: Essays in the State of the Art*. New York: Academic Press.

———. 1983. Ecology of crime. *Encyclopedia of Crime and Justice*. New York: Macmillan.

———. 1985. Crime at any point on the city map. In Robert M. Figlio, Simon Hakim, and George F. Rengert (eds.), *Metropolitan Crime Patterns*. Monsey, N.Y.: Criminal Justice Press.

———. 1986a. Linking criminal choices, routine activities, informal control, and criminal outcomes. In Derek B. Cornish and Ronald V. Clarke (eds.), *The Reasoning Criminal*. New York: Springer-Verlag.

———. 1986b. Routine activities, social controls, rational decisions and criminal outcome. In Derek B. Cornish and Ronald V. Clarke (eds.), *The Reasoning Criminal*. New York: Springer-Verlag.

———. 1987. Routine activities, social controls, rational decisions and criminal outcomes *Criminology*, 25:911–31.

———. 1994. *Crime and Everyday Life*. Thousand Oaks, Calif.: Pine Forge Press.

Felson, Marcus, and Lawrence E. Cohen. 1980. Human ecology and crime: A routine activity approach. *Human Ecology* 8:389–406.

Felson, Marcus, and Michael Gottfredson. 1984. Adolescent activities near peers and parents. *Journal of Marriage and the Family* 46:709–14.

Fernald, Walter E. 1909. The imbecile with criminal instincts. *American Journal of Insanity* 65:731–49.

Ferraris, Maurizio. 1992. Postmodernism and the deconstruction of modernism. In Marco Diani (ed.), *The Immaterial Society: Design, Culture, and Technology in the Postmodern World*. Englewood Cliffs, N.J.: Prentice-Hall.

Ferrell, Jeff. 1992. Making sense of crime: A review essay on Jack Katz's *Seductions of Crime*. *Social Justice*. 19:110–23.

Festinger, Leon. 1957. *A Theory of Cognitive Dissonance*. Stanford: Stanford University Press.

Finestone, Harold. 1976. *Victims of Change: Juvenile Delinquents in American Society*. Westport, Conn.: Greenwood Press.

Fink, Arthur E. 1938. *Causes of Crime: Biological Theories in the United States, 1800–1915*. Philadelphia: University of Pennsylvania Press.

Finsterbusch, Kurt. 1982. Boomtown disruption thesis: Assessment of current evidence. *Pacific Sociological Review* 25:307–22.

Fish, Stanley. 1989. *Doing What Comes Naturally: Change, Rhetoric, and the Practice of Theory in Literary and Legal Studies*. Durham: Duke University Press.

Fishbein, Diana H. 1990. Biological perspectives in criminology. *Criminology* 28:27–72.

———. 1991. Medicalizing the drug war. *Behavioral Sciences and the Law* 9:323–44.

————. 1992. The psychology of female aggression. *Criminal Justice and Behavior* 19:99–126.

Fishbein, Diana H., and Susan Pease. 1996. *The Dynamics of Drug Abuse*. Boston: Allyn & Bacon.

Fishbein, D. H., D. Lozovsky, and J. H. Jaffe. 1989a. Impulsivity, aggression and neuroendocrine responses to serotonergic stimulation in substance abusers. *Biological Psychiatry* 25:1049–66.

Fishbein, D. H., R. Herning, W. Pickworth, C. Haertzen, J. Hickey, J. Jaffe. 1989b. Spontaneous EEG and brainstem evoked response potentials in drug abusers with histories of aggressive behavior. *Biological Psychiatry* 26:595–611.

Fishbein, Diana H., Elizabeth Dax, David B. Lozovsky, and Jerome H. Jaffe. 1992. Neuroendocrine responses to a glucose challenge in substance users with high and low levels of aggression, impulsivity, and antisocial personality. *Neuropsychobiology* 25:106–14.

Fisher, Eric, A. 1975. Community courts: An alternative to conventional criminal justice adjudication. *American University Law Review* 24:1253–91.

Fisher, F. M., and Daniel Nagin. 1978. On the feasibility of identifying the crime function in a simultaneous model of crime rates and sanction levels. In Albert Blumstein (ed.), *Deterrence and Incapacitation: Estimating the Effects of Criminal Sanctions on Crime Rates*. Washington, D.C.: National Academy of Sciences.

Fishman, Mark. 1978. Crime waves as ideology. *Social Problems* 25:531–43.

Fisse, Brent, and John Braithwaite. 1983. *The Impact of Publicity on Corporate Offenders*. Albany: SUNY Press.

Fitzpatrick, Peter. 1984. Law and societies. *Osgood Hall Law Journal* 22:115–38.

————. 1988. The rise and rise of informalism. In Roger Matthews (ed.), *Informal Justice*. London: Sage.

Fletcher, J. 1848. Moral and educational statistics of England. *Journal of the Statistical Society*. 10:193; 11:344; 12:151.

Foley, D. L. 1973. Institutional and contextual factors affecting the housing choices of minority residents. In Amos H. Hawley and V. P. Rock (eds.), *Segregation in Residential Areas*. Washington D.C.: National Academy of Sciences.

Folkman, Susan. 1991. Coping across the life-span: Theoretical issues. In E. Mark Cummings, Anita L. Greene, and Katherine H. Karraker (eds.), *Life-Span Developmental Psychology: Perspectives on Stress and Coping*. Hillsdale, N.J.: Lawrence Erlbaum.

Foucault, Michel. 1977. *Discipline and Punish: The Birth of the Prison*. New York: Pantheon.

————. 1978. *The History of Sexuality*. Vol. I: *An Introduction*. New York: Random House.

————. 1979. *Discipline & Punish: The Birth of the Prison*. Trans. Alan Sheridan. New York: Vintage.

————. 1982. The subject and power. In Hubert Dreyfus and Paul Rabinow (eds.), *Michel Foucault: Beyond Structuralism and Hermeneutics*. Chicago: University of Chicago Press.

————. 1988. The dangerous individual. In Lawrence D. Kritzman (ed.), *Foucault: Politics, Philosophy, Culture (Interviews and Other Writings 1977–1984)*. Trans. Alain Baudot and Jane Couchman. London: Routledge.

Fowles, Don C. 1980. The three-arousal model: Implications of Gray's two-factor learning theory for heart rate, electrodermal activity, and psychopathy. *Psychophysiology* 17:87–104.

Frazier, Charles E. 1976. *Theoretical Approaches to Deviance: An Evolution*. Columbus, Ohio: Charles Merrill.

Frazier, E. Franklin. 1932. *The Negro in the United States*. New York: Macmillan.

Freire, Paulo. 1970. *Pedagogy of the Oppressed*. Trans. Myra Bergman Ramos. New York: Herder and Herder.

Freire, Paulo, and Henry A. Giroux. 1989. Pedagogy, popular culture, and public life: An introduction. In Henry Giroux, Roger I. Simon, and contributors, *Popular Culture, Schooling, and Everyday Life*. Granby, Mass.: Bergin and Garvey.

Freudenburg, W. R. 1984. Boomtown's youth: The differential impacts of rapid community growth on adolescents and adults. *American Sociological Review* 49:697–705.

Friedan, Betty. 1983. *The Feminine Mystique*. New York: Bantam, Doubleday.

Friedlander, Kate. 1947. *The Psychoanalytical Approach to Juvenile Delinquency*. London: International Universities Press.

Friedrichs, David O. 1981. Violence and the politics of crime. *Social Research* 48:135–56.

———. 1996. *Trusted Criminals: White Collar Crime in Contemporary Society*. Belmont, Calif.: Wadsworth.

Frug, Mary J. 1983. Sexual equality and sexual difference in American law. *New England Law Review* 26:665–82.

Gabor, Thomas. 1981. The crime displacement hypothesis: An empirical examination. *Crime and Delinquency* 26:390–404.

Galliher, John F., and John Ray Cross. 1983. *Moral Legislation without Morality*. New Brunswick, N.J.: Rutgers University Press.

Gans, Herbert J. 1962. *The Urban Villagers*. New York: Free Press.

Gansberg, Martin. 1979. *New Jersey Journal. New York Times*. January 21.

Garfinkel, Harold. 1956. Conditions of successful degradation ceremonies. *American Journal of Sociology* 61:420–24.

Garland, David. 1985. *Punishment and Welfare: A History of Penal Strategies*. Brookfield, Vt.: Gower.

Garland, David, and Peter Young (eds.). 1983. *The Power to Punish: Contemporary Penality and Social Analysis*. London: Heinemann.

Gay, Peter. 1966. *The Enlightenment: An Interpretation*. New York: Alfred A. Knopf.

Geis, Gilbert. 1967. The heavy electrical equipment antitrust cases of 1961. In Gilbert Geis and Robert Meier (eds.), *White Collar Crime*. New York: Free Press.

———. 1993. White collar crime. *Annals of the American Academy of Political and Social Science* 525:8–11.

——— (ed.). 1982. *On White-Collar Crime*. Lexington, Mass.: Lexington Books.

Geis, Gilbert, and Colin Goff. 1983. Introduction. In Edwin H. Sutherland, *White Collar Crime: The Uncut Version*. New Haven: Yale University Press.

Geis, Gilbert, and Robert Meier (eds.). 1977. *White-Collar Crime*. New York: Free Press.

Geis, Gilbert, Henry Pontell, and Paul Jesilow. 1987. Medicaid fraud. In Joseph E. Scott and Travis Hirschi (eds.), *Controversial Issues in Criminology and Criminal Justice*. Beverly Hills, Calif.: Sage.

Gelles, Richard J., and Claire P. Cornell. 1985. *Intimate Violence in Families*. Beverly Hills, Calif.: Sage.

Gerber, Jurg, and Susan L. Weeks. 1992. Women as victims of corporate crime: A call for research on a neglected topic. *Deviant Behavior* 13:325–47.

Gersten, Joanne C., Thomas S. Langer, Jeanne G. Eisenberg, and Lida Ozek. 1974. Child behavior and life events: Undesirable change or change per se. In Barbara Snell Dohrenwend and Bruce P. Dohrenwend (eds.), *Stressful Life Events: Their Nature and Effects*. New York: John Wiley & Sons.

Gerth, Hans, and C. Wright Mills. 1953. *Character and Social Structure*. New York: Harcourt Brace Jovanovich.

Ghodsian-Carpey, J., and L. A. Baker. 1987. Genetic and environmental influences on aggression in 4 to 7 year old twins. *Aggressive Behavior* 13:173–86.

Gibbons, Donald. C. 1973. *Society, Crime and Criminal Careers*. Englewood Cliffs, N.J.: Prentice-Hall.

———. 1994. *Talking about Crime and Criminals*. Englewood Cliffs, N.J.: Prentice-Hall.

Gibbs, Jack P. 1975. *Crime, Punishment, and Deterrence*. New York: Elsevier.
———. 1989. *Control: Sociology's Central Notion*. Urbana, Ill.: University of Illinois Press.
Gibbs, Jack P., and Glenn Firebaugh. 1990. The artifact issue in deterrence. *Criminology* 28:347–65.
Giddens, Anthony. 1984. *The Constitution of Society*. Oxford: Polity Press.
Gilmore, Samuel. 1992. Culture. In Edgar F. Borgatta and Marie L. Borgatta (eds.), *Encyclopedia of Sociology*. New York: Macmillan.
Ginsburg, B. E., and B. F. Carter. 1987. *Premenstrual Syndrome: Ethical and Legal Implications in a Biomedical Perspective*. New York: Plenum.
Giordano, Peggy C., and Stephen A. Cernkovich. 1979. On complicating the relationship between liberation and delinquency. *Social Problems* 26:467–81.
Glaser, Barney G., and Anselm L. Strauss. 1967. *The Discovery of Grounded Theory*. Chicago: Aldine.
———. 1971. *Status Passage*. Chicago: Aldine.
Glassner, Barry. 1992. *Bodies: Overcoming the Tyranny of Perfection*. Los Angeles: Lowell House.
Glueck, Sheldon, and Eleanor Glueck. 1950. *Unraveling Juvenile Delinquency*. New York: Commonwealth Fund.
———. 1956. *Physique and Delinquency*. New York: Harper & Row.
———. 1957. Working mothers and delinquency. *Mental Hygiene* 41:327–52.
———. 1968. *Delinquents and Nondelinquents in Perspective*. Englewood Cliffs, N.J.: Prentice-Hall.
Goddard, H.H. 1921. *Juvenile Delinquency*. New York: Dodd, Mead.
Goetting, Ann. 1987. Homicidal wives. *Journal of Family Issues* 8:332–41.
———. 1988. Patterns of homicide among women. *Journal of Interpersonal Violence* 3:3–20.
Goffman, Erving. 1959. *The Presentation of Self in Everyday Life*. Garden City, N.Y.: Anchor.
———. 1961. *Asylums: Essays in the Social Situation of Mental Patients and Other Inmates*. Garden City, N.Y.: Anchor.
———. 1963. *Stigma: Notes on the Management of Spoiled Identity*. Englewood Cliffs, N.J.: Prentice-Hall.
———. 1972. *Relations in Public*. New York: Harper Colophon.
———. 1974. *Frame Analysis*. New York: Harper & Row.
———. 1981. *Forms of Talk*. Oxford: Basil Blackwell.
Gold, Martin. 1970. *Delinquent Behavior in an American City*. Belmont, Calif.: Brooks/Cole.
———. 1987. The social ecology of delinquency. In H. C. Quay (ed.), *Handbook of Juvenile Delinquency*. New York: John Wiley & Sons.
Goldberg, Gertrude S., and Eleanor Kremen. 1987. The feminization of poverty: Only in America? *Social Policy* 17:3–14.
Gordon, Diana R. 1991. *The Justice Juggernaut: Fighting Street Crime, Controlling Citizens*. New Brunswick, N.J.: Rutgers University Press.
Gorecki, Jan. 1985. *A Theory of Criminal Justice*. New York: Columbia University Press.
Gorenstein, E. E., and, Joseph P. Newman. 1980. Disinhibitory psychopathology: A new perspective and a model for research. *Psychological Review* 87:301–15.
Gottfredson, Michael R., and Travis Hirschi. 1987a. The positivist tradition. In Michael R. Gottfredson and Travis Hirschi (eds.), *Positive Criminology*. Newbury Park, Calif.: Sage.
———. 1987b. A propensity-event theory of crime. In Freda Adler and William S. Laufer (eds.), *Advances in Criminological Theory*, Vol. 1. New Brunswick, N.J.: Transaction Publishers.
———. 1990. *A General Theory of Crime*. Stanford, Calif.: Stanford University Press.
Gottfredson, Stephen D., and Ralph B. Taylor. 1983. Person-environment interactions

in the prediction of recidivism. Paper presented at the annual meeting of the American Society of Criminology, Denver.

————. 1986. Person-environment interactions in the prediction of recidivism. In James M. Byrne and Robert J. Sampson (eds.), *The Social Ecology of Crime*. New York: Springer-Verlag.

Gould, Leroy C., Egon Bittner, Sheldon Messinger, Fred Powledge, and Sol Chaneles. 1966. *Crime as a Profession*. Washington, D.C.: U.S. Government Printing Office.

Gould, Stephen J. 1981. *The Mismeasure of Man*. New York: W. W. Norton.

Goulden, Joseph. 1984. *Death Merchant: The Brutal True Story of Edwin P. Wilson*. New York: Simon and Schuster.

Gouldner, Alvin W. 1968. The sociologist as partisan: Sociology and the welfare state. *American Sociologist* 3:103–16.

Gove, Walter R. 1985. The effect of age and gender on deviant behavior: A biopsychological perspective. In Alice Rossi (ed.), *Gender and the Life Course*. New York: Aldine.

Gove, Walter R., and Michael L. Hughes. 1980. Reexamining the ecological fallacy: A study in which aggregate data are critical in investigating the pathological effects of living alone. *Social Forces* 58:1157–77.

Gove, Walter R., and C. Wilmoth. 1990. Risk, crime and physiological highs: A consideration of neurological processes which may act as positive reinforcers. In L. Ellis and H. Hoffman (eds.), *Evolution, The Brain and Criminal Behavior: A Reader in Biosocial Criminology*. New York: Praeger.

Gove, Walter R., Michael L. Hughes, and Omer R. Galle. 1979. Overcrowding in the home. *American Sociological Review* 44:59–80.

Governor's Commission on Science and Technology for the State of New Jersey. 1983. Report of the Governor's Commission on Science and Technology.

Graham, Elspeth. 1992. Postmodernism and paradox. In Joe Doherty, Elspeth Graham, and Mo Malek (eds.), *Postmodernism and the Social Sciences*. New York: St. Martin's Press.

Grasmick, Harold G., Charles R. Tittle, Robert J. Bursik, Jr., and Bruce J. Arneklev. 1993. Testing the core empirical implications of Gottfredson and Hirschi's general theory of crime. *Journal of Research in Crime and Delinquency* 30:5–29.

Gray, Jeffrey A. 1977. Drug effects on fear and frustration: Possible limbic site of action of minor tranquilizers. In Leslie L. Iversen, Susan D. Iversen, and Solomon H. Snyder (eds.), *Handbook of Psychopharmacology*. Vol. 8. *Drugs, Neurotransmitters, and Behavior*. New York: Plenum.

Green, David. 1985. Veins of resemblance: Photography and eugenics. *Oxford Art Review* 7:3–16.

Greenberg, David F. 1977. Delinquency and the age structure of society. *Contemporary Crises* 1:189–223.

————. 1979. Delinquency and age structure of society. In Sheldon L. Messinger and Egon Bittner (eds.) *Criminology Review Yearbook*. Beverly Hills, Calif.: Sage.

————. (ed.). 1981. 1993. *Crime and Capitalism: Readings in Marxist Criminology*. Palo Alto, Calif: Mayfield.

Greenberg, Michael R., and Richard F., Anderson. 1984. *Hazardous Waste Sites: The Credibility Gap*. Piscataway, N.J.: Center for Urban Policy Research.

Greenberg, Stephanie, William M. Rohe, and Jay R. Williams. 1982a. The relationship between informal social control, neighborhood crime and fear: A synthesis and assessment of the research. Paper presented at the annual meeting of the American Society of Criminology, Toronto.

————. 1982b. *Safe and Secure Neighborhoods: Physical Characteristics and Informal Territorial Control in High and Low Crime Neighborhoods*. Washington, D.C.: National Institute of Justice.

————. 1985. *Informal Citizen Action and Crime Prevention at the Neighborhood Level*. Washington, D.C.: National Institute of Justice.

Greenspan, Rosanne. 1988. The transformation of criminal due process in the administrative state. Paper presented at the annual meeting of the Law and Society Association, Vail, Colorado.

Greenwood, Peter. 1982. *Selective Incapacitation*. Santa Monica, Calif.: Rand Corporation.

Gregory, Jeanne. 1986. Sex, class and crime: Toward a nonsexist criminology. In Roger Matthews and Jock Young (eds.), *Confronting Crime*. Beverly Hills, Calif.: Sage.

Grimm, Melchior. 1765a. 1878. Examen de la traduction du *Traite' des De'lits et des Peines de Beccaria par Morellet*. In *Correspondance litteraire, philosophique et critique*. Vol. 6 Paris: Gamier.

————. 1765b. 1878. Sur le traite des *Delits et des Peines, par Beccaria*. In *Correspondance litteraire, philosophique et critique*. Vol. 6. Paris: Gamier.

Gross, Hanns. 1990. *Rome in the Age of Enlightenment*. New York: Cambridge University Press.

Gruder, Charles L. 1977. Choice of comparison persons in evaluating oneself. In Jerry M. Suls and Richard L. Miller (eds.), *Social Comparison Processes*. New York: Hemisphere.

Guerry, A. M. 1833. *Essai sur la Statistique Morale de la France*. Paris: Crochard.

Guest, Avery M. 1984a. The city. In M. Micklin and Harvey M. Choldin (eds.), *Sociological Human Ecology*. Boulder, Colo.: Westview.

————. 1984b. Robert Park and the natural area: A sentimental review. *Sociology and Social Research* 68:1–21.

Gusfield, Joseph R. 1963. *Symbolic Crusade*. Urbana: University of Illinois Press.

Guze, S. B., E. D. Wolfgram, J. K. McKinney, and D. P. Cantwell. 1967. Psychiatric illness in the families of convicted criminals: A study of 519 first-degree relatives. *Diseases of the Nervous System* 28:651–59.

Habermas, Jurgen. 1981. *Theorie des Kommunikativen Handelns*. Frankfurt: Suhrkamp. Published in English translation as *The Theory of Communicative Action*. Boston: Beacon. Vol. 1, 1984; Vol. 2, 1987.

————. 1984. *The Theory of Communicative Action*. Vol 1. *Reason and the Rationalization of Society*. Boston: Beacon Press.

————. 1987. *The Theory of Communicative Action*. Vol. 2. *Lifeworld and System: A Critique of Functionalist Reason*. Boston: Beacon Press.

Hafner, Katherine. 1983. UCLA student penetrates DOD network. *InfoWorld* 5(47):28.

Hagan, John. 1980. The legislation of crime and delinquency: A review of theory, method, and research. *Law and Society Review* 14:603–28.

————. 1989a. Micro and macro structures of delinquency causation and a power control theory of gender and delinquency. In S. F. Messner, M. D. Krohn and A. E. Liska (eds.), *Theoretical Integration in the Study of Deviance and Crime: Problems and Prospects*. Albany: SUNY Press.

————. 1989b. *Structural Criminology*. New Brunswick, NJ: Rutgers University Press.

Hagan, John. 1991. Destiny and drift: Subcultural preferences, status attainments, and the risks and rewards of youth. *American Sociological Review* 56:567–82.

Hagan, John, and Alberto Palloni. 1986. Toward a structural criminology: Method and theory in criminological research. *Annual Review of Sociology* 12:431–49.

————. 1990. The social reproduction of a criminal class in working-class London, circa 1950–1980. *American Journal of Sociology* 96:265–99.

Hagan, John, and Patricia Parker. 1985. White collar crime and punishment: The class structure and legal sanctioning of securities violations. *American Sociological Review* 5:302–16.

Hagan, John, A. R. Gillis, and J. Chan. 1978. Explaining official delinquency: A spatial study of class, conflict and control. *Sociological Quarterly* 19:386–98.

Hagan, John, A.R. Gillis, and John Simpson. 1985. The class structure of gender and delinquency: Toward a power-control theory of common delinquent behavior. *American Journal of Sociology* 90:1151–78.

————— 1987. Class in the household: A power-control theory of gender and delinquency. *American Journal of Sociology* 92:788–816.

Hagan, John, John Simpson, and A. R. Gillis. 1979. The sexual stratification of social control. *British Journal of Sociology* 30:25–38.

—————. 1987. Class in the household: A power-control theory of gender and delinquency. *American Journal of Sociology* 92:788–816.

—————. 1988. Feminist scholarship, relational and instrumental control, and a power control theory of gender and delinquency. *British Journal of Sociology* 39:301–36.

Hagedorn, John M. 1988. *People and Folks: Gangs, Crime and the Underclass in a Rustbelt City*. Chicago: Lakeview.

—————. 1991. Gangs, neighborhoods, and public policy. *Social Problems* 38:529–42.

Haldane, John. 1992. Cultural theory, philosophy and the study of human affairs: Hot heads and cold feet! In Joe Doherty, Elspeth Graham and Mo Malek (eds.), *Postmodernism and the Social Sciences*. New York: St. Martin's Press.

Halevy, Elie. 1928. *The Growth of Philosophical Radicalism*. London: Faber & Gwyer.

Hall, Jerome. 1952. *Theft, Law and Society*. Indianapolis, Ind.: Bobbs-Merrill.

Haller, Mark. 1963. *Eugenics: Hereditarian Attitudes in American Thought*. New Brunswick, N.J.: Rutgers University Press.

Hamid, Ansley. 1992. The developmental cycle of a drug epidemic: The cocaine smoking epidemic of 1981–1991. *Journal of Psychoactive Drugs* 24:337–48.

Hamilton, James A. 1989. Postpartum psychiatric disorders. *Psychiatric Clinics of North America* 12:89.

Hamparin, D. M., R. Schuster, S. Dinitz, and J. P. Conrad. 1978. *The Violent Few: A Study of Dangerous Juvenile Offenders*. Lexington, Mass.: Lexington Books.

Hannerz, Ulf. 1969. *Soulside: Inquiries into Ghetto Culture and Community*. New York: Columbia University Press.

Haraway, Donna. 1990. A manifesto for cyborgs: Science, technology, and socialist feminism in the 1980s. In Linda J. Nicholson (ed.), *Feminism/Postmodernism*. New York: Routledge.

Hare, R. D. 1970. *Psychopathy: Theory and Research*. New York: John Wiley & Sons.

Hare, R. D., and D. Schalling. 1978. *Psychopathic Behavior*. New York: John Wiley & Sons.

Harrer, Tom. 1985. Hackers try to outsmart system . . . as software producers work to foil "pirates." *Gainesville Sun*, July 7, Supplement:6.

Harries, Keith D. 1980. *Crime and the Environment*. Springfield, Ill.: Charles C Thomas.

Harrington, Christine, and Sally Merry. 1988. Ideological production: The making of community mediation. *Law and Society Review* 22:709–35.

Harrington, Christine, and Barbara Yngvesson. 1990. Interpretive sociolegal research. *Law and Social Inquiry* 15:135–48.

Harris, A. R. 1977. Sex and theories of deviance. *American Sociological Review* 42:3–16.

Harrison, G. A., J. M. Tanner, D. R. Pilbeam, and P. T. Baker. 1988. *Human Biology: An Introduction to Human Evolution, Variation, Growth, and Adaptability*. Oxford: Oxford University Press.

Harry, B., and C. Balcer. 1987. Menstruation and crime: A critical review of the literature from the clinical criminology perspective. *Behavioral Sciences and the Law* 5:307–22.

Hart, H. L. A. 1982. *Essays on Bentham*. Oxford: Clarendon Press.

Hartmann, Heidi. 1979. Capitalism, patriarchy and job segregation by sex. In Zillah Eisenstein (eds.), *Capitalist Patriarchy and the Case for Socialist Feminism*. New York: Monthly Review Press.

—————. 1981. The unhappy marriage of Marxism and feminism: Towards a more progressive union. In Lydia Sargent (eds.), *Women and Revolution*. Boston: South End Press.

Haskell, Edward F. 1940. Mathematical systematization of "environment," "organism" and "habitat." *Ecology* 21:1–16.

Haskett, R. F. 1987. Premenstrual dysphoric disorder: Evaluation, pathophysiology and treatment. *Progress in Neuro-Psychopharmacology and Biological Psychiatry* 11:129–35.

Haskins, Ron. 1989. Beyond metaphor: The efficacy of early childhood education. *American Psychologist* 44:274–82.

Havemann, Joel. 1993. The trade secrets of Denmark. *Los Angeles Times*, July 3:A1.

Hawkins, J. David, and Denise M. Lishner. 1987. Schooling and delinquency. In Elmer H. Johnson (ed.), *Handbook on Crime and Delinquency Prevention*. New York: Greenwood.

Hawkins, Keith. 1983. Bargain and bluff: Compliance strategy and deterrence in the enforcement of regulation. *Law and Policy Quarterly* 5:35–73.

———. 1984. *Environment and Enforcement: Regulation and the Social Definition of Pollution*. New York: Oxford University Press.

Hayner, Norman S. 1942. Five cities of the Pacific Northwest. In Clifford Shaw and Henry McKay (eds.), *Juvenile Delinquency and Urban Areas*. Chicago: University of Chicago Press.

Hazelrigg, Lawrence. 1986. Is there a choice between "constructionism" and "objectivism"? *Social Problems* 33:510–13.

Healy, William, and Augusta Bronner. 1926. *Delinquents and Criminals: Their Making and Unmaking*. New York: Macmillan.

———. 1936. 1969. *New Light on Delinquency and Its Treatment*. New Haven: Yale University Press.

Hegtvedt, Karen A. 1990. The effects of relationship structure on emotional responses to inequity. *Social Psychology Quarterly* 53:214–28.

———. 1991. Social comparison processes. In Edgar F. Borgotta and Marie E. Borgotta (eds.), *Encyclopedia of Sociology*. Vol. 3. New York: Macmillan.

Heitgerd, Janet L., and Robert J. Bursik, Jr. 1987. Extra-community dynamics and the ecology of delinquency. *American Journal of Sociology* 92:775–87.

Helvetius, Claude-Adrien. 1758. *De l'esprit*. Paris: Durand.

Henderson, Charles R. 1893. *An Introduction to the Study of the Dependent, Defective and Delinquent Classes*. Boston: D.C. Heath.

Henry, Stuart. 1977. On the Fence. *British Journal of Law and Society* 4:124–33.

———. 1983. *Private Justice*. London: Routledge & Kegan Paul.

———. 1985. Community justice, capitalist society and human agency: The dialectics of collective law in the cooperative. *Law and Society Review* 19:301–25.

———. 1987. Private justice and the policing of labor: The dialectics of industrial discipline. In Clifford Shearing and Philip Stenning (eds.), *Private Policing*. Beverly Hills. Calif.: Sage Publications.

———. 1988a. Can the hidden economy be revolutionary? Toward a dialectic analysis of the relations between formal and informal economies. *Social Justice* 15:29–60.

———. 1988b. Rules, rulers and ruled in egalitarian collectives: Deviance and social control in cooperatives. In James G. Flanagan and Steve Rayner (eds.), *Rules, Decisions, and Egalitarian Societies*. Aldershot, U.K.: Avebury.

———. 1989a. Constitutive criminology: The missing link. *Critical Criminologist*, 1 (Summer):9, 12.

———. 1989b. Justice on the margin: Can alternative justice be different? *The Howard Journal of Criminal Justice* 28:255–71.

———. 1994a. *Inside Jobs: A Realistic Guide to Criminal Justice Careers for College Graduates*. Salem, Wis.: Sheffield Publishing.

———. 1994b. Newsmaking criminology as replacement discourse. In Gregg Barak (ed.) *Media, Process and the Social Construction of Crime: Studies in Newsmaking Criminology*. New York: Garland Publishing.

———. 1994c. *Social Control*. Aldershot, U.K.: Dartmouth.

———. 1996. Criminology. In Joseph Bessette (ed.), *Ready Reference: American Justice*. Pasadena: Salem Press.

Henry, Stuart, and Dragan Milovanovic. 1991. Constitutive criminology: The maturation of critical theory. *Criminology* 29:293–316.

———. 1993. Back to basics: A postmodern redefinition of crime. *Critical Criminologist* 5:1–2, 12.

———. 1994. The constitution of constitutive criminology: A postmodern approach to criminological theory. In David Nelken (ed.), *The Futures of Criminology*. London: Sage.

———. 1996. *Constitutive Criminology: Beyond Postmodernism*. London: Sage.

Herrnstein, Richard J., and Charles Murray. 1994. *The Bell Curve: Intelligence and Class Structure in American Life*. New York: Free Press.

Hersh, Seymour. 1979. Ex-analyst says CIA rejected warning on Shah. *New York Times*, January 7:A10. Cited in Piers Beirne and James Messerschmidt. 1991. *Criminology*. New York: Harcourt Brace Jovanovich.

Hess, H. F., and J. V. Diller. 1969. Motivation for gambling as revealed in the marketing methods of the legitimate gambling industry. *Psychological Reports* 25:19–27.

Heydebrand, Wolf, and Carroll Seron. 1990. *Rationalizing Justice: The Political Economy and Federal District Courts*. New York: SUNY Press.

Hilborn, Robert C. 1994. *Chaos and Nonlinear Dynamics: An Introduction for Scientists and Engineers*. New York: Oxford University Press.

Hill, Gary D., and Elizabeth M. Crawford. 1990. Women, race, and crime. *Criminology* 28:601–23.

Hindelang, Michael J. 1973. Causes of delinquency: A partial replication and extension. *Social Problems* 20:471–78.

———. 1974. Moral evaluations of illegal behaviors. *Social Problems* 21:370–84.

———. 1978. Race and involvement in common-law personal crimes. *American Sociological Review* 43:93–109.

———. 1981. Variations in sex-race-age-specific incidence rates of offending. *American Sociological Review* 46:461–74.

Hindelang, Michael J., Travis Hirschi, and Joseph G. Weis. 1979. Correlates of delinquency: The illusion of discrepancy between self-report and official measures. *American Sociological Review* 44:995–1014.

———., Travis Hirschi, and Joseph G. Weis. 1981. *Measuring Delinquency*. Beverly Hills, Calif.: Sage.

Hirsch, A. R. 1983. *Making the Second Ghetto: Race and Housing in Chicago 1940–1960*. New York: Cambridge University Press.

Hirschel, J. David, Ira W. Hutchison, Charles W. Dean, and Anne-Marie Mills. 1992. Review essay on the law enforcement response to spouse abuse: Past, present, and future. *Justice Quarterly* 9:247–83.

Hirschi, Travis. 1969. *Causes of Delinquency*. Berkeley: University of California Press.

———. [1969]. 1979. Separate and unequal is better. *Journal of Research in Crime and Delinquency* 16:34–38.

———. 1983. Crime and family policy. In Ralph Weisheit and Robert Culbertson (eds.), *Juvenile Delinquency: A Justice Perspective*. Prospect Heights, Ill.: Waveland.

———. 1985. Crime and the family. In James Q. Wilson (ed.), *Crime and Public Policy*. San Francisco: ICS Press.

———. 1994. Theory without ideas: Reply to Akers. *Criminology* 34:249–56.

Hirschi, Travis, and Michael R. Gottfredson. 1979. Introduction: The Sutherland tradition in criminology. In Travis Hirschi and Michael Gottfredson (eds.), *Understanding Crime: Current Theory and Research*. Beverly Hills, Calif.: Sage.

Hirschi, Travis and Michael R. Gottfredson. 1983. Age and the explanation of crime. *American Journal of Sociology* 89:552–84.

———. 1986. The distinction between crime and criminality. In Timothy F. Hartnagel and Robert Silverman (eds.), *Critique and Explanation: Essays in Honor of Gwynn Nettler*. New Brunswick, N.J.: Transaction Publishers.

———. 1987a. Causes of white-collar crime. *Criminology* 25:949–74.
———. 1987b. Toward a general theory of crime. In Wouter Buikhuisen and Sarnoff Mednick (eds.), *Explaining Crime: Interdisciplinary Approaches*. Leiden: Brill.
———. 1989. The significance of white-collar crime for a general theory of crime. *Criminology* 27:359–71.
———. 1993. Commentary: Testing the general theory of crime. *Journal of Research in Crime and Delinquency* 30:47–54.
——— (eds.). 1994. *The Generality of Deviance*. New Brunswick, N.J.: Transaction Publishers.
Hirschi, Travis and Michael J. Hindelang. 1977. Intelligence and delinquency: A revisionist view. *American Sociological Review* 42:571–87.
Hirschi, Travis, Michael J. Hindelang, and Joseph G. Weis. 1980. The status of self-report measures. In Malcolm W. Klein and Katherine S. Teilman (eds.), *Handbook of Criminal Justice Evaluation*. Beverly Hills, Calif.: Sage.
Hirst, Paul Q. 1986. *Law, Socialism and Democracy*. London: Allen & Unwin.
Hobbs, Daniel F., Jr. 1965. Parenthood as crisis: A third study. *Journal of Marriage and the Family* 27:367–72.
Hoffman-Bustamente, Dale. 1973. The nature of female criminality. *Issues in Criminology* 8:117–36.
Holland, John H. 1992. *Adaptions in Natural and Artificial Systems*. Cambridge, Mass.: MIT Press.
Holland, Terrill R., and Norman Holt. 1975. Personality patterns among short-term prisoners undergoing presentence evaluation. *Psychological Reports* 37:827–36.
Hollinger, Richard C. 1984. Computer deviance: Receptivity to electronic rule-breaking. Paper presented at the annual meeting of the American Society of Criminology, Cincinnati, Ohio.
Homans, George C. 1961. *Social Behavior: Its Elementary Forms*. New York: Harcourt, Brace and World.
Hood, Roger, and Richard Sparks. 1970. *Key Issues in Criminology*. London: Weidenfeld and Nicolson..
Hook, Elizabeth F. 1984. Black women, white women: Separate paths to liberation. In Allison M. Jagger and Paula S. Rothenberg (eds.), *Feminist Frameworks*. 2d ed. New York: McGraw-Hill.
hooks, bell. 1984. *Feminist Theory: From Margin to Center*. Boston: South End Press.
Hooton, Earnest Albert. 1939a. *The American Criminal: An Anthropological Study*. Cambridge, Mass.: Harvard University Press.
Hooton, Earnest Albert. 1939b. *Crime and the Man*. Cambridge, Mass.: Harvard University Press.
Hope, Tim J. 1982. *Burglary in Schools: The Prospects for Prevention. Research and Planning Unit Paper 11*. London: HMSO.
Horley, Sandra. 1991. *The Charm Syndrome*. London: Papermac.
Hougan, Jim. 1978. *Spooks: The Haunting of America—The Private Use of Secret Agents*. New York: William Morrow.
———. 1984. *Secret Agenda: Watergate, Deep Throat, and the CIA*. New York: Random House.
House, James S. 1981. *Work Stress and Social Support*. Reading, Mass.: Addison-Wesley.
House, T. H., and W. L. Milligan. 1976. Autonomic responses to modeled distress in prison psychopaths. *Journal of Personality and Social Psychology* 34:556–60.
Howard, R. C. 1984. The clinical EEG and personality in mentally abnormal offenders. *Psychological Medicine* 14:569–80.
———. 1986. Psychopathy: A psychobiological perspective. *Personality and Individual Differences* 7:795–806.
Huesmann, L. Rowell, Leonard D. Eron, Monroe M. Lefkowitz, and Leopold O. Walder. 1984. Stability of aggression over time and generations. *Developmental Psychology* 20:1120–34.

Huff, C. Ronald. 1990. *Gangs in America*. Newbury Park, Calif.: Sage.
Huizinga, David, and Delbert S. Elliott. 1986. *The Denver High-Risk Delinquency Project*. Proposal Submitted to the Office of Juvenile Justice and Delinquency Prevention.
Hume, David. 1739. *A Treatise of Human Nature*. 1967. Oxford: Clarendon Press.
Humphries, Drew, and David F. Greenberg. 1981. The dialectics of crime control. In David F. Greenberg (ed.), *Crime and Capitalism: Readings in Marxist Criminology*. Palo Alto, Calif.: Mayfield.
Hunt, Alan. 1987. The critique of law: What is "critical" about critical legal theory? *Journal of Law and Society* 14:5–19.
———. 1990. The big fear: Law confronts postmodernism. *McGill Law Journal* 35:507–40.
———. 1991. Postmodernism and critical criminology. In Brian D. MacLean and Dragan Milovanovic (eds.), *New Directions in Critical Criminology*. Vancouver, B.C.: Collective Press.
———. 1992. Foucault's expulsion of law: Toward a retrieval. *Law and Social Inquiry* 17:1–38.
———. 1993. *Explorations in Law and Society: Toward a Constitutive Theory of Law*. London: Routledge.
Hutcheson, Francis. 1725a.*An Inquiry Concerning Beauty, Order, Harmony, Design*. 1973. The Hague: Martinus Nijhoff.
———. 1725b. *An Inquiry into the Original of Our Ideas of Beauty and Virtue. In Two Treatises*. 1738. London: Printed for D. Midwinter, A. Bettesworth, and C. Hitch.
———. 1755. *A System of Moral Philosophy*. London: A. Millar and T. Longman.
Huyssen, Andreas. 1986. Mass culture as woman: Modernism's other. In Tania Modleski (ed.), *Studies in Entertainment: Critical Approaches to Mass Culture*. Bloomington: Indiana University Press.
Hyman, Herbert. 1953. The value systems of the different classes: A social-psychological contribution to the analysis of stratification. In Reinhard Bendix and Seymour Martin Lipset (eds.), *Class, Status, and Power*. New York: Free Press.
Ignatieff, Michael. 1978. *A Just Measure of Pain: The Penitentiary in the Industrial Revolution, 1750–1850*. London: Macmillan.
Inciardi, James. 1974. Vocational crime. In Daniel Glaser (ed.), *Handbook of Criminology*. Chicago: Rand McNally.
———. 1975. *Careers in Crime*. Chicago: Rand McNally.
———. (ed.). 1980. *Radical Criminology: The Coming Crises*. Beverly Hills, Calif.: Sage.
Ingraham, Donald G. 1980. On charging computer crime. *Computer/Law Journal* 2:429–39.
Irwin, John. 1985. *The Jail: Managing the Underclass in American Society*. Berkeley: University of California Press.
Jackall, Robert. 1988. *Moral Mazes: The World of Corporate Managers*. New York: Oxford University Press.
Jackson, Bernard. 1988. *Law, Fact and Narrative Coherence*. Merseyside, U.K.: Deborah Charles Publications.
Jackson, Bruce. 1969. *A Thief's Primer*. Englewood Cliffs, N.J.: Prentice-Hall.
Jacobs, James B. 1977. *Stateville: The Penitentiary in Mass Society*. Chicago: University of Chicago Press.
Jacobs, Jane. 1961. *The Life and Death of Great American Cities*. New York: Random House.
Jacobs, John. 1977a. The diaries of a CIA operative. *Washington Post*, September 5:1.
———. 1977b. Turner cites 149 drug-test projects. *The Washington Post*, August 4:1.
Jacobs, P. A., M. Brunton, M. M. Melville, R. P. Brittain, and W. McClemont. 1965. Aggressive behaviour, mental subnormality, and the XYY male. *Nature* 108:1351–52.
Jacoby, Russell. 1987. *The Last Intellectuals: American Culture in the Age of Academe*. New York: Basic Books.

Jaggar, Alison. 1983. *Feminist Politics and Human Nature.* New Jersey: Roman and Allanheld.

Jamieson, Katherine M. 1994. *The Organization of Corporate Crime: Dynamics of Antitrust Violation.* Thousand Oaks, Calif.: Sage.

Jankowski, Martin Sanchez. 1991. *Islands in the Street: Gangs and American Urban Society.* Berkeley: University of California Press.

Janowitz, Morris. 1967. *The Community Press in an Urban Setting.* 2d ed. Chicago: University of Chicago Press.

——. 1976. *Social Control of the Welfare State.* Chicago: University of Chicago Press.

——. 1978. *The Last Half-Century: Societal Change and Politics in America.* Chicago: University of Chicago Press.

Jasso, Guillermina, and Peter H. Rossi. 1977. Distributive justice and earned income. *American Sociological Review* 42:639–51.

Jastrow, Joseph. 1886. A theory of criminality. *Science* 8:20–22.

Jaucourt, Chevalier de. 1751. 1969. Crime (faute, peche, delit, forfait). In Diderot and d'Alembert (eds.), *Encyclopedie, ou dictionnaire raisonne des sciences, des arts et des metiers.* Vol. 1. New York: Pergamon.

Jefferson, Tony. 1990. *The Case for Paramilitary Policing.* Milton Keynes: Open University Press.

Jeffery, C. Ray. 1965. Criminal behavior and learning theory. *Journal of Criminal Law, Criminology and Police Science* 56:294–300.

Jenkins, Philip. 1984. Varieties of Enlightenment criminology. *British Journal of Criminology* 24:112–30.

Jenness, Valerie. 1993. *Making It Work: The Prostitutes' Rights Movement in Perspective.* New York: Aldine de Gruyter.

Jensen, Gary. 1986. Dis-integrating integrated theory: A critical analysis of attempts to save strain theory. Paper presented at the annual meeting of the American Society of Criminology, Atlanta.

Jensen, Gary F., Maynard L. Erickson, and Jack Gibbs. 1978. Perceived risk of punishment and self-reported delinquency. *Social Forces* 57:57–58.

Jesilow, Paul, Henry N. Pontell, and Gilbert Geis. 1993. *Prescription for Profit: How Doctors Defraud Medicaid.* Berkeley: University of California Press.

Jessop, Bob. 1982. *The Capitalist State.* New York: New York University Press.

Jessor, Richard, John E. Donovan, and Frances M. Costa. 1991. *Beyond Adolescence: Problem Behavior and Young Adult Development.* New York: Cambridge University Press.

Joas, Hans. 1981. George Herbert Mead and the "division of labor": Macrosociological implications of Mead's social psychology. *Symbolic Interaction* 4:177–90.

——. 1985. *G. H. Mead: A Contemporary Reexamination of His Thought.* Cambridge, U.K.: Polity Press.

Johnson, B. D., T. Williams, K. Dei, and H. Sanahria. 1985. *Taking Care of Business: The Economics of Crime by Heroin Abusers.* Lexington, Mass.: D. C. Heath.

Johnson, Deborah G. 1985. *Computer Ethics.* Englewood Cliffs, N.J.: Prentice-Hall.

Johnson, Deborah G., and John W. Snapper. 1985. *Ethical Issues in the Use of Computers.* Belmont, Calif.: Wadsworth.

Johnson, Miriam M. 1988. *Strong Mothers, Weak Wives.* Berkeley: University of California Press.

Johnson, Richard E. 1979. *Juvenile Delinquency and Its Origins.* London: Cambridge University Press.

Johnstone, John W. C. 1978. Social class, social areas and delinquency. *Sociology and Social Research* 63:49–77.

Jones, D. Caradog. 1934. *The Social Survey of Merseyside.* Vol. III. Liverpool: University Press of Liverpool.

Jones, David A. 1986. *History of Criminology: A Philosophical Perspective.* New York: Greenwood Press.

Joseph, Gloria I. 1981. Black mothers and daughters. In Gloria I. Joseph and Jill Lewis (eds.), *Common Differences: Conflicts in Black and White Feminist Perspectives*. Boston: South End Press.

Jurik, Nancy C., and Russ Winn. 1990. Gender and homicide: A comparison of men and women who kill. *Violence and Victims* 5:227–42.

Kagan, J., J. S. Reznick, and N. Snidman. 1988. Biological bases of childhood shyness. *Science* 240:167–71.

Kandel, Denise B., and John A. Logan. 1984. Patterns of drug use from adolescence to young adulthood I: Periods of risk for initiation, continued risk and discontinuation. *American Journal of Public Health* 74:660–67.

Kandel, Denise, Mark Davies, and Nazli Baydar. 1990. The creation of interpersonal contexts: Homophily in dyadic relationships in adolescence and young adulthood. In Lee Robins and Michael Rutter (eds.), *Straight and Devious Pathways from Childhood to Adulthood*. New York: Cambridge University Press.

Kandel, E., and S. A. Mednick. 1988. IQ as a protective factor for subjects at high risk for antisocial behavior. *Journal of Consulting and Clinical Psychology* 56:224–26.

Kaplan, Howard B., Cynthia Robbins, and Steven S. Martin. 1983. Toward the testing of a general theory of deviant behavior in longitudinal perspective: Patterns of psychopathology. In James R. Greenley and Roberta G. Simmons (eds.), *Research in Community and Mental Health*. Greenwich, Conn.: JAI Press.

Kaplan, L., and J. Maher. 1970. The economics of the numbers game. *American Journal of Economics and Sociology* 29:391–408.

Kappeler, Victor, Mark Blumberg, and Gary Potter. 1993. *The Mythology of Crime and Criminal Justice*. Prospect Heights, Ill.: Waveland Press.

Kapsis, Robert E. 1976. Continuities in delinquency and riot patterns in black residential areas. *Social Problems* 23:567–80.

———. 1978. Residential succession and delinquency. *Criminology* 15:459–86.

Katz, Jack. 1979a. Concerted ignorance: The social construction of coverup. *Urban Life* 8:295–316.

———. 1979b. Legality and equality: Plea bargaining in the prosecution of white collar crimes. *Law and Society Review* 13:431–60.

———. 1988. *Seductions of Crime: Moral and Sensual Attractions of Doing Evil*. New York: Basic Books.

———. 1991. Criminals' passions and the progressive's dilemma. In Alan Wolfe (ed.), *America at Century's End*. Berkeley: University of California Press.

Keane, Carl, Paul S. Maxim, and James J. Teevan. 1993. Drinking and driving, self-control, and gender: Testing a general theory of crime. *Journal of Research in Crime and Delinquency* 30:30–46.

Kellam, S. G., M. E. Ensminger, and M. B. Simon. 1980. Mental health in first grade and teenage drug, alcohol, and cigarette use. *Drug and Alcohol Dependence* 5:273–304.

Kellam, S. G., J. D. Branch, D. C. Agrawal, and M. E. Ensminger. 1975. *Mental Health and Going to School: The Woodlawn Program of Assessment, Early Intervention and Evaluation*. Chicago: University of Chicago Press.

Kellner, Douglas. 1990. The postmodern turn: Positions, problems and prospects. In George Ritzer (ed.), *Frontiers of Social Theory: The New Synthesis*. New York: Columbia University Press.

Kellor, Frances A. 1901. *Experimental Sociology. Descriptive and Analytical. Delinquents*. New York: Macmillan.

Kemper, Theodore D. 1978. *A Social Interactional Theory of Emotions*. New York: John Wiley & Sons.

Kenrick, Douglas T., and David C. Funder. 1988. Profiting from controversy: Lessons from the person-situation debate. *American Psychologist* 43:23–34.

Kessler, Suzanne J., and Wendy McKenna. 1978. *Gender: An Ethnomethodological Approach*. Chicago: University of Chicago Press.

Kidder, Frederic. 1870. *History of the Boston Massacre*. Albany: Joel Munsell.

Kiloh, L. G., A. J. McComas, and J. W. Osselton. 1972. *Clinical Electroencephalography*. 3d ed. London: Butterworths.

Kirschenman, Joleen, and Kathryn Neckerman. 1991. "We'd love to hire them, but. . .": The meaning of race for employers. In Christopher Jencks and Paul Peterson (eds.), *The Urban Underclass*. Washington, D.C.: Brookings Institution.

Kitsuse, John I. 1962. Societal reaction to deviant behavior: Problems of theory and method. *Social Problems* 9:247–56.

Kitsuse, John I., and Aaron V. Cicourel. 1963. A note on the uses of official statistics. *Social Problems* 11:131–39.

Klang, Daniel M. 1984. Reform and enlightenment in eighteenth-century Lombardy. *Canadian Journal of History/Annales Canadiennes d'Histoire* 19(April):39–70.

Klare, Karl. 1979. Law making as praxis. *TELOS* 40:123–35.

Klein, John F. 1974. Professional theft: The utility of a concept. *Canadian Journal of Criminology and Corrections* 16:133–44.

Klein, Lloyd. 1988. Big brother is still watching Yyou. Paper presented at the annual meeting of the American Society of Criminology, Chicago.

Klein, Malcolm W. 1971. *Street Gangs and Street Workers*. Englewood Cliffs, N.J.: Prentice-Hall.

———. 1987. Watch out for that last variable. In S. Mednick, T. E. Moffitt, and S. A. Stack (eds.), *The Causes of Crime: New Biological Approaches*. New York: Cambridge University Press.

Klein, Malcolm W., and Cheryl L. Maxson. 1993. Gangs and cocaine trafficking. In C. Uchida and D. Mackenzie (eds.), *Drugs and the Criminal Justice System*. Newbury Park, Calif.: Sage.

Klein, Malcolm W., Cheryl L. Maxson, and Lea C. Cunningham. 1991. Crack, street gangs, and violence. *Criminology* 29:623–50.

Kling, Rob. 1980. Computer abuse and computer crime as organizational activities. *Computer/Law Journal* 2:403–27.

Kluegel, James R., and Eliot R. Smith. 1986. *Beliefs about Inequality*. New York: Aldine de Gruyter.

Knorr-Cetina, Karin, and Aaron Cicourel. 1981. *Advances in Social Theory and Methodology: Toward an Integration of Macro- and Micro-Sociologies*. London: Routledge & Kegan Paul.

Kobrin, Solomon. 1971. The formal logical properties of the Shaw-McKay delinquency theory. In Harwin L. Voss and D. M. Peterson (eds.), *Ecology, Crime and Delinquency*. New York: Appleton-Century-Crofts.

Kornhauser, Ruth Rosner. 1978. *Social Sources of Delinquency: An Appraisal of Analytic Models*. Chicago: University of Chicago Press.

Kram, Kathy E., Peter C. Yeager, and Gary Reed. 1989. Decisions and dilemmas: The ethical dimension in the corporate context. In James E. Post (ed.), *Research in Corporate Social Performance and Policy*. Vol. 11. Greenwich, Conn.: JAI Press.

Kreitman, Norman. 1976. The coal gas story: United Kingdom suicide rates, 1960–71. *British Journal of Preventive and Social Medicine* 30:86–93.

Kreitman, Norman, and S. Platt. 1984. Suicide, unemployment, and domestic gas detoxification in Britain. *Journal of Epidemiology and Community Health* 38:1–6.

Kreuz, L. E., and R. M. Rose. 1971. Assessment of aggressive behavior and plasma testosterone in a young criminal population. *Psychomatic Medicine* 34:321–32.

Kroeber, Alfred, and Talcott Parsons. 1958. The concepts of culture and of social system. *American Sociological Review* 73:582–83.

Krueger, R. F., P. Schmutte, A. Caspi, T. E. Moffitt, P. A. Silva, and K. Campbell. 1994. Personality traits are linked to crime among males and females: Evidence from a birth cohort. *Journal of Abnormal Psychology* 103:328-38.

Kruger, Henrik. 1980. *The Great Heroin Coup*. Boston: South End Press.

Kuhn, Thomas. 1962. 1970. *The Structure of Scientific Revolutions.* Chicago: University of Chicago Press.

Kwitny, Jonathan. 1987. *The Crimes of Patriots.* New York: W. W. Norton.

La Questione Criminale. 1981. Dibattito su: Il codice Rocco cinquant'anni dopo. *La questione criminale* 7:3–168, 247–322, 349–89, 435–41.

Laberge, D. 1991. Women's criminality, criminal women, criminalized women? Questions in and for a feminist perspective. *Journal of Human Justice* 2:37–56.

Labouvie, Erich W. 1986a. Alcohol and marijuana use in relation to adolescent stress. *International Journal of the Addictions* 21:333–45.

———. 1986b. The coping function of adolescent alcohol and drug use. In Rainer K. Silbereisen, Klaus Eyfeth and Georg Rudinger (eds.), *Development as Action in Context.* New York: Springer-Verlag.

Lacan, Jacque. 1977. *Ecrits.* Trans. Alan Sheridan. New York: W. W. Norton.

Land, Kenneth C., Patricia L. McCall, and Lawrence E. Cohen. 1990. Structural covariates of homicide rates: Are there any invariances across time and social space? *American Journal of Sociology* 95:922–63.

———. 1991. Characteristics of U.S. cities with extreme (high or low) crime rates: Results of discriminant analyses of 1960, 1970, and 1980 data. *Social Indicators Research* 24:209–31.

Lander, Bernard. 1954. *Toward an Understanding of Juvenile Delinquency.* New York: Columbia University Press.

Landreth, Bill. 1985. *Out of the Inner Circle: A Hacker's Guide to Computer Security.* Bellevue, Wash.: Microsoft Press.

Lane, Paul J., and Jean S. Kling. 1979. Construct validity of the overcontrolled hostility scale of the MMPI. *Journal of Consulting and Clinical Psychology* 47:781–82.

Lang, R. A., R. Holden, R. Langevin, G. M. Pugh, and R. Wu. 1987. Personality and criminality in violent offenders. *Journal of Interpersonal Violence* 2:179–95.

Langbein, John H. 1976. *Torture and the Law of Proof: Europe and England in the Ancien Regime.* Chicago: University of Chicago Press.

Larson, C. J. 1984. *Crime, Justice and Society.* New York: General Hall.

Lasley, James R. 1987. Toward a control theory of white-collar offending. Unpublished manuscript. Claremont, Calif.: Department of Criminal Justice, Claremont Graduate School.

Lather, Patti. 1991. *Getting Smart.* London: Routledge.

Laub, John. 1983. Urbanism, race, and crime. *Journal of Research in Crime and Delinquency* 20:183–98.

Laub, John, and M. Joan McDermott. 1985. An analysis of serious crime by young black women. *Criminology* 23:89–98.

Laub, John H., and Robert J. Sampson. 1993. Turning points in the life course: Why change matters to the study of crime. *Criminology* 31:301–25.

Lauritsen, Janet L., Robert J. Sampson, and John Laub. 1991. The link between offending and victimization among adolescents. Criminology 29:265–92.

Lea, John, and Jock Young. 1984. *What Is To Be Done About Law and Order?* Harmondsworth, U.K.: Penguin.

LeBlanc, Marc, and Marcel Frechette. 1989. *Male Criminal Activity from Childhood through Youth: Multilevel and Developmental Perspectives.* New York: Springer-Verlag.

Lee, Barrett A., Ralph S. Oropesa, Barbara J. Metch, and Avery M. Guest. 1984. Testing the decline-of-community thesis: Neighborhood organizations in Seattle, 1929 and 1979. *American Journal of Sociology* 89:1161–88.

Lemert, Edwin M. 1942. The folkways and social control. *American Sociological Review* 7:394–99.

———. 1951. *Social Pathology. A Systematic Approach to the Theory of Sociopathic Behavior.* New York: McGraw-Hill.

———. 1958. The behavior of the systematic check forger. *Social Problems* 6:141–48.
———. 1967. *Human Deviance, Social Problems and Social Control.* Englewood Cliffs, N.J.: Prentice-Hall.
Leonard, Eileen B. 1982. *A Critique of Criminology Theory: Women, Crime and Society.* New York: Longman.
Leonard, William N., and Marvin G. Weber. 1977. Automakers and dealers: A study of crimogenic market forces. In G. Geis and R. F. Meier (eds.), *White-Collar Crime: Offenses in Business, Politics, and the Professions.* Rev. ed. New York: Free Press.
Lerner, Harriet Goldhor. 1980. Internal prohibitions against female anger. *American Journal of Psychoanalysis* 40:137–47.
Lerner, Melvin J. 1977. The justice motive: Some hypotheses as to its origins and forms. *Journal of Personality* 45:1–52.
Lernoux, Penny. 1984. The Miami connection. *Nation,* February 18:186–98.
Lester, M. L., and D. H. Fishbein. 1987. Nutrition and neuropsychological development in children. In R. Tarter, D. H. Van Thiel, and K. Edwards (eds.), *Medical Neuropsychology: The Impact of Disease on Behavior.* New York: Plenum.
Letkemann, Peter. 1973. *Crime as Work.* Englewood Cliffs, N.J.: Prentice-Hall.
Levin, Yale, and Alfred Lindesmith. 1937. English ecology and criminology of the past century. *Journal of Criminal Law and Criminology* 27:801–16.
Levy, Steven. 1984. *Hackers: Heroes of the Computer Revolution.* New York: Doubleday.
Lewis, D. O., S. S. Shanok, and J. N. Pincus. 1981. The neuropsychiatric status of violent male delinquents. In D. O. Lewis (ed.), *Vulnerabilities to Delinquency.* New York: Spectrum.
Lewis, Diane. 1977. A response to inequality: Black women, racism, and sexism. *Signs* 3:339–61.
———. 1981. Black women offenders and criminal justice: Some theoretical considerations. In Marguerite Warren (ed.), *Comparing Female and Male Offenders.* Beverly Hills, Calif: Sage.
Lichter, Daniel T. 1988. Racial differences in underemployment in American cities. *American Journal of Sociology* 13:771–92.
Lieberman, David. 1989. *The Province of Legislation Determined.* New York: Cambridge University Press.
Lieberson, Stanley. 1985. *Making It Count: The Impoverishment of Social Research and Theory.* Berkeley: University of California Press.
Liebow, Elliot. 1967. *Tally's Corner.* Boston: Little, Brown.
Lilly, J. Robert, Francis Cullen, and Richard A. Ball. 1989. *Criminological Theory: Context and Consequences.* Newbury Park, Calif.: Sage.
Lincoln, Y. S., and E. G. Guba. 1985. *Naturalistic Inquiry.* Beverly Hills, Calif.: Sage.
Linder, R. L., S. E. Lerner, and R. S. Burns. 1981. The experience and effects of PCP abuse. In Ronald L. Linder (ed.), *PCP, The Devil's Dust: Recognition, Management, and Prevention of Phencyclidine Abuse.* Belmont, Calif.: Wadsworth.
Lindesmith, Alfred R. 1967. *The Addict and the Law.* New York: Vintage.
Linnoila, M., M. Virkunnen, M. Scheinin, A. Nuutila, R. Rimon, and F. K. Goodwin. 1983. Low cerebrospinal fluid 5-hydroxyindoleacetic acid concentration differentiates impulsive from non-impulsive violent behavior. *Life Sciences* 33:2609–14.
Linsky, Arnold S., and Murray A. Straus. 1986. *Social Stress in the United States.* Dover, Mass.: Auburn House.
Lipsky, Michael. 1980. *Street Level Bureaucrats.* New York: Russell Sage Foundation
Liska, Allen E. 1987. *Perspectives on Deviance.* Englewood Cliffs, N.J.: Prentice-Hall.
Liska, Allen E., and Mark Reed. 1985. Ties to conventional institutions and delinquency. *American Sociological Review* 50:547–60.
Liska, Allen E., Marvin Krohn, and Steven Messner. 1988. *Theoretical Integration in the Study of Deviance and Crime: Problems and Prospects.* Albany: State University of New York at Albany Press.

Locke, John. 1689. 1727. Essay Concerning Human Understanding, and Of the Conduct of the Understanding. In *The Works of John Locke*. Vol. 1 and 3. London: Printed for Arthur Bettesworth.

Loeber, Rolf. 1982. The stability of antisocial and delinquent child behavior: A review. *Child Development* 53:1431–46.

Loeber, Rolf, and Thomas Dishion. 1983. Early predictors of male delinquency: A review. *Psychological Bulletin* 94:68–99.

Loeber, Rolf, and Marc LeBlanc. 1990. Toward a developmental criminology. In Michael Tonry and Norval Morris (eds.), *Crime and Justice: An Annual Review of Research*. Vol. 12. Chicago: University of Chicago Press.

Loeber, Rolf and Magda Stouthamer-Loeber. 1986. Family factors as correlates and predictors of juvenile conduct problems and delinquency. In Michael Tonry and Norval Morris (eds.), *Crime and Justice: An Annual Review of Research*. Vol. 7. Chicago: University of Chicago Press.

———. 1987. Prediction. In Herbert C. Quay (ed.), *Handbook of Juvenile Delinquency*. New York: John Wiley & Sons.

Loeber, Rolf, Magda Stouthamer-Loeber, Wilmoet Van Kammen, and David Farrington. 1989. Development of a new measure for self-reported antisocial behavior for young children: Prevalence and reliability. In Malcolm W. Klein (ed.), *Cross-National Research in Self-Reported Crime and Delinquency*. Dordrecht: Kluwer.

———. 1991. Initiation, escalation, and desistance in juvenile offending and their correlates. *Journal of Criminal Law and Criminology* 82:36–82.

Lombroso, C. 1911. 1918. *Crimes: Its Causes and Remedies*. Boston: Little, Brown.

———. 1912. Crime and insanity in the twenty-first century. *Journal of Criminal Law and Criminology* 3:57–61.

Lombroso, Cesare and William Ferrero. 1895. 1915. *The Female Offender*. New York: D. Appleton.

Lombroso-Ferrero, Gina. 1911. 1972. *Criminal Man According to the Classification of Cesare Lombroso*. Montclair, N.J.: Patterson Smith.

Lorde, Audre. 1988. Age, race, class, and sex: Women redefining difference. In Paul S. Rothenberg (ed.), *Racism and Sexism: An Integrated Study*. New York: St. Martin's Press.

Loseke, Donileen R. 1992. *The Battered Women and Shelters: The Social Construction of Wife Abuse*. Albany: SUNY Press.

Lowe, Marian, and Ruth Hubbard (eds.). 1990. *Women's Nature: Rationalizations of Inequality*. New York: Pergamon.

Lowell, Josephine Shaw. 1879. One means of preventing pauperism. *National Conference of Charities, 6th Proceedings* 1879:189–200.

Luhmann, Niklas. 1985. *A Sociological Theory of Law*. Boston: Routledge & Kegan Paul.

Lumsden, Charles J., and Edward O. Wilson. 1981. *Genes, Mind, and Culture*. Cambridge, Mass.: Harvard University Press.

Lydston, George F. 1904. 1905. *The Diseases of Society (The Vice and Crime Problem)*. Philadelphia: J. B. Lippincott.

Lykken, David T. 1957. A study of anxiety in the sociopathic personality. *Journal of Abnormal and Social Psychology* 55:6–10.

———. 1995. *The Antisocial Personalities*. Hillsdale, N.J.: Lawrence Erlbaum.

Lynch, Michael J., and W. Byron Groves. 1989. *A Primer in Radical Criminology*. 2d ed. New York: Harrow and Heston.

Lynxwiler, J., N. Shover, and D. A. Clelland. 1983. The organization and impact of inspector discretion in a regulatory bureaucracy. *Social Problems* 30:425–36.

Lytton, Hugh. 1990. Child and parent effects in boys' conduct disorder: A reinterpretation. *Developmental Psychology* 26:683–97.

MacCoun, Robert and Peter Reuter. 1992. Are the wages of sin $30 an hour? Economic aspects of street-level drug dealing. *Crime and Delinquency* 38:477–91.

MacDonald, Arthur. 1893. *Criminology, with an Introduction by Dr. Cesare Lombroso.* New York: Funk & Wagnalls.

MacKinnon, Catharine. 1987. *Feminism Unmodified: Discourses on Life and Law.* Cambridge, Mass.: Harvard University Press.

———. 1989. *Toward a Feminist Theory of the State.* Cambridge, Mass.: Harvard University Press.

MacLean, Brian, and Dragan Milovanovic. 1997. *Thinking Critically about Crime.* Vancouver: Collective Press.

MacLeod, Jay. 1987. *Ain't No Makin' It: Leveled Aspirations in a Low-Income Neighborhood.* Boulder, Colo.: Westview.

Maestro, Marcello T. 1942. *Voltaire and Beccaria as Reformers of Criminal Law.* New York: Columbia University Press.

Magnusson, David, and Lars R. Bergman. 1988. Individual and variable-based approaches to longitudinal research on early risk factors. In Michael Rutter (ed.), *Studies of Psychosocial Risk: The Power of Longitudinal Data.* New York: Cambridge University Press.

———. 1990. A pattern approach to the study of pathways from childhood to adulthood. In Lee Robins and Michael Rutter (eds.), *Straight and Devious Pathways from Childhood to Adulthood.* New York: Cambridge University Press.

Maguire, Kathleen, and Timothy J. Flanagan. 1990. *Sourcebook of Criminal Justice Statistics 1989.* U.S Department of Justice, Bureau of Justice Statistics. Washington, D.C.: U.S. Government Printing Office.

Maguire, Kathleen, Ann L. Pastore, and Timothy J. Flanagan. 1993. *Sourcebook of Criminal Justice Statistics 1992.* U.S Department of Justice, Bureau of Justice Statistics. Washington, D.C.: U.S. Government Printing Office.

Maguire, Mike. 1980. Burglary as opportunity. *Home Office Research Unit Research Bulletin.* 10:6–9.

Maier-Katkin, Daniel, and Robbin S. Ogle. 1993. A rationale for infanticide laws. *Criminal Law Review* (December):903–14.

Maletsky, B.M. 1976. The diagnosis of pathological intoxication. *Journal of Studies on Alcohol* 37:1215–28.

Mann, Coramae Richey. 1987. Black female homicide in the United States. Paper presented at the Conference on Black Homicide and Public Health.

———. 1990. Black female homicide in the United States. *Journal of Interpersonal Violence* 5:176–201.

Mann, Kenneth. 1985. *Defending White-Collar Crime: A Portrait of Attorneys at Work.* New Haven: Yale University Press.

Mann, Kenneth, Stanton Wheeler, and Austin Sarat. 1980. Sentencing the white-collar offender. *American Criminal Law Review* 17:479–500.

Mann, Leon. 1973. Differences between reflective and impulsive children in tempo and quality of decision making. *Child Development* 44:274–79.

Manning, Peter K. 1988. *Symbolic Communication: Signifying Calls and the Police Response.* Cambridge, Mass.: MIT Press.

———. 1991. Critical semiotics. In Brian D. MacLean and Dragan Milovanovic (eds.), *New Directions in Critical Criminology.* Vancouver, B.C.: Collective Press.

Mantsios, Gregory. 1988. Class in America: Myths and realities. In Paula S. Rothenberg (ed.), *Racism and Sexism: An Integrated Study.* New York: St. Martin's Press.

Marinacci, A. A. 1963. Special types of temporal lobe seizures following ingestion of alcohol. *Bulletin of the Los Angeles Neurological Society* 28:241–50.

Markoff, John. 1982. Computer crimes: Lots of money, little ingenuity. *InfoWorld* 4:27–28.

———. 1983. Giving hackers back their good name. *InfoWorld* 5:43.

Marks, Alan. 1977. Sex differences and their effect upon cultural evaluations of methods of self-destruction. *Omega* 8:65–70.

Marris, P., and M. Rein. 1973. *Dilemmas of Social Reform.* 2d ed. Chicago: Aldine.

Marrs-Simon, P. A., M. Weiler, M. C. Santangelo, M. T. Perry, and J. B. Leikin. 1988. Analysis of sexual disparity of violent behavior in PCP intoxication. *Veterinary and Human Toxicology* 30:53–55.

Martens, Frederick T., and Colleen Miller-Longfellow. 1982. Shadows of substance: Organized crime reconsidered. *Federal Probation* 46:3–9.

Martin, Del. 1981. *Battered Wives*. San Francisco: Volcano Press.

Martin, Joanne. 1986. When expectations and justice do not coincide: Blue collar visions of a just world. In Hans Weiner Bierhoff, Ronald L. Cohen, and Jerald Greenberg (eds.), *Justice in Social Relations*. New York: Plenum.

Martin, Joanne, and Alan Murray. 1983. Distributive injustice and unfair exchange. In David M. Messick and Karen S. Cook (eds.), *Equity Theory: Psychological and Social Perspectives*. New York: Praeger.

Martinez, Tomas. 1983. *The Gambling Scene*. Springfield, Ill.: Thomas.

Marx, Gary. 1988. *Undercover: Police Surveillance in America*. Berkeley: University of California Press.

Marx, Karl. 1852. 1984. The eighteenth brumaire of Louis Bonaparte. In K. Marx and F. Engels, *Werke*. In Eugene Kamenka (ed.), *The Portable Marx*. Harmondsworth: Penguin.

———. 1970. *Preface to A Contribution to the Critique of Political Economy*. New York: International Publishers.

———. [1844] 1977. Economic and philosophical manuscripts. In David McLellan (ed.), *Karl Marx: Selected Writings*. Oxford: Oxford University Press.

Marx, Karl, and Frederick Engels. 1976. *The German Ideology*. In Karl Marx and Frederick Engels, *Collected Works*. New York: International Publishers.

Massey, James L., and Marvin Krohn. 1986. A longitudinal examination of an integrated social process model of deviant behavior. *Social Forces* 65:106–34.

Mathieson, Thomas. 1983. The future of control systems—The case of Norway. In David Garland and Peter Young (eds.), *The Power to Punish*. London: Heinemann.

Matsueda, Ross L. 1982. Testing social control theory and differential association. *American Sociological Review* 47:489–504.

Matsueda, Ross L. 1988. The current state of differential association theory. *Crime and Delinquency* 34:277–301.

Matsueda, Ross L., and Karen Heimer. 1987. Race, family structure, and delinquency: A test of differential association and social control theories. *American Sociological Review* 52:826–40.

Mattes, J. A., and M. Fink. 1987. A family study of patients with temper outbursts. *Journal of Psychiatric Research* 21:249–55.

Matthews, Roger, and Jock Young. 1992. Reflections on realism. In Jock Young and Roger Matthews (eds.), *Rethinking Criminology: The Realist Debate*. London: Sage.

Matza, David. 1964. *Delinquency and Drift*. New York: John Wiley & Sons.

———. 1966. The disreputable poor. In Reinhard Bendix and Seymour M. Lipset (eds), *Class, Status and Power*. Glencoe, N.Y.: Free Press.

Matza, David, and Gresham Sykes. 1961. Juvenile delinquency and subterranean values. *American Sociological Review* 26:712–19.

Maurer, David W. 1974. *The American Confidence Man*. Springfield, Ill.: Thomas.

Mawson, Anthony R. 1987. *Criminality: A Model of Stress-Induced Crime*. New York: Praeger.

Mayhew, Henry. 1861. *London Labour and the London Poor*. London: Griffin.

Mayhew, Patricia M., Ronald V. Clarke, Andrew Sturman, and J. M. Hough. 1976. *Crime as Opportunity*. Home Office Research Study. No. 34. London: HMSO.

Maynard, Douglas W., and Thomas P. Wilson. 1980. On the reification of social structure. *Current Perspectives in Social Theory* 1:287–322.

McAdam, Doug. 1989. The biographical consequences of activism. *American Sociological Review* 54:744–60.

McBarnet, Doreen. 1991. Whiter than white collar crime: Tax, fraud insurance and the management of stigma. *British Journal of Sociology* 42:323–44.

McBride, Duane C., and Clyde B. McCoy. 1981. Crime and drug-using behavior: An areal analysis. *Criminology* 19:281–302.

McCaghy, Charles H., and A. Sergio Denisoff. 1973. Pirates and politics: An analysis of interest group conflict. In A. Sergio Denisoff and Charles H. McCaghy (eds.), *Deviance: Conflict and Criminality*. Chicago: Rand McNally.

McCardle, L., and D. H. Fishbein. 1989. The self-reported effects of PCP on human aggression. *Addictive Behaviors* 4:465–72.

McClain, Paula D. 1982. Black females and lethal violence: Has time changed the circumstances under which they kill? *Omega* 13:13–25.

McClelland, Katherine. 1990. The social management of ambition. *Sociological Quarterly* 31:225–51.

McClintock, Anne. 1993. Gonad the barbarian and the Venus flytrap: Portraying the female and male orgasm. In Lynne Segal and Mary McIntosh (eds.), *Sex Exposed*. New Brunswick, N.J.: Rutgers University Press.

McCord, James W., Jr. 1974. *A Piece of Tape*. Rockville, Md.: Washington Media Services.

McCord, Joan. 1979. Some child rearing antecedents of criminal behavior in adult men. *Journal of Personality and Social Psychology* 37:1477–86.

———. 1991. The cycle of crime and socialization practices. *Journal of Criminal Law and Criminology* 82:211–28.

McCoy, Alfred. W. 1973. *The Politics of Heroin in Southeast Asia*. New York: Harper & Row.

McGee, R., S. Williams, D. L. Share, J., Anderson, and P. A. Silva. 1986. The relationship between specific reading retardation, general reading backwardness and behavioural problems in a large sample of Dunedin boys: A longitudinal study from five to eleven years. *Journal of Child Psychology and Psychiatry* 27:597–610.

McGue, Matt, Steven Bacon, and David T. Lykken. 1993. Personality stability and change in early adulthood: A behavioral genetic analysis. *Developmental Psychology* 29:96–109.

McGurk, Barry J., and Rae E. McGurk. 1979. Personality types among prisoners and prison officers. *British Journal of Criminology* 19:31–49.

McKay, Henry D. 1967. A note on trends in rates of delinquency in certain areas in Chicago. In President's Commission of Law Enforcement and the Administration of Justice. *Task Force Report: Juvenile Delinquency and Youth Crime*. Washington, D.C.: U.S. Government Printing Office.

McKenzie, Roderick. 1926. The scope of human ecology. *Publications of the American Sociological Society* 20:141–54.

McKim, W. Duncan. 1900. *Heredity and Human Progress*. New York: Putnam's Sons.

McKnight, Gerald. 1974. *Computer Crime*. London: Joseph.

McManus, M., A. Brickman, N. E. Alessi, and W. L. Grapentine. 1985. Neurological dysfunction in serious delinquents. *Journal of the American Academy of Child Psychiatry* 24:481–86.

Mead, George Herbert. 1934. *Mind, Self and Society*, ed. C. W. Morris. Chicago: University of Chicago Press.

———. [1925] 1964. The genesis of the self and social control. In *George H. Mead: Selected Writings*, ed. Andrew J. Reck. Indianapolis: Bobbs-Merrill.

Mednick, Sarnoff A. 1977. A biosocial theory of the learning of law-abiding behavior. In Sarnoff A. Mednick and Karl O. Christiansen (eds.), *Biosocial Bases of Criminal Behavior*. Beverly Hills, Calif.: Sage.

Mednick, Sarnoff A., W. F. Gabrelli, Jr., and B. Hutchings. 1984. Genetic influences in criminal convictions: Evidence from an adoption cohort. *Science* 224:891–94.

Mednick, Sarnoff A., Terrie E. Moffitt, and Susan A. Stack. 1987. *The Causes of Crime: New Biological Approaches*. New York: Cambridge University Press.

Mednick, Sarnoff A., Terrie E. Moffitt, William F. Gabrielli, and Barry Hutchings. 1986. Genetic factors in criminal behavior. In J. Block, D. Olweus, and M. R. Yarrow (eds.), *The Development of Antisocial and Prosocial Behavior*. New York: Academic Press.

Megargee, Edwin. 1966. Undercontrolled and overcontrolled personality types in extreme antisocial aggression. *Psychological Monographs* 80: No. 3.

———. 1973. Recent research on overcontrolled and undercontrolled personality patterns among violent offenders. *Sociological Symposium* (Spring):37–50.

Meier, Robert. 1985. *Theoretical Methods in Criminology*. Beverly Hills, Calif.: Sage.

———. 1995. Review of Travis Hirschi and Michael R. Gottfredson (eds.), *The Generality of Deviance*. *Social Forces* 73:1627–29.

Meier, Robert and Gilbert Geis. 1982. The psychology of the white-collar offender. In Gilbert Geis (ed.), *On White-Collar Crime*. Lexington, Mass: Lexington Books.

Melossi, Dario. 1976. The Penal Question in "Capital." *Crime and Social Justice* 5:26–33.

———. 1980. Oltre il "Panopticon." Per uno studio delle strategie di controllo sociale nel capitalismo del ventesimo secolo. *La Questione Criminale* 6:277–361.

———. 1985. Punishment and social action: Changing vocabularies of punitive motive within a political business cycle. *Current Perspectives in Social Theory* 6:169–97.

Melossi, Dario, and Massimo Pavarini. 1979. *The Prison and the Factory: Origins of the Penitentiary System*. London: Macmillan.

Menaghan, Elizabeth. 1982. Measuring coping effectiveness: A panel analysis of marital problems and coping efforts. *Journal of Health and Social Behavior* 23:220–34.

———. 1983. Individual coping efforts: Moderators of the relationship between life stress and mental health outcomes. In Howard B. Kaplan (ed.), *Psychosocial Stress: Trends in Theory and Research*. New York: Academic Press.

Merton, Robert K. 1938. Social structure and anomie. *American Sociological Review* 3:672–82.

———. 1957. 1968. *Social Theory and Social Structure*. New York: Free Press.

Messerschmidt, James W. 1986. *Capitalism, Patriarchy, and Crime: Toward a Socialist Feminist Criminology*. Totowa, N.J.: Rowan & Littlefield.

———. 1993. *Masculinities and Crime: Critique and Reconceptualization of Theory*. Boston: Rowman & Littlefield.

———. 1997. *Crime as Structured Action: Gender, Race, Class and crime in the Making*. Thousand Oaks, Calif.: Sage.

Messick, David M., and Keith Sentis. 1979. Fairness and preference. *Journal of Experimental Social Psychology* 15:418–34.

———. 1983. Fairness, preference, and fairness biases. In D. M. Messick and K. S. Cook (eds.), *Equity Theory: Psychological and Sociological Perspectives*. New York: Praeger.

Messinger, Sheldon. 1969. Strategies of control. Ph.D. dissertation, Department of Sociology, University of California at Los Angeles.

Messinger, Sheldon, and John Berecochea. 1990. Don't stay too long but do come back soon. Proceedings, Conference on Growth and Its Influence on Correctional Policy, Center for the Study of Law and Society, University of California at Berkeley.

Messner, Steven F., and Marvin D. Krohn. 1990. Class compliance structures and delinquency: Assessing integrated structural-Marxist theory. *American Journal of Sociology* 96:300–28.

Messner, Steven F., and Richard Rosenfeld. 1994. *Crime and the American Dream*. Belmont, Calif.: Wadsworth.

Messner, Steven F., and Kenneth Tardiff. 1985. The social ecology of urban homicide: An application of the routine activities' approach. *Criminology* 23:241–68.

————. 1986. Economic inequality and levels of homicide: An analysis of neighborhoods. *Criminology* 24:297–316.

Messner, Steven F., Marvin D. Krohn, and Allen E. Liska, eds. 1989. *Theoretical Integration in the Study of Deviance and Crime: Problems and Prospects*. Albany: SUNY Press.

Michalowski, Raymond J., 1993. (De)construction, postmodernism, and social problems: Facts, fiction, and fantasies at the "end of history." In James A. Holstein and Gale Miller (eds.), *Reconsidering Social Constructionism: Debates in Social Problems Theory*. New York: Aldine de Gruyter.

Mickelson, Roslyn Arlin. 1990. The attitude-achievement paradox among black adolescents. *Sociology of Education* 63:44–61.

Mikula, Gerald. 1980. *Justice and Social Interaction*. New York: Springer-Verlag.

————. 1986. The experience of injustice: Toward a better understanding of its phenomenology. In Hans Werner Bierhoff, Ronald L. Cohen and Jerald Greenberg (eds.), *Justice in Social Relations*. New York: Plenium.

Miller, Brent, J. Kelly McCoy, Terrance Olson, and Christopher Wallace. 1986. Parental discipline and control in relation to adolescent sexual attitudes and behavior. *Journal of Marriage and the Family* 48:503–12.

Miller, Eleanor M. 1986. *Street Woman*. Philadelphia: Temple University Press.

Miller, Walter B. 1958. Lower class culture as a generating milieu of gang delinquency. *Journal of Social Issues* 14:5–19.

Mills, C. Wright. 1940. Situated actions and vocabularies of motive. *American Sociological Review* 5:904–13.

————. 1959. *The Sociological Imagination*. New York: Oxford University Press.

————. [1959]1963. *Power, Politics and People*. New York: Oxford University Press.

————. 1972. Situated actions and vocabularies of motive. In Jerome G. Manis and Bernard N. Meltzer (eds.), *Symbolic Interaction: A Reader in Social Psychology*. 2d ed. Boston: Allyn & Bacon.

Milovanovic, Dragan. 1986. Juridico-Linguistic Communicative Markets: Towards a Semiotic Analysis. *Contemporary Crises* 10:281–304.

————. 1988a. Jailhouse lawyers and jailhouse lawyering. *International Journal of the Sociology of Law* 16:455–75.

————. 1988b. 1992. *Primer in the Sociology of Law*. Albany: Harrow and Heston.

Milovanovic, Dragan. 1989. Critical criminology and the challenge ————. *Critical Criminologist* 1:9–10, 17.

————. 1991. Images of unity and disunity in the juridic subject and the movement to the peacemaking community. In Harold Pepinsky and Richard Quinney (eds.), *Criminology as Peacemaking*. Bloomington: Indiana University Press.

————. 1992a. *Postmodern Law and Disorder: Psychoanalytic Semiotics, Chaos and Juridic Exegeses*. Liverpool: Deborah Charles.

————. 1992b. Rethinking subjectivity in law and ideology. In Dawn Currie and Brian Maclean (eds.), *Rethinking the Administration of Justice*. Halifax, Nova Scotia: Fernwood Publishing.

Milovanovic, Dragan, and Jim Thomas. 1989. Overcoming the absurd: Prisoner litigation as primitive rebellion. *Social Problems* 36:48–60.

Minneapolis Star. 1978. Crime's knowledge of computers far outstripping law enforcement, December 5:1.

Minor, W. William. 1980. The neutralization of criminal offense. *Criminology* 18:103–20.

————. Techniques of neutralization: A reconceptualization and empirical examination. *Journal of Research in Crime and Delinquency* 18:295–318.

Mirowsky, John and Catherine E. Ross. 1990. The consolation-prize theory of alienation. *American Journal of Sociology* 95:1505–35.

Mischel, Walter. 1968. *Personality and Assessment*. New York: John Wiley & Sons.

Mischel, Walter, Yuichi Shoda, and Monica L. Rodriguez. 1989. Delay of gratification in children. *Science* 244:933–38.

Mitzman, Arthur. 1969. *The Iron Cage*. New York: Grossett and Dunlap.

Moffitt, Terrie E. 1983. The learning theory model of punishment: Implications for delinquency deterrence. *Criminal Justice and Behavior* 10:131–58.

———. 1989. Accommodating self-report methods to a low-delinquency culture: Experience from New Zealand. In Malcolm W. Klein (ed.), *Cross-National Research in Self-Reported Crime and Delinquency*. Dordrecht: Kluwer.

———. 1993. "Life-course-persistent" and "adolescence-limited" antisocial behavior: A developmental taxonomy. *Psychological Review* 100:674–701.

———. 1994. Natural histories of delinquency. In Hans-Jurgen Kerner and Elmar G. M. Weitekamp (eds.), *Cross-National Longitudinal Research on Human Development and Criminal Behavior*. Dordrecht: Kluwer.

Moffitt, Terrie E., S. A. Mednick, and W. F. Gabrielli, Jr. 1989. Predicting careers of criminal violence: Descriptive data and predispositional factors. In D. A. Brizer and M. Crowner (eds.), *Current Approaches to the Prediction of Violence*. Washington, D.C.: American Psychiatric Press.

Mokhiber, Russell. 1988. *Corporate Crime and Violence: Big Business Power and Abuse of the Public Trust*. San Francisco: Sierra Club Books.

Montesquieu, Charles Louis de Secondat. 1748. De l'esprit des lois. 1973. 2 vols. Paris: Gamier.

Moore, Joan W. 1978. *Homeboys: Drugs and Prison in the Barrios of Los Angeles*. Philadelphia: Temple University Press.

———. 1991. *Going to the Barrio: Homeboys and Homegirls in Change*. Philadelphia: Temple University Press.

Moore, L. S., and A. I. Fleischman. 1975. Subclinical lead toxicity. *Orthomolecular Psychiatry* 4:61–70.

Moore, M. H., S. R. Estrich, D. McGillis, and W. Spelman. 1984. *Dangerous Offenders: The Elusive Target of Justice*. Cambridge, Mass.: Harvard University Press.

Morell, Virginia. 1993. Evidence found for a possible "aggression gene." *Science* 260:1722–23.

Morgan, Rick L., and David Heise. 1988. Structure of emotions. *Social Psychology Quarterly* 51:19–31.

Moyer, Imogeney L. (ed.). 1992. *The Changing Roles of Women in the Criminal Justice System: Offenders, Victims and Professionals*. Prospect Heights, Ill.: Waveland Press.

Moynihan, Daniel P. 1969. *Maximum Feasible Misunderstanding: Community Action in the War on Poverty*. New York: Free Press.

Mueller, Charles W. 1983. Environmental stressors and aggressive behavior. In Russell G. Geen and Edward I. Donnerstein (eds.), *Aggression: Theoretical and Empirical Reviews*. Vol. 2. New York: Academic Press.

Mueller, G. O. W. 1990. Whose prophet is Cesare Beccaria? An essay on the origins of criminological theory. In William S. Laufer and Freda Adler (eds.), *Advances in Criminological Theory*. Vol. 2. New Brunswick, N.J.: Transaction Publishers.

Muhlbauer, H. D. 1985. Human aggression and the role of central serotonin. *Pharmacopsychiatry* 18:218–21.

Mullings, Leith. 1986. Anthropolitical perspectives on the Afro-American family. *American Journal of Social Psychiatry* 6:11–16.

Nader, Ralph, and Mark J. Green. 1972. Crime in the suites: Coddling the corporations. *New Republic* 166:17–21.

Naffine, Ngaire. 1988. *Female Crime: The Construction of Women in Criminology*. Boston: Allen & Unwin.

Nagin, Daniel, and Raymond Paternoster. 1991. On the relationship of past to future participation in delinquency. *Criminology* 29:163–89.

———. 1992. Social capital and social control: The deterrence implications of a theory of individual differences in criminal offending. Unpublished manuscript. Carnegie Mellon University, Pittsburgh.

Nagin, Daniel, and Joel Waldfogel. 1992. The effects of criminality and conviction on the labour market status of young British offenders. Unpublished manuscript. Carnegie Melon University, Pittsburgh.

NARMIC. 1984. *Military Exports to South Africa: A Research Report on the Arms Embargo*. Philadelphia: American Friends Service Committee.

National Center for Children in Poverty. 1987. *Household Statistics on Families and Poverty Rate*. New York: Columbia University Press.

Naughton, James M., John Crewdson, Ben Franklin, Christopher Lydon, and Agie Solpukas. 1977. How Agnew bartered his office to keep from going to jail. In Gilbert Geis and Robert F. Meier (eds.), *White-Collar Crime*. New York: Free Press.

Needleman, Martin L., and Carolyn Needleman. 1979. Organizational crime: Two models of crimogenesis. *Sociological Quarterly* 20:517–28.

David Nelken (ed.). 1994. *The Futures of Criminology*. London: Sage.

Nelson, Bill. 1985. Highlights of Bill Nelson's legislative accomplishments. Handout from Representative Nelson's congressional office, photocopy.

Nettler, Gwynn. 1982a. *Explaining Criminals*. Cincinnati, Ohio: Anderson.

———. 1984b. *Explaining Crime*. 3d ed. New York: McGraw-Hill.

———. 1984. *Killing One Another*. Cincinnati, Ohio: Anderson.

New York Times. 1983. Laws in U.S. called inadequate to block abuse of computers, September 18:1.

———. 1984a. Low Tech, January 5:26.

———. 1984b. Survey outlines computer crimes, June 11:16.

Newcomb, Michael D., and L. L. Harlow. 1986. Life events and substance use among adolescents: Mediating effects of perceived loss of control and meaninglessness in life. *Journal of Personality and Social Psychology* 51:564–77.

Newman, Graeme, and Pietro Marongiu. 1990. Penological reform and the myth of Beccaria. *Criminology* 28:325–46.

Newman, Oscar. 1972. *Defensible Space: Crime Prevention through Urban Design*. New York: Macmillan.

———. 1975. *Community of Interest*. New York: Anchor.

Newsweek. 1983a. Beware: Hackers at play, September 5:42-46, 48.

———. 1983b. Preventing "WarGames," September 5:48.

Nihill, Grant. 1982. Bank links to spies, drugs. *Advertiser*, November 10:1.

Noble, E. P., K. Blum, M. E. Khalsa, T. Richie, A. Montgomery, R. C. Wood, R. J. Fitch, T. Ozkaragoz, P. J. Sheridan, M. D. Anglin, A. Paredes., L. J. Treiman, and R. S. Sparkes. 1993. Allelic association of the D2 dopamine receptor gene with cocaine dependence. *Drug and Alcohol Dependence*. 33:271–85.

Norland, Stephen, and Neal Shover. 1977. Gender roles and female criminality. *Criminology* 15:87–104.

Norland, Stephen, Neal Shover, William Thornton, and Jennifer James. 1979. Intrafamily conflict and delinquency. *Pacific Sociological Review* 22:223–40.

Norris, Pippa. 1984. Women in poverty: Britain and America. *Social Policy* 14:4–43.

Novy, Diane M., and Stephen Donohue. 1985. The relationship between adolescent life stress events and delinquent conduct including conduct indicating a need for supervision. *Adolescence* 78:313–21.

Noyes, William. 1887. The criminal type. *American Journal of Social Science* 24:31–42.

Nycum, Susan. 1976a. The criminal law aspects of computer abuse: Part I—State penal laws. *Rutgers Journal of Computers and Law* 5:271–95.

Nycum, Susan. 1976b. The criminal law aspects of computer abuse: Part II—Federal ———. *Rutgers Journal of Computers and Law* 5:297–322.

Nye, F. Ivan. 1958. *Family Relationships and Delinquent Behavior*. New York: John Wiley & Sons.

O'Neill, R. V., D. L. DeAngelis, J. B. Waide, and T. F. H. Allen. 1986. *A Hierarchical Concept of Ecosystems*. Princeton: Princeton University Press.

Oberman, Michelle. 1992. The control of pregnancy and the criminalization of femaleness. *Berkeley Women's Law Journal* 7:1–12

Olson, Sheryl L., John E. Bates, and Kathryn Bayles. 1990. Early antecedents of childhood impulsivity: The role of parent-child interaction, cognitive competence, and temperament. *Journal of Abnormal Child Psychology* 18:317–34.

Olweus, Dan. 1979. Stability of aggressive reaction patterns in males: A review. *Psychological Bulletin* 86:852–75.

Olweus, D., A. Mattsson, D. Schalling, and H. Low. 1988. Circulating testosterone levels and aggression in adolescent males: A causal analysis. *Psychosomatic Medicine* 50:261–72.

Orwell, George. 1949. *1984*. New York: Harcourt, Brace & World.

Owen, D., and J. O. Sines. 1970. Heritability of personality in children. *Behavior Genetics* 1:235–48.

Owen, John. 1983. *Sleight of Hand: Fine $25 Million Nugan Hand Bank Scandal*. Sydney: Calporteur Press.

Padilla, Felix. 1992. *The Gang as an American Enterprise*. New Brunswick, N.J.: Rutgers University Press.

Palmer, Bryan D. 1990. *Descent into Discourse: The Reification of Language and the Writing of Social History*. Philadelphia: Temple University Press.

Parenti, Michael. 1983. *Democracy for the Few*. New York: St. Martin's Press.

Park, Robert E. 1952. *Human Communities: The City and Human Ecology*. New York: Free Press.

Park, Robert E., and Ernest W. Burgess. 1924. *Introduction to the Science of Sociology*. 2d ed. Chicago: University of Chicago Press.

Park, Robert E., Ernest W. Burgess, and Roderick McKenzie. 1925. *The City*. Chicago: University of Chicago Press.

Parker, Donn B. 1976. *Crime by Computer*. New York: Charles Scribner's Sons.

———. 1979. *Computer Crime: Criminal Justice Resource Manual*. Washington, D.C.: Government Printing Office.

Parker, Donn B. 1980a. Computer abuse research update. *Computer/Law Journal* 2:329–52.

———. 1980b. Computer-related white collar crime. In Gilbert Geis and Ezra Stotland (eds.), *White Collar Crime: Theory and Research*. Beverly Hills, Calif.: Sage.

———. 1983. *Fighting Computer Crime*. New York: Charles Scribner's Sons.

Parker, G. A. 1974. Assessment strategy and the evolution of fighting behaviour. *Journal of Theoretical Biology* 47:223–43.

Parker, J., and Harold G. Grasmick. 1979. Linking actual and perceived certainty of punishment: An exploratory study of an untested proposition in deterrence theory. *Criminology* 17:366–79.

Parmelee, Maurice. 1911. 1918. Introduction to Cesare Lombroso, *Crime: Its Causes and Remedies*. Boston: Little, Brown.

Parsons, Philip A. 1909. *Responsibility for Crime*. New York: Longmans, Green.

Pasquino, Pasquale. 1980. Criminology: The birth of a special savior. *Ideology and Consciousness* 7:17–32.

Paternoster, Raymond, Linda E. Saltzman, Theodore G. Chiricos, and Gordon P. Waldo. 1983. Perceived risk and social control: Do sanctions really deter? *Law and Society Review* 17:457–79.

Paternoster, Raymond, Linda E. Saltzman, Gordon P. Waldo, and Theodore G. Chiricos. 1982. Perceived risk and deterrence: Methodological artifacts in perceptual deterrence research. *Journal of Criminal Law and Criminology* 73:1238–58.

Patterson, Gerald. 1980. Children who steal. In T. Hirschi and M. Gottfredson (eds.), *Understanding Crime: Current Theory and Research*. Beverly Hills, Calif.: Sage.

———. 1982. *Coercive Family Process: A Social Learning Approach*. Eugene, Oreg.: Castalia.

Patterson, Gerald R., and Thomas S. Dishion. 1985. Contributions of families and peers to delinquency. *Criminology* 23:63–80.

Patterson, Gerald R., Barbara D. DeBaryshc, and Elizabeth Ramsey. 1989. A developmental perspective on antisocial behavior. *American Psychologist* 44:329–335.

Patterson, Gerald R., John B. Reid, and Thomas J. Dishion. 1992. *Antisocial Boys.* Eugene, Oreg.: Castalia.

Patterson, Gerald R., J. B. Reid, R. Q. Jones, and R. E. Conger. 1975. *A Social Learning Approach to Family Intervention.* Vol. 1. Eugene, Ore.: Castalia.

Paul, Steven M. 1990. Introduction: Serotonin and its effects on human behavior. *Journal of Clinical Psychiatry (Supplement)* 51:3–4.

Pearce, Frank, and Steve Tombs. 1992. Realism and corporate crime. In Roger Matthews and Jock Young (eds.), *Issues in Realist Criminology.* London: Sage.

Pearlin, Leonard I. 1982. The social contexts of stress. In Leo Goldberger and Shlomo Berznitz (eds.), *Handbook of Stress.* New York: Free Press.

———. 1983. Role strains and personal stress. In Howard Kaplan (ed.), *Psychosocial Stress: Trends in Theory and Research.* New York: Academic Press.

Pearlin, Leonard I., and Carmi Schooler. 1978. The structure of coping. *Journal of Health and Social Behavior* 19:2–21.

Pearson, Frank S., and Neil A. Weiner. 1985. Toward an integration of criminological theories. *Journal of Criminal Law and Criminology* 76:116–50.

Pease, Ken, and Kristiina Hukkila (eds.). 1990. *Criminal Justice Systems in Europe and North America.* Helsinki: Helsinki Institute for Crime Prevention and Control.

Pelfrey, William V. 1980. *The Evolution of Criminology.* Cincinnati, Ohio: Anderson.

People. 1983a. Computers can be robbed, tricked or sabotaged, warns an expert, and their power, if abused, could cause havoc, September 12:49–54.

People. 1983b. The FBI puts the arm on hacker Neal Patrick, September 12:54.

Pepinsky, Harold E. 1991a. *The Geometry of Violence and Democracy.* Bloomington: Indiana University Press.

———. 1991b. Peacemaking in criminology. In Brian D. MacLean and Dragan Milovanovic (eds.), *New Directions in Critical Criminology.* Vacouver, B.C.: Collective Press.

Pepinsky, Harold E., and Paul Jesilow. 1984. *Myths That Cause Crime.* Cabin John, Md.: Seven Locks Press.

Pepinsky, Harold E., and Richard Quinney. 1991. *Criminology as Peacemaking.* Bloomington: Indiana University Press.

Perez, Jacob. 1978. Corporate criminality: A study of the one thousand largest industrial corporations in the United States. Ph.D. dissertation, University of Pennsylvania, Philadelphia.

Perkins, Douglas D., Abraham Wandersman, Richard C. Rich, and Ralph B. Taylor. 1993. The physical environment of street crime: Defensible space, territoriality, and inclivities. *Journal of Environmental Psychology* 13:29–50.

Perlmutter, B. F. 1987. Delinquency and Learning Disabilities: Evidence for compensatory behaviors and adaptation. *Journal of Youth and Adolescence* 16:89–95.

Peterson, R. D., and John Hagan. 1984. Changing conceptions of race. *American Sociological Review* 49:56–70.

Petras, James. 1977. Chile: Crime, class consciousness and the bourgeoisie. *Crime and Social Justice* 7:14–22.

Pfohl, Stephen J. 1977. The discovery of child abuse. *Social Problems* 24:310–24.

———. 1985. *Images of Deviance and Social Control: A Sociological History.* New York: McGraw Hill.

———. 1985. Toward a sociological deconstruction of social problems. *Social Problems* 32:228–31.

———. 1992. Postmodernity as a social problem: Race, class, gender and the new social order. Paper presented at the Annual meeting of the Society for the Study of Social Problems, Pittsburgh.

———. 1993. Twilight of the parasites: Ultramodern capital and the new world order. *Social Problems* 40:125–51.

Pfohl, Stephen J., and Avery Gordon. 1986. Criminological displacements: A sociological deconstruction. *Social Problems* 33:94–113.

Pfuhl, Erdwin H., Jr. 1987. Computer abuse: Problems of instrumental control. *Deviant Behavior* 8:113–30.

Pick, Daniel. 1989. *Faces of Degeneration A European Disorder, c.1848–c.1918*. New York: Cambridge University Press.

Pickles, Andrew, and Michael Rutter. 1991. Statistical and conceptual models of "turning points" in developmental processes. In David Magnusson, Lars Bergman, Georg Rudinger, and Bertil Torestad (eds.), *Problems and Methods in Longitudinal Research: Stability and Change*. New York: Cambridge University Press.

Pielou, E. C. 1975. *Ecological Diversity*. New York: John Wiley & Sons.

Pihl, R. O., and M. Parkes. 1977. Hair element content in learning disabled children. *Science* 198:204.

Pihl, R. O., and D. Ross. 1987. Research on alcohol related aggression: A review and implications for understanding aggression. In S. W. Sadava (ed.), *Drug Use and Psychological Theory*. New York: Haworth Press.

Pihl, R. O., F. Ervin, G. Pelletier, W. Diekel, and W. Strain. 1982. Hair element content of violent criminals. *Canadian Journal of Psychiatry* 27:533.

Pincus, J., and G. Tucker. 1974. *Behavioral Neurology*. New York: Oxford University Press.

Pitch, Tamar. 1975. *La devianza*. Firenze: La Nuova Italia.

Piven, Frances Fox, and Richard A. Cloward. 1979. Hidden protest: The channelling of female innovation and resistance. *Signs* 4:461–70.

Platt, Anthony M. 1969. *The Child Savers*. Chicago: University of Chicago Press.

———. 1978. Street crime: A view from the left. *Crime and Social Justice* 9:26–48.

———. 1982. Crime and punishment in the United States: Immediate and long-term reforms from a Marxist perspective. *Crime and Social Justice* 18:38–45.

Plomin, R. 1989. Environment and genes: determinants of behavior. *American Psychologist* 44:105–111.

Plomin, R., and D. Daniels. 1986. Genetics and shyness. In W. H. Jones, J. M. Cheek, and S. R. Briggs (eds.), *Shyness: Perspectives on Research and Treatment*. New York: Plenum.

———. 1987. Why are children in the same family so different from one another? *Behavioral and Brain Sciences* 10:1–16.

Plomin, R., J. C. DeFries, and G. E. McClearn. 1980. *Behavioral Genetics: A Primer*. San Francisco: W. H. Freeman.

Plomin, R., T. T. Foch, and D. C. Rowe. 1981. Bobo clown aggression in childhood: Environment, not genes. *Journal of Research in Personality* 15:331–42.

Plomin, Robert, Katherine Nitz, and David C. Rowe. 1990. Behavioral genetics and aggressive behavior in childhood. In Michael Lewis and Suzanne Miller (eds.), *Handbook of Developmental Psychopathology*. New York: Plenum.

Plomin, R., N. L. Pedersen, G. E. McClearn, J. R. Nesselroade, and C. S. Bergeman. 1988. EAS temperaments during the last half of the life span: Twins reared apart and twins reared together. *Psychology and Aging* 3:43–50.

Plutchik, R., and H. M. van Praag. 1989. The measurement of suicidality, aggressivity and impulsivity. *Progress in Neuro-Psychopharmacology and Biological Psychiatry (Supplement)* 13:S23–S34.

Polk, Kenneth, Christine Adler, Gordon Bazemore, Gerald Blake, Sheila Cordray, Garry Coventry, James Galvin, and Mark Temple. 1981. *Becoming Adult: An Analysis of Maturational Development from Age 16 to 30 of a Cohort of Young Men*.

Final Report of the Marion County Youth Study. Eugene, Oreg.: University of Oregon.

Pontell, Henry N., and Kitty Calavita. 1993. The savings and loan industry. In Michael Tonry and Albert J. Reiss, Jr., (eds.), *Beyond the Law: Crime in Complex Organizations.* Chicago: University of Chicago Press.

Pontius, A. A., and K. F. Ruttiger. 1976. Frontal lobe system maturational lag in juvenile delinquents shown in narratives test. *Adolescence* XI(44):509–18.

Poole, Eric D., and Robert M. Regoli. 1979. Parental support, delinquent friends and delinquency: A test of interactional effects. *Journal of Criminal Law and Criminology* 70:188–93.

Pope, Alexander. [1734] 1961. *Epistles to Several Persons.* ed. F.W. Bateson 2d ed. New Haven: Yale University Press.

Poremba, C. 1975. Learning disabilities, youth and delinquency: Programs for intervention. In H. R. Myklebust (ed.), *Progress in Learning Disabilities.* Vol. III. New York: Grune & Stratton.

Potter, Gary W., and Bruce Bullington. 1987. Drug trafficking and the contras: a case study of state-organized crime. Paper presented at annual meeting of the American Society of Criminology, Montreal.

Poyner, Barry. 1983. *Design against Crime: Beyond Defensible Space.* London: Butterworths.

Preble, Edward, and John H. Casey. 1969. Taking care of business: The heroin user's life on the street. *International Journal of the Addictions* 4:1–24.

President's Commission on Law Enforcement and the Administration of Justice. 1967. *The Challenge of Crime in a Free Society.* Washington, D.C.: Government Printing Office.

Pyle, Gerald F., Edward W. Hanten, Patricia G. Williams, and Allen L. Pearson III, J. Gary Doyle, and Dwame Kwofie. 1974. The Spacial Dynamics of Crime. Department of Geography Research Paper No. 159. Chicago: University of Chicago Press.

Quay, Herbert C. 1965. Psychopathic personality as pathological stimulation seeking. *American Journal of Psychiatry* 122:180–83.

———. 1986. The behavioral reward and inhibition systems in childhood behavior disorder. In Lewis M. Bloomingdale (ed.), *Attention Deficit Disorder: Research in Treatment, Psychopharmacology and Attention.* Vol. 3. New York: Spectrum.

Quetelet, L. Adolphe. 1831. 1984. *Research on the Propensity for Crime at Different Ages.* Trans. S. Sylvester. Cincinnati, Ohio: Anderson.

Quicker, John. 1974. The effect of goal discrepancy on delinquency. *Social Problems* 22:76–86.

Quinney, Richard. 1970. *The Social Reality of Crime.* Boston: Little, Brown.

———. 1973. *Critique of the Legal Order.* Boston: Little, Brown.

———. 1977. *Class, State, and Crime.* New York: David McKay.

Quinney, Richard, and John Wildeman. 1991. *The Problem of Crime.* 3d ed. Mountain View, Calif.: Mayfield.

Rada, R. T., D. R. Laws, R. Kellner, L. Strivastava, and G. Peake. 1983. Plasma androgens in violent and nonviolent sex offenders. *Bulletin of the American Academy of Psychiatry Law* 11:149–58.

Rafter, Nicole Hahn. 1992. Claims-making and socio-cultural context in the first U. S. eugenics campaign. *Social Problems* 39:17–34.

Raine, Adrian. 1993. *The Psychopathology of Crime: Criminal Behavior as a Clinical Disorder.* New York: Academic Press.

Ramsay, Allan. n.d. Lettre à A. M. Diderot. In *Diderot: Oeuvres completès.* Vol. 4. Paris: Gamier.

Ramsey, Elizabeth, Gerald R. Patterson, and Hill M. Walker. 1990. Generalization of the antisocial trait from home to school settings. *Journal of Applied Developmental Psychology* 11:209–23.

Rankin, Joseph. 1977. Investigating the interrelations among social control variables and conformity. *Journal of Criminal Law and Criminology* 67:470–80.

———. 1983. The family context of delinquency. *Social Problems* 30:466–79.

Ray, Isaac. 1838. *A Treatise on the Medical Jurisprudence of Insanity*. 1983. New York: Da Capo Press.

Reckless, Walter C. 1926. *Publications of the American Sociological Society* 20:164–76.

———. 1940. *Criminal Behavior*. New York McGraw-Hill.

———. 1950. 1967. *The Crime Problem*. New York: Appleton-Century-Crofts.

Reckless, Walter C., Simon Dinitz, and Ellen Murray. 1956. Self-concept as an insulator against delinquency. *American Sociological Review* 21:744–56.

Reichman, Nancy. 1986. Managing crime risks: Toward an insurance-based model of social control. *Research in Law, Deviance and Social Control* 8:151–72.

———. 1992. Moving backstage: Uncovering the role of compliance practices in shaping regulatory policy. In Kip Schlegel and David Weisburd (eds.), *White-Collar Crime Reconsidered*. Boston: Northeastern University Press.

———. 1993. Insider trading. In Michael Tonry and Albert J. Reiss, Jr. (eds.), *Beyond the Law: Crime in Complex Organizations*. Chicago: University of Chicago Press.

Reige, Mary. 1972. Parental affection and juvenile delinquency in girls. *British Journal of Criminology* 12:55–73.

Reiman, Jeffrey. 1979. *The Rich Get Richer and the Poor Get Prison*. New York: John Wiley & Sons.

Reinarman, Craig, and Harry G. Levine. 1990. Crack in context: politics and media in the making of a drug scare. *Contemporary Drug Problems* 16:535-77.

Reiss, Albert, J. Jr. 1951. Delinquency as the failure of personal and social controls. *American Sociological Review* 16:196–207.

———. 1986. Why are communities important in understanding crime? In Albert J. Reiss, Jr., and Michael Tonry (eds.), *Communities and Crime*. Chicago: University of Chicago Press.

Reiss, Albert J., Jr., and Albert Biderman. 1980. *Data Sources on White-Collar Law-Breaking*. Washington, D.C.: U.S. Department of Justice.

Reiss, Albert J., Jr., and Jeffrey A. Roth. 1993. *Understanding and Preventing Violence*. Washington, D.C.: National Academy Press.

Reiss, Albert J., Jr., and Michael Tonry. (eds.) 1986. *Communities and Crime*. Chicago: University of Chicago Press.

Reppetto, Thomas. 1976. Crime prevention and the displacement phenomenon. *Crime and Delinquency* 22:166–177.

Resnick, Phillip J. 1970. Murder of the newborn: A psychiatric review of neonaticide. *American Journal of Psychiatry* 126:1414–20.

Reuter, Peter. 1983. *Disorganized Crime: The Economics of the Visible Hand*. Cambridge, Mass.: MIT Press.

Rich, Adriene. 1979. Toward a woman-centered university. In Adriene Rich (ed.), *On Lies, Secrets and Silence*. New York: W. W. Norton.

Rimland, B., and G. E. Larson. 1983. Hair mineral analysis and behavior: An analysis of 51 studies. *Journal of Learning Disabilities* 16:279–85.

Ritzer, George. 1990. *Frontiers of Social Theory: The New Syntheses*. New York: Columbia University Press.

Rivera, Beverly, and Cathy Spatz Widom. 1990. Childhood victimization and violent offending. *Violence and Victims* 5:19–35.

Roberts, John M. 1960. Enlightened despotism in Italy. In Harold Acton (ed.), *Art and Ideas in Eighteenth-Century Italy*. Rome: Italian Institute of London.

Robins, L. N. 1966. *Deviant Children Grown Up: A Sociological and Psychiatric Study of Sociopathic Personality*. Baltimore: Williams & Wilkins.

Robins, L. N., and K. S. Ratcliff. 1979. Risk factors in the continuation of childhood antisocial behaviors into adulthood. *International Journal of Mental Health* 7:96–116.

Robins, L. N., P. A. West, and B. L. Herjanic. 1975. Arrests and delinquency in two generations: A study of black urban families and their children. *Journal of Child Psychology and Psychiatry* 16:125–40.

Robinson, W. S. 1950. Ecological correlation and the behavior of individuals. *American Sociological Review* 15:351-357.

Robison, Sophia M. 1936. *Can Delinquency be Measured?* New York: Columbia University Press.

Rockefeller Report. 1975. Report to the President by the commission on CIA activities within the United States. Washington, D.C.: U.S. Government Printing Office.

Rogeness, G. A., M. A. Javors, J. W. Maas, C. A. Macedo, and C. Fischer. 1987. Plasma dopamine-B-hydroxylase, HVA, MHPG, and conduct disorder in emotionally disturbed boys. *Biological Psychiatry* 22:1155–58.

Rollins, Boyd, and Darwin Thomas. 1979. Parental support, power, and control techniques in the socialization of children. In Wesley Burr, Reuben Hill, F. Ivan Nye, and Ira Reiss (eds.), *Contemporary Theories about the Family*. Vol. 1. New York: Free Press.

Roncek, Dennis W. 1981. Dangerous places: Crime and residential environment. *Social Forces* 60:74–96.

———. 1987a. Changing crime patterns in two major cities: The cases of Cleveland and San Diego. Paper presented at the annual meeting of the American Society of Criminology, Montreal.

———. 1987b. Racial composition and crime: A comparative analysis of intraurban relationships. Paper presented at the annual meeting of the American Society of Criminology, Montreal.

Roncek, Dennis W., and Antionette Lobosco. 1983. The effect of high schools on crime in their neighborhoods. *Social Science Quarterly* 64:598–613.

Roper. 1982a. *Roper Report 82–6*, June 5–12.

———. 1982b. *Roper Report 87–2*, July 10–17.

Rose, Harold M., Ronald S. Edari, Lois M. Quinn, and John Pawasrat. 1992. *The Labor Market Experience of Young African American Men from Low-Income Families in Wisconsin*. Milwaukee: University of Wisconsin-Milwaukee Employment and Training Institute.

Rosecrance, John D. 1985. *The Degenerates of Lake Tahoe: A Study of Persistence in the Social World of Horse Race Gambling*. New York: Lang.

Rosen, Lawrence. 1985. Family and delinquency: Structure or function? *Criminology* 23:553–73.

Rosen, Lawrence, and Kathleen Neilson. 1982. Broken homes. In L. Savitz and N. Johnston (eds.), *Contemporary Criminology*. New York: John Wiley & Sons.

Rosenau, Pauline Marie. 1992. *Post-Modernism and the Social Sciences: Insights, Inroads, and Intrusions*. Princeton: Princeton University Press.

Rosenbaum, James. 1984. *Career Mobility in a Corporate Hierarchy*. Orlando, Fla.: Academic Press.

Rosenberg, Morris. 1979. *Conceiving the Self*. New York: Basic Books.

———. 1990. Reflexivity and emotions. *Social Psychology Quarterly* 53:3–12.

Rosenfeld, Rachel A. 1992. Job mobility and career processes. *Annual Review of Sociology* 18:39–61.

Roshier, Bob. 1989. *Controlling Crime: The Classical Perspective in Criminology*. Chicago: Lyceum Books.

Ross, Dorothy. 1979. The development of the social sciences. In A. Oleson and J. Voss (eds.), *The Organization of Knowledge in Modern America, 1860–1920*. Baltimore: Johns Hopkins University Press.

———. 1991. *The Origins of American Social Science*. New York: Cambridge University Press.

Ross, E. A. 1901. *Social Control: A Study of the Social Foundations of Social Order*. New York: Macmillan.

Ross, Irwin. 1992. *Shady Business: Confronting Corporate Corruption*. New York: Twentieth Century Fund Press.

Ross, Luana K. 1988. Toward an Indian Study of Indian deviance. Unpublished manuscript, Montana State University, Bozeman.

Ross, Michael, John Thibaut, and Scott Evenback. 1971. Some determinants of the intensity of social protest. *Journal of Experimental Social Psychology* 7:401–18.

Rossi, Peter, and Richard Berk. 1985. Varieties of normative consensus. *American Sociological Review* 50:333–47.

Rothman, David. 1971. *The Discovery of the Asylum: Social Order and Disorder in the New Republic*. Boston: Little, Brown.

Rothman, M., and R. F. Gandossy. 1982. Sad tales: The accounts of white-collar defendants and the decision to sanction. *Pacific Sociological Review* 4:449–73

Rowe, D. C. 1983. Biometrical genetic models of self-reported delinquent behavior: A twin study. *Behavior Genetics* 13:473–89.

———. 1986. Genetic and environmental components of antisocial behavior: A study of 265 twin pairs. *Criminology* 24:513–32.

Rowe, D. C., and D. W. Osgood. 1984. Heredity and sociological theories of delinquency: A reconsideration. *American Sociological Review* 49:526–40.

Roy, A., M. Virkkunen, S. Guthrie, R. Poland, and M. Linnoila. 1986. Monoamines, glucose metabolism, suicidal and aggressive behaviors. *Psychopharmacology Bulletin* 22:661–65.

Roy, Prodipto. 1963. Adolescent roles: Rural-urban differences. In F. Ivan Nye and Lois Hoffman (eds.), *The Employed Mother in America*. Chicago: Rand McNally.

Ruelle, David. 1991. *Chance and Chaos*. Princeton: Princeton University Press.

Rushton, J. P., D. W. Fulker, M. C. Neale, D. K. B. Nias, and H. J. Eysenck. 1986. Altruism and aggression: The heritability of individual differences. *Journal of Personality and Social Psychology* 50:1192–98.

Rutenberg, Sharon. 1981. In ten minutes almost anyone can rob a bank via computer. *Indianapolis Star*, April 5, 4:19–20.

Rutter, Michael. 1987. Psychosocial resilience and protective mechanisms. *American Journal of Orthopsychiatry* 57:316–33.

———. 1989a. Age as an ambiguous variable in developmental research: Some epidemiologicalconsiderationsfromdevelopmentalpsychopathology.International *Journal of Behavioral Development* 12:1–34.

———. 1989b. Pathways from childhood to adult life. *Journal of Child Psychology and Psychiatry* 30:23–51.

Rutter, Michael, David Quinton, and Jonathan Hill. 1990. Adult outcomes of institution-reared children: Males and females compared. In Lee Robins and Michael Rutter (eds.), *Straight and Devious Pathways from Childhood to Adulthood*. New York: Cambridge University Press.

Ryder, Norman B. 1965. The cohort as a concept in the study of social change. *American Sociological Review* 30:843–61.

Samaha, Joel. 1987. *Criminal Law*. 2d ed. St. Paul, Minn.: West Publishing.

Samenow, Stanton E. 1984. *Inside the Criminal Mind*. New York: Times Books.

Sampson, Robert J. 1985. Neighborhood and crime: The structural determinants of personal victimization. *Journal of Research in Crime and Delinquency* 22:7–40.

———. 1986. Neighborhood family structure and the risk of personal victimization. In James M. Byrne and Robert J. Sampson (eds.), *The Social Ecology of Crime*. New York: Springer-Verlag.

———. 1987a. Communities and crime. In Michael R. Gottfredson and Travis Hirschi (eds.), *Positive Criminology*. Beverly Hills, Calif.: Sage.

———. 1987b. Does an intact family reduce burglary risk for its neighbors? *Sociology and Social Research* 71:204–7.

———. 1987c. Urban black violence: The effect of male joblessness and family disruption. *American Journal of Sociology* 93:348–82.

————. 1988. Local friendship ties and community attachment in mass society: A multilevel systemic model. *American Sociological Review* 53:766–79.

————. 1991 Linking the micro and macro-level dimensions of community social organization. *Social Forces* 70:43–64.

Sampson, Robert J., and W. Byron Groves. 1989. Community structures and crime: Testing social-disorganization theory. *American Journal of Sociology* 94:774–802.

Sampson, Robert J., and John H. Laub. 1992. Crime and deviance in the life course. *Annual Review of Sociology* 18:63–84.

————. 1993. *Crime in the Making: Pathways and Turning Points through Life.* Cambridge, Mass.: Harvard University Press.

————. 1996. Socioeconomic achievement in the life course of disadvantaged men: Military service as a turning point, circa 1940–1965. *American Sociological Review* 61:347–67.

Sarup, Madan. 1989. *An Introductory Guide to Post-Structuralism and Postmodernism.* Athens, Ga: University of Georgia Press.

Savitz, Leonard D., Stanley H. Turner, and Toby Dickman. 1977. The origin of scientific criminology: Franz Joseph Gall as the first criminologist. In Robert F. Meier (ed.), *Theory in Criminology: Contemporary Views.* Beverly Hills, Calif.: Sage.

Scheff, Thomas J. 1963. The social role of the mentally ill and the dynamics of mental disorder: A research framework. *Sociometry* 26:436–53.

————. 1966. *Being Mentally Ill: A Sociological Theory.* Chicago: Aldine.

Schelling, Thomas C. 1967. Economics and criminal enterprise. *Public Interest* 7:61–78.

Schiavi, R. C., A. Theilgaard, D. R. Owen, and D. White. 1984. Sex chromosome anomalies, hormones, and aggressivity. *Archives of General Psychiatry* 41:93–99.

Schmid, Calvin F. 1960a. Urban areas: Part I. *American Sociological Review* 25:527–42.

————. 1960b. Urban areas: Part II. *American Sociological Review* 25:655–78.

Schoenberg, Ronald L. 1975. A Structural Model of Delinquency. Ph.D. dissertation. University of Washington, Seattle.

Schoenfeld, A. Clay, Robert Meier, and Robert Griffin. 1979. Constructing a social problem: The press and the environment. *Social Problems* 27:38–61.

Schrager, Laura S., and James F. Short, Jr. 1980. How serious a crime? Perceptions of organizational and common crimes. In Gilbert Geis and Ezra Stotland (eds.), *White Collar Crime: Theory and Research.* Beverly Hills, Calif.: Sage.

Schuckit, M. A., and E. R. Morrissey. 1978. Propoxyphene and phencyclidine (PCP) use in adolescents. *Journal of Clinical Psychiatry* 39:7–13.

Schuerman, Leo A., and Solomon Kobrin. 1983. Crime and urban ecological processes: Implications for public policy. Paper presented at the annual meeting of the American Society of Criminology, Denver.

————. 1986. Community careers in crime. In Albert J. Reiss, Jr. and Michael Tonry (eds.), *Communities and Crime.* Chicago: University of Chicago Press.

Schuessler, Karl F., and Donald R. Cressey. 1950. Personality characteristics of criminals. *American Journal of Sociology* 50:476–84.

Schumpeter, Joseph A. 1954. *History of Economic Analysis.* New York: Oxford University Press.

Schur, Edwin M. 1965. *Crimes without Victims: Deviant Behavior and Public Policy.* Englewood Cliffs, N.J.: Prentice-Hall.

————. 1971. *Labeling Deviant Behavior: Its Sociological Implications.* New York: Harper & Row.

————. 1980. *The Politics of Deviance: Stigma Contests and the Uses of Power.* Englewood Cliffs, N.J.: Prentice-Hall.

————. 1984. *Labeling Women Deviant.* New York: Random House.

Schutz, Alfred. 1967. *The Phenomenology of the Social World.* Evanston: Northwestern University Press.

Schwartz, Gary. 1987. *Beyond Conformity or Rebellion.* Chicago: University of Chicago Press.

Schwartz, Martin D. 1989. The undercutting edge of criminology. *Critical Criminologist* 1 (Spring):1–2, 5–6.
Schwartz, Martin D., and David O. Friedrichs. 1994. Postmodern thought and criminological discontent. *Criminology* 32:221–46.
Schwendinger, Herman, and Julia Schwendinger. 1975. Defenders of order or guardians of human rights. *Issues in Criminology* 7:72–81.
Schwendinger, Julia and Herman Schwendinger. 1983. *Rape and Inequality*. Newbury Park, Calif.: Sage.
———. 1985. *Adolescent Subcultures and Delinquency*. New York: Praeger.
Scott, Marvin B. 1968. *The Racing Game*. Chicago: Aldine.
Scott, Marvin B., and Stanford M. Lyman. 1968. 1972. Accounts. *American Sociological Review* 33:46–62; reprinted in Jerome G. Manis and Bernard N. Meltzer (eds.), *Symbolic Interaction: A Reader in Social Psychology*. 2d ed. Boston: Allyn & Bacon.
Scott, Michael D. 1984. *Computer Law*. New York: John Wiley & Sons.
Scott, P. D. 1973. Parents who kill their children. *Medical Science Law* 13:120–26.
Scott, William Robert. 1900. *Francis Hutcheson*. New York: Cambridge University Press.
Searle, John R. 1969. *Speech Acts*. Cambridge: Cambridge University Press.
Segrave, Kerry. 1992. *Women Serial and Mass Murderers: A World-Wide Reference, 1580 through 1990*. Jefferson, N.C.: McFarland.
Seigal, R. K. 1978. Phencyclidine, criminal behavior, and the defense of diminished capacity. In R. C. Peterson and R. C. Stillman (eds.), *Phencyclidine (PCP) Abuse: An Appraisal. NIDA Research Monograph 21*. Rockville, Md.: National Institute on Drug Abuse.
Sekula, Allen. 1986. The body and the archive. *October* 39:3–64.
Sellin, Thorsten. 1938. *Culture, Conflict and Crime*. New York: Social Science Research Council.
Selva, Lance, and Bob Bohm. 1987. Law and liberation: Toward an oppositional legal discourse. *Legal Studies Forum* 113:243–66.
Shabecoff, Philip. 1979. House unit attacks lags on toxic waste. *New York Times*. October 14.
———. 1985. Toxic waste threat termed far greater than U.S. estimates. *New York Times*. March 10.
Shannon, Lyle W. 1982. The relationship of juvenile delinquency and adult crime to the changing ecological structure of the city. Executive Report to the National Institute of Justice.
———. 1984. The development of serious criminal careers and the delinquent neighborhood. Executive Report, submitted to the National Institute of Justice and Delinquency Prevention.
Shapiro, Susan P. 1980. *Thinking about White-Collar Crime: Matters of Conceptualization and Research*. Washington, D.C.: U.S. Government Printing Office.
———. 1984. *Wayward Capitalists*. New Haven: Yale University Press.
Sharkey, Jacqueline. 1988. The Contra-drug trade off. *Common Cause Magazine*, September–October:23––33.
Shaw, Clifford, and Henry D. McKay. 1942. 1969. *Juvenile Delinquency and Urban Areas*. Chicago: University of Chicago Press.
Shaw, Clifford R., Frederick M. Zorbaugh, Henry D. McKay, and Leonard S. Cottrell. 1929. *Delinquency Areas*. Chicago: University of Chicago Press.
Shea, Tom. 1984. The FBI goes after hackers. *InfoWorld* 6(13):38.
Sheldon, Randall. 1987. The chronic delinquent: Gender and racial differences. Paper presented at the annual meeting of the American Society of Criminology, Montreal.
Sheldon, William H., Emil M. Hartl, and Eugene McDermott. 1949. *Varieties of Delinquent Youth*. New York: Harper and Brothers.
Sheldon, William H., S. S. Stevens and W. B. Tucker, 1940. *The Varieties of Human Physique*. New York: Harper & Row.

Shepelak, Norma J., 1987. The role of self-explanations and self-evaluations in legitimating inequality. *American Sociological Review* 52:495–503.

Shepelak, Norma J., and Duane Alwin. 1986. Beliefs about inequality and perceptions of distributive justice. *American Sociological Review* 51:30–46.

Sherman, Lawrence W. 1992. *Policing Domestic Violence*. New York: Free Press.

Shibutani, Tamotsu. 1962. Reference groups and social control. In Arnold M. Rose (ed.), *Human Behavior and Social Processes*. Boston: Houghton Mifflin.

Shoham, S. Giora, and John Hoffman. 1991. *A Primer in the Sociology of Crime*. New York: Harrow and Heston.

Shonfeld, I. S., D. Shaffer, P. O'Connor, and S. Portnoy. 1988. Conduct disorder and cognitive functioning: Testing three causal hypotheses. *Child Development* 59:993–1007.

Short, James F., Jr. 1960. Differential association as a hypothesis: Problems of empirical testing. *Social Problems* 8:14–25.

———. 1969. Introduction to the revised edition. In C. R. Shaw and H. D. McKay, *Juvenile Delinquency and Urban Areas*. Chicago: University of Chicago Press.

———. 1975. The natural history of an applied theory: Differential opportunity and mobilization for youth. In N. J. Demerath, III, Otto Larsen, and Karl F. Schuessler (eds.), *Social Policy and Sociology*. New York: Academic Press.

———. 1985. The level of explanation problem in criminology. In Robert F. Meier (ed.), *Theoretical Methods in Criminology*. Beverly Hills, Calif.: Sage.

———. 1990. Gangs, neighborhoods, and youth crime. *Criminal Justice Research Bulletin* 5:1–11.

Short, James F., and Fred L. Strodtbeck. 1965. *Group Process and Gang Delinquency*. Chicago: University of Chicago Press.

Shover, Neal. 1973. The social organization of burglary. *Social Problems* 20:499–514.

———. 1985. *Aging Criminals*. Beverly Hills, Calif.: Sage.

Shover, Neal, Donald A. Clelland, and John Lynxwiler. 1986. *Enforcement or Negotiation: Constructing a Regulatory Bureaucracy*. Albany: SUNY Press.

Silberman, Charles. 1978. *Criminal Violence, Criminal Justice*. New York: Random House.

Silbey, Susan, and Austin Sarat. 1988. Dispute processing in law and legal scholarship: From institutional critique to a reconstruction of the juridical subject. *Denver Law Review* 66:437–98.

Silk, L. Howard, and David Vogel. 1976. *Ethics and Profits: The Crisis of Confidence in American Business*. New York: Simon & Schuster.

Silva, Phil A. 1990. The Dunedin multidisciplinary health and development study: a fifteen-year longitudinal study. *Paediatric and Perinatal Epidemiology* 4:96–127.

Silverstein, M. 1977. The history of a short, unsuccessful academic career. In J. Snodgrass (ed.), *For Men against Sexism*. Albion, Calif.: Times Change Press.

Simcha-Fagan, Ora, and Joseph E. Schwartz. 1986. Neighborhood and delinquency: An assessment of contextual effects. *Criminology* 24:667–704.

Simmel, Georg. [1908] 1955. *Conflict and the Web of Group Affiliations*. Glencoe, Ill.: Free Press.

Simon, Herbert A. 1990. A mechanism for social selection and successful altruism. *Science* 250:1665–68.

Simon, Jonathan. 1987. The emergence of a risk society: Insurance law and the state. *Socialist Review* 95:61–89.

———. 1988. The ideological effect of actuarial practices. *Law and Society Review* 22:771–800.

———. 1990. From discipline to management: Strategies of control in parole supervision, 1890–1990. Ph.D. dissertation, Jurisprudence and Social Policy Program, University of California at Berkeley.

———. 1993a. From confinement to waste management: The postmodernization of social control. *Focus on Law Studies* 8:4, 6–7.

————. 1993b. *Poor Discipline: Parole and the Social Control of the Underclass,* 1890–1990. Chicago: University of Chicago Press.

Simon, Rita. 1975. *Women and Crime.* Lexington, Mass.: D. C. Heath.

Simpson, Sally S. 1986. The decomposition of antitrust. *American Sociological Review* 51:859–75.

————. 1987. Cycles of illegality: Antitrust violations in corporate America. *Social Forces* 65:943–63.

————. 1989. Feminist theory, crime, and justice. *Criminology* 27:605–31.

————. 1991. Caste, class, and violent crime: Explaining difference in female offending. *Criminology* 29:115–35.

Simpson, Sally, S., and Lori Elis. 1994. Is gender subordinate to class? An empirical assessment of Colvin and Pauly's structural-Marxist theory of delinquency. *Journal of Criminal Law* 85:453–80.

————. 1995. Doing gender: Sorting out the caste and crime conundrum. *Criminology* 33:47–81.

Singer, Simon I., and Murray Levine. 1988. Power-control theory, gender, and delinquency: A partial republication with additional evidence on the effects of peers. *Criminology* 26:627–47.

Skinner, B. F. 1953. *Science and Human Behavior.* New York: Macmillan.

————. F. 1971. *Beyond Freedom and Dignity.* New York: Alfred A. Knopf.

Skogan, Wesley. 1986. Fear of crime and neighborhood change. In A. J. Reiss, Jr. and M. Tonry (eds.), *Communities and Crime.* Chicago: University of Chicago Press.

Skolnick, Jerome H. 1990. The social structure of street drug dealing. *American Journal of Police* 9:1–41.

Slaby, Ronald G., and Nancy G. Guerra. 1988. Cognitive mediators of aggression in adolescent offenders: 1. *Developmental Psychology* 24:580–88.

Smart, Barry. 1993. *Postmodernity.* London: Routledge.

Smart, Carol. 1976. *Women, Crime and Criminology: A Feminist Critique.* Boston: Routledge & Kegan Paul.

————. 1989. *Feminism and the Power of Law.* London: Routledge.

————. 1990. Feminist approaches to criminology or postmodern woman meets atavastic man. In Loraine Gelsthorpe and Allison Morris (eds.), *Feminist Perspectives in Criminology.* Milton Keynes: Open University Press.

Smith, Carolyn, and Terence P. Thornberry. 1995. The relationship between childhood maltreatment and adolescent involvement in delinquency. *Criminology* 33:451–82.

Smith, Dorothy E. 1976. The ideological practice of sociology. *Catalyst* 8:39–54.

Smith, D.E., and D.R. Wesson. 1980. PCP abuse: Diagnostic and pharmacological treatment approaches. *Journal of Psychedelic Drugs* 12:293–99.

Smith, Douglas A. 1986. The neighborhood context of police behavior. In Albert J. Reiss, Jr. and Michael Tonry (eds.), *Communities and Crime.* Chicago: University of Chicago Press.

Smith, Douglas A., and G. Roger Jarjoura. 1988. Social structure and criminal victimization. *Journal of Research in Crime and Delinquency* 25:27–52.

Smith, Douglas, and Raymond Paternoster. 1987. The gender gap in theories of deviance: Issues and evidence. *Journal of Research in Crime and Delinquency* 24:140–72.

Smith, Dwight C., Jr. 1980. Paragons, pariahs, and pirates: A spectrum-based theory of enterprise. *Crime and Delinquency* 26:358–86.

Smith, Dwight C., Jr., and Richard D. Alba. 1979. Organized crime and American life. *Society* 3:32–38.

Snider, Laureen. 1990. Cooperative models and corporate crime: panacea or cop-out? *Crime and Delinquency* 36:373–90.

Snyder, J., and Gerald Patterson. 1986. The effects and consequences on patterns of social interaction: A quasi-experimental approach to reinforcement in natural interaction. *Child Development* 57:1257–68.

Sokolik, Stanley L. 1980 Computer crime: The need for deterrent legislation. *Computer/Law Journal* 2:353–83.

Soma, John T., Paula J. Smith., and Robert D. Sprague. 1985. Legal analysis of electronic bulletin board activities. *Western New England Law Review* 7:571–620.

Sommers, Ira, and Deborah Basking. 1992. Sex, race, aging, and violent offending. *Violence and Victims* 7:191–201.

Sonnenfeld, Jeffrey and Paul R. Lawrence. 1978. Why do companies succumb to price-fixing? *Harvard Business Review* 56:145–57.

Soubrie, P. 1986. Reconciling the role of central serotonin neurons in human and animal behavior. *Behavioral and Brain Sciences* 9:319–64.

Spelman, Elizabeth V., and Martha Minow. 1992. Outlaw women: An essay on Thelma and Louise. *New England Law Review* 26:1281–96.

Spergel, Irving. 1964. *Racketville, Slumtown, Haulburg: An Exploratory Study of Delinquent Subcultures*. Chicago: University of Chicago Press.

Spergel, Irving A., and G. David Curry. 1990. Strategies and perceived agency effectiveness in dealing with the youth gang problem. In C. Ronald Huff (ed.), *Gangs in America*. Beverly Hills, Calif.: Sage.

Spergel, Irving A., and John Korbelik. 1979. The local community service system and ISOS: An interorganizational analysis. Executive Report, submitted to the Illinois Law Enforcement Commission.

Spoont, M. R. 1992. Modulatory role of serotonin in neural information processing: Implications for human psychopathology. *Psychological Bulletin* 112:330–50.

Sprecher, Susan. 1986. The relationship between inequity and emotions in close relationships. *Social Psychology Quarterly* 49:309–21.

Staats, Gregory R. 1977. Changing conceptualization of professional criminals. *Criminology* 15:49–65.

Stack, Carol B. 1974. *All Our Kin: Strategy for Survival in a Black Community*. New York: Harper Colophon Books.

Stark, Rodney. 1986. *Crime and Deviance in North America: ShowCase*. Seattle: Cognitive Development Company.

———. 1987. Deviant places: A theory of the ecology of crime. *Criminology* 25:893–909.

Stark, Rodney, and William Sims Bainbridge. 1985. *The Future of Religion*. Berkeley: University of California Press.

Stark, Rodney, and James McEvoy. 1970. Middle class violence. *Psychology Today* 4:52–54, 110–12.

Stark, Rodney, Daniel P. Doyle, and Jesse Lynn Rushing. 1983. Beyond Durkheim: Religion and suicide. *Journal for the Scientific Study of Religion* 22:120–31.

Staw, Barry M., and Eugene Szwajkowski. 1975. The scarcity-munificence component of organizational environments and the commission of illegal acts. *Administrative Science Quarterly* 20:345–54.

Steffensmeier, Darrell. J. 1989. On the causes of "white-collar" crime: An assessment of Hirschi and Gottfredson's claims. *Criminology* 27:345–58.

Steffensmeier, Darrell, J., and Emilie Anderson Allen. 1988. Sex disparities in arrest by residence, race, and age: An assessment of the gender convergence/crime hypothesis. *Justice Quarterly* 5:53–80.

Steffensmeier, Darrell J., and Michael J. Cobb. 1981. Sex differences in urban arrest patterns, 1934–1979. *Social Problems* 28:37–50.

Steiner, Henry J. 1987. *Moral Vision and Social Vision in the Court: A Study of Tort Accident Law*. Madison: University of Wisconsin Press.

Stenning, Philip C., and Clifford D. Shearing. 1980. The quiet revolution: The nature, development, and general legal implications of private security in Canada. *Criminal Law Quarterly* 22:220–48.

Stephenson, G. M., and J. H. White. 1968. An experimental study of some effects of injustice on children's moral behavior. *Journal of Experimental Social Psychology* 4:460–69.

Stern, G., and L. Kruckman. 1983. Multidisciplinary perspectives on postpartum depression: An anthropological critique. *Social Science and Medicine* 17:1027.

Stewart, M. A., and C. S. de Blois. 1983. Father-son resemblances in aggressive and antisocial behavior. *British Journal of Psychiatry* 142:78–84.

Stewart, M. A., and L. Leone. 1978. A family study of unsocialized aggressive boys. *Biological Psychiatry* 13:107–17.

Stewart, M. A., C. S. de Blois, and C. Cummings. 1980. Psychiatric disorder in the parents of hyperactive boys and those with conduct disorder. *Journal of Child Psychology and Psychiatry* 21:283–92.

Stone, Christopher D. 1975. *Where the Law Ends: The Social Control of Corporate Behavior*. New York: Harper & Row.

Straus, Murray. 1991. Discipline and deviance: Physical punishment of children and violence and other crimes in adulthood. *Social Problems* 38:133–54.

Strauss, Anselm L. [1959] 1972. Language and identity. In J. Manis and B. Meltzer (eds.) *Symbolic Interaction: A Reader in Social Psychology*. 2d ed. Boston: Allyn & Bacon.

Strauss, Anselm L. 1987. *Qualitative Analysis for Social Scientists*. Cambridge, Mass.: Cambridge University Press.

Strauss, William, and Neil Howe. 1991. *Generations: The History of America's Future, 1584 to 2069*. New York: William Morrow.

Sudnow, David. 1965. Normal crimes: Sociological features of the penal code in a public defender office. *Social Problems* 12: 255–76.

Sugden, Robert. 1986. *The Economics of Rights, Cooperation and Welfare*. Oxford: Basil Blackwell.

Sullivan, Louis. 1992. Violence research NRC panel provides a blueprint. *Science* 258:1298.

Sullivan, Mercer L. 1989. *Getting Paid: Youth Crime and Work in the Inner City*. Ithaca: Cornell University Press.

Suls, Jerry, M. 1977. Social comparison theory and research: An overview from 1954. In Jerry M. Suls and Richard L. Miller (eds.), *Social Comparison Processes*. New York: Hemisphere.

Surette, Ray. 1992. *Media, Crime and Criminal Justice: Images and Realities*. Pacific Grove, Calif.: Brooks/Cole.

Surface, Bill. 1976. *The Track*. New York: Macmillan.

Sutherland, Edwin H. 1937. *The Professional Thief*. Chicago: University of Chicago Press.

Sutherland, Edwin H. 1924. *Criminology*. Philadelphia: J. B. Lippincott.

———. 1939. 1947. *Principles of Criminology*. Philadelphia: J. B. Lippincott.

———. 1949. *White Collar Crime*. New York: Dryden.

———. 1950. The sexual psychopath laws. *Journal of Criminal Law, Criminology and Police Science* 40:543–54.

———. 1951. The diffusion of sexual psychopath laws. *American Journal of Sociology* 56:142–48.

———. 1956. *The Sutherland Papers*, ed. Albert Cohen, Alfred Lindesmith, and Karl Schuessler. Bloomington: Indiana University Press.

———. [1947] 1973a. *On Analyzing Crime*. Edited with an introduction by Karl Schuessler. Chicago: University of Chicago Press.

———. 1973b. A statement of the theory. In Edwin H. Sutherland (ed.), *On Analyzing Crime*. Chicago: University of Chicago Press.

———. 1983. *White-Collar Crime: The Uncut Version*. New Haven: Yale University Press.

Sutherland, Edwin H., and Donald R. Cressey. 1955. 1961. 1966. 1978. *Principles of Criminology*. Philadelphia: J. B. Lippincott.

———. 1980. The theory of differential association. In Stuart H. Traub and Craig B. Little (eds.), *Theories of Deviance*. Itasca, Ill.: F. E. Peacock.

Suttles, G. 1968. *The Social Order of the Slum*. Chicago: University of Chicago Press.
———. 1972. *The Social Construction of Communities*. Chicago: University of Chicago Press.
Swigert, Victoria, and Ronald Farrell. 1980. Corporate homicide: Definitional processes in the creation of deviance. *Law and Society Review* 15:161–82.
Sykes, Gresham M., and David Matza. 1957. 1980. Techniques of neutralization: A theory of delinquency. *American Sociological Review* 22:664–70. Reprinted in
Syndulko, K. 1978. Electrocortical investigations of sociopathy. In R. D. Hare and D. Schalling (eds.), *Psychopathic Behavior: Approaches to Research*. Chichester, U.K.: John Wiley & Sons.
Syndulko, K., D. A. Parker, R. Jens, I. Maltzman, and E. Ziskind. 1975. Psychophysiology of sociopathy: Electrocortical measures. *Biological Psychology* 3:185–200.
Szasz, Andrew. 1982. The dynamics of social regulation: A study of the formation and evolution of the Occupational Safety and Health Administration. Ph.D. dissertation. University of Wisconsin, Madison.
———. 1984. Industrial resistance to occupational safety and health legislation: 1971–1981. *Social Problems* 32:103–16.
Taber, John K. 1979. On computer crime (Senate Bill S. 240). *Computer/Law Journal* 1:517–43.
———. 1980. A survey of computer crime studies. *Computer/Law Journal* 2:275–327.
Talbot, Eugene S. 1898. *Degeneracy: Its Causes, Signs, and Results*. New York and London: Walter Scott.
Tannenbaum, Frank. 1938. *Crime and the Community*. New York: Ginn.
Tarde, Gabriel. 1886. *La Criminalité Comparée*. Paris: Alcan.
Tarter, R. E., A. I. Alterman, and K. L. Edwards. 1985. Vulnerability to alcoholism in men: A behavior-genetic perspective. *Journal of Studies on Alcoholism* 46:329–56.
Tavris, Carol. 1984. On the wisdom of counting to ten. In Philip Shaver (ed.), *Review of Personality and Social Psychology: 5*. Beverly Hills, Calif.: Sage.
Taylor, Carl. 1990. *Dangerous Society*. East Lansing: Michigan State University Press.
Taylor, Ian. 1981. *Law and Order: Arguments for Socialism*. London: Macmillan.
Taylor, Ian, Paul Walton, and Jock Young. 1973. *The New Criminology: For a Social Theory of Deviance*. London: Routledge & Kegan Paul.
——— (eds.). 1975. *Critical Criminology*. London: Routledge & Kegan Paul.
Taylor, Ralph B., and Jeanette Covington. 1987. Gentrification and crime in Baltimore neighborhoods. Unpublished final report. Department of Criminal Justice, Temple University, Philadelphia.
Taylor, Terence, and David C. Watt. 1977. The relation of deviant symptoms and behavior in a normal population to subsequent delinquency and maladjustment. *Psychological Medicine* 7:163–69.
Tellegen, Auke. 1982. *Brief Manual for the Multidimensional Personality Questionnaire*. Minneapolis: University of Minnesota Press.
———. 1985. Structures of mood and personality and their relevance to assessing anxiety, with an emphasis on self-report. In A. Hussain Tuma and Jack Maser (eds.), *Anxiety and the Anxiety Disorders*. Hillsdale, N.J.: Lawrence Erlbaum.
———. 1991. Personality traits: Issues of definition, evidence, and assessment. In W. M. Grove and D. Cicchetti (eds.), *Thinking Clearly about Psychology, Vol. 2: Personality and Psychopathology*. Minneapolis: University of Minnesota Press.
Tellegen, Auke, and Niels G. Waller. In press. Exploring personality through test construction: Development of the Multidimensional Personality Questionnaire. In Steven R. Briggs and Jonathan M. Cheek (eds.), *Personality Measures: Development and Evaluation, Vol. 1*. Greenwich, Conn.: JAI Press.
Tellegen, Auke, David T. Lykken, Thomas J. Bouchard, Kimerly J. Wilcox, Nancy L. Segal, and Stephan Rich. 1988. Personality similarity in twins reared apart and together. *Journal of Personality and Social Psychology* 54:1031–39.

Tennenbaum, Daniel. 1977. Personality and criminality: A summary and implications of the literature. *Journal of Criminal Justice* 5:225–35.

Thibaut, John W., and Harold H. Kelley. 1959. *The Social Psychology of Groups*. New York: John Wiley & Sons.

Thiessen, D. D. 1976. *The Evolution and Chemistry of Aggression*. Springfield, Ill.: Charles C. Thomas.

Thoits, Peggy. 1984. Coping, social support, and psychological outcomes: The central role of emotion. In Philip Shaver (ed.), *Review of Personality and Social Psychology: 5*. Beverly Hills, Calif.: Sage.

———. 1989. The sociology of emotions. In W. Richard Scott and Judith Blake (eds.), *Annual Review of Sociology*. Vol. 15. Palo Alto, Calif.: Annual Reviews.

———. 1990. Emotional deviance research. In Theodore D. Kemper (ed.), *Research Agendas in the Sociology of Emotions*. Albany: SUNY Press.

———. 1991a. On merging identity theory and stress research. *Social Psychology Quarterly* 54:101–12.

———. 1991b. Patterns of coping with controllable and uncontrollable events. In E. Mark Cummings, Anita L. Greene, and Katherine H. Karraker (eds.), *Life-Span Developmental Psychology: Perspectives on Stress and Coping*. Hillsdale, N.J.: Lawrence Erlbaum.

Thomas, Jim. 1988. *Prisoner Litigation: The Paradox of the Jailhouse Lawyer*. Totowa, N.J.: Rowman & Littlefield.

Thomas, Jim, and Aogan O'Maolchatha. 1989. Reassessing the critical metaphor An optimistic revisionist view. *Justice Quarterly* 6:143–72.

Thomas, William I. [1931] 1972. The definition of the situation. In Jerome G. Manis and Bernard N. Meltzer (eds.), *Symbolic Interaction: A Reader in Social Psychology*. 2nd ed. Boston: Allyn & Bacon.

Thomas, William I., and Florian Znaniecki. 1920. *The Polish Peasant in Europe and America*. Vol. IV. Boston: Gorham Press.

Thompson, Michael, Richard Ellis, and Aaron Wildavsky. 1990. *Cultural Theory*. Boulder, Colo.: Westview.

Thornberry, Terence P. 1987a. Reflections on the advantages and disadvantages of theoretical integration. Presented at the Conference on Theoretical Integration in the Study of Crime and Deviance, Albany.

Thornberry, Terence P. 1987b. Toward an interactional theory of delinquency. *Criminology* 25:863–91.

Thornberry, Terence P., and R. L. Christenson. 1984. Unemployment and criminal involvement: An investigation of reciprocal causal structures. *American Sociological Review* 49:398–411.

Thornberry, Terence P., Melanie Moore, and R. L. Christenson. 1985. The effect of dropping out of high school on subsequent delinquent behavior. *Criminology* 23:3–18.

Thornberry, Terence P., Marvin D. Krohn, Alan J. Lizotte, and Deborah Chard-Wierschem. 1993. The role of juvenile gangs in facilitating delinquent behavior. *Journal of Research in Crime and Delinquency* 30:55–87.

Thornberry, Terence P., Alan J. Lizotte, Marvin D. Krohn, Margaret Farnworth, and Sung Joon Jang. 1994. Delinquent peers, beliefs, and delinquent behavior: A longitudinal test of interactional theory. *Criminology* 32:47–83.

Thrasher, Frederick. 1927. 1963. *The Gang*. Chicago: University of Chicago Press.

Tierney, Kathleen J. 1982. The battered women movement and the creation of the wife beating problem. *Social Problems* 29:207–20.

Tilly, Charles. 1985. War making and state making as organized crime. In P. Evans, D. Rueschemeyer, and T. Skocpol (eds.), *Bringing the State Back In*. Cambridge, Mass.: Cambridge University Press.

Time. 1982. Crackdown on computer crime, February 8:60–67.

———. 1983a. The 414 gang strikes again, August 29:75.

————. 1983b. Playing games, August 22:14.

Tittle, Charles. R. 1985. The assumption that general theories are not possible. In R. F. Meyer (ed.), *Theoretical Methods in Criminology*. Beverly Hills, Calif.: Sage.

Tittle, Charles R. 1988. Two empirical regularities (maybe) in search of an explanation: Commentary on the age-crime debate. *Criminology* 26:75–86.

Tittle, Charles R. 1991. Review of Michael R. Gottfredson and Travis Hirschi, *A General Theory of Crime*. *American Journal of Sociology* 96:1609–11.

Tittle, Charles R. 1995. *Control Balance: Toward a General Theory of Deviance*. Boulder, Colo.: Westview.

Tittle, Charles R., and Robert F. Meier. 1990. Specifying the SES delinquency relationship. *Criminology* 28:271–99.

Tittle, Charles R., Wayne J. Villemez, and Douglas A. Smith. 1978. The myth of social class and criminality: An empirical assessment of the empirical evidence. *American Sociological Review* 43:643–56.

Toby, Jackson. 1957. Social disorganization and stake in conformity: Complementary factors in the predatory behavior of hoodlums. *Journal of Criminal Law, Criminology and Police Science* 48:12–17.

Toby, Jackson and Marcia L. Toby. 1961. *Law School Status as a Predisposing Factor in Subcultural Delinquency*. New Brunswick, N.J.: Rutgers University Press.

Tong, Rosemary. 1989. *Feminist Thought*. Boulder, Colo.: Westview.

Tonry, Michael L., Lloyd E. Ohlin, and David P. Farrington. 1991. *Human Development and Criminal Behavior*. New York: Springer-Verlag.

Tornblum, Kjell Y. 1977. Distributive justice: Typology and propositions. *Human Relations* 30:1–24.

Totman, Jane. 1978. *The Murderess: A Psychosocial Study of Criminal Homicide*. San Francisco: R. and E. Research Associates.

Tracy, Paul E., Marvin E. Wolfgang, and Robert M. Figlio. 1990. *Delinquency Careers in Two Birth Cohorts*. New York: Plenum.

Traub, Stuart H. and Craig B. Little (eds.), *Theories of Deviance*. Itasca, Ill.: F. E. Peacock.

Tremblay, Pierre. 1986. Designing crime. *British Journal of Criminology* 26:234–53.

Trunnell, E. P., and C. W. Turner. 1988. A comparison of the psychological and hormonal factors in women with and without premenstrual syndrome. *Journal of Abnormal Psychology* 97:429–36.

Tuchman, Gaye. 1978. *Making News: A Study in the Social Construction of Reality*. New York: Free Press.

Turk, Austin. T. 1966. "Conflict and Criminality." *American Sociological Review* 31:338–52.

————. 1969. *Criminality and Legal Order*. Chicago: Rand McNally.

Turner, Bryan S. (ed.). 1990. *Theories of Modernity and Postmodernity*. Newbury Park, Calif.: Sage.

Turner, Stansfield. 1985. *Secrecy and Democracy: The CIA in Transition*. New York: Houghton Miflin.

Twito, T. J., and M. A. Stewart. 1982. A half-sibling study of aggressive conduct disorder. *Neuropsychobiology* 8:144–50.

U.S. Bureau of the Census. 1988. *Median Income Levels by Sex. Current Population Reports*, Series P-60. Washington, D.C.: U.S. Government Printing Office.

————. 1992. *Women as Part of the Labor Force. Current Population Reports*. Washington, D.C.: U.S. Government Printing Office.

————. 1993. *Statistical Abstract of the U.S., 1993*. Washington, D.C.: U.S. Government Printing Office.

U.S. Congress, House. 1982. *Hearing before the Subcommittee on Civil and Constitutional Rights of the Committee on the Judiciary on H.R. 3970: Federal Computer Systems Protection Act*. 97th Cong., 2d Sess. (September 23). Washington, D.C.: U.S. Government Printing Office.

————. 1983a. *Hearing before the Subcommittee on Antitrust and Restraint of Trade Activities Affecting Small Business: Small Business Computer Crime Prevention Act, H.R. 3075.* 98th Cong., 1st Sess. (July 14). Washington, D.C.: U.S. Government Printing Office.

————. 1983b. *Hearing before the Subcommittee on Civil and Constitutional Rights of the Committee on the Judiciary: Computer Crime.* 98th Cong., 1st Sess. (November 18). Washington, D.C.: U.S. Government Printing Office.

————. 1983c. *Hearing before the House Subcommittee on Transportation, Aviation and Materials of the Committee on Science and Technology: Computer and Communications Security and Privacy.* 98th Cong., 2d Sess. (September 26). Washington, D.C.: U.S. Government Printing Office.

————. 1984. *Counterfeit Access Device and Computer Fraud and Abuse Act of 1984 (H.R. 5616).* Report 98–894, 98th Cong., 2d Sess. (July 24). Washington, D.C.: U.S. Government Printing Office.

U.S. Congress, Senate. 1978. *Hearings before the Subcommittee on Criminal Laws and Procedures of the Committee on the Judiciary on S. 1766: Federal Computer Systems Protection Act.* 95th Cong., 2d Sess. (June 21 and 22). Washington, D.C.: U.S. Government Printing Office.

————. 1980. *Hearing before the Subcommittee on Criminal Justice of the Committee on the Judiciary on S. 240: Federal Computer Systems Protection Act.* 96th Cong., 2d Sess. (February 28). Washington, D.C.: U.S. Government Printing Office.

————. 1976. *Hazardous Waste Management: Public Meetings.* December 2–11. Washington, D.C.: U.S. Government Printing Office.

————. 1979. *Public Hearings on the Proposed Regulations Implementing Sections 3001 to 3004 of the Resource Conservation and Recovery Act.* February 22–23. Washington, D.C.: U.S. Government Printing Office.

U.S. Department of State. 1985. *Revolution Beyond our Border: Information on Central America.* State Department Report N 132. Washington D.C.: U.S. Department of State.

U.S. General Accounting Office. 1976. Computer related crimes in federal programs. Reprinted in *Problems Associated with Computer Technology in Federal Programs and Private Industry, Computer Abuses.* Senate Committee on Governmental Operations, 94th Cong., 2d Sess. 71–91. Washington, D.C.: U.S. Government Printing Office.

————. 1981. NORAD's Missile Warning System: What went wrong? GAO Report MASAD 81–30 (May 15). Washington, D.C.: U.S. Government Printing Office.

————. 1985. *Illegal Disposal of Hazardous Waste: Difficult to Detect or Deter.* Comptroller General's Report to the Subcommittee on Investigations and Oversight, Committee on Public Works and Transportation, House of Representatives. Washington, D.C.: U.S. Government Printing Office.

U.S. House of Representatives. 1975. *Waste Control Act of 1975. Hearings Held by the Subcommittee on Transportation and Commerce, Committee on Interstate and Foreign Commerce.* April 8–11, 14–17. Washington, D.C.: U.S. Government Printing Office.

————. 1976. *Resource Conservation and Recovery Act of 1976. Hearings Held by the Subcommittee on Transportation and Commerce, Committee on Interstate and Foreign Commerce.* June 29–30. Washington, D.C.: U.S. Government Printing Office.

————. 1980. *Organized Crime and Hazardous Waste Disposal. Hearings Held by Subcommittee on Oversight and Investigations, Committee on Interstate and Foreign Commerce.* December 16. Washington, D.C.: U.S. Government Printing Office.

————. 1981a. *Hazardous Waste Matters: A Case Study of Landfill Sites. Hearings Held by Subcommittee on Oversight and Investigations, Committee on Energy and Commerce.* June 9. Washington, D.C.: U.S. Government Printing Office.

————. 1981b. *Organized Crime Links to the Waste Disposal Industry. Hearings Held by*

Subcommittee on Oversight and Investigations, Committee on Energy and Commerce. May 28. Washington, D.C.: U.S. Government Printing Office.

————. 1983. *Hazardous Waste Disposal. Hearings Held by Subcommittee on Oversight and Investigations. Committee on Science and Technology.* March 30 and May 4. Washington, D.C.: U.S. Government Printing Office.

U.S. Public Law 98–473. 1984. *Counterfeit Access Device and Computer Fraud and Abuse Act of 1986.* Amendment to Chapter 47 of Title 18 of the United States Code (October 12). Washington, D.C.: U.S. Government Printing Office.

U.S. Public Law 99–474. 1986. *Computer Fraud and Abuse Act of 1986.* Amendment to Chapter 47 of Title 18 of the United States Code (October 16). Washington, D.C.: U.S. Government Printing Office.

U.S. Senate. 1974. *The Need for a National Materials Policy. Hearings Held by the Subcommittee on Environmental Pollution, Committee on Public Works.* June 11–13, July 9–11, 15–18. Washington, D.C.: U.S. Government Printing Office.

————. 1979. *Oversight of RCRA Implementation. Hearings held by the Subcommittee on Environmental Pollution and Resource Protection, Committee on Environmental and Public Works.* March 28–29. Washington, D.C.: U.S. Government Printing Office.

————. 1986. *Senate Select Committee on Assassination, Alleged Assassination Plots Involving Foreign Leaders. Interim Report of the Senate Select Committee to Study Governmental Operations with Respect to Intelligence Activities.* 94th Cong., 1st sess., November 20. Washington, D.C.: Government Printing Office.

United Nations Asia and Far East Institute and Australian Institute of Criminology (UNAFEI). 1990. *Crime and Justice in Asia and the Pacific.* Tokyo: UNAFEI. Washington, D.C.: U.S. Government Printing Office.

Unnever, James D. 1987. Review of James M. Byrne and Robert J. Sampson, *The Social Ecology of Crime. Contemporary Sociology* 16:845–46.

Useem, Bert, and Mayer N. Zald. 1982. From pressure group to social movement: Organizational dilemmas of the effort to promote nuclear power. *Social Problems* 30:144–56.

Vaillant, George. 1983. *The Natural History of Alcoholism.* Cambridge, Mass.: Harvard University Press.

Valentine, Bettylou. 1978. *Hustling and Other Hard Work.* Glencoe, N.Y.: Free Press.

Valzelli, L. 1981. *Psychobiology of Aggression and Violence.* New York: Raven Press.

Van Houten, Ron. 1983. Punishment: From the animal laboratory to the applied setting. In Saul Axdrod and Jack Apsche (eds.), *The Effects of Punishment on Human Behavior.* New York: Academic Press.

van Praag, H. M., R. S. Kahn, G. M. Asnis, S. Wetzler, S. L. Brown, A. Bleich, and M. L. Korn. 1987. Denosologization of biological psychiatry or the specificity of 5-HT disturbances in psychiatric disorders. *Journal of Affective Disorders* 13:1–8.

Vaughan, Diane. 1983. *Controlling Unlawful Organizational Behavior.* Chicago: University of Chicago Press.

Vaughn, Brian E., Jeanne H. Block, and Jack Block. 1988. Parental agreement on child rearing during early childhood and the psychological characteristics of adolescents. *Child Development* 59:1020–33.

Vaux, A. 1988. *Social Support: Theory, Research, and Intervention.* New York: Praeger.

Vaux, A. and M. Ruggiero. 1983. Stressful life change and delinquent behavior. *American Journal of Community Psychology* 11:169–83.

Venables, P. H. 1987. Autonomic nervous system factors in criminal behavior. In Sarnoff A. Mednick, Terrie E. Moffitt, and Susan A. Stack (eds.), *The Causes of Crime: New Biological Approaches.* New York: Cambridge University Press.

Vila, Bryan J. 1990. Exploring the evolutionary ecology of crime: a preliminary assessment and extension of a general theory of expropriative crime. Ph.D. dissertation, University of California, Davis.

————. 1994. A general paradigm for understanding criminal behavior: Extending evolutionary ecological theory. *Criminology* 32:311–59.

————. 1997a. Human nature and crime control: Improving the feasibility of nurturant crime control strategies. *Politics and the Life Sciences* 16:1–19.

————. 1997b. Motivating and marketing nurturant crime control strategies. *Politics and the Life Sciences* 16:x–xx.

Vila, Bryan J., and Lawrence E. Cohen. 1993. Crime as strategy: Testing an evolutionary ecological theory of expropriative crime. *American Journal of Sociology* 98:873–912.

Virkkunen, M., and S. Narvanen. 1987. Plasma insulin, tryptophan and serotonin levels during the glucose tolerance test among habitually violent and impulsive offenders. *Neuropsychobiology* 17:19–23.

Virkkunen, M., A. Nuutila, F. K. Goodwin, and M. Linnoila. 1987. Cerebrospinal fluid monoamine metabolite levels in male arsonists. *Archives of General Psychiatry* 44:241–47.

Virkkunen, M., J. DeJong, J. Bartkko, F. K. Goodwin, and M. Linnoila. 1989. Relationship of psychobiological variables to recidivism in violent offenders and impulsive fire setters. *Archives of General Psychiatry* 46:600–603.

Visher, Christy. 1983. Gender, police arrest decision, and notions of chivalry. *Criminology* 21:5–28.

Vold, George B. 1958. 1979. *Theoretical Criminology*. New York: Oxford University Press.

Vold, George B., and Thomas J. Bernard. 1986. *Theoretical Criminology*. 3d ed. New York: Oxford University Press.

Von Hentig, Hans. 1942. The criminality of the colored woman. *University of Colorado Studies* (Series C1):231–60.

Wahler, R. 1980. The insular mother: Her problems in parent-child treatment. *Journal of Applied Behavior Analysis* 13:207–19.

Waldo, Gordon P., and Simon Dinitz. 1967. Personality attributes of the criminal: An analysis of research studies, 1950–1965. *Journal of Research in Crime and Delinquency* 4:185–202.

Waldorf, Dan. 1993. *Final Report of the Crack Sales, Gangs and Violence Study: NIDA Grant 5#R01DA06486*. Alameda: Institute for Scientific Analysis.

Waldorf, Dan, Craig Reinarman, and Sheigla Murphy. 1991. *Cocaine Changes: The Experience of Using and Quitting*. Philadelphia: Temple University Press.

Walker, Andrew. 1981. Sociology and professional crime. In Abraham Blumberg (ed.), *Current Perspectives on Criminal Behavior*. New York: Alfred A. Knopf.

Walker, Lenore E. 1989. *Terrifying Love: Why Battered Women Kill and How Society Responds*. New York: Harper & Row.

Waller, Irwin. 1979. What reduces residential burglary: Action and research in Seattle and Toronto. Paper presented at the Third International Symposium on Victimology, Munster, West Germany.

Wallgren, H., and H. Barry. 1970. *Action of Alcohol*. Vols. 1 and 2. New York: Elsevier.

Walster, Elaine, Ellen Berscheid, and G. William Walster. 1973. New directions in equity research. *Journal of Personality and Social Psychology* 25:151–76.

Walster, Elaine, G. William Walster, and Ellen Berscheid. 1978. *Equity: Theory and Research*. Boston: Allyn & Bacon.

Walters, Gary, and Joan Grusec. 1977. *Punishment*. San Francisco: W. H. Freeman.

Walters, Glenn D., Roger L. Greene, and Gary S. Solomon. 1982. Empirical correlates of the overcontrolled hostility scale and the MMPI 4–3 highpoint pair. *Journal of Consulting and Clinical Psychology* 50:213–18.

Walters, Glenn D., and T. W. White. 1989. Heredity and crime: Bad genes or bad research? *Criminology* 27:455–86.

Wandersman, Lois, Abraham Wandersman, and Steven Kahn. 1980. Social support in the transition to parenthood. *Journal of Community Psychology* 8:332–42.

Warr, Mark, and Mark Stafford. 1991. The influence of delinquent peers: What they think or what they do? *Criminology* 4:851–66.

596   *References*

Watson, David, and Leanna A. Clark. 1984. Negative affectivity: The disposition to experience aversive emotional states. *Psychological Bulletin* 96:465–90.
Weiner, Neil Alan, and Marvin E. Wolfgang. 1985. The extent and character of violent crime in America. In Lynn A. Curtis (ed.), *American Violence and Public Policy*. New Haven: Yale University Press.
Weingartner, H., M. V. Rudorfer, M. S. Buchsbaum, and M. Linnoila. 1983. Effects of serotonin on memory impairments produced by ethanol. *Science* 221:472–74.
Weinstein, D., and L. Deitch. 1974. *The Impact of Legalized Gambling: The Socio-economic Consequences of Lotteries and Off-track Betting*. New York: Praeger.
Weis, Joseph G., and John Sederstrom. 1981. *The Prevention of Serious Delinquency: What To Do?* Washington, D.C.: U.S. Department of Justice.
Weiss, Robert P. 1987. From "slugging detectives" to "labor relations." In Clifford D. Shearing and Philip C. Stenning (eds.) *Private Policing*. Beverly Hills, Calif.: Sage.
Weisser, Michael R. 1979. *Crime and Punishment in Early Modern Europe*. Atlantic Highlands, N.J.: Humanities Press.
Weitzman, Lenore J. 1985. *The Divorce Revolution: The Unexpected Social and Economic Consequences for Women and Children in America*. Glencoe, N.Y.: Free Press.
Welch, Kevin. 1983. Community development and metropolitan religious commitment: A test of two competing models. *Journal for the Scientific Study of Religion* 22:167–81.
Wells, L. Edward, and Joseph Rankin. 1985. Broken homes and juvenile delinquency: An empirical review. *Criminal Justice Abstracts* 17:249–72.
———. 1988. Direct parental controls and delinquency. *Criminology*. 26:263–85.
Werkentin, Falco, Michael Hofferbert, and Michael Baurmann. 1974. Criminology as police science or: How old is the new criminology? *Crime and Social Justice* (Fall–Winter):24–41.
Werner, Emily E., and Ruth S. Smith. 1992. *Overcoming the Odds: High Risk Children from Birth to Adulthood*. Ithaca: Cornell University Press.
West, Donald and David Farrington. 1977. *The Delinquent Way of Life*. London: Heinemann.
Wethington, Elaine, Jane D. McLeod, and Ronald C. Kessler. 1987. The importance of life events for explaining sex differences in psychological distress. In Rosalind Barnett, Lois Biener, and Grace K. Baruch (eds.), *Gender and Stress*. New York: Free Press.
Wey, Hamilton D. 1888. A plea for physical training of youthful criminals. *National Prison Association, Proceedings 1888*:181–93.
———. 1890. Criminal anthropology. *National Prison Association, Proceedings 1890*:274–90.
Wheeler, Stanton. 1984. Sitting in judgment: Judicial perspectives on sentencing of white-collar offenders. Paper presented at the annual meeting of the American Society of Criminology, Cincinnati.
———. 1992. The problem of white-collar crime motivation. In Kip Schlegel and David Weisburd (eds.), *White Collar Crime Reconsidered*. Boston: Northeastern University Press.
Wheeler, Stanton, David Weisburd, and Nancy Bode. 1982. Sentencing the white-collar offender. *American Sociological Review* 47:641–59.
White, Jennifer L., Terrie E. Moffitt, Avshalom Caspi, Dawn J. Bartusch, and Douglas J. Needles. 1994. Measuring impulsivity and examining its relationship to delinquency. *Journal of Abnormal Psychology* 103:192–205.
White, Jennifer L., Terrie E. Moffitt, Felton Earls, Lee N. Robins, and Phil A. Silva. 1990. How early can we tell? Predictors of childhood conduct disorder and adolescent delinquency. *Criminology* 28:507–33.
Whiteside, Thomas. 1978. *Computer Capers: Tales of Electronic Thievery, Embezzlement and Fraud*. New York: Crowell.
Whyte, William Foote. 1943. *Street Corner Society*. Chicago: University of Chicago Press.

Wiatrowski, Michael, David Griswold, and Mary Roberts. 1981. Social control theory and delinquency. *American Sociological Review* 46:525–41.

Wickman, Peter, and Phillip Whitten. 1980. *Criminology: Perspectives on Crime and Criminality.* Lexington, Mass.: D. C. Heath.

Widom, Cathy S. 1978a. An empirical classification of the female offender. *Criminal Justice and Behavior* 5:35–52.

———. 1978b. Toward an understanding of female criminality. In Brendan A. Maher (ed.), *Progress in Experimental Personality Research.* Vol. 8. New York: Academic Press.

———. 1979. Female offenders: Three assumptions about self-esteem, sex-role identity and feminism. *Criminal Justice and Behavior* 6:365–82.

———. 1989. The cycle of violence. *Science* 244:160–66.

Widom, Cathy S. 1992. The cycle of violence. *National Institute of Justice Research in Brief* (NCJ136607). Washington D.C.: U.S. Government Printing Office.

Wilkins, Leslie T. 1964. *Social Deviance.* London: Tavistock.

———. 1973. Crime and criminal justice at the turn of the century. *Annals of the American Academy of Political and Social Science* 408:13–29.

Wilkinson, K. P., J. G. Thompson, R. R. Reynolds, Jr., and L. M. Ostresh. 1982. Local social disruption and western energy development: A critical review. *Pacific Sociological Review* 25:275–96.

Wilkinson, Paul. 1977. *Terrorism and the Liberal State.* London: Macmillan.

Will, George. 1987. Keep your eye on Giuliani. *Newsweek* March 2:84.

Williams, Bruce A., and Albert R. Matheny. 1984. Testing theories of social regulation: Hazardous waste regulation in the American states. *Journal of Politics* 46:428–58.

Williams, Carolyn L., and Craige Uchiyama. 1989. Assessment of life events during adolescence: The use of self-report inventories. *Adolescence* 24:95–118.

Williams, Terry. 1989. *The Cocaine Kids.* Reading, Mass.: Addison-Wesley.

Willis, Paul. 1977. *Learning to Labor.* Farnborough: Saxon House.

Willis, Susan. 1991. *A Primer for Daily Life.* London: Routledge.

Wills, Garry. 1978. *Inventing America: Jefferson's Declaration of Independence.* Garden City, N.Y.: Doubleday.

Wilson, James Q., and Richard J. Herrnstein. 1985. *Crime and Human Nature.* New York: Simon and Schuster.

Wilson, William J. 1982. *The Declining Significance of Race.* Chicago: University of Chicago Press.

———. 1987. *The Truly Disadvantaged: The Inner City, the Underclass, and Public Policy.* Chicago: University of Chicago Press.

Wise, James. 1987. Personal communication with Marcus Felson.

Wolff, P. H., D. Waber, M. Bauermeister, C. Cohen, and R. Ferber. 1982. The neuropsychological status of adolescent delinquent boys. *Journal of Child Psychology and Psychiatry* 23:267–79.

Wolfgang, Marvin E. 1958. *Patterns of Criminal Homicide.* Philadelphia: University of Pennsylvania Press.

———. 1972. Cesare Lombroso. In Herman Mannheim (ed.), *Pioneers in Criminology.* 2d ed. enlr. Montclair, N.J.: Patterson Smith.

Wolfgang, Marvin, and Franco Ferracuti. 1967. *The Subculture of Violence.* New York: Barnes and Noble.

Wolfgang, Marvin E., Robert Figlio, Paul E. Tracy, and Simon T. Singer. 1985. *The National Survey of Crime Severity.* Washington, D.C.: U.S. Government Printing Office.

Wolfgang, Marvin E., Robert M. Figlio, and Thorsten Sellin. 1972. *Delinquency in a Birth Cohort.* Chicago: University of Chicago Press.

Wolfgang, Marvin E., Terence P. Thornberry, and Robert M. Figlio. 1987. *From Boy to Man—From Delinquency to Crime: Follow-up to the Philadelphia Birth Cohort of 1945.* Chicago: University of Chicago Press.

Wood, P. B. 1989. The natural history of man in the Scottish Enlightenment. *History of Science* 28:89–123.

Woodiwiss, Anthony. 1990. *Social Theory after Postmodernism: Rethinking Production, Law and Class*. Winchester, Mass.: Unwin and Hyman.

Woolf, Stuart. 1979. *A History of Italy, 1700–1860*. London: Methuen.

Woolgar, Steve and Dorothy Pawluch. 1985. Ontological gerrymandering: The anatomy of social problems explanations. *Social Problems* 32:214–27.

Wuthnow, Robert. 1987. *Meaning and Moral Order: Explorations in Cultural Analysis*. Berkeley: University of California Press.

Wuthnow, Robert, and Kevin Christiano. 1979. The effects of residential migration on church attendance. In Robert Wuthnow (ed.), *The Religious Dimension*. New York: Academic Press.

Wylie, Ruth. 1979. *The Self-Concept*. Vol. 2. Lincoln: University of Nebraska Press.

Yeager, Peter C. 1987. Structural bias in regulatory law enforcement: The case of the U.S. Environmental Protection Agency. *Social Problems* 34:330–44.

———. 1991. *The Limits of Law: The Public Regulation of Private Pollution*. New York: Cambridge University Press.

———. 1993. Industrial water pollution. In M. Tonry and A. J. Reiss, Jr. (eds.), *Beyond the Law: Crime in Complex Organizations*. Chicago: University of Chicago Press.

———. 1995. Management, morality and law: Organizational forms and ethical deliberations. In Frank Pearce and Laureen Snider (eds.), *Corporate Crime: Contemporary Debates*. Toronto: University of Toronto Press.

Yeager, Peter C., and Kathy E. Kram. 1995. Fielding hot topics in cool settings: The study of corporate ethics. In Jonathan B. Imber and Rosanna Hertz (eds.), *Studying Elites Using Qualitative Methods*. Thousand Oaks, Calif.: Sage.

Yeudall, L. T., O. Fedora, and D. Fromm. 1985. *A Neuropsychosocial Theory of Persistent Criminality: Implications for Assessment and Treatment. Research Bulletin 97*. Edmonton: Alberta Hospital.

Yochelson, Samuel and Stanton E. Samenow. 1976. *The Criminal Personality*. Vol. 1. *A Profile for Change*. New York: Jason Aronson.

———. 1977. *The Criminal Personality*. Vol. 2. *The Change Process*. New York: Jason Aronson.

Young, David. 1983. Cesare Beccaria: Utilitarian or retributivist? *Journal of Criminal Justice* 11:317–26.

Young, Jock. 1975. Working-class criminology. In Ian Taylor, Paul Walton, and Jock Young (eds.), *Critical Criminology*. London: Routledge & Kegan Paul.

Young, Jock. 1981. Thinking seriously about crime: Some models of criminology. In Mike Fitzgerald, Gregor McLennan, and Jennie Pawson (eds.), *Crime and Society: Readings in History and Society*. London: Routledge & Kegan Paul.

Young, Jock. 1994. Incessant chatter: Recent paradigms in criminology. In Mike Maguire, Rod Morgan, and Robert Reiner (eds.), *The Oxford Handbook of Criminology*. Oxford: Clarendon Press.

Young, T. R. 1992. Chaos theory and human agency: Humanist sociology in a postmodern era. *Humanity and Society* 16:441–60.

Young, Vernetta D. 1980. Women, race, and crime. *Criminology* 18:26–34.

Zeman, Thomas E. 1981. Order, crime, and punishment: The American criminological tradition. Ph.D. dissertation. University of California, Santa Cruz.

Zillman, Dolf. 1979. *Hostility and Aggression*. Hillsdale, N.J.: Lawrence Erlbaum.

Zimring, Franklin, and Gordon Hawkins. 1991. *The Scale of Imprisonment*. Chicago: University of Chicago Press.

Zimring, Franklin E., Satyanshu K. Mukherjee, and Barrik Van Winkle. 1983. Intimate violence: A study of intersexual homicide in Chicago. *University of Chicago Law Review* 50:910–30.

Zingraff, Matthew T., Jeffrey Leiter, Kristen A. Myers, and Matthew C. Johnsen. 1992. Child maltreatment and youthful problem behavior. *Criminology* 31:173–202.

Zipf, George K. 1949. *Human Behavior and the Principle of Least Effort: An Introduction to Human Ecology.* Cambridge: MA: Addison-Wesley.

———. 1950. *The Principle of Least Effort.* Reading, Mass.: Addison-Wesley.

Zuckerman, Marvin. 1983. A biological theory of sensation seeking. In Marvin Zuckerman (ed.), *Biological Basis of Sensation Seeking, Impulsivity and Anxiety.* Hillsdale, N.J.: Lawrence Erlbaum.

———. 1989. Personality in the third dimension: A psychobiological approach. *Personality and Individual Differences* 10:391–418.

Index

Abel, R. xv, xvi, 9
Academy of Criminal Justice Sciences (ACJS) xxi, xxiii, 10
Accounts xv, 3, 11, 57, 69, 70, 140, 141, 155, 199, 245-251, 253, 257, 258, 259, 261, 262, 266, 273, 274, 294, 297, 305, 314, 316, 320, 339, 342, 346, 362, 367, 387, 391, 399, 417, 438-440, 457
Actuarial Criminology 446, 449, 453, 454, 459, 463, 464
Adaptations 176, 178, 187, 188, 190, 191, 194, 496
Adler, F. xv, xvi, 176, 384, 401
Adoption studies 97
Agency 20, 43, 130, 176, 278, 343, 356, 358, 365, 374, 430, 431, 434, 437, 448, 452, 520; *see also* human agency
Agger, B. 422, 429
Agnew, R. vi, xvii, 4, 7, 176-181, 184, 185, 187-189, 191, 192, 247, 401, 402, 405, 413, 484, 510
Akers R. vii, xvii, 3, 4, 6, 193, 216, 228, 229, 236-238, 240, 266, 296, 303, 321, 471, 477, 482
Alcohol abuse 295, 296, 495; *see also* drinking
Alienation 114, 116-118, 269, 393, 397, 406
Allport G. 77, 409
Amateurs 223, 225
American Dream 151, 206
American Society of Criminology (ASC) xi, xii, xiii, xv, xvii, xviii, xxi, xxii, xxiii, xxiv, 10
Anarchist 7, 336
Anger 95, 114, 115, 122, 178, 179, 181, 182, 185, 186, 193, 249, 385, 397, 402, 405-408, 410-412

Anomie 6, 175, 176
Anthropology vi, xxii, 3, 76, 78-82, 81, 83-86, 88-91
Antisocial personality 93, 97, 99, 276
Antitrust violations 64, 247, 248, 253-262, 299, 303, 307
Arson 64, 312, 379
Aspirations 52, 176, 180, 181, 183, 185, 188, 193, 197, 205, 206, 208, 455, 457, 459, 483
Assault xxiii, 57, 146, 182, 232, 283, 284, 301, 360, 388, 391, 408, 450, 513, 517
Atavism 86
Autonomic Nervous System (ANS) 107, 408

Bandura, A. 6, 134, 184-186, 191, 192, 495, 503, 506
Barak, G. 2, 3, 8, 450
Battered women xxii, 401, 410, 412, 430, 431, 434
Baudrillard, J. 420, 421, 425, 434, 435
Beccaria, C. v, 5, 17, 19-44
Becker, H. 6, 291, 317, 326, 335, 337, 338, 498
Beirne, P. v, xvii, 17, 19
Belief 9, 19, 25, 40, 46, 70, 79, 106, 111, 147, 189, 230, 249, 255, 263, 266, 277, 278, 323, 396, 417, 421, 466, 473, 474, 476, 477, 480, 481-483, 485, 487, 490, 491
Bennett, T. 52, 54, 55
Benson, M. vii, xvii, 245, 247, 249, 296, 297, 306, 307, 309, 514
Bentham, J. 5, 17, 20, 21, 43
Bequai, A. 301, 316-318, 432
Bernard, T. viii, xviii, 3, 19, 177, 180, 185, 186, 191-194, 229, 385 *(Cont'd)*